Mass Media II

AN INTRODUCTION TO MODERN COMMUNICATION

RAY ELDON HIEBERT
Dean
College of Journalism
University of Maryland

DONALD F. UNGURAIT
Associate Professor
College of Communication
Florida State University

THOMAS W. BOHN
Chairman
Faculty of Communication
University of Tulsa

LONGMAN
New York and London

MASS MEDIA
An Introduction to Modern Communication

Second Edition

Longman Inc., New York
Associated companies, branches, and representatives throughout the
world.

Developmental Editor: Edward Artinian
Editorial and Design Supervisor: Linda Salmonson
Design: Antler & Baldwin, Inc.
Manufacturing and Production Supervisor: Louis Gaber
Composition: The Composing Room of Michigan, Inc.
Printing and Binding: The Book Press

Library of Congress Cataloging in Publication Data

Hiebert, Ray Eldon.
  Mass media.

  Bibliography: p.
  Includes index.
  1. Communication. 2. Mass media. I. Ungurait,
Donald F., joint author. II. Bohn, Thomas W., joint
author. III. Title.
P90.H48 1978   301.16   77-17721
ISBN 0-582-28070-2

Manufactured in the United States of America

Part One   The Process of Mass Communication

Contents

Part Three   Media of Mass Communication

Part Four Uses of Mass Communication

Part One The Process of Mass Communication

A s the erstwhile farmer from rural Georgia placed his left hand on the Bible and raised his right hand to take the oath of office, millions of people looked over his shoulder. He was about to be inaugurated as President of the United States.

A battery of reporters, cameramen, photographers, directors, and producers helped to communicate the inauguration of President Jimmy Carter to the world. In addition to the huge audience that saw the event on television, there were untold others who listened to it on their radios or read about it in their newspapers and magazines. Later, there would be detailed analyses of the proceedings in books and documentary films. The mass media covered this day, as they do all important events, pervasively.

Through high-speed printing, computer technology, modern electronics, and space satellites, mass communication has grown into a worldwide phenomenon. In recent decades, for example, as the technology has improved and expanded, each new presidential inauguration has had a larger world audience than the one before.

It is entirely fitting that Jimmy Carter was inaugurated before such an audience; without the mass media, he probably would not have become President. Despite his single term as governor of Georgia, he was all but unknown to the American public when he decided to run for the most powerful office in the world. And, at the outset, he did not have the backing of the Democratic party.

1

Introduction: Mass Media and the Critical Consumer

But he and his advisers planned a campaign that brought him to the attention of the mass media, and the media in turn made him known to Americans and the world.

The news media also played an important role in bringing about the resignation of a previous occupant of the White House, Richard M. Nixon. It was the press and not the government—not the FBI, CIA, Secret Service, Justice Department, or any other government agency that is supposed to protect the people—that made public the wrongdoings in the Nixon administration. The exposure started with the persistent investigations of newspaper reporters such as Robert Woodward and Carl Bernstein of the *Washington Post*. Soon other newspapers and news magazines were amassing more facts. As this public information stirred Congress into holding hearings on the "Watergate crisis," the radio and television coverage of those hearings went out to a concerned audience of millions.

Richard Nixon turned to the mass media to plead his case. He went before the cameras on all the national networks, with the transcripts of his tape-recorded conversations stacked around him, to say that he was not a common criminal. But when the feedback from his television appearances came in, the President knew that he had lost the faith of the American people. Richard Nixon was forced to resign his office, the first American President in history to do so.

What Are the Mass Media?

The powerful forces we call mass media are the means of public communication that surround us. Newspapers are one medium. Together with magazines and books, they make up the print media. Radio is an electronic medium, as is television. The motion picture is an audiovisual medium. The phonograph recording is an aural medium.

These media (or "mediums," as they are sometimes called) are the subject of this book. They exist all over the world; but in American society they are unique because the mass media in America are privately owned, influential, and exist at the local as well as the national level.

One thing is essential to state at the outset. In America the mass media are not part of the government apparatus, as they are in many other countries of the world. In America the mass media are private businesses, and our Constitution guarantees their freedom and the noninterference of government in their activities. Indeed, in America there is a custom that government should be completely separated from public communication. That tradition is almost as strong as the belief in separation between church and state.

The Role of Mass Media

In a democratic society the mass media play a central role. Since nothing in democracy can succeed without the will of the people, informing and shaping that will is a major undertaking.

Take, for example, the enormously expensive operation that put a man on the moon. Why were American taxpayers willing to put billions of dollars into that venture rather than, say, to clean up the inner cities or build low-cost housing? Part of the answer may be in the fact that the space program benefited from compelling mass communication. The officials in NASA, the American agency responsible for space exploration, realized early that in order to get sufficient congressional appropriations of funds to send a man to the moon, they would have to inform the American people of their intentions and persuade people to support the space program.

NASA welcomed full media coverage of the space effort. Television, radio, and the other mass media were there when the first rocket went into orbit; through the media, millions participated in the event. Mass communication stimulated public interest, allowing NASA to build its case with Congress, the President, and the people. By the time of the Apollo flights that did put a man on the moon, worldwide interest had been captured.

An estimated 528 million people around the world witnessed the moon landing on live television. In nations where home television sets were not yet common, great crowds gathered in public squares to watch the event on communal TV. James Clayton, a *Washington Post* writer, called the Apollo 11 flight "the most massive publicity effort in the history of the world." He meant that, without the tremendous public exposure, NASA would not have been so successful.

One can even argue that the moon landing could not have been undertaken without mass media. Could such a journey have taken place before we had perfected a portable television camera and the electronic capability to transmit words and pictures 238,856 miles back to earth? One might go back into the past and conjecture that Columbus could not have discovered the New World until the invention of the printing press. For it was only after the invention of the printing press that word could be spread about scientific discoveries, explorations, hypotheses, charts, and maps, without which few would have dared the dangerous voyage.

The media can also get people to take action against an issue, as in the Vietnam war. In retrospect, it seems clear that the battles in Vietnam were never able to generate much support from the American people. The war in Vietnam was the first war that was reported live and in color by television, without government censorship. Perhaps seeing the war so intimately, in all its gruesome detail, made the majority of Americans decide against it.

In a democratic society, the public must be informed and their opinions shaped by facts and ideas. That's the role of the media. But the media themselves are inanimate objects; it is people who put them to various uses. The uses we are concerned with in this book are information, persuasion, interpretation, entertainment, education, and economic promotion. But before we analyze those uses in depth, we need to look at mass communication as a process, examine its parts, and describe the media themselves.

The Medium Is the Message

The act of mass communication has many parts, and these can be broken down into components for study. Traditionally, we have been most concerned with the message, the message sender, the audience, and the effects of the mass communication process. These are all valid areas of scholarship.

Nevertheless, increased emphasis has been placed on the medium itself as an important element in the mass communication process. Indeed, the medium may be the key component in the process. Marshall McLuhan, in his book *Understanding Media: The Extensions of Man*, coined the phrase "The medium *is* the message." What this means is that the carrier of communications— whether human voice or printed page, neon sign or electronic impulse— influences the message, the sender, the audience, and the effects of mass communication far more than was previously understood.

The medium shapes the message. A neon sign can sell a hot dog, but it cannot very well express an abstract political idea—unless the political idea is reshaped to fit the preferences of neon signs for simple and concrete notions.

The medium shapes the message sender. The technical considerations inherent in the production of a TV series or the publication of a metropolitan newspaper are so complex that they require a team of communicators to accomplish mass communication. The individual sender has been replaced by the conglomerate media communicator.

The medium shapes the audience because it alters perceptual habits. The dominant medium of any society conditions the thought processes of that society and shapes its culture.

Because the media affect the message, the message sender, and the audience, we can say without hesitation that if we do not know the medium, we cannot really understand the communication. Canadian anthropologist Dr. Edmund Carpenter has written:

"You see, Dad, Professor McLuhan says the environment that man creates becomes his medium for defining his role in it. The invention of type created linear, or sequential, thought, separating thought from action. Now, with TV and folk singing, thought and action are closer and social involvement is greater. We again live in a village. Get it?"

The new mass media—film, radio, TV—are new languages, their grammars as yet unknown. Each codifies reality differently; each conceals a unique metaphysics.[1]

In an age of mass communication, perhaps nothing could be more vital than the study of mass media. This book introduces the student to the grammars of the mass media as we currently know them. We need to see how each medium codifies reality differently; we have to learn each medium's individual metaphysics; we must understand the media biases of our culture. We also need to know what the media have in common as mass media rather than

[1]Edmund Carpenter, "The New Languages," in *Explorations in Communication,* ed. Edmund Carpenter and Marshall McLuhan (Boston: Beacon Press, 1960), p. 166.

Introduction: Mass Media and the Critical Consumer   7

personal media. Such a study can help us understand ourselves and our environment. For mass media have undoubtedly shaped us. They are the message.

The Scope of Mass Media

We have moved into an age where mass communication is a major human activity, one on which people spend more time and money every year. As never before, we have the time and the need to be informed, persuaded, educated, and entertained. We need an increased amount of information merely to exist in our complex modern society, and we need help in having that information interpreted. We also need to escape from the burdens of our complicated days through the entertainment that mass media can provide. Our needs have made mass media growth industries in our society. We have surrounded ourselves with mass media.

Television has become the baby-sitter for our young and the constant companion for our old and lonely. Most of us catch TV over breakfast, watch the evening news before dinner, perhaps take in a movie or variety show several nights a week or a sporting event or a special on the weekend. In all, the average American family spends more than six hours a day with television.

Radio occupies a different time, place, and function but is nonetheless important. We would hardly think of getting in the car without turning on the radio, and we listen to news and music as we drive to and from work, go to the shopping center, or take a Sunday drive. The radio and the phonograph, because they do not require our complete attention, have become necessary background and filler. We are apt to turn on a radio or phonograph while we read and study, while we clean the house, while at a party or at work. Even at the White House, background music is piped in.

Contrary to some opinion, radio and television have not taken away much time from newspapers. Many metropolitan areas have both morning and evening dailies, thicker than ever with news and advertising, and more people than ever are reading them. Americans spend about one and a half hours a day reading newspapers. They depend on them for background and interpretation of the news of the day, to learn who among their friends is alive or dead, to check on the progress of their stock at the market, to see where they should shop for groceries, to look for a house or apartment, to keep up with the statistics of their favorite team.

Magazines, too, are bigger than ever and come in all shapes and sizes. More than 10,000 magazines are published every year in the United States. Increasingly they are aimed at specialized audiences. The large general-interest magazines of the past, such as *Collier's*, have died. But their places have been taken with news, travel, men's, women's, opinion, cultural, professional, and romance magazines. You name it, and there is probably a magazine that specializes in the subject crowding newsstands, drugstore counters, and racks in supermarkets.

Book production has also increased in this age of mass communication. Most college students spend hundreds of dollars on books, for a book is still one of the handiest ways to package, store, and retrieve information. With its table of contents and index, a book allows readers to flip through its pages and find exactly what they want, and they can spend as much time with it as they want. With the development of the soft-cover book, which can be produced quickly and cheaply, books have found a new life as a mass medium as well as a tool of education.

The movie industry, too, is playing an ever-larger role in our society. Americans are spending $2.5 billion each year to see films. Hollywood no longer has a monopoly on motion-picture production. Movies are now made in every corner of the world, with independent production units turning out over half of American feature-length films. Most TV series are filmed. Film is increasingly used for education and information, too. The U.S. Department of Defense, to name only one example, has made more than 4,000 films a year for troop education and information.

Disk and tape sound recording has also increased, with sales of about $3 billion a year. And at every turn we are exposed to other forms of mass media—billboards, subway and bus cards, bumper stickers, pamphlets, leaflets, brochures, booklets, neon signs, and skywriting. Even the newsletter, an ancient form of journalism, has been revived in the twentieth century and seems to be everywhere. Each delivery of mail brings another mass communication, perhaps from our church group, alumni association, social club, political party, congressman, stock broker, or professional society.

The Global Village?

America is by far the largest producer and consumer of mass communication. Americans use four times as much newsprint as Japan, which is second in the world in newsprint consumption. Almost half the world's telephones belong to Americans. The ratio of television sets per person in the United States is far above that of any other country. There are more radio sets in America than there are people. America is a mass communication society.

American mass media have a great impact not only on our own society, but also on the rest of the world. Herbert Read, in his study of international communication entitled *Mass Media Merchants*, noted that "commercial

American mass media are permeating human activity on an unprecedented scale." In Africa, for example, one is more apt to hear American music on radio, television, in discos and nightclubs, and on home phonographs than African music. In India, American movies are shown more often than Indian movies. In Latin America, the *Reader's Digest* is more popular than any locally produced magazine. Mass media are one of America's biggest exports.

While the masses are entertained in a global village of American mass media, a worldwide "information elite" is getting a greater amount of its information and interpretation from American news media. A United States Information Agency survey found that 15 to 30 percent of elite audiences in noncommunist countries read *Time* magazine. More than 200 of the world's leading newspapers subscribe to the *New York Times* or the *Washington Post–Los Angeles Times* news services. And United Press International, one of the two major America wire services (Associated Press is the other), sends its stories out to more than 62 foreign countries in more than 48 foreign languages.

This surely supports Marshall McLuhan's notion that electronic media are creating a global village, one in which the mass of humanity are joined together by a common television set watching the same program.

The Rise of the Mass Communicator

In the past, the journalist and mass communicator were not always highly regarded by society, in spite of the important role they have always played. A newspaperman was sometimes considered little more than an itinerant printer, or low-paid social gadfly. That attitude is changing rapidly.

Today's reporters and editors are important and influential members of their communities. They are not only criticized and feared; they are also admired, sought after, and often rewarded. In part this change in attitude may have resulted from the introduction of reporters on television. For the first time, people could see journalists at work, often in a setting where they were asking tough questions of important public officials. When the journalists became the equal of the officials, a new status was conferred upon them. Indeed, some journalists have become stars in our new age of mass media. The two reporters who exposed the Watergate affair, Woodward and Bernstein, produced best-selling books and were immortalized in a successful feature film, *All the President's Men* (1976), based on one of their books. Book and film royalties, television appearances, lecture fees, and new free-lance opportunities have made them millionaires. Barbara Walters, on the staff of ABC News, was the first journalist to be paid a straight salary of $1 million a year. Some of her colleagues—Walter Cronkite, David Brinkley, and Frank Reynolds, among others—had been paid hundreds of thousands of dollars a year, and with Ms. Walters' competition, their salaries would probably rise.

These are more or less isolated cases, the big stars at the top. But even at lower levels, salaries and working conditions for mass communicators have improved substantially in the past decade, making them solid, middle-class citizens. Starting salaries for reporters and photographers at the *National Enquirer* range from $30,000 to $38,000 a year. At the *New York Times*, similar jobs offer a starting salary of about $23,500 a year. At the *Washington Post*, the minimum salary after four years is about $25,000. The average minimum salary for a newspaper reporter is $16,000 a year, compared to $4,600 a year in 1950. And these are just beginning-level jobs; as one moves up, the salaries go considerably higher. Curiously, in 1950 printers were paid more than reporters. Reporters are now paid an average of about 40 percent more than printers.

Journalists and mass communicators more and more think of themselves as professionals, in the same mold as doctors, lawyers, and engineers. Increasingly, these mass communicators adhere to professional codes of conduct and standards of practice. They increasingly need professional education required to be experts and specialists in their individual tasks.

The Critical Consumer

In our discussion so far, a basic question remains: if the media play such an important role in our lives, are we their victims or their masters? That is, are we managed, manipulated, massaged, and brainwashed by the mass media, or do the media simply reflect us and our wishes, our purchases in the marketplace, our attention, our dial-twirling, and our page-turning?

The best answer is probably a combination of both. We still do not know enough about the process to make final judgments. Though we speak of communication science, we have far to go to arrive at answers to some basic questions. One thing seems clear, however: the more we know about a subject, the less we can be misled about it.

During the Korean war, when the problems of brainwashing in communist prison camps became a great concern of Americans, a team of psychologists at the University of Illinois undertook an experiment. Two groups were tested to see how their opinions on a subject could be changed. One group was given advance information about the subject, while a control group was not. Test results showed that the ideas of the group with the advance information were less likely to be changed about the subject than those of the control group. The experimenters concluded that the more information a person had about a subject, the less likely that he or she could be brainwashed.

It seems certain that the mass media will play an ever-increasing role in our lives; therefore, the consumer of mass communication must have greater knowledge of the process. The educated person in modern society should be informed about mass media whether he or she becomes a participant or remains an observer or consumer. This book, then, is written for the critical consumer as well as the future communicator.

Educated people must develop a critical attitude toward mass media. They must be able to make judgments beyond their likes and dislikes. They must know why something is of high quality and when it is not. They must develop a critical awareness about mass media. Universities have offered courses on art appreciation, music appreciation, and literary appreciation in which students are taught to be critical of these forms. We need courses in mass media appreciation that will allow students—and all consumers of mass communication—to be critically aware of the problems and processes of mass media.

Today, an understanding of mass media is as important for full community participation and active citizenship as a knowledge of civics and government. Knowing the processes of human communication is as important for our minds as knowing about nutrition and diet is for our bodies.

Uncritical audiences are more likely to believe everything they see in print, hear on radio, watch on television or at the movies. The power of print has intimidated human beings for hundreds of years, and the power of live-action pictures on television can be even more intimidating. Individuals who have believed so completely in what they read in the newspaper or observe on television are apt to become disillusioned and suspicious when they discover that what they read and see is not always 100 percent true. They begin to listen to voices of suspicion and become easy victims of the prophets of doom. They settle into a deep-seated suspicion that they are being manipulated and man-handled by those distant puppeteers behind the scenes, by mass media newsmen and Madison Avenue advertisers.

Those who understand the process can achieve greater perspective. The critical consumer can put what is artificial in mass communication into better balance with the reality of life. The study of mass media is important, then, because it helps the educated person understand one of the crucial processes of modern life. Such understanding not only helps the participant in mass communication perform more effectively, but it can also enable the critical consumer to make more effective use of mass communication.

As you begin to read this page you are participating in the basic social process of human society—communication. When you think about someone you love, or have an argument, or listen to a lecture, or call the "time-temperature" number, or write home, or go to a movie, you are involved in the process of communication. Communication is the human cement that holds a society together; it links each of us to other individuals, groups, and institutions and is the basic tool of a culture. Without communication there would be no society.

A large vocabulary has grown up around our attempts to describe and define communication. "Credibility gap," "loss of identity," "global village," "other-directed man," "hot and cool media," and other catch phrases attempt to popularize communication concepts. These terms are so common that we sometimes accept and use them without understanding what they represent. Yet what is communication? What are its distinct characteristics? How does it occur? And how does it break down?

Communication Defined

Many definitions of communication are available, but as John Newman remarks in "A Rationale for a Definition of Communication," no generally accepted definition exists, not because of a lack of knowledge about communica-

2

The Process of Mass Communication

tion, but because of a lack of understanding about the nature of a definition. Newman further states that communication is so diverse and discursive that the attempt to create a generally accepted definition becomes involved and hinders rather than helps further thought on the subject. That is why this book does not try to define communication as a single act but examines it as a cultural phenomenon.

Some of the more functional definitions of communication describe it as "the transfer of meaning," "the transmission of social values," or "the sharing of experience." Communication is all these things, but it is more than the sum of them.

It is best to think of communication as a *process*, which is a series of actions or operations, *always* in motion, directed toward a particular goal. Communication is not a static entity fixed in time and space. It is a dynamic process used to transfer meaning, transmit social values, and share experiences.

Kinds of Communication

All of us engage in a variety of communication processes. *Intrapersonal* communication involves one individual thinking or talking to himself or herself. *Interpersonal* communication involves an individual with another individual. *Group* communication involves an individual with more than one person in close physical proximity. Finally, *mass* communication involves a communicator (who may or not be a single individual) with large numbers of people using a mass medium. These four levels of the communication process can be visualized in the form of a V-shaped continuum, as shown in figure 2.1.

As you move from left to right along the continuum, the communication process is modified in a number of ways. The number of people involved in it increases from one to millions. The messages become less personal and more

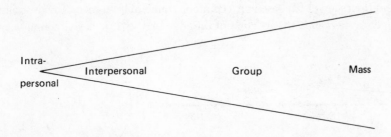

FIGURE 2.1. *The V-shaped Continuum of the Levels of the Communication Process. From Eugene L. Hartley and Ruth E. Hartley,* Fundamentals of Social Psychology *(New York: Alfred A. Knopf, 1959), p. 163.*

general. The persons involved become physically separated. Machines and organizations become involved in the process. Nevertheless, all four levels have essentially the same basic components.

One useful way to analyze communication is to develop a model of the process. We can better show the dynamic, ongoing, ever-changing aspect of the process if we visualize it much as a football coach diagrams a football play. Such a model can help break down communication into its components, allowing us to study the role each part plays in the total process.

Models of Interpersonal and Group Communication

There are many models of the various levels of communication, but all of them contain three basic elements. In every communication situation, someone (A) sends something (m) to someone else (B). The labels attached to each of these three basic elements vary, but the intent is the same.

(A) Someone	*(m) Something*	*(B) Someone Else*
Communicator	Communiqué	Communicatee
Sender	Message	Receiver
Encoder	Content	Decoder
Source	Signal	Destination

One of the basic concerns of scholars in communication has been to emphasize that the message sent is not always the message received. Wilbur Schramm visualizes (models) this concept two different ways (see figure 2.2). Schramm's linear model emphasizes that both the communicator (A) and the communicatee (B) act on the message (m). It is important to understand that receiving is not a passive act; it requires action by the receiver on the message. The circular model emphasizes that the message (AB) is shared by the sender (A) and the receiver (B) based on a common frame of reference. The destination (B) only understands that portion of the idea (AB) that it has in common with

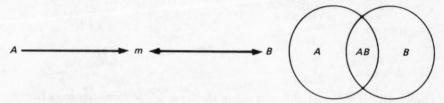

FIGURE 2.2. *Two Visualizations of the Sender-Message-Receiver Relationship. Developed by Wilbur Schramm*

the source (A). In intrapersonal communication the two circles overlap completely, because the sender is also the receiver; but in mass communication the two circles sometimes barely touch, because of the differences in the two frames of reference.

In an early attempt to explain how communication works, Claude E. Shannon and Warren Weaver developed a "Mathematical Model of Communication" (see figure 2.3). This model interposes a device (a telephone) in the form of a transmitter-receiver and within that device indicates that a breakdown in the process may occur in the form of noise. This model emphasizes how the message moves from source to destination. It is, in effect, a technical system.

Charles E. Osgood models the process somewhat differently to emphasize the interactive nature of communication. The Osgood model, shown in figure 2.4, visualizes the interpersonal communication process with each individual as both sender and receiver. In this model it is the interpretation of the other's intent that is the key to successful communication. In most interpersonal situations the individual is often sending and receiving at the same time.

A very basic visualization of the process of communication is the model developed by Andrew Weaver and Ordean Ness in figure 2.5. The Weaver-Ness model adds codes, which are written, visual, or verbal symbol systems, broadens noise to mean any interruption of the process, and includes a feedback loop or the response of the receiver. Interpersonal communication becomes a circular or response-oriented activity through channels of communication.

The components of interpersonal communication then are generally (1) a sender or encoder or communicator; (2) a personal, intimate message; (3) a code in the form of a commonly accepted symbol system; (4) a channel, such as airwaves or paper and pencil; (5) a limited number of receivers; (6) feedback, or

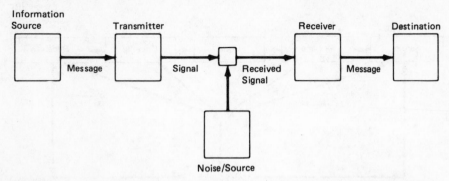

FIGURE 2.3. *The Shannon-Weaver Schematic Diagram of a General Communication System*

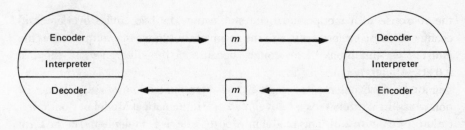

FIGURE 2.4. *The Charles E. Osgood Model of Communication*

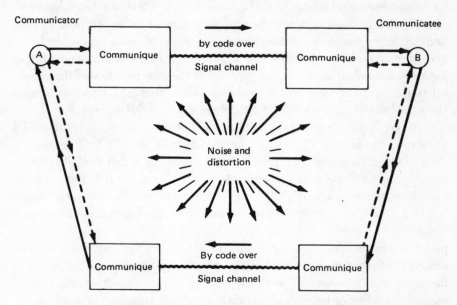

FIGURE 2.5. *The Weaver-Ness Model of Speech Communication*

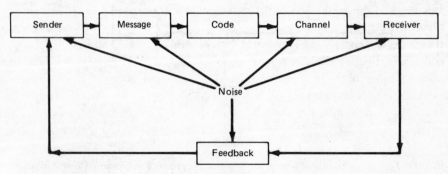

FIGURE 2.6. *Summary Model of Interpersonal Communication*

the response to a message (usually the sender and the receiver constantly change roles using feedback as a means of interacting); and (7) noise or any interruption that breaks down communication. The summary model in figure 2.6 attempts to visualize all the basic parts of interpersonal-group communication as simply as possible so as to set up a comparison of the mass communication models that follow.

Models of Mass Communication

Many different kinds of models are also used to diagram mass communication. One of the most widely used is Harold Lasswell's model. This simple and graphic description is somewhat limited, however. Several essential elements necessary to an understanding of the mass communication process, such as feedback and noise, are omitted. Nevertheless, it identifies a continuing interest in the impact or effect of the mass communication process.

Who?
Says What?
In Which Channel?
To Whom?
With What Effect?[1]

Another model, constructed by Melvin DeFleur, outlines a more complete process (figure 2.7). In this model, source and transmitter are seen as different phases of the mass communication act carried out by the originator of the message. The channel is a mass medium through which the information passes. The receiver functions as an information recipient and decoder, transforming the physical events of the information into a message. The destination functions to interpret messages into meaning. This is a function of the brain. Feedback is the response of the destination to the source. The model reemphasizes the fact that noise may interfere at any point in the mass communication process and is not solely identified with the channel or medium. The major concern of the DeFleur model is to achieve isomorphism or a commonly shared understanding of the meaning of the message between source and destination.

The model of mass communication developed by Bruce Westley and Malcolm MacLean emphasizes the role of gatekeepers in the mass communication

[1]Harold D. Lasswell, "The Structure and Function of Communication in Society," in *Mass Communication*, ed. Wilbur Schramm (Urbana: University of Illinois Press, 1960), p. 117.

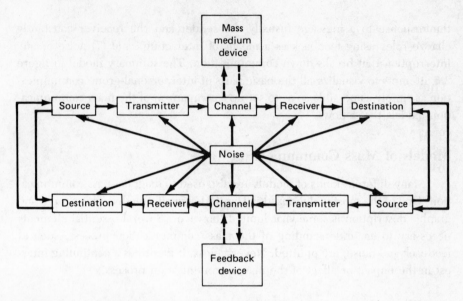

FIGURE 2.7. *The DeFleur Model of Mass Communication, or The Component of a General System for Achieving Isomorphism of Meaning*

process (figure 2.8). This model visualizes the ways in which individuals and organizations within the media system decide what messages are to be transmitted and the content that is to be modified or deleted.

The gatekeeper (C) serves as an agent of the audience (B) and selects messages and transmits them to receivers from the senders (A). The gatekeeper can amplify or interfere with messages sent by the communicator before the

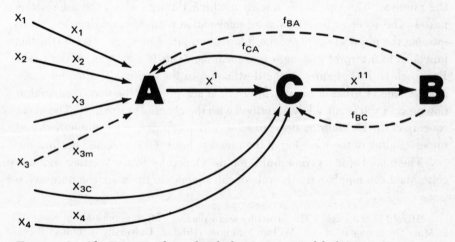

FIGURE 2.8. *The Bruce Westley and Malcolm MacLean Model of Mass Communication*

THE PROCESS OF MASS COMMUNICATION

content reaches the audience because the gatekeeper is interposed between them with the power to modify message content.

The HUB Model of Mass Communication

All the models previously shown are satisfactory ways to analyze the communication process. For our purposes we use an alternative method of modeling mass communication to show the process more completely as a circular, dynamic, ongoing progression. We have chosen to visualize the process as a set

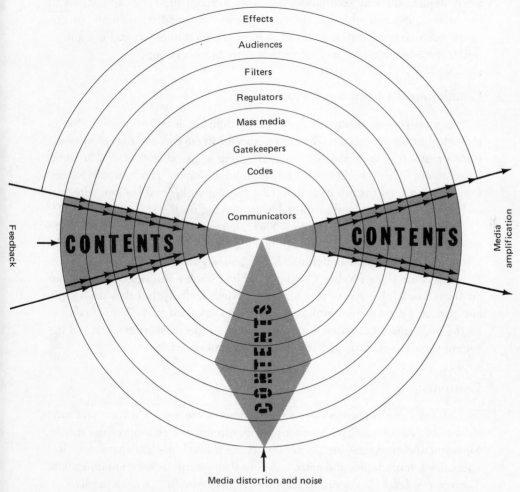

FIGURE 2.9. *The HUB Model of Mass Communication*

of concentric circles, describing communication as a series of actions and reactions.

The HUB model (figure 2.9) pictures communication as a process similar to the series of actions that take place when one drops a pebble into a pool. The pebble causes ripples that expand outward until they reach the shore and then bounce back toward the center. The content of communication (an idea or an event) is like a pebble dropped into the pool of human affairs. Many factors affect that message as it ripples out to its audience and bounces back. Those factors are the components of the total process.

The HUB model is formed of concentric circles because this more accurately depicts the way communication flows through the various elements in the process and resembles the physical process of sound conduction. In this model mass communication is simply a form of communication and not a mysterious process unknown and uncontrolled by human beings.

Conglomerate Communicators

In mass communication it is extremely difficult, if not impossible, for an individual to be the sender. The communicator in "mass comm" is a conglomerate or group of individuals each performing a specialized task. The communicator of "The Tonight Show Starring Johnny Carson" is not simply Johnny Carson but a total organization involving the network, local station, director, and technical staff, as well as the talent appearing on the show.

The communicators of the *New York Times* or the *Cumberland Advocate* are not just the managing editors but include reporters, copyeditors, photographers, and many others. Individuals have dominated and have become symbols for a television show (Walter Cronkite), a film (Stanley Kubrick), a newspaper (William Randolph Hearst), or a magazine (Hugh Hefner), but they are simply one part of the total communicator, albeit an important part. Individuals can be the predominant creative force, but a team of specialists is at work and the sum of their talents form the conglomerate communicator.

Content

All mass media serve a variety of functions or are used in a variety of ways by society. These uses and functions are in essence the content of the media. Mass media messages are generally characterized as less personal, less specialized, more rapid, and more transient than interpersonal communication. There are at least six important uses, or kinds of content, of mass media.

News and Information. The mass media are used to provide timely and important facts that have consequences in our daily lives. They survey events in the society and report them to the publics they serve.

Analysis and Interpretation. The mass media also provide us with an evaluation of events, placing them in perspective. In effect, the media can be used to take editorial positions and provide insights beyond the single event itself.

Education and Socialization. The mass media are used to perform educational functions such as socialization, general education, and classroom instruction. The media can serve to reinforce, modify, and replace the cultural heritage of the parent society.

Persuasion and Public Relations. The mass media serve as instruments of propaganda and public persuasion. Government, business corporations, pressure groups, and individuals seek to establish or improve relationships through mass media.

Sales and Advertising. The mass media are used in the marketing and distribution processes of our economic system. Advertising informs the public about new products, convinces them of their value, and persuades them to buy.

Entertainment and Art. The mass media help people relax during their leisure time. This escapist use of media is an overlay function, which means that media entertain as they inform, analyze, persuade, educate, and sell. Entertainment is the popular art of our time, but the media also contribute to the bettering of our cultural heritage through artistic achievement.

Codes

Mass communication has modified and expanded the codes (or languages and symbol systems) used in communication. For example, in the motion picture, new visual symbol systems often replace verbal language. Camera angles, freeze frames, and editing broaden rather than limit film's communicative capacities. As Edmund Carpenter has stated:

> The new mass media—film, radio, TV—are new languages, their grammars as yet unknown. Each codifies reality differently; each conceals a unique metaphysics. Linguists tell us it's possible to say anything in any

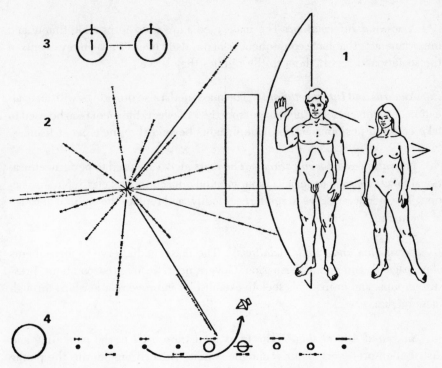

FIGURE 2.10. *The Plaque on Board the Pioneer 10 Spacecraft*
1. A drawing of the life forms who send the spacecraft message with the male's hand raised in greeting.
2. A sketch of our sun radiating pulsars or sources of cosmic radio energy.
3. The hydrogen atom which can be used as a universal clock.
4. A diagram of our solar system with the path of Pioneer 10 indicated.

language if you use enough words or images, but there's rarely time; the natural course is for a culture to exploit its media biases.[2]

Slow motion, split screen, and instant replays have resulted in new ways of looking at athletic events on television. We no longer need to wonder "How did he manage to make that catch?" or "I wish I could see that one again!" We are given the opportunity to recapture the event from several different camera angles.

Variations in typography and design of the printed page can affect the way we view information on the page. These variations become part of the code of

[2]Edmund Carpenter, "The New Language," in *Languages of the Mass Media*, ed. Irving and Harriet Deer (Boston: D. C. Heath, 1965), p. 1.

the communication. Thus new symbols may result in new ways of looking at events and can modify meaning.

An interesting problem was faced in the launch of the Pioneer 10 spacecraft in 1972. It was to be the first earthcraft to leave our solar system. A message plaque on board was coded using a variety of symbols (figure 2.10). The code used assumed that an intelligent life form existed that would have enough of a universally shared frame of reference to decode the message. It was code designed for inter-being communication. It was a "new" code just as the mass media are new codes.

Gatekeepers

Gatekeepers are individuals within the media, such as wire-service editors, TV network continuity personnel, or theater owners, who make decisions about what is communicated, and how. They are not usually originators of content but function as creative evaluators more often than censors. In other words, gatekeepers can be positive forces creating as well as eliminating content. They can delete, insert, emphasize or deemphasize messages in the mass media.

Mass Media

Mass communication *always* requires a mass medium; *without* a mass medium, mass communication can *never* occur. This mass medium is not simply a mechanical device for sending messages—a printing press, paper, transmitter, camera, or projector. By mass medium we mean a total system or institution—newspapers, magazines, books, radio, television, motion pictures, and the phonograph—utilizing these mechanical devices for transmission. Three mass media characteristics—velocity, complex technology, and amplitude—alter and modify the process.

Mass media sometimes send messages with such *velocity* that the measure of their speed becomes meaningless. It would almost be more meaningful to speak of instantaneousness, both in transmission and content. A television signal can be sent around the world in less than a second. While not all mass media are that fast, notably motion pictures and the print media, all mass media emphasize timely content. Thus speed directly affects the message.

A second characteristic of mass media is *complex technology*. The mass media use complicated hardware such as transmitters, printing presses, microphones, and motion-picture cameras. A technically complex medium affects the sender, the message, and the audience. Complex technology creates mass audiences. It separates communicators from audience. The conglomerate communicator rarely interacts with the audience since feedback is so difficult to achieve. Many communicators accustomed to live audiences find it difficult to act, speak, or sing before a microphone or camera because they depend upon feedback for effective performance.

The complex technology of media requires *amplitude*. The media need vast numbers of machines to produce, distribute, and exhibit their products. Great sums of money must be spent in providing a structure for the production, distribution, and exhibition of the product. One obvious effect of this size is the alteration of the communicator from a single person into a complex institution.

Regulators

The regulators of the mass media, such as courts, government commissions, consumers, professional organizations, and public pressure groups, are external in the sense that they function outside the media institution. Their regulation consists of laws, rules, restrictions, and informal pressures that control both the content and structure of the media. Regulators of the mass media have the ability to close down a theater, delete content, and revoke TV or radio licenses. Although these powers are not often overtly used, regulators have considerable impact on decisions of the media because no one wants to incur the "wrath of regulators."

Filters

Filters are the frames of reference through which audiences receive messages. In effect, filters are the eyeglasses through which we view the world. Four types of filters affect an individual's ability to handle content:

Informational. Does the audience understand the symbols or codes being used? When a black man raps about "Mr. Charlie," does an *ofay* have the necessary data to understand that he is talking about white people? In other words, does the receiver have the same set of symbols in his head as does the sender?

Physical. If the room is too hot, or the receiver is "running a fever," or the projector bulb is too dim, or the chair is uncomfortable, those physical conditions can affect the message.

Psychological. Is the audience member emotionally committed on that issue? A woman who has been sexually assaulted will respond differently to a television program on rape than a woman who has not had the same experience and therefore has a different psychological set. A man who has been divorced

"GENTLEMEN OF THE PRESS! I SUPPOSE YOU'RE ALL WONDERING WHY I'VE ASKED YOU HERE TODAY!!"

will respond differently to a magazine article on "ingredients for a successful marriage" than a man who is married or a man who has never been married.

Audiences

Audiences have always fascinated sociologists and are the most studied component of the mass communication process. Charles Wright considers the nature of the audience to be crucial: "Mass communication is directed toward a relatively large, heterogeneous, and anonymous audience."[3] A British sociologist, Denis McQuail, finds that "the relationship between communicator and audience is impersonal."[4] In effect, mass media audiences are isolated and fluid. They normally cannot be defined according to the standard parameters of time and space. It is important to emphasize that such negative terms as the "masses" or the "mass audience" are not really applicable. All of us remain individual human beings while being audience members.

[3]Charles R. Wright, *Mass Communication: A Sociological Perspective* (New York: Random House, 1975), p. 5.
[4]Denis McQuail, *Towards a Sociology of Mass Communication* (London: Collier-Macmillan, 1969), p. 9.

Feedback, Noise, and Amplification

Feedback is the communicated response of the audience to a message. In an interpersonal-communication situation, *feedback* is immediate. The sender and the receiver constantly change roles using feedback as a means of interaction. A speaker sees his audience and its feedback in a variety of forms: people sleeping, applauding, booing, or walking away. Feedback enables the communicator to alter his message.

In mass communication, feedback is delayed and diffused. TV ratings are a form of feedback, but even with ratings, a television-program producer has no way of knowing if he lost his audience halfway through the program. He must wait for the ratings, at least overnight for ratings reports. Thus, lack of speed in mass communication feedback has distinct implications for mass communicators.

Feedback in mass communication is often expressed quantitatively: a rating of 15 (which means 15 percent of the more than 72 million U.S. television homes), or circulation figures of 10 million, or box-office receipts of $5 million. Some letters are written to editors and performers, but these are generally few in number and carry less weight than audience numbers. A program, periodical, book, or motion picture generally succeeds or fails on the basis of its quantitative feedback.

Mass communication has an increased possibility of *noise*, and noise in the mass communication process can occur at any point, not simply in the medium. Because of its public nature, mass communication allows more interruption on a far broader level than interpersonal communication. Noise can occur in a variety of forms: static on radio or television, a poorly printed newspaper, an out-of-focus motion picture. When the consuming process is in the home, interference from noise is greatly increased and intensified. Competing stimuli from other media, the family, and the outside environment can and do interfere with message reception.

Message *amplification* is also increased by the mass media. Television amplifies a speech by President Carter before a small group of people in Georgia. It is amplified physically because it is broadcast into millions of homes. It is also amplified psychologically because anything on which the media focus attention becomes news.

Effects

The study of the impact of the mass communication process on our lives is a topic of ever-growing importance. The key in this area is that the mass media do not function in isolation; they are a part of the total society.

Historically, the media have played an important political role in our society. "Freedom of the press"remains a central issue. The whole "Watergate" phenomenon was a media event because the media participated in the political events that led to President Nixon's resignation. The media did have an impact on those events, and the "press" significantly affected the process by which the Chief Executive was toppled.

Culturally, the mass media are changing our society. The civil rights and women's movements of the past twenty years are media phenomena that have had a great impact on the entire society.

Behaviorally, the mass media are being studied to determine the individual effects that violence, pornography, and other media content are having on children and adults. We know there are effects but are having difficulty measuring them.

The effects of mass communication are real, but our ability to study them has frankly not kept pace with other aspects of the process. Effects may well be the central issue in the future of mass communication.

These, then are the component parts of mass communication when we view it as a process. The HUB model pictures communicators, codes, gatekeepers, media, regulators, filters, audiences, and effects as concentric circles through which the content (or the message) must pass. Feedback is the response that comes back to the communicator, while noise and amplification can both affect the message and feedback as they travel through these steps in the process.

The remainder of part 1 describes other aspects of the process: the way media systems develop and the economics of media systems. In part 2 we focus on the various component parts of the process—communicators, codes, gatekeepers, media, regulators, filters, audiences, feedback, amplification, and noise. Part 3 narrows our focus to the media themselves—books, newspapers, magazines, radio, television, motion pictures, sound recordings, and other media. In part 4 we discuss the content of the media or the uses to which mass media are put—news, analysis, persuasion, education, advertising, and entertainment. And part 5 analyzes both the behavioral and the social impact of the media, and suggests avenues for future research by students of the mass media.

A young boy scuffles down a dusty road in East Africa as his Japanese-made transistor radio blares out the latest American rock 'n' roll. A middle-aged man in a South America "banana republic" picks up a copy of one of the few newspapers that survive the strict censorship of the current junta to read about the earthquake that has ravaged his native Rumania. A matron in Tokyo rocks back and forth in pleasure at the antics of a dubbed-in Lucille Ball. An erudite young man intones the words of a little-known English poet to a minuscule "high culture audience" of the BBC's Third Programme. An old-line Russian bureaucrat of the Moscow Central Television station worries about the problems in the program-distribution pattern he is responsible for executing. All these people are using national media to interact with the world at large. Although the mass media experience is an international phenomenon, each nation-state has evolved its own mass communication system based on unique conditions as well as common problems. The uses made of mass media are based in part on the type of media institutions that have evolved, and in order to understand fully the merits and faults of the American system, it is necessary to examine mass communication media in other nations as well.

3 Philosophies of Mass Communication

One method used to describe, analyze, and compare media systems was outlined in the mid-1950s by Frederick Siebert, Theodore Peterson, and Wil-

The Development of Media Systems

bur Schramm in their book, *Four Theories of the Press*. These four theories for characterizing the press are (1) the authoritarian theory; (2) the Soviet-Communist theory; (3) the libertarian theory; and (4) the social-responsibility theory. Every nation's press (all mass media institutions) could then be analyzed and assigned to a given category.

The authoritarian theory of the press emerged in Europe during the sixteenth century. This media philosophy is based on the political assumption that absolute power should rest in the hands of a monarch, military dictator, or an elite, a political idea as old as humankind. Direct criticism of the government by the press is forbidden under this concept because media are key instruments of the state and are used to voice its policies. A limited group controls all media, operating by permission of the state, which directly licenses, supervises, or censors media content. Ownership is normally in the hands of the government or those private citizens whose support of the regime is unquestioned. The fascist states, especially Nazi Germany, are modern examples of this media philosophy.

The Soviet-Communist theory of the press developed from application of Marxist-Leninist-Stalinist philosophy to mass communication in the twentieth century. The major thrust of the press operating under this theory is to implement long-range political, social, and economic policies of the government and support current party decisions. The media are a political arm of the state and are directed by high-ranking, orthodox party members. The press never criticizes a specific goal, although it may discuss means used to reach it. The media are owned by the state. Party control of the media presumably ensures that public interests will be served and that the masses will not be exploited. Party dissidents, as well as those who do not belong to the party, are denied access to the media. The Soviet Union operates the prototype system after which most Communist states pattern their press institutions.

The libertarian theory of the press grew out of the writings of rational-humanitarian philosophers such as John Stuart Mill, John Milton, and John Locke in England. According to this theory, media serve as watchdogs *on* the government and at the same time search for truth. Under this system media functions become important to political action. Limited control is generally exercised by the state through the judicial system, which steps in only when it can be demonstrated that a given book, newspaper, film, or broadcast is harmful to the people (obscenity, defamation of character, sedition, and so on). In theory the media are available to anyone with the financial and technical resources to operate them and are privately owned. Sweden, England, and the United States are examples of this philosophy in action.

The social-responsibility theory of the press, which began to emerge in the

United States after World War II, has as its main thrust the idea that freedom of the press carries with it a responsibility to the society that nurtures it. In essence, this philosophy is a refinement of the libertarian theory and seeks to provide access to the media for every sector of society, not only to those who can afford it. Theoretically, media are controlled by community action, but everyone, including unpopular minorities, has an equal opportunity to express views when vital social issues are involved. The media are privately owned and operated for a profit, but the press must function for the general welfare. If a medium fails to operate in a socially responsible fashion, someone (media industry or government) must correct that course of action. Broadcast operations in the United States exemplify this theory in part.

The four theories of the press serve as a starting point for the analysis of media systems; however, some countries fail to fit neatly into any of the four groupings. For example, Spain and Portugal seem to be shifting away from their traditional authoritarian systems of control. In terms of the individual media, print media in the English-speaking democracies tend to reflect the libertarian theory, whereas broadcast media in most of these countries reflect the social-responsibility philosophy. Censorship of the press, be it under Hitler, Stalin, or Idi Amin Dada, is not significantly different whether it is called totalitarian or communist. In fact, considerable repressive control of the media is exercised in some democracies during periods of civil strife or under wartime conditions. In other words, there are too many deviant national media systems to rely exclusively on the "four theories" approach to media systems analysis.

The Political Continuum

Some individuals prefer to analyze media systems according to a political continuum in which the overriding influence on the development of media is the amount of political control exercised by the state. At one end of the political continuum there is absolute freedom for media, and at the other end there is absolute control.

The Political Continuum

ABSOLUTE   ABSOLUTE
FREEDOM   CONTROL

Each nation is placed on the continuum at the point that describes the limits imposed by the state on its media. Thus the continuum is a comparative device that assesses the relative freedom of various countries' media systems.

This method of analysis sometimes works well when we compare nations with significantly different political systems. Nevertheless, if we compare many of the outspoken films of Czechoslovakia with some of the "new wave" films of France in the 1960s, we would consider France (a democracy) and Czechoslovakia (a communist dictatorship) to be equally free of government restriction. In other words, the amount and type of actual political control may not be reflected in the kinds of media content produced because more than political considerations affect a nation's media institutions.

Models of Media Systems

Wilbur Schramm has developed a model of the structure and function of mass media based on principles of management or organizational components (figure 3.1). Schramm points out key factors that affect media that can be applied to any nation's mass communication system. This model indicates that political control, sources of content, organizational grouping, and economic support affect the mass media and in turn the content produced for audience consumption.

The mass media have also been examined as social systems by Melvin DeFleur and Sandra Ball-Rokeach. They have developed a model (figure 3.2) into which any mass medium can be placed. This model visualizes a political, economic, and production system that distributes content to three levels of audience taste (highbrow, middlebrow, or lowbrow). The process as depicted is influenced by government agencies, media associations, advertising groups, and research teams, who are interested in economic and cultural decisions of

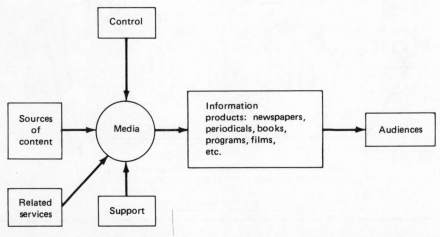

FIGURE 3.1. *A Diagrammatic View of the Structure and Function of the Mass Media*

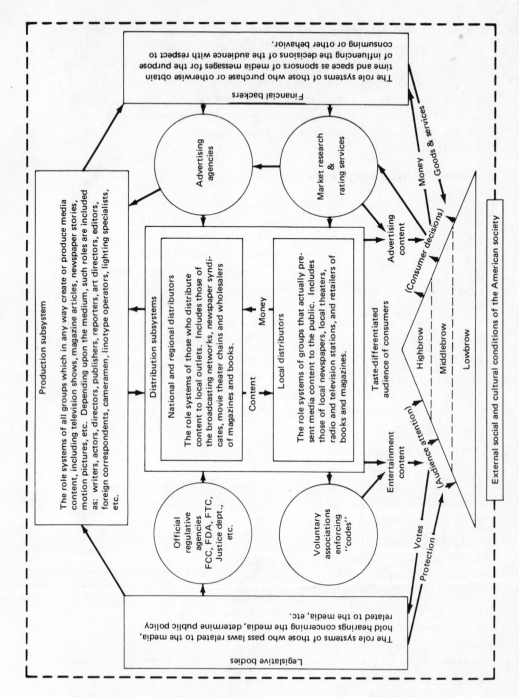

FIGURE 3.2. *Schematic Representation of the Mass Media as a Social System*

the consumer-audience. The system is viewed as being inside "the social and cultural conditions of American society."

Both the Schramm model and the DeFleur/Ball-Rokeach model add important perspectives to any analysis of mass communication systems.

The Media Systems Paradigm

The relationship between media and societies is reciprocal: a country creates a national media system, and this media system in turn modifies that society. Since every nation is different and media systems vary from nation to nation, the interaction between a given country and its media is unique. Because this relationship is not static, media and societies constantly change each other. For example, the deaths of Mao Tse-tung and Chou En-lai were political events of significance. In the People's Republic of China the media and society interacted so that the nation, the people, and the media system were all bound to be "massaged." Consequently, what may have been a correct observation a short time ago may no longer be accurate.

For our purposes, then, it seems advisable to analyze every national media system as a distinct entity. In order to perform this analysis, we must develop a standard model or paradigm as the basis for comparison. The Media Systems Paradigm (figure 3.3) is designed to reflect the interplay between media and societies as well as to help describe similarities and dissimilarities in national media systems. The Media Systems Paradigm is based on the theory that in every country, special *factors* or social forces interact in unique ways: (a) to create a national *media system* that is used (b) to perform a variety of *functions* (c) which eventually *participate in reshaping* that society. This paradigm is action-oriented (dynamic vs. static) to emphasize the changing nature and interaction of media and societies.

Six social factors or forces interact in the development of a media system: (1) physical and geographical characteristics, (2) technological competencies, (3) cultural traits, (4) economic conditions, (5) political philosophies, (6) media qualities. The interaction of these six factors, rather than their independent action, is crucial in media systems' evolution.

Within every nation's media system there is a variety of individual media institutions. Seven major media merit special consideration: (1) three print media—the book, the newspaper, and the magazine; and (2) four electronic media—radio, television, the motion picture, and sound recording.

These media institutions and others are used to perform six basic functions: (1) news and information, (2) analysis and interpretation, (3) education and socialization, (4) persuasion and public relations, (5) sales and advertising, (6) entertainment and art.

As these functions are performed, the media change the societies that created them. The extent and kinds of effect the media have on us are debatable, but it is commonly agreed that the media do participate in modifying our nation and every other industrial society of the world.

Factors That Influence the Development of Media Systems

Before examining each of the six social forces that affect media development as separate entities, it is important to reemphasize that these factors

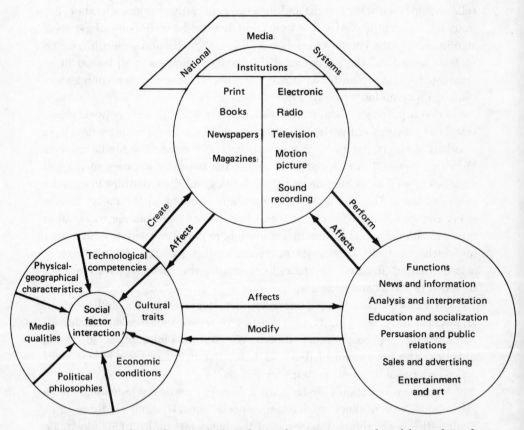

FIGURE 3.3. *The Media Systems Paradigm. This action-oriented model visualizes the theory that in every country social factors interact in unique ways to create a national media system to perform a variety of functions which eventually participate in reshaping that society.*

seldom operate independently. It is their interaction that stimulates significant differences in media systems. All six are influential to varying degrees in different situations. In fact, it is impractical to designate one factor as the only variable influencing any one aspect of a given media system.

Physical-Geographical Characteristics. A country's climate, geography, and other physical characteristics affect the development of its media system, just as they alter population patterns and economic development. For example, many nations have developed frequency modulation (FM) rather than amplitude modulation (AM) radio because the technical characteristics of the FM signal are better suited to mountainous regions. Film stock tends to deteriorate more rapidly in the tropics than in temperate zones; nations located in tropical areas must take this into consideration when setting up film production, distribution, and exhibition facilities. In most regions of the United States winters are less hospitable than summers for outdoor activity. For this reason, audiences available for television viewing in warmer months are decidedly smaller than in colder months. Climate, audience size, and TV economics have interacted to require the use of reruns or low-cost replacements during the summer quarter of the television year.

Technological Competencies. In order for a mass communication system to evolve in a nation, four technological competencies are needed. First, a society must have a basic scientific capability, as both pure and applied research are necessary to develop media. Early research in electricity was not aimed at creating television, just as initial experiments to prove that "for every action there is an equal and opposite reaction" were not designed to send men to the moon. But the results of that research were essential to its application. This ability to apply research findings to improve mass communication is a critical technological competence for media development.

Second, a nation needs raw materials to develop mass media or the economic resources to obtain them. In order to have books, magazines, and newspapers, you must have paper, ink, and the machinery to print pages. Paper requires suitable trees, rice, rags, or another source of fibrous material that can be turned into pulp. Ink requires acids, tints, resins, oils, drying agents, and other chemical components. Machines to produce print media need lead for type, aluminum for offset plates, various steels for presses, rubber for belts and rollers, and lubrication oils to keep the presses rolling. Electronic media make similar demands on a nation's natural resources.

Third, a country must have the industrial capability to mass-produce media products or the money to buy these finished goods. Mass communication systems cannot operate unless they have sophisticated industrial complexes to support them. A nation must have vast quantities of transistors, cameras, linotype machines, film stocks, presses, TV sets, inks, vacuum tubes, and other components if its media are to function optimally.

Fourth, trained personnel are needed who can make these complex systems function. A medium cannot function satisfactorily without a technical staff to operate the equipment, a production staff to create content, and a managerial staff to handle the day-to-day operations of the system. This process requires an ongoing program to recruit and train new personnel.

Cultural Traits.　Every society has unique ways of doing things, of evaluating what is important, and of modifying behavior. There are social laws, taboos, norms, mores, values, and attitudes. All these cultural traits and social characteristics are important in the development of media systems.

In Czechoslovakia two national groups, the Czechs and the Slovaks, each have a distinct language. Films are made in each of the two national languages to reflect the differences in these two cultures. In Switzerland the government recognizes four national languages. Broadcasts are provided in German, French, Italian, and Romansch.

Danish cultural values allow pornographic material to appear in some media. Films, books, and magazines that are banned as obscene in most countries are openly available in Denmark. In the United States there is considera-

"DISGUSTING!"　"OBSCENE!"　"WITHOUT REDEEMING SOCIAL VALUE!"

ble disagreement on the sexual content of the mass media. Recent Supreme Court decisions have not always followed a consistent pattern, and the various media voices have not been unanimous in their thinking. The civil rights and women's movements have changed American cultural attitudes tremendously; the mass media as well as business and industry are hiring minorities and women in senior positions throughout their organizations. Her ability as a journalist aside, Barbara Walters' position with ABC News can be cited as a reflection of this cultural change.

A variety of cultural or social factors deeply influences media development; these include urbanization, population, specialization, sexual taboos, religion, race relations, labor organizations, youth culture, and education. Every mass society is a mixture of stability and change—the resulting conflict involves and affects the development of media systems.

Economic Conditions. The physical devices, content, and personnel that make mass communication systems possible cost vast sums. A country's or an individual's attitude toward a given medium can in part be assessed by the economic commitment made to that medium. The nation's economic philosophy, structure, and conditions determine in great measure the ways and the extent to which media are funded. Capitalist countries are more likely to allow the media to be profit-oriented, while communist nations are less likely to have advertising in their media.

The economic condition of a state also determines how the audience gains access to media. Are television sets purchased by individual viewers or does the state provide communal receivers for group use? If a family buys a receiver, its members tend to exercise somewhat more control over how, when, and where their viewing takes place than those in a communal audience. This makes communal viewing decidedly different from family or individual viewing.

In the United States campus newspapers that are distributed free of charge have wider circulation than those that students must purchase. Nevertheless, the student press that supports itself is less likely to bend to administrative pressure when sensitive issues arise.

One thing is certain: a complex, sophisticated media system cannot thrive in economically impoverished nations. A poor country faced with starving people can only support media that help alleviate immediate problems. In most modern states media survive because mass communication is a very valuable asset to the complete economic process.

Political Philosophies. A country's political structure and attitudes influence the development of a media system. The amount and kinds of control over mass communication are determined by the nature and structure of the government in power. Political forces establish the laws under which media institutions must operate. Media regulations may be repressive or permissive depending on the political atmosphere of a particular society.

In the People's Republic of China the media system is a political arm of the state used to implement party policy. The system is restricted to party officials in good standing—they alone have access to the media. All mass communication is directly supervised by government officials who are also party members.

During times of severe political stress, such as war, governments tend to exercise greater political control over media systems than in normal times. Both the Arab and Israeli governments exercised censorship over all media content, foreign as well as domestic, during their military confrontations. During the war in South Vietnam, newspapers that disagreed with political policies of the Thieu government were shut down in the name of national security. After the war, that policy continued, but the types of papers that were permitted to publish changed. Those newspapers which were not a part of the "reunification" effort ceased operation when the North Vietnamese and Viet Cong assumed power.

The events of "Watergate" led to a major political struggle, which impacted on and involved the mass media of this country. Significant pressures from a variety of political sources affected the news media during the eclipse of the Nixon administration. The "fairness" tradition of the press was and remained a political force throughout this dark period in American political history.

The degree and kind of political controls vary in each country depending on that nation's political philosophies and goals. This aspect may well be the most potent single factor influencing media development, because political power is often a physical as well as philosophical pressure.

Media Qualities. Technical features, media-use patterns, and overall institutional characteristics affect the development of media systems. For example, development of commercial television radically changed radio and motion-picture institutions. The men who ran radio stations and motion-picture companies had to reevaluate and change their roles in the total U.S. media system. This form of media interaction is constantly reshaping the total media system of the United States and every other nation.

Some media are inherently more expensive to operate than others: television is a more costly medium than radio; high-quality magazines have a higher per-copy production cost than newspapers; it costs less to produce a phonograph record than a motion picture. The unique qualities of each of these media contribute to the per-unit cost, and this cost affects the way the medium is used and its place in the overall system.

To illustrate: Print media can be highly effective only in literate societies; electronic media require no more than a speaking knowledge of a given language. However, print media are more portable and do not require high-cost playback equipment. Every medium has a different speed at which it can produce and distribute its messages. Radio, television, and newspapers have the fastest turnaround times, and the speed of these three media is very important in disseminating news.

The Media System

By definition, a system is an arrangement of things, events, and people in an organized way. Media systems, then, are organized or prearranged methods of mass communication. For example, radio transmitters and receivers are mechanical devices around which the radio medium has been organized. A medium (radio) is more than a physical device (a radio receiver); it is an institution. When a group of these institutions (publishing and broadcasting) interact with a society, they create a media system.

The media system of the United States is divided into two classes: (1) print media, which include the book, newspaper, magazine, and other publishing industries; and (2) electronic media, which include radio and television broadcasting, the recording industry, and the motion-picture industry. Chapter 8 explores the complex nature of media institutions, and chapters 13–20 explore each of the seven media in detail.

Uses of the Media

Every medium is used in a variety of ways by the society in which it evolves. These functions of mass media are the content of mass communication. Because our society uses mass media to both reinforce and change itself, a key thrust of any evaluation of mass communication must be the following six functions: (1) news and information (chapter 21); (2) analysis and interpretation (chapter 22); (3) education and socialization (chapter 23); (4) persuasion and public relations (chapter 24); (5) sales and advertising (chapter 25); (6) entertainment and art (chapter 26).

External Media Systems Impact

Forces within a country affect its media systems, but other nations' media systems also have their impact. Marshall McLuhan speaks of a "global village" whose size has been overcome by the speed of "electric" media and their ability to penetrate national boundaries. An example would be the cold war "jamming" of radio signals. Today, the cultural manipulation by large industrialized states of smaller industrial states and Third World cultures is the major concern.

Figure 3.4 visualizes the concern of many governments that external media encourage a lessening of traditional beliefs and substitute a value system that may be unsuitable for their societies. The foreign content (especially movies and television) that is imported has considerable impact on the goals and aspirations of the people. For example, the significant postwar change in Japan was in part media-enhanced. Japan was "Westernized" by foreign media content. The Middle East is another battleground for competing media cultures and ideologies.

People desire what they observe individuals in other cultures enjoying; e.g., the urban explosion in Latin America was stimulated by the media reinforcing "urban values." The amount of foreign content in local media is bound to have an impact on the society and its peoples' attitudes about the "old" culture. But the parent society cannot always cope with externally created aspirations. And "new" cultures may not necessarily be appropriate changes for a society.

People want what they see. The media carry an inherent status conferral that gives value to the contents displayed. For example, in the United States today there is concern over the amount of "imported theater" on public television. Is American theater dead? The amount of British theater on American

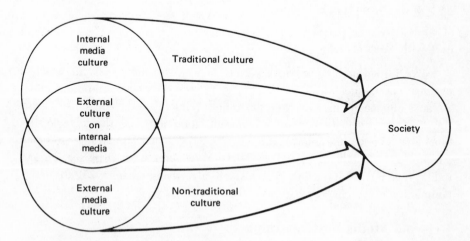

FIGURE 3.4. *Model of Cultural Impact of Mass Communication on Small Industrial States and Third World Nations*

screens gives the impression that England's television is culturally "better" than America's. This creates an uneasy feeling among some critics of public television regardless of whether they live "upstairs or downstairs."

Outside content on inside systems is both functional and dysfunctional depending on the amount and uses to which it is put and the perceptions and changes it may create in a society.

Media Systems Analysis

The Media Systems Paradigm forms the basis for a brief analysis of national media systems in Guatemala, the Netherlands, and the Union of Soviet Socialist Republics. These three nations were selected because they provide distinct patterns of development. Each media system is unique and is intended to provide a general basis for comparison with the United States.[1]

Guatemala

Factors That Influence Development.   Guatemala, with an area of 42,000 square miles, is the most northern and most populous (6 million) Central American nation. It has a tropical climate along its coastline and in the lowlands; but the population is concentrated in the highlands, where the climate ranges from subtropical to temperate. With a population of 700,000, Guatemala City is the nation's only urban area and its capital. Most of the people (52.5 percent) are involved in agriculture. Service and manufacturing industries are of less importance than land use. Technology is not advanced and nearly all imported. Severe earthquakes in 1976 caused heavy loss of life and severely retarded industrial development.

Economically, Guatemala is underdeveloped ($3.25 billion GNP). Large investments by foreign entities in national companies exploit the country's considerable natural resources. The per capita income is $600 per year, and the nation consistently imports more than it exports. Less than 600 miles of railroads and 1,600 miles of paved roads limit transportation and further restrict economic growth.

There are two major ethnic groups in Guatemala: Indians (41.4 percent) and Latinos, or mixed bloods (58.6 percent). Spanish is the official language, but over 40 percent of the population speaks Quiché or another of the twenty-

[1]This section relies on statistics collected by the Central Intelligence Agency and published semiannually in *National Basic Intelligence Factbook* (Washington, D.C.: Government Printing Office, 1976) and on Unesco's *World Communications*, 1975.

odd Indian dialects. The educational system is inadequate; only 30 percent of the population is literate.

Politically, Guatemala has traditionally been an unstable republic dominated by the military. The current constitution went into effect in 1966 and has been plagued by guerrilla activities from both rightists and leftists, although the Communist party is outlawed. Sufferage is compulsory for literates and optional for illiterates over eighteen; five major parties vie for public support. The 1974 elections saw a renewal of violence and repression, and the opposition press came under considerable pressure after its allegations of voting fraud. What political stability does exist depends in considerable degree on military action and foreign aid.

The Media System. Guatemala has eight daily newspapers—seven in Guatemala City (one is in English, published for tourists) and one in Quetzaltenango—with a combined national circulation of less than 150,000, or 27 copies per 1,000. The newspapers offer only a limited spectrum of political opinion but are not directly controlled by the government. Twenty-eight papers are printed two or three times each week, and there are 10 weeklies, but there is no national news service. Modern magazines, which require extensive capital and technological skills, are nonexistent, but 86 periodicals are published by government agencies, professional, industrial, and commercial associations, and university faculties. Approximately 300 book titles are published in Spanish each year, but they have small sales. The severe transportation problems and high illiteracy limit the effectiveness of all print media.

Lack of money, poor transportation facilities, and electric-power shortages have hindered the growth of the electronic media. In Guatemala there are 57,000 telephones, 360,000 radios, and 110,000 TV receivers. Three commercial television stations operate in Guatemala City: Radio-Television Guatemala (12 hours per day), Tele Once (6 hours per day), and Televicentro (6 hours per day). Radio-Television Guatemala also has a relay installation in Quetzaltenango that is connected with the Mexican microwave network. Less than 10 percent of Guatemala's programming, mainly news and public-affairs programs, is of local origin; more than half of it comes from the United States. In reality, Guatemala has little control over the content of TV except in selecting programs to import.

Radio, because it is a less expensive medium, is more highly developed. Of the 75 radio stations, six are government-owned and operated. These stations offer a full range of locally produced content. Five noncommercial stations, run by cultural and religious organizations, broadcast in Spanish and in Indian dialects and offer educational and adult literacy content as well as religious programs. Half the commercial stations are in Guatemala City and are primarily entertainment systems supported in part by a tax on receivers.

A film-production industry has just begun in Guatemala. There are 105 movie theaters, with an average seating capacity of less than 75 persons. The average Guatemalan attends a movie less than once a year. All 35-mm features shown in the country are imported primarily from the United States, Britain, France, Germany, Spain, and Mexico. The recording industry is also in its infancy, so most recorded music is imported.

Uses of the Media. Who is being served by media institutions in Guatemala? One thing is certain: the Indian population is not, because of a high illiteracy rate and the fact that most Indians reside in remote rural areas. The media do, however, serve the wealthy, European, and Latino groups in the capital and the larger towns. News media do provide the urban population with a restricted supply of information but fail to meet the information needs of most citizens outside Guatemala City. With regard to the cultural uses of the media, the local culture is not being reinforced because so much of the media's content is imported. There seems to be little attempt in the print media—and only a beginning being made in the electronic media—to correct the educational deficiencies of the poor, rural citizens. Some political control of the media is exercised by the Ministry of Communication and Public Works; but by law, radio and television may not be used for political purposes, although most media are used to persuade the populace to support the current regime. Advertising is permitted, but the severe poverty of most citizens restricts its effectiveness. Those without money and power in Guatemala have no access to the media.

The Netherlands

Factors That Influence Development. The Kingdom of the Netherlands is a small (13,000 square miles), densely populated (14,000,000) nation with 70 percent of its land mass under cultivation and 80 percent of its population in urban areas. It is a modern, heavily industrialized trading country with 30 percent of its labor force involved in manufacturing. Jobs in services, commerce, agriculture, construction, and transportation and communication follow in that order. The unemployment rate is around 5 percent.

Economically, the Netherlands has a very high standard of living ($5,279 per capita income), a positive balance of trade, and a GNP of $72 billion. There are over 1,800 miles of railroads, 63,000 miles of paved roads, and almost 4,000 miles of navigable waterways. The oil shortage has had a negative impact on the Netherlands, as it has on all the small industrial states of Europe. Nevertheless, it is still one of the most stable trading nations in the world.

Culturally, the population is 99 percent Dutch; a small but growing Indonesian population has experienced some strain in adapting to the dominant culture, and a militant faction of Moluccans within that minority has committed internationally publicized acts of terrorism. Established religious groups play an important role in the country with a division of 41 percent Protestant, 40 percent Roman Catholic, and 19 percent unaligned. The national language is Dutch, but a large percentage of the population is multilingual. Literacy is above 98 percent, and the Dutch educational system is one of the strongest in Europe.

The political system reflects an urban society: it is democratic, pluralistic, and attempts to accommodate a wide range of ideologies. Of the fifteen political parties active in recent elections, no party received more than 27 percent of the vote. There are a number of strong political pressure groups: unions, religious groups, trade associations, and multinational corporations. The 1976 Lockheed scandal led to the resignation of Prince Bernhard, Queen Juliana's husband, from military and business posts and has affected the executive branch. The constitution of 1815 remains in effect.

The Media System.   Because of the almost total literacy of the population, the Dutch are strongly print-oriented. With numerous urban areas, an excellent transportation system, and a citizenry with a high standard of living, print media have flourished. Newspapers can be divided into three classes: (1) papers allied with a particular religious or political group and nationally distributed; (2) provincial newspapers operating in areas larger than a single community, but which do not have significant national circulation; (3) local newspapers, which are found in Dutch cities and towns. Amsterdam and Rotterdam each have 10 daily newspapers, and 53 other Dutch cities have at least one daily paper. Most papers express the views of a given political faction. Of the eight papers with nationwide readership, two have circulation in excess of 300,000. There are a total of 95 dailies and 138 nondailies, or over 300 copies per 1,000 people for dailies and 79 per 1,000 for nondailies. Nearly all Dutch papers devote a high proportion of their space to national and international events. The press is capitalistic, sober in tone, nonsensational, family-oriented, and politically committed. A staff of 700 runs the Dutch national news agency, Algemeen Nederlands Persbureau (ANP), which is cooperatively owned and controlled by a group of newspapers of various persuasions. A smaller Catholic news agency,

Katholik Nederlands Persbureau (KNP), has a branch in Rome as well as The Hague, and is run by Catholic daily papers. Nearly every family subscribes to at least one newspaper, and only 5 percent of all newspaper purchases comes from street sales.

The magazine industry is well run and economically sound but does not have the same mass appeal found in the United States. Magazines, as well as newspapers, actively solicit advertising. There are four major types of magazines in Holland, each seeking out specialized audiences: (1) radio-TV magazines, which are published by the various broadcast-program services and have a combined circulation of almost 3 million; (2) women's magazines, with a combined circulation of more than 3 million; (3) family magazines, which are published by religious and cultural groups and serve more than 1 million homes; (4) opinion magazines, which are politically oriented and distribute over 300,000 copies per issue. The Dutch magazine industry publishes over 15 million copies of its 421 magazines annually.

The print-oriented Dutch publish more than 10.5 million copies of books each year, and the publishing business is one of the soundest industries in the economy.

The broadcast system of the Netherlands is unique and mirrors the pluralism of the society. Most programs are produced by private organizations and reflect the specific political or religious viewpoints of that group. The broadcasting law of 1967 created an open system that allows all major social and political groups access to broadcast time if they have an initial enrollment of 15,000 subscribers. However, the number of subscribers must reach 100,000 at the end of two years if the group hopes to continue. They must demonstrate the ability to meet community needs, must provide a wide range of program content, and must not operate for profit. These broadcasting associations must affiliate with the Dutch broadcast foundation, Nederlandse Omroep Stichting (NOS), which includes the Nederlands Televisie Stichting (NTS) and Nederlands Radio Unie (NRU). There are seven broadcasting groups in NOS.

Broadcasting operates under the Ministry of Cultural Recreation and Social Work, but no person or group has censorship power. The programmers are required by law, however, to avoid broadcast material that is seditious, immoral, obscene, or might create public disorder. Currently there are two operational television services (Nederlands I and II) and three national radio services (Hilversum I, II, and III) and a system of regional FM stations that are shared by the Dutch Broadcast Foundation and the programming organizations. There are three sources of income: (1) a tax on 9 million radio and 3.65 million TV receivers, which supports the entire system; (2) revenue from program guides, which is used by individual program producers; (3) advertising revenue, which goes directly to an independent foundation, Stichting Ether Reclame (STER), which produces and sells all commercials. This revenue is used to improve programming and compensate print media for any losses in advertising. The 5 AM, 12 FM, and 13 TV transmitters literally blanket the country with broadcast programming.

The Dutch film industry is small: 41 companies affiliated with the Netherlands Cinema League produce about 75 short and 5 feature films each year. The Dutch government encourages the industry with grants for short films and subsidies for theatrical releases. To ensure a wide range of product, members of the Cinema League are required to show 12 non-American films each year. Roughly 350 films are imported annually, with about a third coming from the United States. There are 321 cinemas, which serve over 25 million moviegoers a year. As in other countries with improving television systems, film attendance is down from levels of 10 to 15 years ago.

Uses of the Media. The overriding concern of all Dutch media institutions is education, both in terms of cultural reinforcement and classroom use. Formal education is a major industry in Holland, with extensive print materials in use. In the mid-1960s the Netherlands began actively producing TV classroom materials in a wide range of subject areas, and the program has succeeded in supplying educational materials to religious as well as non-denominational schools. Radio has long provided a similar service. The media institutions actively function as cultural reinforcers in the home. Nearly 10 percent of all air time is devoted to religious programming. The media actively participate in political activities; political groups across the spectrum use media to influence citizens.

News and editorial standards in all Dutch media are high. Broadcast news is prepared by an independent organization and is responsible to no political or social group. Although print media are allied with special interests, they maintain high standards of fairness and accuracy. Analysis and interpretation provided by broadcast-program groups, newspapers, and magazines reflect the views and opinions of the various factions within this pluralistic society.

Newspapers and magazines have always been involved in the sales function, but advertising was banned from broadcasting until the late 1960s. After the Dutch government closed down offshore "pirate" stations in the North Sea, which sold advertising, businessmen forced acceptance of limited advertising on the national broadcast services.

The strength of the economy and the political and social pluralism have created a mass media system in the Netherlands that serves a wide range of units within the total society. Each major subgroup is able to avail itself of editorial, cultural, political, educational, and entertainment content from a wide range of viewpoints.

The Union of Soviet Socialist Republics

Factors That Influence Development. The Union of Soviet Socialist Republics (USSR) is the largest nation in the world (8,600,000 square miles) and has a population of 260,000,000. It has the complete range of topography and climate from arctic to temperate. The USSR's largest land unit, Siberia, is still very lightly populated, and the highest population centers remain primarily in Old Russia. Less than 10 percent of land is cultivated and only 2.6 percent is used for urban areas. Forests (37.1 percent); pastureland (16.8 percent); and desert, swamp, and wasteland (34.2 percent) dominate the landscape.

Technologically, this nation is a twentieth-century success story. The Soviet Union has moved rapidly to develop a sound scientific base and uses a highly skilled work force to exploit vast natural resources within its huge industrial capability. Roughly one-fourth of the work force is involved in agriculture; the rest work in industry, service, and government. Unemployment figures are not reported in the Soviet Union. The economic condition of the average Soviet citizen has improved significantly in recent years because consumer goods are now major goals of economic five-year plans. Despite agricultural failures, the USSR has been able to import foodstuffs to improve diets. Highly diversified light and heavy industries are moving the Soviet Union toward a favorable balance of trade; over 30 percent of the country's trade is now done with the West. More than 91,000 miles of railroad, a million miles of paved roads, and 90,000 miles of navigable waterways plus 63 major ports have enhanced trading and industrial growth over the past 20 years. Per capita income is about $2,800; GNP is $710 billion with an ever-increasing emphasis on consumer and luxury items.

Culturally, the Soviet Union is diverse. Most of the population is Slavic (74 percent), but the remainder are from 170 other ethnic groups. Approximately 70 percent of the population adheres to the atheist party policy, but substantial Russian Orthodox and Moslem minorities coexist. Segments of the Jewish minority have been trying to emigrate in recent years, with mixed success. Although Russian is the national language, 200 other languages and dialects are used. Literacy now extends to 98 percent of the population. The traditional arts (ballet, music, theater) have been preserved, and newer "political arts"— especially film—have been nurtured.

Politically the USSR is a socialist-communist state made up of 15 union republics, 20 autonomous republics, 6 krays, 120 oblasts, and 8 autonomous oblasts. Its civil law is based on the constitution of 1936 with three branches of government: (1) the executive (Council of Ministers), (2) the judicial (the Supreme Court of USSR), and (3) the legislative (the Supreme Soviet). The Communist party (CPSU) is the only legal political force in the nation and has 15.5 million members. The political structure is vertical and dominated by top-ranking party members and bureaucrats. Political and cultural dissension are not well tolerated, although the image of the Stalinist police state has softened. Despite intense internal pressures on dissidents, a minority of individuals continues to defy imprisonment and deportation. The political facts of life are that the system has yet to achieve its utopian goals regarding individual freedom. Détente with the West has met with only partial success, and considerable tension still exists between the USSR and its communist competitor China.

The Media System. There are no privately owned media in the USSR, and no private advertising, although some information on commodity availability is allowed. All newspapers are published by the Communist party or allied associations such as trade unions, collective farms, and sports clubs. Because of the massive size and the diversity of cultural subgroups in the Soviet Union, very distinct "layers" of newspapers have evolved, which include (1) a central all-union press, national in scope; (2) a regional system for each of the republics; (3) papers that serve special local functions. Tremendous growth in both numbers and circulation of newspapers has occurred since 1960. There are 639 daily newspapers (608 morning and 31 evening papers) and 8,000 non-dailies. Circulation figures are 82 million for dailies and 59 million for non-dailies. Many major national and regional papers in the Soviet Union are published in both Russian and the regional language. Newspapers are published in 57 languages native to the USSR as well as nine foreign languages.

All newspapers are controlled by the central government to ensure "correct" interpretation of current policies. The Central Committee controls the press through its "propaganda and agitation department," which has sections responsible for each level of the press. The national press speaks for the Presidium, which informs the regional press, which passes the word along to local papers. *Pravda* ("Truth"), the voice of the party and the most important paper in the USSR, is printed in 28 cities and has more than 60 percent of its circulation outside Moscow. *Izvestia* ("News") serves a similar function for the government on foreign policy. Many national ministries publish their own papers; of these *Red Star*, published by the defense department, is the most famous. Each republic has a regional version of *Pravda* (such as *Pravda Ukraina*) printed in Russian and of *Izvestia* (in the Ukraine *Radyanska Ukraina*) printed in the

"ONE OTHER THING, SOLZHENITSYN — TURN OUT THE LIGHTS WHEN YOU LEAVE!"

local dialect. In effect there are two dailies, one government and one party paper, in each republic. Regional ministries also publish weekly regional papers. The local press consists of small community papers that deal with local problems. They are policy rather than politically oriented. A major section of Russian newspapers features letters or reports from the general public as well as industrial and agricultural experts criticizing the progress of projects. The press is regarded as the voice of the people.

A variety of Russian magazines are published along the same lines as the newspapers. Estimates place the number of Soviet periodicals as high as 5,600, and 141 magazines are published in 23 foreign languages specifically for foreign consumption. There are approximately 1,200 consumer magazines and 2,300 scientific journals in the total listed above; the remainder are pamphlets and bulletins published irregularly by various organizations. Book publishing in a variety of languages is a Soviet industry of major proportion. Both magazines and books are subject to strict government censorship.

Telegrafnoie Agentsuo Sovetskovo Soyuza (TASS) is the national communist news agency and serves to disseminate news and state policy to all media. TASS, which serves as Russia's foreign news agency, has a permanent staff of 2,000 in Moscow with more than 500 correspondents in major centers throughout Russia. A worldwide staff of 180 correspondents in 100 locations is linked with Moscow by two-way teleprinter. Of the 10,000 subscribers to

TASS, 300 are in foreign countries. Interestingly, TASS is self-supporting; payments from subscribers finance it. Since 1961, a second agency, Novisti (APN), organized by several journalistically oriented societies, has served primarily as a feature service for all media.

The structure of broadcast operations is almost identical to that of the print media except for the fact that the chairman of the State Television and Radio Committee is now a member of the Council of Ministers (executive branch) and is a high-ranking government official and party member. A central (national) radio service emanates from Moscow with local longwave service and a shortwave transmission to other parts of the country. Some republics have regional microwave and wired systems, which originate considerable amounts of programming. Few regional programs are exchanged, however, in part because they are produced in 67 different local languages. The local wired system provides tight control and effectively limits outside, i.e., international, interference. The wired system of 52 million sets provides the same high-quality reception found in most U.S. cable-TV systems. Nearly 33 million wireless radios are in use in the Soviet Union, and more than half of them are equipped to receive shortwave broadcasts from outside Russia.

The Soviet Union is rapidly expanding both its wired and wireless systems and now has over 3,000 radio and 1,460 TV transmitters in operation. The Central Radio Service in Moscow broadcasts seven programs, each with an individual style and content. Educational, cultural, and news content is emphasized; entertainment is deemphasized. Shortwave broadcasts for foreign audiences are carried in 64 languages and are a major political-propaganda instrument of the state. The Central Television Service produces five programs for a total of 33 hours of programs a day. Color TV is moving ahead slowly, and international exchange of TV content is definitely on the upswing as a part of the overall government policy of détente.

Russia has traditionally had a brilliant film industry. Directors such as Eisenstein, Vertov, and Pudovkin set the style in the 1920s. Today, the USSR has over 47,000 fixed cinema theaters and mobile units, with a yearly attendance in excess of 4.5 billion serviced by 39 studio production centers. Russia is one of the ten largest film producers in the world, and the high artistic level of Russian films has influenced many film directors, especially in Eastern Europe. The film industry is supervised by the Cinematography Committee of the USSR Council of Ministers, and the government funds all films. Russia produces more than 230 feature films each year, plus 700 documentaries, educational films, and other short films. The motion picture is a major teaching resource in the Russian school system, as are radio and television programs. By international standards, the film industry is the USSR's major media achievement.

Uses of Media.   The primary function of the media in the USSR is political persuasion. The media are structured specifically to advocate policies of the Communist party and the state. Individuals and groups in opposition to these policies are denied access to the media.

V. I. Lenin quickly recognized the power of the mass media and formulated a general theoretical framework for communication in a communist society. Three political-cultural ideas dominate the uses to which media are put in a communist nation: (1) agitation and propaganda must be used as underground phenomena during the struggle for power and must be intensive instruments once power has been attained; (2) mass solidarity, party-mindedness, and economic reeducation of the people must be developed using all available mass media; (3) improvement of the total proletariat culture—in effect, raising the nation's cultural aspirations and standards—must be achieved via the mass media. The mass media are openly used as direct instruments of the party's political, social, and cultural policies.

News and editorial functions are performed by professional journalists committed to party goals. The primary thrust of the press is not to handle fast-breaking news events but to provide interpretation of events in the perspective of party commitments. More than 25 percent of all radio programs are news-oriented. Theoretically, news in the Soviet Union is carefully planned and executed to serve the best interests of the state.

The Soviets have a definite commitment to using the media for educational purposes, particularly socialization. The artistic and cultural levels of entertainment series are designed to preserve classical cultural traditions and communist political values. Over half of the broadcast music is classical. Print production units seek to assimilate minorities into the larger cultural mainstream. Significantly, however, large nationalities within the state have their own ethnic-language papers and broadcasts. The media are designed to meet the changing needs of the people as perceived by the state. Entertainment is seen as useful when it improves the audience's taste.

Advertising in this socialist state is not highly developed, but all media provide information about new products when they appear on the market. In addition, the media are also used to stimulate distribution of specific goods in oversupply. When shoes are overstocked at GUM stores in Moscow, a news story appears to tell the people about it.

In the Soviet Union, then, the political, cultural, and economic policies of the state are intertwined with media institutions and the specific functions performed. The media are strictly controlled to advance state policies and improve the society. Every function of the media involves the party and its policies.

Comparison of the Three Media Systems

It is apparent that each of the nations discussed develop and use mass media in different ways. Guatemala is small, poor, and illiterate; it is racked with political, economic, and cultural problems; the mass media apparently do not serve most of the people but are the transmitters of outside culture. The Netherlands, also small, is economically sound and politically stable, which allows a diverse culture to share access to a mass media system that serves a variety of subgroups and helps to preserve a national identity. The USSR is a massive, technologically advanced superpower that uses a sophisticated media system to advance party policies internally and the cause of international communism worldwide.

The physical and geographical conditions, the technological competencies, the cultural traits, the economic conditions, the political philosophy, and the quality of the media interact to create unique media systems. The media are then used by the society to perform tasks that are essential to that society including news, analysis, education, persuasion, advertising, and entertainment.

The roles that the media perform in a nation cannot help but modify that nation, and as the parent society changes, the social forces and the uses made of media also change. This interaction of media systems and societies is critical to the development and well-being of the modern industrial state.

In the film *Cabaret* (1972), Joel Grey and Liza Minnelli perform a stunning rendition of "Money Makes the World Go Around." The intensity and style of the number bring into critical focus the economic condition of the cabaret, which serves as a symbol for Germany during the Nazi rise to power.

In a very real sense, "money makes the *media* go around." For in every nation, the relationship between the economy of the country and its mass media system is significant.

Dimensions of Media Economics

The gross national product (GNP) of the United States is close to $1.8 trillion, and per capita income is about $6,500. The personal-consumption expenditure by Americans is $1.2 trillion. Whatever do we spend all that money on? One answer is the mass communication system and the goods and services it produces. Consider these economic events and their impact on media costs:

1. Oil is used to produce phonograph records. Because the price of crude oil rose dramatically on the world market, list prices on popular record albums rose over $1.00. Despite this price increase, the record industry

The Economics of Mass Communication

grossed $2.7 billion in 1977 in the United States and is expected to climb over $3 billion in the next two years.[1]

2. Over 10 million automobiles are sold annually in the United States. Consider the money it costs to put AM and AM-FM radios, tape decks, and CB units in those cars. "Ten-four, good buddy, but that's economic impact."

3. *Star Wars* has earned over $200 million in domestic rentals, topping the *Jaws* bonanza in 1975. Both films have earned over $25 million more than the next three blockbusters: 1972's *The Godfather* ($86 million), 1973's *The Exorcist* ($82 million), and 1964's *The Sound of Music* ($79 million). The "big films" each year earn "megabucks" and literally change the stock market value of corporate stock of parent companies.

4. The Radio Corporation of America is the world's leading entertainment company with over $5 billion in sales for all of its units.

5. In a bidding war that inflated prices, 72 newspapers were sold in 1976. The largest purchase price, $300 million, was paid by Samuel I. Newhouse for Booth Newspapers, which includes *Parade* magazine and 8 daily newspapers. Chains are no longer buying up independent newspapers. Now the big chains are swallowing smaller chains.

6. An estimated $250 billion will be spent on advertising in the United States in this decade. The top 100 advertisers spend a combined total of over $6.5 billion a year.

Economic Theory and Media

Without question, the economic dimension of mass communication is overwhelming; Americans are the world's biggest spenders on media activities. To establish a framework of analysis, the media need to be examined as part of the total economic system in terms of how we use them and the values assigned to them.

Media Goods and Services.   In popular economic language, there are two kinds of goods: (1) free goods supplied by nature; (2) economic goods, to which human effort has added utility. Mass communication industries use free goods to produce economic goods. Trees, a free good, are used to produce newsprint, an economic good. Industrial diamonds are used to make phonograph needles. Within the economic goods category, there are two classes: (1) *producer goods*

---

[1]Roman Kozak, "CBS Exec Predicts U.S. 1977 Music Sales $3.6 Bil," *Billboard* 89, no. 9 (5 March 1977): 3.

and services, which are used in the production of other goods and services; (2) *consumer goods and services*, which are used directly by the buyer without significant modification. Using the previous example and extending it—free goods (e.g., trees and diamonds) are used to make producer goods (e.g., newsprint and phonograph needles), which in turn are used to make consumer goods (e.g., newspapers and record players).

The distinction between media goods and services, at its simplest level, is that media goods are physical things (e.g., TV sets, transistor radios, copies of books and magazines), and media services are the content or activities that supplement or supply goods (e.g., the stories in magazines and books, the programs on radio and television).

Media Supply and Demand.   The law of supply and demand is always at work in the media marketplace. Consumer demand is the desire to use and the ability to pay for goods and services. Producer supply refers to the quantity of goods available for purchase at a particular time for a set price. When the consumer demand for color television sets exceeds the producer supply, the price tends to increase. When the supply of color TV receivers exceeds the demand, the price tends to drop. Media people, like any other businesspeople, seek to supply the demand at the most economically rewarding level for themselves (and sometimes even for the consumers). Newspapers, magazines, and TV series that consistently misread the media marketplace are probably headed for economic disaster and oblivion.

Consumer Decisions and Media.   The individual's decision to spend money and time on the media is significant because that decision determines whether a medium will succeed or fail. The consumer has three levels of purchasing power in regard to media consumption:

1. The consumer can choose between media and nonmedia goods and services. A family has to decide whether to spend its $500 on a new living-room sofa, a week's vacation, or a new media product.

2. The consumer can choose between various media. If the family decides to spend its money on media goods and services, its members must determine whether they want a color TV, $500 worth of books, or a stereo system.

3. The consumer can choose between competing issues or programs in a given medium. Once the decision is made to buy the color television receiver, the family must then choose between competing brands.

Dual Consumers of Media

When any individual or corporation buys and consumes the goods and services of the newspaper, television, recording, magazine, radio, motion-picture, or book industries, they become media consumers. Media consumers use their time and money to purchase mass communication goods and services. These consumers are divided into two distinct categories: (1) audiences and (2) advertisers.

Audience as Consumer. The audience buys media products so that it can avail itself of media content. Its members use their financial resources to buy the electric hardware so that they can spend time listening to and viewing the content. Audiences buy issues of newspapers and magazines in order to read the content. Money buys media goods. Time is spent consuming media services.

Short-term and long-term consumption are the realities of the media marketplace, and the quicker a given item is consumed, the sooner it must be replaced. This rapid turnover is one of the major factors that makes media businesses viable economic enterprises. Audiences' constant willingness to spend more money and time on media is one indicator of the value they place on them.

Advertiser as Consumer. Traditionally, advertisers have been said to be buyers of time in the electronic media and space in the print media. This labeling process is technically accurate but somewhat misleading as to what is actually being bought. The purchase of a 30-second spot on ABC's "Happy Days" or a page in *People* is a meaningless act—and a poor business decision—unless there are audiences involved. In reality, advertisers buy the audience, which is a byproduct in the mass communication process. The estimated audiences for commercial broadcasting stations and most newspapers and magazines are more valuable in the end than the original product—the pages and the minutes of content. Although a time-buyer talks about buying a 30-second spot on ABC's "Happy Days" or a page in *People*, his major concern is the audiences who consume these pages and seconds. Advertisers buy people because people consume the products advertised in the media.

Models of Media Support

There are essentially four categories or types of financial support systems for American media: (1) media supported by audiences; (2) media supported by advertisers; (3) media supported by both advertisers and audiences; (4) media supported by public and private groups or other nonconsumers.

Media Supported by Audiences. Record companies, the film industry (with the exception of those films made expressly for television), and book publishers derive practically all their revenue from audiences, who bear the full brunt of the cost of producing these goods and services. The audience is not resold to advertisers. Commercials could be inserted between chapters of books or cuts on LP records or scenes in motion pictures (as indeed they are when shown on TV), but the traditions of our media system have established that the audience pays the entire cost of these three media.

Media Supported by Advertisers. Radio and television stations produce programs that they provide "free of charge" to audiences. Stations and networks earn their money by selling these audiences to advertisers, who must recoup their ad costs when they sell their products to the public.

Media Supported by Advertisers and Audiences. Most general-circulation newspapers and magazines derive revenue from both advertisers and audiences. Audiences buy media content through subscriptions or newsstand purchases—advertisers pay for audiences. Although the exact amount varies from publication to publication, usually audiences provide less than one-third of the total revenue earned by general-circulation newspapers and magazines.

Media Supported by Public and Private Groups. Some media are supported by groups such as state and federal agencies, foundations, nonprofit organizations, and private corporations. These media obtain little or no consumer support. Public television and radio stations, student newspapers, corporate house organs, and some subsidized government publishing are supported in this manner. The public indirectly pays part of the bill through local, state, and federal taxes, tuition, or support of those corporations involved with the media.

In order to develop an understanding of media economics, this examination divides media into three classes: (1) media that are supported solely by advertising (radio, television); (2) media that derive support from advertisers and audiences (newspapers, magazines); (3) media that are supported solely by audiences (motion pictures, sound recordings, books).

Advertising Media

Value in Advertising. The value of a magazine, newspaper, radio, or television advertisement depends on both the size and the characteristics of the audience. To an advertiser, the most important audiences are composed of those individuals most likely to buy the product being advertised. These *target audiences* are critical to the media because they have real economic value based on the following dimensions:

1. If Union 76 does not have many service stations in a given state, it is not worthwhile to advertise there. The *geographical* location of the audience-consumer is critical to the advertiser.

2. Frequent airline travelers live mainly in metropolitan areas, so United Airlines will advertise in large urban newspapers. *Population density* is an important dimension.

3. The Kellogg Company sells most of its presweetened cereals to children. Saturday morning is a good time to advertise its products on TV. *Age* is the relevant dimension here.

4. Women buy Revlon's cosmetics, so advertising in men's magazines would be foolhardy. *Sex* is a dimension of the target audience.

5. The purchase of convenience foods and already prepared foods are affected by *family size, income,* and *employment patterns.* Large families eat more and spend a larger portion of the family income for food. Working women use more of these food products than do women who remain at home.

Research methods are also beginning to report media usage based on *product category.* For example, in Atlanta, Georgia, how many heavy users of coffee read *Family Circle* or watch "The Mike Douglas Show"? This type of information could have significant impact on traditional advertising patterns.

Advertising Efficiency. Advertisers seek the largest possible target audience at the lowest possible price. Advertisers tend to use media vehicles that provide the best cost efficiency. This cost efficiency, or cost per-thousand (CPM) readers or viewers, is determined simply by dividing advertising cost by audience size. Cost efficiency is a means of assigning relative value to media audiences.

Advertising cost

$$\frac{\text{Advertising cost}}{\text{Audience size (in audience units of 1,000)}} = \begin{array}{c} \text{Cost efficiency} \\ \text{or} \\ \text{CPM} \end{array}$$

The Effect of Audience Size on Advertising Costs.   Under normal conditions, newspapers with larger circulations have higher advertising rates; and when a newspaper's audience increases, its rates go up. For example, the *Chicago Tribune* charges a one-time advertiser about $9,000 to use a full-page ad to reach its approximately 750,000 daily readers. On Sunday, the *Tribune* charges about $12,500 for the same-size ad because Sunday circulation exceeds 1,111,000.[2] When the cost efficiency of the two editions of the *Tribune* is compared, the CPM is actually reduced because the increase in cost is offset by the larger audience.[3]

Cost Efficiency

Daily Tribune	*Sunday Tribune*
$\dfrac{\$9,000 \text{ (cost)}}{748(000) \text{ circulation}} = \dfrac{\$12.03}{\text{(CPM circulation)}}$	$\dfrac{\$12,500}{1,111(000)} = \$11.25$

In terms of advertiser cost, the Sunday editions of the *Chicago Tribune* are more efficient, based on paid circulation estimates made by the Audit Bureau of Circulation.

The Effect of Audience Characteristics on Advertising Costs.   Advertisers need to know what kinds of people use a given newspaper, magazine, radio, or television station. In television, for example, total audience size may be less important than the characteristics or composition of a program's audience. If we compare two network programs, this point may become clearer. For example, advertisers could buy one 30-second spot during a situation comedy for $40,000

[2]All cost and circulation figures are rounded estimates of information provided by Standard Rate and Data Service, *Daily Newspaper Rates and Data*, 12 July 1976, pp. 216–21.

[3]Normally, newspaper efficiency is computed using milline rate, but for the purposes of this example the page cost efficiency format is clearer.

and another during a football game for $50,000. The situation comedy reaches 12.9 million viewers while the football game reaches only 11.5 million viewers. Comparing CPMs, the "sit-com" ($3.10) seems to be a better buy than the football game ($4.35) because it has a larger total audience.

CPM Total Audience

Variety show	Football game
$\dfrac{\$40,000}{12,900(000)} = \dfrac{\$3.10 \text{ CPM}}{\text{total audience}}$	$\dfrac{\$50,000}{11,500(000)} = \dfrac{\$4.35 \text{ CPM}}{\text{total audience}}$

If an advertiser's target audience is men aged 18–49, however, the situation changes markedly. The situation comedy has only 3.6 million male viewers (18–49) while the football game has 5.1 million male viewers (18–49). At this point the football game ($9.80 CPM men 18–49) becomes a more efficient buy than the "sit-com" ($11.11 CPM men 18–49). Football is a better buy for this advertiser because it reaches more of the target audience at a lower unit cost.

CPM Men (18–49)

Variety show	Football game
$\dfrac{\$40,000}{3,600(000)} = \dfrac{\$11.11 \text{ CPM}}{\text{men (18–49)}}$ men (18–49)	$\dfrac{\$50,000}{5,100(000)} = \dfrac{\$9.80 \text{ CPM}}{\text{men (18–49)}}$ men (18–49)

In the current television season the average 30-second commercial costs approximately $50,000, with a "CPM homes" of $2.75 to $3.50. In the summer quarter network television prices for 30 seconds may drop to between $25,000 to $35,000. Since available audiences are smaller in the summer months, commericial prices are decreased to keep CPM homes at about the same level.[4]

Both audience size and characteristics make a TV show or newspaper economically valuable. *A quality audience for an advertiser is one that meets his marketing criteria.*

Expenditures by Medium. Table 4.1 examines advertising volume in 1976 for all media; from the table, several interesting points can be made: (1) ad

[4]These data are from a draft copy of the annual media report of the Leo Burnett Company, which is developed from a variety of sources.

TABLE 4.1. ADVERTISING VOLUME 1976 (*in millions of dollars*)

MEDIUM	1975	1976	1976 TOTAL	PERCENT OF INCREASE OVER 1975
Newspapers				
Total	8,442	9,910	29.6	17.4
National	1,221	1,502	4.5	23.0
Local	7,221	8,408	25.1	16.4
Magazines				
Total	1,465	1,789	5.3	22.1
Weeklies	612	748	2.2	22.2
Women's	368	457	1.4	24.2
Monthlies	485	584	1.7	20.4
Farm Publications	74	86	.2	16.2
Television				
Total	5,263	6,622	19.8	25.8
Network	2,306	2,857	8.5	23.9
Spot	1,623	2,125	6.4	30.9
Local	1,334	1,640	4.9	22.9
Radio				
Total	1,980	2,277	6.8	15.0
Network	83	104	.3	25.3
Spot	436	493	1.5	13.1
Local	1,461	1,680	5.0	15.0
Direct Mail	4,181	4,754	14.2	13.7
Business Publications	919	1,035	3.1	12.6
Outdoor				
Total	335	383	1.1	14.3
National	220	252	.7	14.5
Local	115	131	.4	13.9
Miscellaneous				
Total	5,571	6,604	19.7	18.5
National	2,882	3,453	10.3	19.8
Local	2,689	3,151	9.4	17.2
Total				
National	15,410	18,450	55.1	19.7
Local	12,820	15,010	44.9	17.1
GRAND TOTAL	28,230	33,460	100.0	18.5

Source: *Advertising Age*, July 1977.

revenue increased 18.5 percent and crossed the $30 billion mark for the first time; (2) the 15 to 20 percent growth in television ad rates, coupled with a greater demand for TV ads, caused two phenomena: TV revenue went up and some advertisers transferred dollars to other media to increase their revenue;

(3) the single highest percentage increase was in spot TV because some advertisers were forced by cost or lack of availability of network time; (4) radio had its second boom year in a row, with network revenues up 25 percent; (5) combined network and spot TV billings now account for 14.9 percent of all national advertiser revenue, which moved television ahead of direct mail (14.2 percent) for the first time in national ad revenue; (6) newspapers continue to dominate local advertising with one out of every four ad dollars spent in 1976 coming from local retailers to local newspapers, which is about six out of every ten dollars of retail advertising; (7) because of lower unit costs, local radio ad revenues continue to exceed dollars spent by local merchants on TV; (8) the miscellaneous category, which includes everything from ball point pens to skywriting, continues to earn one out of every five advertising dollars.[5]

Preliminary indications are that the 1980s will continue to show increases, but that the increases will be far less dramatic than the pattern of the late 1970s.

Economic Patterns in Broadcast Media. Table 4.2 lists television revenue, expenses, and income. Three important facts are incorporated in the table: (1) the networks showed a 37.4 percent increase in income over 1976; (2) the networks and their affiliated stations accounted for under 40 percent of the income but had 50 percent of the revenues, and 55 percent of the expenses; (3) local stations earned 50 percent of the revenue and had 47 percent of the expenses, but they had 61 percent of the income.

Of the 458 VHF stations reporting financial data, 422 showed a profit, with 49 stations having profits in excess of $5 million. Of the 173 UHF stations reporting, 127 showed a profit, but only 3 stations had profits of $3 million or more. This was the best year for UHF stations as a group.

Table 4.3 reports radio revenue, expenses, and income. The important facts to be noted from this table are: (1) unlike television, radio networks do not dominate the medium economically: the seven networks (ABC's 4 networks, CBS, MBS, and NBC) made their first profit in 5 years; the income of their owned-and-operated stations was up 24 percent over the previous year; (2) AM and AM/FM stations do dominate the medium economically and account for 65 percent of all income; (3) the total income for FM stations ran $41.6 million, only their second annual profit ever.

Public Broadcasting. Although public broadcasting is not funded through advertising, their economic situation can best be understood when examined

---

[5]Robert J. Coen, "No Let Up in Boom," *Advertising Age* 48, no. 28 (1978): 1.

TABLE 4.2. TELEVISION REVENUE, EXPENSES, AND INCOME, 1977

	REVENUE		EXPENSES		INCOME	
	($ millions)	(%)	($ millions)	(%)	($ millions)	(%)
Networks (ABC, CBS, NBC)	2,581.4	(21.9)	2,175.3	(19.4)	406.1	(37.4)
Stations (15) owned and operated by networks	503.5	(3.4)	354.2	(8.0)	149.3	(−6.1)
All other stations	2,804.1	(8.1)	1,958.5	(8.9)	845.7	(6.3)
Totals	5,889.0	(13.3)	4,488.0	(13.7)	1401.1	(12.1)

SOURCE: *Broadcasting*, 22 August 1978, p. 34.

in relation to commercial broadcast operations. The Corporation for Public Broadcasting (CPB) budget for the 1977 fiscal year was $103 million. The budget was allocated as follows: (1) public radio, $15.38 million; (2) public television, $77.32 million; (3) CPB operations, research, and planning, $10.3 million. This was a $24 million budget increase over 1976.

Public radio spent: $6.38 million for National Public Radio (NPR) and other productions, $1.83 million for local station expansion grants, $.3 million for satellite interconnection, and $.35 million for membership awareness.

Public television spent: $13.32 million for production, $51.5 million for local stations, and $12.5 million for satellite interconnection. These figures do not include local station budgets or fund-raising projects.

In effect, 15 percent of this national budget went to radio; 75 percent to TV; and 10 percent for CPB's management and research costs. The manage-

TABLE 4.3. RADIO REVENUE, EXPENSES, AND INCOME, 1977

	REVENUE	EXPENSES	INCOME
	($ millions)	($ millions)	($ millions)
Networks	84.5	59.2	25.3
AM stations (17) affiliated with networks	98.4	79.4	19.0
All other stations AM & AM/FM stations	1,663.0	1,502.8	160.2
FM stations	428.6	387.0	41.6
Total	2274.5	2,028.0	246.1

SOURCE: From data information in *Broadcasting*, 11 December 1978, p. 36.

ment cost is very high and has raised protest from critics both within and outside the organization.

Economic Patterns in Newspapers and Magazines.

Most newspapers and magazines earn advertising and circulation revenue from single-copy sales and subscriptions. Total revenue for these industries are about $10 billion in newspaper publishing and $5 billion in magazine publishing.

In terms of advertising revenue, newspapers are primarily a local ad medium; magazines a national medium. The significant factor in newspaper advertising is that individual newspapers' major ad competitors are not other newspapers—many markets are newspaper monopolies—but television stations and networks. Magazine competition for dollars is very intense within each magazine type, however. Although newspapers and magazines have seen their share of the total ad market drop, total revenue has generally increased.

In recent years, newspapers and magazines have asked their readers to pay a larger share of publishing costs. The street-sale price of newspapers is about $.15 for daily editions and $.35 for Sunday editions. At the same time the average price for magazines is $.96 per copy and $10.69 per annual subscription. The average daily newpaper prices are expected to rise to $.25–$.35 and the Sunday edition will cost $.75 in a few years. Magazines already receive over 40 percent of their publication cost from readers vs. about 60 percent from advertisers.

Several observations should be made about the economics of newspaper and magazine publishing.

1. The 1974–75 recession had an impact on newspapers. In fact, "all of the revenue gain came from higher advertising rates... and the negative impact was particularly severe for metropolitan dailies."[6] Nevertheless, ad lineage has since increased.

2. The urban newspaper is facing a change in its market as middle-class families continue their migration to the suburbs and are replaced by lower-income groups who are less attractive to advertisers.

3. Cost increases for newsprint and equipment are major factors in newspaper economics. Automation will continue to accelerate to cut labor costs.

4. Advertising and readership pressures are hardest on afternoon papers, and the gradual move to the morning edition even in small markets continues. The afternoon position of the *Chicago Daily News* was one of the problems in its economic collapse.

[6]"Communication," *Industry Surveys* (New York: Standard & Poors, 1976), p. c-73.

5. Increases in postal rates hit magazines very hard. Alternate delivery systems will be a major thrust in the next few years.

6. The 1974–75 recession hit magazine advertising the hardest. Both ad rates and issue prices were reduced; however, the current picture has improved.

7. Special-interest magazines will continue as the most economically viable vehicles, and general magazines will decrease further over the next several years. "Store books" like *Family Circle* and *Woman's Day* have gone to a 13th issue to meet advertising demand during the Christmas holidays.

8. The "majors" in both publishing businesses are doing very well economically, and many are diversifying to improve economic interests. The groups are definitely consolidating even further.

Nonadvertising Media

Three of the mass media are supported directly by their audiences: book publishing, motion pictures, and sound recordings. Because of this, they have different problems and different outlooks from newspapers and magazines.

Book Publishing. Total book sales were $4.6 billion in 1977, and sales for the future are expected to be greater than the 7.8 percent average annual increase from 1971 to 1976 because of higher prices for books and a stronger economy.

One of the larger percentage increases was 10.7 percent in religious publishing—God is certainly *not* dead in the book business—and six categories of the business had increases of over 10 percent. Mass market paperbacks and mail order books led in terms of dollar increases, but five other categories increased sales over $24 million (trade books, professional books, book clubs, college texts, and subscription reference books). Education remains one of the dominant sales areas for book publishing, although elementary and high school texts decreased in sales in 1976.

In the general book business (trade, religious, professional), the booklist developed over the years is the backbone of the company. Nevertheless, new titles can produce high income in short periods to improve profits measurably. Hardcover sales have increased only 6.8 percent in the past five years, but juvenile paperbacks have increased sales by 50.8 percent in the same period. Paperbacks, a merchandising phenomenon, continued to improve dramatically in the late 1970s.

The economical purchase of multiple titles from specialty book clubs continues to expand this area. The Book-of-the-Month-Club remains the leader in the field, but most clubs are subsidiaries of the major publishers.

In terms of volumes published, the industry's total booklist decreased in 1976 as unprofitable books were dropped; 25,000 hardcover and 11,000 paperbacks were printed. In terms of cost, the average list price of a hardcover book in 1976 was $16.32. Mass market paperbacks increased by $.14 per copy, to $1.60. Trade paperbacks saw a sharper price increase, $.29, for an average per copy price of $5.53.

Book sales were made by the 1,013 wholesalers, 191 book clubs, and 11,717 bookstores that serve the American public.

The major event of 1976 in print communication was the passage of the copyright bill and the impact was immediately felt in the photocopying of published material (see chapter 9).

The Motion-Picture Industry. Perhaps in no industry is the economic situation more complex or Machiavellian than the "Hollywood" film industry. The business cannot be predicted nor is it well reported.

Business is booming with more tickets sold at very inflated prices ($4 and up in New York)—the highest number in 15 years. Deal makers are the kingpins of the industry, and it is not easy to track down costs or profits. But if we use the year 1975 as a benchmark, we can begin to understand movie economics. Film box-office receipts reached $2.5 billion. This amounted to two-thirds of all spectator-amusement expenditures and 3.5 percent of all recreation dollars. To earn this money, 21 principal distributors released 182 films to 16,000 (3,800 drive-in and 12,200 indoor) theaters, and they earned over $1.2 billion in film rentals.

The motion picture is the most economically volatile mass medium because it depends on annual production of product that no one can predict in terms of economic sources. The Music Corporation of America (MCA) led the industry with sales of about $812 million and income of $96 million. MCA's success was due to $200 million in worldwide rental sales of *Jaws* and 14 weekly hours of television-film production in network television prime time. Although MGM ranked eighth in sales ($255 million), it ranked fourth in net income ($32 million). Conglomerates are in control of four of the major producers: Warner Communications (Warner Brothers), Walt Disney (Buena Vista), Transamerica (United Artists), and Gulf & Western (Paramount).

In terms of individual motion pictures, two measures of economic success are of interest: the total gross and the gross in the year of release. Considering U.S.-Canadian film rentals only, only two of the all-time "Top 50" moneymakers are from the "golden age" of Hollywood—*Gone With the Wind*, and

Snow White and the Seven Dwarfs. Over 60 percent of the "Top 50" were released since 1970. Only three low-budget motion pictures made the list— *American Graffiti*; *The Trial of Billy Jack*; and *The Love Bug.* The individual product rather than the stars, directors, source, or type of film dominates this list.

In terms of specific releases in 1976, and again limited to the United States and Canada, every film on the "Top 25" list made more than $7 million in its first year of release. *Jaws*, reissued the year after its 1975 release, made another $16 million in rentals. In fact, four reissues—*Jaws* (No. 9), *Blazing Saddles* (No. 10), *The Exorcist* (No. 16), *The Other Side of the Mountain* (No. 23)—made the "Top 25" list. Eight comedies made the list, which is unusual.

Both the all-time "Top 50" and the annual "Top 25" lists need to be understood in light of the fact that films make 30 to 40 percent of their rental income outside North America. Recent currency devaluations in Australia, Europe, and South America have had an impact on this percentage factor. Additional income is made from merchandising in the form of paperbacks, T-shirts, games, and so forth. *Star Wars* has become a merchandising phenomenon, and the ancillary rights to the *Saturday Night Fever* album alone could amount to $20 million.

Figure 4.1 reveals that two periods in the year account for major box-office receipts: (1) the spring–summer period (April–August) accounts for 40.5 percent of all ticket sales; (2) the holiday months of December, January, and February account for 26.3 percent. Because of this, many feature films with large anticipated box offices are timed for release in December (family or children's films) or June (adult films and blockbusters.)

Ticket prices now average about $2.25 per person because of recent price increases at drive-ins and increases in ticket prices for children. Average ticket prices for major first-run features in metropolitan areas are around $3.50. Audiences are still dominated by young people, who account for over 60 percent of all tickets sold. Moviegoers now selectively attend films instead of "going to the movies" as a habit.

Several observations about the film industry can be made:

1. Production costs for films now average about $4.0 per feature film, largely due to increased labor costs, and require roughly 2.5 times their production budget in ticket sales to show a profit. Some film businessmen argue that economic facts of life may soon lead to a 4 to 1 ratio before profits will appear.

2. With costs increasing, audiences changing, and revisions in tax laws

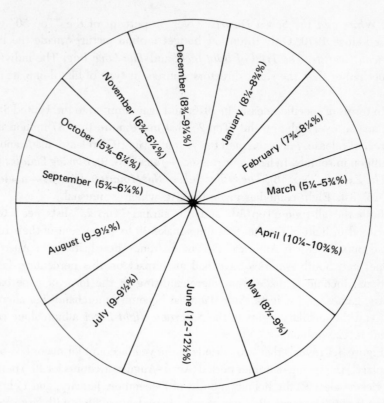

FIGURE 4.1. *Annual U.S. Key City Box Office (month-by-month average share)*

(which eliminated films as tax shelters in 1977), the economic future of the industry is uncertain, although very "bullish" at present.

3. It also appears that fewer feature films will be produced while the number of theaters will continue to go up in the future; reissues will be more important than ever.

4. The balance of power is swinging from exhibitors to distributors. Most films are beginning their runs at a 90%–10% split favoring distributors. Local movie theaters earn 50 percent of their profit at the candy counter and are forced to operate at the 1 to 2 percent profit margin, which is not a significant return on investment in today's marketplace.

5. Home video systems should have considerable feature-film content available on disk or tape by 1980.

6. Time Inc.'s Home Box Office (HBO) is heavily dependent on Hollywood product as its major source of content. HBO is more "pay movie" than "pay TV."

7. The conglomerate entertainment corporation is a reality and will grow.

8. In 1978, the film industry faced something of a scandal regarding shady economic practices that came to light in the form of embezzlement, kickbacks, and financial gimmickry, as well as charges of "block booking" (outlawed in 1948), a practice forcing exhibitors to take the "dogs" to get the box-office winners. Furthermore, talent is beginning to sue "studios" to ensure proper accounting of profit-sharing.

9. The "blockbuster" policy of economic planning is the current vogue in the picture business. *Star Wars'* success was the primary reason for 20th Century-Fox's 500 percent increase in profits over the previous year. The average film budget today is over $5 million, which is twice what it was five years ago. The "big hit" rather than consistent business is the dominant economic pattern

10. Six major producers (United Artists, Universal, 20th Century-Fox, Paramount, Warner Brothers, and Columbia Pictures) account for $.85 of every admission dollar. More and more independents are moving under distributor umbrellas.

The Sound-Recording Business.   The "hype" in the "platinum age" music business certainly rivals the "hoopla" of the "golden age" of Hollywood studios. The Beatles, for example, are constantly reported to be planning a second coming. Bill Sargent offered $50 million for the rock legends to "come together." It did not happen.

The economic data compiled by industry sources is based on list prices rather than actual over-the-counter prices paid by consumers; sales figures may thus be somewhat inflated. Retail sales volume is currently over $3.0 billion.

The sales of "singles" fell off sharply because the $1.29 list price made them less of a bargain compared to albums. In addition, the youth market, so important to single sales, is shrinking as the "baby boom" passes along to the next age bracket. Record clubs, premiums, and mail orders are losing their share of the market. "Rack-jobbers" and "low margin retailers" are the major sales forces at work in the retail marketplace today. The 8-track tape accounts for 84 percent of all nonrecord sales of music.

The record industry is similar to the motion-picture business in that it depends on immediate purchase of current product for financial well-being. Both records and movies can make an individual rich in a short period of time, but four out of five singles and three out of four albums never make back their production costs. And an album averages $30,000 to $70,000 to produce.

Representative album costs would break down somewhat as follows: Using an average list price of $6.98, there is a markup of $.46 between the producer price and distributor price, and the list price is double what the distributor pays. Contract and production schedules are extremely diverse, but even album-cover artwork has emerged as a major cost ($3,000). The variable costs include artist royalties of 5 to 15 percent; songwriter mechanicals, about $.28 an album under the new copyright law; roughly $.07 an album to union pension funds; and manufacturing costs of about $.52 per album. Production costs for tapes are roughly 25 percent higher than for records, and these costs are reflected at each level of the distribution chain.

The gross profit on an individual record album can run as high as $2.00, but that has to cover: (1) overhead and interest, (2) records that "flop," (3) distribution, (4) variable costs, and (5) location and development of new talent.

Business is booming; there were over 30 platinum and 182 gold singles and albums in 1977. Nevertheless, in the future there are going to be significant changes in phonograph industry economics with continued adjustment of content for aging audiences, the significant changes brought about in the new copyright law, and the continuation of the fierce retail price-cutting wars of the past few years.

Media Expenses

With all the dollar amounts that have been used to measure advertising, sales, rentals, profits, incomes, and the like, it is important to keep in mind that every medium and business unit within that medium also has labor and material costs to meet.

The revenue derived from consumers and nonconsumers alike goes to pay media's bills. Media industries incur initial costs when they begin; they incur operating expenses as they continue to pay for (1) production costs involved in making media products; (2) distribution costs incurred in selling and delivering goods and services to the consumer.

Initial Costs. Some media businesses can start with relatively little capital investment, while others require enormous amounts. A phonograph record can be produced for whatever a local band can scrape together to rent a studio, cut the necessary tracks, and produce a "demo." Small-town newspapers can be started with little capital outlay. Books can be inexpensively produced using aluminum plates or typed masters, offset printing, and plastic binders.

However, low initial costs are not the rule in media economics. A textbook such as this one can require a commitment up to $100,000 on the part of the publisher in terms of total investment in editorial, manufacturing, and promotion costs as well as the advance payment to the authors. One episode of most hour-long television series costs more than $325,000 to make. Even bargain-basement films such as *Joe* or *Easy Rider* cost $300,000 to $400,000, while films such as *Apocalypse Now, King Kong, The Wiz, Superman,* and *Close Encounters of the Third Kind* cost many millions. To start a newspaper in a major metropolitan area would require an investment of $5 million to $10 million. Moderately successful TV stations sell for millions of dollars.

Operating Expenses.   Most media enterprises involve long-term commitments in the form of operating expenses: supplies, labor, overhead, interest, as well as modernization and expansion. Newspapers alone spend more than $150 million annually to improve their operations.

All media must produce and distribute their products if they are to survive economically. Radio operations depend on music, news, and sports formats for content because of economic and audience considerations. Newspapers use newsprint rather than high-gloss paper to cut production costs. Magazine publishers depend on 750 wholesalers and more than 100,000 retail outlets to help sell their wares. The phonograph industry uses record clubs, distributors, retailers, and rack-jobbers to get their records into the hands of the public.

Network Television: A Case Study in Production and Distribution

Television advertisers incur three costs when they use the networks: (1) the cost of producing programs, (2) the cost of distributing programs to local stations, and (3) the cost of making commercials.

Program-Production Costs.   Programs can be aired live, but most are videotaped or filmed. TV economics has been a primary reason for the death of live programming. High production costs forced the industry to use reruns, and that meant recording programs. Today, most prime-time TV series produce about 22 new shows each season, which means it is possible for each episode to be run twice each year. In theory, this practice cuts production costs for a season by 60 percent.

In prime time (8:00 P.M. to 11:00 P.M. EST) nearly all variety series are videotaped and dramatic series are filmed. In recent years, situation comedies, under impetus from Norman Lear, have turned from film to electronic production techniques. Without international markets and the ability to be use reruns as syndicated series, few, if any, network prime-time shows would be economically successful. *Star Trek* is a syndication rather than a network success story.

Production costs fall into two basic categories: (1) above-the-line costs cover all items related to creative elements of production, including writing, directing, acting, and producing the show; (2) below-the-line costs relate to physical or technical elements of the program, including the production staff, scenery, costumes, location costs, equipment rental, editing, processing, and overhead.

For videotaped variety shows, above-the-line elements account for 50 to 65 percent of the total production cost because of high talent costs. Below-the-line items account for 50 to 65 percent of film-drama production charges because of high labor, scenery, location, and equipment costs.

The high cost of production, over $350,000 per hour, must be distributed over a large actual audience to develop satisfactory cost efficiency.

Program-Distribution Costs. The cost of producing a TV series remains the same whether 1,000, or 10,000, or 10,000,000 people see it. Network interconnection of local stations spreads costs over an extremely larger audience base, thereby providing a lower unit cost (CPM).

Network-time charges are based on the available audience, that percentage of U.S. TV homes with their sets on—not the actual audience turned to a specific program in a specific time slot. The available audience (and therefore network distribution costs) is affected by five variables: (1) the number of U.S. homes equipped with TV sets; (2) the coverage of the stations affiliated with the network; (3) the scope of the available interconnection system; (4) the season of the year; (5) the day-part (time segment, e.g., daytime, prime time).

The cost of one hour of time on a TV network of 200 stations has risen little in the past few years, but still costs over $160,000. Of this amount, network operations use 10 percent to 20 percent; the affiliated stations in the lineup get 20 percent to 30 percent; American Telephone and Telegraph gets 3 percent to 6 percent for use of its distribution system of coaxial cables and microwave relays; a 15-percent commission is paid to the advertising agency of record; 20 percent to 40 percent is rebated to the advertiser through seasonal and day-part discounts; overhead eats up 5 percent to 10 percent; and if anything is left, it is profit.

Commercial Costs. A 30-second color TV commercial of high quality costs from $20,000 to $30,000 to produce, and commercials with detailed production values now cost national advertisers over $100,000. Because commercials are recorded, their cost can be prorated over a period of time on both the national networks and local stations.

    The High Cost of Failure.   Let us assume an advertiser sponsors a 30-minute TV program. It could cost $150,000 to make six 30-second color commercials, another $80,000 for network distribution, over $150,000 for program production—the total cost could run to $380,000. No advertiser can afford a failure of this sort. Such an investment requires a huge audience of potential consumers week after week. The possibility that a TV program may fail to attract a large audience has led advertisers to the practice of using scatter plans (placing ads in a large number of programs). This enables advertisers to hedge their bets with a few winners and some losers. The high costs of production and distribution make it harder and harder to try something new in programming. The high cost of failure has made advertisers very cautious television consumers. However, the recent demand for network TV spots is forcing prices up, creating long-term commitments, and forcing advertisers to make very early decisions about what they will buy. At the present time the networks are definitely in the driver's seat on commercial prices. All three networks are consistently sold out in nearly all their time periods regardless of who is winning the current ratings battle.

Effects of Media Economics

    High initial costs and operating expenses have had far-reaching effects on the American media system. Many people are becoming concerned that not all these changes are for the better. For example:

1. Entry into media ownership is becoming increasingly difficult because of the large sums required to start and operate a medium.

2. Those groups already involved in media operations are, in general, succeeding at a rapid rate. Successful companies seem to get bigger and bigger with ever-increasing power accruing to them. Because of the economics, media have become "big business" with chain and crossmedia ownership dominant. In the most lucrative "Top 100" TV markets, over 70 percent of the stations are licensed to group owners.

3. Because of the enormous sums being risked in the media marketplace, the media in general have become more competitive in trying to capture the largest, most valuable audience available, rather than striving to meet

the special needs of all segments of society. Even "public" broadcasters now struggle to reach the mass audience in many of their content offerings.

4. Some media businessmen seem to be sensitive only to the demands of the marketplace. Some media investors refuse to take anything other than mild positions on sensitive issues. The very rich and the very poor in media need to be somewhat timid in order to retain or improve their economic positions.

5. Today, 71 percent of newspaper circulation comes from papers controlled by 168 multiple ownerships, and the top 25 chains control over half the newspaper business. Fewer than 50 cities have more than one newspaper; in 97.5 percent of America's 1,500 cities there is but one newspaper. It often seems economically unsound for newspapers to compete for local revenue. In all cities, however, there still are competing media.

6. Networks, syndicates, news services, and other corporate giants operate increasingly within media oligopolies. A limited number of powerful competitors exist in every media institution.

7. Financial wealth seems to accrue to limited media groups in major metropolitan areas. Broadcast profits for some stations in the large markets have been reported to return close to 100 percent on annual tangible investments. Similar profits come to successful record and film producers as well as publishers.

Group Ownership of Media.   Media ownership has significant impact on what Americans will read, hear, and watch, and control of content in the media is in an ever-shrinking number of hands. The chains are getting bigger, and there are fewer and fewer independents. Conglomerates must be of special concern because of the power they now hold and because they are increasingly involved in many media rather than one medium. The marketplace of ideas is shrinking as the numbers of independent viewpoints are reduced through sales and mergers.

Most other media conglomerates pale by comparison, but RCA is the prototype. An analysis by Ben H. Bagdikian raises an important concern:

> The RCA Corporation, for example, owns NBC. The parent corporation does more than $5 billion of business a year, of which NBC represents less than 20 percent. RCA owns Random House, the book publisher, together with its subsidiaries which include Ballantine Books, Alfred A. Knopf, Pantheon, Vintage, and Modern Library. It owns the Hertz Corporation. It is a major defense industry, producing military radar, electronic-

warfare equipment, laser systems, instruments that guide aerial bombs to targets, hardware that does intelligence processing, guidance for surface-to-air missiles, and it has wholly owned subsidiaries around the world. It controls telecommunications among 200 nation states through its RCA Global Communications, Inc. RCA is also a subcontractor on the Alaska pipeline project, and it has produced guidance systems for Apollo and Skylab spacecraft. One wonders what might have been lost to RCA in its multimillion-dollar Apollo and Skylab space contracts if its wholly owned broadcasting arm, NBC, had produced a convincing documentary against spending all that money on space exploration.[7]

It must be understood that ABC and CBS are also conglomerates; RCA-NBC is not alone. But the conglomerates are not limited only to parent broadcast companies. Time Inc., for example, publishes magazines (*Time, People, Fortune, Money,* and *Sports Illustrated*) and in 1978 bought the *Washington Star* for $20 million to add to the 17 weekly newspapers it already controlled. Time Inc. also runs Time-Life Films, Home Box Office, Manhattan Cable Television, a Grand Rapids, Michigan, TV station (WOTV), Time-Life Books, Little, Brown publishers, Book-of-the-Month Club, the New York Graphic Society, interests in foreign publishers, a paper company, and marketing research companies. The real concern is that lucrative media operations have become prime targets for big investors who were not previously involved with public communication systems. And since their major concern is business, the functions of the media may suffer at the hands of individuals whose training is in business rather than in mass communication. Corporate conflicts of interest and the economics of media influence are very real issues in American society. Mediamen can be resocialized by businessmen, and vice versa.

Current Concerns

High costs and enormous profits can lead to a concentration of economic power and information control in the hands of a limited number of huge corporations. Some critics have said that the regional domination of the Northeast has led to the development of an elite corps of media businessmen who exercise undue influence over the content of the media. These critics have referred to "media barons" who can exercise undue influence on the political structure of the United States, limiting government controls that might cut profits.

[7]Ben H. Bagdikian, "Newspaper Mergers—the Final Phase," *Columbia Journalism Review* 15, no. 6 (March/April 1977): 20.

One of the leaders of the attack on media conglomerates is Nicholas Johnson, a former member of the Federal Communications Commission, who writes:

> In general, I would urge the minimal standard that no accumulation of media should be permitted without a specific and convincing showing of a continuing countervailing social benefit. For no one has a higher calling in an increasingly complex free society bent on self-government than he who informs and moves the people. Personal prejudice, ignorance, social pressure, and advertiser pressure are in large measure inevitable. But a nation that depends upon the rational dialogue of an informed electorate simply cannot take any unnecessary risk of polluting the stream of information and opinion that sustains it. At the very least, the burden of proving the social utility of doing otherwise should be upon him who seeks the power and profit which will result.[8]

Economic problems are the consequences of the high initial costs and operating expenses of the mass media. The rise of media giants and corporate conglomerates has been the natural economic consequence of a media system in which operation and control is private rather than governmental. The alternative seems to be government ownership and control of the media, and this, of course, has always been rejected by a free and democratic society.

In a free society two courses of action have been suggested: (1) easier access to the media should be available to all segments of the society; (2) the media must continue to serve in a responsible fashion all the functions required of them. Access and responsibility are the two key issues of the 1980s. Fear has been expressed in some quarters that economic pressure will negatively affect free and easier access as well as responsible action on the part of the media.

Signs on the horizon indicate that the picture may not be as dire as it may seem. Cheaper means of publication and production are becoming available. Photo-offset lithography, cold-type composition, and inexpensive paper are bringing newspaper publishing back within reach of the average person. In many towns and cities of the United States new publications are springing up, mostly weeklies, that are being published on a low-budget basis through offset printing. The so-called underground press is included in this category.

Even the electronic media are getting less expensive. Hand-held cameras and videotape equipment are now being manufactured at a price that many people can afford. This has brought about so-called people's TV, in which small,

[8]Nicholas Johnson, *How to Talk Back to Your Television Set* (Boston: Little, Brown, 1970), p. 65.

closed-circuit telecasting is produced by neighborhood and inner-city groups for their own information and education. These developments, too, will help to overcome the economic imbalance of mass media.

Finally, it should be noted that, in spite of these dire economic warnings, mass media in America are more varied in their ownership and ideological commitment than in any other country in the world. In one study undertaken in the greater Washington, D.C., metropolitan area, more than 250 discrete and separately owned media were found to be available to the average citizen—counting daily and weekly newspapers, regularly published local newsletters and magazines, AM and FM radio, commercial television, and educational television.

In other words, the average American has a vast array of media available to him. The value our society places on its media institutions can be determined in part by the amount of money spent on them. Obviously, the media are important to the United States or its citizens would not spend the sums they do. The economics of mass media create problems of some concern, however, and it is of increasing importance that both citizen and mass communicator respond to the problems with a growing sense of responsibility.

Demands of Media Users

Demands made upon the media are crucial to their survival. The extensive media system serving our society would not exist without consumer demands and the willingness to pay for mass communication goods and services. When audiences buy magazines or spend their time listening to the radio, they affect the success of these media, whether they want to or not. A few advertisers occasionally feel they have a right to influence some media because they are paying bills. But the economy and the mass media are interlocked in a life-and-death relationship, and the United States has the most sophisticated total media system in the world because of it. Economically sound media are less likely to acquiesce to consumer pressures. In a free society the media must respond to intelligent criticism but reject unreasonable demands.

Part Two The Elements of Mass Communication

The process of mass communication starts with a communicator. But the mass communicator is quite different from the individual communicator in interpersonal communication. When we exchange messages on a person-to-person basis, the sender and the receiver are individual entities. In mass communication, the receiver may be flesh and blood, but an individual sender is more myth than reality.

Simply stated, the communicator or sender in mass communication is rarely one individual. The people we identify as mass communicators are for the most part only the visible portion of a vast and complex network of people. Many people, not simply those we actually see or hear, play an important role in shaping the media message.

For example, the mass communicators of "The NBC Nightly News" are not simply David Brinkley and John Chancellor but include, among others, a production team involving writers, directors, producers, engineers, and reporters. The CBS program "60 Minutes" has four familiar and very visible communicators in Mike Wallace, Dan Rather, Morley Safer, and Harry Reasoner. Nevertheless, as the credits roll by at the end of the program, we see that over 40 other people are involved in the program's production. In reality, Chancellor, Brinkley, Wallace, Rather, Safer, and Reasoner are representatives of a communication team. They take the efforts of many people and represent these people to the audience. On a large scale, a television network or a motion-picture

5

Communicators

studio does the same thing when it assembles a series of programs or films from a wide variety of sources.

The mass communicator in American media is usually a complex organization; at its simplest level, it is a small group of independent workers. Individuals may at times seem to function as mass communicators. The animated films of Norman McLaren, for example, are essentially the result of a single individual. Because of McLaren's association with the Canadian Film Board, however, key characteristics of most mass communicators, such as complexity, specialization, and a high degree of organization, are still evident.

Many people assume that the performers on a TV program are the senders, but usually they are only a part of the total message created, packaged, and sold by other senders—the writers, producers, and directors of a program. For example, in some parts of "The Today Show," both Tom Brokaw and Jane Pauley are the content as well as the communicators of what the audience sees and hears. They perform material created by someone else, under the direction of still another person. Performers, then, are only one part of the conglomerate mass communicator.

A similar generalization can be made about print media communicators. Bob Woodward and Carl Bernstein could not have functioned as newspaper reporters without a battery of secretaries, clerks, editors, accountants, publishers, and newsboys.

Characteristics of the Mass Communicator

Many factors characterize the mass communicator in the United States, but two of the most significant are complexity and competitiveness, which result in high cost. Complexity and competition obviously influence cost. Large organizations that are competing with one another for audiences spend large amounts of money to ensure that they reach those audiences. Total radio-TV revenue f 1977 alone was over $8 billion. The three major TV networks spend more than $1 billion annually on network programming. A half-hour pilot (a test program used to sell a series idea to a network or sponsor) costs anywhere from $100,000 to $300,000. The most tightly budgeted commercial motion-picture feature, including production, distribution, and promotion, costs a minimum of $1,000,000. Starting a small daily newspaper today would require at least $500,000, and a major metropolitan daily would take well over $7,000,000. Mass communicators must spend a great deal of money, and this affects what they do and how they function within the mass media.

Competition in mass communication is a major force that has great impact on the communicator. In interpersonal communication individuals compete for

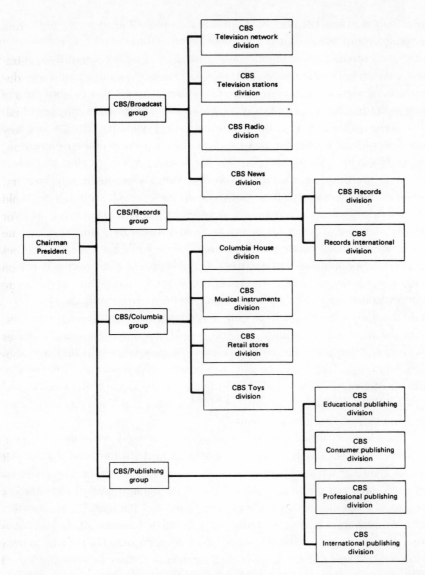

FIGURE 5.1. *The CBS Organization. CBS is engaged in a number of businesses in leisure and consumer fields, all of which involve the communication of ideas, information, or entertainment. The company began as a radio broadcasting service in 1927 and today operates one of the nation's three commercial television networks, five television stations, a nationwide radio network, and fourteen AM and FM radio stations. In 1938 CBS entered the recorded music field and is now the world's largest producer, manufacturer, and marketer of recorded music. Since 1964 the company has broadened its activities into other consumer product and service areas: the manufacture and distribution of musical instruments and toys; the retailing of audio equipment and other products; and the publishing of books and magazines for educational, consumer, and professional markets. Three key CBS businesses are international in scope: recorded music, musical instruments, and publishing.*

the attention of another person. A busy signal on the telephone suggests communicator competition. But this is minor compared to the intense competition in the mass media. This competition is created by economic forces that require most mass media organizations to seek the largest possible audience. For example, newspapers compete with one another in terms of circulation figures; motion pictures compete for box-office gross. Perhaps the most intense competition occurs in network television, where it is best symbolized by the emphasis placed on ratings. One rating point representing 1 percent of the American TV homes is worth millions of dollars to a network. ABC's signing of Barbara Walters represented an attempt to win the ratings' race among the three networks' evening news programs. Entire companies, such as A. C. Nielsen and the American Research Bureau, are devoted to research concerning the comparative standing of programs, magazines, advertisements, and the like.

Successful mass communicators remain alive while their weaker competitors lose their opportunity to speak out. Complexity and size are closely related in mass media organizations. The economic necessity to reach large audiences in order to survive requires a large organization. As size increases, complexity quite naturally emerges. A large daily newspaper has many separate divisions to handle its work; an incomplete listing could cite news reporting, editorial, advertising, circulation, promotion, research, personnel, production, and management groups. CBS is known primarily as a television network. But the CBS "Broadcast Group," as it is called, is only one of five separate divisions including CBS Records, CBS Columbia, and CBS Publishing. The Broadcast Group itself has four separate subdivisions.

These factors form the base from which the most common mass communicator patterns emerge. Industrialization is perhaps the most obvious pattern. A glance at the stock-market section of a newspaper reveals the extent of industrialization of the mass media. Many mass communication organizations are part of large industrial conglomerates. NBC and Random House are small parts of a corporate giant, the Radio Corporation of America (RCA). Almost all major film studios are subsidiaries of larger corporations. Gulf-Western owns Paramount; Warner Brothers films are a product of Kinney Leisure Services. A high level of organization is revealed by the CBS corporate structure with its 4 major groups, 14 divisions, and almost 80 subsidiaries. This structure not only reveals the nature of industrialization, but also, and most dramatically, reveals the complexity and specialization of the mass communicator.

Specialization is an *internal* fragmentization and is perhaps nowhere more apparent than in the motion-picture industry. Most feature films credit between 50 and 60 people performing the many jobs required to produce a motion picture. As Paul Mayersberg points out in his book *Hollywood: The*

Haunted House, many of these jobs are subdivided even further by the unions. For example, under painters there may be a foreman, a color mixer, a sign writer, and a marbelizer. An organizational chart of a typical daily newspaper reveals approximately 25 areas of specialization including three different sub-units under advertising covering display, national, and classified advertising. The photography department may have as many as 20 photographers, each one specializing in different aspects of the job.

Still another concept emerging from this view of the mass communicator is representation. Representation is basically an *external* fragmentization of the mass communicator. Mass communicators have become so complex and must deal with so many different audiences that they often find it impossible to contact and make arrangements with all individuals and organizations necessary to a smooth functioning of the organization. Mass communicator representatives include talent agents, managers, unions, program distributors, broadcast station representatives, and music licensing services.

In order to examine further the nature of the mass communicator, let us look at some of the mass media in greater detail.

Broadcasting

The radio and television industries have three basic groups of communicators: network, package, and local. Within each of these groups individual communicators perform a wide variety of tasks.

Networks are organizations that provide a diverse supply of television programming and a limited supply of radio news and special-information services. On network television the idea for a program or a program series can, and often does, originate outside the network. By the time most programs or series are broadcast, however, they have come in contact with and have been influenced by many network people, all the way from a stagehand to the chief executive of the network.

Today the networks actually create very few programs, primarily news, sports, and some documentaries. Ninety percent of all television network prime-time entertainment comes from program production or package agencies working in conjunction with the network programmers. The function of the package agency is to develop a program and/or program series. It employs writers, producers, actors, and technical personnel. This team of creators does everything short of broadcasting the program. Some production companies independently produce a pilot program and attempt to sell a series to the network on the basis of the pilot. A more common practice is to produce a feature-film pilot with financial and creative support provided by the network

"Hi! I assemble visual and verbal elements and package and market the result."

on which the series is intended to appear. Showcases for this material have been developed by the networks, for example, ABC's "Movie of the Week" and NBC's "World Premiere Movie." Package agencies also produce material directly for local television station syndications. In this case, series such as "The Lawrence Welk Show" are sold on a station-by-station basis rather than to the network.

A wide variety of people are involved with producing a single program. To use the CBS program "60 Minutes" again as an example, there are 15 full-time producers, 3 researchers, 15 film editors, and more than 20 assorted secretaries and administrative assistants, plus, of course, the four anchormen. Many of the people involved in producing the program do not receive on-air credit.

Although the individual communicators vary from program to program, the process of production is similar. A writer creates the script, writing not only actors' lines but also descriptions of what the viewer will see. A producer takes the script and assembles a creative staff to produce the show. A director coordinates the artistic efforts of the creative performers and technicians; these include actors, cameramen, soundmen, set designers, and musicians, among others. The actors add their dimension as they work with the total company. Thus, a large number of specialists work together as a corporate communicator in the form of a program production or a package agency.

Program syndicators are also a form of broadcast communicators. They are "passive" senders in that they usually take off-network programs or feature motion pictures and sell them to individual stations in a package. They do not sell the programs as such but merely the right to show the programs. They do not usually engage in program creation but simply distribute programs. Some of the major program syndicators are the three networks and many of the major package agencies. But there are also companies, such as Association Films, that do nothing but distribute programs to stations.

At the local level, radio stations depend on two outside creators for the bulk of their content: (1) the recording industry, which includes, among others, artists who write, arrange, and perform popular music and recording engineers who mix sound tracks to produce a master tape; and (2) the jingle-package companies that produce such items as station-break announcements, weather spots, and station identifications. Radio has also, however, taken on some attributes of a personal medium through the presence of the disk jockey, who is the bulwark of local radio programming. The disk jockey is the individual thread that weaves together all the material supplied by other creative teams; often, his individuality is a major force in the station's popularity.

Radio stations vary greatly in staff size. WABC in New York, for example, has 50 employees, but more than half of all AM and FM stations employ fewer than 11 people full-time. Television staff size ranges from over 100 at major market stations to less than 20 at smaller organizations. The average staff size for a television station today is 50 people.

A local television station generally employs its own staff in producing local programs; however, such stations also rely on outside senders such as the phonograph industry, jingle-package agencies, syndicators, and the networks. "Romper Room" for example, is a syndicated creative idea that is produced by local stations under guidelines established by the syndicator, who trains each of the local teacher-talents who appear in the series.

On the local level, news programs are the major effort of most radio and television stations. Senders on this level include local broadcast reporters who not only seek out the news but also present it to the audience, photographers, cameramen, film editors, directors who control the flow of the program, technicians, and, of course, the Associated Press (AP) and United Press International

(UPI). These two wire services are key communicators for virtually every news program on television and radio as well as for newspapers.

Motion Pictures

The communicator in motion pictures assumes many of the characteristics and performs many of the functions of the broadcaster. In fact, the amount of television production done by motion-picture studios increases the similarity. Basically, the role of motion-picture communicators is not as complex as in broadcasting because of the absence of such elements as networks and thousands of individual stations. Although theaters serve as a local outlet for film production, they are primarily passive outlets as contrasted with the active involvement of stations in broadcast production.

Motion pictures have almost come full circle in terms of production. In the early twentieth century, production involved a few people. Often one man, a Chaplin, a Sennett, or a Griffith, would conceive an idea, write the script, direct the film, and sometimes play the leading role. Only a cameraman and a few extras were needed. The emergence of studios in the 1920s changed this. Huge organizations were built to produce an assembly-line product. Thousands of people became involved with the making of one motion picture.

The conglomerate communicator role in motion pictures is perhaps the most specialized in all mass media. Figure 5.2 reveals some of the major and minor communicators involved in the production of a motion picture. Each person in these roles has a different task. The producer is an organizer; he creates a structure in which other communicators can work effectively. The screenwriter produces a working film script. The film editor reviews the "raw" footage from the director and assembles the film into a meaningful form. The director has overall artistic control of the film's actual production.

In the late 1960s, films began to be made with fewer people primarily due to the relaxtion of union rules governing participation of various crafts in film making. Such films as *Easy Rider* (1969) and *Billy Jack* (1971) were written, directed, and acted in by small groups of people and formed what many called a "new wave" in American film. For years we had the individualistic (auteur) film styles of Ingmar Bergman, François Truffaut, or Akira Kurosawa. The experimental films of Andy Warhol, Jonas Mekas, and Kenneth Anger often involved little more than the creator and strips of film.

Nevertheless, major motion pictures, such as *King Kong* (1976) and *Star Wars* (1977), with their huge casts, high costs, and complex organizations illustrate that American films are still the product of a variety of people working together. The real change in motion pictures has been in the deemphasis of the

City Official	JOHN AGAR	Illustrators	MENTOR HUEBNER
Ape Masked Man	KENY LONG		DAVID NEGRON
Petrox Chairman	SID CONRAD	Sound Mixer	JACK SOLOMON
Army Helicopter Pilot	GEORGE WHITEMAN	Re-Recording Mixers	HARRY W. TETRICK
Air Force Colonel	WAYNE HEFFLEY		WILLIAM McCAUGHEY
		Key Grip	ROBERT SORDAL
Assistant to the Producer	FREDERIC M. SIDEWATER	Gaffer	ED CARLIN
		Property Master	JACK MARINO
Casting by	JOYCE SELZNICK AND ASSOCIATES	Makeup Artist	DEL ACEVEDO
		Hair Stylist	JO McCARTHY
Director	JOHN GUILLERMIN	Wardrobe	ARNY LIPIN
Producer	DINO DE LAURENTIIS		FERN WEBER
Screenplay by	LORENZO SEMPLE, JR.	Special Effects	GLEN ROBINSON
Based on the Screenplay by	JAMES CREELMAN AND RUTH ROSE		JOE DAY
		Set Painters	ROBERT CLARK
From an idea Conceived by	MERIAN C. COOPER AND EDGAR WALLACE		CURTIS "RED" HOLLINGSWORTH
Executive Producers	FEDERICO DE LAURENTIIS, CHRISTIAN FERRY	Greensman	KEN RICHEY
		Hair Design for Kong	MICHAEL DINO
		Sculptor of Kong	DON CHANDLER
Director of Photography	RICHARD H. Kline, A.S.C.	Kong Mechanical Coordinator	EDDIE SURKIAN
		Construction Coordinator	GARY MARTIN
In Charge of Production	JACK GROSSBERG	Miniature Coordinator	ALDO PUCCINI
Music Composed and Conducted by	JOHN BARRY	Transportation Coordinator	JOE SAWYERS
		Stunt Coordinator	BILL COUCH
Film Editor	RALPH E. WINTERS, A.C.E.	Costume Designer	MOSS MABRY
Production Designed by	MARIO CHIARI AND DALE HENNESY	Gowns and Native Costumes by	ANTHEA SYLBERT
Second Unit Director	WILLIAM KRONICK	Post-Production Supervisor	PHIL TUCKER
Production Manager	TERRY CARR	Supervisor of Photographic Effects	FRANK VAN DER VEER
Unit Production Manager (Hawaii)	BRIAN FRANKISH	Photographic Effects Assistant	BARRY NOLAN
		Matt Artist	LOU LICHTENFIELD
Unit Production Manager (New York)	GEORGE GOODMAN	Sound Effects by	JAMES J. KLINGER
		Music Editor	KENNETH J. HALL
Assistant Directors	DAVID McGIFFERT KURT NEUMANN	Music Recording	DAN WALLIN
		Music Re-recording	AARON ROCHIN
Second Assistant Director	PAT KEHOE	Assistant Film Editors	ROBERT PERGAMENT
Second Unit Assistant Director	NATE HAGGARD		MARGO ANDERSON
Production Coordinator	LORI IMBLER	Publicity Coordinator	GORDON ARMSTRONG
Production Secretary	CHARLOTTE DREIMAN	Unit Publicist	BRUCE BAHRENBURG
Set Decorator	JOHN FRANCO, JR.	Production Auditor	ROBERT F. KOCOUREK
Script Supervisor	DORIS GRAU	Production Accounting	MERYLE SELINGER
Camera Operator	AL BETTCHER	Messengers	SCOTT THAYLER
Assistant Cameraman	ROBERT EDESA		JEFFREY CHERNOV
Additonal Photographic Effects	HAROLD WELLMAN, A.S.C.		MICHAEL WINTER
		Native Dance Choreography by	CLAUDE THOMPSON
Still Photographer	ELLIOTT MARKS	Extra Casting by	SALLY PERLE AND ASSOCIATES
Art Directors	ARCHIE J. BACON DAVID A. CONSTABLE ROBERT GUNDLACH	Titles by	PACIFIC TITLE AND ART STUDIO

FIGURE 5.2. *Partial credits for* King Kong (1976)

studio and the elimination of many elements of general studio overhead that at times cluttered and overburdened a film with too many communicators.

Print Media

As in other mass media, print communicators work within a large, organized, specialized, competitive, and highly expensive environment. Creative producers of print messages include researchers and reporters who find basic facts; writers who assemble material into effective messages; and editors who create ideas, manage their production, and evaluate the results.

In the jargon of the newspaper profession, the legman is a researcher whose main task is to get the facts. He might station himself at police headquarters and simply telephone leads into the home office. The reporter is both researcher and writer. Within the magazine or book industry, the researcher is often a fact-checker who verifies the authenticity of the work of reporters and writers.

Writers play the key creative role in the production of print media. They often are the people with the original ideas, although some magazine and book writers are word technicians who take the ideas of others and dress them in effective language. The reporter is the key writer within the newspaper organization, the person who gathers the facts and composes the story. Indeed, the reporter is often the essential communicator in deciding whether any given event warrants mass communication.

The editor—whether copyeditor, assignment editor, or managing editor—is more an evaluator, or gatekeeper, of communication than its originator. But editors are part of the sending process to the extent that they supervise the entire package of communication through imaginative management and evaluation.

The masthead from *Time* (figure 5.3) indicates the variety of mass communicators who participate in each issue, showing that, like other mass media, hundreds of people are necessary to the process of print mass communication.

There are few do-it-yourself handymen anymore in the area of mass communication. Of course, in numerous small media units, such as a weekly newspaper or a small-market radio station, one person performs a variety of tasks. The editor of a small weekly newspaper may also be a reporter, salesman, copywriter, and photographer. Even here, the conglomerate communicator concept is expanded beyond this single individual through the wire services, syndicated columnists, advertisers, and local stringers. Thus, the mass communication sender as an individual is at best the rare exception. Most media organizations follow the pattern of hiring an expert; some people do little but write headlines, others specialize in creating station-identification jingles.

TIME

Founders: BRITON HADDEN 1898-1929
HENRY R. LUCE 1898-1967

Editor-in-Chief: Hedley Donovan
Chairman of the Board: Andrew Heiskell
President: James R. Shepley
Group Vice President, Magazines: Arthur W. Keylor
Vice Chairmen: Roy E. Larsen, Arthur Temple
Corporate Editors: Ralph Graves, Henry Anatole Grunwald

MANAGING EDITOR: Ray Cave
EXECUTIVE EDITOR: Edward L. Jamieson
ASSISTANT MANAGING EDITORS: Richard L. Duncan, Jason McManus
SENIOR EDITORS: James D. Atwater, Ruth Brine, Martha M. Duffy, John T. Elson, Timothy Foote, Otto Friedrich, Timothy M. James, Leon Jaroff, Stefan Kanfer, Ronald P. Kriss, Marshall Loeb.
International Editor: Jesse Birnbaum
Chief of Research: Leah Shanks Gordon
ART DIRECTOR: Walter Bernard
SENIOR WRITERS: George J. Church, Michael Demarest, Robert Hughes, T.E. Kalem, Ed Magnuson, Lance Morrow, R.Z. Sheppard.
ASSOCIATE EDITORS: William Bender, Gerald Clarke, Spencer Davidson, William R. Doerner, Frederic Golden, James Grant, Paul Gray, Dorothy Haystead, Marguerite Johnson, Frank B. Merrick, Mayo Mohs, Donald M. Morrison, Frederick Painton, B.J. Phillips, Burton Pines, William E. Smith, David B. Tinnin, Frank Trippett, Marylois Purdy Vega, Edwin G. Warner.
STAFF WRITERS: James Atlas, Patricia Blake, Christopher Byron, Andrea Chambers, John S. DeMott, Walter Isaacson, Michiko Kakutani, John Leo, Richard N. Ostling, Jay D. Palmer, Kenneth M. Pierce, Frank Rich, George Russell, Annalyn Swan, Evan Thomas, Jack E. White.
CONTRIBUTORS: A.T. Baker, Gilbert Cant, Jay Cocks, Thomas Griffith, Melvin Maddocks, Richard Schickel, John Skow.
REPORTER-RESEARCHERS: Senior Staff: Audrey Ball, Amanda MacIntosh Berman, Peggy T. Berman, Nancy McD. Chase, Eileen Chiu, Ursula Nadasdy de Gallo, Patricia N. Gordon, Anne Hopkins, Gaye McIntosh, Sara C. Medina, Nancy Newman, Gail Perlick, Sue Raffety, Betty Satterwhite, Raissa Silverman, F. Sydnor Vanderschmidt, Genevieve A. Wilson-Smith, Rosemarie T. Zadikov.
Edward Adler, Peter Ainslie, Janice Castro, Oscar Chiang, Barbara B. Dolan, Rosamond Draper, Elaine Dutka, Cassie T. Furgurson, Tam Martinides Gray, Georgia Harbison, Allan Hill, Carol A. Johmann, Adrianne Jucius, John Kohan, Ellie McGrath, Laurie Upson Mamo, Elizabeth D. Meyer, Jamie Murphy, Brigid O'Hara-Forster, Bliss Inui Rand, Susan M. Reed, Elizabeth Rudulph, Victoria Sales, Marion H. Sanders, Zona Sparks, John Tirman, Susan Tribich, Jane Van Tassel, Joan D. Walsh, Susanne S. Washburn, Sandra A. Wilson, Linda Young.

CORRESPONDENTS: Richard L. Duncan (Chief), William Stewart (Deputy).
Washington Contributing Editor: Hugh Sidey
Diplomatic Correspondent: Strobe Talbott
Senior Correspondents: James Bell, Ruth Mehrtens Galvin, Sandy Smith, John L. Steele.
Washington: Robert Ajemian, R. Edward Jackson, Laurence I. Barrett, Stanley W. Cloud, William Drozdiak, Simmons Fentress, Hays Gorey, Jerry Hannifin, Richard Hornik, Neil MacNeil, Johanna McGeary, Christopher Ogden, Jeanne Saddler, Eileen Shields, Don Sider, John F. Stacks, George Taber, Gregory H. Wierzynski. **Chicago:** Benjamin W. Cate, Patricia Delaney, Barry Hillenbrand, David S. Jackson, J. Madeleine Nash, Roberto Suro. **Los Angeles:** William Rademaekers, William Blaylock, Edward J. Boyer, Robert L. Goldstein, Joseph J. Kane, Marion Knox, James Willwerth. **New York:** Donald Neff, Gisela Bolte, Mary Cronin, Dorothy Ferenbaugh, Marcia Gauger, Robert Geline, Jeff Melvoin, Robert Parker, James Shepherd, Peter Stoler, John Tompkins. **Atlanta:** Rudolph S. Rauch III, Anne Constable. **Boston:** Marlin Levin. **Detroit:** Barrett Seaman, Paul A. Witteman. **San Francisco:** Joseph N. Boyce, James Wilde. **Houston:** Robert C. Wurmstedt. **Miami:** Richard Woodbury. **United Nations:** Curtis Prendergast.
London: Bonnie Angelo, Erik Amfitheatrof, Arthur White. **Paris:** Henry Muller, Sandra Burton. **Bonn:** B. William Mader. **Eastern Europe:** David Aikman. **Brussels:** Friedel Ungeheuer. **Madrid:** Karsten Prager, Gavin Scott. **Rome:** Jordan Bonfante, Roland Flamini. **Jerusalem:** Dean Fischer, David Halevy. **Cairo:** Wilton Wynn, Dean Brelis. **Moscow:** Bruce W. Nelan. **Hong Kong:** Marsh Clark, Richard Bernstein, David DeVoss, Bing W. Wong. **Nairobi:** David Wood, Eric Robins. **Johannesburg:** William McWhirter. **New Delhi:** Lawrence Malkin. **Tokyo:** Edwin M. Reingold, S. Chang, Frank Iwama. **Melbourne:** John Dunn. **Canada:** John M. Scott (Ottawa), Ed Ogle (Vancouver). **South America:** Lee Griggs (Buenos Aires). **Mexico City:** Bernard Diederich.
News Desk: Minnie Magazine, Margaret G. Boeth, Al Buist, Susan Lynd, Blanche Holley, Jean R. White, Arturo Yanez. **Administration:** Emily Friedrich, Linda D. Vartoogian.

OPERATIONS MANAGER: Eugene F. Coyle; Mary Ellen Simon (Deputy)
PRODUCTION: Charles P. Jackson (Makeup Editor); John M. Cavanagh (Deputy); Sue Aitkin, Stephen A. Bertges, Manuel Delgado, Agustin Lamboy, Leonard Schulman, Alan Washburn.
ART DEPARTMENT: Arturo Cazeneuve, Rudolph Hoglund, Irene Ramp (Assistant Art Directors), Rosemary L. Frank (Covers), Leonard S. Levine, Anthony J. Libardi, William Spencer (Designers). **Layout Staff:** Burjor Nargolwala, Steve Conley, John P. Dowd, Carroll Dunham, John F. Geist, Modris Ramans, Kenneth Smith. **Maps and Charts:** Paul J. Pugliese, Joseph Arnon, Nigel Holmes. **Researchers:** Nancy Griffin, E. Noel McCoy, Sara Paige Noble.
PHOTOGRAPHY: Arnold H. Drapkin (Picture Editor); Alice Rose George (Assistant Picture Editor); Demetra Kosters (Administration). **Researchers:** Evelyn Merrin, Nancy Baye, Sue Considine, Gay Franklin, Francine Hyland, Rose Keyser, Julia Richer, Carol Saner, Elizabeth Statler, Mary Themo. **Photographers:** Walter Bennett, Sahm Doherty, Dirck Halstead, Neil Leifer, Kit Luce, Ralph Morse, Stephen Northrup, Bill Pierce, David Rubinger, Ted Thai, John Zimmerman.
COPY DESK: Anne R. Davis (Chief), Eleanor Edgar, Susan Hahn (Deputies). Frances Bander, Minda Bikman, Madeline Butler, Joan Cleary, Leo Deuel, Lucia Hamet, Evelyn Hannon, Katherine Mihok, Marilyn Minden, Emily Mitchell, Maria Paul, Linda Pocock, Shirley Zimmerman.
LETTERS: Maria Luisa Cisneros (Chief)
EDITORIAL SERVICES: Norman Airey (Director), George Karas, Michael E. Keene, Benjamin Lightman, Carolyn R. Pappas, Elizabeth G. Young.

PUBLISHER: John A. Meyers
Associate Publisher: Reginald K. Brack Jr.
Assistant Publisher: Stephen S. LaRue
General Manager: Donald L. Spurdle
Promotion Director: Robert D. Sweeney
Circulation Director: S. Christopher Meigher III
Business Manager: Ronald J. Dronzek
ADVERTISING SALES DIRECTOR: William M. Kelly Jr.
U.S. Advertising Sales Manager: George W. McClellan
Associate U.S. Adv. Sales Directors: Kenneth E. Clarke, John A. Higgons

FIGURE 5.3. *Masthead from* Time

Summary

The foreign operations of CBS give an indication of the complexity of the mass communicator role. About 60 of CBS's subsidiaries are foreign. As wholly owned or majority-owned companies they carry out part of CBS's international business. The CBS Records International Division, through 27 wholly owned subsidiaries and 14 licensees, has distribution facilities in nearly 100 countries and each year markets over 50 million records outside the United States. CBS Enterprises, Inc., distributes syndicated television programs and program series in almost 100 foreign countries. In addition, CBS has minority interests in offshore television operations (in program production) in Argentina, Peru, Venezuela, Trinidad-Tobago, and Antigua.

Given this enormous industrial complexity, the communicator in mass media has difficulty being an individualist. Nevertheless, complexity and size do not diminish the contributions made by the many specialists who make up the conglomerate communicator. A corporate structure is not some sort of infernal machine that runs itself. It is run by individuals who are vital parts of the communication process at all levels.

Essential attributes of individual mass communicators are the ability to think, to see things accurately, to organize their thoughts quickly and express themselves articulately and effectively. Mass communicators have to be curious about the world, and the people in it. They are called upon to make judgments, sometimes of vast importance, and they should be able to distinguish the significant from the insignificant, the true from the false. Mass communicators need to have a broad view of the world, but increasingly they must specialize within communication. Finally, they must know how to communicate. In mass communication this seemingly simple act becomes exceedingly complex, requiring many kinds of talents, abilities, and specialties. Above all, the sender must understand and respect the medium that he or she uses and works in.

The training and education necessary to become a part of mass media institutions and the personal attributes of mass communications are things that are often misunderstood. A great many potential mass communicators believe that technical training is the key to understanding the process of mass communication. The technology of mass media often blinds "students" to the fact that the *process* of mass communication involves more than pushing a button or flipping a switch.

In his book *The Information Machines: Their Impact on Men and Media*, Ben Bagdikian writes about "printed and broadcast news as a corporate enterprise." He says that news is both an intellectual artifact and the product of a bureaucracy. Distinguished journalism, he writes, requires strong individual leadership, yet such journalism is often at odds with the demands of corporate efficiency. He predicts that daily newspapers will find themselves increasingly in a new corporate enterprise. As Edward Jay Epstein writes in his excellent study *News From Nowhere: Television and the News*: "Before network news can be properly analysed as a journalistic enterprise, it is necessary to understand the business enterprise that it is an active part of, and the logic that proceeds from it."

One must add, of course, that our costly, complex, and competitive corporate media enterprises have produced more information and entertainment than any simplistic, individual, altruistic effort could achieve. There is both good and bad in the system. But one cannot understand the mass communicator without seeing the individual as part of a much larger organism.

One August evening in 1974, four men broke into the Watergate complex in Washington, D.C. Shortly after, two *Washington Post* reporters wrote a routine news story about the incident, which the *Post* handled in a normal way. But the two reporters began to investigate the story further, and wire stories and headlines soon carried the events to a national audience. Radio and television broadcast the story on their news programs, and soon documentaries were being filmed. "Watergate" became a household word as magazines began to publish feature stories about the investigation. After the investigation was complete, the *Post* reporters published two books detailing the events. Soon theater marquees advertised a new motion picture, *All The President's Men*, starring Dustin Hoffman and Robert Redford.

Each of the media that carried elements of this story structured the communication in a different form. We refer to these differences in form as *codes*. The key questions raised here are (1) what are these codes? (2) how are they different? and (3) what meaning do these differences have for an understanding of mass communication?

6 Differences between Content and Codes

At the outset, we must make a clear distinction between the content of mass communication and its code. *Content* refers to the substance or data of a

Codes

message, be it information about President Carter, a humorous monologue by Johnny Carson, or an advertisement for toothpaste. The *code* is the symbol system used to carry the data, whether in the form of the spoken word, the written word, the photograph, music, or the motion picture. In mass communication the code and the content interact to produce the meaning of the message. The different codes of different media can modify the audience's perception of the message, even when the content is the same. For example, watching *Gone With the Wind* on a 12-inch black-and-white TV set is very different from seeing it in a 70-mm wide screen format amplified by stereophonic sound.

Mass media codes add a new set of symbols to traditional language structure. In other words, books, newspapers, magazines, radio, television, film, and recordings employ new languages. Each codifies reality differently; each makes its own statement in its own way. Edmund Carpenter has pointed out that, like the theater, film is a visual-verbal medium presented before a theater audience. Like the ballet, it relies heavily on movement and music. Like the novel, it usually presents a narrative depicting characters in a series of conflicts. Like painting and photography, it is two-dimensional, composed of light and shadow and sometimes color. But its ultimate definition lies in its unique qualities.

Print-Media Codes

As Marshall McLuhan and others have pointed out, when writing was introduced it did not simply record oral language; it was an entirely new, distinct language. It utilized an alphabet as code. Nevertheless, the bits and parts of the alphabet had no meaning in themselves. Only when these components were strung out in a line in a specified order could meaning be created.

Printing is basically an extension of this code with even more uniform linear order. Using this linear order a book's code proceeds from subject to verb to object, from sentence to sentence, from paragraph to paragraph, from chapter to chapter. What this implies is that print codifies reality in a linear manner. Events take place one after the other in print, rather than all at once as they often happen. A football play involves an explosion of simultaneous action that print cannot adequately describe. To do so, it must restructure the reality in linear form.

Books. Because of its coded form, the book is an individual medium generally read silently and alone. A book is usually conceived of as a "serious" mass medium with a definite author or authority. The content is generally placed in some sequential order, either narrative, descriptive, or chronological.

Thus, a book tends to be read in a standard progression rather than selectively as are most magazines and newspapers. The code by which a book is structured also enables the audience to consume content at its own pace, even to reread portions of the content. A book therefore can deal with complex ideas and plots involving many issues or people because its language and code are best able to handle this complexity effectively.

Newspapers. Here, rather than a single line-by-line development of the same idea, there is an explosion of headlines and stories all juxtaposed and all competing for attention. The front pages from the *New York Times* (see figure 6.1) give some idea of the simultaneity of ideas competing for the reader's attention. They also suggest that code systems are manipulated in different ways to reach different readers with different information. The *New York Times* front page is designed to carry "heavy" information. The *New York Daily News*, by contrast, is coded to attract a different reader and to accommodate the type of news it prints. The overall newspaper code does not require sequential use but encourages selective reading by the audience. Through a balanced page make-up using mulitcolumn headlines, with stories developed vertically beneath them, the newspaper gives the reader a choice.

Other noticeable coding characteristics are evident in the newspaper. The inverted pyramid style of writing a story is one. With this coding style, the important information is given first. Less important items follow in the order of descending importance. The reader can stop anywhere and will still have the essence of the story. The editor can cut the story easily at any point without destroying its meaning.

Short paragraphs and narrow columns are also characteristic of newspaper codes. The format of the newspaper and the audience dictate this. Newspaper columns are narrow because a short line is easier to read. Short paragraphs are easier to read than long ones and aid readers in assessing meaning. By breaking up a story, they permit an audience to skim and read selectively.

Another newspaper code characteristic is the use of banners and headlines in different type sizes. Headlines in different type size (see figure 6.2) perform two functions. They indicate the importance of the articles and give the reader a quick summary of the contents.

This coding process and characteristics—inverted pyramid, story structure, narrow columns, short sentences and paragraphs, and headlines in different type size—extend naturally from the way people consume newspapers. We do not generally sit down with a newspaper for hours, but instead read selectively for short periods of time, such as on the subway, in the office, or over breakfast. Few people read a newspaper from cover to cover. Some people

"All the News That's Fit to Print"

The New York Times

LATE CITY EDITION

VOL. CXXVIII . . . . No. 44,120 — NEW YORK, TUESDAY, FEBRUARY 6, 1979 — 20 CENTS

KHOMEINI APPOINTS A DISSIDENT TO LEAD PROVISIONAL REGIME

WARNS AGAINST OPPOSING HIM

Prime Minister Bakhtiar Is Said to Accept It as 'Shadow' Cabinet but Vows Not to Resign

By JAMES M. MARKHAM

Continued on Page A7, Column 1

Congress Urged To Avoid Clash On China Policy

Administration Opens Its Defense of New Stance

By BERNARD GWERTZMAN

Continued on Page A8, Column 3

FARMERS RALLY IN WASHINGTON: 20 were arrested as tractors tied up traffic in protest on prices. Page A12.

S.E.C. ENDS INQUIRY ON CITY'S FINANCES; SAFEGUARDS SOUGHT

NO ENFORCEMENT IS PROPOSED

Agency Names No Names, but It Says Improvements Are Still Needed Despite Gains

By JUDITH MILLER

Excerpts from report are on page B8.

Continued on Page B8, Column 1

Koch Backs New Juvenile Agency; 4 Centers Would Replace Spofford

By CHARLES KAISER

Continued on Page B3, Column 1

RELEASE OF OFFICER IN KILLING IS UPSET

Court Orders That Robert Torsney Be Kept in a Mental Hospital

By JOHN KIFNER

Continued on Page B4, Column 3

Ayatollah Ruhollah Khomeini with Mehdi Bazargan, whom he named prime minister of his provisional government

New Troupe Will Stage Classics in Repertory At Brooklyn Academy

By RICHARD F. SHEPARD

Continued on Page C7, Column 4

Fink Drops 215 Jobs in Assembly; Expects $1.2 Million Yearly Saving

By RICHARD J. MEISLIN

Assembly Speaker Stanley Fink

Continued on Page B8, Column 5

Stocks and Dollar Fall on Iran News

By ROBERT D. HERSHEY Jr.

Continued on Page D15, Column 1

INSIDE

Policeman Kills IND Bystander

Sara Jane Moore Escapes

News Summary and Index, Page B1

FIGURE 6.1 *Front page of the* New York Times

The Washington Post

Defiant Khomeini Names Prime Minister

By William Claiborne
Washington Post Foreign Service

TEHRAN, Feb. 5—Ayatollah Ruhollah Khomeini took a major step toward the creation of an Islamic republic in Iran today by naming a prominent moderate political leader as its prime minister.

MEHDI BAZARGAN
...veteran opponent of shah

Protesting Farmers Snarl City's Traffic

By Douglas B. Feaver
Washington Post Staff Writer

The American Agriculture Movement brought 3,500 people, hundreds of tractors and the worst traffic snarl in memory to metropolitan Washington yesterday morning as part of their economic protest.

Traffic Outlook Today Unclear

A tractor ran into a row of police scooters at Pennsylvania Avenue and John Marshall Place, then went a half a block till it hit police cars in its path.

By Linda Wheeler—The Washington Post

Wagonmaster Cannot Control a Group of Equals

By Blaine Harden
Washington Post Staff Writer

Gerald McCathern, a broad-shouldered farmer from Texas, is the head man in a volunteer organization that has no dues and claims there are no head men.

Senators Insist U.S. Give Strong Support to Taiwan

By Robert G. Kaiser
Washington Post Staff Writer

Five Prosecutors Vow to Resign If Cowhig Returns

By Stephanie Mansfield
Washington Post Staff Writer

Social Security: Some Good News

First of two articles

By Peter Milius
Washington Post Staff Writer

FIGURE 6.2.   *Headline from the* Washington Post

read only one or two sections, such as sports or the comics, the front page, or the women's section. Thus, newspaper-code characteristics are a natural outgrowth of the uses made of the medium.

Magazines. The magazine follows a variety of formats that are quite dissimilar to the newspaper. Instead of many stories that hit the reader simultaneously, articles are published in a sequential plan according to the publication's philosophy. Most magazines print a table of contents that demonstrates their use of sequential organization (see figure 6.3). Within the page, however, magazines adopt a different style demonstrating the creative use of juxtaposition, one story vs. another, advertisements vs. stories, photographs vs. print, and color vs. black and white.

A magazine's use of typography, paper (texture and weight), and page design all add to its code. The slick appearance of *Playboy* is designed to reinforce its "contemporary" content. The code of the *Atlantic Monthly* is staid, in keeping with *Atlantic Monthly* messages; the symbol system used in *Confidential* is exploitative and harsh. Every magazine develops a coding system that augments or enhances its particular message.

Index

Cover: Painting by Roy Andersen.

70
Cover: It's a global outbreak of Einstein fever as all the world joins in a centennial celebration honoring the father of relativity, and scientists everywhere find new relevance in his revolutionary theories. *See* SCIENCE.

12
Nation: Carter flies to Mexico to mend relations strained by Secretary Schlesinger's hard line on oil and gas. ▶ Tax-cut fever brings a move for a Constitutional Convention. ▶ In newly chic Key West, the natives are restless.

84
Roots II: Excitement, fine acting and historical sophistication help *Roots II* outshine its successful parent. ABC's new mini-series climaxes in 1967, the year Alex Haley went to Africa to find Kunta Kinte. *See* TELEVISION.

30
World
In Iran, troops battle supporters of the Ayatullah Khomeini, who names a popular new provisional Prime Minister. ▶ A rare interview with a man from SAVAK. ▶ Israel is accused of mistreating terrorist suspects. ▶ Thailand worries about becoming another domino. ▶ Tales of Tito's love for music.

6
American Scene
At the world's biggest truck stop, drivers eat, sleep, wash and yarn about dope smoking and the hated "four wheels" (cars).

80
Medicine
An insurer hits unneeded diagnostic tests. ▶ European blood pours into the U.S. ▶ Test-tube-baby doctor tells all.

44
Economy & Business
Financial fallout from Iran. ▶ More bad price news. ▶ Bill Buckley on the SEC's firing line. ▶ Dickering with the Chinese.

90
Books
The Ides of August teaches the lessons of the Berlin Wall. ▶ *Dress Gray* catches West Point with its guard down.

54
Religion
In Jonestown's wake, charges of mind control are leveled during a raucous Capitol Hill session on religious cults.

97
Law
A lone holdout hangs the jury in a Congressman's bribery trial, and the Government probes for jury tampering.

59
Cinema
Hardcore is a grim look at the world of porno film making. ▶ *Murder by Decree* does injustice to Sherlock Holmes.

98
Education
With a hard-earned doctorate in heroism, ex-P.O.W. James Stockdale teaches moral philosophy to a class of naval officers.

65
Theater
Playwright Michael Weller is addicted to the young. In *Loose Ends*, his characters suffer growing pains without growing up.

4 Letters
69 People
97 Milestones

FIGURE 6.3. *Contents from* Time

STAR TRACKS

Chip shot∨

With his dad tied up preparing for the Camp David summit with Menachem Begin and Anwar Sadat, Chip Carter, 28, was the designated pinch hitter at Cleveland's annual AFL-CIO Labor Day picnic. However the union folks feel about the Administration these days, they politely didn't shoot the messenger. One spectator, Deborah Davis, representing a vote and a half, flatteringly even asked for an autograph. Of course, Chip is the nephew of Billy Carter.

Douglas chugs∧

Michael Douglas logged a lot of mileage on the streets of San Francisco, but nothing to equal the workout he's getting on the pavements of New York, where he's shooting a movie, *Running*. He plays a 30ish man questing for Olympic gold in the marathon after his marriage and career have gone ka-flooey. When Douglas, who is executive producer as well as the star of the flick, recently did some early morning roadwork on the Queensboro Bridge, he found one rival he could outrun: Manhattan-bound rush-hour traffic.

Carroll caroms‹

It was tee-off time for the Diahann Carroll Celebrity Invitational Golf Tournament at the Woodlands Inn and Country Club near Houston, but the lure of the great indoors was too much for contestants. Especially when Claude (*Movin' On*) Akins, Carroll and Joey Bishop got some education in body English from former world champ Willie Mosconi (second from left). The lesson apparently didn't help his pupils with the nonfelt greens: The winning team was led by old (58) TV comic George Gobel.

CONTINUED
77

FIGURE 6.4. *A typical page from* People

reached 110 stations and organizations.

In the opinions of INTV Chairman Bob J. Wormington (KBMA-TV Kansas City, Mo.) and President Herman W. Land, the site of last week's meeting turned out to be an especially good one. Mr. Land called the meeting the "beginning of political recognition" for INTV.

Mr. Land noted that INTV was considering an expansion of its regular Washington operations, saying the group was contemplating hiring a lobbyist there.

What government officials who were in attendance at the convention last week heard was that independent television broadcasters have put the children's advertising issue—the Federal Trade Commission's proposed rulemaking and the FCC's inquiry—at the top of its list of priorities. The independents are convinced they are "disproportionately affected" by the plans now before the regulatory agencies. According to Mr. Land, for example, about half of independent broadcasters' schedules could be affected by any government-imposed restrictions on advertising in children's television.

Mr. Wormington was especially critical of an FTC staff proposal that children's programs be redefined along the lines of audience composition and not target audience. (The proposal is that any program with an audience composed 20% or more of children would be defined as a "children's program.") Mr. Wormington said such a redefinition "impacts tremendously on family programing," the bread-and-butter of many local independent stations. INTV is "opposed to an audience-composition type of redefinition of

Wormington

Land

children's programing," Mr. Wormington said.

The INTV board met during the convention and reaffirmed its "determination to go all the way" in fighting the proposed children's advertising restrictions.

The board has yet to come up with a firm position on the other issue of the meeting—superstations. "This was the superstation convention," Mr. Land declared, admitting that the broadcasters are still "groping our way, trying to find a position on it."

The broadcasters' feelings on the subject were buoyed considerably by Mr. Bortz's call for "retransmission con-

sent"—a plan that would require the superstations to negotiate with copyright holders before cable systems could receive their signals.

If the independents felt they had found a friend at NTIA, they were less enthusiastic with the FCC—which one participant said had become an acronym for "First Comes Cable."

Delayed a full hour by what the local papers said was the worst snow storm to strike Washington in five years, Chairman Ferris met with the broadcasters Wednesday morning and for 45 minutes fielded questions from the audience. And one broadcaster, Harry J. Pappas of KMPH-TV

In Brief

Three commercial networks are said to be **close to agreement** with Public Broadcasting Service on system of providing **closed captioning for deaf viewers.** Joseph Califano, secretary of health, education and welfare, who has taken lead on issue for administration, is expected to announce within next four weeks that four networks will **put new system into effect early next year.** With negotiations continuing, some details remain to be settled. But it's understood that three commercial networks would each contribute $500,000 to establishing center where programing would be coded for captioning that could be seen only on sets equipped with decoders. It wasn't clear last week how much of its programing each commercial network would encode, but PBS, which has pioneered captioning system and is providing administration with negotiating aim and technical expertise, is said to be committed to 10 hours weekly. Still to be determine is cost of decoding device, but estimates put price at $100 and higher.

□

Elizabeth Hanford Dole, resigned from Federal Trade Commission last Friday (Feb. 9), effective March 9. Commissioner Dole has occupied position since Dec. 4, 1973, with term due to end Sept. 26, 1980. In resignation letter to President Carter, Mrs. Dole said he looked forward to continuing her "commitment to consumer protection and robust competition." No official reason for resignation was given, but spokesman for husband, presidential hopeful Senator Robert Dole (R-Kan.), said, "It would be fair to speculate that this makes it more likely he will run." Commissioner took leave of absence from post in 1976 when Senator Dole ran for Vice President.

□

FCC this week considers what is understood to be staff recommendation that renewal of WDAS-AM-FM **Philadelphia be designated for hearing,** reportedly on **payola and plugola charges** that are said to

involve management. Also pending is application for sale of stations to black group—National Black Network—for $5 million. Complicating matter further is opposition that has been filed by black groups in Philadelphia, who say station should be owned by local blacks.

□

Mobil Corp., currently backing *Edward the King* on ad hoc network of affiliates and independents (BROADCASTING, Jan. 29) has **bought rights to Edward and Mrs. Simpson,** seven-hour miniseries about Edward's grandson, Duke of Windsor, who abdicated British throne in 1936. Latest buy comes from Thames Television and is expected to be scheduled next season similarly to current "Mobil Showcase."

□

The Journal Co. has reached agreement to buy ABC-affiliate KSHO-TV **Las Vegas** (ch. 13) from Arthur P. Williams and family for **$13.5 million.** Buyer publishes *Milwaukee Journal* and *Sentinel* and owns WTMJ-AM-TV and WKTI-FM Milwaukee. Broker: Blackburn & Co.

□

Television Bureau of Advertising estimates that **total TV advertising expenditures in 1978 rose by 18% to $8.97 billion** (for similar Commerce Department estimates, see page 23). Roger D. Rice, TVB president, said bureau placed local TV up 24% at $2.415 billion; spot TV at $2.645 billion, up 20%, and network TV at $3.91 billion, up 13%. He reaffirmed earlier industry projections for 1979 and 1980. He called 1979 "hammock year," hanging between high political years of 1978 and 1980 and said this year local will increase by about 13%; spot by 8% and network by 10%. Mr. Rice said 1980, both Olympic and presidential year, is expected to show gain in local TV of 24%, and in network and in spot of 15% each, with total TV gain of 17%.

□

While **Senate Communications Subcommittee** Democrats and Republicans have had respective staffs working on **separate omnibus bills** amending Communications Act up to this point, they plan to get

FIGURE 6.5. *A typical page from* Broadcasting

Again, much of this use of a particular code system comes from the type of readership and how the reader consumes the magazine. For example, the page structure and layout of *Broadcasting* are much different from those of *People*. *Broadcasting* is a trade magazine read by media professionals interested in the content. The coding system of the magazine does not have to function to attract the reader as much as does *People* magazine's system. *People* makes extensive use of color, boxed inserts, graphics, and white space to attract the reader to a page. Figures 6.4 and 6.5 illustrate these two different coding styles, each designed according to the magazine's content and audience.

Still Photograph.   The still photograph has obvious validity as a separate and distinct form of communication. It is not a mass media as such, however, because it has to be "carried" by another media in order to reach a mass audience. The photograph exists as mass communication primarily as photojournalism in newspapers and magazines. Photography in this sense forms part of the code structure of the print media and is a powerful language. It is used primarily to communicate a sense of reality to the reader. In some cases it is used simply to break up a page and add variety. Increasingly, photographs, especially in magazines, are printed in color, which adds another code structure to the medium. The photo page from *Time* in figure 6.6 illustrates the creative use of the photograph as part of the code structure of this magazine.

Radio–TV–Film Codes

Radio.   Radio departs from the various linear structures of the book, newspaper, and magazine. The ear rather than the eye is the key factor of awareness and interpretation. When radio began as a broadcast medium in 1920, its structure was linear and sequential. Programs were scheduled in 15- and 30-minute formats. All programs were tightly written and performed live. With the advent of television, radio was forced to abandon its program-oriented structure and develop a more flexible nonlinear format. People didn't listen to radio the way they used to, sitting for periods of a half hour or more concentrating on the program. Radio became a companion to people, something they could take with them and tune in and out when they pleased. Today, radio literally bombards the listener with data on a constant and continuous level. For example, a 10-minute time block on a typical "Top 40" station may contain the following content units:

8:00.00–8:00.10   Station Identification
8:00.10–8:00.25   Commercial

Formal portrait of the Shah in full military dress; Western-equipped Iranian troops on parade in Tehran, the capital

Crowd of 25,000 Muslims in the well-to-do Gheytariyeh sector of Tehran in a celebration last week of 'Id al Fitr, ending the Ramadan fast

Religious protestors with anti-Shah banners marching through the capital last week; Shi'ite Spiritual Leader Ayatullah Sharietmadari

FIGURE 6.6. *A photo page from* Time

8:00.25–8:00.50	Disk-Jockey Talk
8:00.50–8:03.50	Music
8:03.50–8:04.20	Weather
8:04.20–8:04.40	Commercial
8:04.40–8:05.00	Talk
8:05.00–8:08.00	Music
8:08.00–8:08.20	Commercial
8:08.20–8:08.35	Station Identification
8:08.35–8:09.00	Talk
8:09.00–8:11.30	Music

With this change, the code of radio has developed into a syntax of words, music, sound effects, and electronically created noise. This coding process affects the content and our perceptions of it. For example, on rock-music radio stations the coding speed contributes to the medium functioning as background "noise"; the slower and less complicated pace of many FM classical-music stations enables the medium to function as a primary activity. One of the problems with the speed and structure of radio's code today is something called "clutter." Clutter is interference created by too many short message units following each other in a short time. In order to cut through clutter, most radio advertisements are stylized with a jingle or ear-catching tune.

Recordings. The code of recordings is aural, of course, consisting of speech, music, and sound effects. This code is now manipulated and stylized in radically different ways than in the past. The Beatles probably did more to create and popularize this new sound as they began to experiment with electronic music and multiple-track mixing of various sounds. Today, recorded music often consists of more than 40 different sound tracks. Often the real creator of this music is the sound mixer, who sits in a studio manipulating dials to produce a complete recording. Individuals or groups on tour often sound very different from their records primarily because the code system of recordings is stylized differently from a live performance.

Motion Pictures and Television. Television and motion pictures have incorporated the most complex code structure of any mass medium. Sight, sound, and motion are combined to produce a dynamic and energetic style. We do not see television and film in the same way that we see a newspaper. As we look at the printed page, our eyes are active scanners of information, engaging in a highly selective process. With film and television our eyes are bombarded by moving, visual images, and because of this, the film and television process includes more of a total sense involvement. McLuhan goes so far as to label television a "tactile" medium. Almost all television programs, with the exception of local and networks news and sports events, are on film and videotape. Therefore, as we discuss the film code, both motion pictures and television are included. The separate process of live television will be considered later.

The film code includes the symbol systems of speech, music, movement, color, and lighting as well as camera composition and editing techniques. The visual components of film language can be broken down into two categories: (1) intrashot elements, which take place within a shot, such as camera movement and composition, lighting, and setting; (2) intershot elements, which include the methods by which separate shots are joined together by means of various transitional devices.

INTRASHOT ELEMENTS.   Perhaps the most important factor in this category is composition. The camera photographs every object from a particular viewpoint, and this viewpoint helps shape the audience's view of the object both intellectually and emotionally.

FIGURE 6.7.   *Nuremburg rally sequence from* Triumph of the Will

The still from the 1936 German propaganda film *Triumph of the Will* (figure 6.7) shows Hitler and two top aides walking through massed columns of soldiers at the 1934 Nuremberg rally. The angle and distance of the shot indicates the immensity of the rally and also serves to isolate and emphasize Hitler's importance. Shooting a subject from below looking up creates a sense of strength or size. James Arness as Matt Dillon in "Gunsmoke" was consistently shot in this manner to emphasize his strength and importance.

Camera distance from the object and lens length are also important. The close-up is an especially powerful element in film and television codes. The close-up of Jack Nicholson in *One Flew Over the Cuckoo's Nest* (1976) aids the viewer in gaining emotional and intellectual insight into the nature of his world (figure 6.8). By limiting the camera's viewpoint, the film maker provides the reality that he feels is critical to an understanding of the message being presented. Milos Forman, the director, wanted to establish an emotional identity for Nicholson and create a feeling for Nicholson's world in the asylum. The film code allows the film maker to intensify the audience's experience by visually isolating critical visual dimensions of the content.

The Museum of Modern Art/Film Stills Archive

FIGURE 6.8. *Jack Nicholson in* One Flew Over the Cuckoo's Nest

A slightly different use of camera perspective is found in a shot in *The Graduate* (1968) that shows Dustin Hoffman running to a church trying to stop a wedding. He is frustrated and desperate, and the camera emphasizes that he is getting nowhere despite his furious, exhaustive running. The director, Mike Nichols, could have represented this by letting Hoffman express the feeling verbally, but he chose to do it "filmically." In this instance, using a telephoto lens, the camera is focused on a close-up of Hoffman running. As he runs toward the camera, he seems to be getting nowhere. Because of the optical characteristics of the telephoto lens, he does not change size during the shot.

In Alain Resnais' *Night and Fog* (1955), a gripping study of the horrors of a Nazi concentration camp, the director creates a powerful effect by slowly pulling the camera back from a close-up of a small mound of woman's hair, to reveal a huge mass. We feel growing horror as this small mound becomes a mountain.

The film code also incorporates special optical effects, among them reverse, fast or slow motion, and freeze frames. These devices are used sparingly because they tend to draw attention to themselves and may distract the viewer from the meaning of the scene. Used correctly, however, they can be a powerful tool. In the television special "Roots," slow motion is used very effectively as the young captured black struggles against the chains that bind him. Extensive use of slow and stop motion does occur in sports programming, adding to spectator insight and enjoyment. This results in new ways of looking at a game or event. We can verify a referee's decision and focus on often unnoticed aspects of a play or piece of action. As used by ABC in televising the XXI Olympiad from Montreal, these effects allowed viewers to analyze a performance or event and gain a perspective that would have been impossible if they were actually there.

Lighting and settings are elements of a visual code that convey a great deal of meaning. The shot in figure 6.9, taken from Ingmar Bergman's film *The Seventh Seal* (1957), illustrates how lighting is used to convey mood and heighten the relationship between Death and the Knight as they play chess.

Color is an important part of a visual code system. Most products, including motion pictures and television programs, come packaged in bright colors designed to attract the consumer. There are times, however, when absence of color amid color can add to the message. Black-and-white public service announcements for CARE are designed to present an image that is thoughtful, quiet, and sober. The film *The Last Picture Show* (1971) reveals how a subject can be as powerful filmed in black and white as in color. The film's director, Peter Bogdanovich, actually shot test scenes in color but decided they looked too beautiful and that black and white photography would best convey the bleak atmosphere of a small Texas town.

INTERSHOT ELEMENTS.   The basis of this element is editing, or the connection of shots, scenes, and sequences in a meaningful pattern. Often the effect and meaning of a scene is communicated by the manner in which shots are combined. Editing links episodes in time and place, and it can present a concept by selecting certain shots or scenes or both instead of allowing the spectators to pick out what they want.

Editing separate shots in specific ways can create a definite sense of rhythm. Joining ten long shots, for example, can create a slower pace. A series of flash cuts or jump cuts can communicate chaos or disorder. This is evident in the scene in *The Graduate* in which the audience looks at a nude Mrs. Robinson as Benjamin sees her, or at least in the way that his mind sees her—in quick, almost imperceptible, flashes of her anatomy. Benjamin is almost afraid to look and yet cannot help but look, and the editing pattern communicates this psychological dilemma.

The editing in Sergei Eisenstein's classic film *Potemkin* (1925) conveys a sense of intellectual and emotional juxtaposition, a radical departure from tradi-

FIGURE 6.9.   *Still from* The Seventh Seal

tional narrative continuity. Eisenstein's methodology, however, was not influential on other film makers. Editing is used by most film makers today to construct narrative stories, to connect scenes, time, and places.

Live Television. Live television, unlike film or edited videotape, is a continuous process. The story is told with a multicamera setup, used by a director who first designs the shots and then edits by selecting among them. In live TV there is no chance to go back over a scene again or shoot out of context. Although traditionally a less flexible process than film or videotape, live television is increasing this flexibility, especially at sporting and other special events, through large numbers of cameras, many of them portable "mini cams." Television news has benefited greatly from the revolution in miniaturization because live remote broadcasts are now possible within the time frame of an actual news program.

There are special effects in television as well as film that add to the medium's flexibility. Such techniques as superimposition, chroma key, wipes, and video feedback, among others, are widely used in television today.

Perhaps the major difference between television and motion pictures today is their exhibition. Seeing an event on television—especially live television—is simply not the same as seeing it in a motion-picture theater. Watching President Carter's inauguration on live television as it was occurring, seeing him step out of the car and walk down Pennsylvania Avenue, is quite different from watching it two days or even two hours later via film or videotape. At this "distance" the event becomes history, bound in time and without, as Edmund Carpenter has said, "potentiality."

Yet another difference is the size of the screen: television uses a small screen, film uses a large one. The huge screen of a motion-picture theater is better suited for spectacles such as *Gone With the Wind* or *Star Wars*. In contrast, television has room for two, perhaps three, faces comfortably.

Code Preferences

Different media have different codes, and often these differences mean that a message may not be suitable for a particular medium. Each medium tends to select or even create its own messages.

For example, Marshall McLuhan makes a strong case for the fact that baseball was popularized by the nineteenth-century newspaper. Baseball is the perfect game for print; it is absolutely linear, with only usually one main action occurring at any given time, so the story of the game can be told chronologically. Football, however, might be considered the national pastime created by twentieth-century television. In football the action is not linear; in fact, the action is literally an explosion, with men scattering in all directions, each carrying out a different assignment simultaneously. Such multidimensional action is more suitable for the code of television, which involves the viewer and absorbs him in many levels of action and experience at once.

We need to go beyond content when assessing the impact of a medium's code. We can understand what McLuhan means when he says the medium is the message when we see how media codes change not only the message but man and his society. For example, the introduction of the alphabet and printing press changed an oral tradition. As Tom Wolfe, in his interpretation of McLuhan, has put it:

> The printing press brought about a radical change. People began getting their information primarily by seeing it—the printed word. The visual sense became dominant. Print translates one sense—hearing, the spoken word—into another sense—sight, the printed word. Print also converts sounds into abstract symbols, the letters. Print is orderly progression of abstract, visual symbols. Print led to the habit of categorizing—putting everything in order, into categories, "jobs," "prices," "departments," "bureaus," "special ties." Print led, ultimately, to the creation of the modern economy, to bureaucracy, to the modern army, to nationalism itself.[1]

And McLuhan himself says:

> All that ends now in the electronic age, whose media substitute all-at-onceness for one-thing-at-a-timeness. The movement of information at approximately the speed of light has become by far the largest industry of the world. The consumption of this information has become correspondingly the largest consumer function in the world. The globe has become on one hand a community of learning, at the same time, with regard to the tightness of its interrelationships, the globe has become a tiny village. Patterns of human association based on slower media have become overnight not only irrelevant and obsolete, but a threat to continued existence and sanity.[2]

[1]Tom Wolfe, "The New Life Out There," in New York *Herald Tribune*, 21 November 1965; idem, *McLuhan: Hot and Cool*, ed. Gerald E. Stearn (New York: New American Library, 1969), p. 36.

[2]Marshall McLuhan, Harley Parker, and Robert Shafer, "The Gutenberg Galaxy: A Voyage Between Two Worlds"; idem, *Report on Project on Understanding New Media*

Media messages derive much of their meaning from three factors: environment, media codes, and media uses. Media reflect the environment in which they are created and the conditions governing that creation. That reflection, however, is conditioned by the codes the media employ and the uses to which they are put. In essence, a medium's environment, code, and uses are its content. The six primary uses of media are discussed at length in part 4. While these are referred to as uses, they are also media content. Content is essentially an extension of a medium's use at a particular point in time and should be treated in a broader perspective.

Thus, what do media say? They say what their particular environments, codes and uses permit them to say. A study of content is inherent throughout this book, as we review the history of media, as we analyze media codes and languages, and as we review media's uses.

(Washington, D.C.: Office of Education, U.S. Department of Health, Education, and Welfare, 1960), Appendix; idem, *McLuhan: Hot and Cool*, p. 151.

Nearly everyone has played the communication game in which someone whispers a statement that is passed from person to person. By the time the message gets back to the originator, the content is usually distorted and sometimes totally different from the original. Each person in this communication chain has acted as a resistor or booster, emphasizing certain aspects of the message while deemphasizing others. In interpersonal communication each of us receives, makes judgments about, and modifies messages before we pass them along. Each of us acts as a checkpoint in the communication process—we refuse to transmit some messages, overemphasize others, and play down still more. All of us, in effect, serve as gatekeepers—as checkpoints in the flow of communication. In the mass communication process these checkpoints are extremely important and have assumed formalized roles.

The Concept of the Gatekeeper in Mass Communication

It should be noted that the word *gatekeeper* is essentially a sociological term used in mass communication research and may not even be recognized by many media professionals. The term was originally coined by Kurt Lewin in 1947 in *Human Relations* to describe the process by which a news item, traveling through channels, gains clearance at certain checkpoints along the way. Lewin calls these checkpoints *gates*. The individuals or organizations who give clearance he labels *gatekeepers*.

7

Gatekeepers

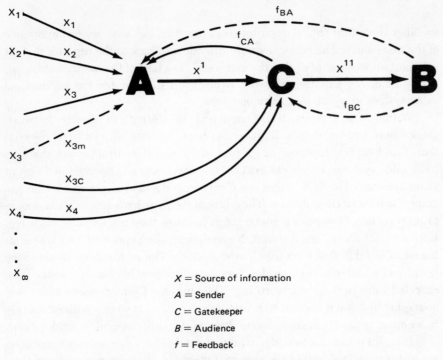

X = Source of information
A = Sender
C = Gatekeeper
B = Audience
f = Feedback

FIGURE 7.1. *The Westley and MacLean Model*

In the mass communication process gatekeepers take many forms. They are magazine publishers, newspaper editors, radio station managers, television news directors, or movie producers. The gatekeeper's function is to evaluate media content in order to determine its relevance and value to audiences. What is most important is the fact that gatekeepers have the power to cut off or alter the flow of certain kinds of information.

The Westley-MacLean model introduced in chapter 2 and shown again here (figure 7.1) visualizes the concept of the gatekeeper in the mass communication process.[1] The Xs refer to events or sources of information (e.g., a fire or a copy of a speech released prior to its actual presentation). The mass communicator A in this example is a reporter who describes the fire and speech in the form of news stories. The gatekeeper C is the editor who deletes, deemphasizes, or adds to the reports of the fire and speech based on data that may or may not have been available to the reporter. The audience B then reads the news reports of the fire and speech in the newspaper. The reader may respond

[1]Bruce Westley and Malcolm S. MacLean, Jr., "A Conceptual Model for Communications Research," *Journalism Quarterly* 34 (Winter 1957): 31–38.

to either the editor *fBC* or reporter *fBA* regarding the accuracy or importance of the news story. The editor may also provide feedback to the reporter *fCA*. It is important to remember that the gatekeeper is a part of the media institution, and most of the gatekeeper's work is designed to reinforce the institutional value system in which he or she operates.

Within this context it is important to distinguish clearly between gatekeepers and regulators. Both act to check, restrain, or clarify media content. Gatekeepers, however, are a part of the media institution and share its basic value systems; regulators exist outside the media and operate on different value systems. The U.S. Supreme Court may declare a certain film pornographic and halt its distribution. The editor of the *Evansville Courier* may decide to drop certain *Doonesbury* comic strips because they are sexually offensive. Each acts as a check, as a restraint. Nevertheless, the Supreme Court is operating on values different from the *Courier* editor's. The editor drops *Doonesbury* because of possible adverse reader reaction and/or possible loss of revenue from canceled subscriptions or advertising. The Supreme Court declares a film pornographic because it appeals to prurient interest and is wholly without socially redeeming value. Its decision has nothing to do with economic considerations.

It is also important to understand that gatekeepers in mass communication are institutionalized within the system. Often, they are not personally visible. They are so vital to the proper functioning of the mass communication process that they are institutionalized into formal roles and responsibilities. Mass media systems do not simply *tolerate* gatekeepers, they create them. Historically, gatekeepers existed in the press in the singular form of owners, men like Hearst, Pulitzer, Scripps, Luce, and Greeley. Today, however, gatekeepers are not so socially visible and rarely do they exist in the form of a single person. Rather, gatekeeping in mass media today is behind the scenes. Rather than individuals, there are departments staffed by publicly faceless but enormously powerful people. The motion picture *All the President's Men* presented an excellent example of the gatekeeping process as we witnessed the *Washington Post* editorial board sitting around a desk making decisions on what would make up the news in the *Post* that day.

Today's gatekeepers assume a variety of roles. Let us examine a few of them.

Roles of Gatekeepers

All mass media have a large number of gatekeepers. They perform a variety of functions and play several roles. They can simply stop a message by refusing to "open the gate." The program practices department of a television network can do this by simply refusing a proposed script. Local stations can also delete content, and in recent years the television networks have assisted the stations by feeding affiliates up to 20 hours a week of program material that might be controversial. Gatekeepers can alter the message by deleting limited portions of it, as they sometimes do on late-night talk programs when certain words and even phrases are "bleeped."

Sometimes one medium serves a gatekeeping function that affects another medium. For example, the *Detroit Free Press* and several other newspapers refuse to accept advertising of X-rated films—newspaper editors in several major cities deleted a series of *Doonesbury* strips from their papers because they were "objectionable." The critic for a magazine can refuse to review a new book on the market. A radio station may refuse to play a recently released record because it deals with a controversial subject. Several radio stations routinely ban all records with drug-oriented lyrics. All these gatekeeping decisions affect the ability of an audience to avail itself of specific media experiences, and deleting or stopping a message is the most powerful force a gatekeeper has. But gatekeepers are not simply passive-negative forces opening or closing the gate on a message or a portion of it. They can also be a creative force adding to the message.

The news editor can add to messages by combining information from other sources as well as his reporter, or by adding a story at the beginning of a newscast. The magazine-layout editor can increase the impact of a story by adding a significant number of pictures. The artist-and-repertoire person in a record company can send the master tape back for additional background music to improve the total sound. The movie producer can send a work print back to the editor or director to have scenes added or deleted. This process of adding to a message makes the role of a gatekeeper similar to a communicator's, and indeed gatekeepers can be looked at as part of the mass communicator concept in that they affect content. The key distinction, however, is that gatekeepers do not originate content; they alter it.

The gatekeeper also modifies the emphasis of the message. Murray Schumach notes this function in the film *Breakfast at Tiffany's*. The heroine, Holly Golightly, was an amusing girl with few moral inhibitions. Part of her humor was based on her indifference to promiscuity. But when Audrey Hepburn was cast in the role, it was considered improper to let the public see her depicted this way. As the director, Blake Edwards, said: "In the movie we don't exactly say what Holly's morals are. In a sense she can be considered an escort service for men. . . . Risqué dialogue was deleted and she no longer discusses her affairs with men. Holly is now a patroness of the arts."[2] In newspapers, message emphasis is changed by headline size and story placement. Some radio station managers have "soul" programs for black listeners, but many such programs are slotted late at night when smaller audiences are available.

Gatekeepers, then, serve three basic functions in the mass communication process: (1) they have the power to delete a message; (2) they can increase the amount and importance of a certain kind of information; (3) they can decrease the amount and importance of a specific kind of information.

There is little question that gatekeeping represents enormous power and control. Nevertheless, gatekeepers retain that power only by exercising it within the shared value system of the media institution in which they work. A film editor who consistently cuts out a director's best scenes or an actor's most appealing camera angle will soon be out of a job.

The various gatekeeping functions are usually accomplished through three means: economic control, individual taste or bias, or an ideology or value system. Economic control can exist in the form of broad policy, such as a corporation vice president allowing no motion picture to cost more than $1 million. Clearly, this would place restraints on content and how it was presented. More often, however, economic control takes the form of simple space/time restrictions. A publisher may decide the news hole for today's paper will be 75 columns. The editor may have enough news to fill 125 columns but to no avail. The producer of "The CBS Evening News" has only a limited amount of time to present the news of the day and must make hard decisions about which news stories get on the air.

Individual personality is historically the most common and most visible form of gatekeeping. Henry Luce determined much of what went into each issue of *Time*. Ben Bradlee made a critical decision by allowing stories by Woodward and Bernstein to appear in the *Washington Post* despite great pressure to drop the stories. Rupert Murdoch has clearly changed the style and content of *New York* magazine and the *New York Post*. There will always be key people in any media organization who will shape and influence media content. Bill Jackson, former editor of the *Sunday Courier Press* in Evansville, Indiana, stated that what got printed on the front page of his paper was what he decided was news.

The influence of an ideology or value system is a little more difficult to recognize but is perhaps the most powerful gatekeeping method. The conservative ideology of the *New Republic* clearly influences its content, as does the

[2]Murray Schumach, *The Face on the Cutting Room Floor* (New York: William Morrow, 1964), pp. 142–43.

"*I deem thee newsworthy.*"

liberal philosophy of the *New York Times*. Les Brown comments in his book *Television: The Business Behind the Box*, "The ruling powers at the networks are decidedly Establishment in their politics and in general closer to the right of the political center than to the left." This would seem to affect the content broadcast by the networks.

A variety of people perform the gatekeeping function. Nevertheless, certain people or positions function more often and with greater influence as gatekeepers than others. Let us review individual media and their major gatekeepers.

The Gatekeeper and News. The major gatekeeper in the news media is the editor. In the face of today's tremendous news output, every news medium must be selective. Studies indicate that a typical large-city daily newspaper can carry as little as one-tenth of the news that comes into the newsroom on any given day. The same is true for news magazines because much more material is available to their editors than space limitation permit them to use. Editors determine which stories should reach the public. They also decide what emphasis to give the stories. Placement of a story on the front page of a newspaper or as the lead article in a magazine can have a significant influence on the number of persons who read it. The use of a larger size of type for a headline can give a story more importance than it would otherwise have and thus attract more readers.

Although the editor is the most easily identifiable gatekeeper in a news operation, other persons assist in the gatekeeping function. To emphasize the complexity of this aspect of mass communication, let us examine the steps a story on President Carter vetoing a congressional bill goes through before it appears in a local newspaper. The news sources—in this case President Carter or his press secretary and certain congressmen—serve as the first gatekeepers. They are the witnesses to and participants in an attempt to veto the piece of congressional legislation. They view the operation selectively; they see some events, miss others, forget some, and misinterpret others. Significantly, the fact that they are involved in the action affects their perception.

The reporter gathering information is the next step in the gatekeeping process. He may choose to believe President Carter, who viewed the legislation as ill conceived although Congress viewed the legislation as necessary. The reporter has to decide which facts to pass along, how to write or photograph them, what perspectives he should offer from his previous experiences in covering the federal government.

By the time the report gets to a wire service, it has become part of a large amount of information flowing to wire-service editors who must decide what copy is worth passing along to regional and state bureaus, where a similar decision is made.

Finally, the story is pulled from the wire by a local newspaper's wire editor or a TV station's news director. Literally hundreds of stories are competing for space in the newspaper, and if President Carter's action is deemed important, and if there is space for it or no local news that might take precedence, it will be used. The key to understanding the process is that the story can be kept out of the news by any gatekeeper along the line.

Gatekeepers also operate in radio and television news. While newspapers have a space problem, broadcasters are limited by time. The editor of the "NBC Nightly News" faces a selection and emphasis problem that is even more severe than that faced by the editor of the *New York Times*. Wire services and staff reporters provide much more news than can possibly be used. Most television network news programs are 30 minutes long, including commercials and credits. At most, only 10–15 stories can be covered in this time period. Thus, program length becomes a critical factor in news selection by broadcast gatekeepers.

The Gatekeeper and Entertainment. Broadcast-entertainment gatekeepers include writers, directors, producers, actors, editors, designers, musicians, and many other persons associated with a production. "60 Minutes," for example, as noted earlier, had more than 60 people involved in the production of a single episode including 15 producers, 3 researchers, 15 film editors, and 4 correspondents. Not all these people serve as gatekeepers, but most of them have the gatekeeping potential to evaluate and alter the flow of communication. Perhaps the key persons are the program producers. In "60 Minutes" these are Don Hewitt, the executive producer, and Palmer Williams, the senior producer. Stephen Zito notes some of the two men's functions in his article, "Inside 'Sixty Minutes'": "He [Williams] constantly keeps an eye out for story ideas and draws inspiration from a variety of sources—CBS producers and correspondents, newspaper clippings, and people at the regional news bureaus and affiliates. Williams's desk is piled high with mail. He reads most of it himself and estimates that perhaps twenty-five percent of the segments that reach the air have their origin in viewer suggestions. . . . Hewitt makes up the show each week in much the same way a magazine editor assembles an individual issue of a magazine, giving thought to length, tone, and contrast."[3] Hewitt himself gives an excellent explanation of his gatekeeping role in "60 Minutes": "It's all instinctive . . . I'm the least intellectual person I know. A lot of times I say to a producer, 'I see it and I hear it but I don't feel it in the pit of my stomach.' I don't make decisions intellectually, I make them viscerally. . . . When I get bored, I figure other people will get bored. I have the ability to put myself in the place of the viewer because I have the same short attention span he has.

"When an idea comes in, my first reaction is always, 'Does anybody care? Is anyone gonna watch this?' It's not important in TV what you tell people; it's only important what they remember of what you told them. If you bombard them with a lot of facts in a dull fashion just to discharge your public duty, you perform no service at all. There is a certain entertainment value to this broadcast, but that doesn't detract from the fact that America is now better informed. If you can entertain people, you can keep them close to the show and they'll come back next week. I don't want to broadcast in a vacuum."

[3]Stephen Zito, "Inside Sixty Minutes," *American Film* 2, no. 3 (December–January 1977): 31–36, 55–57.

Once a television program is shot, the editor—a key gatekeeper—comes into play. This person can completely alter the message of the director. A fascinating glimpse of this process and its influence is found in the short film *Interpretations and Values*. The film shows how three editors cut a sequence from the television series "Gunsmoke" and reveals how each editor saw the raw footage a little differently and stamped the film with his own interpretation.

Much the same gatekeeping process is involved in making a motion picture, although some differences occur because of the expanded scope and budget of a feature film. Whereas an episode of a television series usually takes less than a week to shoot, a motion picture may involve months, even years, of work. A brief glimpse at some of the people involved in the 1976 production of *King Kong* as described by Bruce Bahrenburg in his book *The Making of King Kong* will illustrate this point.

The film began with a press conference January 14, 1976 in which producer Dino De Laurentiis introduced the major participants in the film, and ended on December 17, 1976 when the film opened simultaneously in 1,500 theaters. The film's permanent production crew numbered over 400 people, and including extras, assistants, and location personnel, the actual number of people involved in the making of the film was well over 1,000. There were a number of key gatekeepers on the film, including the screenwriter Lorenzo Semple, Jr., the director John Guillermin, and two men who did not even speak the same language, special effects designers Carlo Rambaldi of Italy and Glen Robinson of the United States. Other important gatekeepers were the film's editor Ralph Winter, the production designers Mario Chiari and Dale Hennesy, and director of photography Richard H. Kline. However, the major influence on the film was De Laurentiis. As he stated in an interview while still filming: "A producer does too much. If the picture is a flop, a hundred-percent responsibility belongs to the producer. He selects the script, cast, editor and director. But if the picture is a success, it belongs to everyone, including the producer."

The Impact of the Gatekeeper

From the previous discussion it becomes clear that the identity of the gatekeeper blurs with that of the communicator. When is the copyeditor or film editor a communicator rather than a gatekeeper? The distinction lies in terms of *what* the person is doing. An individual who is creating is serving as a communicator. An individual who is evaluating another's creation is a gatekeeper. Obviously, the same individual may perform both functions at the same time: one person can evaluate a director's visual output and add a creative dimension to the film. A copyeditor's evaluation of a reporter's story also involves the creative editing of the total newspaper.

The regulator and gatekeeper roles are similar in one respect—both can stop messages from reaching audiences. The significant difference is that the *gatekeeper is a part of the media institution,* but the *regulator is an external agent* of the public or government. Gatekeepers are further distinguished from regulators in that the gatekeeper can, as noted, add to as well as delete from mass communication messages.

The gatekeeper can have a potent effect on the mass communication process—especially if a society's media are controlled by an elite minority intent on restricting the public's right to know. Former Vice-President Spiro Agnew brought this concern to the public spotlight in his Des Moines, Iowa, speech in 1969. Although overstating the issue, he did create controversy within the news media and focused attention on those individuals functioning as gatekeepers in television network news. In a free society, however, where television news is in competition with newspapers and magazines as well as with other broadcast journalists, this potential misuse of the gatekeeping role is less likely to occur. Obviously, the reactionary right and radical left sometimes feel that the media's gatekeepers in the United States devote too little time and space to these groups' views of what is news.

In practice, the gatekeeper's power is diffuse because in mass communication the message is usually meant for such a large audience that one single cut from a script or a news story cannot produce a fundamental change in the nature of the communication event or in the society itself. Nevertheless, live television coverage of news events has demonstrated that gatekeepers can have a significant impact on mass communication. This fact was dramatically brought to light by television coverage of the 1968 Democratic National Convention in Chicago. The interpretation and the subsequent impact of the convention were created by the selective coverage given the demonstrations outside the convention headquarters. Videotape editing demonstrated the impact gatekeepers can have by presenting a selected view of events.

The concern expressed over the Chicago coverage has also been raised over television handling of riots in some large cities. Television cannot and does not simply "tell it like it is." It may record, but it does so under the influence of many communicators and gatekeepers who filter, amplify, or interfere with the message. The amplifying role used on television for news coverage has been severely criticized. Critics claim that by emphasizing looting and destruction, television gatekeepers may actually encourage observers to participate.

The same basic gatekeeping effects occur with an entertainment program, with the exception that the public probably does not feel the same concern over the deletion of a particular song or spoken vulgarity that it does when it suspects that what is being offered as news is untrue or that part of the truth is being withheld. After an initial furor, the gatekeeping incident involving the "Richard Pryor Show" was seemingly forgotten. On the other hand, questions are still being raised about news coverage of events in Vietnam that happened years ago.

Thus, the basic effect of gatekeeping is that the message is altered in some way. Only when this alteration seriously distorts the public's view does the gatekeeping function become unsatisfactory. The media can and do distort reality. This distortion can occur in one of two ways: (1) systematic distortion or (2) random distortion. Systematic distortion can occur through deliberate bias; random distortion can occur through carelessness or ignorance. A study of wire-news editors revealed a degree of systematic distortion at work when it was found that some editors, because of their particular bias and predisposition, would not carry certain stories. This can usually be corrected because it is highly visible to many people within and outside the particular mass media institution. Random distortion, usually caused by carelessness or ignorance, is often more dangerous and harmful. Here the role of the gatekeeper is not as easily discernible. Gatekeepers who operate by random distortion seldom have reasons for their decisions because their job may be so routine, so institutionalized, that they do not actually feel they are making decisions.

It is clear that some gatekeepers are more important than others. Robert K. Merton has described several types of "influentials"—that is, certain types of individuals in any society who receive an unusually large number of messages. He further breaks down this category into "cosmopolitans" and "locals."[4] The cosmopolitan receives his information from outside the community while the local functions within the local society. These kinds of influentials exist as gatekeepers on a movie set, in a newspaper office, or a television studio. What is important about their presence in mass communication is that they are so numerous, are fragmented into highly specialized positions, and may have an effect disproportional to their relative position and power.

Gatekeepers are a normal part of any communication process. Ordinarily, they create no great concern. With mass communication chains organized in the way that they are, however, gatekeepers assume importance because they have the power to alter, delete, or stop media content altogether.

---

[4]Robert K. Merton, "Patterns of Influence: A Study of Interpersonal Influence and Communications Behavior in a Local Community," in Robert K. Merton, *Social Theory and Social Structure* (Glencoe, Ill.: Free Press, 1957), pp. 387–420.

What is as important is the fact that gatekeepers may be invisible to most people and may be barely aware that they are making decisions affecting the lives of millions of people. Gatekeepers have enormous power and control in the mass communication process. It is critical that we understand who they are and how they function.

An essential element of communication is the medium that carries the message. In this sense the medium refers to the element that provides for the actual physical transmission of the message. When we communicate person to person, the medium is sound waves in the air, a letter delivered through the mail, or telephone wires and receivers. In mass communication, however, a vast and complex fabric of specialized machinery makes up the medium.

The machines and technology by which media messages are physically transmitted have become institutionalized in the form of huge industrial organizations. We cannot really separate the machines of mass communication from the institutions that control them. Because of this, when we speak of the media of mass communication we are referring to both the machinery and the institutions controlling this machinery.

Figure 8.1 indicates in brief form the extent and complexity of mass communication as a part of American society. Seven principal mass media *institutions*—newspapers, magazines, books, radio, television, motion pictures, and recordings—are composed of basic media *units* that are the producers of communication *products*—publications, pictures, programs, and records. The basic media units are themselves dependent on a system of media service units that produce, distribute, exhibit, sell, manufacture, and represent communications, communication facilities, and communicators. In addition, a large network of management and professional associations represents the managers

8

The Media

and communicators in their relations with one another and with other institutions in society.

Media Institutions

Let us examine and describe briefly the seven primary mass media institutions, the physical medium surrounded by the industrial organization.

The Book.　Books come in a fairly standardized format, although there is variation in page size, binding, type of cover, and length. The institutions encompassing the book normally take the form of publishing companies. About 1,500 publishing firms produce about 40,000 book titles in America each year. But only about 300 publishers produce the majority of books, and most of them are concentrated in New York City.

The Newspaper.　Newspapers are also fairly standardized in format. They are printed on large sheets of paper, either blanket size (about 22 inches by 15 inches) or tabloid size (about 15 inches by 12 inches). About 1,800 daily newspapers and about 10,000 weekly newspapers are published in the United States, although many are "chains," owned by larger corporations. In America, only a small handful of newspapers, such as the *Christian Science Monitor*, have national circulations; most are geographically confined to distinct metropolitan areas or communities.

The Magazine.　Magazines come in all sizes and shapes. They are usually printed on heavier and higher-quality paper than newspapers and are bound by staple with soft covers. About 10,000 different magazine publication units exist in the United States, with many under chain ownership. Magazines have a broader range than newspapers, both in subject matter and in geographical distribution, and can reach specialized audiences.

The Motion Picture.　Although this label usually refers to feature-length dramatic films running 90 to 180 minutes in duration, there are many different types of motion pictures. Production has shifted away from large Hollywood-studio corporations to small, independent producers who use the old units such as Warner Brothers and MGM primarily for financing, promotion, and distribution services. Motion-picture studios are today heavily engaged in producing film for another medium—television—which uses motion-picture film for news and documentaries, series programs, and commercials, as well as feature-length dramas.

Media Institutions	Media Products	Basic Media Units
Newspaper	Daily newspapers Weekly newspapers Sunday supplements	*New York Times* *Christian Science Monitor* *Baltimore Afro-American* *Bakersfield Californian* *National Observer*
Magazine	Weekly magazines Monthly magazines Quarterly magazines Comic books	*Newsweek* *Sports Illustrated* *Playboy* *Horizon* *Journalism Quarterly*
Book	Hardcover books Paperback books	Acropolis Books David McKay Company Dodd, Mead, and Company University of Illinois Press Bantam Books

Motion picture	Feature-length
	  motion pictures
	Cartoons
	Documentaries
	Industrial films
	Television commercials
	  and programs
		Columbia Pictures
		Walt Disney Productions
		Metro-Goldwyn-Mayer
		Hearst Metrotone Telenews
		Avco-Embassy

Radio	Radio programs and commercials	WGN, Chicago KYW, Cleveland WNEW, New York WXHR-FM, Boston WUEV-FM, Evansville
Television	Television programs and commercials	KTTV, Los Angeles WOR-TV, New York WMAL-TV, Washington, D.C. KGO-TV, San Francisco KRLD-TV, Dallas
Sound recording	Disk recordings Tape recordings Cassette recordings Cartridge recordings	Capitol Records, Inc. Columbia Record Company Decca Recordings RCA Victor Records
Various	Personal, graphic, audiovisual, mixed- multi, and computer media	Kiplinger Washington Letter Academic Media Services, Inc.

Media Service Units	Media Associations
Associated Press United Press King Features	American Newspaper Publishers Association American Society of Newspaper Editors
Publication retailers Advertising agenties	Magazine Publishers Association Society of Magazine Writers
Printing–press manufacturers	American Book Publishers Council American Institute of Graphic Arts
Motion-picture exhibitors Film laboratories Directors Guild	Motion Picture Association of America National Academy of Motion Picture Arts & Sciences
ABC MBS American Federation of R–TV Artists	National Association of Broadcasters R–TV News Directors Association
NBC CBS TV set manufacturers	National Association of Broadcasters National Academy of R–TV Arts & Sciences
Broadcast Music Inc. (BMI) Record distributors Talent agencies	Recording Industry Association of America
Public-relations agencies	Public Relations Society of America

FIGURE 8.1.   *HUB Structural Chart of Mass Media*

Radio. Like TV, this medium requires special equipment both for transmission and reception. Transmission equipment is expensive and complex, but radio receivers using solid-state transistors are relatively inexpensive. Ownership and operation of the over 4,400 amplitude-modulation (AM) and 3,400 frequency-modulation (FM) stations in the United States are regulated by the federal government. Radio is oriented toward local rather than regional or national operations even though there are four national networks (ABC, CBS, MBS, NBC), which provide mostly news programming. More than 98 percent of all homes in the United States have radio receivers, most of them capable of receiving at least six to eight stations in the average listening area.

Television. This medium is composed of two basic types of transmission systems: very high frequency (VHF—channels 2 to 13) and ultra-high frequency (UHF—channels 14 to 83). VHF stations normally reach more people because their signals cover a larger area using less power than UHF stations. This is reflected in the greater number of VHF stations (more than 500 commercial and 95 noncommercial) compared to UHF stations (almost 200 commercial and 160 noncommercial). As with radio, TV stations are licensed by the federal government. The three national television networks (ABC, NBC, and CBS) dominate the medium because they supply 70 to 90 hours of programming per week out of their affiliated stations' total program schedule of 100 to 110 hours.

Sound Recording. Like broadcast media, records and tapes require special production and playback equipment. Approximately 80 percent of all U.S. homes have phonograph or tape recorders, which use records and tapes produced by over 1,500 record companies. Five companies—led by Columbia—dominate record production in the United States. Record companies are also the largest suppliers of programming for radio.

Other Media. Although few of what are described as other media are as completely institutionalized as the seven described above, their day may soon be at hand. Newsletters and direct-mail companies are growing, and new graphic and audiovisual media are coming into widespread use, particularly in education and advertising. Experiments with mixed- and multimedia styles are producing new forms, usually combining still and motion pictures with recording and publications. Newest and most important of all are the computer-based media, which can publish, broadcast, store, retrieve, and manipulate communication in a variety of new ways.

Communication Products

The end results of the labors of mass communicators are products not completely dissimilar from products of other producers in society. The products have substance, monetary value, social and intellectual value, and a limited lifetime. Print-media goods and services include issues of publications, either periodic, such as daily or weekly newspapers and monthly or quarterly magazines, or one-time issues of publications, such as books.

Film-media products are motion pictures.[1] Broadcast media produce programming for radio or television, often using the products of other institutions—films and sound recordings in particular. These programs, too, have a substance—even if not recorded on sound or videotape. But since the substance is magnetic fields in the air, broadcast services are fleeting unless recorded. The recording industry produces disk and tape recordings that are similar to books in their distribution. Media products acquire distinctive style and identity aside from their technological reality by the manner in which they are used. Television programs, magazines, motion pictures, and the like achieve individual identity chiefly through code and use manipulation.

Basic Media Units

The mass communication industry resembles the operational organization of other corporate enterprises in our country. Media products are produced, distributed, and exhibited through national corporations as well as local retailers. The basic media unit may be national or local, but whatever its primary function, the *basic media unit is that part of mass media held responsible for content*, even though the unit may not have produced or distributed the content. In fact, some basic media units actually create a relatively small portion of the content for which they are held accountable.

The local newspaper is held responsible for the news and entertainment it prints, even though much of its content may come from outside sources such as syndicated feature or wire services. Most papers also seek to create a specific editorial policy on issues affecting their communities. They seek to create a distinct identity through layout, content, style, and coverage. The same is true of magazines. The responsible party is the particular staff that carries out the production of a publication that appears periodically under one title.

The book publisher—Longman, Harper & Row, Hastings House—is the

[1]Although the production of still photographs has not resulted in a separate medium, independent still photographers provide photographic service to other media.

basic media unit in the book industry. The publisher not only serves as producer and distributor, but in a few metropolitan markets one or two also operate retail bookstores.

The motion picture's traditional pattern of having the studio serve as the basic media unit is beginning to change as the movie industry moves through a transitional period. For example, in the case of the new 16-mm, sexually explicit films operating in many metropolitan areas, the exhibitor may be the producer, and no formal distribution chains may exist. Because of the costs involved in production and the complex system of distribution, however, most feature films still rely on studio organizations (20th Century-Fox, Paramount, MGM, and so on) as the basic media unit.

Radio and television stations licensed by the Federal Communications Commission are directly responsible for all content broadcast, despite the fact that they create only a small part of it. In radio, the phonograph record, wire services, network news operations, advertisers, and packaging agencies produce the content of radio. The station organizes and supplements it but is still the responsible party and required by law to serve "the public interest, convenience, and necessity" of the community. The networks, syndication companies, and advertisers dominate the content of television, but the station assumes responsibility for all programs telecast.

Sound-recording companies producing records are the basic media units and the responsible party in this medium.

Media Service Units

In many ways, media service units are more important to mass communication than the basic units that carry their own imprint and reach the consumer directly. Although these service units rarely are identified by name—and only indirectly touch the lives of the consumer—nevertheless they often produce the bulk of the communication, exercise control over its production, or provide the necessary technical equipment and talent.

Press Associations. These organizations are the primary news gatherers and processors for mass media. The largest American associations are (1) the Associated Press (AP), a cooperative that sends teletype news and features to more than 8,500 newspaper, magazine, TV, and radio media units that are members of the association; and (2) United Press International (UPI), a private association that has more than 7,000 media unit subscribers. These press associations, or wire services as they are also called, do not produce material directly for the public but only for media units. They have widespread bureaus and experienced reporters, writers, and editors to process the news. The mass media are largely dependent upon them for nonlocal news and information.

Syndicates. These service units provide feature and interpretative material, particularly for the print media. More than 200 syndicates exist that own the rights to the production of individual writers and commentators. These syndicates package, promote, and sell columns, analyses, comic-strip cartoons, and other features to individual newspapers, magazines, or other media units.

Networks. In radio and television the networks play a complicated and involved role. The chief networks in the United States are the American Broadcasting Company, the National Broadcasting Company, the Columbia Broadcasting System, and the Mutual Broadcasting System (radio only). They have become wealthy and powerful units of mass communication, buying and producing programs that they distribute to their affiliated radio and television stations. They do not, however, broadcast or distribute programs directly to the public—all programs are transmitted to local stations, which then transmit them into homes. The networks do own some stations of their own, but FCC regulations limit network ownership to seven stations, of which five may be in the VHF channel. These five VHF stations serve as a critical element in the total corporate enterprise of ABC, CBS, and NBC.

Networks function by working out an affiliation agreement with local stations willing to carry their programs. Fundamentally, the station gives the network the right to sell certain hours of the station's time at established rates to national advertisers. In return the network agrees to provide programs and from 20 percent to 40 percent of the money normally charged by the local station owner when he sells the time himself. Network affiliation is dominant in television, while only 25 percent of all radio stations are network affiliated. Most radio stations receive a free program service—primarily news—but little or no income from the networks.

Advertising Agencies. These service organizations work for their clients' marketing operations. They produce advertisements and place them in the media. Leading agencies represent a variety of clients but normally do not represent competing products. For example, the Leo Burnett Company, Inc., services accounts for nearly 40 companies, including United Air Lines, Procter and Gamble, Maytag, Kellogg's, and Pillsbury, none of which competes with the other. More than 5,500 advertising agencies operate in the United States, with a majority of the largest agencies that handle national accounts located in New York City.

*"Good evening. This is TBC, bringing you the best
from ABC, NBC, CBS, and BBC."*

Public Relations. Firms that specialize in handling public relations are
also concentrated in New York City. But while ad agencies serve their clients'
marketing needs by purchasing time or space in the mass media, public-
relations firms concern themselves with their clients' total communication
problems. They counsel their clients on the communication results of their
actions; provide advice on the course of action needed to win public acceptance;
and seek to publicize their clients to their publics (and publics to the clients)

through communication, most often mass communication. While public-relations firms may produce advertising, they engage primarily in publicity (free space and time in the mass media) and promotion (other communication efforts over a period of time) to persuade the public on their clients' behalf. Some attempts to determine the extent of public-relations work have shown that a large percentage of mass media content originates with public-relations firms.

Independent Production Companies. These media service units perform a service for broadcast, film, and record media similar to that which syndicates perform for print media. Independent companies exist because of the great degree of production complexity in broadcasting. While the idea for a program often originates with an individual, the programs are developed by program-package agencies. Today, with the exception of network news, sports, and some documentaries, 90 percent of all television network prime-time entertainment is produced by these package agencies.

The package agency develops the program, employs writers, producers, and actors—doing everything short of broadcasting. The packaging concept also extends to commercials for network and national spot advertising. Production companies generally subcontract all the production details to the ad agencies that create the specific advertisements. Program consultants, especially in radio, perform a significant function in selecting format and content for individual stations. In addition, some companies supply specific audio and video effects, including canned laughter, applause, and elaborate artwork (for station ID slides, program credits) for television programs.

Distribution and Exhibition. Unlike radio and television, where the networks serve as the distributor and the station as exhibitor, the other media—especially motion pictures, publications, and records—require complicated marketing, distributing, or exhibiting operations and facilities. Newspapers sometimes contract with a local dealer to distribute the papers through a system of newsstands, delivery boys, and the mail. Magazines make widest use of the mail system for distribution, but they often hire commercial firms to sell subscriptions. Book publishers in recent years have engaged in direct-mail selling and distributing, but they are still closely tied to bookstores, book dealers, and book clubs for distribution—often with complicated arrangements and large discounts. The middleman as distributor has increasingly entered the book and magazine fields; jobbers sell books to bookstores, and distribution companies sell books and magazines to newsstands, drugstores, supermarkets, and department stores. A similar apparatus exists for phonograph records and tapes.

Distribution and exhibition are even more complicated in the motion-picture medium. Because of court rulings on antimonopoly procedures, no film company can engage in more than two of the following activities: production, distribution, and exhibition—unless it can be demonstrated that the third activity will *not* restrain trade. With the dwindling supply of feature films, some distributor-exhibitors have begun limited film production. But this activity has not been judged to be in restraint of trade.

Today there are over 12,200 indoor movie theaters and about 3,800 drive-in theaters. These exhibitors are sometimes chain-owned by large exhibition companies, and they in turn rent the films from distribution companies, many of which are affiliated with large production studios based in Hollywood. Currently, over 700 chains, each with four or more theaters, control over 50 percent of all theaters in this country.

Manufacturing. The equipment and materials necessary for mass communication provide the basis of a large industry of its own. One large newspaper, the *Los Angeles Times*, has more than $65 million invested in printing-press equipment alone. The *New York Times* uses up more than 100 acres of trees to provide the pulp for the paper necessary for one Sunday issue. Ink, chemicals, plastics, precision optical equipment, and complex electronic gear are all necessary for the operation of mass media.

Separate companies exist to provide printing and binding services for magazine and book publishers; separate film-processing companies develop and print film for motion pictures and television; and separate record-pressing companies manufacture disks and tapes for the phonograph industry. Finally, separate companies produce radio and television sets for the individual home consumer, and these firms have become giant corporations in the American business world. Such companies as RCA, General Electric, and Zenith earn a far larger share of the market by producing radio and television hardware than the software media industries they serve.

Representation. Mass communicators are people with special talents, skills, and abilities. Increasingly, like artists, they need special help in promoting their interests and protecting the value of their work. A variety of "talent" agencies have grown to be a part of mass media. Writers' agents help find publishers for authors' works, oversee the legal protection of their rights and properties in contracts, and help promote their fame. In return these agents receive a share (usually 10 percent) of the author's profits. For actors and performers—particularly in the fields of radio, television, motion pictures, and phonograph recordings—talent agents play a crucial role: often all dealings are with the agent rather than the performer, with the agent receiving 10 to 15 percent of his client's earnings.

Special note should be made of the work of representation in the field of music, which provides a bulk of the programming in the electronic media. Two giants—the American Society of Composers, Authors, and Publishers (ASCAP) and Broadcast Music Incorporated (BMI)—dominate the field. They exercise considerable control over published, recorded, and broadcast music, protecting the rights of their artists and charging a fee to every media unit that uses their clients' work through recordings or sheet music. This process is simplified by having the media unit pay a percentage of some of its income for the right to play the music licensed by ASCAP and BMI. For example, a small market, top 40-format radio station may have to pay up to 5 percent of its gross time sales as "payment" for the music it plays on the air.

Labor unions have become an increasingly important part of mass media. The American Newspaper Guild, founded in the 1930s, represents newspaper editorial personnel in salary negotiations and seeks to help improve working conditions. Largely through its efforts, the salaries of reporters, photographers, copyeditors, and other professional staffers have risen to professional levels. For example, in 1976 the Guild had a minimum guaranteed salary at the *Washington Post* of $25,000 per year for all editorial staffers with at least four years' experience. The *New York Times* editorial staff had a $23,500 minimum for all staffers with two years' experience. Of course, many newspeople earn more than the minimum salary. The American Federation of Television and Radio Artists, the American Guild of Variety Artists, the Screen Actors Guild, among many others, perform similar services for mass communicators in the electronic media. The mass communication industry is one of the most heavily unionized in this country. Almost all the various crafts and skills used in the mass communication process are unionized. While in general this is beneficial to both labor and management, union policies regarding wages, work performed, and hiring practices have caused problems, especially in the motion-picture industry. Low-budget feature films were virtually impossible to produce until unions relaxed some of their rules.

Media Associations

Professional and management associations represent a final aspect of mass media, and one of growing importance. Increased recognition of the role of professional standards and responsibilities for mass communication in a free society has placed more emphasis on such associations. In some countries striving for a free and responsible press—especially in Western and Northern Europe—such press associations or societies of journalists have been given considerable power to approve or license journalists, admitting only those properly prepared and talented for the profession and barring those who willfully violate the standards of the profession. Such societies act for journalism in the same manner as the medical association, bar association, and accounting association act for doctors, lawyers, and accountants.

In America, however, these associations do not have, and perhaps never will have, such power over individual journalists, simply because the constitutional guarantee of freedom of speech and press for all individuals would make any attempt to approve or reject journalists illegal.

Nevertheless, many associations have come into being, and these groups influence the profession and speak for their members in a variety of ways. The owners of the media units are well organized. Newspapers, magazine and book publishers, broadcasters, and film producers all have active associations that serve their needs, collect information, lobby for sympathetic laws, and promote their interests. In addition to national organizations, these bodies often have state, country, or city groups as well—such as the Maryland-Delaware-D.C. Press Association, or the Montgomery County Press Association.

In broadcasting, the National Association of Broadcasters (NAB) functions as a lobby for broadcast stations with Congress, as a public relations firm with the public, and as a supervisor of both the NAB Radio and Television Codes. The National Association of Educational Broadcasters (NAEB) serves similar functions for public broadcasters as well as teachers and scholars in broadcast education.

In the film industry the Motion Picture Producers Association serves a very important public-relations effort, and its production-code division has created film ratings (G, PG, R, or X) for all films submitted by its members.

The Recording Industry Association of America (RIAA) serves as a public-relations arm as well as arbiter of production standards and controls.

Media workers, too, have professional associations that promote their interests and advance their standards. The largest of these is Sigma Delta Chi, the national society of journalists, which has both campus chapters (at colleges where journalism and mass communication are taught) and professional chapters (for those working in the media). Other associations represent almost every individual type of communication profession; from editors and editorial writers to photographers, public-relations people, advertisers, and cartoonists.

The mass media, as institutions in our society, are composed of an intricate fabric of people, products, institutions, production units, service units, and associations, all of which are based on a form of technology. At the root of all mass media is a technical process that must be understood and respected if efficient and successful communication is to take place. No doubt, media institutions are among the most complex in society, and this makes their study intriguing, their operation demanding, their role vital, and their impact difficult to determine.

In mass communication, regulation of the media is a complicated operation involving a number of groups. The role of the regulator is similar to that of the gatekeeper, but the regulator operates outside the basic media and media service units that create the messages. We might think of regulators as resistors in an electric circuit or valves in a fluid system, which control the quantity as well as direction of the current.

In many national systems government censorship is the major type of regulation and precludes others from attempting to control media activities and content. In the United States, the government cannot censor the news media but, along with other institutions in our society, can apply some pressure to regulate and control quantity, quality, and direction. This statement must be carefully qualified.

In the United States five regulators are at work in the mass communication process:

1. *The government* is the key regulator, even in a system where the Constitution guarantees freedom of communication.
2. *The source* of the message can, of course, affect the flow, by deciding what to make public through the media.
3. *The advertiser* regulates; if he pays the bills, he can exercise some influence on content.

9

Regulators

4. *The profession* acts as a self-regulator of individual members as well as basic media units and media service units.

5. *The consumer* of communication is a regulator, exercising control through purchase in the marketplace, through public pressure groups, and through establishing rights in the courts.

The Government as Regulator

In American society, devoted to freedom of the press and speech, government is the only agency capable of protecting those guarantees of freedom. Most American government regulations, but by no means all, are concerned with maintaining an environment of freedom of communication and with protecting the individual's rights in the communication process.

Constitutional Guarantees. Mass media are unique as business enterprises in our society because they alone operate with special sanctions and freedoms guaranteed by the U.S. Constitution. The First Amendment to the Constitution, which Congress adopted in 1791, states:

> Congress shall make no law respecting an establishment of religion, or prohibiting the free exercise thereof; or abridging the freedom of speech, or of the press; or the right of the people peaceably to assemble, and to petition the government for a redress of grievances.

This expression of freedom of the press was the result of a long struggle for individual rights and freedoms under Anglo-Saxon law. The way had been paved by previous landmarks such as the Magna Carta of 1215, the Petition of Rights in 1628, the English Bill of Rights in 1689, and the American Declaration of Independence in 1776. In the New World of the American colonies, where communication and independence were both important, freedom of speech and press had become key factors.

The First Amendment to the Constitution does not define limits of freedom. Court and legislative decisions have defined the meaning of that amendment, usually in the light of current trends and social conditions. The Constitution as it is interpreted by the courts and lawmakers controls the regulators and determines which of their actions are permissible and constitutional under the American system.

Censorship. Censorship, meaning prior restraint or suppression of communication, has been held to be unconstitutional in all its many forms, save

Drawing by Dana Fradon; © 1977 The New Yorker Magazine, Inc.

"To paperback rights, movie rights, TV rights, and human rights."

one. Government agencies, both local and national, have from time to time attempted to censor communication, sometimes for the best motives. A Minnesota state legislature, for example, passed a "gag law" in the 1920s aimed at restricting newspapers that were "public nuisances," specifically scandal sheets that made scurrilous attacks on the police and Jews. But the U.S. Supreme Court found this, as it has most other attempts at censorship, illegal, in its interpretation of the First Amendment.

The famous "Pentagon Papers" incident in 1971 provides another case in point. A multivolumed study made by the Department of Defense entitled *History of U.S. Decision-making Process on Viet Nam Policy* was classified as top secret but was leaked to the press. The *New York Times* and the

Washington Post both decided to publish stories based on the material in the 47 volumes. The Justice Department got a temporary court injunction to prevent further publication of the material. Because of the significance of the case, it quickly went to the U.S. Supreme Court. The Court, in a 6–3 landmark decision, ruled in favor of the newspapers and freedom of the press.

The Court's ruling hinged on the question of the constitutionality of prior restraint. Although the decision clarified the First Amendment, it did not really broaden the protection of freedom. The newspapers hoped that the Court would rule that the First Amendment guaranteed an absolute freedom. In the Pentagon Papers case, however, the Court held that the government had not provided sufficient evidence justifying prior restraint of the publications. This left the door open for future cases to decide how much justification the government must provide in order to censor a publication. But the six concurring opinions of the Supreme Court justices all gave ample support for the general theory of freedom from prior restraint by the government.

The one exception is in the area of motion pictures. In 1915 the Supreme Court in the case *Mutual Film Corporation* v. *Industrial Commission of Ohio* upheld the right of individual states to censor motion pictures, on the grounds that they were "a business pure and simple." They were a "spectacle or show and not such vehicles of thought as to bring them within the press of the country." In 1952, however, a Supreme Court decision changed this somewhat and laid the groundwork for increasing freedom for motion pictures. In the case of *Burstyn* v. *Wilson* involving the film *The Miracle*, the Supreme Court stated: "We conclude that expression by means of motion pictures is included within the free speech and free press guaranty of the First and Fourteenth Amendments. To the extent that language in the opinion in the Ohio case is out of harmony with the views here set forth, we no longer adhere to it." Decisions since then have continually brought movie censorship into question. However, by 1979 only one state, Maryland, still had a censorship board that could review motion pictures and restrict their public showing, either in part or in whole. Only two communities—Chicago and Dallas—still require motion pictures to be submitted for examination prior to public showing. A 1970 decision of the U.S. Supreme Court upheld the Maryland board's legal right to determine which motion pictures were obscene.

It should be noted that when we speak of movie censorship, we are referring primarily to obscenity, and obscenity is not protected by the First Amendment. To some extent, the movie review boards that exist view themselves as consumer-protection agencies, not merely censors of obscenity. The Dallas Motion Picture Classification Board, for example, gives films a public rating to warn the moviegoer in advance; ratings are for explicit sex (S), excessive violence (V), drugs (D), rough language (L), nudity (N), and perversion (P).

Other forms of censorship, which exist in some countries and have been tried in the United States, have from time to time been declared unconstitutional. The print media, for example, are constitutionally protected from discriminatory or punitive taxes and from licensing that would amount to censorship.

Restrictions on Importation, Distribution, and Sale. It is legal to regulate some aspects of mass communication without causing prior restraint or suppression. The government has generally held that the morals of the community should be protected against certain types of communication that could be objectionable to the average person. These kinds of restrictions pertain primarily to obscene publications, gambling and lottery information, and, in some cases, treasonous propaganda.

The Customs Bureau of the U.S. Treasury Department has the right to impound obscene material or gambling and lottery information. But a recent Supreme Court decision declared unconstitutional the role of Customs in restricting the importing of propaganda materials.

The U.S. Postal Service exercises the right to restrict the distribution of obscene publications or lottery advertisements through the public mails and can stop the mailing of such material and issue an order to refrain from further mailings.

Local courts and legislatures have the right to forbid the sale of obscene material. The Supreme Court has upheld the right of communities to protect themselves from the sale of materials they feel are harmful. A person who violates a local ordinance against the sale of such material would be subject to arrest and punishment as called for in the ordinance.

It is important to note that in all cases of such restrictions by the Customs Bureau, the Postal Service, and local authorities, none has the right to censor or prevent publication. It should also be noted that social mores are changing rapidly, and certainly in the 1980s many forms of obscenity might not be considered as socially harmful as in previous decades and generations.

Criminal Libel. Government has assumed the right to protect society and the public welfare from libel. Criminal libel is interpreted as false and malicious attack on society that would cause a breach of the peace or disrupt by force the established public order. In wartime, sedition laws are more explicit about communication that might damage the state. Criminal libel might also apply to libelous statements made against groups or against dead persons who cannot defend themselves in a civil action; thus the state becomes the prosecutor and the libel a crime. Cases of criminal libel, however, have become extremely rare.

Libel of Government and Public Officials.   Governments in totalitarian countries can suppress the critical press with criminal prosecution for seditious libel, but this is not possible in America. The trial of John Peter Zenger in New York in 1735 first established the unqualified right of the press to criticize the government, even if the facts are false and the criticism malicious. Various attempts have been made by government to protect itself from such criticism, for example the Alien and Sedition Acts of 1798–1800. But the courts have steadily upheld the impunity of the press as goad and critic of government.

One of the most far-reaching U.S. Supreme Court decisions was *The New York Times Co.* v. *Sullivan* ruling in 1964. This ruling gave the press almost as much right to libel public officials as it has the right to criticize government. The case came about as the result of an advertisement appearing in the *Times* in 1960; the ad, it was claimed, libeled one L. B. Sullivan, commissioner of public affairs for Montgomery, Alabama, among others. The Court ruling extended the privilege of publishing defamatory falsehoods about public officials, if the statements were made in good faith, if they concerned the official's public rather than his private life, and if they were not made in reckless disregard of the truth.

Contempt.   Government also exercises the right to protect the administration of justice against the interference of mass media. If a journalist, for instance, in the course of professional work, disobeys a court order, disturbs a courtroom, attempts to influence court decisions or participants, or (in some states) refuses to testify as to sources of news, that journalist can be cited for contempt of court. Court officials have used this power to subpoena newsmen's notes, tapes, photographs, and film in an effort to use this material in court cases. However, at least 25 states have laws protecting the journalist's right not to reveal confidential sources of information.

The Supreme Court, in a 5–4 decision in 1972, ruled that journalists have no absolute privilege to protect their sources of information if they are subpoenaed to testify in court proceedings. Medical doctors do not have to reveal the nature of their relationships with their patients, nor lawyers with clients, nor ministers with parishioners, nor teachers with students. But the Court held that such a privilege does not apply to the relationship between a journalist and a news source. The ruling was made on the basis of three different cases. Paul Pappas of WTEV-TV (New Bedford, Massachusetts) had refused to tell a grand jury what he had seen in a Black Panthers headquarters. Earl Caldwell, a *New York Times* reporter, also had refused to testify about a Black Panther case. And Paul M. Branzburg, reporter for the *Louisville* (Kentucky) *Courier-Journal*, had refused to tell a state grand jury the names of individuals he had written about in a drug story.

An increasing number of journalists have gone to jail since that ruling for contempt of court after failing to divulge information in court proceedings. For example, Peter Bridge, a former reporter for the *Newark* (New Jersey) *News*, was sentenced to an indefinite jail term for refusing to answer grand jury questions beyond his story about an alleged bribe attempt. He was ultimately released. In Fresno, California, four journalists from the *Fresno Bee*—the managing editor, the newspaper's ombudsman, and two court reporters—went to jail in 1976 for an indefinite term for refusing to tell a judge the source of secret grand jury testimony used in a news story. They, too, were ultimately released; but the basic problem remains unresolved.

Congress can cite journalists for contempt, as it did in the 1976 case of Daniel Schorr, the CBS reporter who refused to tell the House of Representatives how he obtained a copy of the congressional committee's report on intelligence activities. Congress ultimately decided not to punish Schorr.

Restrictions on Court Coverage.   The judicial branch of government can also restrict news media in their coverage of court news by closing the courtroom to reporters. For example, in 1975 a Nebraska judge ordered restrictions on news coverage in a mass-murder trial on the grounds that it was too sensational. But in 1976, the Supreme Court, in a unanimous decision, ruled that the Nebraska gag order, as it was called, was an unconstitutional restraint of freedom of the press. The Court did not rule out the possibility that such orders could be issued to protect the right of a defendant to a fair trial, but such orders should be made only when there is a clear threat to the fairness of the trial.

The problem of "free press versus a fair trial," the First Amendment versus the Sixth Amendment, has posed difficulties for both the news media and the courts. Journalists and lawyers have increasingly debated the problems of prejudicial publicity on the one hand versus censorship of the news on the other, without resolution. Some restrictions have been eased, however. Longstanding rules forbidding cameras and broadcast equipment in the courtroom have been changed in some states; cameras and microphones are now allowed on a limited and experimental basis. Some state bar and press associations have joined together to adopt guidelines for court coverage that would be acceptable to both sides, but national guidelines have thus far not been established.

Protection of Property. The government also regulates communication by protecting the property rights of communicators. The present copyright law was revised in 1976 for the first time since its original passage as a federal statute in 1909. The copyright law protects the property rights of authors, composers, artists, and photographers and establishes a system of punishments and a method of redress for violations of those rights. Among other restrictions, the 1976 revision also limits the amount of photocopying that can be done on copyrighted works and extends the life of a copyright. Thus it is a form of restriction of the media as well as a protection for the owner. It is important to note that facts and ideas cannot be copyrighted, only the order and selection of words, phrases, clauses, sentences, and the arrangement of paragraphs.

The government has also used protection of property as a means of restricting news media access to a news event. In a few cases, the media have been cited for trespass in covering such events as fires. The news media contend that they should not have to obtain permission of a property owner to enter the scene of a news event, but court rulings on such cases have not yet established clear precedents.

The government also protects property rights through the application of antitrust laws to the mass media. For example, newspaper mergers that eliminated actual or potential competition in a newspaper-market area were formerly considered a violation of the antitrust laws, but a new "Failing Newspaper Act" gives newspapers special antitrust privileges.

Regulation of Broadcasting. Unlike other mass media, only radio and television stations are licensed by the government. It should be noted, however, that the government cannot censor or suppress any broadcast once the broadcaster has a government license. Two reasons can be given for the more direct form of government regulation of broadcasting. One is that major broadcasters in the 1920s requested government help to maintain order in the scramble for limited frequencies and channels. The other is the idea that broadcasters are using public property—the airwaves—and government has an obligation to administer property that is not private. In 1927 the Federal Radio Commission was established, and in 1934 it became the Federal Communications Commission (FCC) charged with regulating radio, telephone and telegraph, and later television.

The Federal Communications Act of 1934 is the basis of the commission's regulatory power. Like the courts, the commission interprets rather than makes the law. A broadcast station must be licensed by the FCC, and the license must be renewed every three years. At the time of renewal, the station and its programming are reviewed, and if the commission rules that the station has not acted in the public interest, the license may be rescinded. The FCC also has the power to issue cease-and-desist orders, and short-term license renewals, revoke licenses, and levy fines up to $10,000 for specific violations of its rules and regulations. These regulatory powers do not give the FCC the right to censor. Nonrenewals of licenses are rarely assessed for single violations; it is the station's overall performance that is evaluated.

Few cases exist where licenses have been revoked, since the burden of proof falls upon the FCC, and the definition of "public interest" is vague. Nevertheless, the government does have more power to regulate a broadcaster than to regulate a publisher.

The FCC also controls the extent of broadcast ownership, so that it can prevent monopolies. No one can own more than one AM, one FM, and one TV station in any one listening area. And no one can own more than a total of seven of each of these stations in the entire country. In television no more than five of these outlets may be very high frequency (VHF—channels 2 to 13) stations. More recently, the FCC limited new acquisitions to forbid cross-ownership of TV and radio or daily newspaper and broadcast stations in the same market.

The FCC also regulates some broadcasting program content, especially in the areas of politics and public affairs. Section 315 of the FCC code requires the broadcaster to furnish equal time and equal opportunity to all political candidates for a given office, with the exception of news programs, which have been carefully qualified to allow debates between candidates of principal parties when covered as a bona fide news event. The so-called Fairness Doctrine of the FCC also charges broadcasters with the duty of seeking out and broadcasting contrasting viewpoints on controversial issues of public importance.

The constitutionality of the Fairness Doctrine has been upheld by the Supreme Court in the famous *Red Lion Broadcasting Co.* v. *FCC* case of 1969. The Court in effect ruled that the public's right to hear all points of view was more important than the broadcaster's right to express only one point of view. We should also mention that the FCC has adopted specific regulations for cable television. Until the mid-1960s, the FCC paid little attention to cable TV, regarding it as a passing phenomenon. But the FCC increasingly became aware that cable was a meaningful new method of television transmission, and in 1972 the commission adopted a set of rules specifically for cable. The rules established which broadcast stations the cable systems could transmit and which ones they could not; it required the systems to have a minimum 20-channel capacity; and it made provisions for an access channel (discussed later in chapter 22). The commission also required that cable systems build in the capacity for two-way circuitry, allowing for feedback from a subscriber to the system, among other regulations. Not all the rules for cable have been consistently applied, however, in an effort not to discourage a fledgling industry.

Regulation of Advertising. The Federal Trade Commission Act passed in 1914 was meant to regulate unfair competition in business, but checking dishonest advertising has become an important aspect of its work. The FTC is chiefly concerned with advertising that has a tendency to deceive. Other government commissions have more specific tasks in the regulation of advertising. The Food and Drug Administration controls labeling and branding in the important area of food and drugs. The FCC does not regulate advertising on radio and television, but it does note whether a station is complying with the profession's own codes (the National Association of Broadcaster's code, which seeks to limit advertising for hard liquor, for example, or overcommercialization). An act of Congress denied broadcasters the right to advertise cigarettes, although broadcasters can advertise pipe tobacco, cigars, and snuff.

The Postal Service controls fraudulent advertising sent through the mails. And the Securities and Exchange Commission can regulate advertising about stocks and bonds.

In all these cases, there is still no censorship or suppression on the part of the government. It can ask for voluntary compliance and, if not agreed to by the advertiser, can issue a cease-and-desist order. Violation of such an order can bring about a $5,000 fine, six months in jail, or both. The FTC can also publicize deceitful advertising and thus warn the public.

In sum, the government can and does regulate and restrict mass media in certain areas, and in these areas the Court has interpreted this regulation as not in violation of the First Amendment of the Constitution. These regulations are aimed at protecting society from damage by mass media as well as protecting the rights of the media from damages by competing media, individuals, or the state itself.

The Content Source as Regulator

The content source is also a regulator in the communication process, providing a form of regulation at the very beginning of communication. And as the process of communication has grown massive and complicated, the forms of regulation that are used by the content source can be analyzed into fairly distinct patterns.

Strategic Releasing. The content source regulates communication by strategically timing and packaging the message in a letter, a publication, or (if the content source has enough money) radio, television, or motion-picture production. Or the content source might release a communication to the established mass media through a news release, a press conference, or an exclusive interview.

Strategic Withholding. The content source can also regulate the flow of communication by strategically withholding the message and blocking the media from getting it. The government can do this by classifying documents or claiming executive privilege. The Freedom of Information Act of 1967 set forth the legal rationale for what can be withheld by the federal government and what cannot, and it established the judicial procedures to make the government prove in court why something should be withheld if challenged. Many states have statutes that set forth the categories of public records to which the media can have access, and what may be legally withheld.

Another form of withholding has been to deny news media access to meetings. But in 1976 the "Government in Sunshine Act" was passed, requiring about 50 federal agencies, boards, and commissions with two or more heads or directors to open their meetings and their records to the public. There are ten exceptions under which meetings may be closed, but in those cases, transcripts must be kept for scrutiny in case of legal action. Some states have passed sunshine laws to apply to open meetings at state and local government levels as well.

Strategic Staging. The content source can also regulate the flow of communication by deliberately and strategically staging a situation or an event in such a way that a certain kind of message gets into the media. Again using government as an example, a senator might wish to express his point of view about a particular issue, so he holds a hearing and calls a group of witnesses from whom he can elicit the type of fact and opinion that will get news headlines. The President, not wanting to see this point of view expressed in the media, announces a trip to Europe to take place at the same time as the Senate hearing, taking many reporters with him, attracting daily coverage in the newspapers and news shows, and overshadowing the hearing called by the senator. Meanwhile, a citizen's group holds a rally on the steps of the Capitol to get media (and public) attention for its views of the problem. These are staged situations used to regulate the flow of news and opinion.

The Advertiser as Regulator

Advertisers obviously play a role in the regulation of mass media, but this can be a subtle and unspecific type of control. David Potter, a historian who made a study of advertising as a force in molding the American character, wrote in his book *People of Plenty*:

> . . . in the mass media we have little evidence of censorship in the sense of deliberate, planned suppression imposed by moral edict (by advertisers) but much evidence of censorship in the sense of operative suppression of a great range of subjects. . . . The dynamics of the market . . . would seem to indicate that freedom of expression has less to fear from the control which large advertisers exercise than from the control which these advertisers permit the mass market to exercise.[1]

Individual instances can be cited in which advertisers used their economic power to "regulate" the media. For example, advertisers in a Wisconsin town withdrew their advertising from the local newspaper when it used its shop to print an underground newspaper. But the newspaper stood its ground and ultimately won the battle. The news offices of most mass media are separate from the advertising offices, and news officials rarely want to accept the dictates of the advertising offices.

Theoretically, the more independent the medium can be from advertising, the less power of regulation the advertiser will have. Radio and television, receiving 100 percent of their revenue from advertising, run the risk of greater pressures from sponsors. Newspapers and magazines, for the most part, receiving a third to a half of their revenue directly from subscribers, have less direct obligation to sponsors. Books, the phonograph-record industry, and motion pictures—which receive 100 percent of their revenue directly from their audiences—can afford to ignore Madison Avenue.

The Profession as Regulator

The gatekeeper, who as we have seen plays a key role in the flow of mass communication, voluntarily accepts codes of conduct that act as regulators of his or her actions. This is less important in the United States than in most other countries because the First Amendment prevents such codes from being absolutely binding on the communicator. In Sweden, for example, a journalist could be thrown out of the profession for violating a journalistic standard, but in the United States—since the Constitution guarantees anyone the right to practice journalism—such codes can be used only as voluntary guidelines.

[1]David M. Potter, *People of Plenty* (Chicago: University of Chicago Press, 1954), p. 184.

Examples of important professional codes are the "Code of Ethics" or "Canons of Journalism" of the American Society of Newspaper Editors, "The Television Code" and "The Radio Code" of the National Association of Broadcasters, and the "Code of Professional Standards" of the Public Relations Society of America. See the representative codes on pages 155–59.

Self-censorship has long been an important concept in the motion-picture and broadcast media. A motion-picture code was adopted by the industry in the 1920s in an effort to avert government censorship. The ratings of movies today is a form of voluntary self-censorship. The G (family), PG (parental guidance), R (restricted to those under age 17 without an accompanying parent), and X (restricted to all under age 17) ratings are self-applied and not required by government.

Self-regulation is also practiced in broadcasting. The major networks each have a "standards and practices" division that establishes standards and sees that they are followed. NBC's broadcast standards department has more than 40 people in it. Since television views itself as a family medium, it has usually adopted stricter standards than the movie industry, with the result that, as television shows more and more movies, it has more and more work to do in censoring various aspects of these movies. In 1976, for example, when CBS showed the movie *Smile*, a satirical comedy about young women embroiled in a California beauty pageant, it had to remove certain scenes and words. A scene in which a plucked chicken got smooched by hooligans at a fraternal initiation was cut by CBS. The words "sanitary napkin" were censored from a scene in which plumbers were complaining about discarded sanitary napkins clogging the pipes. This is media self-censorship, not government censorship.

The so-called family viewing policy of the National Association of Broadcasters is an interesting example of government interference in professional codes. "Family viewing" stated that prime-time television periods should be restricted to programs that were appropriate for a general family audience, including children. A suit was brought against the FCC by Hollywood writers, actors, and program producers, who said that "family viewing" restricts their freedom of expression, and they claimed it was the FCC that inspired the policy, not the NAB. A district court in California agreed with the writers, actors, and producers, saying that "family viewing" violates the First Amendment and need not be enforced or followed by networks or stations.

Much more discussion and litigation will without doubt be produced during the 1980s regarding the role of the profession or the media as regulators of media content.

Code of Ethics or Canons of Journalism
(American Society of Newspaper Editors)

The primary function of newspapers is to communicate to the human race what its members do, feel and think. Journalism, therefore, demands of its practitioners the widest range of intelligence, or knowledge, and of experience, as well as natural and trained powers of observation and reasoning. To its opportunities as a chronicle are indissolubly linked its obligations as teacher and interpreter.

To the end of finding some means of codifying sound practice and just aspirations of American journalism, these canons are set forth:

I.

RESPONSIBILITY—The right of a newspaper to attract and hold readers is restricted by nothing but considerations of public welfare. The use a newspaper makes of the share of public attention it gains serves to determine its sense of responsibility, which it shares with every member of its staff. A journalist who uses his power for any selfish or otherwise unworthy purpose is faithless to a high trust.

II.

FREEDOM OF THE PRESS—Freedom of the press is to be guarded as a vital right of mankind. It is the unquestionable right to discuss whatever is not explicitly forbidden by law, including the wisdom of any restrictive statute.

III.

INDEPENDENCE—Freedom from all obligations except that of fidelity to the public interest is vital.

1. Promotion of any private interest contrary to the general welfare, for whatever reason, is not compatible with honest journalism. So-called news communications from private sources should not be published without public notice of their source or else substantiation of their claims to value as news, both in form and substance.

2. Partisanship, in editorial comment which knowingly departs from the truth, does violence to the best spirit of American journalism; in the news columns it is subversive of a fundamental principle of the profession.

IV.

SINCERITY, TRUTHFULNESS, ACCURACY—Good faith with the reader is the foundation of all journalism worthy of the name.

1. By every consideration of good faith a newspaper is constrained to be truthful. It is not to be excused for lack of thoroughness or accuracy within its control, or failure to obtain command of these essential qualities.

2. Headlines should be fully warranted by the contents of the articles which they surmount.

V.

IMPARTIALITY—Sound practice makes clear distinction between news reports and expressions of opinion. News reports should be free from opinion or bias of any kind.

1. This rule does not apply to so-called special articles unmistakably devoted to advocacy or characterized by a signature authorizing the writer's own conclusions and interpretation.

VI.

FAIR PLAY—A newspaper should not publish unofficial charges affecting reputation or moral character without opportunity given to the accused to be heard; right practice demands the giving of such opportunity in all cases of serious accusation outside judicial proceedings.

1. A newspaper should not invade private rights or feeling without sure warrant of public right as distinguished from public curiosity.

2. It is the privilege, as it is the duty, of a newspaper to make prompt and complete correction of its own serious mistakes of fact or opinion, whatever their origin.

DECENCY—A newspaper cannot escape conviction of insincerity if while professing high moral purpose it supplies incentives to base conduct, such as are to be found in details of crime and vice, publication of which is not demonstrably for the general good. Lacking authority to enforce its canons the journalism here represented can but express the hope that deliberate pandering to vicious instincts will encounter effective public disapproval or yield to the influence of a preponderant professional condemnation.

CODE OF BROADCAST NEWS ETHICS
RADIO TELEVISION NEWS DIRECTORS ASSOCIATION

The members of the Radio Television News Directors Association agree that their prime responsibility as journalists—and that of the broadcasting industry as the collective sponsor of news broadcasting—is to provide to the public they serve a news service as accurate, full and prompt as human integrity and devotion can devise. To that end, they declare their acceptance of the standards of practice here set forth, and their solemn intent to honor them to the limits of their ability.

Article One

The primary purpose of broadcast journalists—to inform the public of events of importance and appropriate interest in a manner that is accurate and comprehensive—shall override all other purposes.

Article Two

Broadcast news presentations shall be designed not only to offer timely and accurate information, but also to present it in the light of relevant circumstances that give it meaning and perspective.

> This standard means that news reports, when clarity demands it, will be laid against pertinent factual background; that factors such as race, creed, nationality or prior status will be reported only when they are relevant; that comment or subjective content will be properly identified; and that errors in fact will be promptly acknowledged and corrected.

Article Three

Broadcast journalists shall seek to select material for newscast solely on their evaluation of its merits as news.

> This standard means that news will be selected on the criteria of significance, community and regional, relevance, appropriate human interest, service to defined audiences. It excludes sensationalism or misleading emphasis in any form; subservience to external or "interested" efforts to influence news selection and presentation, whether from within the broadcasting industry or from without. It requires that such terms as "bulletin" and "flash" be used only when the character of the news justifies them; that bombastic or misleading descriptions of newsroom facilities and personnel be rejected, along with undue use of sound and visual effects; and that promotional or publicity material be sharply scrutinized before use and identified by source or otherwise when broadcast.

Article Four

Broadcast journalists shall at all times display humane respect for the dignity, privacy and the well-being of persons with whom the news deals.

Article Five

Broadcast journalists shall govern their personal lives and such nonprofessional associations as may impinge on their professional activities in a manner that will protect them from conflict of interest, real or apparent.

Article Six

Broadcast journalists shall seek actively to present all news the knowledge of which will serve the public interest, no matter what selfish, uninformed or corrupt efforts attempt to color it, withhold it or prevent its presentation. They shall make constant effort to open doors closed to the reporting of public proceedings with tools appropriate to broadcasting (including cameras and recorders), consistent with the public interest. They acknowledge the journalist's ethic of protection of confidential information and sources, and urge unswerving observation of it except in instances in which it would clearly and unmistakably defy the public interest.

Article Seven

Broadcast journalists recognize the responsibility borne by broadcasting for informed analysis, comment and editorial opinion on public events and issues. They accept the obligation of broadcasters, for the presentation of such matters by individuals whose competence, experience and judgment qualify them for it.

Article Eight

In court, broadcast journalists shall conduct themselves with dignity, whether the court is in or out of session. They shall keep broadcast equipment as unobtrusive and silent as possible. Where court facilities are inadequate, pool broadcasts should be arranged.

Article Nine

In reporting matters that are or may be litigated, the journalist shall avoid practices which would tend to interfere with the right of an individual to a fair trial.

Article Ten

Broadcast journalists shall not misrepresent the source of any broadcast news material.

Article Eleven

Broadcast journalists shall actively censure and seek to prevent violations of these standards, and shall actively encourage their observance by all journalists, whether of the Radio Television News Directors Association or not.

The Consumer as Regulator

In a system of free mass communication, the consumer is perhaps the most important regulator of the media. In two areas consumers can resort to court procedures to help protect themselves from the media as well as help keep the media within acceptable boundaries. These areas are civil libel and right of privacy.

Civil Libel.   Libel is the false defamation of a person's character through printed or broadcast means. Slander is false defamation through spoken words. Defamation is communication that exposes a person to hatred, ridicule, or contempt, lowers him in the esteem of his fellows, causes him to be shunned, or injures him in his business or calling. The concept of defamation as a punishable act has a long history; the ancient Egyptians cut out the tongues of those who were found guilty of lying maliciously about their neighbors.

Those who feel that damage has been done them by communication can bring a civil suit against those responsible and seek payment for damages. The legal action is not much different from a lawsuit in which a person seeks to be paid for the actual damage to a car fender in an auto accident. In a libel suit tradition holds that a person's reputation is a priceless commodity, unlike an auto fender, and little just compensation can be paid for actual damages. Thus the plaintiff can ask for punitive damages, an amount of compensation so great that it will punish the libeler. Some punitive damages for libel have run into the millions of dollars, especially when the libel was shown to have been published with malicious intent.

The publisher or broadcaster of a defamatory statement can defend the publication or broadcast under certain conditions that might absolve the defamer completely or mitigate the damages. Truth is now accepted as an absolute defense for the publication of a defamation, and a defamer who can prove the truth of a statement can be absolved. Certain statements are privileged, that is, the publisher has a right to repeat them without fear of libel suits; such privileged statements are records of legislative, judicial, and other official public proceedings. Also, statements made as a matter of fair comment or criticism about public matters are defensible, even if defamatory.

The Right of Privacy.   Individuals have the right to be private, even from mass media. Unlike libel, however, this is a relatively new concept of communication regulation. Citizens have the right to recover damages from the media for intruding on their solitude, publishing private matters violating ordinary decencies, having their names publicly used in a false manner, or having their names or likenesses used for commercial purposes. Individuals can bring a civil action in court to seek compensation for damages done to them from such invasion of privacy.

There are areas, however, where the individual might lose the right of privacy. For example, a person involved in a newsworthy act or a person who becomes newsworthy by virtue of public actions, loses the right to privacy in those matters. Or someone who gives consent to an invasion of privacy—for example, by signing a waiver upon entering a studio to become a member of a television audience—cannot recover any damages through loss of privacy.

Some states have passed laws that have added to the privacy of individuals but may cause abuses in secrecy. For example, Oregon passed a law in 1975 preventing police from disclosing names and addresses of people arrested, detained, indicted, charged, sentenced, serving time, and released, in an effort to protect those individuals who might have been falsely arrested or charged or sentenced. But the law in reality allows the police to carry out secret arrests, secret trials, or secret jailings in the name of protecting the few. Certainly no greater abuse could be perpetrated in a free and open society than police action without the scrutiny of the public, through the watchdog eyes of the press. In such cases, it would seem, the right to know would be more important to a free society than the right to privacy.

Control through Consumption.   No doubt the greatest area of consumer regulation is in the marketplace itself. Those publications that sell stay in business, and those that cannot obtain or maintain an audience do not. Broadcast programs that do not attract large audiences go off the air. Because the media are in business to make a profit, they are usually sensitive to their customers and pay careful attention to the moods and habits of their readers, listeners, and viewers. Of course, what the audience wants may not always be the best or most constructive content for the social good. Violence and sex seem to be more popular than news analysis and interpretation of public issues. Thus, control by the marketplace has to be balanced against other considerations to achieve social well-being.

Control through Pressure Groups.   Although mass media are sensitive to individual responses, nevertheless, as media grow, the individual voice gets weaker. Increasingly, people have joined together in groups and associations to make their voices heard and their opinions felt. These groups have been able to pressure mass media, thus serving as regulators of mass communication. Nearly every religious, ethnic, occupational, and political group has an association that can speak for the members of the group, such as exerting pressure on television to stop portraying Italians as criminals, on newspapers to publish stories about gun laws, on radio to present antismoking commercials, on magazines to stop obscenity. One such pressure group, started by some women from Boston, Action for Children's Television (ACT), has petitioned the FCC for a rule barring advertisements on children's shows. The efforts were a major force behind the appointment by all three networks of executives to supervise children's programming. Such pressure is also often brought to the media through regulatory agencies of the government. For example, the FCC's Fairness Doctrine is largely enforced through the complaints of individuals and groups.

One group that is increasingly applying pressure on all media is women. A number of women's groups have lobbied in various forums for more equal coverage and less discriminatory practices by the mass media. For example, a number of women complained about the first edition of this textbook, saying that it contained too many sexist references, such as the constant use of the term "newsman." As a result, the authors were encouraged (not forced) by their editor to change or modify such references in the new edition. We were happy to comply with the request, for the earlier edition did reflect outdated usage and, more importantly, the changes have improved the book.

In 1976, the National Commission on the Observance of International Women's Year, after study by a committee, produced a set of guidelines for mass media coverage of, and practices for, women (see Ten Guidelines for Mass Media). No doubt, these guidelines will be studied seriously by mass media communicators and gatekeepers, for the mass media would certainly not continue to be mass if they offended so large a segment of their audience.

Thus we have an array of regulators and regulations that apply to the mass communication process in a free society. For the most part, these regulations are meant to strengthen the freedom of mass communication while protecting the communicator and the audience as well as those who happen to become part of the message itself.

Ten Guidelines for Mass Media on the Employment and Portrayal of Women

(National Commission on the Observance of International Women's Year, 1976)

1. The media should establish as an ultimate goal the employment of women in policymaking positions in proportion to their participation in the

labor force. The media should make special efforts to employ women who are knowledgeable about and sensitive to women's changing roles.

2. Women in media should be employed at all job levels and, in accordance with the law, should be paid equally for work of equal value and be given equal opportunity for training and promotion.

3. The present definition of news should be expanded to include more coverage of women's activities, locally, nationally, and internationally. In addition, general news stories should be reported to show their effect on women. For example, the impact of foreign aid on women in recipient countries is often overlooked, as is the effect of public transportation on women's mobility, safety, and ability to take jobs.

4. The media should make special, sustained efforts to seek out news of women. Women now figure in less than 10 percent of the stories currently defined as news.

5. Placement of news should be decided by subject matter, not by sex. The practice of segregating material thought to be of interest only to women into certain sections of a newspaper or broadcast implies that news of women is not real news. However, it is important to recognize and offset an alarming trend wherein such news, when no longer segregated, is not covered at all. Wherever news of women is placed, it should be treated with the same dignity, scope, and accuracy as is news of men. Women's activities should not be located in the last 30–60 seconds of a broadcast or used as fillers in certain sections or back pages of a newspaper or magazine.

6. Women's bodies should not be used in an exploitative way to add irrelevant sexual interest in any medium. This includes news and feature coverage by both the press and television, movie and movie promotion, "skin" magazines, and advertising messages of all sorts. The public violation of woman's physical privacy tends to violate the individual integrity of all women.

7. The presentation of personal details when irrelevant to a story—sex, sexual preference, age, marital status, physical appearance, dress, religious or political orientation—should be eliminated for both women and men.

8. Hopefully, the day will come when all titles will be unnecessary. But in the meantime, a person's right to determine her (or his) own title should be respected without slurs or innuendoes. If men are called Doctor or Reverend, the same titles should be used for women. And a woman should be able to choose Ms., Miss, or Mrs.

9. Gender designations are a rapidly changing area of the language, and a

decision to use or not to use a specific word should be subject to periodic review. Terms incorporating gender reference should be avoided. Use firefighter instead of fireman, business executive instead of businessman, letter carrier instead of mailman. In addition, women, from at least the age of 16, should be called women, not girls. And at no time should a female be referred to as "broad," "chick," or the like.

10. Women's activities and organizations should be treated with the same respect accorded men's activities and organizations. The women's movement should be reported as seriously as any other civil rights movement; it should not be made fun of, ridiculed, or belittled. Just as the terms "black libbers," "Symbionese libbers," or "Palestine libbers" are not used, the term "woman's libbers" should not be used. Just as jokes at the expense of blacks are no longer made, jokes should not be made at women's expense. The news of women should not be sensationalized. Too often news media have reported conflict among women and ignored unity. Coverage of women's conferences is often limited solely to so-called "splits" or fights. These same disputes at conferences attended by men would be considered serious policy debates.

In any description of the elements of mass communication, we must consider the problem of how the message is received. The message in mass communication is sent out with as much if not more regard for how it is received than it is in personal communication, and the problem of reception is vital. The audiences of mass media vary in age, sex, race, religion, social status, occupational group, income level, nationality, psychological makeup, or physical condition, yet they receive the same message. Obviously, they do not bring the same experience to decoding the message, so the meaning is apt to vary from individual to individual.

In spite of mass communication on all sides today, we speak increasingly of a communication gap. The rich do not seem to communicate with the middle classes, and the middle classes seemingly cannot speak or listen to the poor. Whites and blacks seem unable to overcome communication barriers. Ghetto residents of the inner city, suburbanites, and country squires seem to have little ground for communion. Protestants, Catholics, and Jews still seem to have difficulty finding many common areas for discourse. Even within families, gaps develop as fathers and mothers fail to speak the language of their children; nor can they often speak the language of their own parents.

Anthropologists have taught us much about these communication gaps. In studying the cultures of mankind, they have found that human beings are creatures of their environments, their attitudes and opinions shaped by forces

Filters

of which they may be only dimly aware and over which they may have little control.

Our Senses as Filters

No two people see the world alike. The way in which we see the world depends upon what sociologists call our "frame of reference." We perceive the world only through our own senses—our own eyes, ears, nose, mouth, and fingers.

We might more appropriately call this phenomenon of perception a filtering system, like a filter used on a camera lens, a fine screen to remove particles in water purification, or that bit of substance at the end of a cigarette designed to remove tars and nicotine from tobacco smoke. Using the analogy of filters in photography, we might say that these filters are color lenses that absorb certain rays of light to color the picture; they might be lenses ground with distortions and blind spots, or they might be lenses that polarize light and only let in rays slanted in a certain direction.

Our senses, which serve as communication filters, are affected by three sets of conditions: (1) cultural, (2) psychological, (3) physical.

How Filters Are Affected

Culture. These filters—our senses—are colored, distorted, or polarized by our culture. Edward T. Hall, a cultural anthropologist, has written effectively about the role of culture in human communication efforts, especially in his book *The Silent Language*, in which he shows how culture affects the way a person sends and receives messages. We are not fully aware, he says, of "the broad extent to which culture controls our lives. Culture is not an exotic notion studied by a select group of anthropologists in the South Seas. It is a mold in which we are all cast, and it controls our daily lives in many unsuspected ways."

One can identify ten separate kinds of human activity that are "primary message systems." These are interaction, association, subsistence, bisexuality, territoriality, temporality, learning, play, defense, and exploitation (or use of materials). These systems vary from individual to individual and from culture to culture, and they constitute a vocabulary and a language of their own, a silent language of which most of us are not aware.

Consider temporality, for example. To the average American of European origin, time exists as a continuum, with a past, a present, and a future. Such a person is able to compartmentalize time, to see distinctions in time, to do one thing at a time. The American-European culture is basically linear, and that is perhaps one cultural reason for this perceptual phenomenon. But to the Navajo Indian, time has no limits. The American Indian culture, without written language, is not linear. For the Navajo, time has no beginning, middle, or end. Time starts when the Navajo is ready, not at a given point. The future has little reality because it does not exist in the Navajo's time, nor does the past.

Territoriality is also a cultural message system. The average American of European origin has a strong sense of space and knows where things belong and to whom they belong. Individuals with this cultural background establish their rights to territory. For example, students take a certain seat in a classroom; it then becomes *their* seat, and they might well return to the same seat throughout a semester, as if they had established a right to it. But to typical Hopi Indians, space does not belong to anyone; they are apt to settle down wherever it suits them, regardless of whose territory they are invading.

Obviously the Hopi and the Navajo have different message systems regarding time and space from those exhibited by Americans of European origin. And this could not help but affect their message intake and output on any subject where temporality and territoriality are involved. We could make an almost endless list of cultural traits and subcultural habits of mind that influence our patterns of communication and our ability to make the act of communication a mutual sharing of a common understanding.

Psychological Sets. We structure our perception of the world in terms that are meaningful to us, according to our frames of reference or our filters. This process has been described as selective exposure, selective perception, and selective retention. Wilbur Schramm defines three problems in this regard that communicators must expect as they try to communicate meaning. First, the receivers will interpret the message in terms of their experiences and the ways they have learned to respond to them. For example, a jungle tribesman who has never seen an airplane will tend to interpret the first one he sees as bird. Second, the receivers will interpret the message in such a way as to resist any change in strong personality structures. For instance, a person strongly committed to the Democratic party will tend to ignore the campaign information of the Republicans. And third, the receivers will tend to group characteristics from their experiences so as to make whole patterns. To illustrate, notice how we need just a few strokes of a cartoonist's brush, creating a steel helmet, to enable us to summon up an image of a conservative hardhat.

Physical Conditions. Our sensory perceptions are altered by both internal and external physical conditions and help heighten, diminish, accept, or reject mass messages.

Internal physical conditions refer to the well-being or health of the individual audience member. When physically ill, a person filters messages differently from the way he or she does in good health. A migraine headache, a bleeding ulcer, or an abcessed tooth can radically alter message filtering. The pain of a smashed thumb affects the sense of touch so intensely that sight and sound are impaired. In some cases physical discomfort may heighten the communication experience. For example, Pepto-Bismol commercials are filtered differently when we have upset stomachs from the way they are when we are feeling well. A beer commercial is filtered one way by a person who is hot and thirsty, but another way by someone suffering from a "morning after." In the extreme the absence or impairment of one sense significantly heightens the effectiveness of another. Blind individuals tend to develop acute hearing—blindness filters motion-picture messages negatively but may increase positive filtering of phonograph music.

External physical conditions refer to the environment or surroundings in which we receive messages. If the room in which you are reading this book is too hot, too cold, too dark, or too noisy, this environment will affect your senses and the way you filter the content of this page. The purpose behind the construction of most motion-picture theaters is the development of the most satisfactory environment possible for viewing films. The seats are comfortable. The building is air-conditioned in the summer and heated in the winter. The theater is darkened, and the screen has excellent visual definition as well as a superior sound system. Every sense is catered to in order to improve the way movies are filtered. Compare this situation to the way you watch a movie on TV. The room is lighted. People wander in and out. The phone rings. Commercials interrupt. The senses are bombarded by a competing array of stimuli. No wonder seeing a movie in a theater is a different experience from seeing that same movie at home. We filter these two experiences in entirely different physical environments. Every medium is affected in significantly different ways by the way people feel and the physical surroundings in which they use a given medium.

Stereotypes and Public Opinion

The process we are describing here was discussed at length by Walter Lippmann in a pioneering work, *Public Opinion*, first published in 1922. He called the process "stereotyping," a term he borrowed from the printing industry. It refers to the plates, molded from type, that are used to reproduce printed copies, each one exactly the same as the original. Lippmann used the term to characterize the human tendency to reduce our perceptions into convenient categories, cataloging people, ideas, and actions according to our frames of reference for the purpose of easy recognition.

"The pictures inside people's heads," Lippmann wrote, "do not automatically correspond with the world outside." Yet those pictures in our heads are our public opinions, and when those pictures "are acted upon by groups of people, or by individuals acting in the name of groups, they are Public Opinion with capital letters." This "Public Opinion" is the "National Will" that is supposed to govern democratic societies; and mass media are supposed to inform the public about the truth of the world outside. But communicators themselves cannot keep from shaping the news in terms of the pictures in their heads and the stereotypes of their audiences.

We can see one example of stereotyping in our attitudes toward the people of other nations. Two social psychologists, William Buchanan and Hadley Cantril, studied the image that one national group has of another and found a definite tendency to ascribe certain characteristics to certain people. For example, Americans think of Russians as cruel, hardworking, domineering, backward, conceited, and brave; Americans think of themselves as peace-loving, generous, intelligent, progressive, hardworking, and brave; the British think of Americans as intelligent, hardworking, brave, peace-loving, conceited, and self-controlled. Buchanan and Cantril found that countries that were on friendly terms tended to use less derogatory adjectives in describing each other's characteristics, and that people invariably described their own nation in flattering terms.

Media Formulas and Styles Produce Stereotyped Views

The mass media actually reinforce our stereotyped view of the world, for a variety of reasons. First, the media have to simplify reality. Because of the limits of time and space, the mass communicator must reduce most messages to their simplest elements. There is never enough time on the air or enough space on the page to tell everything in detail. Audiences themselves usually do not have enough time or energy to digest great detail; so they, too, demand a simple version.

Second, the message must be framed in terms that are understandable and acceptable to the audience. In general, the media give favorable presentation to those ideas that their audiences approve, and unfavorable presentation to those that are not approved. For example, during the 1930s and 1940s, the American media never pictured President Franklin D. Roosevelt on crutches, in a wheelchair, or in any other posture that emphasized his disability. Most Americans knew that Roosevelt was a cripple, but they had difficulty accepting the notion that their President was not a powerful figure physically. In the 1970s, the media seemed bent on full coverage of every slip and fall made by President Gerald Ford. The American people had undoubtedly changed their notion about their President and wanted to see him as an ordinary human being. The view of life that the mass audience gets from mass media reflects audience values and behaviors, fits frames of reference, or matches filters.

Mass media achieve simplification and audience identification by resorting to easily structured molds and readily recognizable formulas, themes, and attitudes. The news story is a highly structured message with a lead and a body usually composed in an inverted pyramid style, almost always containing the answers to certain questions such as who, when, where, why, what, and how. Not only does this enable the reporter, editor, copyreader, and even printer to deal with the material quickly and easily, but it also aids readers in quickly and easily filtering from the news story that part of the message meaningful to them. The same is true of the editorial, the feature story, the column, and other parts of the printed newspaper or magazine.

As we show in chapter 6 the print media are highly structured, highly stylized even in makeup and layout. A particular newspaper will always contain the same number of columns, with the same flag (title of the newspaper) at the top of the first page, same type style, and similar handling of the news on the page from day to day. The editorial page appears in approximately the same place in each issue, the comic strips in the same section, and classified ads and stock-market quotations in the same location. Magazines and books, too, share this structured makeup. Imagine a book that did not start with a title page. Most nonfiction books have a contents page at the beginning and end with a bibliography or an index, or both.

Electronic media are also structured, stylized, and standardized. Programs are segmented throughout the programming day and timed to the split second. News programs tend to be in 5-, 15-, or 30-minute segments, whether the news warrants it or not. Dramas are put into segments of 30, 60, or 90 minutes. To be sure, electronic media have made great attempts to create a nonlinear structure, but even these attempts often end in standardization. "Laugh-In," for example, attempted to get away from a story line in dealing with comedy material, but the show still was cast in a 60-minute format, with segments broken up with commercials at well-timed intervals.

Fictional material in the mass media is also usually reduced to simple themes and formulas that are manifestations of our culture. The good guys win and the bad guys lose, and the good guys are apt to wear white hats and the bad guys black hats for easy and quick recognition. Soap operas on television repeat basic themes that we want to believe in, such as "love conquers all" or "work hard and you will succeed" or "nature is good." Even a soap like "Mary Hartman, Mary Hartman," which tried to present a more realistic view of life, often must reduce complex behavior to simple terms to cope with time limitations, ending up using quick formulas to get across an idea.

These formulas and themes vary with the times and the patterns of culture.

But they reinforce the culture and enhance the stereotyped view through our filters. We might say that the mass media, because of limitations of time, space, and audience, deal largely in caricature rather than in portraiture, deliberately selecting features for quick recognition and easy identification in a few strokes, rather than presenting a full picture, rich in detail and complexity, which might be closer to reality.

Public Relations and Filters

The problem of the proper perception of meaning is so great in a mass society that in the twentieth century a profession has grown up devoted to providing counsel on communication between groups with varied interests and cultures. This is the profession of public relations, which seeks to develop and utilize expertise in relating one public to another through communication. It is a profession devoted to the task of making sure that the right image of the sender penetrates the filters of the receiver.

To do this, the public relations man structures the message in a particular manner. As early as 1922, Walter Lippmann noted that in modern life:

> . . . many of the direct channels to news have been closed and the information for the public is first filtered through publicity agents. . . . The development of the publicity man is a clear sign that the facts of modern life do not spontaneously take a shape in which they can be known. They must be given a shape by somebody, and since in the daily routine reporters cannot give a shape to facts, and since there is little disinterested organization of intelligence, the need for some formulation is being met by the interested parties.

Public relations is the professionalization of the activity of getting others to see the world as one's sponsor sees it. Essential to effective public relations is not only a clear understanding of one's own frame of reference, biases, and filters, but also those of one's audience. This two-way communication effort requires careful listening as well as distinct speaking.

Specialized Media as Polarizers

As the world grows more complex, the problems of cross-cultural communication, in one sense at least, grow greater rather than smaller. As people become more specialized in the functions they perform, their filters become more specialized. They acquire a specialized vocabulary and language for their

tasks. Engineers do not speak the language of doctors. In fact, eye doctors do not speak the language of foot doctors. And different kinds of eye doctors do not communicate with other kinds of eye doctors. The people who live in a neighborhood may have less in common with one another than they have with professional colleagues whom they meet only occasionally. We have to make new maps of the world sociologically and psychologically.

Specialized media have developed to accommodate the growing specialization of people. Various forms of engineers and doctors, to name only two professional groups, have new and growing specialized media to serve their communication needs. Almost every day, a new publication is born in America to serve a distinct audience, whether it is a group of prosthetics specialists or an association of terrazzo and mosaic experts.

In the 1960s and 1970s, the emergence of new "black media" to serve the black minority in American society is an example of new specialized media adapting to the specialized filters of one group. Another example is the development of the so-called underground press, which serves a particular segment of society, a particular age group, and, within that group, a specialized subculture. The underground press uses a specialized language that is understood best only by those within the subculture.

Thus the specialized media of modern times help to polarize groups in society along new lines, perhaps of age, skin color, or professional specialization. They adapt themselves to those specialized filters.

Mass Media and Acculturation

The opposite side of this coin is the role of mass media in bringing people together. Mass communication can have the effect of providing common filters for people of diverse backgrounds and interests, allowing them to learn from one another and grow together.

Mass communication can make possible the consensus and understanding among individual components of society, bringing people together on some common ground, even if stereotyped, oversimplified, and structured. The mass media are important to the process of acculturation, where one culture modifies another.

An excellent example is the 8-part television show "Roots" adapted from the novel by Alex Haley, about the search of a black man for his ancestors in Africa and in American slavery. The show was one of the most widely viewed and popular television presentations in the history of television, gaining a larger audience than the television showing of *Gone With the Wind* or the Super Bowls. "Roots" probably could not have attracted such a popular audience in the 1940s or 1950s; the mood in America about racism and blacks has been changing, and in the 1970s this change made it possible not only to elect a President from the Deep South who scorned racism, but also to produce a popular program about the evils of slavery. The program itself, however, was presented in terms that whites could understand; the blacks spoke in English throughout, not in African dialects or pidgin English derivations. The situations and characters were dramatized in stereotypes with which both blacks and white could readily identify.

Indeed, it has been pointed out that "Roots" is the story of African blacks, slavery, and American blacks told in terms of the typical American stereotypes and the American dream. The story has been simplified to the struggle of good versus evil; in this case the good people are the blacks, and the bad people are the whites. But it is the orthodox story of American values, the struggle for freedom with courage, honor, family, and mercy. The conclusion of the series presents the old American ideal—the black families head west in a wagon train to freedom—so blatantly that it seems a direct descendent of a thousand Hollywood movies, almost a parody.

And yet the dramatic marvel of "Roots" was that it told the story of the evils of slavery and racial discrimination in such a way that millions of whites could identify with it and say, "That's my story, too." Thus, white attitudes toward blacks and black history will no doubt be modified by "Roots"; in the same way, blacks will see themselves in different terms as a result of molding the story in terms demanded by mass media.

In such ways, mass media quicken the historical process of acculturation, with the mutual interpenetration of minds and cultures going forward at a rapid pace.

Perhaps in no society yet known to humankind has the process of acculturation gone forward so quickly as in America. Here, the great melting pot has taken people with different filters from diverse backgrounds and environments of Europe, Africa, and Asia, and made of them one new culture where the vast majority of them, regardless of what their grandparents did or where they came

The concluding episode of the eight-part series was seen by more viewers than any other program in the history of television. With a 51.1 rating and a 71 percent share of the viewing audience, the program was seen in 36,380,000 homes, or 2.4 million more homes than tuned in the previous all-time winner, *Gone With the Wind*.

All told, 130 million viewers, or 85 percent of all homes in the United States with television sets, watched some or all of the series. The week-long ratings averaged 44.9 with a 66 percent share of the viewing audience. That did not include the opening segment on Sunday, Jan. 23.

Eight of the 14 most watched programs in the history of television were the eight episodes of "Roots." And instead of losing audience as the week progressed, almost every installment's audience exceeded that of the previous night, until the climax Sunday pulled in the most viewers of all.

FIGURE 10.1. *"Roots," an Example of Acculturation in the Mass Media. An all-black television drama reached the largest audience in television history for a single-network production. In one week, from January 23 to January 30, 1977, "Roots," as reported here by the* Washington Star, *made television history.*

from, now speak the same language, live in the same kind of split-level house or high-rise apartment, study in the same kind of school, drive the same kind of car, and eat the same kind of hamburgers and apple pie at the same kind of drive-in restaurant.

For this, mass media are largely responsible. They have increasingly modified our filters, changed our frame of reference, given us a way of looking at and perceiving the world around us.

Mass media in the United States provide more accurate and better mass communications than any media system in the world. The focus of the entire "mass comm" process is on the destination—the audience. Why else would a conglomerate communicator send content, if it were not for audiences and the reactions of individuals that make up audiences? The audience is the most studied and analyzed component in mass communication.

The *public* refers to a total pool of available people, whereas *audience* refers to the individuals who actually use the content produced by a basic media unit. For the mass communicator, the public is an abstraction; but the audience is a reality because audience members actually consume what the media produce. An individual has only to exist to be a part of the public, but a person must take action to become a part of an audience. The individual must buy or read or listen or watch. The members of the audience are *active participants* in mass communication. They select, consume, are affected by, and act on mass media content. Human beings are not vegetables in the media cooker. Audiences interact with the media, and the results are stunning.

No mass medium through its basic media units serves all parts of the public. In fact, most basic media units serve only a tiny fraction of the total American populace. Even radio and television stations that use the public's airwaves, which theoretically belong to all Americans, serve only those people who listen to or view their programs. Although stations are licensed to serve the

Audiences

public interest, convenience, and necessity, in reality they serve basically *audi-ence* interests, conveniences, and necessities. No medium reaches all the people, but the total media system attempts to accomplish the feat of reaching most of the people, most of the time.

Implosion and the Audience

Marshall McLuhan describes the audience situation in terms of the concept *implosion.* In this description the audience is central to mass communication and is under constant bombardment from the media (see figure 11.1). Instead of talking about an information explosion, we may need to refer to an information *implosion.*

McLuhan argues that it is the medium itself, not the content of that medium, that "massages" the audience.

> Societies have always been shaped more by the nature of the media by which men communicate than by the content of the communication. The alphabet, for instance, is a technology that is absorbed by the very young child in a completely unconscious manner, by osmosis so to speak. Words and the meaning of words predispose the child to think and act automatically in certain ways. The alphabet and print technology fostered and encouraged a fragmenting process, a process of specialism and of detach-

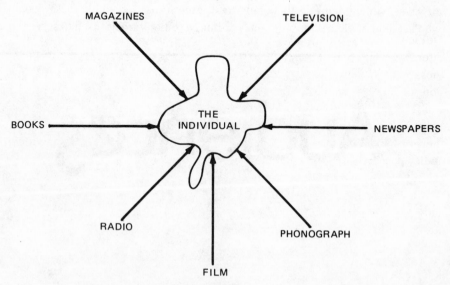

FIGURE 11.1. *An Implosion Model of Mass Communication*

ment. Electric technology fosters and encourages unification and involvement. It is impossible to understand social and cultural changes without a knowledge of the workings of media.[1]

Actually, it is the medium, the content, how it is presented, how it is received, and a multitude of other factors that affect individuals in the audience; but the media are *imploding* on all of us, all the time.

The media distribution of information implodes inwardly on the individual. The media are so pervasive, they are almost impossible for audiences to escape. In addition, each individual is a member of a great number of audiences and receives thousands of mass messages daily. The American Association of Advertising Agencies estimates that an average of 1,500 advertising messages alone reach an individual each day; the average person pays attention to only 75 of these, however. We have developed psychological barriers that filter out most mass communication and filter in those messages that might be helpful for a particular need.

There are physical, psychological, and cultural limits to our ability to perceive and understand. As the mass media provide more and more information and entertainment and implosion increases, an audience's filtering systems become more complex and difficult to penetrate.

Theories of Mass Communication Audiences

In the third edition of their *Theories of Mass Communication*, Melvin DeFleur and Sandra Ball-Rokeach analyze three perspectives of how audiences interact with the mass media and the messages the media carry.[2] In effect, these two sociologists are looking at the effects of mass media–audience interaction, or how the audience acts on the content of the media.

The *Individual-Differences Perspective* describes audiences in terms of behaviorism, where learning takes place on a stimulus-response basis. Here there is no uniform mass audience—the mass media effect each individual audience member differently in terms of that individual's personal psychological makeup derived from past experiences.

Using the Individual-Differences Perspective in figure 11.2, the individual audience members in (A_1, A_2, A_3) act on the media content by selectively attending and perceiving the same messages using different, individual filters.

[1]Marshall McLuhan, *The Medium Is the Message* (New York: Bantam Books, 1967), p. 8.
[2]Melvin DeFleur and Sandra Ball-Rokeach, *Theories of Mass Communication* (3rd ed.; New York: Longman, 1975), pp. 202-15.

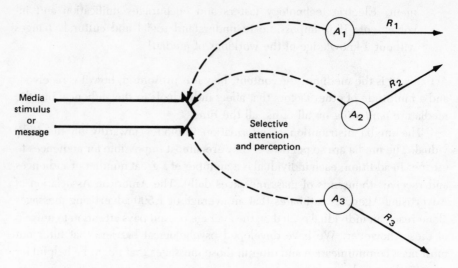

FIGURE 11.2. *A Visualization of the Individual-Differences Perspective*

Therefore, each individual responds differently (A_1 produces R_1; A_2 reacts as R_2; A_3 responds as R_3). This perspective suggests that each of us responds independently to the same message.

The *Social-Categories Perspective* takes the position that there are social aggregates in American society based on the common characteristics of sex, age, education, income, occupation, and so forth. Since these social aggregates have had commonly shared experiences, audience members have similar social norms, values, and attitudes. Here there are broad audience groups (e.g., working mothers, males aged 18–49, southern white females with two children) who will react similarly to specific message inputs.

Using the Social-Categories Perspective in figure 11.3, the members of the audience (A_1, A_2, A_3) are culturally linked and share a common frame of reference; therefore their responses to the same message are similar given that other conditions remain the same.

The Individual-Differences and the Social-Categories perspectives, in combination, produce the "who says what to whom with what effect" approach to mass communication. DeFleur and Rokeach evaluate this approach in the following manner:

> While these two perspectives on mass communication remain useful and contemporary, there have been further additions to the set of variables intervening between media stimuli and audience response. One additional elaboration of the S-R formula represents a somewhat belated

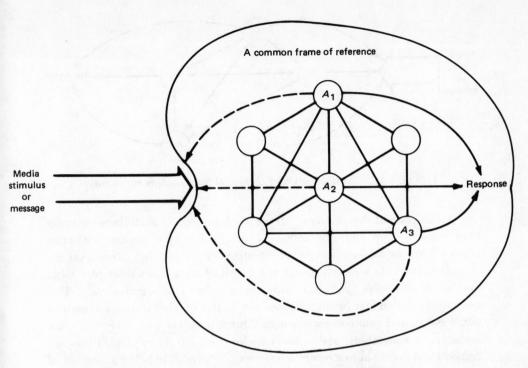

FIGURE 11.3. *A Visualization of the Social-Categories Perspective*

recognition of the importance of patterns of interaction *between* audience members.[3]

The *Social-Relationships Perspective*, based on the research of Paul Lazarsfeld, Bernard Berelson, Elihu Katz, and others, suggests that informal relationships significantly affect audiences. The impact of a given mass communication is altered tremendously by persons who have strong social relationships with the audience member. As a result, the individual is affected as much by other audience members' attitudes as by the mass communication itself.

Using the Social-Relationships Perspective in figure 11.4, the audience members in (A_1, A_2, A_3, and an opinion leader [OL]) receive a message. Here, however, it is not the media stimulus that has the significant impact: the informal interaction with others and a significant other (opinion leader) creates a common response. Audience member A_3 has no observable reaction, but an individual (NA) who did not receive the media message but did interact with audience members now reacts as they do. The interaction, rather than the message in isolation, has the significant impact.

[3]Ibid., p. 208.

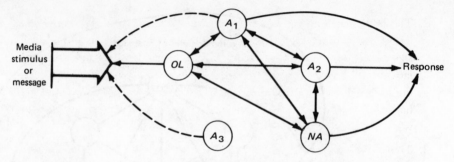

FIGURE 11.4. *A Visualization of the Social-Relationships Perspective*

Audiences and Perspectives. If we combine aspects of all three perspectives we come up with the following description of a possible audience "theory": No *one* mass audience of our media system exists, but rather a variety of audiences exists for each media event. All of us are members of a large number of audiences, and each audience member reacts individually. This individual reaction may be similar, however, to that of other audience members who have shared common experiences. Our interaction with other audience members, nonmembers, and opinion leaders also has an impact on how we respond and may lead to a common reaction. As a result of being a member of an audience, an individual is changed by the total media experience, not just the content of that experience.

Characteristics of Audiences

In the interpersonal communication process the receiver is normally one individual. In mass communication the receiver is part of a larger audience (listeners, readers, and viewers). Mass communication audiences exhibit five basic characteristics:

1. The audience tends to be composed of *individuals* who are apt to have commonly shared experiences and are affected by similar interpersonal social relationships. These individuals choose the media products they use by actual conscious selection or habitual choice. Some people react to audiences as unthinking masses, following the line of thought developed by Gustave LeBon in *The Crowd*, where the masses (*the* mass audience) follow a leader (a TV program or magazine) in zombielike obedience. The "crowd mentality" and "mass audience" are not well-thought-out concepts. The audience member remains an individual throughout the "mass comm" process.

2. The audience tends to be *large*. Charles Wright says: "We consider as 'large' any audience exposed during a short period of time and of such a size that the communicator could not interact with its members on a face-to-face basis."[4] There is no numerical cutoff point intended in the definition of *large*. Audience size is relative. A "large" audience for a hardback textbook might be a "small" audience for a prime-time, network, television special.

3. The audience tends to be *heterogeneous* rather than homogeneous. Individuals within a given audience represent a wide variety of social categories. Some basic media units increasingly seek specialized audiences, but even these groups tend to be more heterogeneous than homogeneous. In actuality, audiences for some basic media units are relatively narrow in scope. For example, the target audience for "Soul Train" is young black Americans in predominantly urban markets. The audience of *Ms.* magazine is a selective audience with a relatively limited audience based on sex, age, and sociopolitical views. The younger, college-educated female is more likely to read *Ms.* than is her older, grade-school-educated grandmother. The audience for this textbook is very specialized, but its readers are still part of a mass communication audience. To coin a phrase, audiences exhibit a "selective heterogeneity." Certainly most mass media are available to a heterogeneous public if not actually used by a heterogeneous audience.

4. The audience tends to be relatively *anonymous*. Communicators normally do not know the specific individuals with whom they are communicating, although they may be aware of general audience characteristics. For example, Elton John does not personally know the individuals who are listening to his latest record.

5. The audience tends to be *physically separated* from the communicator. Thus, "Mary Hartman, Mary Hartman" came into the audience members' environment weeks after the episode was videotaped and miles from the studio where it was produced. Audiences are separated from the conglomerate communicator in both time and space.

Once again, the word *mass*, when modifying audience, creates problems because it has the negative connotation of the great unwashed, antiintellectual, and unthinking masses. The implication is that audience members are automa-

[4]Charles Wright, *Mass Communication: A Sociological Perspective* (2nd ed.; New York: Random House, 1975), p. 6.

tons readily available for media manipulation. Unfortunately, some people still regard audience behavior as automatic, routine, and indiscriminate. Few Americans spend their time and money automatically, routinely, and indiscriminately on the mass media, however.

Audiences of Media

Print Media. Every time we commit ourselves to newspapers, books, and magazines, we become part of the audience of that specific book or given issue of a magazine or newspaper. When business people talk about print readership, they normally refer to circulation, i.e., those who buy the product. Media people, in point of fact, do not know exactly *what* is read or *who* reads it. So when we talk about readership, we are referring to those people *who do not necessarily buy but whom we hope read* the media product in question. Financial commitment generally precedes actual consumption, however, so we can assume that the buyers have a high probability of becoming readers. The buyer and his immediate family are *primary readership*. If someone outside the buyer-household uses the issue in question, we call them *pass-along readership*. Pass-along readership is an important aspect of the magazine audience because every reader is a potential reactor to the messages and a potential customer for the products advertised.

The readers of books, newspapers, and magazines meet the audience criteria established earlier:

1. Each basic media unit has a variety of audiences, not just one audience.

2. The audiences for books, newspapers, and magazines are very large. Many sell millions of copies even though they specialize in a select body of content.

3. Although specialized books and magazines seek specific audiences, they are available and used by a wide variety of individuals. Newspaper audiences are heterogeneous even for a selective newspaper like the *Los Angeles Free Press*, which is an example of what has been called an "underground newspaper" and is, in effect, a part of a subcategory of alternate media. The *Los Angeles Free Press* is different from the *Los Angeles Times* and has a more selective clientele.

4. Print media audiences are relatively anonymous. Publishers try to identify the characteristics of prospective audiences but seldom personally know the users.

5. The reader is physically removed from the writer. The audiences read after something is written (time). The audiences do not read over the author's shoulder (space).

Reading is individual, private, and personal. Words are written to be read by one person at a time. Reading is the act of one person, which makes print audiences a collection of individuals.

Recorded and Broadcast Media.   Broadcast and record audiences are collections of groups and individuals. These electronic audiences may listen as individuals (as is usually the case in radio and phonograph-record listenership), in small family groups (as is usually the case with TV), and in small-to-large nonfamily gatherings (party or discothèque use of the phonograph or the jukebox).

Record listenership is assessed by record sales. Radio and TV audiences are determined by audience-rating services, which attempt to determine not only the size but also the characteristics of the individuals using these media. Unlike what happens with print media, audiences frequently use radio, television, and recordings as a group, although individual members maintain their personal identity.

The Motion-Picture Medium.   Movies are seldom viewed by a solitary individual and almost always by group audiences, although drive-in motion pictures provide something akin to a solitary experience. Even though the individual may become deeply involved in a given film, he remains an individual. There is a variety of movie audiences that is massive, heterogeneous, relatively anonymous, and physically removed from the communicator.

Audiences in Media Environments

Each medium creates or modifies the environment in which it is used. Likewise, physical conditions in which media are used affect audience response.

Reading Environments. The print media are highly mobile; they can be used almost anywhere if the user is literate and there is light to read by. Interestingly, some print-use environments establish a variety of physical constraints on the user. The library, presumably a place where intense concentration is required, usually demands quiet. Reading a textbook or studying for a test normally requires low-level sound. Freedom of movement is not restricted, however. It is amazing how irritating noise can be in a library but how unobtrusive it becomes on the subway ride to work. The rider-reader conditions himself to the use of magazines, newspapers, and books in this noisy environment.

All of us learn to use media in a variety of environments. When these environmental conditions are altered, the audience member may become upset. Today's older generation learned to study quietly, and parents cannot fathom their children's use of rock music for background purposes while doing homework. The amount of retention required affects the reading situation. Reading for pleasure and reading for school are quite different acts and require different levels of concentration because each requires us to acquire different amounts and kinds of information.

The reading of a magazine, newspaper, or book can take place in a variety of environments. Studying, however, tends to require environments that have less distraction. Nevertheless, the tremendous mobility of most printed matter allows readers to function anywhere they can establish satisfactory physical and psychological environments.

Listening and Viewing Environments. Radio has great mobility if the audience member owns a portable radio or has a car radio. In addition to having the physical device, the radio user must also have an electrical source, be it dry-cell batteries, the car battery, or the standard alternating current. The automobile environment requires primary concentration on driving. For this reason, the radio hopefully gets less attention than the road. Despite this, the audience member is captive unless the driver turns the radio off or leaves the car. The portable radio has no single physical setting for its use, but portable use is inhibited where radio volume would disrupt others. The development of the earplug has solved this problem, however.

Television tends to be located in a specific place, often modified for that experience, generally the living room or family room. If there are two or more sets in a household, the second generally goes into a bedroom. There are portable TV sets, but the television receiver tends to be less portable than radio or print. The TV room is often the focus of family activity, and normal distractions and interruptions are accepted as part of viewing. Americans use television as a social activity, and interaction during viewing is not only permissible but encouraged.

The record environment depends greatly on whether the phonograph in use is the portable that belongs to the youngsters or the family stereo. The portable usually gets around more, and because it has little sound quality it needs to be played louder. The stereo, however, is often housed in a visible area—immovable and supreme. The portable and 45-rpm. record are adapted to new environments by means of an increased volume. The album and the stereo modify the environment in which they are kept. Perhaps the best phonograph environment might be provided by headsets, which eliminate other aural stimuli.

The motion-picture environment is the least portable and most institutionalized of all media. Watching a movie at home, on TV, or in the classroom is completely unlike the experience we have in the movie theater. The movie house is created to increase the involvement of the audience with the film experience. The screen is huge; the place is dark; the seats are designed for comfort; the interruptions are minimal; the sound is usually good. Without question, the motion picture operates in the best of all possible controlled media environments.

Multimedia Audiences. Some audience members make use of the same content coded by a variety of media. As the message is translated into different media environments, it has a kind of cumulative impact on the environment itself. For example, *Jesus Christ, Superstar* is a 45-rpm. single; a 33⅓-rpm. album; a record on Scott Muni's show on WNEW-FM; a concert tour; a broadway hit; a movie; a television movie; a review in a magazine; an article in the newspaper; and a book.

Because ideas such as *Jesus Christ, Superstar* are multiple media events, the impact and response of each audience is predicated on previous exposure to the content in other media environments. In these situations, the audience becomes part of the environment, and the "feeling" of the audience is intensified (massaged) by the familiarity and repetition of the experience. In effect, it is "extraeffective" because the audience is a participant in the production.

The Effects of Audiences on Media Content

The audience-consumer influences the content of media in a variety of ways. The audience-consumer can change the content by personally communicating with the people who produce it. The buyer of a southern newspaper can write a letter to ask the editor to get the hockey scores printed in that paper. The consumer can telephone the local television station to complain about the inaccuracy of the weather reports. The audience member can go to see the general manager of the local radio station to ask that the station cease to play certain records. Obviously, the basic media unit can reject these requests outright. But when the communicator feels that the complainer may speak for a sizable portion of the audience, changes may be made.

The audience-consumer can join with others to form pressure groups that, as a body, attempt to change the media content, as did the Legion of Decency (a Roman Catholic organization that rated the moral tone of motion pictures and had a powerful influence on the decision-making process of the Motion Picture Code Office and Hollywood film makers) in the 1930s, '40s, and '50s. The audience-consumer can refuse to spend time or money on the basic media unit. The buyer can refuse to subscribe to the local newspaper. The consumer can refuse to watch a television series. The audience member can refuse to listen to the local radio station. If audience size decreases appreciably, the media content will change.

This method is the most effective because it is the hardest on the media economically. The newspaper, TV station, and radio depend on audiences to attract advertisers. The size of a basic media unit's audience affects its revenue, and this may be the most accurate index of the value our society places on that particular newspaper or station. For example, when a movie becomes a smash hit, similar films are produced until the public fails to support them financially. Thousands of records are produced annually, and the public selects those that it finds valuable from the ones "plugged" on their favorite radio stations.

Theoretically at least, the media have a responsibility to meet the needs of American audiences. When a basic media unit succeeds in satisfying the wants of one or more audiences, it will be rewarded financially. The audience affects the content of books, films, television programs, and records by financially rewarding or punishing the people who produce them. The Rolling Stones are a cultural success because the consumers deemed it so. Harold Robbins is an economic success because audiences buy his books. *Star Wars* succeeded because movie audiences bought the tickets.

The Education of the Consumer-Audience

Audiences are consumers of media content, and they spend time and money on media messages. There is growing concern about the education of "critical consumers"—consumers who may or may not choose "better" content but who are critical in the sense of knowing about the mass media and making a conscious choice about why and how they use the media.

It is not a matter of "improving the media" because media are changing in many ways for the better. Certainly audiences are becoming more sophisticated. The concern must be in "improving the audience" so that it can handle the content and put it to the desired use. A media-educated audience is also better prepared to eliminate negative media effects.

Communication, by its very definition, is a two-way process, a cooperative and collaborative venture. It is a joint effort, a mutual experience, an exchange between two parties—a sender and a receiver. The communication experience is not complete until an audience is able to respond to the message of the communicator. That response is called feedback.

Characteristics of Feedback

In interpersonal communication the receiver usually responds naturally, directly, and immediately to the message and sender. We might flutter our eyelids or raise an eyebrow, ask for explanation or repetition, or even argue a point. In this way the message is shaped and reshaped by the participants until the meaning becomes clear. The sender and receiver interact and constantly exchange roles.

Many responses to mass communication resemble those in interpersonal communication. An audience member may respond by frowning, yawning, coughing, swearing, throwing down the magazine, kicking the TV set, or talking back. None of these responses is observable to the mass communicator, however, and they are all ineffective responses unless they lead to further action—writing a letter, making a phone call, canceling a subscription, or turning off the TV set.

Feedback

Because of the distance in time and space between communicator and audience in the mass communication process, feedback in mass communication assumes different characteristics from interpersonal feedback. Instead of being individual, direct, immediate, one-time, and personal, mass communication feedback is representative, indirect, delayed, cumulative, quantitative, and institutionalized.

Despite what might seem to be complicating obstacles—obstacles not worth the effort in overcoming—feedback for mass communicators is extremely important. All of us want our communication to be efficient; that is, we want to achieve the goals of our communication with as little effort as possible. Mass communicators are similarly concerned. Communicating by mass media involves enormous expense. These expenses have to be justified to executives and stockholders. The communicator must bring a return on the investment, must prove to be efficient, and feedback is necessary to provide the proof.

Therefore, feedback in mass communication is not simply desirable; it is required. And because it is required, the mass media have gone to elaborate lengths to ensure that it is received on a regular basis; so much so that the process of obtaining and communicating feedback has been institutionalized. This is just one characteristic of mass communication feedback, however.

Representative Feedback. Because the audiences of mass media are so large, it is impossible to measure feedback from each member. Instead, a representative sample of the audience is selected for measurement, and the response of this sample is projected scientifically to the whole. A letter to the editor or a change of channels may be noted by the mass communicator, but these responses would have little significance unless they could be shown to be statistically representative of the feelings of a large portion of that medium's total audience. In measuring the response of the mass media audiences, specific responses of every individual are replaced by representative sampling of the audiences.

Sampling is perhaps the least understood and most controversial aspect of mass communication survey research. Sampling is a statistically valid technique in which a portion of the total population is used in order to arrive at answers about the entire population. In determining the size of the sample, the idea is to use as few units as possible and still maintain reasonable accuracy. What makes for "reasonable accuracy" varies, but the standard rule of thumb is that samples of less than 100 are extremely dangerous and samples of more than 1,000 are seldom needed. Nevertheless, the more quantitative the results, the larger the sample should be. A. C. Nielsen, for example, uses a national sample of about 1,500 households to determine national television ratings. It may be difficult to accept that 1,500 homes can represent all the television homes in the United States, but sampling technique is a proven method that has stood the test of time.

Indirect Feedback.   Rarely does a performer on television or a reporter for a newspaper receive any direct response from audience members. Rather, the feedback comes through a third party, a rating organization or polling company. Even when a performer or reporter receives a telephone call from a listener or a letter from a reader, the response seldom offers much opportunity for direct interaction or substantially changes specific media content—unless that response is felt to be representative of a large part of the total audience. Because mass communication feedback is filtered through a third party, such as a rating organization, there is less variety in form and type of feedback. As we discuss later, one form—quantitative feedback—dominates.

Delayed Feedback.   The response is also delayed in time from the moment of transmission. There are some overnight television ratings, but most ratings are not published until about two weeks after the original program transmission. Letters to the editor must go through the mail. Surveys and polls take time to conduct and study. The reaction of the communicator to feedback is also delayed by the way that medium operates. For example, once a motion picture is "in the can" it can be modified in only minor ways after audience reaction to preview screenings. Even in the more flexible daily newspaper, immediate modifications and corrections are played down and put in the back pages because they are not timely and newsworthy. Before the first episode of a new network television series appears in the fall, 13 episodes of that series have usually been completed. Thus, because of the financial investment and contractual commitments involved, poor ratings (negative feedback) almost never spell the immediate termination of a new TV program; this occurs at the end of the first or fall quarter (the 13-week period from September to December).

Feedback to this book occurred primarily through published reviews and letters to the authors. Response to this feedback was delayed until a second edition was published. The effect of delay, for this book or for other forms of mass communication, is the necessity of continuing inefficient communication beyond a natural stopping point. So, despite the mass communicator's great concern over efficiency, by the very nature of the feedback process, a great deal of inefficiency is built into the original message.

Cumulative Feedback.   In mass communication, the immediate and individual response is not as frequent, and therefore not as important, since emphasis is placed on the collective or cumulative responses over a substantial period of time. Since the response is delayed, there is seldom any chance for immediate reaction; thus the communicator accumulates data over a period of time from a variety of sources. The communicator stores these data, and they influence future decisions—especially concerning what the public wants in the way of media content. The "spinoff" concept in television programming is evidence of this. "The Mary Tyler Moore Show," for example, was very successful. Some of this success was attributed to the various characters in the series—including Mary's two female friends, Rhoda and Phyllis. Consequently, series were created around both these characters. The enormous success of "Rich Man, Poor Man" stimulated the use of the anthology drama on primetime television. Motion pictures such as *Airport 75*, *Airport 76*, *Godfather II*, and *Jaws II* are the result of cumulative feedback on the original motion picture.

Quantitative Feedback. For the most part, feedback is sought and measured in quantitative terms. Examples include box-office figures for motion pictures, ratings for television programs, sales figures for records and books, and circulation figures for newspapers and magazines. Critics of the mass media provide some qualitative judgments via book, phonograph, movie, and television reviews. But the mass communicator is more interested in knowing how many people responded rather than how one person (e.g., a critic) responded, unless the critic's view can be shown to have affected a number of people. The review of a book, a record, or a movie can seriously affect purchases or attendance, but in television the review of a particular program has little impact because it usually takes place after the telecast. Little or no consistent critical evaluation of newspapers, magazines, or radio is available to audiences. Numbers are what count in mass communication. As the A. C. Nielsen Company states in one of its promotional brochures: "... these are quantitative measurements. The word rating is a misnomer because it implies a measurement of program quality—and this we never do. Never!"

This fact creates some problems. When you consistently measure the success or efficiency of your message in terms of how many responses, rather than what kind of response, you are severely limiting your ability to judge the quality of your message. A television program may have a large audience at 9:00 P.M. on Tuesdays, not because it is inherently good, but because the competition is weak. Placed in another time slot or on another day, it may fail.

Communication research firms today are also analyzing the "whys" as well as the "whos." A. C. Nielsen supplements its audimeter figures with diary responses, and more and more communicators are utilizing interviews and detailed questions to go beyond a simple quantitative measure of response.

Institutionalized Feedback.   Finally, mass communication feedback is institutionalized. That is, it requires large and complex organizations to accomplish meaningful feedback to mass communication. Research organizations such as the A. C. Nielsen Company, the American Research Bureau, and Pulse, Inc., provide quantitative feedback data for broadcasting in the form of ratings. Companies such as Simmons and Politz survey print-media audiences. Market research and public opinion survey groups such as Gallup, Harris, and Roper go directly to the public to find out what messages have come through and what changes have resulted in levels of information, attitudes, and actions.

Most media institutions not only purchase the raw data but also seek an analysis of the information by the research institution. In fact, little feedback is developed or interpreted directly by the majority of mass communicators.

This "third party" function regarding the indirect nature of mass communication feedback further complicates the issue. Because an organization is collecting responses and then communicating them back to the sender, a gatekeeping function sets in with all of its potential concerns and problems. In essence, mass communication feedback is mass communication in reverse, with many of the same characteristics such as conglomerate communicators, gatekeepers, regulators, and so forth.

Techniques of Obtaining Feedback

It should be obvious by this point that feedback is essential for communicators using mass media. Whether the originator of the message is an advertiser, a public relations official, a politician, or an entertainer, all need to ask questions concerning the responses to their message. Examples of the type of information desired by mass communicators includes radio-TV set counts, audience size, audience characteristics or demographics, buying habits, product use, station image, and public opinion.

The answers to these questions are obtained through research, using scientific methods developed by sociologists, psychologists, and survey researchers. As noted, correct sampling procedures are a critical aspect of such research. Although there are many ways to conduct mass communication research, four techniques are common to most research organizations:

1. The *personal interview* is frequently used in media research because it can provide lengthy, detailed responses that involve personal interaction of the respondent and the interviewer. It offers the greatest flexibility in questioning methods, and the sample can be designed so that it is fully

representative of the entire population under study. The drawbacks of this method are that it is time-consuming, relatively expensive, and often depends on recall rather than the immediate responses of audience members.

2. The *telephone coincidental* is a method that provides immediate feedback as to what the individual is doing at the time of the phone call. It is fast, simple, and relatively inexpensive. Extremely lengthy and detailed answers are difficult to obtain, however, and because of the prevalent use of the telephone as a sales tool, many people called in such surveys are suspicious and refuse to cooperate. This method also automatically limits the sample to people with phones, to those who have not moved recently, and to those at home or not using the phone when called.

3. The *diary* method, whereby respondents keep a log of their own or family use of media, has the advantage of providing a continuous record over a substantial period of time (usually one week). Detailed information regarding viewer habits and consumer behavior can also be obtained. Major disadvantages are failure to maintain the diary, thus depending on recall to fill in data, and forgetting to return the diary. It is also more expensive than the telephone technique although not as expensive as the personal interview.

4. The *mechanical device*, such as the audimeter used by the A. C. Nielsen Company, records the minute-by-minute use of the television set. But the audimeter only supplies information as to whether the set is on and the station to which it is tuned. No data are provided as to who the viewers are or how many viewers are involved.

Another technique that is beginning to be used by a number of mass communication organizations is the so-called preview theater. Here a random sample of people are shown various television programs and/or advertisements in a theater and respond to the messages by pushing buttons or turning dials signaling like–dislike feelings. The American Research Institute of Los Angeles uses this technique. It is gaining in popularity because it provides data that show how people react at different stages of the message, not simply at the end.

The ways in which these research methods have been used tend to fall into general patterns. The diary and the mechanical device are used almost exclusively in providing feedback for the broadcast media. The personal interview and telephone coincidental serve as essential methods in public opinion surveys. The telephone-coincidental survey is also used as a fast method of obtaining broadcast-audience information, and the personal interview is used almost exclusively for print feedback.

The quality of the quantitative feedback varies with the questions being asked. In terms of *how many people are exposed*, media research data are excellent within the limits of statistical error. As to *who the audience is*, the feedback is also superior within these statistical limits. In terms of *how messages are perceived* and *the effects of this perception*, reliable feedback is extremely limited.

Forms of Feedback

The Motion-Picture and Sound-Recording Media. For both commercial films and records, the most critical form of feedback is how audiences spend their money. Record sales and box-office receipts are key determinants in the kinds of feature-length movies and singles or albums that will be produced in the future. For both films and records, critics have some impact, but the communicator usually focuses on ticket and record sales rather than reviews.

TITLE	DISTR	THIS WEEK $	RANK	LAST WEEK $	RANK	TOTALS CITIES	FIRST RUN	SHOW CASE	ROAD SHOW	THE- ATRES	WEEKS ON CHART	TOTAL TO DATE $
NATL LAMPOONS ANIMAL HOUSE	U	2,022,990	1	1,438,934	3	19	21	61		82	5	6,629,876
REVENGE OF THE PINK PANTHER	UA	1,583,585	2	852,673	8	20	16	151		167	6	8,453,177
HEAVEN CAN WAIT	PAR	1,486,410	3	1,707,521	2	19	21	126		147	9	15,410,355
GREASE	PAR	1,330,946	4	1,363,483	4	20	25	109		134	11	27,888,990
PIRANHA	NW	1,151,384	5	82,700	28	10	4	115		119	5	1,715,805
HOOPER	WB	1,011,711	6	1,747,842	1	18	15	151		166	6	7,984,405
EYES OF LAURA MARS	COL	982,212	7	1,191,500	5	20	18	105		123	4	4,596,794
FOUL PLAY	PAR	926,218	8	1,066,265	6	21	21	72		93	6	6,035,933
STAR WARS	FOX	651,736	9	864,904	7	14	7	169		176	66	73,681,140
DOGS	MRV	450,000	10			1	1	48		49	15	2,868,159
WHO LL STOP THE RAIN	UA	449,000	11	125,400	25	13	9	44		53	4	768,725
SGT PEPPERS LONELY HEARTS	U	315,583	12	297,019	11	19	20	63		83	5	3,174,786
MAGIC OF LASSIE	IPS	299,500	13	245,000	14	3	4	4		8	4	1,148,566
YOUNG FRANKENSTEIN	FOX	270,000	14	400,000	9	1		51		51	56	16,047,867
CORVETTE SUMMER	UA	235,000	15	124,000	26	5	2	26		28	5	1,194,224
HOT LEAD & COLD FEET	BV	202,450	16	262,200	12	13	10	40		50	8	1,569,095
BUDDY HOLLY STORY	COL	193,644	17	238,400	15	15	18	17		35	11	2,047,601
INTERNATIONAL VELVET	UA	174,400	18	49,101	39	4	3	17		20	7	902,692
LOVE BUG	BV	150,000	19			1		46		46	26	5,632,412
CHEAP DETECTIVE	COL	119,265	20	17,316		10	4	30		34	9	8,813,448
SATURDAY NIGHT FEVER	PAR	97,424	21	33,656	42	8	7	12		19	37	33,809,347
CAT FROM OUTER SPACE	BV	88,285	22	142,177	22	6	3	23		26	9	1,973,444

FIGURE 12.1. *Top-grossing films from* Variety

Figures 12.1 and 12.2 are from *Variety* and *Billboard* magazines. These figures represent a major form of feedback for movie and record producers in that they reveal the number of people buying a particular product.

Although this feedback cannot alter the content of a film or a recording already produced, it can affect the booking and distribution of a film or record and can greatly influence future production of films and records with similar themes. Economic feedback is also critical in the careers of the talent employed in the film and recording media. Unless the efforts of a singer or director sell, that individual cannot remain in the business, no matter how accomplished he or she may be.

One other form of feedback important to both media is professional recognition of excellence in the form of awards. The Oscars and Grammys are important forms of feedback to the artists involved. They can and often do serve as recognition of a specific film or recording, or they can be used as a reward for exceptional careers. The most important effect of this feedback, however, is monetary. An award brings increased sales for a film or record and gives the performers additional leverage with future employers. They can, in some instances, help turn around a declining career. Frank Sinatra's Oscar for his supporting role in *From Here to Eternity* is an example of this effect. Consequently, awards are rarely an end in themselves; they are usually means to a more significant end—monetary reward.

Broadcasting. For both radio and television, critics' feedback has little impact, and awards in the form of Emmys are often used by actors and other talent to criticize TV business decisions.

Feedback in the form of volume of radio or TV-set sales as well as subscriptions to community-antenna television systems (cable TV, or CATV) also has little direct effect on programming practices of stations or networks because it provides no information about specific content; it merely implies that the medium is popular.

In both radio and TV, ratings provide the most important form of feedback. Considerable confusion surrounds what ratings are, how they are used, and the impact this form of feedback has on the decision-making process in broadcast programming. Ratings are a percentage; in the case of TV, ratings represent a percentage of homes with TV sets. The ratings most of us are familiar with are the national ratings compiled by the A. C. Nielsen Company. Actually, Nielsen compiles four different types of ratings, the most important being those involving network TV programs.

The national television ratings, obtained by Nielsen, are a percentage of the estimated number of U.S. TV households watching certain programs. A

Billboard HOT 100

© Copyright 1979, Billboard Publications, Inc. No part of this publication may be reproduced, stored in a retrieval system or transmitted, in any form or by any means, electronic, mechanical, photocopying, recording or otherwise, without the prior written permission of the publisher.

*Chart Bound

WATCH OUT FOR LUCY—Eric Clapton And His Band (RSO 910)
UNLOVED—Walter Egan (Columbia 310916)
SEE TOP SINGLE PICKS REVIEWS, page 86

THIS WEEK	LAST WEEK	WKS. ON CHART	TITLE—Artist (Producer) Writer, Label & Number (Distributing Label)
☆1	1	9	DO YOU THINK I'M SEXY—Rod Stewart ● (Tom Dowd), R. Stewart, C. Appice, Warner Bros. 8724 WBM
2	2	18	Y.M.C.A.—Village People ▲ (Jacques Morali), J. Morali, H. Belolo, V. Willis, Casablanca 945 CPP
4	4	13	A LITTLE MORE LOVE—Olivia Newton-John (John Farrar), J. Farrar, MCA 40975 ALM
☆5	5	15	FIRE—Pointer Sisters ● (Richard Perry), B. Springsteen, Planet 45901 (Elektra/Asylum)
7	7	10	I WILL SURVIVE—Gloria Gaynor (Dino Fekaris), D. Fekaris, F. Perren, Polydor 14508 ALM
6	6	15	EVERY 1'S A WINNER—Hot Chocolate ● (Mickie Most), E. Brown, Infinity 50002 (MCA) MCA/CPP
7	3	17	LE FREAK—Chic ● (Bernard Edwards, Nile Rogers), N. Rogers, B. Edwards, Atlantic 3519 WBM
☆10	13		LOTTA LOVE—Nicolette Larson (Ted Templeman), N. Young, Warner Bros. 8664 WBM
11	10		SOMEWHERE IN THE NIGHT—Barry Manilow (Barry Manilow and Ron Dante), W. Jennings, R. Kerr, Arista 0382 ALM
12	12	15	I WAS MADE FOR DANCING—Leif Garrett (Michael Lloyd), M. Lloyd, Scotti Brothers 403 (Atlantic) CPP
11	8	14	SEPTEMBER—Earth, Wind & Fire ● (Maurice White), M. White, A. McKay, A. Willis, Arc 310854 (Columbia) ALM
☆14	12		GOT TO BE REAL—Cheryl Lynn ● (Marty Paich, David Paich), C. Lynn, D. Paich, D. Foster, Columbia 310808 WBM
15	14		SHAKE IT—Ian Matthews (S. Roberton, I. Matthews), T. Boylan, Mushroom 7039 WBM
☆16	11		SOUL MAN—Blues Bros. (Bob Tischler), D. Porter, I. Hayes, Atlantic 3545 ALM
☆17	6		HEAVEN KNOWS—Donna Summer & Brooklyn Dreams (Giorgio Moroder, Pete Bellotte), D. Summer, G. Moroder, P. Bellotte, Casablanca 959
18	9		NO TELL LOVER—Chicago (Phil Ramone), L. Loughnane, D. Seraphine, P. Cetera, Columbia 10891 CPP
☆20			BLUE MORNING, BLUE DAY—Foreigner (Keith Olsen, Mick Jones, Ian McDonald), L. Gramm, M. Jones, Atlantic 3543 WBM
☆19	16		THE GAMBLER—Kenny Rogers (Larry Butler), D. Schlitz, United Artists 1250 CPP
☆29	2		TRAGEDY—Bee Gees ● (Bee Gees), Karl Richardson, Albhy Galuten, B. Gibb, R. Gibb, M. Gibb, RSO 913 CHA
☆22			DON'T CRY OUT LOUD—Melissa Manchester (Harry Maslin), C.B. Sager, P. Allen, Arista 0373 ALM/CHA
☆24	10		SHAKE YOUR GROOVE THING—Peaches & Herb (Freddie Perren), D. Fekaris, F. Perren, Polydor 14514 CPP
☆25	10		DANCIN' SHOES—Nigel Olsson (Paul Davis), C. Storie, Bang 740 CHA
23	9	14	TOO MUCH HEAVEN—Bee Gees ● (Bee Gees/Albhy Galuten, Karl Richardson), B. & M. Gibb, RSO 913 CHA
☆30	9		EVERY TIME I THINK OF YOU—The Babys (Ron Nevison), R. Kennedy, J. Lowell, Chrysalis 2279 CLM
☆27	11		BABY I'M BURNIN'—Dolly Parton (Gary Klein), D. Parton, RCA 11420 CPP
☆31	7		LADY—Little River Band (John Boylan & Little River Band), G. Goble, Capitol 4667 WBM
☆32	5		WHAT A FOOL BELIEVES—Doobie Brothers (Ted Templeman), M. McDonald, K. Loggins, Warner Bros. 8725 CPP
☆33	9		WHAT YOU WON'T DO FOR LOVE—Bobby Caldwell (Ann Holloway), Caldwell & Kettner, Cloud 11 (TK) CPP
29	16		TAKE ME TO THE RIVER—The Talking Heads (Talking Heads), A. Green, L. Hodges, Sire 1032 (Warner Bros.) CPP
☆37	4		I JUST FALL IN LOVE AGAIN—Anne Murray (Dortt, Skinner-Lloyd, Herbstritt), Jim Ed Norman, Capitol 4675 CPP
☆38	5		CRAZY LOVE—Poco (Richard Sanford Orshoff), R. Young, ABC 12439 WBM
32	23	16	MY LIFE—Billy Joel ● (Phil Ramone), B. Joel, Columbia 3-10853 ABP/BP
☆47			SULTANS OF SWING—Dire Straits (Dire Straits), M. Knopfler, Warner Bros. 8736 ALM
☆40	7		HAVEN'T STOPPED DANCING YET—Gonzalez (Richard Jones & Gloria Jones), G. Jones, Capitol 4674 CPP
35	13	19	NEW YORK GROOVE—Ace Frehley (Eddie Kramer, Ace Frehley), R. Ballard, Casablanca 941 ABP/BP
☆42	7		STORMY—Santana (Dennis Lambert, Brian Potter), B. Blue, J.R. Cobb, Columbia 310873 CPP
37	39	9	YOU CAN DO IT—Dobie Gray (Nick Hall), E. Sands, B. Weisman, R. Germinaro, Infinity 50003 (MCA) B-3
☆45	4		SONG ON THE RADIO—Al Stewart (A. Stewart), Alan Parsons, Arista 0389 WBM
☆46	4		FOREVER IN BLUE JEANS—Neil Diamond (Bob Gaudio), N. Diamond, R. Bennett, Columbia 3-10897 WBM
☆44	6		YOU MAKE ME FEEL MIGHTY REAL—Sylvester (Harvey Fuqua, Sylvester), Sylvester, Wirrick, Fantasy 846 CPP
41	34		SING FOR THE DAY—Styx (Styx), T. Shaw, A&M 2110 ALM
☆49	4		STUMBLIN' IN—Suzie Quatro & Chris Norman (Mike Chapman), M. Chapman, N. Chinn, RSO 917 WBM
43	21	15	DON'T HOLD BACK—Chanson (David Williams, James Jamison Jr.), D. Williams, J. Jamison Jr., Ariola America 7717
☆51	4		KNOCK ON WOOD—Amii Stewart (Floyd-Cropper), D. Long, Ariola 7736 ALM
☆54	4		MAYBE I'M A FOOL—Eddie Money (Ramone), L. Chiate, L. Garrett, B. Taylor), Bruce Botnick, Columbia 3-10905 ALM
☆52	4		I GO TO RIO—Pablo Cruise (Bill Schnee), P. Allen, A. Anderson, A&M 2112 ALM
☆53	5		EVERY WHICH WAY BUT LOOSE—Eddie Rabbitt (Snuff Garrett), S. Dorff, M. Brown, T. Garrett, Elektra 45554 CPP
48	50	5	YOU STEPPED INTO MY LIFE—Melba Moore (Gene McFadden, John Whitehead), B. Gibb, R. Gibb, M. Gibb, Epic 850600 CHA
☆55			I DON'T KNOW IF IT'S RIGHT—Evelyn "Champagne" King (Not Listed), T. Life, J.H. Fitch, RCA 11386 CLM
☆57	5		GOODBYE, I LOVE YOU—Firefall (Tom Dowd, Ron Albert, Howard Albert), R. Roberts, Atlantic 3544 WBM
51	28	12	HOME AND DRY—Gerry Rafferty (Hugh Murphy, Gerry Rafferty), G. Rafferty, United Artists 1266 CPP
52	34	20	HOLD THE LINE—Toto (Toto), Paich, Columbia 310830 WBM
53	56	7	GET DOWN—Gene Chandler (Carl Davis), J. Chapman, 20th Century 2386 CPP
☆64	4		MUSIC BOX DANCER—Frank Mills (F. Mills), Frank Mills, Polydor 14517 CHA
☆62	5		THE CHASE—Giorgio Moroder (Giorgio Moroder), G. Moroder, Casablanca 956 CPP
☆65	6		SUPERMAN—Herbie Mann (Patrick Adams, Herb Mann), S. Ito, Atlantic 3547 PSP
☆67	4		LIVIN' IT UP—Bell & Jamas (L. Bell, C. James), LeRoy Bell, Casey James, A&M 2069 CPP
☆69	2		BIG SHOT—Billy Joel (Phil Ramone), B. Joel, Columbia 3-10913 ABP/BP
60	35	15	HE'S THE GREATEST DANCER—Sister Sledge (Bernard Edwards, Nile Rodgers), B. Edwards, N. Rodgers, Cotillion 44245 (Atlantic) WBM
☆71	3		OOH BABY BABY—Linda Ronstadt (Peter Asher), W. Robinson, M. Moore, Asylum 45546 CPP
☆71	3		DOG & BUTTERFLY—Heart (Mike Flicher, Heart, Michael Fisher), A. Wilson, N. Wilson, S. Ennis, Portrait 70025 (CBS) WBM
☆72	5		ALL THE TIME IN THE WORLD—Dr. Hook (Ron Haffkine), E. Stevens, S. Silverstein, Capitol 4677 CPP
63	63	8	BABY I NEED YOUR LOVIN'—Eric Carmen (Holland, Dozier), Eric Carmen, Arista 0384 CPP
☆74	3		BUSTIN' LOOSE—Chuck Brown & The Soul Searchers (James Purdie), C. Brown, Source 40967 (MCA)
☆75	2		TAKE ME HOME—Cher (Bob Esty), M. Allen, B. Esty, Casablanca 965 ALM
77			SURVIVOR—Cindy Bullens (Tony Bongiovi, Lance Quinn), C. Bullens, United Artists 1261 CPP
☆80			OH, HONEY—Delegation (Ken Gold), Gold, Denne, Shadybrook 1048 (Janus)
100	81		OUR LOVE IS INSANE—Desmond Child & Rouge (Richard Landis), D. Child, Capitol 4669

THIS WEEK	LAST WEEK	WKS. ON CHART	TITLE—Artist (Producer) Writer, Label & Number (Distributing Label)
69	43	11	DANCIN' IN THE CITY—Marshall Hain (Christopher Neil) Hain-Marshall, Capitol 4648
☆80	2		JUST ONE LOOK—Linda Ronstadt (Peter Asher), G. Carroll, D. Payne, Asylum 46011
71	73	6	RUN HOME GIRL—Sad Cafe (John Punter), Young & Stimpson, A&M 2111 ALM
☆82	3		FOUR STRONG WINDS—Neil Young (Neil Young, Ben Keith, Tim Mulligan), Reprise 1396 (WB) WBM
73	59	5	POPS, WE LOVE YOU—Diana Ross, Stevie Wonder, Marvin Gaye, Smokey Robinson (Sawyer & McLeod), Sawyer & McLeod, Motown 1455 CPP
☆			CONTACT—Edwin Starr (Edwin Starr), E. Starr, A.K. Pullan, R. Dickerson, 20th Century 2396 (RCA) WBM
☆87	2		PRECIOUS LOVE—Bob Welch (Carter), B. Welch, Capitol 4685 CPP
☆86	2		I'LL SUPPLY THE LOVE—Toto (Toto), D. Paich, Columbia 312898
77	78		FANCY DANCER—Frankie Valli (Bob Gaudio, Larry Brown), Brown-Crewe, Warner/Curb 8734 CPP
☆88	2		I WANT YOUR LOVE—Chic (Nile Rodgers, Bernard Edwards), B. Edwards, N. Rogers, Atlantic 3557 WBM
☆89	2		NOW THAT WE FOUND LOVE—Third World (Alex Sadkin, Third World), K. Gamble, L. Huff, Island 8663 (WB) CPP
☆90	2		LOVE STRUCK—Stonebolt (Walter Stewart, Ray Roper), R. Roper & D.J. Willis Parachute 522 (Casablanca) ALM
NEW ENTRY			SINNER MAN—Sarah Dash (W. Gold, J. Siegel, G. Knight, G. Allan), H. Hegel, C. George, Kirshner 6-4278 (CBS) WBM
NEW ENTRY			SHAKE YOUR BODY—Jacksons (The Jacksons), M.J. Jackson, R. Jackson, Epic 50656
83	84	4	BAD BREAKS—Cat Stevens (C. Stevens, A. Davies), Paul Samwell-Smith & Cat Stevens, A&M 2109 CPP
NEW ENTRY			HEART OF GLASS—Blondie (Mike Chapman), D. Harry, C. Stein, Chrysalis 2275 WBM
NEW ENTRY			KEEP ON DANCIN'—Gary's Gang (Eric Matthews), E. Matthews, G. Turnier, Columbia 3-10884
NEW ENTRY			WHEELS OF LIFE—Gino Vannelli (Gino Vannelli, Joe Vannelli), G. Vannelli, A&M 2114 ALM
NEW ENTRY			DON'T STOP ME—Queen (Queen), Ray Thomas Baker), Mercury, Elektra 46008
NEW ENTRY			MAN WITH THE CHILD IN HIS EYE—Kate Bush (Andrew Powell), K. Bush, EMI 8006
NEW ENTRY			SOUVENIRS—Voyage (Roger Tokarz), M. Chantereaux, P. Dahan, S. Pezin, Marlin 3330 (TK)
NEW ENTRY			I GOT MY MIND MADE UP—Instant Funk (Bunny Sigler), R. Miller, S. Miller, R. Earl, Salsoul 72078 (RCA) CPP
91	91	4	SHOOT ME—Tasha Thomas (J.R. Glaser), James R. Glaser & Peter Buglie, Atlantic 3542
92	68	11	LOVE DON'T LIVE HERE ANYMORE—Rose Royce (Norman Whitfield) M. Gregory, Whitfield 8712 (Warner Bros.) WBM
93	58	14	FREE ME FROM MY FREEDOM—Bonnie Pointer (Jeffrey Bowen, Barry Gordy), A. Bond, T. Thomas, B. Polatier, Motown 1451 CPP
94	60	5	LONELY WIND—Kansas (Kansas), S. Walsh, Kirshner 84280 (CBS) WBM
95			YOU DON'T BRING ME FLOWERS—Barbra Streisand & Neil Diamond (Bob Gaudio), N. Diamond, A. Bergman, M. Bergman, Columbia 310840
96	93	11	WE'VE GOT TONIGHT—Bob Seger (Bob Seger & Muscle Shoals Rhythm Section), B. Seger, Capitol 4653
97	85	3	FOR YOU AND I—10cc (Eric Stewart, Graham Gouldman), E. Stewart, G. Gouldman, Polydor 14528
98	48	10	SHATTERED—Rolling Stones (Glimmer Twins), M. Jagger, K. Richards, Rolling Stones 19310 (Atlantic)
99	79	6	TAKE THAT TO THE BANK—Shalamar (Dick Griffey & Leon Sylvers), L. Sylvers, K. Spencer, Solar 11379 (RCA)
100	81		SUPERMAN—John Williams (J. Williams), Not Listed, Warner Bros. 8729 WBM

A reflection of National Sales and programming activity by selected dealers, one-stops and radio stations as compiled by the Charts Dept. of Billboard.

FIGURE 12.2. *Record sales from Billboard*

program rating of 20 means that 20 percent of all U.S. TV-equipped homes are watching that program. In 1978 there were about 72 million TV homes. Thus a rating of 20 meant that almost 15 million homes were tuned to that program.

$$\frac{\text{A program's}}{\text{rating}} \times \frac{\text{U.S. TV}}{\text{homes}} = \frac{\text{The number of homes}}{\text{tuned to that program}}$$

$$20\% \times 74{,}000{,}000 = 14{,}800{,}000$$

It should be reemphasized that these ratings represent households, not individuals, and are based only on those homes with television sets.

The Nielsen Television Index Reports also carry ratings (percentages) for various audience groups based on age, sex, family size, location, income, and so forth. For example, if we consider women aged 18–49 (a primary target audience of a large number of advertisers), a rating is a percentage of that universe—women aged 18–49 who reside in a TV household. Figure 12.3 provides feedback in the form of ratings—percentages for the syndicated program "To Tell the Truth" according to a specific kind of audience. The program was viewed, for example, in Providence by 32 percent of all TV households in the station's market area. The 43 percent share figure indicates the percentage of households watching television at that time who were tuned to "To Tell the Truth." The information is further broken down by estimating figures (in thousands) for people aged 18–49 and 18–34, and for two groups of housewives. This type of information is obtained by using diaries, because it deals with *viewers* rather than *sets*. In using this feedback, mass communicators place as much importance on the share a program receives as on the rating because a share indicates how many households watching TV tuned into a program, thus providing a more significant measure of head-to-head popularity.

The most specialized ratings are based on product usage, a practice initiated in the mid-1960s by the Brand Rating Index (BRI). Here, viewers are reported as percentages (ratings) of users of a product class. For example, a BRI rating of 20 indicates that 20 percent of the viewers are heavy users of a product class (e.g., gasoline, prepared cereal, beer). The rationale for this system is that the advertiser on TV is more interested in feedback that indicates results in terms of product use than audience characteristics and demographics. This feedback is obtained through personal interviews as a means of getting product information, and diaries to get viewer information.

Radio- and television-rating feedback for local network programs are also prepared by Singlinger, Pulse, Trendex, and the American Research Bureau

Market	Station	ADI		METRO		Homes				Housewives	
		RATING	SHARE	RATING	SHARE		TOTAL	18–49	18–34	TOTAL	UNDER 50
Providence (WED)	WJAR	32	43	38	51	215	218	61	34	183	51
Chattanooga (THURS)	WDEF	25	36	29	48	60	51	20	11	47	20
Spokane (MON)	KXLY	24	39			64	52	20	14	46	17
Memphis (6:30 CST) (WED)	WREC	29	41	29	42	159	161	68	37	137	55
Albany (FRI)	WTEN	23	36	27	42	97	93	43	25	79	37
Columbus, O. (FRI)	WTVN			20	39	98	87	39		77	
Phoenix (6:30 CST) (MON)	KOOL	23	43	24	45	93	85	24		80	
Indianapolis (WED)	WISH	22	33	25	38	162	155			138	
St. Louis (6:30 CST) (THURS)	KTVI	20	33	18	31	184	163	58		145	49
Fresno (THURS)	KMJ	22	37	25	42	54	50	24		46	21
Roanoke (MON)	WSLS	28	39	35	49	91	90	44	21	77	36

FIGURE 12.3. *Selected Market Ratings Analysis of "To Tell the Truth"*

(ARB). Each of these organizations uses a different method of obtaining feedback. Sindlinger uses the telephone-coincidental method for network-radio research. Pulse, Inc., uses the personal interview. Trendex uses the telephone coincidental. ARB uses the diary and is the major competitor of Nielsen in providing local TV feedback.

Local TV ratings for more than 200 markets are reported in November and March. The largest markets are surveyed as frequently as once a month, but the smaller markets are covered only in the two annual "sweeps." In New York, Chicago, and Los Angeles, Nielsen provides overnight ratings based on a small sample of homes with audimeters linked directly to computers.

The main criticism leveled at ratings is the emphasis placed upon them by networks, stations, and advertisers. Low ratings bump programs off the air because a program with a rating of 10 costs its sponsor twice as much for each home reached as does a program with a 20 rating. This cost per home is, of course, the critical form of feedback for the television industry. CPM (cost per thousand) has been discussed extensively in chapter 4; suffice it to say that this is the bottom line. A television program stays on the air or is canceled almost exclusively according to how much it costs the sponsor of the program to reach a thousand people. CPM figures of $5 and under are desirable. Figures of $5–$10 are acceptable. Figures of over $10 are unacceptable.

As long as we have a commercial system of broadcasting in the United States, ratings will play an important role in the medium. Broadcasters and advertisers must know what they are getting for their money in TV as in any other advertising medium.

Print Media. Feedback for books comes from critics, award committees, and sales. All three provide a good indication of a book's success.

For newspapers and magazines, feedback as to the number of copies sold comes from the Audit Bureau of Circulation. This information indicates *only* the newspaper's and magazine's paid circulation. Additional feedback on both media is provided by readership studies conducted by companies such as Politz and Simmons, but these studies are not made with the regularity of broadcast ratings. In terms of advertisers, considerably more feedback on a repetitive basis would be helpful.

The effect of telephone calls and letters from audiences has seldom had significant impact on the print media. This form of feedback is often considered "crank mail," unless the media are barraged by a huge quantity of mail over a period of time. The media are so complex that the audience often feels powerless to change them. In spite of the competition in the media marketplace, subscription cancellation or even advertiser boycott of print media are often relatively ineffective forms of feedback.

The Impact of Feedback

Given the reliance on institutionalized and largely quantitative feedback, it is no wonder the average viewer feels helpless in terms of having any impact on specific programs or programming practices. Still, individual or group feedback can have an effect if directed at the right target. Often this takes the form of going beyond the local communicator to other agencies or groups, which in turn can exert pressure on the particular medium.

Many dissatisfied audience members of radio and TV stations write to the Federal Communications Commission rather than the specific station. The FCC—under public pressure—then will provide the station with indirect feedback that might be more effective than that of the local audience. For example, WLBT-TV in Jackson, Mississippi, lost its license because of indirect feedback on that station's policy in regard to racial issues. FCC action can also serve as feedback for other stations, indicating that certain actions are frowned upon. Television is not the only medium where this type of feedback is effective. The action by the Motion Picture Producers Association in establishing a production code and self-regulating agency was a result in part of public feedback to Congress, which was retransmitted to the film industry. In addition, public reaction to increased violence and nudity in film has been communicated to other media, the local newspapers, and national magazines, which in turn transmit it to the film industry.

Public feedback over references to drugs in rock-music lyrics led the FCC to send a notice in 1971 to radio stations, reminding them that they were responsible for putting this material on the air. The stations, in turn, pressured the recording industry for changes in the music or printed lyrics of all new releases so they could be evaluated in light of the FCC policy statement.

There is some indication that the public feels its direct, negative feedback goes unheeded when sent directly to the media. Letters alone usually cannot keep a TV series on the air, change the content of movies or the lyrics of rock music. This is, in part, correct—a few letters are ineffective—but a massive barrage of letters, telephone calls, or a boycott by regular users of a medium can have some effect. Reform feedback in mass communication must consist of extensive long-term pressure on the appropriate source in order to be successful in accomplishing major change.

Interference

All along the route of a message from communicator to audience and back, there are many possibilities for distraction, and this element of the communication process should not be minimized. This breakdown in mass communication is called interference, static, or noise. In person-to-person communication, these distractions occur in various ways: one person may look away, or another person may interrupt the flow of conversation.

In mass communication the possibilities of interference are greatly multiplied. Noise or static can result from weak signals, clutter, or competing messages, distractions in the environment, and audiences burdened by information overload.

Weak signals, such as poor sound levels in radio, distorted pictures on television, poor quality of paper and printing in newspapers, magazines, and books, can all result in a message reaching an audience in distorted form or not at all. This type of technical noise is the most easily controlled since the sender has direct influence on the source of the noise.

Clutter, such as the variety of sounds and images in broadcasting, the jumble of stories splashed on the newspaper page, or the profusion of books and magazines lined up on the newsstand rack, can cause so much competition for the mind of the audience that it turns off and receives no messages or receives so many different and conflicting messages that none makes any impression. This is especially prevalent in commercial radio where a five-minute segment can contain as many as seven or eight message units.

Information overload also can interfere with the message. The audiences of mass media receive so much continuous information that the barrage often distracts from the meaning of the message. The difference between clutter and information overload is that information overload results primarily from the continuous barrage of messages. We are surrounded by mass media messages, and given the number of exposures bombarding the audience, it is remarkable that any messages come through at all.

It is important to distinguish between interference, or noise, and filters. Both elements have the ability to distort the sender's message. The key difference is the ability of the sender to control noise partially and the inability to control filters. In other words, a sender can work to eliminate noise by reducing static, or increasing power, or reducing the number of messages. However, distortion can still occur because of audience filters. The sender has little or no control over filters.

Amplification

Those messages that actually do get through the maze of mass communication do so because they are amplified. Somewhere along the line a message gets amplified so that it stands out from the other facts and ideas clamoring for our attention. Amplification might be the result of front-page banner headlines, frequent reproduction of the same message in many media over a period of time, or the approval of a third party. The very fact that one message gets into the media, while others do not, serves to emphasize that message and deemphasize others.

Strong signals can amplify the message. Bold, black type in a front-page headline can make one item stand out more loudly than another. Powerful radio transmission, color television, technicolor-stereophonic-wide-screen movies, slick paper, and artful typography all can add to the effectiveness of a message.

Repetition of the message over a period of time can also amplify it. A person whose name is mentioned in the headlines day after day becomes a household word, acquires status and prestige; people listen to that person more carefully than they would if they had never heard the name. Products, ideas, and events, too, can be amplified if they are repeated in the mass media.

Endorsement may be one of the most important elements in achieving amplification of a message. An attractive woman is often used to endorse an idea. A baseball hero, movie star, or popular politician can also amplify a message by verifying it for the sender, or approving it. Joe Namath is paid very well for his effectiveness in selling popcorn poppers.

The Completed Process

Finally, let us put all the elements of mass communication together again in the HUB model (figure 12.4), and picture once again how the process might look if we could diagram it like a football play. In this figure, three different types of messages are pictured.

Message *A* might be the transmission of a newspaper story. As it goes from the original source to the communicator, who encodes it into the proper language, the message becomes amplified. It has no trouble passing through the gatekeepers, and the medium, too, amplifies the message. There is some interference with the message at the filter stage, however, since the story is about an event that does not quite fit our cultural concepts. Nevertheless, it reaches most of its intended audience, and there is some feedback to the communicator commenting in both negative and positive terms.

Message *B* might be the transmission of news about a violent campus protest. The message has no trouble passing through all the elements of the mass communication process and is enlarged upon, amplified, and repeated all along the way. The message is coming through loud and clear, we might say. The feedback, too, is strong. Action is taken as a result of the message in almost direct proportion to the strength of the message.

Message *C* might be the release of a press statement by a political candi-

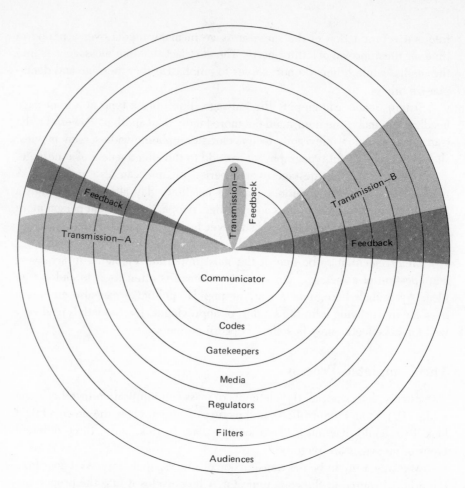

FIGURE 12.4. *HUB Model of Mass Communication*

date. The message was amplified by a communicator, but somehow it was not put into the proper code, or did not have sufficient news or communication value, and it did not pass the barrier of the gatekeeper and get into the mass media. Nevertheless, there was some feedback; the communicator of the message at least got the message that the message was not perceived as important by the gatekeepers.

Using such a model, we could draw a diagram of every communication act, for all messages that get communicated by mass media are affected by all elements we have described in this unit. This, of course, is only a rudimentary picture of the process, and we should not be fooled into thinking that such a complex process as mass communication is, in all its ramifications, as simple as we have tried to show it.

Part Three
Media of Mass Communication

Clarence Day, the famous author and playwright, once wrote:

> The world of books is the most remarkable creation of man. Nothing else that he builds ever lasts. Monuments fall, civilizations grow old and die out. After an era of darkness new races build others; but in the world of books there are volumes that live on, still as young and fresh as the day they were written; still telling men's hearts of the hearts of men centuries dead.

That is still true, for the book, oldest of the mass media, remains one of the most important. For a time, there might have been some feeling that, with the advent of the popular press and the electronic media, books would pass from the scene. But books play a greater role in our society than ever before. The book is still the most convenient and most permanent way to package information for efficient storage, rapid retrieval, and individual consumption. With the new media to compare with it today, we can recognize the special qualities of the book as a valuable communication vehicle.

Historical Perspectives

Books have had a long history. As far back as 2400 B.C., clay tablets about the size of shredded-wheat biscuits were used as we use books today. In

13

Books

Babylonia these clay tablets were inscribed with cuneiform characters recording legal decisions or revenue accounts; the clay was baked and the tablets placed in jars, arranged on shelves, and the jars labeled with still other tablets attached by straw. In 700 B.C., an entire library of literary works written on such tablets existed in Nineveh in Asia Minor.

Technical Advances. The development of paper was the first great technical advance in book production. The earliest form of paper was papyrus, made from the pith of a reed found chiefly in Egypt and believed to have been used as a writing material in Egypt as early as 4000 B.C. In the second century B.C., finding papyrus difficult to procure because of conflict with the Egyptians, the king of Pergamon sought improvements in the preparation of animal skins for writing purposes, leading to the development of parchment. Parchment became the chief medium for writing until the tenth century A.D., which saw the introduction of a new writing material made from the pulp of linen.

Developments in bookbinding were also important. The earliest form of paper books, called *volumen*, were rolls of long pieces of papyrus or parchment, wound around a stick. Such scrolls were difficult to handle and impossible to index or shelve for ready reference. They were more useful for inspiration than information. In the fourth century A.D. a new form of binding was developed by the Romans, called *codex*, in which scrolls of paper were cut into sheets tied together on the left side, between boards of wood, forming the kind of book we still use today. Codex binding opened a new world for books; the reader could leaf through the book and find the passage he wanted; he could begin to compare passages of books; he could set up a table of contents and an index and put material into some order. The Romans used this form of book to organize and codify their laws. With this development, the book started to become an important medium of information.

The Development of Printing. The most important single innovation for book publishing was the invention of the printing press and movable type. Until the middle of the fifteenth century most books were hand copied. The Chinese were the first to develop printing, sometime during the ninth century, and the oldest known printed book is *The Diamond Sutra*, printed in China in 868 and made up of seven sheets pasted together to form a 16-foot scroll. But the Chinese did not carry their invention much further. Printing did not develop in the Western world until the fifteenth century, when Johannes Gutenberg, in Mainz, Germany, put together a wine press and movable type to make a usable printing system.

Book distribution improved with printing, but mass distribution came slowly. Two of the first books to be printed with movable type were a book of masses, *The Constance Missal*—believed to have been printed by Gutenberg in 1450—and a Latin Bible—completed about August 1456. The art of printing spread rapidly in Europe, with more than 30,000 different books produced in printing's first 50 years. Most of these books were religious or Latin classics, printed in Latin or Greek. As more people came into contact with books and learned to read, printers slowly began to produce common or vulgar versions of these classics in native languages, and they began to publish more popular subjects, such as works on history, astronomy, and supernatural phenomena.

Developments in typography followed the spread of printing. The first printed books looked much like the hand-copied volumes of the Middle Ages. The style of type was *text,* or Old English, resembling the handwriting of the monks who had copied manuscripts in florid letters. This type design was useful for religious or inspirational purposes, but because it was not easy to read, it was not as useful for information. The spread of the printed word caused new type styles to be designed, and families of type styles began to grow. As more people began to read books, type style itself began to be vulgarized or simplified. Gothic type, made up of black, bold, square letters, was easier to read than ornate text type. This new type expressed a feeling of simplicity and directness. Roman type was a combination of text and Gothic, with some ornateness and some simplicity in the design of the letters, much like the type we use most today.

Each development in the production of books—whether in paper, binding, printing, typography, or broader distribution through vulgar translations—brought the book closer to the common person, and each development paved the way further for the ultimate mass production and dissemination of the book as a mass medium.

Books in Early America. Books were, of course, important to the discovery of the New World and the development of America. They allowed explorers and discoverers to pass along their discoveries, and accelerated accumulation and distribution of this knowledge.

Nineteen years after the Pilgrims first set foot at Plymouth Rock, Stephen Daye became the first printer in North America, establishing himself at Cambridge; and a year later, 1640, he published his first book, *The Whole Book of Psalms*. The first American Bible was published in 1663; it was soon translated into the language of the Massachusetts Indians for missionary work.

More popular works gradually made their appearance. Most famous of these was *Poor Richard's Almanac,* published by Benjamin Franklin every year from 1733 to 1758. Franklin wrote the almanac under a pseudonym, Richard

Saunders, and, between meteorological reports, filled the books with wise and witty sayings. In 1731 Franklin had started the first subscription library in America, the Library Company of Philadelphia. One of the first American inventors, a scientist as well as an eminent statesman, Franklin was also one of America's pioneer mass communicators, making important innovations not only in book publishing but in magazine and newspaper publishing as well.

Until the nineteenth century, however, books were relatively scarce, and the elite and affluent were the most likely possessors or readers of books. A man's library was often a mark of his place in society. The aristocrats of Virginia, for example, prided themselves on their leather-bound volumes of classics. One of the best collections belonged to one of the greatest statesmen among them, Thomas Jefferson, and his personal library was purchased by Congress in 1815 to start the Library of Congress.

Development into a Mass Medium.   For the first 350 years of printing, the production of books changed very little. The type was set by hand, the paper was handmade, and the wooden press was hand operated. At the beginning of the nineteenth century, such slow production did not matter since only about 10 percent of the population was able to read. But by the end of the nineteenth century 90 percent of America's population had become literate. As literacy increased, the demand for books soon exceeded the supply, and during the nineteenth century mass production techniques came to the book business.

The first technological innovation was the invention of a machine in France in 1798 that could make paper in a continuous roll rather than in single sheets. Innovations in the press were also made during the same time. First, an iron press was developed to replace wood in England about 1800. Then, in Germany in 1811, steam power was added to replace hand production, and the press was changed from a flat bed to a cylinder which could make impressions. It was not until 1846 that an American invented a rotary press where the type also was put on a cylinder. And in 1865 another American put paper rolls together with a rotary press for the first high-speed printing. Type continued to be hand set until 1884 when Ottmar Mergenthaler in Baltimore invented the linotype to set type by machine.

These developments in technology were accompanied by rapid change in the editorial side of book publishing. To fill the rising demand for books that could be produced more quickly and cheaply, book publishing became a more organized business, and a few major publishers began to emerge. They sought writers to produce books quickly for the new market.

The nineteenth century saw the emergence of the popular book, a cheaply produced and often sensational treatment of some popular theme, either fictional or nonfictional. The development of fast printing methods and cheap paper in the 1840s opened the way for the dime novel. Thus the world of books, which had formerly been devoted primarily to works of philosophy, religion, literature, and science, also became inhabited, during the latter half of the nineteenth century, by popular heroes of adventure, romance, the wild West, and Horatio Alger success stories.

While the emerging book publishing industry continued to devote its primary editorial attention to producing books that would add significantly to man's storehouse of knowledge, it was the less important type of book that often sold the most copies. Indeed, the concept of "best seller" became important to book publishing in the latter half of the nineteenth century. Books came to be judged by the book industry not so much on their intrinsic merit as their popularity—how many copies were sold? How much money did they make? The best-seller concept was to become basic to all mass media.

Current Developments in Book Publishing.   Until the end of World War II, book publishing in America remained essentially the same kind of industry it was in the late nineteenth century. Most firms were still relatively small, family-owned publishing houses, usually specializing in one type of book, such as adult trade books, specialized professional books, e.g., books for medicine, law, or science; or textbooks for elementary or secondary schools or colleges.

In 1945 the volume of sales of the entire book publishing industry was comparatively modest. At wholesale prices, the industry grossed $293 million in 1945, of which $60 million was earned in textbooks and $85 million in encyclopedias. By 1947 the gross sales had increased to $464 million, but this was still far behind the gross sales in the same year by the magazine industry, which were $1.086 billion, and the newspaper industry, which grossed $1.917 billion.

In the half dozen years immediately after World War II, changes began to take place that resulted in massive improvement and a sustained growing period for book sales. From 1952 to 1970, the book industry increased at a rate of more than 10 percent each year. In the 1970s, the industry grew at a slightly slower 7 percent a year. By 1978, the gross sale of books had exceeded $4.7 billion a year. Textbooks accounted for by far the largest share of that market. See figure 13.1 for comparative statistics on different parts of the book industry in the mid-1970s.

The growth in book publishing over the past 25 years is due in large part to four specific developments within the book industry and American society: (1) development of book clubs, (2) emergence of paperback books, (3) changes in organization of publishing firms, and (4) the boom in American education.

The development of the book club provided a new mechanism for the distribution of books. Unlike magazines and newspapers, books cannot depend upon subscription sales, which will guarantee that the consumer will purchase and receive continuing installments of the publication over a regular period. The purchase of a book is not habitual; rather, it is usually a one-time action to fill a specific need. Books generally have been sold in bookstores or through direct mail, and the sale is often accidental. Book clubs began to develop in the 1920s, providing a kind of automatic subscription for books and regular ordering each month through the mail, in a habit-forming pattern. The book club thus became a new distribution technique that has revitalized book publishing. In the late 1970s, more than $350 million was grossed annually by the industry through book-club sales.

A second element in the growth of book publishing was the emergence of the paperback book. Europeans were the first to publish cheaply bound books on a large scale, giving readers access to a much broader range of books than they could otherwise afford; if a reader wanted to keep any one book permanently, he could have it bound in leather for his personal library. The growth of paperback publishing spurted during World War II, when millions of men needed inexpensive reading material that could easily be carried in their pockets. Today, paperback books are a staple item at almost every newsstand, drugstore, corner grocery, supermarket, bus depot, train station, and airport. Paperbacks are no longer limited to the 75-cent variety; the average trade paperback costs $5.53.

A new dimension was added to book publishing in the mid-1970s: the development of the managed book. Publishers began to put books together in the same way that movie producers and magazine executives assemble their products. A managed book begins in editorial board rooms, not in an author's imagination. Editors and publishers look at demographic charts and opinion polls and decide what kind of book is needed and what will sell. They then hire out various pieces of the job in order to get it done rapidly. Good examples of this type of publishing are the books produced by Time-Life and American Heritage.

The growth of the industry has been marked by important changes in the organization of publishing firms. What used to be largely family businesses and privately held firms are now large public corporations with wide distribution and public listing on the stock market. Often these corporations have diversified their publishing activities into broad ranges of books, including trade, juvenile, elementary, secondary, college-textbook, scientific, and technical-book publication. In addition, these corporations have been steadily merging into giant conglomerates, which often include other media as well.

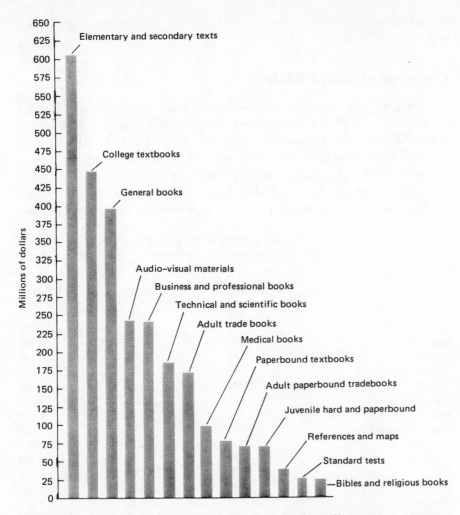

FIGURE 13.1. *Comparative Share of the Book Market by Different Types of Books, 1975. Based on figures prepared by the Association of American Publishers, Inc.*

The most important development in the growth of book publishing has been the boom in American education. Textbooks now account for more than one-third of the total gross sales of books; in 1945 they had accounted for only one-fifth. If we added together all books falling generally within the educational category, including encyclopedias and professional books, they would account for more than half the publishing industry's sales. Among the mass media, the book has a particular usefulness for conveying information instead of providing entertainment. As a tool of education, it is still far superior to other media, and this fact has been an essential element in the growth of publishing in the United States.

The Scope of Book Publishing

Even with the growth of book publishing in the past 30 years, it is still a comparatively small and concentrated field; Bowker estimates that almost 36,000 different titles were published in 1977 (see table 13.1). About three-fourths of these were new; one-fourth were revisions and reprints.

Book publishers are concentrated primarily in New York City, with some important publishing also taking place in Boston, Philadelphia, and Chicago. San Francisco and Washington, D.C., also have growing book companies, and

TABLE 13.1.   AMERICAN BOOK TITLE OUTPUT 1977

CLASSIFICATION	NEW BOOKS	1977 NEW EDITIONS	TOTALS[a]
Agriculture	379	116	495
Art	1,198	255	1,453
Biography	1,310	472	1,782
Business	721	211	932
Education	789	178	967
Fiction	2,001	1,250	3,251
General Works	917	252	1,169
History	1,169	513	1,682
Home Economics	551	85	636
Juveniles	2,326	237	2,563
Language	336	122	458
Law	576	182	758
Literature	1,006	578	1,584
Medicine	1,861	499	2,360
Music	172	137	309
Philosophy, Psychology	898	249	1,147
Poetry, Drama	826	291	1,117
Religion	1,375	312	1,687
Science	1,982	454	2,436
Sociology, Economics	4,538	1,027	5,565
Sports, Recreation	766	174	940
Technology	1,443	342	1,785
Travel	273	120	393
Totals	**27,413**	**8,056**	**35,469**

[a]Not counted are U.S. government publications, or publications of other governmental units, or university theses. In addition, certain classes of books are known to be underreported: textbooks and mass market paperbacks.

of course small publishers are scattered across the country, often in university towns, but these constitute an insignificant percentage of the industry. By the late 1970s, there were about 1,500 book publishers in the United States, but of these it is estimated that about 300 produced more than 80 percent of the total volume, and most of those 300 are headquartered in New York City.

The book market is still limited as a mass medium, but the number of outlets where one can obtain a book is steadily growing. Some 12,000 bookstores, including specialty shops like college bookstores, serve the country, and there are more than 80,000 retail outlets for paperbacks.

The average American still does not spend much leisure time reading books for pleasure. It is estimated that the average American adult purchases and reads only 4 to 12 books a year. The amount of time spent each day by the average American on book reading as compared with television viewing is infinitesimal.

The Structure and Organization of Book Publishing

The book publisher is essentially a middleman between author and reader. In most small firms, the publisher contracts for all the services necessary for the production and distribution of his publications—including the work of artists, designers, copyeditors, paper dealers, printers, binders, salesmen, and distributors. Even some of the largest book publishers use outside services for some production aspects, and only a handful of major publishers have their own printing facilities.

As figure 13.2 shows, the publisher operates at the center of a large number of services and specialists between the author and the reader. Within the publisher's offices, generally speaking, writes Henry Z. Walck, "no more than forty to forty-five percent of the publisher's staff work is in the editorial, manufacturing, advertising, and selling departments. The shipping clerks, invoice clerks, accountants, yes, the top executive officer, frequently find their particular operations not much different from those in a plumbing business or that of selling cornflakes."

A typical publishing office, employing about 50 persons, would have the following organization and components (figure 13.3). It has a head editor, an officer manager, a sales manager, and a manufacturing man. It has one assistant editor, one advertising manager, two salesmen (plus "commission salesmen" who also sell other lines), one publicity director, one person in charge of subsidiary rights and permissions, one production assistant, one manuscript reader, one proofreader, and four secretaries. The remaining staff personnel are clerical workers such as stenographers and typists, file clerks, bookkeepers,

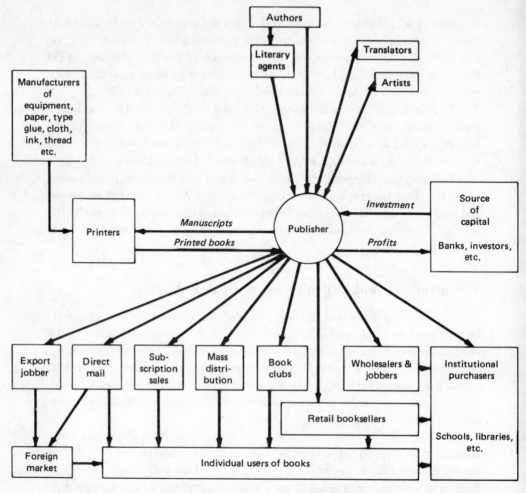

FIGURE 13.2. *The Book Publishing Industry. This diagram depicts the structure of the book industry and visualizes the interaction of a variety of institutions with publishers. From Datus Smith*, A Guide to Book Publishing *(New York: R. R. Bowker, 1966), p. 16.*

billing clerks, shipping clerks, switchboard operators, keypunch and duplicating-machine operators. The larger the firm, the more specialized each individual's function must become.

Editors themselves have increasingly specialized tasks. Managerial editors are responsible for planning and managing publishing programs. These editors are decision makers, deciding what books to publish, what authors should write the books, and how the product should be packaged and promoted. Production editors are technicians rather than planners, performing the technical steps necessary to convert a manuscript into a finished book. This includes such tasks as supervision of copyediting, rewriting if needed, and supervision of preparation of front matter, registering copyright, proofreading, and indexing.

The other jobs in book publishing are also specialized, whether in selling, promoting, distributing, or producing. Artists, designers, advertising copywriters, and promotion specialists are of increasing importance and concern. There are many different and challenging jobs in book publishing, and, as one publisher says: "The qualifications necessary for many of these positions are not unique to publishing; they are the same as required by most other business enterprises for similar jobs. Book publishing is a business, and as such it offers opportunity to almost anyone who has a business skill or professional talent."

Types of Book Publishing

Today we speak of book publishing in terms of three broad types: general, professional, and educational.

General Books. These are also often called "trade" books because most of them are sold to the public by the trade, meaning bookstores. General trade books include reference works, children's books, "how-to-do-it" books, fiction, poetry, humor, biography, and religion. Children's books, or "juveniles" or "junior books," represent a rapidly growing segment of the trade field.

Where do trade books come from and how are they distributed? Often ideas or completed manuscripts come from free-lance writers, except in the reference-book field. There seems to be no dearth of people with ideas for books, and the typical large publisher may receive annually up to 25,000 unsolicited manuscripts or book outlines and ideas. Only a small fraction of these ever get published. Trade books are generally sold through bookstores and to libraries for general public consumption. Reference works and encyclopedias are more often sold by subscription, through the mail, or by house-to-house salesmen.

Professional Books. These have become increasingly important because of our constantly changing and rapidly developing society. The professional person, no matter what the occupation, must continue to keep up with the changes in his field or run the risk of obsolescence. Hundreds of books are published each year for lawyers, doctors, engineers, scientists, businessmen, teachers, and executives. These might be how-to-do-it books, specialized monographs with a highly limited audience, handbooks, manuals, special reference works, and learned dissertations.

These books are most often written by experts and specialists in the various

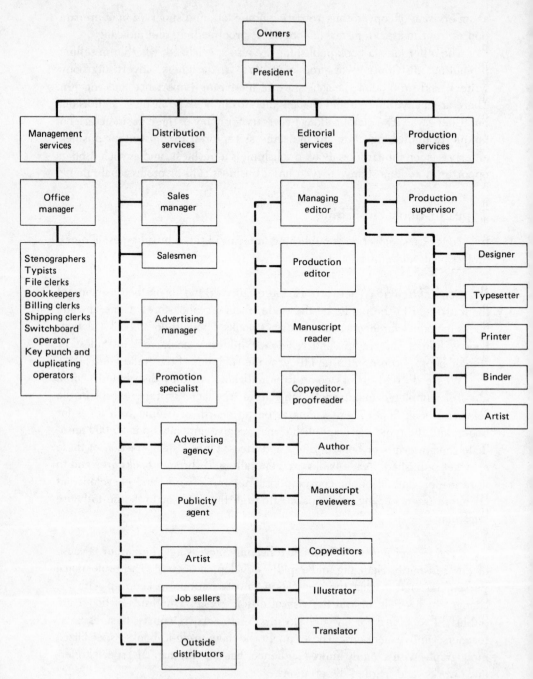

Organization of a Typical Small Publishing House

professions and are often produced at the suggestion of the book publisher. The professional book editor has a responsibility to keep up with a particular field, to know where there are needs for certain kinds of information or interpretation in that field, and to know who can produce the needed product. Such books are usually sold through direct mail or in special technical or campus bookstores, and almost always at prices higher than those of trade books.

Educational Books. These comprise the largest area of publishing. There are over 50 million students in primary and secondary schools, about 11 million in colleges, universities, and technical institutes, and more than 25 million adults enrolled in evening courses, on-the-job training, or home-study programs. This represents a giant audience for educational textbooks, workbooks, supplementary-reading books, reference works, and laboratory materials.

Most of these books are written by teachers, college professors, or specialists. As with professional books, they are often written at the suggestion of a particular editor or publisher who sees the need for a particular text, but educational-book ideas often come from educators who have developed new materials or new ways of looking at old subjects. The essential element of distribution for educational books is the adoption. Textbooks are not selected by the individual student but usually adopted by the teacher for an entire class. In some cases, a book can be adopted for an entire school, an entire school system, or even a statewide school system.

The Book as a Journalistic Medium

The book is becoming an important medium of journalism and is being rediscovered by journalists. Because of improvements in the speed of production, books are increasingly being used for timely news and interpretation, especially when a subject needs more in-depth development.

This has stimulated the relationship between literary writing and journalism, and between journalists and literary techniques. Novelist Truman Capote, for example, used the techniques of the journalist to produce *In Cold Blood,* a factual work of literary merit that was the forerunner of many similar books. And journalists have increasingly used literary techniques to bring color and action to their books, for example, Theodore H. White's *The Making of the President* books about recent presidential elections. Using the book as their medium, journalists can add dialogue, description, and dramatic pacing that bring factual events to life.

Robert Woodward and Carl Bernstein, the *Washington Post* reporters who broke the Watergate story, turned to books to tell the full story of the events leading to the downfall of the Nixon administration. *All the President's Men* and *The Final Days* are journalistic books that read like fiction. The authors have been criticized for overdramatization, for imagining scenes, for lack of sufficient attribution, and for failure to document their sources fully. These are all journalistic sins; but by using these novelists' techniques, in book form, the writers were probably able to show the whole Watergate episode better than other media could.

The work of such writers as Robin Moore represents another dimension in the new role of books in journalism. Moore is the author of *The French Connection*, *The Green Berets*, *The Happy Hooker*, and *The Washington Connection*. He employs a team of investigative reporters to research all the facts about a current public problem or situation—in the books mentioned, drug addiction, combat elites, prostitution, political scandal. He then puts all the facts together in the form of a novel.

Moore calls his form of journalism *faction*, halfway between fiction and fact, halfway between a magazine and a book. The key to it is speed. For example, *The Kaufman Snatch*, Moore's book based on the Bronfman kidnapping, took just six weeks to research, write, manufacture, and deliver as a paperback to the newsstands. The subject was still topical, and the book could thus add another facet to the reporting of the event.

Characteristics and Roles of Books

Books are marked by several distinguishing characteristics. They are, first of all, the only medium to which we attach some *permanence*. We throw away magazines and newspapers; the sound of radio and sight of television passes immediately; phonograph records are a bit more permanent, but they wear out, break, become dated, and are hard to store. Movie film is also difficult for the private individual to store. But any person can put together bookshelves and keep books for a lifetime. The permanent storage of books has been institutionalized through libraries. All this gives books a reusage rate that is far higher than that for most other media. The book can be retrieved, referred to, and reused better than other forms of communication.

The book, more than most other media, is an *individual medium*. A person can sit alone with a book, at leisure, whenever the mood strikes. One can read a book at one's own speed—can stop and start at will—can leaf through the book and find a special passage. Because the reading of a book is individual and there is no need for speed, time is of little concern; the author of a book can develop a subject much more completely and deeply than can the originator of any other mass communication medium.

The book carries with it an aura of more dignity and respect than most other media, perhaps because it is the oldest medium or because it has been so closely identified with education, intellectual activity, and the recorded wisdom of mankind. People who would not think twice about wrapping their garbage with the "Week in Review" section of the *New York Times* might keep on their bookshelves a superficial romance bound in book form. We tend to have a reverence for the book that transcends all other media.

The book is one medium of mass communication that increasingly will be able to combine creative writing and news reporting to give greater meaning and impact to the swift-paced and complicated occurrences in today's changing world.

Although the book is the oldest medium in use today, the newspaper is the oldest *mass* medium, for it was the first form of communication to reach a mass audience. The newspaper's early identification with the masses, with the man on the street, made it the medium of democracy, so newspapers have played a unique role in the development and continuation of a democratic form of government in America. Thomas Jefferson summed up the political philosophy of the role of newspapers in a free society when he said:

> The basis of our governments being the opinion of the people, the first object should be to keep that right; and were it left to me to decide whether we should have a government without newspapers, or newspapers without a government, I should not hesitate a moment to prefer the latter.

As a medium of the masses, the newspaper has often been suppressed by those in power and authority, and the history of the newspaper is a story of a continuing struggle to be free to publish news, facts, information, and opinion.

Historical Perspectives

The regular publication of news goes back more than 2,000 years to at least 59 B.C. when the Romans posted public news sheets called *Acta Diurna*. The

Newspapers

word *diurna*, meaning "daily," has been an important part of news ever since. The words *journal* and *journalism* have their roots in the same word, "day," and the daily, current, or timely aspect of news has always been an essential factor in newspapers.

But for much of the past 2,000 years, the communication of news has been carefully guarded. Through most of the empire days of Rome and the centuries of dark ages, the distribution of news came under the strict control of both secular and ecclesiastical authorities. Even after the development of the printing press in the mid-fifteenth century, it took another 150 years before the political climate could change sufficiently to allow the first beginnings of the modern newspaper.

Early Development of the Newspaper. During that 150 years following the mid-fifteenth century (and long thereafter), printers had to fight monarchs for the right to publish. William Caxton, the first English printer, set up his press in 1476 and worked in relative freedom for 50 years, largely because he did not print any news. When Henry VIII came to the throne of England, he feared the power of the press, and by 1534 he had set up strong measures to control printing. For more than a hundred years after that, the British maintained repressive restrictions on printers; some were hanged and many were imprisoned for defying the authority of the Crown.

As Edwin Emery points out in his history of journalism, *The Press and America*, "It is significant that the newspaper first flourished in areas where authority was weak, as in Germany, at that time divided into a patchwork of small principalities." The first prototype newspaper, a rudimentary version, to be sure, was published about 1609, probably in Bremen, Germany. In that same year a primitive newspaper appeared in Strasbourg, and in 1610 another in Cologne. By 1620, infant newspapers were being printed in Frankfurt, Berlin, Hamburg, Vienna, Amsterdam, and Antwerp.

The first English prototype newspaper was printed in London in 1621. From that year to 1665, various *corantos* and *diurnals* ("current" and "daily" forms of publication) made their appearance. These often were tracts and broadsides in format, rather than newspapers. Their production accompanied a growing political and philosophical climate of freedom from governmental control, climaxed by the ringing declarations of the poet John Milton. In 1664, in his essay *Areopagitica*, he expressed the basic rationale of a free press in a democratic society, when he wrote:

> . . . though all the winds of doctrine were let loose to play upon the earth, so truth be in the field, we do injuriously by licensing and prohibiting to misdoubt her strength. Let her [truth] and falsehood grapple; who ever knew truth put to the worse, in a free and open encounter?

In 1665 the first true English-language newspaper, in form and style, was published in Oxford, then the seat of the English government; it was called the *Oxford Gazette*. When the government moved to London some months later, the newspaper moved too, and became the *London Gazette*. Thirty-seven years later, in 1702, the first daily newspaper, the *Daily Courant*, was published in London. In those 37 years, English printers of newspapers had won many rights, including the freedom to publish without a license.

Newspapers in Early America.   In the British colonies, where people did not have full British citizenship, printers did not yet enjoy the same rights and freedoms. Thus, the first newspaper in the American colonies, *Publik Occur-ances, Both Forreign and Domestick*, published on September 10, 1690, was banned after its only issue because its printer, Benjamin Harris, did not have an appropriate license from the Crown.

Fourteen years later, the *Boston News-Letter* was started, published with the authority of the Massachusetts governor. Nevertheless, in its lifetime from 1704 to 1776—when it ended publication during the American Revolution—it was rebuked by the government on occasion, and publication was suspended several times.

Most early colonial newspapers, like their European counterparts, existed primarily for the purpose of spreading information about business and commerce. Produced by printers, not journalists, they contained some local gossip and stories; but many of them were concerned chiefly with advertising and often had the word "advertiser" in their title. They told about ship comings and goings, market information, import and export news, and trade tips. But the colonial printers who published these newspapers could not help but inject stories about political conditions that affected their businesses, and they expressed their opinions on such political matters. As they increasingly smarted under their second-class British-citizenship status, they expressed their bitterness over the policies of the Crown with increasing frequency in their editorials.

In 1721 James Franklin, a colonial printer, began publication of the *New England Courant*. When he made a sarcastic comment in his paper about the British governor, he was thrown into jail and his 13-year-old brother, Benjamin, took over. This started Ben Franklin on a lifetime of writing, printing, and publishing. Later Ben went to Philadelphia to start his own print shop and newspaper, and before he was 40 he had become the first "press lord" in America, having founded a chain of print shops and newspapers in which he held part ownership.

Another colonial printer who ran afoul of the Crown was John Peter

Zenger, printer of the *New York Weekly Journal,* who in 1734 was thrown into jail for libeling the governor. But a jury of colonists ultimately freed Zenger when a shrewd Philadelphia lawyer, Andrew Hamilton, made a convincing argument of the point that Zenger's facts had been true, and that men should be free to print the truth, even if libelous.

The case eventually led to the legal interpretation that newspapers could print anything, even attacks on the follies and abuses of government, if they could prove their criticism was based on true facts. This gave journalists an unprecedented kind of power in the modern world.

The Zenger case emboldened the colonial newspapers to take up the attack against the colonists' status as second-class citizens. Increasingly, political activists among them used the pages of the colonial newspapers to arouse public opinion against the abuses of British authority, leading finally to the Declaration of Independence and the Revolutionary War.

Historian Arthur M. Schlesinger, Sr., in his book *Prelude to Independence: The Newspaper War on Britain 1764–1776,* clearly establishes the fact that colonial newspapers were powerful weapons in the battle for freedom from the Crown. Some of the Founding Fathers were newspaper writers and press agents who used their communication abilities to stir the fight for independence through the pages of the colonial press. Among them were men such as Samuel Adams, Thomas Paine, Thomas Jefferson, John Adams, John Dickinson, Benjamin Franklin, and Richard Henry Lee.

After the Revolution, the colonial newspapers again served to encourage social action, helping to persuade the liberated citizens to ratify the Constitution and adopt a democratic form of government. Another historian, Allan Nevins, in a booklet titled *The Constitution Makers and the Public, 1785–1790,* describes how James Madison, Alexander Hamilton, and John Jay sent essays to the colonial newspapers urging support for the new constitution. Today we know those "press handouts" as *The Federalist Papers.* It was, says Nevins, "the greatest work ever done in America in the field of public relations." Little wonder, then, that newspapers were so important to the new nation of America.

The Penny Press—The First Mass Medium. Although the first "daily" newspaper, the *Pennsylvania Evening Post and Daily Advertiser,* was started in 1783, it was not until half a century later that newspapers began to reach a truly mass audience. Until the 1830s, newspapers were fairly high-priced and aimed at a relatively elite audience of political influentials. They were politically biased, often functioning as organs for a particular party or political viewpoint.

Technical advances in printing early in the nineteenth century made communication for the masses more feasible. Most important was the development of the cylinder press, which speeded the printing process enough to allow for mass production. One New York printer, Benjamin Day, used the new, fast press to start a new trend in journalism. In 1833 he began the *New York Sun* and sold it for one penny rather than the usual six cents. By hiring newsboys to hawk the newspapers on the streets, he succeeded in making up in volume what he lost in individual sales. The *New York Sun* became the publishing success of journalism and started the era of the "penny press," the first mass circulation medium.

In order to sell penny papers on a mass basis, the newspapers had to contain material of interest to many people. This economic factor led to the development of the profession of news-gathering. The man most responsible was James Gordon Bennett, a printer, like Day, who started the *New York Herald* in 1835, two years after Day had started the *Sun*. Day and Bennett both realized that to sell papers on the streets of New York, they had to have good stories and interesting headlines.

Bennett started the practice of hiring men to go out and find the stories, and the modern news reporter was born. He sent men to the police stations to get stories about crime, to the city hall for stories about politics. He sent men in boats out into the New York harbor to meet ships coming in from Europe so that his paper could be the first with foreign news. And when the telegraph became a possibility in the 1840s, he was the first to station a Washington correspondent in the nation's capital to send back to New York City telegraphed stories about Congress and government.

The penny press proved to be a great business success. Only 15 months after Bennett's *Herald* was born, it had a circulation of more than 40,000, and the number of readers grew steadily. Other newspapers were started, such as Horace Greeley's *New York Tribune*, and Henry Raymond's *New York Times*. With circulation ultimately reaching the hundreds of thousands, these papers and their editors became powerful forces in society in the mid-nineteenth century, playing an influential role in the Civil War, the industrial revolution, western expansion, and American urbanization. Similar newspapers soon were started in cities across the country.

Yellow Journalism and Muckrakers. Mass circulation newspapers became big business by the end of the nineteenth century. The papers were highly competitive, and for the most part independent, no longer tied to any one political party or group. Circulation was built largely through sensational news coverage or spicy features, with bold headlines and extra editions for latest news.

"Newspaper barons" emerged toward the end of the nineteenth century, men who had built newspaper empires through aggressive promotion. Joseph Pulitzer developed a strong *St. Louis Post-Dispatch* and then bought the *New York World* in 1883. The *World* had a circulation of 20,000 when Pulitzer took it over; less than a decade later, by 1892, he had raised its readership to 374,000. Pulitzer stressed sound news coverage combined with crusades and stunts to win his readers; in 1889 he sent a young female reporter with the pseudonym of Nellie Bly around the world to beat the record of the fictitious Phineas Fogg, hero of Jules Verne's *Around the World in Eighty Days.* Nellie completed the trip in 72 days, and circulation of the *World* soared as readers kept up daily with her trip.

In that same year, Pulitzer's *World* produced the first regular comic section in a Sunday paper, soon printed in color. The most popular cartoon was a strip called *The Yellow Kid,* a feature that gave the name of yellow journalism to the whole era of sensational newspaper practices.

Another press lord, William Randolph Hearst, entered journalism as the student business manager of the *Harvard Lampoon* and then received the *San Francisco Examiner* as a gift from his wealthy father. In 1895 he purchased the *New York Journal* and copied many of Pulitzer's techniques to compete with the *New York World.* Knowing that headlines would sell papers, Hearst not only reported news—he sometimes made news to get banner stories. Some historians have accused Hearst and the *Journal* of fomenting the Spanish-American War in 1898 to get more subscribers.

Yellow journalism, according to newspaper historian Frank Luther Mott, was based on sensationalized coverage of crime news, scandal and gossip, divorces and sex, disasters, and sports. Its distinguishing features were scare headlines, sensational pictures and photographs, stunts and faked stories, comic strips, Sunday-supplement features, and crusades for the downtrodden and the lower classes. Similar elements often have been part of other new mass media.

The crusading element was most important. The yellow press, with hundreds of thousands of regular readers, exercised great influence on public opinion. By exposing graft and corruption in society, newspapers found they not only could sell more papers but they could also perform a social service. A new breed of reporter began to develop who was interested in investigating the sins of society and the hidden perversions of power. These men, to use Teddy Roosevelt's expression, raked the muck of society.

The so-called muckrakers did much social good. For example, reporter and writer Lincoln Steffens exposed graft and corruption in city governments and helped bring about municipal reform. Ida Tarbell's exposé of the Standard Oil

Company helped to strengthen antimonopoly laws. Samuel Hopkins Adams's investigation of the patent-medicine business led to federal food and drug regulations. These writers worked in the magazine and book fields as well as newspapers, but they typified a new breed of newspaper journalist.

By the beginning of the twentieth century, the daily newspaper had become a power for good and evil in society. It was the first and most influential mass medium.

The Modern Newspaper. In the twentieth century the American newspaper has grown into more maturity and responsibility. During the first 30 years of the new century, some of the old newspaper giants of the nineteenth century declined and fell, including ths *World* and *Sun*. In *The Compact History of the American Newspaper*, John Tebbel says this marked "the transition from propaganda and personal journalism to the conservative newspapermaking of a new generation of businessmen soon to rise." In the twentieth century, corporate caution replaced the old individual newspaper flamboyance.

One of the reasons for the change was economic. James Gordon Bennett had started the *New York World* in 1835 for an investment of $500. By 1900 it would have taken $1 million to start a New York newspaper, and by mid-century at least $6 million. The amount of investment required for a large metropolitan newspaper plant today is usually in the millions of dollars. The *Los Angeles Times*, for example, estimates that it has more than $65 million invested in printing equipment alone. Enterprises with that sort of money at stake cannot afford to be reckless.

One consequence of rising costs and big-business operations has been the death of many newspapers and the merger of many others. In New York City, most of the giants of the nineteenth century merged, becoming the *New York World, Telegram,* and *Sun;* the *New York Herald Tribune;* and the *New York Journal-American*. And all of these ultimately merged in the 1960s into the *New York World-Journal Tribune;* and then died. The same happened, though perhaps less dramatically, in other American cities.

Sensational journalism did not die completely in the twentieth century. An important manifestation of it was the so-called jazz journalism of the 1920s, marked by the rise of tabloid newspapers, smaller in size than regular "blanket" newspapers. These papers usually made extensive use of photographs and concentrated coverage on one or two major headline stories. Such a paper was the *New York Daily News;* started in 1919, it grew swiftly in the 1920s, with sex and sensation as its stock in trade, and became the largest-circulation newspaper in the country, a position it still holds.

In the twentieth century, daily newspapers have had to withstand rising competition from many sides. The new mass media—radio, television, and movies—have grown to challenge the number-one place of the newspaper as mass communicator in society. The automobile revolution, the suburban exodus, the death of the inner city, and growing leisure time for sports, recreation, and entertainment, have also changed the place of the newspaper in the daily life of the twentieth-century man.

To offset rising costs and growing competition, another phenomenon of the twentieth century has been the increase in newspaper chains, a form of newspaper organization that goes back to Ben Franklin, in which different newspapers are owned by a single corporation and gain the advantage of management efficiency. Among the larger and more important newspaper chains in the United States are those of Hearst, Scripps-Howard, Copley, Gannett, Newhouse, Thomson, Knight-Ridder, Dow Jones, Harte-Hanks, and Tribune Company newspapers.

By the 1970s a number of great newspapers emerged in America as economically sound, politically independent, and socially responsible organs, despite competition and high costs. The *New York Times* has maintained a position for nearly a century as the newspaper of record. (It is kept in libraries as the official record of the day's events.) Two other great newspapers claiming a national audience are the *Wall Street Journal* and the *Christian Science Monitor*, both of which have won wide respect for their coverage of important news and their penetrating analysis of events. The *Washington Post* rose rapidly during the 1950s and 1960s to challenge the premier position of the *New York Times*, as did the *Los Angeles Times* on the West Coast, under the dynamic leadership of Otis Chandler. Other great newspapers of the twentieth century are the *Baltimore Sun*, *Kansas City Star*, *Louisville Courier-Journal*, *Milwaukee Journal*, *Minneapolis Star-Tribune*, and *St. Louis Post-Dispatch*, to name a few.

The Scope of Newspapers

The number of daily newspapers reached its high point in the United States immediately before World War I, in 1914, with 2,250 individual papers, and its low point immediately after World War II, with 1,749 papers. The number of newspapers stabilized after 1945, with some slight growth, but at the beginning of 1978 the number of dailies in America stood at 1,765 (see table 14.1).

Since the mid-1960s, newspaper circulation has stabilized at around 60

TABLE 14.1.
TOTAL NUMBER OF MORNING, EVENING, AND SUNDAY NEWSPAPERS AND THEIR CIRCULATION
Editor & Publisher

YEAR	MORNING	EVENING	TOTAL M&E	CIRCULATION	TOTAL SUNDAY	TOTAL SUNDAY CIRCULATION
1920	437	1,605	2,042	27,790,656	522	17,083,604
1925	427	1,581	2,008	33,739,369	548	23,354,622
1930	388	1,554	1,942	39,589,172	521	26,413,047
1935	390	1,560	1,950	38,155,540	518	28,147,343
1940	380	1,498	1,878	41,131,611	525	32,371,092
1945	330	1,419	1,749	48,384,188	485	39,860,036
1946	334	1,429	1,763	50,927,505	497	43,665,364
1950	322	1,450	1,772	53,829,072	549	46,582,348
1955	316	1,454	1,760	56,147,359	541	46,447,658
1960	312	1,459	1,763	58,881,746	563	47,698,651
1965	320	1,444	1,751	60,357,563	562	48,600,090
1966	324	1,444	1,754	61,397,252	578	49,281,852
1967	327	1,438	1,749	61,560,952	573	49,224,125
1968	328	1,443	1,752	62,023,323	578	49,660,143
1969	333	1,443	1,758	62,059,589	585	49,674,847
1970	334	1,429	1,748	62,107,527	586	49,216,602
1971	339	1,425	1,749	62,231,258	590	49,664,643
1972	337	1,441	1,761	62,510,242	605	50,000,669
1973	343	1,451	1,774	63,147,280	634	51,717,465
1974	340	1,449	1,768	61,877,197	641	51,678,726
1975	339	1,436	1,756	60,655,431	639	51,096,393
1976	346	1,435	1,762	—	650	—
1977	351	1,414	1,765	—	669	—

million copies of each issue. Circulation hit a peak of 62.5 million in 1972 and then declined, perhaps because of inflation and recession in the mid-1970s or, in some cases, because of combining of morning and evening papers.

Despite stabilized numbers of newspapers and circulation, and despite competition from other media, newspaper advertising, both national and local, has continued to grow. In 1975 newspapers had almost as much advertising revenue as magazines, radio, and television combined (figure 14.1). Total newspaper advertising was $8.4 billion in 1975 and rose to more than $10 billion in 1976 (figure 14.2).

Newspaper readership has remained fairly stable even though people allot more and more time to television. Today's newspapers are read by 77 percent

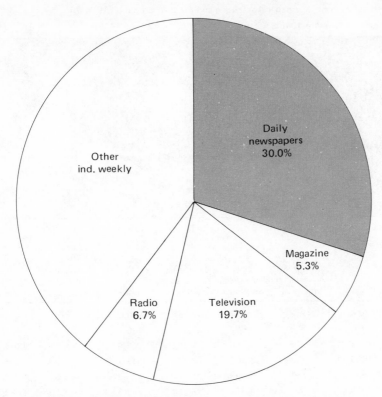

FIGURE 14.1. *Major Media Shares of Advertising Dollar, 1976*

of the adult population, with higher percentages recorded for college graduates and higher-income groups; 3.5 persons read each daily newspaper, and the average reader spends 34 minutes a weekday on each paper.

Newspapers are fatter than ever. The average morning newspaper had 60 pages per issue in 1978, and many large metropolitan dailies regularly ran more than 100 pages every day. In an average-size (60 page) morning paper, more than 20 pages were devoted to editorial content and the remainder to advertising. Sunday editions were awesome; an average of 180 pages and sometimes more than a million words of copy.

By the late 1970s, more cities than ever had at least one daily newspaper. In 1977 there were 1,545 cities with a daily newspaper, an increase of 45 over 1972. But fewer cities had competing newspapers; at the beginning of 1977 only 42 cities had two or more dailies under separate ownership and published separately.

The problem of "one-newspaper towns" has become a major issue among

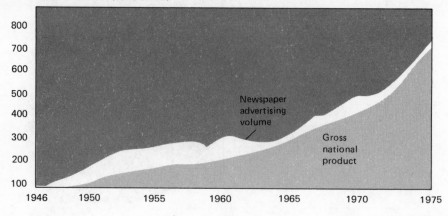

The Growth of Newspaper Advertising and the U.S. Economy, 1946-75.

Index of Growth (1946 BASE)

Year	National Advertising (millions)	Local Advertising (millions)	Total Newspaper Advertising (millions)	Index	Gross National Product (billions)	Index
1946	$ 238	$ 917	$1,155	100.0	$ 208.5	100.0
1950	518	1,552	2,070	179.2	284.8	136.6
1955	712	2,365	3,077	266.4	398.0	190.9
1960	778	2,903	3,681	318.7	503.7	241.6
1965	784	3,642	4,426	383.2	684.9	328.5
1970	891	4,813	5,704	493.9	977.1	468.6
1975	1,210	7,220	8,430	729.9	1,498.8	718.9
1976						

FIGURE 14.2. *Index of Growth (1946 BASE)*

American journalists. A growing number of media competes in almost every American urban area, however, if one counts weekly newspapers, metropolitan magazines and newsletters, and radio and television stations.

Weekly newspapers have declined throughout the twentieth century. In 1892 about 11,000 weeklies published in the United States, and by 1914 the total had grown to 12,500. Since then, the number of papers has declined, although total weekly circulation continued to increase until recently. Fewer weekly newspapers were going to more people until 1975, when weeklies experienced their first decline in circulation in more than a decade, a decline attributed to the fact that some strong weeklies converted to a daily basis while weak papers were forced out of business by rising costs. In general, however, the field of weekly newspapers in the late 1970s was healthy (see table 14.2).

The number of employees working in the newspaper industry also rose in

TABLE 14.2. U.S. WEEKLY NEWSPAPERS AND THEIR CIRCULATION

YEAR	TOTAL WEEKLY NEWSPAPERS	AVERAGE CIRCULATION	TOTAL WEEKLY CIRCULATION	ESTIMATED READERSHIP
1960	8,138	2,606	21,327,782	85,311,128
1965	8,003	3,260	26,088,230	104,352,920
1970	7,610	3,866	29,422,487	117,689,948
1971	7,567	4,030	30,495,921	121,983,648
1972	7,553	4,236	31,997,341	127,989,364
1973	7,641	4,572	34,938,800	139,935,200
1974	7,612	4,702	35,792,409	143,569,636
1975	7,486	4,698	35,176,130	140,704,520
1976	8,506	—	—	—
1977	7,980	—	—	—

SOURCE: American Newspaper Association.

the 1970s. Total employment in 1977 was estimated at 383,000, making newspapers one of the largest employing segments of the manufacturing industry, ranked third behind the automotive and steel industries. The number of women employees in the newspaper industry increased by 25 percent from 1970 to 1975.

The Structure and Organization of Newspapers

Like all mass media, the newspaper is a highly structured, carefully organized, and exceedingly complex mechanism. Literally millions of words come into the large metropolitan daily each day, from many sources. These words must be sorted, selected, checked, evaluated, edited, rewritten, laid out, set in type, made up into pages, printed, and distributed to readers, all in less than 24 hours. In order to accomplish this task with a maximum of reader interest and a minimum of error, the newspaper mechanism must work like a well-oiled machine, with each part running in its place and operating in smooth relationship to the next.

The operation of a newspaper is usually divided into three parts—editorial, business, and production. Although the most important of these, for our purposes, is the editorial side, the newspaper could not function without the other two. The business manager is in charge of both classified and display advertising. Without these the newspaper as we know it could not exist. The business manager is also in charge of selling or promoting the newspaper and is responsible for getting it properly distributed, through a circulation department, which is usually made up of independent distributors and a network of newspaper carriers. And the business manager has general charge of the bookkeeping and accounting for the entire organization.

The production manager, also essential to the operation, is in charge of the printing plant, which usually includes composition or typesetting; engraving or photographic platemaking; stereotyping or casting of the type into curved plates to fit on the cylinders of the press; and finally the press itself, usually a gigantic machine with more than a million moving parts.

Most mass communicators, however, work on the editorial side of the newspaper. The typical daily newspaper with a circulation of 100,000 has about 75 full-time editorial staff members. The main function of the editorial department is to gather information, judge its importance, evaluate its meaning, process it into forms that will attract and hold the attention of readers, and put it through the cycle of production until it reaches the printed page.

As figure 14.3 indicates, this process requires a complex organization for the typical newspaper. It also requires organized action rather than individual caprice. The important decisions are often made in committee. The editors meet at the start of each news day to draw up a list of assignments from their knowledge of events that have taken place or will soon occur. As the reporters complete their assignments, they and the editors together in further conferences during the day develop the way in which the news and opinions will be played in the newspaper. This kind of constant team effort is an essential aspect of newspaper work.

The organizational chart shows that a career in newspapers can advance within the organization in two directions, horizontally or vertically. Vertically, a person can go up the editorial ladder, starting as a news assistant or copy assistant and working up to reporter, copyeditor, city editor, managing editor, and editor. "While many of today's top editors," says the American Newspaper Publishers Association, "started as copyboys, large papers now have intern programs which recruit students and graduates of journalism schools."

A newspaper career can also be successful in a horizontal path. A reporter, for example, may succeed, not by becoming a city editor, but by specializing in one field and becoming a special editor, in business, for example, or entertainment, science, or politics. Such a specialist can ultimately command considerable respect and be in demand as a lecturer, magazine and book writer, and consultant. A reporter assigned to cover a union strike, for example, became interested in the labor field. He asked for more assignments to that type of story and soon was named the newspaper's labor editor. He then was asked to write major magazine articles about labor strikes. Several book publishers asked him

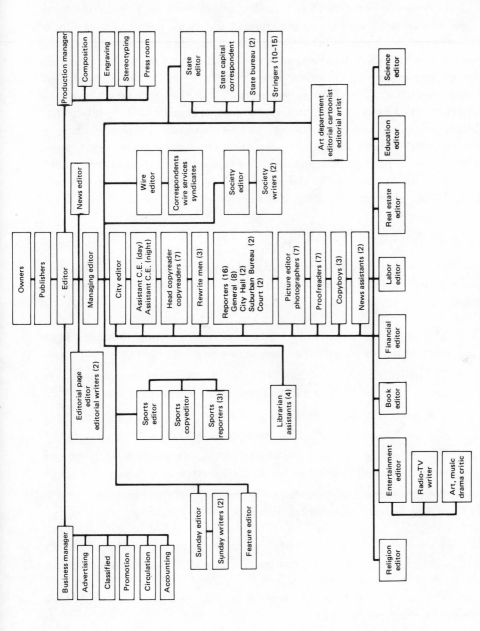

FIGURE 14.3. *Organizational Chart for a Typical Newspaper with a Circulation of 100,000. Based on The Structure and Layout of Editorial/News Departments, ANPA Research Institute Bulletin 1008, 26 January 1970.*

to write books about unions. Ultimately, the government appointed him to a high position on a key labor-negotiating commission.

As the world becomes more complex, newspapers will increasingly need such specialists in addition to generalists. The news department of future newspapers, according to ANPA, might well be organized along lines that would permit greater specialization. An urban affairs unit might have reporters specializing in coverage of urban renewal, sewers, water, building and real estate, zoning, and city planning. A governmental affairs unit might have special reporters for city hall, politics, civil courts, criminal courts, county courthouse, and the highway department. The economic affairs unit might have a farm reporter, a labor and industry reporter, a financial reporter, and a news clerk to handle stock-market quotations and tables. The social affairs unit might have reporters assigned to special coverage of civil rights and poverty, health and welfare, children, education, and religion.'

The Technological Revolution

A series of technical and electronic developments in the past few decades have brought about a revolution in the editing and production of the newspaper. They are:

1. The perfection of photo-offset lithography, a technique of printing from photo-sensitive plates rather than with raised letters.

2. The perfection of photo-composition to set type by photographing letters rather than casting type with hot metal on a linotype machine.

3. The perfection of an optical character reader (OCR) that can scan letters on a page or videoscreen and automatically set the material in type.

4. The introduction of the computer to automate many of the functions of composition and printing and to store and retrieve material.

5. The development of video display terminals (VDT) for direct transmission of copy into an automated system.

By the end of 1977, two out of three dailies and nine out of ten weeklies had switched to offset printing, and the U.S. Department of Commerce predicted that by 1980 every major daily in the country should have changed from hot-metal composition to photo-composition with place plates or should fully convert to offset production.

Not as many newspapers had adopted VDT systems by 1978, but many were in the planning stages. VDT promises to be the most significant change that newspapers should make in the late 1970s and 1980s. Many major American newspapers such as the *Washington Post, Washington Star, Baltimore Sun, Baltimore News-American, New York Times,* and *New York News* have already revolutionized their newsrooms with the new equipment. Many other papers use VDT systems for circulation, accounting, and advertising and will convert them to editorial uses.

In a VDT system, the reporter types the story on a typewriterlike keyboard, but the words appear on a videoscreen in front of the reporter rather than on a sheet of paper. Editing copy on the screen can be done much faster than editing on paper because a reporter can add or delete words, sentences, or paragraphs with a single push of a key. The reporter transmits the story to the memory bank of the computer, where it can later be retrieved by the copyeditor for further editing. The story then goes to the automatic typesetter, which can produce camera-ready copy, in the prescribed typeface and size, with headline, to be pasted up for a negative from which the final plates are made for printing. Throughout this process, no paper is used until the camera-ready copy is produced.

Systems are already developed that will automate layout and pagination as well. In 1977 the *New York Daily News*, the nation's largest newspaper, installed a complete pagination system, with page view terminals to display full-size representations of a tabloid newspaper page. The next development will be the use of satellites to transmit full newspaper pages.

Characteristics and Roles of the Newspaper

With the development of new media in the twentieth century, the role of the newspaper in society has changed. The newspaper is no longer the fastest medium, and its responsibility for carrying bulletins and headlines of the day has been taken over by radio and television. The "extra" edition that typified newspaper publishing through World War II for any major news break has all but vanished. Radio and television can do a better job of skimming the surface of events around the world and providing hourly "extra" editions of the news.

But the newspaper has the advantage of being a better display case or bulletin board of news. At a glance readers can survey the layout of the newspaper and quickly know what is happening. They have better control over what elements of the news on which they want to spend their time. Readers can be more selective, choosing items that are important to them and pursuing them as far as time will allow. Thus the newspaper can offer a greater variety of information, and it can go into greater depth with the information.

Daily and weekly newspapers play an essential role in the community, therefore, providing the small details of day-to-day and week-to-week information that sew together the fabric of society. They announce births, marriages, and deaths; tell what is for sale; explain laws and customs; help form opinions that touch local citizens; and provide some escape from the heavier issues of the day with the picture of a winsome child or a sentimental story about someone's old dog.

Not only can the newspaper cover the less significant elements of local stories, it can also go into far greater depth on national and international events. While radio and television can provide the surface bulletins, and while movies and phonograph records can provide greater entertainment, the newspaper can, on a daily or weekly basis, explain in detail and provide penetrating analysis of issues and events of great concern.

Newspapers are turning more and more to investigative and interpretive reporting, forms of journalism that are not as adaptable to radio and television. Newspaper stories are getting longer and are going into greater depth; increasingly, newspapers let radio and television serve the function of providing spot news and headlines.

Thus, as we move into the last two decades of the twentieth century, the problem of competition among the media has changed considerably as the various media have found their own special advantages and disadvantages. For the newspaper of the future, the key role will increasingly be local community reporting, specialized and in-depth coverage, and information and advertising display.

While books have a particular appeal as a medium to fill individual needs, and newspapers have a role as informers and interpreters on a local and regional basis, magazines are increasingly providing communication for special-interest groups. As competition has forced specialization among media, and with the rise of television as a national medium for general communication, magazines have found their strength in their ability to reach readers who are related by interest—whether professional, occupational, avocational, sexual, or regional.

"The rise of special-interest magazines and the related decline of general interest magazines has been the most significant development in publishing since the end of World War II," according to Arnold Gingrich, former publisher of *Esquire*. "Television has hastened the growth [of special magazines] by making people aware of all that there is to be aware of. The age of the Renaissance man is over. There is just too much to know for a man to be satisfied with claiming a little knowledge in many areas," he said. "The time is passing when a magazine can succeed by only scraping lightly on every possible surface."

This does not mean that all general-interest magazines, such as *Reader's Digest*, are doomed. There is still room for the successful popular magazine with wide general appeal. The word "magazine" itself means a general

15

Magazines

storehouse; it comes from the French word *magasin*, meaning store or shop. Indeed, the earliest magazines, appearing in France, were really catalogues of booksellers' storehouses. These were issued periodically, and after a while essays, reviews, and articles were added. The names of early magazines, often called "museums" and "repositories," reflected their nature as collections of varied items of general interest.

Historical Perspectives

Magazines have often been started by young men with new ideas and little money. And that seems to have been true of the medium from the very beginning. The first English publication of magazine type was really a cross between a newspaper and a magazine; called the *Review*, it was published in London starting in 1704. It had four small pages in each issue and was printed as often as three times a week for nine years. Daniel Defoe, who went on to become one of the great men of British letters, was the author, editor, and publisher. A nonconformist and dissenter, he was in debt and in prison when he started the *Review*, sentenced for having libeled the Church of England. Defoe wrote and published news, articles on domestic affairs and national policy, and essays on literature, manners, and morals.

In the fifth year of the *Review's* publication, 1790, an imitator was started, testimony to the fact that Defoe's idea had been a good one. The *Tatler* was produced by Richard Steele, who was later joined by Joseph Addison; together they also published the *Spectator*. They printed political, international, and theatrical news, coffeehouse gossip, and moralistic essays. They also carriie extensive advertising, a feature that was to become a necessary aspect of almost all magazine publishing. The *Tatler* and the *Spectator* provided some of the first magazine contributions to English literature as well: the informal essay and the short story.

More than 500 issues of the *Spectator* were published between 1711 and 1750, and numerous imitators sprang up, including six periodicals founded by Steele himself, and at least one, the *Grub Street Journal* (1730–38), ostensibly inaugurated by Alexander Pope. In 1731 the first publication was started that carried the name magazine; this was the *Gentlemen's Magazine*, founded by Edward Cave. He produced varied reading fare, but perhaps his most important contribution was his publication of reports of debates in Parliament. Eventually Cave hired the famous Dr. Samuel Johnson to write these reports, and Johnson ultimately used this experience to found his own magazine, the *Rambler* (1750–52). By 1750, the *Gentlemen's Magazine* had the amazing circulation of 15,000 copies, and a number of imitators were being published in London.

Half a century after the first magazine appeared, more than 150 periodicals were being printed in England.

Magazines in Early America. About 35 years after the first English magazine was published, the new medium appeared in the American colonies, and Benjamin Franklin was again one of the pioneers. In 1740 he announced his plans to publish the *General Magazine and Historical Chronicle, for All the British Plantations in America.* A competitive printer in Philadelphia, Andrew Bradford, seizing upon Franklin's idea, rushed his own magazine into print and beat Franklin by three days. Thus American magazine journalism was born in a state of competitiveness that has marked it ever since.

Bradford's *American Magazine, or a Monthly View of the Political State of the British Colonies* lasted for only three issues, and Franklin's lived for only six. But they inspired more than a dozen other magazine efforts in colonial America. No American magazine before 1800 lasted more than 14 months, and advertising support was scarce. Average circulation was about 500 copies, although each issue passed into many hands and each page was widely read. Magazines covered a large range of general topics—including religion, philosophy, natural science, political affairs, and literature. These magazines were a unifying force in the new nation, and they numbered among their authors and editors many of the great names of early America, including Franklin, Noah Webster, Philip Freneau, and Thomas Paine as editors; and George Washington, Alexander Hamilton, John Jay, Benjamin Rush, John Hancock, and Richard Henry Lee as authors. Paul Revere was the foremost magazine illustrator of the day.

After the turn of the nineteenth century, magazines blossomed into a national force, and some were started that would last a century and a half. They influenced education, spreading the new nation's ideas and culture, building literacy, and shaping public opinion. In the 1820s, 1830s, and 1840s magazines played the same role that radio would later play in the 1920s, 1930s, and 1940s. "This is the age of magazines," wrote a poet in the *Cincinnati Literary Gazette* in 1824. Edgar Allan Poe, magazine editor and writer, wrote in the 1830s: "The whole tendency of the age is Magazineward. The magazine in the end will be the most influential of all departments of letters. . . ."

Most famous among these magazines was the *Saturday Evening Post*, started in 1821 (although it claimed lineage back to 1728 and Ben Franklin's *Pennsylvania Gazette*). It lasted until the late 1960s, when it became a victim of the trend away from general-audience magazines. Another was the *North American Review*, founded in 1815. It lasted until 1938, numbering among its contributors the literary figures of the nation for more than a century.

As literacy spread in the nineteenth century, magazines became a literary force, building a national literature of American fiction, poetry, and essays. *Harper's Monthly* and the *Atlantic Monthly*, both founded in the 1850s, were among several dozen widely influential literary magazines. These publications provided the launching pad for most American literary giants of the nineteenth century, including William Cullen Bryant, Henry Wadsworth Longfellow, Washington Irving, Ralph Waldo Emerson, Henry David Thoreau, Mark Twain, William Dean Howells, Henry James, Richard Henry Dana, Nathaniel Hawthorne, John Greenleaf Whittier, James Fenimore Cooper, Oliver Wendell Holmes, Edgar Allan Poe, and many others.

The Magazine as a National Medium. With the coming of the Civil War, magazines played an increasingly journalistic role, informing the nation and influencing public opinion. Magazines were widely used by antislavery groups to spread information about slavery and antislavery activities and to mold public opinion on the issue. Most famous among them was William Garrison's *Liberator*, started in 1831 and ended in 1865, when its goal of liberation had been attained.

Magazines became reporters and interpreters of the social and political scenes, increasingly dealing with public affairs. *Harper's Weekly*, founded in 1857 (sister publication to *Harper's Monthly*), got its great chance to further magazine journalism during the Civil War. It sent a staff of writers and artists to the battlefronts for firsthand coverage of the war. Included on its staff was photographer Matthew Brady, whose Civil War pictures are still regarded among the best in photojournalism. During Reconstruction, magazines were in the forefront in the fight against political corruption, led by such publications as the *Nation*, whose militant editor, E. L. Godkin, made his magazine a leading commentator on current affairs and a fighter for democratic principles.

After the Civil War, magazines began to reach a national audience, particularly for special-interest groups. Magazines for farmers had already emerged as a separate publishing field. Among them was the *Tribune and Farmer*, published by Cyrus H. K. Curtis—who would go on to establish one of the largest magazine empires in history. Magazines for women also came into their own, particularly with the founding of the *Ladies' Home Journal*, published by Curtis and edited by Edward Bok, one of the great innovative editors of magazine history. Other women's magazines that grew to nationwide circulation by the end of the century were *Good Housekeeping*, *Woman's Home Companion*, *McCalls*, *Harper's Bazaar*, *Vogue*, and *Vanity Fair*.

By the end of the nineteenth century, magazines were a mass medium. Improvements in printing, especially the automatic typesetting machine of

Ottmar Mergenthaler, perfected in 1884, sped production. Prices were lowered, and the "dime magazine" became a counterpart to the penny press. The number of magazines increased by nearly 500 percent in a 20-year period, going from 700 in 1865 to 3,300 in 1885. By 1900 there were at least 50 well-known national magazines, many of them with circulations of more than 100,000. One had a circulation over a million; it was Curtis's *Ladies' Home Journal*. By 1908, another Curtis publication, the *Saturday Evening Post*—which he had taken over as a failing magazine—had also reached a circulation of 1 million copies per issue.

With a nationwide audience, magazines became a vital political and social force. Nowhere can this be seen better than in the socially conscious magazine writing of the muckrakers. Magazines actually were ahead of newspapers in using their pages to expose crime and corruption, fraud and manipulation. Chief among such publications was *McClure's Magazine*, founded by S. S. McClure in 1894. He used his pages to expose oil monopolies, railroad injustices, political shenanigans, and life-insurance trickery (among others). He was so successful, both in winning audiences and in reforming society, that other magazines followed McClure's muckraking—including *Cosmopolitan*, *Munsey's Magazine*, *Collier's*, and *Frank Leslie's Popular Monthly*, which became the *American Magazine*.

Between 1894 and 1904, the American magazine came of age as a mass medium and proved itself to be a powerful institution in society.

The Magazine in the Twentieth Century.   Magazines have continued to change and enlarge their scope in the twentieth century. Innovation in the magazine field seems to have come particularly from individual genius, often the vision of the young with new ideas and fresh talent.

In the twentieth century the digest has become a major publishing phenomenon, having as its basic purpose the fundamental proposition of all mass media—saving people time by giving them the cream off the top, making it appetizing, palatable, and easily digestible. None has achieved this better than the *Reader's Digest*, which before the middle of the twentieth century was the largest circulation magazine in existence; but by the mid-1970s, its position was challenged by *TV Guide*. The *Reader's Digest* was the product of a young man, DeWitt Wallace, and his wife, Lila, both children of poor Presbyterian ministers. In 1922, while still in their twenties, the Wallaces borrowed the necessary funds to give their idea a try. In the 1970s their magazine was being sent each month to more than 18 million subscribers in the United States alone, and other editions were sent all over the world by the millions.

More important even than the digest phenomenon has been the

emergence in the twentieth century of the news magazine as a national force. Another far-from-wealthy son of a Presbyterian missionary, Henry Luce, founder of *Time, Life, Fortune,* and *Sports Illustrated,* must be given much of the credit for building the weekly news magazine into a viable journalistic medium. Luce was a young man just out of Yale in 1923 when he and Briton Hadden founded *Time.* Like the *Reader's Digest,* it has not changed much since its early editions. And its imitators, including *Newsweek* and *U.S. News & World Report,* follow its format.

Luce was also a pioneer in modern photojournalism, founding *Life* magazine to report news through pictures. *Life* was not the first picture magazine, but it was the first to use photography as a regular journalistic tool to inform, entertain, persuade, and sell. *Life* earned its imitators, too, including such magazines as *Look,* and had an influence on the pictorial aspects of dozens of other modern magazines. Although *Life* is again in print, *Look* became a casualty of the rising costs in the magazine business in December 1972.

The city magazine, once the only form of magazine, has come back into its own in the twentieth century. The most successful and most influential of these has been the *New Yorker,* founded in 1925 by former newspaperman Harold Ross. He built it into a magazine that has lived up to his own original prospectus, which described it as a sophisticated "reflection in word and picture of metropolitan life. It will be human," Ross wrote at the beginning. "Its general tenor will be one of gaiety, wit, and satire. . . . The *New Yorker* will be the magazine which is not edited for the little old lady in Dubuque. . . ." It has not reached the circulation heights of some magazines that are edited for "those little old ladies," but it has influenced scores of other metropolitan magazines. By the end of the 1970s, the city magazine was enjoying unusual growth. Standard Rate and Data Service in 1977 listed over 75 major metropolitan magazines, from Baltimore to San Francisco. In the Washington, D.C., area alone, a half dozen city magazines were flourishing.

The twentieth century has seen the rise of magazines devoted to higher culture, too. Some of these magazines, in their articles on art, science, history, philosophy, and current affairs, are similar to some of the earliest magazines. Chief among these have been *American Heritage* and *Horizon.* Often produced without advertising, in a book binding with hard covers, and with lengthy articles and lavish illustrations, these magazines have aimed at a level higher than the common denominator and have been successful far beyond their publishers' original dreams.

Other trends in the twentieth century should not be overlooked. True-confession and movie-fan magazines reach an enormous audience. More important are the specialized publications, covering subjects from *Farm Journal* and *Presbyterian Life* to *Hairdo & Beauty.* The "little magazine" of poetry and criticism is another twentieth-century phenomenon, as is the esoteric or scientific journal such as *Biotechnology & Bioengineering* or *Journal of Applied Polymer Science*. The association magazine, the trade journal, and the house organ are all growing types of magazine journalism in the twentieth century.

Perhaps the most remarkable development in the magazine field has been the increasing growth and success of specialized magazines aimed at a narrow target audience. Ethnic groups are increasingly being served by their own magazines, such as *Ebony* and *Sepia* for blacks. In 1977, a slick new magazine called *Identity*, directed toward Italian-Americans, went on the market. Specialized groups of every sort were turning to magazines as a means of providing communication among those with similar interests, including such magazines as *Advocate*, the largest and most influential news magazine for the gay community, and *High Times*, a slick magazine for marijuana users.

One of the most successful magazine stories since World War II is that of men's magazines, which began to come into their own in much the same way that women's magazines did in the latter half of the nineteenth century. The women's group is still far out in front in circulation, but some men's magazines are catching up, especially *Playboy*. This magazine was started by Hugh Hefner when he was only a few years out of the University of Illinois, with some experience at *Esquire*. *Playboy* has ushered in a new era of hedonism in American popular culture, with stress on sophisticated food, drink, and frank sexual pleasure. Begun in 1953, *Playboy* had a circulation of over 5 million by the 1970s, having long since outstripped Hefner's forebears at *Esquire*. *Playboy* also had profound influence on other men's magazines, many of which left hunting, fishing, and sports cars behind to follow Hefner's nude Playmates. To what extent the "Playboy philosophy" has influenced America's manners and morals or to what extent it simply reflects them remains for historians to determine.

In the 1970s, a new kind of women's magazine emerged, representing the liberated female. Unlike earlier magazines for women, such as *Good Housekeeping* and *Ladies' Home Journal*, these new periodicals did not carry articles on cooking, homemaking, sewing, housecleaning, and child rearing. They published articles on such subjects as politics, career development, and sex. Some, like *Playgirl*, an imitation of *Playboy*, published centerfold full-color pictures of nude men. Others, like *Ms.*, aimed at spreading the news of the women's movement.

Table 15.1 provides a comparative basis of analysis of circulation figures for the top 50 magazines in the United States today.

Special Problems. In the 1950s and 1960s television threatened to capture advertising dollars from the general-consumer magazine, causing some to predict that the mass magazine would be killed. Magazines fought back by

TABLE 15.1.

TOP-46 MAGAZINE CIRCULATION FIGURES, 1978

RANK		CIRCULATION
1	TV Guide	19,881,726
2	Reader's Digest	18,300,843
3	National Geographic	9,960,287
4	Family Circle	8,277,077
5	Better Homes & Gardens	8,032,920
6	Woman's Day	8,002,758
7	McCall's	6,503,187
8	Ladies' Home Journal	6,001,578
9	National Enquirer	5,719,918
10	Good Housekeeping	5,198,082
11	Playboy	4,824,789
12	Penthouse	4,510,824
13	Redbook	4,431,266
14	Time	4,311,084
15	Star	3,008,948
16	Newsweek	2,958,851
17	Cosmopolitan	2,658,571
18	American Legion	2,597,816
19	Sports Illustrated	2,336,344
20	People	2,319,097
21	U.S. News & World Report	2,100,796
22	Field & Stream	2,042,764
23	True Story	2,000,791
24	Popular Science	1,862,418
25	Workbasket	1,814,486
26	Glamour	1,795,596
27	Outdoor Life	1,746,025
28	Midnight Globe	1,736,886
29	Mechanix Illustrated	1,704,774
30	Smithsonian	1,682,831
31	V.F.W. Magazine	1,681,561
32	Popular Mechanics	1,670,832
33	Today's Education	1,667,888
34	Boy's Life	1,620,673
35	Elks Magazine	1,613,226
36	Southern Living	1,594,117
37	Parents' Magazine	1,516,333
38	Hustler	1,507,901
39	Seventeen	1,457,871
40	Farm Journal	1,417,030
41	Sunset	1,391,140
42	Sport	1,305,219

TABLE 15.1.   *continued*

RANK		CIRCULATION
43	Ebony	1,264,718
44	Psychology Today	1,172,440
45	Grit	1,096,234
46	House & Garden	1,031,324
	Total	**171,331,840**

playing what they called "the numbers game," building circulation figures to compete with television for national advertising. Some magazines turned from their traditional newsstand sales to concentrate on subscription selling. They hired high-powered subscription sales organizations to sell subscribers at any cost. These organizations often used young people for door-to-door, high-pressure selling campaigns, offering long-term bargain prices or package deals with many publications for the price of one. The sales organization owned the subscription, collected the money from the subscriber, and sold the subscription to the magazine publisher.

In effect, such magazines were buying subscribers in order to produce large numbers of readers to attract advertisers. They earned no money from the subscriber; indeed, they had to pay to get the subscriber. And they had to lower their price far below value to keep the subscriber. In 1968 the average magazine cost the buyer 54 cents, but it cost the publisher perhaps four or five times that amount to produce the 54-cent copy. The publisher hoped to make up for the difference in large advertising sales.

Such economics ultimately put some of the large mass-consumer magazines out of business. *Colliers*, the *Woman's Home Companion*, and the *Saturday Evening Post* failed in the 1950s and 1960s. They did not go under from lack of readers, however. When the *Saturday Evening Post* died, it had more than 4 million regular subscribers. But the magazine did not have the right type of audience (young, with discretionary income) and could not attract advertisers to its older, more conservative audience.

In spite of these failures, the magazine field is not by any means dying. In the ten-year period from 1962 to 1971 the number of magazines that went out of business was 160. But in the same period, 753 magazines were born; they developed new ideas and used new approaches to succeed. By the mid-1970s, magazine circulation and advertising revenues were at an all-time high. In 1976, the American public was paying a larger share of magazine costs, spending $2.3 billion annually for magazines, more than ever before in history.

The public's willingness to pay high costs for magazines changed the "numbers race" of the postwar decades. Magazine publishers were no longer selling their product cheaply to attract masses of subscribers in order to get advertising. They were looking for circulation for its own sake. They raised magazine prices to an average $.96 per issue from 1960 to 1976 (a 246 percent increase) and $10.69 per annual subscription (a 233 percent increase). In 1966, circulation produced about 30 percent of all revenue while advertising produced about 70 percent. By 1976, circulation provided 43.5 percent and advertising 56.5 percent; many publishers predicted the ratio would soon be 50–50.

Advertising revenues for magazines increased in the 1970s, too. One reason for this was that advertisers acknowledged what the publishers called *media imperatives*. The publishers divided the adult population into four segments: (1) the heavy magazine reader and the light television viewer (the *magazine imperative*), (2) the light reader and the heavy viewer (the *television imperative*), (3) the heavy reader and heavy viewer, and (4) the light reader and light viewer. Through audience research, publishers demonstrated that the "magazine imperative" group were better educated, more affluent, greater consumers, and more apt to buy the products advertised than were the "television imperative" group. Obviously, then, it was in the advertisers' interest to do more of their advertising in magazines.

Publishers also encouraged single-copy sales, which have a larger margin of profit than subscriptions. A single copy of *Newsweek*, for example, costs $1.25 at the newsstand, with 52 issues a year; this is twice as much as the annual subscription rate of $30. More people will buy magazines on a single-copy basis when they are available not just at corner newsstands, but also in drugstores and supermarkets. Supermarket sales turned out to be remarkably profitable, so much so that magazine distributors have developed "family reading centers" in stores. Other magazines are sold only as single copies. *Family Circle* and *Woman's Day*, for example, the fourth and sixth largest circulation magazines in the country, are sold only in grocery stores and supermarkets; there are no mail subscriptions. Other magazines are moving in this direction.

Another reason for encouraging single sales has been the rising cost of postage. The U.S. Postal Service started a phased increase for second-class mailing in 1970; by 1979, publishers will be paying 317 percent more for mailing than they did at the start of the decade. Naturally, publishers must look to other means of selling and distributing their products.

Increasingly, magazines are using computers and new demographic techniques to make their advertising and editorial content more selective rather than massive. For less money, the advertiser is able to reach a more appropriate market for the product, either on a regional or reader-interest basis. For example, a magazine's production and circulation can be coordinated so that circulation can be broken out into "25 magamarkets, 50 magastates, and a group of Top Spot Zip-coders." Advertising can even be placed by selected geographical regions to reach any one or any number of predetermined markets.

This kind of distribution will increase, not only on a regional but on a reader-interest basis as well. *Time* magazine, for example, now has the technology available to custom-make its production, to the extent of giving the reader at least one article an issue that meets one of his or her preselected interests. Thus, the same issue of *Time* might bring to a sports fan an issue with an article on pro football, while her next-door neighbor, a science buff, will get an article on electronic engineering. Such magazines can have mass and selectivity, both, with wide appeal to advertisers as well as consumers.

The ability to target one's audience also has made possible the controlled-circulation magazine. The magazine is sent to a certain type of person only, sometimes on application by the reader, sometimes on identification by the publisher. For example, two magazines in Washington, D.C., *Washington Calendar Magazine* and *Washington Dossier*, are sent free to 175,000 households targeted by market research and demographic studies as the "most active households," with annual incomes over $25,000. These are supposedly the big consumer spenders that advertisers are anxious to reach—and the magazines are full of ads—even though the addressee has never indicated an interest in the publication. To beat rising mail costs, the *Washington Calendar Magazine* uses a private delivery service, which might also be an increasing trend.

Magazines are also making improvements in the product itself, with experimentation in hard and plastic covers; looseleaf and book bindings; more opaque, smoother, and lighter paper; full-color printing; faster presses; shorter closing times; three-dimensional visual effects; and "scratch-'n'-sniff" for olfactory appeal. These extensions of magazine production will aid in the economic battle for survival in the jungle of mass media.

The Scope of Magazines

Over 9,500 magazines are published each year in the United States. Monthlies make up the largest group of magazines, with almost 3,900 individual publications. Weeklies make up the next-largest group, comprising over 1,800. The third-largest are the quarterlies, numbering more than 1,000. There are even some daily magazines, 175 at most recent count, and more than 700 that are issued periodically but without any specific time schedule. See table 15.2 for a more detailed breakdown.

TABLE 15.2.
NUMBER OF MAGAZINES PUBLISHED IN THE
UNITED STATES, 1970, 1972, 1974, AND 1977

TYPE	1970	1972	1974	1977
Daily	182	180	187	175
Triweekly	18	73	29	24
Semiweekly	89	105	99	84
Weekly	1,856	1,675	2,105	1,827
Biweekly	273	208	224	257
Semimonthly	316	312	334	284
Monthly	4,314	4,426	4,463	3,846
Bimonthly	957	955	1,031	1,031
Quarterly	1,108	1,201	1,262	1,172
Miscellaneous	460	715	767	882
Total	**9,573**	**9,850**	**10,501**	**9,582**

SOURCE: *Ayer Directory of Publications,* 1978.

Usually, binding rather than timing is the important difference in distinguishing between newspapers and magazines. Both must be published regularly and periodically. But a magazine, in the accepted definition of Frank Luther Mott, is "a bound pamphlet," while newspapers are unbound. A magazine is "issued more or less regularly . . . containing a variety of reading matter," according to Mott.

In all, more than 6 billion issues of magazines are purchased by Americans every year. The average adult is exposed to at least two magazines a week. Nearly four persons read an average magazine issue, and together those four persons spend more than six hours reading that issue (see table 15.3).

Magazine publication is not as widespread as that of newspapers but far

TABLE 15.3.
TOTAL ADULT READING OF THE AVERAGE
MAGAZINE ISSUE

Number of Adult Readers	3.9
Number of Reading Days per Reader	3.3
Reading Time per Reader	93 Minutes
(3.9 Adults × 3.3 Reading Days Each)	362 Minutes
Total Adult Reading Time	
(3.6 Adults × 83 Minutes Each)	(6.05 Hours)

SOURCE: W. R. Simmons, 1976–77 Report and Target Group Index, 1976.

more geographically dispersed than book publication. More than a quarter of all magazines are published in New York, but Chicago, Washington, D.C., Philadelphia, Boston, Los Angeles, and San Francisco are also publishing centers. Every state in the union publishes magazines of some type.

The Structure and Organization of Magazines

Because magazines come in different sizes and shapes and are aimed at different kinds of readers, no one organizational or operational pattern could fit them all. Each magazine develops its own way of organizing and operating to get its special job done. Some magazines—those that deal heavily in news and timely subjects—are organized in much the same manner as newspapers. Others that deal in less time-bound material are set up much like book publishing firms.

Unlike most newspapers, most magazines do not own their own printing plant. Because they do not have to worry about daily printing schedules, they do not need an expensive investment in printing equipment but can accomplish the same purpose by contracting with established printers. Some magazines, even famous ones such as the *Atlantic Monthly,* operate out of a few small offices, with a few editorial hands, a couple of typewriters, some furniture, and a supply of typing paper. Everything else, including production and distribution, can be handled by outside help.

The editorial staff of a magazine usually includes as chief executive an editor who has overall responsibility for establishing policies and making final decisions. A managing editor or executive editor has the responsibility for carrying out the editor's policies and for running the day-to-day operation. Staff editors head various departments within the magazine or handle various functions, such as picture editing, copyediting, or layout and production. Often staff writers on magazines are called editors.

Many magazines have contributing editors, who work either full time or part time either in the office or out in the field; they often are specialists or experts in certain categories and help the magazine discover material, find appropriate writers, approve the authenticity of the writer's copy, or do some writing themselves.

Another distinguishing feature of many magazines is the editorial board, a fixture that has not been used by newspapers or book publishers to the same extent. The editorial board is often composed of leaders in the field to which the magazine is directed, and they serve to give the magazine both direction and authority.

In the past magazines have depended largely on free-lance contributions for their editorial content. The editor could sit back and wait for the mailman and then publish the best of what contributors sent in. There are literally hundreds of thousands of people who would like to be free-lance writers for magazines, and many of them try. *Harper's,* for example, receives more than 20,000 unsolicited manuscripts each year, even though the magazine does not publish unsolicited material. While many free-lancers can supplement their incomes from part-time magazine writing, only a handful of professionals make a substantial full-time salary from writing.

Increasingly, magazines are using staff-developed and staff-written material. Schedules are too demanding and story development too complicated to allow the editors to wait and see what comes in "over the transom." Editor and staff determine the audience they are reaching, the type of material the audience needs and wants, and the subjects available for development into appropriate magazine articles and stories. Then they produce the material to make sure it fits their needs and their time schedules.

Even the *Reader's Digest,* ostensibly a selection of the most interesting articles from other magazines, in reality cannot depend upon other magazines to produce all the material they need to fulfill the demands of their readers. The *Digest* editors often produce their material themselves, sometimes placing it in other magazines and then "borrowing" it for the *Reader's Digest,* or sometimes writing an article for a famous person and then "buying" it from that person for *Digest* publication.

Types of Magazines

Generally, magazines are divided into two types: consumer (or general interest) and specialized (including children's, professional, and trade publications).

Consumer magazines are generally broken down further into at least 13 categories, including women's (e.g., *Redbook*), men's (*Esquire*), sophisticated (*New Yorker*), quality (*Atlantic Monthly*), romance (*Modern Screen*), news (*U.S. News & World Report*), sports (*Sports Illustrated*), travel (*Holiday*), exploration (*National Geographic*), humor (*Mad*), shelter (*Better Homes & Gardens*), class (*American Heritage*), and city (the *Washingtonian*).

Specialized magazines can also be broken down into different kinds of publications as follows: juvenile (e.g., *Boys' Life*), comic (*Superman*), little literary (*Prairie Schooner*), literary (*Paris Review*), scholarly (*Journalism Quarterly*), educational (*College & University Journal*), business (*Nation's Business*), religious (*Christianity Today*), industrial or company (*Western Electric World*), farm (*Farm Journal*), transportation (*Railway Age*), science (*Scientific American*), and discussion (*New Republic*).

The specialized magazines, aiming their editorial fare at specialized reading audiences, have been growing at a rapid rate. In a 20-year survey of this group, entertainment guides grew 256 percent, sports publications grew 247 percent, and business magazines expanded by 76 percent. According to *Advertising Age*, "publishers themselves believe that the future of specialized magazines is the rosiest of any industry group."

The business-publication field, one of the fastest-growing specialties in magazine journalism, expanded from 1,974 magazines in 1955 to 2,336 just 13 years later. Some magazine-publishing houses have developed large groups of such magazines, serving varied trade and business groups from automobile dealers to zoo keepers. Many such magazines are distributed to a prime list of readers, some free of charge. The publisher makes his profit by selling advertising to merchants who want to reach these specific groups.

The Comics

One popular form of mass communication that deserves special consideration is the comic, which is either a cartoon, comic strip, or comic book. Although the comic strip and cartoon often appear in newspapers, we treat this form of communication as part of the magazine medium. The comic as a form has most of the characteristics of the magazine even in its form as a supplement to newspapers.

To qualify as a comic the item must meet certain specific criteria. A comic must develop a narrative within the panel, strip of panels, or pages. A comic must use continuing characters from one panel strip or page to the next panel strip or page. A comic must include dialogue or descriptions as part of the panel, rather than serve as a pictorial adjunct of another feature in the newspaper, magazine, or book. Most comics are printed by high-speed, low-definition presses on newsprint, which affects the degree of subtle detail possible.

Five classes of comics serve mass communication functions: (1) the single-picture (panel) newspaper features such as *Grin and Bear It*, *The Family Circus*, or the cartoons in the *New Yorker*, *Playboy*, and other magazines; (2) the black-and-white multipanel, daily newspaper comic strip, such as *Dick Tracy*, *B.C.*, or *Mary Worth*; (3) the multicolor, weekly, Sunday supplement, which is a collection of strips either continuing the daily newspaper feature's story line or a separate story—nearly all strips are both daily and Sunday features, but many papers will carry more comic strips on Sunday than during the week; (4) multipage, color narratives in magazine form, which are issued monthly, bimonthly, or quarterly, and are called comic books (*Action Comics, Superman, Batman, Captain America,* and so on); (5) the antiestablishment, social-political-economic commentary comics, or underground comic books, which are usually published irregularly in black and white (*Zap, Despair,* and the like).

Historical Background. From 1890 to 1914, three American artists—Richard Felton Outcault, James Swinnerton, and Frederick Opper—and two newspaper press lords—Joseph Pulitzer and William Randolph Hearst—battled to create newspaper comics. Outcault's *Down Hogan's Alley* appeared in Pulitzer's *New York World* in the early 1890s and featured a nightshirted ragamuffin involved in unsavory lower-class goings-on. In 1896 the newspaper experimented with the use of yellow ink on the ragamuffin's nightshirt. The color test became a regular feature—*Down Hogan's Alley* became *The Yellow Kid.* Hearst hired Outcault away from Pulitzer, and both Pulitzer's *World* and Hearst's *Journal* ran *Yellow Kid* comics. Eventually the "yellow" carried over to the phraseology used to identify the Pulitzer-Hearst style of newspaper reporting; thus the designation "yellow journalism" was born. Hearst printed the first comics section in 1896. The daily strip format emerged in the mid-1900s as the comics became a strong circulation builder.

During the period from 1914 to 1929, syndicates such as King Features emerged, supplying a large selection of syndicated strips by a stable of creators. Nearly every newspaper in the country carried a comics section, and "funny papers" were a major part of the industry.

At this time, intellectual content began to appear within the comic form, most noticeably in the *Krazy Kat* strip of George Herriman. This comic's surrealistic style and content revolutionized the relatively realistic strip story lines. During this period most of the strips emphasized a humorous view of family life and its problems. By 1925, the *New Yorker* had begun its now-famous one-line panels of cartoons. Today such cartoons appear in most general-reader magazines.

The most creative development to emerge in the depression and war years (1930–45) was the adventure strip, beginning with Harold Foster's work based on Edgar Rice Burrough's *Tarzan.* The movies had developed a visual sensitivity in the public, and Foster incorporated film "perspectives" into the strip. In 1936 Burne Hogarth took over *Tarzan* and developed the comic strip into an exciting art form.

In the 1930s, three major creators began careers: Milton Caniff's *Terry and the Pirates* and later *Steve Canyon* participated in and sometimes predicted political and military events; Al Capp's *Li'l Abner* became a sharp satirical comment on American society—nothing was sacred—and his attacks were savage; the Walt Disney organization contributed two great characters to American pop culture—*Mickey Mouse*, the gentle helpful, playful, and somewhat inept caricature of Americans, and *Donald Duck*, a satirical picture of the rascally, distempered, and ornery man, constantly attacking his fate.

The comic book emerged during the depression. First came strip reprints in a format called *Funnies on Parade*. *Detective Comics* (1937) was the first to structure its content upon one theme. Then in 1938 the most popular superhero of all time, *Superman*, appeared in *Action Comics*. By 1940 there were more than 40 comic-book titles; in 1941, 168 titles. At U.S. Army bases during World War II, comic books outsold all other magazines ten to one.

Like many other Americans, comic characters went to war, thus contributing mightily to the propaganda effort. Some of the strips' heroes even entered the war before the United States did, joining the RAF or the Flying Tigers. In this way the comics may have helped psychologically to prepare the American public to support the war effort and glorify the American fighting man. Special "war" strips appeared, including *Male Call*, *G.I. Joe*, *The Sad Sack*, and *Johnny Hazard*. Possibly the most important comic characters of the war years were Bill Mauldin's dogfaces, Willie and Joe. These single-panel cartoons depicted the seriocomic life of the average GI. In 1945 Mauldin won the Pulitzer Prize for his work.

From 1946 to the present, three major events characterize the development of the comics. First, the attacks on comic books because of the excesses of some led to the development of the Association of Comic Magazine Publishers (ACMP) in 1947, with a membership that included the 35 leading companies in the field. A code was drafted to safeguard children from comic books that presented nudity, torture, sadism, and frightening monsters. The code also banned racial, ethnic, and religious slurs, negative marital story lines, ridicule of law officers, profanity, and detailed descriptions of criminal acts. The public outcry continued, however, aided by professional reformers who sought outright censorship at the local level via store boycotts. The major thrust of the anticomics campaign was to link comics to increased incidences of juvenile delinquency. Under this pressure, the ACMP regrouped as the Comics Magazine Association of America (CMAA) and developed a 41-point code. Today, 90 percent of the industry submits materials for code approval, which allows them to display the code seal on their products.

The second characteristic evident in the postwar era was the emergence of the gentle comic strips of anxiety which contain strong social comment. *Pogo* (1949) by Walt Kelly revolutionized both the style and political scope of the

strips, becoming so important as to incur the wrath of Senator Joseph McCarthy. *Miss Peach* (1957), *B.C.* (1958), and *The Wizard of Id* (1964) provided gentle fantasies, but the most spectacular comic of all times is *Peanuts* (1950) by Charles Schulz. Schulz's creations seem to speak to the anxieties of our times through the eternal loser, Charlie Brown. The commercialism of religious holidays in the Great Pumpkin, the vagaries of life in Linus and his blanket, Lucy and her front-lawn psychiatry booth, Peppermint Patty's tomboy hangups, and Snoopy's constant battle with the Red Baron are part of millions of Americans' daily experiences. Charlie Brown and his friends may be the best literary explanation of American life styles in the 1960s. Early in the 1970s emerged *Doonesbury* by Garry Trudeau, with its vivid portrayal of generational conflict and swift satiric attacks on politics and social mores.

The final development was the growth of the *underground* comic, which surfaced as a voice of radical movements. Its morbidity, vulgarity, crude physical makeup, antiestablishment themes, and sexual deviance attack the most hallowed traditions of the time. Underground comics sought an audience quite different from that of the straight comic books. The "sick" humor attacked what the author-publishers felt was a sick society.

The Scope of Comics.   One of the most-read parts of the daily newspaper is the comics section; six of every ten readers read the comics every day. Over 100 million persons read the Sunday comics section. A major strip may appear in more than 1,000 papers across the world. Nearly every paper has a comics section supplied by the syndicates. The business is dominated by 25 syndicates led by King Features, which handles about 65 of the available 300 strips. *Puck*, a Sunday comics section, has a multinewspaper circulation of 14.5 million.

More than 100 comic-book publishing companies (dominated by the 25 largest) publish 300 titles and sell over 250 million copies annually. Pass-along readership of these comics is estimated to be three readers to every buyer. Normally a company prints about 200,000 copies of an issue, but *Classics Illustrated*, which are skeletal versions of important literary works, remain on the stand indefinitely, and most titles have sold 1 million copies or more. The heavy users of comic books are youths aged 7 to 14, and they tend to be good readers rather than poor ones.

The comic form is used for religious, educational, and political messages as well as such promotional campaigns as antismoking, antidrinking, and antinarcotics causes.

Despite continuing complaints about them, the comics are a dynamic part of pop culture. They are easy to read, socially relevant, entertaining, and present wish fulfillment and escape for the reader. The comics have influenced broadcast programming, films, plays, art forms, and advertising.

Characteristics and Roles of Magazines

Of all the media, magazines have the largest number of individual and diverse production units. They require the least investment of organized business and the smallest budget to operate. "Find me a list of names and I'll create a magazine for it," said one bold magazine entrepreneur. He was not far off base. Magazines have been published for almost every group in our society.

In addition to this sort of selectivity, magazines have greater flexibility than all media other than books. The magazine publisher can create a package in almost any size, shape, or dimension and can achieve change and variation with ease.

In timing, the magazine has the advantage of a greater intensification than newspapers, radio, or television can usually manage. With a longer lead time and less-pressing deadlines, magazine editors can afford to take a longer look at issues, to penetrate more deeply into problems in order to do a better job of interpretation and analysis. On the other hand, magazines have an advantage over books in that they are usually timely enough to deal with the flow of events. And they have the power to sustain a topic over a period of time in a series of issues, achieving a cumulative impact while books must settle for a single impression.

One of the primary roles of magazines as mass communicators is the role of custom-tailoring mass communications. Magazines, unlike other media, are ideally suited to small groups, whether they are organized by culture, race, religion, geography, or subject. Even the mass general-consumer magazines, as we have seen, are finding ways to specialize in tailoring their product for a specific region or interest group.

Magazines do not have the permanence of books, but they are not as transient as newspapers and not nearly as fleeting as broadcast messages. While the newspaper's lifetime is usually one day, weekly magazines often last two or three weeks, monthlies for several months, and quarterlies are often bound and kept permanently.

It is very difficult to "place" motion pictures in today's society. Traditionally movies have always been identified with eras or styles or "ages"—films of the 30s, film noir, musicals, Westerns, science fiction—but contemporary films refuse to be typecast in this manner. Time is telescoped to the point where one or two films represent a trend or style and then disappear. The large production studios, for years symbols of power and prestige, have been reduced to performing a financing and distributing role, occasionally producing a film. Production companies are set up for individual films, and while the independent film is here to stay, it bears little resemblance to the low-budget shoestring films of a decade ago. *King Kong* (1976) and *A Star Is Born* (1976) were both independent productions, but in form, style, and content they are little different from the "blockbusters" churned out by the studio system for decades. Motion pictures today in some sense resemble what they were at their beginning—products of individual taste and concern reflecting both what the audience wants and what individual communicators want to say. This, of course, was not always so. That brings us to the beginning of our discussion—a brief historical overview of the medium.

Historical Perspectives

The motion picture is the child of science. Many traces of antiquity, such as cave drawings and shadow plays, are evidence of the universal quest to

16

Motion Pictures

reproduce what is seen in nature. Very early this quest was taken up by the scientist as well as the artist.

The Prehistory of the Motion Picture. A number of discoveries, inventions, and theories occurred with some regularity throughout history that demonstrated man's continued fascination with reproducing motion. A variety of camera-projectionlike devices were constructed, including Alberti's *camera lucida,* della Porta's use of da Vinci's *camera obscura,* and most importantly, Kircher's magic lantern. Nevertheless, none of these developments went beyond the ability to project drawn pictures of still life. There was no photography and no motion.

Before motion pictures could actually exist, therefore, several major discoveries had to take place. Five such discoveries formed the scientific base for cinematography: (1) discovery of the persistence of vision; (2) development of photography; (3) development of a motion-picture camera; (4) development of motion-picture projection techniques; (5) integration of motion, projection, and photographic concepts in order to develop motion-picture film, cameras, and projectors.

This final evolutionary process began with Peter Mark Roget's theory of the persistence of vision in 1824. Roget demonstrated that through a peculiarity of the eye, an image is retained on the retina for a fraction of a second after it actually disappears. Since they depend upon this physiological phenomenon for their existence, motion pictures are nothing more than a series of motionless images (still frames) presented before the eye in rapid succession. Persistence of vision allows these still images to blend, thus creating the illusion of motion.

Soon after Roget published the results of his findings, a variety of motion devices incorporating this discovery were invented. They carried such fanciful names as the stroboscope and the phenakistiscope; but the important fact was that drawn pictures had begun to move.

The next component required was the development of a system of projection. This had existed for some time (1646) in the form of Kircher's magic lantern, but it was not until 1853 that Baron Franz von Uchatius projected moving images visible to large numbers of persons. However, this was accomplished by a series of individual projectors each containing a phase drawing. It was not until the 1890s that the motion-picture projector as we know it today developed, out of experiments by Thomas Edison and Thomas Armat in the United States and the Lumière brothers in France.

Despite these advances in projection, the pictures used to simulate motion were still being drawn. The next step toward cinematography actually involved two separate steps: the development of photography and the development of

motion-picture photography. Still photography resulted from the efforts of two men, Nicephore Niepce and Louis J. M. Daguerre, who presented copper-plate photography to the public for the first time in 1839.

Soon, photographs were being used in the available projection devices instead of drawings. In 1870 Henry Heyl projected photographs onto a screen before 1,600 people in Philadelphia.

In order for these developments in motion, projection, and photography to be integrated, special cameras, film, and projectors were needed. A camera that would take pictures faster than the still camera was essential. A number of attempts were made in this direction, including Eadweard Muybridge's famous demonstration of the gait of a galloping horse in 1877. The most successful step came in 1882 when Dr. E. J. Marey developed what he called a "photographic gun," which could take a series of pictures in rapid succession. But this camera still used individual plates. Flexible-roll film was necessary for the complete development of a motion-picture camera.

An American preacher, Hannibal Goodwin, invented roll film, but George Eastman became its greatest promoter. In 1888 Eastman brought out his Kodak camera, which used roll film. He was not concerned with cinematography, however, and did nothing to develop motion-picture film.

It remained for William Laurie Dickson, an assistant of Thomas Edison, to perfect the first motion-picture camera using roll film. There is some confusion as to exact dates, but it appears that by 1889 Dickson and Edison were taking moving pictures. In 1891 Edison applied for patents on the kinetograph as a photographing camera and the kinetoscope as a viewing apparatus and soon began producing short-story film strips.

Edison's kinetoscope was only a "peep show" device and did not involve projection. The final step was the motion-picture projector. Here Edison was lax, for he soon turned to other projects. At least a dozen other men were working on projection, including brothers August and Louis Lumière in France. In 1895 they demonstrated a projection device, the cinematographe, and shortly after began producing films. Edison soon realized his shortsightedness and, taking advantage of the efforts of the Lumières and American inventor Thomas Armat, developed the Vitascope projector. On April 23, 1896, in Koster and Bial's Music Hall in New York, Edison's Vitascope projector was used for the first public showing of motion pictures in the United States.

The Beginnings. The first subject matter of the newly developed "art" of motion pictures was simple pictorial realism. The motion-picture medium began as a recording device—nothing more. The Lumières' *Arrival of the Paris Express* and other films, such as *Venice Showing Gondolas, Kaiser Wilhelm Reviewing His Troops,* and *Feeding the Ducks at Tampa Bay*, emphasized the ability of the camera to record reality. Few of these films ran more than a minute, and they were often run backward to pad the presentation and amaze the audience.

Nevertheless, people soon tired of various versions of Niagara Falls, fire engines racing down the street, and babies smearing their faces with porridge.

Motion pictures next moved into themes involving a story and sustained narrative. An important factor in this rather quick development was that film, unlike some of the more traditional art forms, had the solid traditions and skills of photography and the theater behind it. In addition, when a new technique was discovered, it was quickly imitated by other film makers.

As early as 1896 George Melies, a French film maker, began to create motion pictures with a story line, becoming the first artist of the cinema. Melies discovered new ways of seeing, interpreting, and even distorting reality. He contributed much to the development of the motion picture, including the invention or development of many standard optical devices such as the dissolve, split screen, jump cut, and superimposition. Melies' most important contribution was his approach to film as a means of telling a story, not simply recording reality. In the final analysis, however, he was unable to move beyond his theatrical and magical background. His films were always a series of artificially arranged scenes shot from the fixed view of a spectator in a theater.

Developments in England and America soon propelled the motion picture into its unique means of cinematic expression. In America it was Edwin S. Porter who is credited with the intial development of narrative films. In two films, *The Life of an American Fireman* (1902) and more importantly *The Great Train Robbery* (1903), he demonstrated the power of editing as a means of film construction. According to Nicholas Vardac, the significance of *The Great Train Robbery* lay not only in its technique of building up an effective continuity of action through editing but also in the timeliness of its arrival. Despite the camera trickery of Melies, audiences had begun to tire of films that simply moved. *The Great Train Robbery* presented a fresh approach and offered the public new excitement.

Narrative Development.   The years between 1906 and 1916 were the most important period of artistic development in motion-picture history. It was the time of the feature film, the first film star, the first distinguished director, the first picture palaces, a place called Hollywood, and above all, the development of film as a unique and individual means of expression.

Some historians have aptly labeled this time "the age of Griffith." It was David Wark Griffith who took the raw material of film and created a language, a syntax, an art. His contributions were many, but more than anything else Griffith made film a dynamic medium. Beginning with *The Adventures of Dolly* (1908) and culminating with *The Birth of a Nation* (1915) and *Intolerance* (1916), Griffith freed the motion picture from strictly theatrical bounds. He pioneered a more natural acting style, better story organization, and most important, a true filmic style. He developed a language that emphasized the unique characteristics of the film medium, such as editing, camera movement, and angle, rather than simply using film as a moving photograph or portable theater.

To say that these years were the age of Griffith is not to deny the emergence of other notable film styles and important artists. Mack Sennett and his Keystone company developed their unique brand of slapstick comedy. Charlie Chaplin began to move beyond Sennett's slapstick into humor with a deeper, more philosophical edge. William S. Hart made realistic Westerns, and Mary Pickford was the screen's most popular personality.

The businessman also played an important role in this period. Since most inventors of cinematic devices did little to exploit these devices commercially, it remained for individual entrepreneurs like B. F. Keith, Major Woodville Latham, and Thomas Talley, among others, to bring showmanship to the motion picture. Essentially, there were four stages in the early commercial development of film:

1. The first stage involved vaudeville houses, the first real home of the American motion picture. Films started out as "headliners" but soon ended up as "chasers" moving patrons out of the theater between shows.

2. The second stage involved the move to a slightly more permanent home as projectors were installed in empty stores, music halls, back rooms, and attics. There were also a number of traveling film shows, "electric theaters" as they were called. This was strictly an itinerant operation, however; something more permanent was needed.

3. A new surge began in 1905 with the development of the nickelodeon, so named because of the five-cent price of admission. By this time films had improved in quality and equipment had become more plentiful. By 1907 there were more than 3,000 of these small theaters, and by 1910 over 10,000 nickelodeons were scattered over the eastern half of the country. Motion pictures were now a prosperous and thriving enterprise. Between 1905 and 1910 narrative films grew longer and more costly as well as more popular and more profitable. Porter's *Dream of a Rarebit Fiend* (1906) cost $350 to make and grossed more than $350,000. The Vitagraph Company, which started in 1896 with capital of $936, showed profits of over $900,000 by 1912. The trappings of an industrial empire were not yet apparent, however. There was no star system, no million-dollar salaries, no Hollywood. These would all come about as a reaction against a monopoly called the Motion Picture Patents Company (MPPC). Formed

in 1909 through the pooling of 16 patents, it controlled virtually every aspect of motion-picture production, distribution, and exhibition in the United States for more than three years.

4. The final stage of development witnessed a savage war between the film trust and independent and foreign producers. It was a battle with one of these producers, Adolph Zukor, that precipitated the final stage of development. Zukor acquired the rights to the French film *Queen Elizabeth* (1912), starring Sarah Bernhardt. In order to exhibit it, he had to apply to the MPPC for permission. They refused, and as a result he went to an independent exhibitor. The picture was a success; and the experience led Zukor to form his own company, Famous Players in Famous Plays (the forerunner of Paramount Pictures).

Heartened by Zukor's stand, others began showing films without permission of the trust. Pressure was applied by the MPPC, and as a result many individuals moved west to escape its control. The move to California came gradually, but by 1914 the state had attracted such men as Cecil B. DeMille, Jesse Lasky, Zukor, and others. Some prospered and many failed. Nevertheless, most of Hollywood's major studios trace their origins back to the independents who between 1910 and 1914 fought the MPPC.

One important effect of the war with the trust was the establishing of Hollywood as the center of motion-picture production. Other important results were the introduction of feature-length films and the rise of the star system. For obvious financial reasons, the trust had limited all films to one reel and had blocked actor identification. For the independents, longer films and stars became an effective way of attracting customers. To accommodate the influx of star-studded, feature-length films, elaborate new theaters were constructed. With such films as *The Birth of a Nation*, motion pictures moved out of the nickelodeons and into their own grand palaces.

By 1917, the MPPC had been dissolved by the courts. Even though short-lived, the fight produced lasting results including the founding of an industrial empire, the birth of a multitude of companies, feature-length films, the star system, Hollywood, and above all, a new respectability for film.

International Awakenings. By World War I, motion pictures were firmly established as an artistic and economic reality. The war further strengthened America's position in the international film market because virtually all the major film industries of Europe were either shut down or had had their production severely curtailed. By 1919, 80 percent of the world's motion pictures were made in Southern California. By 1920, average weekly movie attendance in the United States was 40 million and growing rapidly.

Following World War I, there was a great deal of international development in film. The war-ravaged film industries of Germany, France, and Russia were quickly reconstructed and began producing films. Movements in these three countries were especially important because of the contributions they made to film theory and aesthetics. In Germany, for example, two types of film emerged: the expressionistic film, a part of the art movement of the same name, and the realistic "street films," so named because city streets played an important part in them. The street films had a distinct impact in bringing to film a new sense of naturalism and realism. The camera was also used with a new sense of personal perspective and movement. Important films of the movement were *The Cabinet of Dr. Caligari* (1919) and *The Joyless Street* (1925).

The Russians, most notably Lev Kuleshov, Sergei Eisenstein, and V. I. Pudovkin, contributed greatly to the theory of film editing. The Russian concept of montage—the creation of meaning through shot juxtaposition—had a significant impact upon Russian film and was used by Eisenstein and Pudovkin especially to produce films of stunning force and deep meaning. Key films here were Eisenstein's *Potemkin* (1925) and Pudovkin's *Mother* (1927).

In France, the motion picture moved toward an abstract and surrealistic form, chiefly through the efforts of interested intellectuals and creative film makers such as René Clair, Jacques Feyder, and Luis Buñuel. In such films as *Entracte* (1925) and *Un Chien Andalou* (1929), these men extended the boundaries of film beyond the narrative into the realms of deep symbolism and pure form.

All this international energy had a distinct yet diffused impact upon the American film industry. Few of the actual film forms and theories developed were totally incorporated by Hollywood; however, the talent that produced them was. Not long after they had achieved an international reputation, such directors and film stars as Emil Jannings, F. W. Murnau, Greta Garbo, and Marlene Dietrich came to the United States to make films. The result was the gradual weakening and ultimate destruction of most of the national foreign movements.

Hollywood in the 1920s. Meanwhile, Hollywood was busy providing films that were essentially a reflection of the roaring twenties. Companies became studios, which grew in size and power. Salaries rose, huge stages were constructed, and many backlots contained entire towns. By the mid-1920s, a full 40 percent of a film's budget went to pay for studio overhead.

Three types of films dominated this final decade of silent film: the feature-length comedy, the Western, and the comedy of manners. In this era, many critics believe, film comedy reached its zenith. The comedic style of the time moved away from the broad, farcical slapstick of Sennett and his Keystone cops toward a more subtle, sophisticated format, characterized so brilliantly by Charlie Chaplin, Buster Keaton, Harold Lloyd, and others.

The Western came into its own at this time with the move toward the "big" feature best represented by John Ford's *Covered Wagon* (1923), James Cruze's *Iron Horse* (1924), and William S. Hart's *Tumbleweeds* (1925). The "B" Western also became prominent, providing contrast not only to the spectacular Westerns of Ford and Cruze, but more importantly to the stark realism used so effectively by Hart. This was the era of the romantic Western so ably characterized in the films of Tom Mix.

The third film form was a direct result of the social conditions of the time. The mores of the country were freer and more open than at any time in its history. The comedy-of-manners film was a reflection of this increased sophistication. These films concentrated on high society, glittering wealth, and personal freedom. Such films as Cecil B. DeMille's *Male and Female* (1919) and *Why Change Your Wife* (1920) appealed directly to this new sense of freedom.

The Arrival of Sound.

Despite the fact that the 1920s were years of increased prosperity for moving pictures, the end of the era found Hollywood experiencing a profound uneasiness. As the result of a series of major scandals in the early 1920s, a motion-picture-code office was formed to police both the content of films and the behavior of the people who made them. This, coupled with the increasing popularity of radio and the automobile, created an attendance problem. In order to save the industry and win back the lost audience, something new was needed.

Warner Brothers was a small studio on the verge of bankruptcy in 1926. Having little to lose, it invested its remaining capital in a new sound system called Vitaphone. On October 26, 1927, it presented the first talking feature, *The Jazz Singer*, starring Al Jolson. The motion-picture industry, reluctant at first to abandon silent film completely, soon recognized the public's acceptance as permanent and moved to total sound production.

The effect of sound on motion pictures was profound and lasting. Sound's impact upon content was evident from the start with a rush toward the musical. The more a film talked, sang, or shouted, the better it was. Swept aside in the rush were many unique forms, most notably silent comedy.

Individual stars were also greatly affected. Buster Keaton, Charlie Chaplin, and Harold Lloyd, whose basic comedic style was visual, were hampered.

In addition, many stars found that their voices were displeasing to audiences. The careers of John Gilbert, Charles Farrell, and Norma Talmadge were greatly limited because of unsatisfactory vocal quality.

The impact upon audiences was most important. In 1927 an average of 60 million people attended motion pictures every week. By 1929, this figure was over 110 million. This success gave the industry a tremendous financial boost and helped it over the worst years of the depression.

The expense of making sound films also brought a new financial domination in the form of such companies as Western Electric, RCA, and their respective financial backers, Kuhn-Loeb and the First National Bank of New York. RCA, which made sound equipment, bought a film company and theater corporation and set up a powerful new studio, RKO. The eastern banking interests gained a significant hold on the entertainment industry and its products. Despite Hollywood's domestic success, its dominance of the world market diminished. Whereas silent films had a universal language, sound films required dubbing of foreign languages for overseas distribution.

Hollywood in the 1930s.　　Like other elements of the culture, film reflected the tensions, crises, and deepening social awareness in the United States. One reaction to the time was the documentary film, beginning with Robert Flaherty's work in the early 1920s and continuing under John Grierson's influence in England. The United States initially failed to exploit the documentary's potential, but in 1936 Pare Lorentz produced *The Plow That Broke the Plains*. Lorentz was soon made head of the U.S. Film Service, and he—along with other directors—created several powerful films, including *The River* (1937), *Ecce Homo* (1939), and *The Power and the Land* (1940). For a variety of political reasons, however, the service was legislated out of existence in 1940, and it took the catastrophe of World War II to revitalize the documentary form.

Hollywood produced two other responses to the needs of the time. The first was the social-consciousness film, a form in which the action was, as John Howard Lawson states, "specifically motivated and rooted in social circumstances." Such films as *The Public Enemy* (1931) and *I Was a Fugitive from a Chain Gang* (1933) asked their audiences to view men and their actions as a part or result of the social conditions of the time. The other response was escapism. As the depression deepened, more films turned toward musical and comedic themes in an attempt to provide their audiences with another reality. Hollywood produced a wave of Busby Berkeley and Fred Astaire–Ginger Rogers singing-dancing spectacles, such as *Footlight Parade* (1933), *Gold Diggers of 1935* (1935), and *Flying Down to Rio* (1936). These were soon accompanied by "screwball" comedies, such as *It Happened One Night* (1934), directed by

Frank Capra, and "The Thin Man" series starring William Powell and Myrna Loy. The 1930s were the golden age of the studio system. Production was almost completely centered in seven dominant companies: MGM, Paramount, Warner Brothers, RKO, Universal, Columbia, and 20th Century-Fox. Each studio had its own stars and unique style.

World War II.   Toward the end of the 1930s, with war imminent in Europe, American studios began to produce strongly patriotic films, and some cautious steps were taken in portraying future allies and enemies in such films as *Foreign Correspondent* (1940) and *The Ramparts We Watch* (1939). Until Pearl Harbor, however, the United States was technically a neutral nation, and most film companies were wary of economic reprisals by Axis governments.

After Pearl Harbor, the gloves were off. Hollywood began to produce patriotic war films with the Japanese and Germans immediately becoming stock, stereotyped villains. The image of the American fighting man was equally stereotyped; American audiences did not want realistic war dramas detailing the horrors they read about in the newspapers or heard on the radio. As a result of this activity, the studios enjoyed a war boom and profits reached new heights. As the war continued to wear on, however, the studios turned to more and more escapist fare. More than half of the 1,300 films produced from 1942 to 1944 had nothing to do with the war.

The Postwar Era.   The story of postwar film is essentially a chronicle of decline and frustration for Hollywood and the major studios but rebirth and growth for foreign and independent films. After the war, American studios resumed standard operating procedures, producing a great many films designed for the mass public's tastes and habits. Before the 1940s were spent, however, four events occurred that forced major changes in the traditional Hollywood structure: (1) the rise of television, (2) the House Un-American Activities Committee hearings, (3) the Supreme Court divorcement ruling, and (4) the emergence of a vigorous international film movement.

The advent of network television in 1948 diverted much of the audience from its traditional twice-a-week motion-picture habit. Between 1950 and 1960 the number of television sets in the United States increased by 400 percent; motion-picture attendance fell by 50 percent.

The concern about communism in the United States, tagged the "red scare," had a number of effects. One was the congressional hearings into alleged communist activities in the entertainment field that began in 1947 and quickly established a climate of fear over all aspects of American life, especially for motion pictures. Many talented craftsmen and artists were blacklisted because of alleged communist activities and lost to the American screen. Experimentation and initiative in content were discouraged, and producers either fell back on old patterns or grasped at experimental technological straws.

The third blow was the 1950 *Paramount* decision of the U.S. Supreme Court, which forced the Hollywood studios to end vertical integration whereby one corporation produced, distributed, and exhibited films. The High Court ruled that this setup restrained trade. Film companies were forced to divest themselves of one of the three operations. Most major companies sold off their theater chains and stayed in the production-distribution end of the business. This, in effect, caused the collapse of the basic industry monopoly and ended the absolute control the major Hollywood studios held on the American film market for 30 years.

Coincidental to these domestic happenings, and to a certain extent because of them, a strong international film movement emerged. Beginning with neorealism in Italy, vital national cinemas developed in the late 1940s and early 1950s. Japan walked off with the Venice Film Festival award with Akira Kurosawa's *Rashomon* in 1951, and suddenly American audiences became aware of other sources of motion pictures. Foreign films were available not only from Japan, but England, France, Italy, Sweden, and India; and with this availability yet another aspect of studio monopoly was undermined.

Motion pictures in the United States were no longer *the* mass medium, and at the time their future as *a* mass medium looked shaky. Attendance figures dropped off sharply. The industry frantically responded with technological innovations; stereophonic sound, wide screens, and 3-D—anything television could not duplicate. These attractions were built on passing fancies, however, and the basic fact of a changing audience was ignored. Attempts to inject new vigor or themes were fought consistently. This is clearly illustrated by Otto Preminger's unsuccessful fight to obtain the industry's seal of approval for two films, *The Moon Is Blue* (1953), an innocuous comedy about adultery, and *The Man with the Golden Arm* (1956), a film dealing with drug addiction. Hollywood clung to a "blockbuster" policy, emphasizing spectacular film productions with fantastic budgets such as *Around the World in Eighty Days* (1956) and *Ben-Hur* (1959).

The Film Revolution. The 1960s witnessed the further decline of Hollywood and its traditional picture values and saw the emergence of a new cinema, a cinema difficult to characterize except perhaps in what it rejected. The films of the 1960s and early 1970s were the products of a changing society, a society in which relevance, awareness, and freedom of expression became watchwords. Motion pictures no longer existed exclusively as a product to be passively consumed by a mass audience. A new audience was seeking a new kind of involvement in the film experience.

The studio system had controlled American film for over 50 years, and it was not until cracks began to appear in that monopolistic control that any hope for significant change could occur. The change can be dated from the events of the late 1940s and early 1950s already noted. One result of these events was the reorganization of United Artists in 1951. Originally organized in 1919 as an independent outlet for the films of D. W. Griffith, Charlie Chaplin, Douglas Fairbanks, and Mary Pickford, United Artists was revamped in 1951 in order to carry out precisely the same function, that of providing distribution for independently produced films. With such films as *The African Queen* (1951) and *Marty* (1955), it began to provide new hope for the independent film maker. From this beginning, the roots of the "new American cinema" emerged.

Hollywood did not die in the 1960s, but it did experience a radical change. Most of the major studios were used as financing and distributing agents for independently produced features. But the traditional system of motion-picture production, distribution, and exhibition did not undergo transformation easily. Hollywood tried to win back its lost audience and regain some of its former prestige by emphasizing bigness. The spectacle has been a part of Hollywood ever since *Birth of a Nation* (1915). But in the 1960s this film form was looked upon as the savior of the Hollywood system. *Cleopatra* (1963) should have been a warning signal; it was the most expensive and most publicized film made up to this time and was a box-office failure. But two years later *The Sound of Music* (1965) became one of the biggest box-office successes in history, earning more than $80 million in rentals. The major studios, with their confidence bolstered by *The Sound of Music*'s success, set into motion a series of spectacles, among them *Dr. Dolittle* (1968), *Star* (1969), *Goodbye Mr. Chips* (1970), and *Tora! Tora! Tora!* (1971). All were failures that plunged many of the studios to the point of bankruptcy and led to their eventual takeover by non-Hollywood business interests.

It was not simply the rush to duplicate the success of *The Sound of Music* that pushed many of the studios over the brink. Other forces were at work as well. Perhaps the most important was the so-called New American Cinema, which was essentially the surfacing of what used to be called underground films. There have always been films that were shot away from normal production sources. They have been called art, avant-garde, experimental, "new wave," or even pornographic. Perhaps the major film trend of the 1960s was that such films acquired a legitimacy that saw them exhibited virtually without restriction. Essentially, what happened was a juncture of the art/experimental film with the underground film through the normal channels of production, distribution, and exhibition.

One of the first underground features to surface and receive wide public distribution was Shirley Clarke's *The Connection* (1961). This was soon followed by Jonas Mekas's *The Brig* (1964), and Kenneth Anger's *Scorpio Rising* (1966). By the late 1960s, this movement, coupled with the troubles of the major studios, had catapulted the independent film maker into a position of prominence. Dennis Hopper's *Easy Rider* (1969) was the watershed of this trend, as it finally convinced the major studios that a low-budget, independently produced film (cost $370,000) could be a blockbuster ($50+ million in rentals).

The significance of *Easy Rider* is not in its artistic merits, although it certainly possessed them, but that talents outside the Hollywood mainstream (Dennis Hopper, Peter Fonda, Jack Nicholson, Karen Black) could produce a good film with massive audience appeal on a skeletal budget. It showed a new way to mine gold in the American audience.

New audiences are basic to a new cinema. They were and are the driving force behind it. Motion pictures today must appeal to an audience no longer composed of a cross section of the American population. It is estimated that some 75 percent of today's film audience is between the ages of 16 and 30. This is obviously a young and flexible audience. Their effect on motion pictures has been dramatic. On the one hand, many of them have demanded that film do more than simply provide escape; it should in their view make statements, take sides, and promote causes. On the other hand, they *are* using film as escape, as pure entertainment.

There was a great deal of talk in the mid-1960s of a new film generation, of an audience that was more sophisticated and would demand more from film than entertainment. An indication of this growing awareness was and is the expanding film curriculum in high schools, colleges, and universities. The American Film Institute's guide to college film courses lists over 5,000 courses being offered at over 800 schools. Film majors now number over 30,000 at over 200 schools. This new awareness coupled with formal instruction in film production and consumption has produced an audience that is more perceptive and more knowledgeable about film than ever before. As Robert Evans, former head of production at Paramount, said in 1971: "The main change has been in the audience. Today people go to see *a* movie, they no longer go to *the* movies. We can't depend upon habit anymore." This trend continued into the 1970s with films often combining social statement with traditional entertainment values.

They Shoot Horses Don't They? (1969), for example, revealed a sordid side

to the often fondly remembered dance marathons of the 1930s. The outstanding success of such films as *Tell Them Willie Boy Is Here* (1969), *Five Easy Pieces* (1970), *Z* (1969), *Joe* (1970), *M*A*S*H.* (1969), *Little Big Man* (1970), *Dirty Harry* (1971), *The Last Picture Show* (1971), *A Clockwork Orange* (1972), and *Cabaret* (1972), among others, pointed to an increased awareness of film as a medium for social comment.

Nevertheless, what was looked upon as a permanent trend turned out to be simply another cycle. The social-consciousness film movement begun with *Easy Rider* quickly faded. By 1973–74, a new cycle of films appeared—the disaster film. Headed by *The Poseidon Adventure*, this cycle dominated film production for two years with such films as *The Towering Inferno, Earthquake, Airport 75*, and *The Hindenburg*. Several blockbuster films defied this strategy and made money including *The Exorcist, Godfather II, The Sting, Young Frankenstein, That's Entertainment*, and, of course, the usual run of Walt Disney films.

When one looks at the top films today, the only word that comes to mind is diversity. Perhaps the only significant trend has been the decline of foreign films. The 1960s saw a tremendous surge in foreign films, but by 1972 Ingmar Bergman's *Cries and Whispers* could not find an American distributor. In 1976, the top films were *One Flew Over the Cuckoo's Nest, All the President's Men, The Omen, Bad News Bears, Silent Movie, Midway*, and *Dog Day Afternoon*. Clearly, there is no trend here. There is a mixture of strong social drama, the occult, slapstick comedy, war, and Little League baseball. The only type of film conspicuous by its absence is the musical. Minicycles continue to be a part of the industry as witnessed by the swift emergence of science fiction, or outer space, films following the record-breaking success of *Star Wars* (1977). These cycles, however, are short lived, ready to be replaced by another trend.

The money spent on production also fluctuated tremendously from such low-budget (under $1 million) films as *Easy Rider, Bonnie & Clyde,* and *Good-bye Columbus* to a $50 million *Superman.* It is clear that the 1970s were a time when few rules applied. There were no real formulas for success, only individual films from individual film makers.

This individuality has led to new technical and thematic freedom. This is illustrated by the motion-picture industry's code, which no longer censors films but simply suggests suitable age levels for particular films. These ratings include G for general audiences, PG for parental guidance suggested, R for restricted to individuals at least 17 years old or those accompanied by parent or guardian, and X for no one under 17 admitted.

The results of this new freedom have been a dramatic increase in the sexual and violent content in motion pictures. Sex and violence have been a part of motion pictures from the beginning, but industry codes and/or state and local laws always checked "excesses." The new rating code and changes in society led to new standards. Nudity and sexual themes were "open," but most actual sexual activity was suggested. Nevertheless, in 1972 a movie entitled *Deep Throat* changed all this, and "hard-core" sex films appeared. By the end of 1972, it was estimated that more than 700 theaters were showing "porn" films exclusively. This, too, was a cycle that quickly faded. The lasting results are not to be found in the occasional hard-core film that makes the national circuits but in the more open and freer treatment of sex as a theme and activity in most contemporary films.

Much the same could be said regarding violence. It, too, has had a long history in films, and there were "rules" that normally governed its use. These rules were graphically broken in the late 1960s by such films as *Bonnie & Clyde, Bullit, The Wild Bunch,* and *The French Connection.* Violence was now explicit; audiences saw bullet holes, blood, and torn flesh. The effect of this is still open to question. Endless debate has occurred with no true answers in sight. Violence in films is a clear and consistent theme, and as long as films continue to reflect society, it is likely to remain so.

In the end result, it is difficult to say where motion pictures are; they are ultimately in the heads of the people who make them and the people who view them. This constant interaction reflects change and growth, and if anything is a constant for this medium it is change.

The Scope of the Motion-Picture Industry

Motion pictures have long been one of the primary recreational outlets for the American people, although no longer as significant as they were 25 years ago. The industry hit its peak in 1946 with box-office receipts estimated at $1.7 billion on the basis of 90 million admissions per week. Receipts currently are estimated at $2.5 billion, up from a postwar low of $900 million in 1962. This figure reflects higher admission prices rather than increased attendance, however. Some 23 million people attend motion pictures in the United States annually, but various sources put the rise in admission prices between 1960 and 1970 anywhere from 90 to 108 percent. The average admission price is over $2.20 compared with $.75 in 1956. The number of theaters has also declined from over 19,000 in 1946 to an estimated 16,000 at present. In 1977, about 225 feature motion pictures were either started or distributed by the major companies and independents; this represents a 50 percent decline in 20 years.

One of the reasons for this product shortage is the amount of money being spent on each production. This figure has increased despite the decrease in the number of productions. Although the multimillion-dollar spectaculars are less frequent, the average cost for a feature film is over $4 million.

Thus, from all indications, the scope of the American motion-picture industry is diminished. But it continues to be an economic force, with capital investments of $3.5 billion, an annual payroll of more than $1.2 billion, and box-office receipts of over $4 billion (including foreign rentals). Despite current problems, U.S. films still account for 60 percent of all world screen time.

The Structure and Organization of the Motion-Picture Industry

The film industry is divided into three major parts: (1) production—the creation of films; (2) distribution—the supplying of films to markets; (3) exhibition—the displaying of films to the public. In the past all three functions were performed by one company. But in 1950 the Supreme Court ruled that the practice of vertical integration (control of production, distribution, and exhibition by one company) restrained free trade. Today most companies only produce and distribute films with exhibition controlled by individual theaters or chains.

Production. The making of films is a complex operation involving the talents of many people, including directors, cinematographers, producers, editors, lighting and sound crews, designers, musicians, costumers, makeup crews, choreographers, as well as actors. Size is one of the key reasons that production budgets are high.

In recent years, the industry's unions, long one of the prime contributors to exorbitant production costs, have relaxed many of their requirements to allow skeletal crews and lower minimum wages for low-budget films. This shift in policy was forced upon the unions by economic conditions—if Hollywood was to survive, labor costs had to be reduced. Still, personnel costs account for much of a production budget. Labor costs for *King Kong* amounted to 65 percent of the total $25 million budget.

Because of rising personnel costs, film makers have been forced to cut back their nonproduction expenses. In the 1940s, almost 40 percent of a film's budget went to cover studio overhead, which involved upkeep of the backlots, maintenance of huge stockpiles of costumes, props, sets, and equipment, as well as an extensive bureaucracy of production and nonproduction personnel. Today a typical independent production company's permanent staff consists of a small secretarial pool, a good accountant, and the producer. Studio overhead currently accounts for barely 20 percent of production costs.

The heart of the motion-picture business in the 1980s lies beyond the studio gates. More and more films are being shot on location in the United States and Europe rather than on Hollywood backlots. In fact, only one such backlot exists, that being the part-working lot, part-tourist attraction at Universal Studios. With the advent of portable equipment, location shooting is much easier and less expensive than in the past. For most films the sound stage has become unnecessary, especially since the Cinemobile Mark IV was developed by cinematographer Fouad Said for his work on the TV series "I Spy." This 35-foot studio-bus contains dressing rooms, bathrooms, space for a large crew, and a full complement of lightweight equipment. The Cinemobile Mark IV or equipment similar to it was used to produce more than 75 films in 1975. For such films as *The Towering Inferno* or *King Kong*, however, a studio is still a necessity.

The key word today in film production is *independent*. Currently, independent film makers account for over 75 percent of all American films. Thirty years ago they accounted for 8 percent, and as late as 1960 they produced less than one-third. It was such nonestablishment film makers as John Cassavetes, Andy Warhol, Dennis Hopper, Peter Bogdanovich, and Francis Ford Coppola who proved to Hollywood that magical names on the marquee are not necessary for success. With 75 percent of box-office revenues coming from people under 30, it is the independent talent, often young itself, which is currently succeeding. Independent film makers also have achieved financial independence. Directors such as Francis Ford Coppola, Frank Perry, Robert Altman, and Martin Scorsese have persuaded financial backers to allow them almost total artistic and budgetary control. Accountability is still a key word, however, and film makers who don't make money don't make films. The studios with their moguls have simply been replaced by banks with their boards of directors.

This trend has given rise to a new leadership in film, not only among directors, but producers and executives as well. New financial arrangements call for a star and even a director to take a percentage of a film's potential profit rather than a high salary, making them partners in a collaborative enterprise. Of course, only major stars can command such a contract.

Today a great deal of money to finance films is from a variety of nontraditional sources. David L. Wolper signed an agreement with the Quaker Oats Company for a series of family movies that included the very successful *Willie Wonka and the Chocolate Factory* (1971). Reader's Digest funded *Tom Sawyer* (1973) and *Huckleberry Finn* (1974). The advertising agency Wells, Rich and Greene backed *Dirty Little Billy* (1973), and Mattel Toys provided funds for *Sounder* (1973). One of the more unusual sources of outside money was for the film *Gunfight* (1971). The Jicarilla Apaches, a tribe of about 1,800 New Mexico Indians, put up $2 million that they had received from income on oil and gas investments. As Chief Charles Vigil stated: "We consider ourselves a corporation like any other."

Distribution. The primary distributors of motion pictures are the old studios that have traditionally produced films. Most independent producers release their films through one of these established major studios in two major markets, foreign and domestic.

The foreign market is extremely important, since it accounts for over 50 percent of the total annual revenue for most American films. In a great many nations of the world, U.S. films dominate both the exhibition schedule and box-office receipts. The popularity of the American film product is so great that most European nations limit the number of weeks U.S. films may be shown in local theaters. Rights to American films shown abroad are normally retained by the parent company. This contrasts with the practice of foreign film producers, who sell American distribution rights to their films.

Domestic distribution of films involves the normal channels used to move any product from producer to consumer. Seven major studios dominate film distribution in the United States: Columbia, MGM, Warner Brothers, 20th Century-Fox, Paramount, United Artists, and Universal. A group of minor studios are also important, especially in the distribution of low-budget independent films. These include Avco-Embassy, American-International, Cinerama, Allied Artists, and National General. The majors and minors account for 80 to 90 percent of annual film revenue in the United States.

Film-distribution operations involve the booking of films into theaters.

Licenses between the distributor and exhibitor include both price and nonprice agreements. The process of block booking—requiring theaters to buy groups of films rather than individual films—has been outlawed, so every film is leased separately.

Local theater owners bid competitively for films. This usually involves a specific guaranteed minimum against a percentage of the gross receipts. For example, the theater owner pays an amount ($1,000 per week) or a percent of the gross receipts (60 percent of one week's ticket sales), whichever is higher. This procedure saves the exhibitor from losing too badly if the film is a flop and helps the distributor if the film is a major success.

In the motion-picture business in the 1970s the distributor is still the major risk-taker. This is the case because distributors are the prime borrower of funds to produce films. They finance or provide the collateral for nine of every ten films. If the cost of the movie exceeds production estimates, it is the distributor who provides the necessary capital to complete it. Because of this, the distributor receives his return before the producer does. One-third of the distribution gross (total receipts minus the exhibitors' share) is retained to cover distribution costs; the remainder is sent to the bank to retire the standard two-year loan. Before the producer earns any sizable sum, the film must earn roughly 2.5 times its production costs. Thus, a film like *The Wiz* with a cost of approximately $33 million would have to earn over $80 million before the producer could realize any profit. In effect, interest and distribution costs of a film run about 150 percent of the production costs. Marketing costs in film are among the highest—if not *the* highest—for any major consumer product. The risk in film is increased by the fact that the economic life of a film is extremely short; in most cases about 25 weeks account for two-thirds of its total gross. Maximum gross in the shortest period of time is a critical aspect of film distribution.

Exhibition. The 12,200 local theaters and 3,800 drive-ins are the final link in the structure of the motion-picture industry. Here, also, concentration of ownership is dominant. More than half the theaters in the United States are owned by 700 theater chains. Some 70 percent of an average film's gross comes from 1,000 key theaters. These bookings in major population areas mean the difference between financial success or failure for a film. The larger theaters (over 400 seats) account for 80 percent of the total dollar volume of most features. Nine of every ten large houses are owned by the theater chains with the largest, ABC-Paramount, owning over 500 theaters, most of them in metropolitan areas.

Films are exhibited in either roadshow popular-release or four-walling patterns. Roadshow is used only for blockbuster films, such as *Jaws*, *One Flew Over the Cuckoo's Nest*, or *Star Wars*. It requires a large marketing investment and must have a good long-run potential. Tickets are usually sold at only one theater per market. If the film does not do well in this hard-ticket exhibition, it is immediately changed to popular release, whereby the film is booked in as many theaters as possible. The trend today is away from roadshow exclusive releases and toward limited popular release. *King Kong*, for example, was saturation booked into all the medium and large markets. This was done primarily to recoup the investment as quickly as possible and to lessen the effect of poor reviews and word-of-mouth reaction.

The most recent trend in exhibition patterns is "four-walling," whereby the film's producer bypasses normal distribution channels and contracts directly with the local theater owner. For low-budget, limited-audience-appeal films, this is a popular method because the costs normally given to the distributor are put into local advertising. The exhibition pattern of any film is designed to reach the right prospective audience and to take advantage of its particular entertainment value.

Success in film exhibition depends on a number of factors including trade advertising, word of mouth, critical reviews, the weather, local publicity, previous box-office results, season of the year, number and quality of competing films in the area, the content of the film, and its rating by the code authority. Thus the predictability of a film's success is difficult to assess until it is released for public appraisal.

In a poll of audience preferences taken for the motion-picture industry, it was found that 80 percent of the audience rated subject matter most important, and 83 percent prefer color films to black and white. The best month of the year for exhibition is June and the best day of the week is Saturday.

Newer theaters in the United States reflect the changes taking place in our society. They are often twin or multicinemas of 200 to 500 seats per theater located in peripheral shopping centers or malls; they are leased rather than owned. The theater often seeks identification with the shopping area, has fewer parking problems, gains maximum traffic and exposure, and does not face inner-city problems. The multitheater operates with one lobby, one concession stand, and one projection booth to cut costs. Important features can be run in both theaters, or the theaters can cater to two audiences with different films. Interestingly, the concession stand accounts for half the revenues in many theaters.

Characteristics and Roles of the Motion Picture

The role and function of motion pictures has changed greatly in the past 25 years. Once a major source of recreation, motion pictures today serve as a primary source of content for another medium, television. Before the advent of videotape recording in the mid-1950s, television reruns were possible only when films were used or when filmed kinescopes were made of a live performance. In the early 1970s most regular evening network dramas were filmed. Feature films made up an important block of network schedules with all three networks running multiple "nights at the movies" and "movies of the week." Motion pictures today are made with one eye clearly focused on television as a source of income. The average feature film on television costs the sponsoring network almost $1 million; for special films, such as *Gone With the Wind*, the cost can rise to $5 million.

Audiences go to *a movie* now rather than to *the movies*. Nevertheless, despite increased competition from television, motion pictures hold a unique position in American leisure patterns. Many singular elements make the motion picture attractive. For one, the film experience is of a high technical quality that stimulates strong involvement. The picture is a large, high-definition, colored, visual image. The sound is also one of high quality. The theater is designed to encapsulate the viewer. It is dark, the chairs are comfortable, there are relatively few interruptions, food is often available. Every aspect of filmgoing is designed to heighten the impact of film experiences and create viewer involvement. Film is the most realistic of all media, and it is primarily this attribute that contributes to the great persuasive power inherent in film.

The primary function of feature films is entertainment, but motion pictures are also used for information, persuasion, education, and advertising.

The motion picture is perhaps the most international of the media; its primarily visual symbol system and easily dubbed sound make the entire world a film marketplace. It has become a highly selective medium catering to the tastes of a fragmented audience that is becoming more discriminating. The industry is youth oriented, and current film themes reflect this audience's ambitions and tastes. Films have become a primary source of acculturation for the young.

In summary, motion pictures have changed greatly over their relatively short history. But they still function as they always have, in providing entertainment to a large number of people in a unique and involving way.

Thrill to the adventures of the Green Hornet, the Shadow, and Johnny Dollar. Follow the day-by-day episodes in the life of Ma Perkins or Helen Trent. Laugh with Fred Allen or Joe Penner. Listen to Rudy Vallee or Al Jolson sing. These are unfamiliar names to most of us, and yet, for almost 30 years, they and countless other personalities like them made up what is affectionately known as radio's "golden age." Today, we know radio more by the type of recorded music it plays than by specific programs or personalities.

In the 1950s and 1960s, the radio industry in the United States changed radically in order to survive the competition of television. And radio did much better than just survive; by the 1970s it had evolved into a new and highly successful form completely different from what it was less than 15 years earlier.

There are now more radio stations than ever. FM radio has grown from an experimental toy to a powerful vehicle for many different and unique sounds. Radios are in 99 percent of American homes and 95 percent of American cars. Radio is a flexible, adaptable, individual, personal medium. Although it functions primarily as a medium for playing recorded music, it is as alive, dynamic, and popular as it was 30 years ago. Radio experienced one golden age and, unlike most mass media, grew and changed to experience yet another. How it got where it is today is the subject of history, and it is here we begin.

Historical Perspectives

This brief history of radio will be broken into time periods of irregular but logical length corresponding to the medium's major developments. Oddly

Radio

enough, for a medium less than 60 years old, we start in the early nineteenth century.

1840 –1919. Radio developed out of scientific advances made in the fields of electricity and magnetism. The first transmission of an electromagnetic message over a wire was in 1844 by Samuel F. B. Morse. A country expanding rapidly westward saw the enormous potential of the telegraph, and by 1861 a transcontinental, high-speed, electric communication medium was dot-dashing messages across the United States. The first transatlantic cable was laid in 1858, and by 1870 a web of underseas cables linked the Western world and its economic outposts. The replacement of Morse code with voice transmission occurred in 1876 when Alexander Graham Bell used undulations in electric current to activate vocal communication via wire. The telephone's ability to code, transport, and decode voice transmissions personalized electric communication in a way that was impossible with the telegraph.

During the same period that the telegraph and telephone were being demonstrated and perfected, James Clark Maxwell predicted (1864) and Heinrich Hertz demonstrated (1887) that variations in electric current produced waves that could be transmitted through space without wires at the speed of light. These theories stimulated much experimentation—the most successful being Guglielmo Marconi's in the late 1890s. Marconi received a patent for his wireless telegraph in 1897 and by 1901 was transmitting wireless dot-dash transmissions across the Atlantic. With the invention of the audion tube by Lee DeForest in 1907, high-quality wireless *voice* communications carried by electromagnetic waves were possible and set the stage for radio broadcasting. There is evidence, however, to support the idea that Reginald Fessenden, among others, was transmitting voice messages prior to this date.

The advent of radio broadcasting, however, required more than equipment. People had to change their thinking about communication. Two individuals talking back and forth is not broadcasting. The intellectual retooling needed to transform radio *telephoning* into radio *broadcasting* had to wait until people thought in terms of one person talking to a mass audience. Public and industrial appetites had to be whetted to create the demand for the radio medium.

From 1910 to the outbreak of World War I, radio amateurs, or "ham" operators, brought new noise to the night sky as they chattered to each other from their basements, attics, or pantries. It was the time of the neighborhood experimenter who pieced together a radio sender-receiver in order to carry on conversations with others of the same inclination.

During this period, the U.S. government passed two major laws concerned with the use of radio. The first was the U.S. Wireless Ship Act of 1910, which required all passenger ships to carry radio-transmission equipment. The second was the 1912 Radio Act, which required all radio operators to be licensed by the Secretary of Commerce. The Radio Act of 1912 was the first comprehensive attempt to regulate all phases of radio communication. With the involvement of the United States in World War I, the federal government took over all radio operations; the medium marked time until the end of the war.

1920–28. With the cessation of hostilities, an organized attempt was made to develop radio broadcasting as opposed to point-to-point communication. With less than 1,000 radio sets in the entire nation, regular radio programming began with the broadcast of the Harding-Cox election returns over KDKA in Pittsburgh on November 2, 1920. Almost immediately, hundreds of stations began to broadcast music, politics, sports, drama, and vaudeville. By the end of 1922, 690 stations had been licensed by the Secretary of Commerce. By 1923, over a million people a year listened to programs broadcast from the concert halls, theaters, and athletic fields of this nation.

As programming grew, the public bought more radio sets. With the increase in the audience, stations expanded their program schedules. As additional hours of programming became available, the ever-growing audience became more discriminating. Listener tastes soon changed and broadcasters had to provide a greater variety of entertainment. In improving the listening fare, the industry expanded.

As the broadcast industry grew, the revenue from the sale of radio sets proved to be insufficient to support radio's mass entertainment and information services. A new method had to be found to pay the bill for the public's insatiable appetite for radio programming. To solve this problem two developments occurred: (1) radio stations were linked together into networks so that the increased cost of expanded programming could be shared; (2) merchants were asked to support the system by advertising their goods and services on the stations. The American Telephone and Telegraph Company (AT&T) and set manufacturers formed a network in 1923 to provide expanded program-distribution service. After a lengthy, fratricidal war over use of Bell transmission facilities, AT&T withdrew from the program-distribution business in 1926. RCA immediately consolidated its position and formed the National Broadcasting Company (NBC). In 1927 the Columbia Broadcasting System was formed and with its 16 affiliates set out to do battle with NBC's 48 affiliates and two networks, the Blue and the Red.

Now that radio was becoming big business, something had to be done about the chaotic state of the art so that it could more efficiently serve the public and economic interests involved in broadcasting. As more and more stations went on the air, they began to interfere with one another. In 1926 a series of court cases ruled that Secretary of Commerce Herbert Hoover did not have legal jurisdiction under the Radio Act of 1912 to regulate broadcasting. Chaos ruled the airwaves, and it was obvious that immediate legislative action was needed if broadcasting was to survive.

The broadcast media, unlike other media, are physically limited by the number of channels or spaces available in the radio spectrum. The Berlin Conference (1903) and the Havana Treaty (1925) had established international rules for using radio frequencies, but internal use of the allocated channels was left to individual governments. A growing awareness that the airwaves were a natural resource that belonged to the public also began to affect the legal decision-making process.

Congress passed the Radio Act of 1927, which created a Federal Radio Commission to straighten out the radio mess. The Federal Communications Act of 1934 expanded and clarified the act of 1927 and established the Federal Communications Commission to regulate telephone, telegraph, as well as radio communication systems in the public's interest, convenience, and necessity. This act remains in effect today, modified, of course, by prevailing political, social, and economic conditions.

1929–45. With its technical problems solved, radio was free to grow almost unrestricted. By the late 1920s, the medium had achieved a high degree of program sophistication and was on the verge of entering a new stage of development. One of the major areas of growth was in broadcast advertising. Broadcast historian John Spaulding has suggested that the 1928–29 program year marks the point at which radio became a mass advertising medium. That year, four necessary requirements were met by radio: (1) the industry's technical competence had reached a level where station signals could be received dependably, (2) a sizable audience was listening to radio on a regular basis, (3) broadcasters were willing to accept advertisers as partners in program production, and (4) program formats had been developed into satisfactory advertising vehicles. The economic stability provided by advertising set the stage for the advent of the golden age of network radio.

During the first five years of the 1930s, a number of new radio-program types evolved. Network programs drew increasingly large audiences as living rooms became the entertainment centers of a nation locked in the squeeze of the Great Depression. Advertising revenues increased during this period of economic crisis, rising from over $25 million in 1930 to more than $70 million in 1940. The depression affected programming and advertising styles, and as networks and national advertisers came to dominate program content, selling commercials and spot announcements emerged as a major type of radio advertising.

The network economic picture was so good in 1934 that a fourth radio network, the Mutual Broadcasting System (MBS), was formed to challenge NBC-Red, NBC-Blue, and CBS. By 1935 MBS had 60 affiliates competing with the 80 to 120 affiliates of the established networks. As network competition intensified and program costs increased, broadcasters needed to know the audience size of both their programs and their competitors' programs. By 1935, a number of research organizations were providing data on the size and composition of radio audiences. With more than 22 million American radio homes available, programming successes became advertising bonanzas.

The second half of the 1930s was a time of refining and polishing established formats rather than attempting extensive innovation. The networks continued to dominate the period, especially in the areas of advertising revenue and program production. Over 50 percent of all radio-advertising dollars were spent with the four national networks. In 1941 alone, that sum was $75 million.

Two major legal actions also occurred during this period. In 1935 the American Bar Association in Canon 35 ruled that at the discretion of the judge, broadcast journalists could be prohibited from using radio equipment in the courtroom to cover trials. In 1941 the FCC's Mayflower decision forbade broadcasters to editorialize. These two decisions reflected to some extent the print bias of society, which identified print as information media and radio and television as entertainment media. The Mayflower ruling was overturned and broadcasters may now editorialize, but to this day most judges bar radio and television coverage in courtrooms.

Of the 850 stations on the air in 1941, 700 were affiliated with one of the four networks that dominated radio broadcasting. Only three corporations made up the radio oligopoly at that time, however, since the National Broadcasting Company had both a Red and a Blue network. The Federal Communications Commission, recognizing the long-range consequences of the situation, forced NBC to divest itself of one network under the chain-broadcasting rules. The Supreme Court upheld this duopoly decision of the FCC, and NBC sold its Blue network operation to a group of businessmen who formed the American Broadcasting Company (ABC) in 1943.

World War II brought domestic production of radio equipment to a standstill. Despite the fact that the number of radio receivers decreased during the war years, advertising revenue continued to climb. The public demand for war information doubled the number of news programs in the first half of the war, but as war weariness set in during the last 18 months of the conflict, entertainment programs began to squeeze the news out of time slots as Americans sought to escape from reality.

1946–59.   When the war ended, electronics firms returned to radio man-ufacturing. In the period from 1946 to 1948, over 50 million sets were sold for $2.5 billion. During this same time television began its phenomenal rise to preeminence as America's major leisure-time activity. By 1948, the handwrit-ing was on the economic wall, but radio was saved temporarily by the FCC's four-year freeze on television-station allocation. Two other actions by the FCC also changed the face of radio during the postwar period. The first made FM frequencies available for commercial use, and by 1948 over 600 FM stations had been licensed. The second adjusted the distance required between AM stations to allow for multiple use of channels previously used by clear-channel stations.

As a result, when the restrictions on TV's growth were removed by the FCC in 1952, radio's economic situation was further strained by the fact that 3,000 stations were now competing for audiences and revenue. The networks' domination of radio programming ended because their programming lost its economic base as reduced audience size brought in fewer advertising dollars. Also, the networks were busy establishing dominance over television pro-gramming, and radio was quickly shuttled to the back of the bus. The once all-powerful radio networks were suddenly relegated to minor programming roles. By 1960, even the networks' daytime series were defunct.

The networks no longer provided revenue to affiliates, only a national news and speciality service, and they accounted for only 5 percent of the total radio-advertising revenue in 1960. The only major network-programming innovation of the period was NBC's "Monitor" weekend service, which was, in reality, a modification of the disk-jockey format for a national audience.

Into this vacuum leaped the local stations, mostly out of necessity rather than chance. Nevertheless, once the reality of having to provide local pro-gramming and still make money sunk home, local-station programming rapidly developed, primarily around the omnipresent disk jockey, a stack of records, a skeletal news and sports operation, and anything else that provided for and attracted audiences at a low cost. Total advertising revenue stumbled along from 1953 to 1956, as local salesmen attempted to make up the slack created by the continued slide of network revenue, which hit an all-time low of $35 million in 1960. Despite the network crash, additional AM stations plunged into the business so that by 1960, 3,500 AM stations were competing for the radio audience. Over 1,000 of these stations reportedly lost money from 1956 to 1960. FM stations grew to 700 but were chiefly used as an auxiliary service that simulcast the programming service of the AM-FM station combines.

1960 to the Present.   The 1960s were the period of radio's greatest eco-nomic growth. More than 150 million radios were sold at a retail value of $6 billion. Advertising revenue totaled more than $8 billion during the ten years from 1960 to 1969. Network radio stabilized, and revenues increased slowly. The increasing flow of revenue, coupled with intelligent management decisions and low-cost programming, made for a sound AM industry of over 4,500 licensed stations by the late 1970s. One major network innovation occurred in 1968 when ABC Radio developed four separate radio services for affiliates. Although some broadcasters objected, the FCC ruled that the system did not violate the chain-broadcasting rules. More than 1,200 stations are now ABC radio affiliates, which makes ABC the largest U.S. broadcasting network, NBC developed an all-news and information service in the early 1970s that was initially successful but was phased out in 1976 because it had only 62 affiliates.

FM radio has grown at a phenomenal rate since 1960. By 1978 there were over 2,800 commercial FM stations, an increase of 400 percent from 1960. Economic fortunes improved also. Although $3 million was lost in 1968 by all FM stations, this represented a significant improvement in FM fortunes because many individual licensees began to show substantial profits. There are many reasons for this growth. In 1961, the Federal Communications Commission permitted FM stereo broadcasting, for example, and by the mid-1960s, more than 50 percent of all FM stations were stereo operations. Then, in 1965 the FCC ruled that AM-FM combinations in cities of over 100,000 population could no longer duplicate more than 50 percent of either station's programming. Businessmen with only FM licenses had been held in a competitive disadvantage because many combined AM-FM operations used FM merely as another outlet for their AM programming. The AM-FM salesmen then sold the double audience for a unit price. This 50-50 ruling, as it was called, affected approximately 330 stations and greatly opened up the FM market. A wide variety of station operations and formats appeared in the late 1960s because FM could now exist on extremely low-cost programming appealing to very specialized audiences. There were and are stations that broadcast nothing but classified ads, stations with programming for the blind, stations that play only "golden oldies," all-talk stations, and all-news stations. *Broadcasting Yearbook* lists 61 different radio-program formats alone. The 1960s gave birth to a revitalized radio. A tough hybrid had emerged from the ashes of radio's golden age. Today, radio is more powerful and pervasive than ever.

The Scope of Radio Today

Using any measure as a means of comparison, radio is more massive today than at any other time in its history. There are more than 420 million radio receivers in use in the United States. Over 99 percent of all U.S. households are radio equipped. There are five radios for every home and over 1.3 radios for every man, woman, and child. Over $2 billion is spent by Americans each year to purchase nearly 50 million radio receivers. Over $2 billion is spent annually by radio advertisers. Major research studies agree that radio reaches nine out of ten people over 12 years of age every week. Over 75 percent of the adult population listens to radio every day, and studies indicate that the mythical "average adult" (aged 18 and over) listens to the radio 2.5 hours each day from an average of six to eight stations.

The important thing to realize is that the overwhelming share of this growth occurred after the so-called golden age of network radio. The radio-set count is over 200 percent higher today than it was in 1952, and Americans purchase twice as many radios now as they did in 1960. Radio's annual advertising revenue today is double what it was in 1960 and 400 percent above the 1948 level.

Any way the data is evaluated, "new radio" is more massive than "old radio," whether it be dollars, sets, or listeners. Significantly, the bulk of this growth has taken place since 1960.

The Structure and Organization of Radio

A variety of factors affect radio's structure and organization. The local radio station is the basic media unit responsible for almost all content. However, several media service units are deeply involved in radio programming. The phonograph or music industry provides the bulk of most stations' programming at *no* cost for the records, but stations are charged an annual fee for music rights by BMI and ASCAP. Networks provide a free service of national news and features. The wire services (AP and UPI) are the backbone of most radio news departments.

Station organization varies greatly, depending on the size of station, type of programming, size of market, and type of competition (see figure 17.1). At very large stations, specialized tasks and departments exist in the news, sales, and programming areas. At medium-sized stations announcers double as newsmen, salesmen, or engineers, as well as entertainers. At small stations the program manager might also be the sales manager; there is often no news staff, and, normally, all announcers are licensed engineers (see table 17.1).

Radio is highly competitive for audiences, especially in the big markets, and staff members' pay reflects their responsibilities and the size of the market they work in (see table 17.2). High salaries and specialized roles exist only in the very large stations. Radio's high-paid "stars" are extremely rare and exist only in the largest markets.

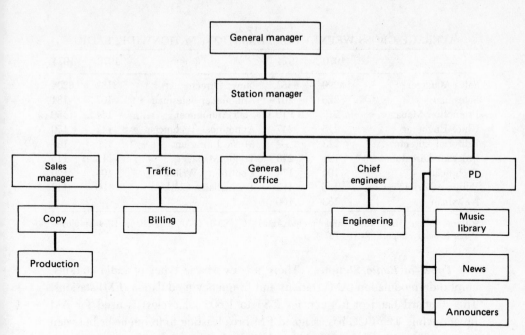

FIGURE 17.1. *Organization Chart for a Small Market Radio Station*

TABLE 17.1.
RADIO AVERAGE NUMBER
OF EMPLOYEES

FULL-TIME	PART-TIME	MARKET SIZE BY POPULATION
17	4	Over 2.5 million
13	3	1–2.5 million
17	3	500,000–1 million
13	4	250,000–500,000
12	3	100,000–250,000
12	3	50,000–100,000
11	3	25,000–50,000
9	3	10,000–25,000
6	3	Less than 10,000
(10)	(3)	(Nationwide avg.)

TABLE 17.2.

AVERAGE GROSS WEEKLY COMPENSATION, NATIONWIDE: RADIO

	1970	1974		1970	1974
Sales Manager	$299	$353	News Director	$182	$234
Salesman	225	207	Announcer-Salesman	167	181
Promotion Manager	217	216	Staff Announcer	154	150
Chief Engineer	215	247	Announcer-Technician	147	150
Editorial Director	213	—	Music Librarian	126	137
Program Director	191	218	Traffic Manager	112	115
Technician	190	174	Continuity Writer	104	120
Public Affairs Director	186	185	Traffic/Sales Clerk	96	112
Newsman	183	160			

SOURCE: "Wages, Hours and Employment/Radio 1970" (NAB, 1970), p. 3; "Radio 1974/Employee Wage & Salary Report" (NAB, 1974), p. 3.

Types of Radio Stations. There are two basic types of radio stations, amplitude-modulation (AM) stations and frequency-modulation (FM) stations. The standard band of frequencies (535 to 1,605 kilocycles) is used for AM broadcasting. The FCC has assigned FM broadcasting to frequencies between 88 and 108 megacycles (1,000 kilocycles equals 1 megacycle).

Within AM broadcasting, there are four classes of stations:

1. Class I stations operate on clear channels and usually with 50,000 watts of power. These stations are designed to serve remote rural areas as well as large urban populations. There are 45 authorized clear channels with only one or two stations on each channel.

2. Class II stations are secondary clear-channel stations also designed to serve a large area. These stations operate at lower power so as not to interfere with the major clear-channel stations. There are 29 channels reserved for Class II stations.

3. Class III stations are regional stations of 500 to 5,000 watts that share 41 channels with many (over 2,000) similar stations.

4. Class IV stations operate on local channels and use a maximum power of 1,000 watts during the day and 250 at night. There are six local frequencies, each used by 150 or more stations.

Three classes of FM stations are in operation today: Class A, under 3,000 watts; Class B, 5,000 to 50,000; Class C, 100,000 watts and antenna heights to 2,000 feet. The reason for the exceptionally high antennas and power is that FM signals do not travel as far as AM signals under the same conditions.

Radio stations are identified by call letters; those in the United States use letters beginning with K or W. Except for a few early stations, such as KDKA in Pittsburgh, stations east of the Mississippi River have call letters beginning with W; K is assigned to stations west of the Mississippi. Most early broadcast call signs used three letters, but these were quickly exhausted and stations were assigned four letters.

Types of Radio Networks. There are four commercial radio networks: CBS, NBC, Mutual, and ABC. ABC provides four distinct radio services to fit the specific formats of local-station operations. The networks provide little more than a national news service to their affiliates. Unlike television stations, the vast majority of radio stations are not affiliated with a national radio network. The financial conditions of network radio operation dictate that only a limited number of stations in the lineup receive payments from the national service, and those that do receive only a nominal sum.

In 1970 National Public Radio began the development of a network radio service designed to provide programming for noncommerical educational stations. Funded through the Corporation for Public Broadcasting, NPR has over 170 interconnected stations. At one time educational radio was little more than a classical jukebox or huge lecture platform, but today it provides a unique alternative to commercial radio. There are over 740 educational radio stations on the air—almost all of them FM.

Station Programming. Most radio programming is based on a limited number of inexpensive components:

1. Recorded music is provided free of charge by most record companies as a means of exposing the public to their new releases. The kind of music played has come to serve as a label for stations and to indicate the kind of audience who listens to them. "Top 40" rock stations program popular music to young audiences. Middle-of-the-road stations program show tunes, light, classical music, milder forms of pop music, or more traditional versions of rock music to older, middle-class people. Country-and-western stations, once located primarily in the South and Southwest, are now major operations in every metropolitan market as population and music alike have migrated north. Soul stations program the latest rhythm-and-blues music to predominantly black audiences in larger cities. There are also commercial as well as educational stations that program classical music for well-educated, upper-income groups.

2. News is the second-most-important part of radio. National news and features are provided by the networks (usually five-minute reports on the hour or half hour). Some stations (usually owned in conjunction with a TV station) have extensive local news operations, but most depend on wire services for nearly all the news they broadcast.

3. Talk by disk jockeys serves as the cement that binds the music, news, sports, weather, and advertising into a cohesive unit. But the creativity of these announcers is limited by the style of the station. In fact, many "rock-jocks" seem to be made on an assembly line, and they are very much replaceable parts—any member of a station's stable of announcers sounds similar to all the others.

4. Local sports, especially high school and college sports activities, are major features on many stations.

5. Finally, advertising is the content aspect that pays the stations' bills. In radio, the most lucrative times of the day are the two "drive-time" periods when people are going to, or coming from, school and work.

Characteristics and Roles of Radio

At present radio is a massive medium with a highly fragmented audience and revenue base. Radio is a local rather than a national medium both in terms of its sources of audience and income. Radio-listening habits are personal, and stations program selectively to satisfy individual needs within a relatively homogeneous group. Radio, adapting to the nature of our society, has used technological advances to become mobile. Listeners use radio as a secondary activity to accompany the work or play of the moment, and advertisers use radio to supplement the primary medium in their advertising mix.

The Fragmented Quality. Radio's massiveness is tempered, however, by two major factors: (1) television siphons off most of the available audience and the lion's share of national advertising dollars; (2) the increase in the number of radio stations has fragmented the audience and revenue available in a given market. Radio advertising has doubled since 1950, but the number of stations has increased by 350 percent. In addition, station expenses for equipment and talent have both increased appreciably since the early 1950s. There are more than 4,500 AM and 2,860 FM stations seeking advertising revenue today. Another 740 educational radio stations swell the number of stations competing for audiences to well over 8,000.

Radio stations must keep their advertising rates at a level that makes them more than competitive with other media. To ease the economic strain, the National Association of Broadcasters' Radio Code has raised the advertising limits to 18 commercial minutes per hour, but this is self-regulation rather than a federal law. The cost efficiency of radio throughout the United States is very good, with a cost per thousand listeners of less than a dollar available in most metropolitan markets. Generally, 65 percent of radio's revenue is from local advertising.

With the improvement in FM economics, frequency-modulation stations have experienced greatest growth. Although many FM and some AM stations lose money every year, economic conditions have continued to improve despite ever-increasing fragmentation of audiences and monies. The typical radio station today shows revenues of $180,000 and expenses of $165,000, for an average profit of $15,000, or about 8 percent.

The Local Quality. Radio has become a local as opposed to a national medium in terms of its sources of audiences, income, and programming. Until the 1950s radio had been the prestige mass medium, controlled by national advertisers and networks. Network affiliation in the past had assured affiliated stations of extensive programming, audience, and revenue. Throughout the golden age, the national-distribution services accounted for at least one-third of all radio-advertising dollars. Today networks account for less than 5 percent of all advertising dollars spent in radio.

In the 1970s, local stations provide the programming, attract the audiences, and earn the revenue. This is not to say that network radio is defunct, because it does provide a valuable news service. What it does say is that local stations are the driving force in radio broadcasting today.

The Selective Quality. In the mid-1950s radio broadcasters were in the position of needing more programs with less money to pay for them. Since both talk and music were relatively cheap, radio rebuilt its programming around music, news, and sports. What evolved has come to be called formula, or format, radio.

Very quickly, AM and FM broadcasters realized that general radio was dead. The more variety a specific station offered, the more its audience dwindled. Television had assumed the general-entertainer role. Stations began to develop variations of the music, news, and sports formula, based on types of recorded music. Audience research indicated that certain formats attracted select segments of the available audience. "Top 40" stations held a virtual monopoly on the teen and subteen groups, while the country-and-western stations had strong appeal, not only in the South and the Southwest but also for vast numbers in the large, northern, metropolitan areas. Middle-of-the-road stations attracted another segment.

Broadcasters began to program selectively to serve one portion of the population. The FCC granted licenses for racially and ethnically oriented stations, which specifically set out to establish themselves as radio service for minority groups within the community. Every station seeks to create a distinct personality, on a program formula, and disk jockeys on formula stations must conform to that personality.

The radio station today programs selectively in order to corner a special segment of the listener-consumer market. Then, if any advertiser wants to reach the black market, the teen-age market, or the young-housewife market in a given area, that advertiser must deal with the station that programs selectively for the consumer-audience in question.

The Personal Quality. Closely allied to radio stations' selective programming is the fact that listening to radio has become a personal activity. No longer does the family unit gather around the console radio to be entertained in a group situation. People tend to listen to the radio as individuals, and radio-station announcers attempt to develop "personal" listening relationships with radio audiences. How many times have you heard a disk jockey single out specific individuals for attention? "I'm sending this song out to Tom and Mary, and Ray and Roz." The radio talk show builds a loyal audience of individuals who call to express their personal views or argue with those individuals with whom they disagree. Entire formats are now built in the talk-show concept.

You might see a couple of teen-agers stroll down the street as they listen as individuals to the same station on two personal radios. This personal orientation is possible because there are 1.3 radios for every individual in the United States; in 1946 there were three people for every radio. In the kitchens, mothers listen for weather reports in order to send their children off to school properly dressed. Upstairs, teen-agers tune in on the latest number-one hit in the country. On their way to work, fathers listen to traffic reports on the automobile radio. The individual listens in relative mental and/or social isolation, seeking to gratify a personal entertainment or information need of the moment.

The Mobile Quality. The United States has been called "a nation a go-go," a "society on wheels," and radio has the ability to get out and go with its American audiences. This ability to participate in the individual's daily routine has been made possible by the new mobility of the medium.

The phenomenal increases in radio sales in recent years are the result in great measure of production of three specific types of radio receivers: the car radio, the portable, and the clock radio. Home radios, usually small AM-FM sets, constitute little more than 15 percent of all radio sales.

This tide toward radio's mobility began immediately following World War II, although production of car radios had been an important part of total radio production as early as 1930, when 34,000 car-radio sets were manufactured. By 1951, auto-set production exceeded that of the home-receiver class for the first time and has continued to be the leading type of set manufactured for the past 15 years. Today 95 out of every 100 new cars are radio equipped and more than 114 million radio-equipped cars are on the road.

During the 1950s and 1960s, portable production also topped home-receiver production, excluding clock radios. The tremendous surge in popularity is due to the advent of the transistor, which reduced set size and cost. The sale of transistor radios exceeds $30 million per year, which is 200 percent above the 1952 level, and Americans spend more than $100 million per year just to keep transistor radios going in a mobile society.

The Secondary and Supplementary Qualities. The final characteristics of radio are that radio is used as a secondary activity by listeners and a supplementary medium by advertisers. Radio today is to drive a car by, study by, or relax at the beach by. No longer does an audience eagerly cling to the radio for every sound. Radio is no longer used as the primary entertainment activity in our society, and with the added mobility of the "new" radio it goes along as a companion for the activity of the moment. An automobile radio is secondary to the prime function of the car itself—to go somewhere. We need traffic reports to get there, and radio provides them. The most recent development that enhances radio's usefulness as a secondary item is the clock radio. It does not jolt you awake; it sings or talks you out of the bed and into the day. Its primary function is not to entertain or provide information—it is basically an alarm clock.

Most national and local advertisers with sizable budgets use radio to supplement the major medium of an advertising campaign. Most local advertisers use newspapers primarily but keep the campaign supported with radio ads. Most major national advertisers spend only a small portion of their total budget on radio. Nevertheless, Radio Advertising Bureau studies have shown that radio can effectively and efficiently reach consumer prospects that television misses. Most of the nation's top 50 advertising agencies spend less than 10 percent of their national clients' budgets on radio. The major exceptions to the rule are the automobile and related industries, which extensively use "drive time" to hit the available audience going to or coming from work.

In summary, radio has clearly survived the competition from television and has evolved into a new and remarkably solid medium. Radio is now a companion medium, fine-tuned to meet almost any need. This unique ability will continue to provide it with an audience and revenue capable of sustaining future expansion.

Have you attended a football game recently and yearned for an instant replay? Have you ever been called to the supper table and turned up the volume so that you wouldn't miss Walter Cronkite? Do you know Archie Bunker, Mr. Green Jeans, Maude, Uncle Miltie, The Fonz, Kojak, Fat Albert, or the Cookie Monster? Did you see the Army-McCarthy hearings, the funeral of President Kennedy, the killing of Lee Harvey Oswald, "The Selling of the Pentagon," the flight of Apollo 11, the first Super Bowl, the invasion of Cambodia, the last cigarette commercial (January 2, 1971), the Watergate hearings, Nixon's resignation, the election of Jimmy Carter, "Voyage to the Bottom of the Sea," "Dragnet," "East Side/West Side," "I Spy," "Maverick," "Ding Dong School," or "Gilligan's Island?" When was the last time you had a TV dinner? Do you have a subscription to *TV Guide*? Did you watch "Roots"? How many hours a week do you watch the tube?

All these questions pertain to television—the uses you make of it and the impact it has had on your life. For many Americans, television is *the* source of entertainment, the most reliable source of news, an important educational experience, the most dynamic form of advertising, and an integral part of the total American life style. This is even more impressive when you consider that television is barely thirty years old. If there are such things as historical periods, one title for the second half of the twentieth century must surely be the Age of Television.

18

Television

Historical Perspectives

Prehistory (1884–1923). The history of television in the United States breaks down into several fairly well defined units. The first encompasses the prehistory of television, the early theoretical research leading up to the first experiments in the mid 1920s.

Television, like radio, grew out of intense experimentation in electricity in the late nineteenth century. Basic research in electromagnetic theory by James Clark Maxwell and Heinrich Hertz led to more practical experimentation culminating in the work of Guglielmo Marconi. Coincidental with this research in wireless communication in the 1880s was the work of Paul Nipkow and Charles Jenkins, who experimented with mechanical scanning-disk methods of sending pictures by wire. Most of the early experiments in television employed the mechanical method. Research in television slowed down somewhat with the tremendous surge of radio in the early twentieth century. Nevertheless, in 1923 Vladimir K. Zworykin patented an electronic camera tube, the iconoscope.

Early Development (1923–47). Barely three years after radio broadcasting became a reality, a crude, all-electronic television was available, although much of its early use was not successful. The first real transmission of television occurred in 1925 with Jenkins's mechanical method. Zworykin's method of electronic scanning was simpler, however, and eventually produced a better picture. Experiments with electronic television were conducted throughout the world in the 1920s, including the work of Alexanderson and Farnsworth in this country and Baird in England. The Federal Radio Commission (later the Federal Communications Commission) granted the first experimental license for visual broadcasting to RCA's W2XBS in April 1928. That same year, the General Electric Company broadcast the first television drama over W6X in Schenectady, New York.

Experimentation continued throughout the 1930s, and by 1937, 17 stations were operating under noncommercial experimental license. The 1939 World's Fair in New York City was the setting for television's coming-out party. President Franklin D. Roosevelt's appearance on television became the hit of the fair.

Commercial television operations were slated to begin September 1, 1940, but the FCC rescinded its original authorization in March 1940. The delay was ordered by the commission because it felt that RCA had indulged in an unwise promotional campaign (to sell its transmission and receiving equipment) that would retard further television research and experimentation.

In January 1941 the National Television System Committee (NTSC) suggested television standards to which the FCC reacted favorably, and the start of commercial telecasting was rescheduled for July 1, 1941. On that date both the DuMont and CBS stations aired programming. But it was RCA's WNBT that ran the first spot commercial (Bulova Watch Company) and sponsored programs, Lowell Thomas's news program (Sunoco), "Uncle Jim's Question Bee" (Lever Brothers), and "Truth or Consequences" (Proctor and Gamble).

By the end of 1941, some ten commercial stations were serving approximately 5,000 to 10,000 television homes. Throughout the first six months of commercial operation, all licensed stations operated at a loss. In its first six months WNBT lost about $7,000.

World War II interrupted TV's growth, delaying its national appearance. Commercial telecasting ended in early 1942, although experimental telecasts continued on an irregular basis. Advertisers were encouraged to use the facilities free of charge. The war was detrimental to the immediate development of television, but the war had its positive effects as well. Chief among them was the development of better electronic techniques and equipment, most importantly the image-orthicon tube.

The single most important event affecting TV's future during World War II was the 1943 duopoly ruling that forced NBC to divest itself of one of its two radio networks. This decision created another economically strong national radio operation (ABC) that enabled the ABC-TV network to evolve and survive during its early years.

Following World War II, the rapid development of television was further retarded by problems involving the placement of television in the electromagnetic spectrum and the $1 million price tag attached to building and equipping a television station. In 1945 there were six commercial stations, and by 1947 only 11 more had been added for a meager total of 17. At this time many broadcasters thought that FM radio would be the next important medium.

By March 1947, the FCC had set aside channels 2 to 13 in the VHF (very high frequency) band, and more and more receivers were appearing on the market. The rush for television facilities was now on, and CBS, because of misplaced television priorities during World War II, belatedly joined in. There was a definite need for more stations because people were buying the high-priced sets as fast as they were being produced. Over one million were sold in 1948 at an average price of $400. By early 1948, 19 stations were on the air, 81 had FCC authorization, and a total of 116 applications were before the FCC. At this time it became obvious that the commission would have to reevaluate TV broadcasting to prevent station interference.

The Formation of the American Television System (1948–52). During this four-year period of television history, three major factors significantly affected the future of video broadcasting: (1) the Federal Communications Commission's "freeze" on TV station allocations, (2) the development of the TV networks, and (3) the evolution of programming formats. All three events influenced and were influenced by public response to the medium.

THE FREEZE. By the fall of 1948, there were 36 TV stations on the air in 19 markets and another 73 licensed in 43 more cities. In order to solve technical-interference problems, provide for the increased demand for licenses, and study color television systems, the Federal Communications Commission froze new-station allocations from September 30, 1948 to July 1, 1952. During these years the RCA compatible-color system was adopted, UHF channels 14 to 83 were added to VHF channels 2 to 13 for telecasting purposes, and 242 station allocations were reserved for educational television (ETC). This third class of stations—public, noncommercial, and educational—was established through the efforts of Commissioner Frieda B. Hennock, despite the lack of support from most educators and universities.

While the freeze was on, 108 of the 109 commercially licensed stations went on the air, and TV homes jumped from 1.5 million to 15 million. Between 1948 and 1952 one of every three American families bought a television set at an average cost of $300. Growth was possible during this period, although no new licenses were being granted, because almost every major population area was being served by at least one television station.

THE NETWORKS. The generally accepted date of the arrival of national television networking is the 1948–49 television season (September to August). In January 1949 the Midwest and the Eastern Seaboard were linked by coaxial cable. The West Coast link-up occurred in September 1951. But it was some time before every station was able to carry "live" feeds, so many new stations had to depend on kinescopes (films of electronically produced pictures) for network productions.

The birth and survival of the television networks depended on four factors: (1) the network needed a financially sound parent company that could survive the lean years of television development; (2) the network required ownership of key stations in the largest population centers to provide local revenue and guarantee that network's series would be aired in those markets; (3) the network needed expertise in national radio operations that provided both financial support and a ready-made lineup of affiliates to carry its programs; (4) the network needed to have a backlog of, or quickly develop, talent and programs that would attract large audiences for national advertisers.

The American Broadcasting Company, the Columbia Broadcasting System, and the National Broadcasting Company were able to meet these four criteria and survived. The key, of course, was financial strength. NBC lost over $18 million in its first four years of network TV operation. The Mutual Broadcasting System, which did not own any radio stations, was the weakest national radio operation and was never able to muster its limited resources to enter the TV network business. The DuMont Television Network, owned by Allen B. DuMont Laboratories, an early pioneer in television operations, did not have the radio network, the financial strength, the station ownership, or programming experience necessary. Although the DuMont operation struggled along through the "freeze," it collapsed completely in 1955.

PROGRAMMING.   In these early years of network and station development most of television's content came from radio-programming formats. The quiz shows, suspense programs, Westerns, variety shows, soap operas, and comedies were direct descendants of developments in radio. In fact, most of television's early hits were exact copies of radio series transposed intact to television, such as "Suspense," "The Life of Riley," "The Aldrich Family," "The Lone Ranger," "Break the Bank," and "Studio One." Television's first stars were radio personalities, including Red Skelton, Burns and Allen, Arthur Godfrey, Jack Benny, and Edgar Bergen. The networks also adopted other traditional radio programming, such as news, sporting events, and live coverage of special events like the 1948 and 1952 political conventions and election returns. The most consistent quality about network programming in the first four years was change; nearly one-third of the network's lineup changed each year—a practice that continues today.

The local stations also attempted to provide programming in those early years to fill the gaps left in the network schedules; much of this was of poor quality, however. As a result, the syndicator emerged very early as an important source of TV content. In 1950 the first package of theatrical films found its way into the local market.

The financial bases of television were clear from the start. The public was acclimated to radio commercials and accepted them as the means of paying for their programs. There were other reasons also, such as an existing network structure complete with contractual agreements with sponsors. Structurally, television economics was simply an extension of radio economics, and because of this TV developed much faster than expected.

Television, despite its affinities to radio, was still a new medium. Its own particular pattern of adoption in society coupled with its unique properties were prime factors in the rapidly changing pattern of programming. Television, like newspapers and radio before it, was not initially a household medium. As newspapers were first read in the "coffeehouses," television was first viewed by many in local bars and taverns. This factor plus the inherent "visualness" of television were strong reasons for sports programming making up as much as 30 percent of all sponsored network evening time in 1949. As the television set became more of a household item, the programming changed to reflect this. Children's and women's programming became more important, as did such family entertainment as variety shows.

The end of television's birth and its push into childhood came in 1952 with the FCC's Sixth Order and Report. The report did more than simply end the freeze. It was essentially a master plan for television development in the United States. Television was beginning to fulfill its destiny as the dominant leisure-time activity for most Americans.

The Golden Age of Television (1952 –60).   This eight-year slice of television history contained the most fantastic growth spurt ever experienced by a mass medium. As one would expect, there was a great rush to obtain station licenses immediately following the end of the freeze. By 1955 there were 439 stations on the air. This number grew to 573 by 1960. Set sales mushroomed as more stations began broadcast operations. The 15 million TV homes in 1952 expanded to 26 million in 1954, 42.5 million in 1958, and reached 45 million homes by 1960. In this eight-year stretch the percentage of TV-equipped homes in the United States grew from 33 percent to 90 percent. Station and network profits kept pace with this growth pattern as gross industry revenues increased from $300 million in 1952 to $1.3 billion in 1960.

CBS and NBC were the dominant networks of this period, primarily because of their network radio experience, available capital assets, and top-quality talent. ABC had many problems. The death of the DuMont network in 1955, however, eased ABC's need for more affiliates to a limited degree. This factor, plus the merger of ABC with United-Paramount Theaters, helped increase its competitiveness, but throughout the 1950s ABC ran a poor third to both CBS and NBC.

The FCC's Sixth Order and Report had sought to ease problems that faced the industry, but the implementation of these changes took considerable time. The UHF (ultra high frequency) band had been opened to increase the number of stations, but since most TV sets were built to receive only VHF signals, special adapters and antennas had to be purchased in order to receive these stations. Although 126 UHF stations were operating in 1954, they were in an extremely poor competitive position, and that number fell to only 77 in 1960. Throughout the 1950s most UHF stations had financial problems, and the failure rate was more than 50 percent because the lack of UHF receivers meant small audiences and little advertising. This situation continued until 1962 when Congress passed the all-channel legislation, which required that all sets produced after January 1, 1964, be capable of receiving both UHF and VHF stations.

Color television in the form of RCA's system began to emerge slowly following FCC approval in 1953. The first color sets were manufactured in 1954 and sold for about $1,000. The high cost of both receivers and broadcast equipment dictated a slow growth, however. The season of 1954–55 was the first color season, with NBC programming 12 to 15 hours a week. It was not until the season of 1964–65 that color television programming became dominant.

Several factors were responsible for the public's slow response to color television: (1) set costs were extremely high; (2) both ABC and CBS refused to move into color programming because it would have given NBC the competitive edge, because most compatible-color patents were held by NBC's parent company, RCA; (3) the electronics industry already had a boom business in black-and-white sets, and they too would have to do business with RCA. These manufacturers chose to experiment with, rather than produce, color sets. In 1960 there were no color series on ABC or CBS; NBC was carrying the full color-programming load.

Another important technical development that occurred in the 1950s was the move toward film and videotape programming. With the development of videotape in 1956, live telecasting, with the exception of sports, specials, and some daytime drama, soon became a thing of the past. By 1960, virtually all network prime-time programming was on film or videotape. Much of the daytime programming on both the network and the local level was still live, however. The two reasons for the rise of recorded programming were that (1) errors could be corrected before they were broadcast, thus improving the artistic quality of the program; and (2) the program could be rerun, and this reuse cut the skyrocketing costs of program production.

Programming in the 1950s continued the trends of the early years. Two important additions were the adult, or psychological, Western, starting with "Gunsmoke" in 1955, and the big-prize game shows, beginning with "The $64,000 Question" in 1956. Westerns reached their peak in 1959–60 with 32 Westerns in prime time and gradually declined; by the mid 1970s, none were on network schedules. The quiz scandals in 1959–60 revealed that some participants had received answers prior to their appearance on the shows or had been coached in their responses to heighten the tension. This notoriety killed off the prime-time big-money quiz shows.

"Live" drama reached its zenith in the middle 1950s with such programs as "Studio One," "Playhouse 90," and "The Armstrong Circle Theater." But television's voracious appetite for new material soon made it impossible to sustain any extremely high standards. The form began to blend with other dramatic types and gradually faded from the scene. Today, with the exception of "The Hallmark Hall of Fame" and limited network specials, quality drama on commercial television is rare.

Program experimentation began to dwindle as network competition set in. In the late 1950s, Westerns, situation comedies, and crime-detective dramas accounted for over 50 percent of all prime-time programming. Everyone seemed to be jumping on the program bandwagon, duplicating whatever was popular at the moment.

The quiz scandals in TV seemed to herald an end to television's age of euphoria. According to the *Tenth Annual Videotown Report* made in 1957 by Cunningham and Walsh, television had become accepted as a routine part of life. It had lost much of its former novelty and excitement. A public opinion poll taken by Sindlinger in 1959 revealed a sharp drop in the public's estimation of television following the quiz scandals. Congress began a series of investigations focusing particular attention upon the relationship between advertisers, agencies, and broadcasters. Much of this concern was strikingly capsulated by FCC Chairman Newton Minnow in 1961, when he criticized television, calling it "the vast wasteland."

The 1950s were a time of experimentation and change. They were witness to the rise and fall of a whole new generation of programs, stars, and techniques. By 1960, the "trial period" was over.

Progress and Criticism: 1961 to the Present. The two words "progress" and "criticism" sum up much of what television has been in the period since 1960. Criticism of television became the "in" thing as politicians, educators, social scientists, minority groups, and parents all took turns attacking the medium. Of particular public concern was television's role in the violence that seemed so much a part of America in the 1960s and '70s. Countless studies were, and still are, being conducted assessing television's effects, especially on children. The results have generally concluded that everyone knows television has an effect, but few are sure just exactly what this effect is and how it works. The medium's advertising effectiveness, however, is clearly evident by the $2 billion investment made annually by advertisers.

Television's impact on the political process became apparent in the 1960s, beginning with the Nixon-Kennedy debates in 1960, continuing in 1968 with TV's coverage of the Democratic convention in Chicago, and highlighted further by the Carter-Ford debates in 1976. Television's advertising role in the presidential campaign was dramatically described in Joe McGinnis's book *The Selling of the President* (1968).

Networks continued their domination of the airwaves. By 1969, they provided almost 64 percent (77.5 hours per week) of their affiliates' programming. As revenues and profits increased, the criticism seemed to keep pace. The FCC proposed a plan whereby 50 percent of all prime-time programming would have to be nonnetwork originated, but this proposal was never implemented. In the 1971–72 season, however, the FCC did institute a ruling cutting network prime-time programming from 3.5 hours to three hours per evening in the 7:30-to-11:00-P.M. (EST) time block.

Pressure groups also succeeded in altering programming. Violence on television was somewhat curtailed because of pressure brought to bear following the assassinations of President John F. Kennedy, Martin Luther King, and Robert Kennedy. An overhaul of Saturday morning cartoon shows occurred in the 1970–71 season to appease critics. Perhaps the most dramatic and effective attack came against the cigarette industry by the Surgeon General's Office with its claims that cigarette smoking was dangerous to a person's health. Pressure by the Surgeon General resulted in all cigarette advertising being taken off the air on January 2, 1971. A short-lived "family hour" was implemented in 1975–76 with less than successful results. The idea was to limit the first hour of prime-time programming to material suitable for the entire family, but the result was a mishmash of weak comedies and variety programs that proved to be poor lead-ins for later programs. The concept was phased out in 1976.

Any historical overview of television in the 1960s finds itself overwhelmed by the sheer number of events, people, and issues in the television spotlight. In this mass, three events stand out: the Vietnam war, the assassination and funeral of President Kennedy, and the Apollo 11 moon landing. All three events are competitors for the label of television's finest hour. It was primarily because of television that these events achieved the drama they did. Instead of simply hearing or reading about the war, the President's funeral, or the moonwalk after they happened, the American public was able—through television—to witness and participate in the events as they were happening. At times this witnessing was inspiring, as when television went to the moon. At times it was frightening, as when suspected presidential assassin Lee Harvey Oswald was murdered in full view of the nation by Jack Ruby, or when a captured Vietcong soldier was shot in the head as cameras recorded the scene, or when dogs and water hoses were turned on civil rights demonstrators and police fought with protestors in Chicago during the 1968 Democratic convention. The 1960s were anything but peaceful, and television was on hand providing dramatic witness, perhaps even dramatic stimulation, to the turmoil. Much of the world was watching and being changed in the process.

In the area of program content, motion pictures became a major part of the network's prime-time fare. In addition, programs such as "That Was the Week That Was," "The Smothers Brothers Comedy Hour," and "Laugh-In" began to challenge a number of taboos, and television in general got in step with a more permissive society. Perhaps the single most important commercial programming development was the appearance of the adult situation comedy. It started in 1970 with "All in the Family" and proliferated throughout the first half of the decade until it made up over 25 percent of the nation's prime-time schedule in 1976–77. Such programs as "Maude," "Soap," "Sanford and Son," "Alice," "Mary Hartman, Mary Hartman," and "Family" regularly used abortion, premarital sex, narcotics, and religious evangelism, to name a few, as comic material. Blacks such as Bill Cosby, Diahann Carroll, Redd Foxx, and Flip Wilson became successful series stars when the entertainment industry responded to the civil rights movement by integrating programs and commercial spots. Professional football became the national television sport, and NBC made it possible for the AFL to survive economically by exposing the junior league to national audiences and by paying large sums for TV rights to the games. Late-night talk shows became part of the three-network competition but were quickly reduced to one as no one could compete against the long established "The Tonight Show." "Sesame Street" emerged as public broadcasting's first "star" and helped focus attention on the almost anonymous fourth network. Late in the decade, with the appearence of "Rich Man, Poor Man," "Roots," and "Holocaust," the miniseries became a strong programming factor threatening to alter television's long-standing seasonal structure built on 13- and 26-week series.

The 1960s and '70s were important years for technical development as well. It was the first full decade of videotape, satellites, widespread color, active UHF stations, and community-antenna television.

With the passing of the Communication Satellite Act of 1962, the United States officially got into international television. The bill provided for the creation of the Communications Satellite Corporation (COMSAT), a private corporation, which came into existence on February 1, 1963. The first satellites, Telstar and Relay, went up in 1963 and provided intercontinental coverage of the funerals of Pope John XXIII and President Kennedy, among other events. In 1965 another satellite, Early Bird, was launched, becoming the first satellite to be used for full-scale commercial operation. By 1969, satellite usage had increased to a total of 779 hours of transmission and 1,050 hours of receiving, much of it being Vietnam coverage via Lanai Bird, the Pacific counterpart of Early Bird. By 1971, a full-scale international communication system existed, with three synchronous satellites in fixed positions over the Atlantic, Pacific, and Indian oceans as well as a large network of earth stations. Recent developments have focused on the domestic use of satellites. The United States entered the field in 1973 with RCA leasing transmission time on Canada's ANIK II to relay signals between the two coasts. In 1974 ABC Radio began transmitting service to its four radio networks via satellite. Further exploration of domestic use includes PBS converting to full satellite transmission by the late 1970s.

These developments are not occurring without great concern over their effect. Satellite relays in the sky compete directly with AT&T's ground networks and, in the case of direct transmission to individual receivers, with local stations. The economic consequences are great, but the potential for expanded program service at a reduced cost makes the risk worthwhile.

Cable television, CATV (Community Antenna Television), has made even more dramatic strides. In 1960 there were only 640 operating systems with a total of 650,000 subscribers. By 1970 it had grown to almost 2,500 systems and 1.3 million subscribers. Today there are over 3,600 systems serving over 7,000 communities and 12 million subscribers, approximately 16 percent of the nation's TV households.

What had begun in the late 1940s as simply a master receiving antenna for isolated communities has grown to the point where it clearly poses an economic threat to local broadcasters. CATV no longer exists simply to serve rural areas. Cable TV is now a growing and lucrative business in which a local station's signal is sold to individuals willing to pay for the cost of bringing the signal into their homes. With FCC-required local-origination programming by large (3,500+ subscribers) systems, cable TV is now competing directly with the local broadcaster in providing alternative programming to local communities. At present, almost 700 systems originate programming in their own studios for an average of 13.5 hours a week.

Many factors cloud the future of cable, not the least of which is the FCC's ambiguous jurisdiction over CATV systems. Nevertheless, it seems clear that cable will succeed only to the extent that it provides a strong alternative to existing programming. If cable chooses to utilize its potential for minority-interest programming, two-way transmission multichannel programming capacity, and "custom tailored" programming, it will not only survive but prosper. If it chooses merely to relay existing signals, performing the role of conduit, it will most likely fail. Clearly, cable TV has a present reality and a future potential. Its direction and growth will be watched with great interest by producers and consumers alike.

With the tremendous growth in cable TV, the potential for pay TV/cable increased greatly. Pay TV has been around since the early 1950s, but most systems lost money and quickly folded. Two major "experiments" existed in the 1960s, one in Hartford, Connecticut, the others in Los Angeles and San Francisco. Both proved moderately successful but were clearly exploratory attempts. The FCC finally instituted rules in 1970 permitting pay TV over the air or by cable. By 1974 at least eight major pay TV systems had begun operations and by 1977 there were over 1 million subscribers. The leading company is Home Box Office with over 1 million subscribers. Programming typically includes first-run motion pictures and sporting events. A greater variety is emerging, including X- and R-rated films on "adult cable." Systems showing these films exist in Ann Arbor, Michigan; Columbus, Ohio; Buffalo, New York; and Thief River Falls, Minnesota; to name a few. The prices vary according to the event, but most subscribers average $15–$20 a month in fees for all types of programs.

Whether or not "fee TV" will pose a threat to free TV is open to question. Siphoning off the most popular events on TV and asking an audience to pay directly for them opens up a large number of issues. Like cable TV, pay TV must be acknowledged by today's broadcaster as a definite reality.

Color television programming replaced black and white in the 1960s. At first, ABC and CBS were reluctant to commit the time and money to convert to color but, following a research report indicating a rating edge for color programs over black and white, both ABC and CBS revised programming plans for 1964–65 with significant increases in color programming. By 1965–66, all three networks were running a complete all-color, prime-time schedule. This growth in available color programming led to a boom in color-set sales. Today, 80 percent of American TV homes have a color-TV set. Just as importantly, color-equipped homes use their sets approximately 20 percent more than black-and-white homes.

Important changes in the structure and organization of TV occurred in the 1960s, as many companies merged or diversified. Educational television (ETV) took on a new name, "public broadcasting." With it, and with long-awaited governmental support, it also acquired new life. The Public Broadcasting Act of 1967 ranks with the 1952 Sixth Order and Report as one of the most important events in educational television. In effect, the 1967 act provided for the first interconnected network of ETV stations. Most importantly, it provided educational television with the long-needed financial support necessary for it to become a vital force in American life. Without that act, many ETV stations would never have been built or modernized.

The act established the Corporation for Public Broadcasting, which in turn established the Public Broadcasting Service (PBS) in 1970. PBS manages programming production, distribution, and station interconnection. Various production centers were set up across the country. The most important single programming development was the creation of The Children's Television Workshop, producers of "Sesame Street" and "Electric Company," among others. It is an independent nonprofit corporation whose only ties to public broadcasting are partial funding by CPB. Another important programming source is the British Broadcasting Corporation, which has supplied such important series as "Civilisation," "The Forsythe Saga," and "Upstairs, Downstairs."

Financing, of course, is at the heart of public broadcasting's present role and future potential. Throughout the Nixon administration, there was controversy. This resulted primarily from CPB's increasing development of public affairs programming, including several controversial programs and series. New legislation under President Ford provided for a federal matching plan and five-year financing. This $634 million bill became law in 1976 and assured public broadcasting of a relatively stable financial base for the first time in its history. Currently, over 250 public television stations are in operation. The late 1970s witnessed a tremendous surge in new forms of video technology, including home video cassette record systems, video games, and the possibility of even more uses of the TV screen with videodisks, home computers, and multiband cable systems. TV audiences will have the opportunity for a broader choice of content, and this will have great impact on the television industry.

The 1960s and '70s have been witness to the most intense and dynamic media-society relationship in history. Television was said to have created a "new" politics, a "new" generation, and a "new" society. In turn, the events of this time forced television to mature, to expand its role beyond that of entertainer to become a positive social force. Some say it did not mature enough. That is probably true. But television is young as a national medium. The 1940s saw its birth, the 1950s its childhood, the 1960s its stormy adolescence. In the 1970s and '80s the medium seems headed toward adulthood, and with it some possibly radical changes in its structure and content.

The Scope of Television

Television is massive in every aspect. Over 73 million homes (97 percent of all U.S. households) are equipped with television sets. More than 75 percent of these families own a color set. More than 50 percent own two sets. About 16 percent are connected to a CATV system. According to the A. C. Nielsen Company, the average TV household uses its set more than 40 hours per week. Top-rated network programs consistently attract more than 40 million viewers during the winter quarter. For special events, television viewing is truly phenomenal. The eight-part series "Roots" is a good example. Over 130 million people watched at least part of the series; the last episode drew an audience of 80 million people, making it the most watched television program in history.

Of the total $5.5 billion spent annually on consumer electric products including radios, phonographs, tape recorders, musical instruments, hearing aids, and software, television-set sales account for more than $1.3 billion of that volume.

The industry providing the programming for this consumer investment is in itself huge. There are almost 40,000 television broadcasters in the United States, with thousands more in allied fields. They work at over 725 commercial television stations, three national networks, and a variety of regional networks. Thousands of others are employed at many related businesses, including almost 550 program producers and distributors, 300 commercial producers, 240 station representatives, and 40 processing labs. Also, over 260 educational television stations are served by one national network and many program suppliers.

A typical television station is on the air 18 hours a day all year long with approximately 65 percent of this time's programming provided by the networks. A television network provides almost 90 different series in any one week.

In order to support this production schedule, television takes in an enormous amount of advertising. Eighteen cents out of every advertising dollar is spent in television. TV advertising revenue has run about $2.5 billion throughout the 1970s; advertising is the third-largest content form on television in terms of amount of time. The average 30-second commercial in network prime time now costs from $30,000 to $50,000 depending on the network and the particular program. For special programs, the cost is even higher. One-minute spots during the Super Bowl cost over $250,000. Production costs for network series now average about $125,000 for each 30-minute program, $250,000 per 60-minute show, $500,000 for 90-minute movies, and $900,000 for 120-minute movies.

The costs, audiences, and advertising revenues make television one of the greatest growth industries of the postwar era. Without doubt, television is the dominant force in American leisure time.

The Structure and Organization of Television

Television's basic function is programming, and the ways in which programs are produced, distributed, and exhibited are the basis for the organization of the TV industry.

Program production is the responsibility of networks, stations, and program-production companies. Distribution is the critical function of the networks using the ground facilities of the American Telephone and Telegraph Company and satellite transmission. The exhibition of programs is the primary role of local stations. The best analysis of the structure of television in the United States can be accomplished by analyzing the two critical participants in programming: the networks and local stations.

The Networks.   At the present time the primary forces in commercial television programming are the national networks: the American Broadcasting Company (ABC), the Columbia Broadcasting System (CBS), and the National Broadcasting Company (NBC). These three commercial networks produce much of their programming in conjunction with package agencies owned by film companies or corporations set up by the talent that appears in the specific series. Approximately 90 percent of the networks' prime-time schedule is produced cooperatively with these program-production agencies. For an annual program season, over 30 separate production companies prepare programs for the networks.

The networks currently provide about 65 percent of all programming hours broadcast by their affiliates during the four blocks of time that make up the television week. The rest is filled by the local stations with local or syndicated programs.

PRIME TIME   (8:00–11:00 P.M. EST daily). This is the most important time period in television, and it is dominated by the three networks. The networks may provide up to three hours of programming per night. During these hours the most expensive and elaborate programs are aired, and the average audience for the average network program in prime time is 32 million persons during the winter quarter. The dominant forms of prime-time network programming today is the action/adventure series (over 30 percent), with situation comedies second (25 percent), and movies third (16 percent). Specials and miniseries are becoming more prominent as the networks are experimenting with program stunting and other strategies to win the audience rating race. The only "live" programming—transmitted at the time of the event—are various sports events such as ABC's "NFL Monday Night Football." All other programs are either filmed or videotaped. The one "innovation" in recent years is to tape programs before a live audience to try and achieve a certain degree of spontaneity. Programs such as "All in the Family" and "The Jeffersons" utilize this process. All programs are telecast in color.

FRINGE TIME is divided into two classes: (1) early fringe (5:00–8:00 P.M. daily) and (2) late fringe (11:00 P.M.–1:00 A.M. daily). The early period usually features network and local news; late-fringe programming consists of network talk shows, network and local movies, and syndicated programs.

WEEKDAY DAYTIME (7:00 A.M.–5:00 P.M. Monday through Friday) is the domain of videotaped quiz shows, soap operas, film reruns of network situation comedies, news shows, and children's programs. Program decisions are dominated by the fact that audiences are composed primarily of women and children.

WEEKEND DAYTIME (7:00 A.M.–5:00 P.M. Saturday and Sunday) offers children's programs on Saturday mornings, public service religious programs, and cartoons on Sunday mornings. Weekend afternoons are dominated by live sports broadcasts.

Besides exercising production control, the networks also assume economic responsibility for distributing the programs, using coaxial cable and microwave facilities of AT&T and satellites. This cost alone amounts to over $50 million.

Each network owns five VHF (very high frequency) stations in major metropolitan areas. These network-owned-and-operated stations, along with the other 700 affiliates, provide for the exhibition of network TV programs.

The dominance of the networks in programming is further strengthened by the fact that successful network series often turn up in syndication programming carried by the local station.

In addition to national networks, there are about 15 regional and special-program networks that offer programs for local broadcast. These networks service national, regional, and local advertisers.

Stations. The actual broadcasting or airing of programs is done by stations in each market. Stations affiliated with networks are paid approximately 30 percent of their hourly rate by the network to carry a prime-time program. No network payments are made for most sports, news, and late-night programs. In addition, a specific number of advertising slots in these programs are left open for local sales, usually at the station break.

The local network-affiliated station's schedule usually consists of 65 per-

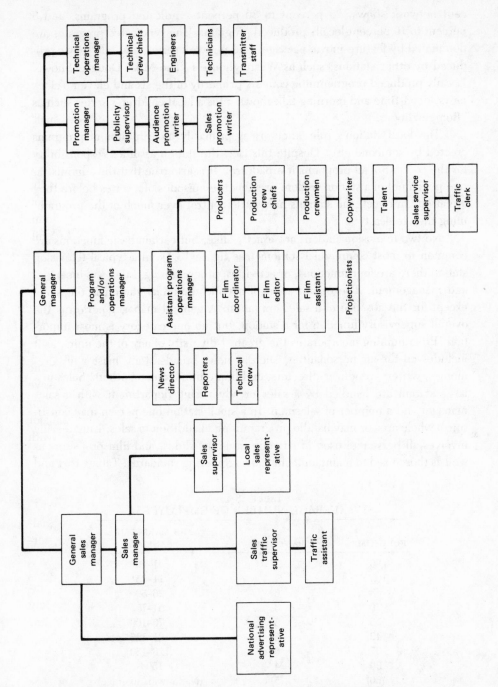

FIGURE 18.1. *Structure of a Typical Large Television Station*

cent network shows, 25 percent to 30 percent syndicated programs, and 5 percent to 10 percent locally produced programs. The syndicated programs are dominated by feature-movie packages, old network series, and talk shows produced by other stations, such as Westinghouse's "The Mike Douglas Show." Locally produced programming consists primarily of the six and eleven o'clock news, noon-time and morning talk shows, plus a local children's series such as "Romper Room."

The local station's role, then, is as primarily an exhibitor of programs created by someone else. Despite this fact, the station assumes responsibility for the content of all programs it broadcasts. It is also true that the administrative personnel of a station seldom preview the episodes of a series before they are aired. In effect, the stations have little control over much of the programming they telecast.

No two television stations are exactly alike, but certain basic functions are common to most commercial stations (see figure 18.1). In a typical television station there are four functions, or activities: programming, sales, engineering, and management. The organization of a noncommercial station is the same except for the absence of a sales operation. A general manager performs the overall supervisory function for a station, but no one category is most important. Programming incorporates the greatest diversity of any of the units, as it includes on-the-air personalities, such as news broadcasters, master of ceremonies, writers, producer-directors, and film editors, among others. Sales in a large station are handled by a sales or advertising department with a sales manager and a number of salesmen. In a small station one person may constitute a whole area or may handle programming in addition to sales. Engineering involves all personnel used in running cameras, slides, and film projectors as well as those used to maintain technical engineering standards. Tables 18.1 and

TABLE 18.1.
TV: AVERAGE NUMBER OF EMPLOYEES

FULL-TIME	PART-TIME	ARB MARKETSIZE RANKING
90	8	1–10
103	7	11–25
88	6	26–50
70	3	51–75
55	5	76–100
42	5	101–125
37	6	126–150
30	4	150+
(60)	(5)	(Nationwide average)

TABLE 18.2.
AVERAGE GROSS WEEKLY COMPENSATION, NATIONWIDE: TELEVISION

	1969	1974		1969	1974
Sales Manager	$452	$572	Staff Announcer	$174	$229
National Sales Manager	409	467	News Cameraman	166	184
Local Sales Manager	377	484	Film Department Head	162	194
Head of TV Engineering	270	319	Art Director	160	217
Head of TV Programming	267	321	Staff Photographer	147	—
Salesman	262	270	Filmman	136	155
Head of TV News Operation	254	325	Studio Cameraman	133	129
Promotion Manager	207	234	Productionman	129	146
Newsman	184	196	Traffic Manager	124	188
Technician	179	213	Floorman, Unskilled	119	126
Producer/Director	176	189	Continuity Writer	112	128

SOURCE: "Wages, Hours and Employment/Television 1969" (Washington, D.C.: National Association of Broadcasters,, 1969), p. 4; "Television 1974/Employee Wage & Salary Report, (Washington, D.C.: NAB, 1974), p. 3.

18.2 provide some data on local station employment. Total employment figures for the 726 local stations are over 37,000 people; over 11,000 people are employed by the three networks.

Unlike radio, all television stations are classified as local outlets. As local outlets they can be typed according to several classifications: technical, market size, or network affiliation.

Technically, television stations are grouped according to where their signal falls in the electromagnetic spectrum. The two bands into which all television signals are placed are very high frequency (VHF) and ultra high frequency (UHF). Channels 2 to 13 are VHF. Channels 14 to 83 are UHF. Of the 726 commercial television stations on the air today, 517 are VHF and 209 are UHF. This technical classification is very important because stations located in the VHF band reach a greater geographical area with less power and a clearer signal than stations in the UHF band. Thus, almost without exception, VHF stations are more powerful, better established, and more profitable.

Another important classification is market size, or the number of households a television station reaches. Generally there are three basic market-size groups: (1) major, the 100 or so largest cities in the country; (2) secondary, cities with populations ranging from 50,000 to 125,000; (3) small, cities of less than 50,000 population. Market size is vital in television broadcasting. National advertisers buy time on stations according to market size; thus stations in major markets get most of the nonlocal advertising dollar while the small-market station must depend greatly on local advertising.

The third important basis for television station classification is whether the station is independent or network affiliated. Most television stations want network affiliation because networks are capable of providing the more popular types of programs and hence attract a larger audience. More than 93 percent of all U.S. television stations are network affiliated. A station is seldom independent unless it is in a market of four or more outlets and all three networks already have affiliates.

Characteristics and Roles of Television

Television today is huge, complex, costly, continuous, and competitive. It is a mass entertainer, mass informer, mass persuader, and mass educator.

Television is universal; more than 97 percent of America's homes have TV and viewing television is the dominant leisure-time activity in our society, occupying almost 6.5 hours per day.

TV viewing is an in-home activity and, although multiset homes are increasing, TV usage is still a family or small-group activity rather than individual or large-group experience. The content of the medium is dominated by national organizations that seek to provide general programming for massive, heterogeneous audiences rather than special content for limited, homogeneous minorities.

The medium is the costliest of the electronic media because of the demand placed on it by the 18-hour-per-day schedule of most stations. Only television among the advertising media has sight, sound, motion, and color, which makes it a dynamic sales tool. This accounts for the fact that today it costs advertisers an average price of $90,000 a minute to advertise on network prime-time television.

As we have pointed out, the primary role of the magazine is the custom tailoring of mass communication. Television's primary role is just the opposite. It specializes in the mass distribution of mass communication. It is the channel through which stream mass-produced messages for the widest-possible dissemination. With virtually the entire population having access to television 18 hours a day, 365 days a year, it is the mass medium for reaching most of the people most of the time. Because of this, television is perhaps the least flexible of the mass media. While it can and does provide instant coverage of many important national and international events, the majority of its time is taken up with programs in schedules that have been put together a year or two in advance.

In a more critical sense, television has been looked upon as having two primary roles: reflecting society and evaluating society. Aubrey Singer, a leading executive of the British Broadcasting Corporation, has stated that television's most common role as practiced today is that of "one of the many windows through which we observe, transmit, and reflect our valuation of society to each other. It has little to do with the initial creation of a spiritual trade wind. It is only a sort of air conditioner that processes and gets this wind into homes more quickly."

Nevertheless, Singer and others feel that television has another potential role. Despite television's essentially passive nature, there are times when it does act in its own right; when, according to Singer, it "uses its power of communication not merely to convey other people's images, but rather to create out of its potentialities its own genuine statement." Many people feel that television's coverage of the assassination and funeral of President Kennedy, along with the coverage of the Apollo 11 moon landing, were times when television did create genuine statements, perhaps not so much out of its particular design or structure, but merely by being there to record the event as it was happening. Perhaps the most fitting description of television's role was given by Herbert S. Schlosser, former president of NBC, when he said that "television is a source of fun and laughter. It is the bearer of good news and bad. It is a teacher and it is also a salesman. It is theater and sports arena. It is a political forum, and it is a course in government."

When was the last time you and your parents agreed as to whether the stereo was on loud enough? When was the last time you took your grandparents to a discothèque? How long has it been since you sat alone feeling sorry for yourself with that special private album that belonged to only you and a million other teen-agers? How old were you when you bought your last 45-rpm. record? How much did you pay for the last record album you bought?

Nowhere is the cultural gap between young and old so evident as it is in rock music. No medium is more involved in the All-American games of dating, romance, and heartbreak than is the phonograph. No purchase other than an automobile is more time-consuming, costly, and used by students than the "ultimate" sound system. If any medium belongs to young people, it is the sound-recording industry.

Historical Perspectives

Sound recording celebrated its 100th year in 1977, which makes it the oldest of the electronic media. But, until recently, the potential of sound recording had not been fully exploited. The use of the term "recording" is generic and refers to a variety of sound-reproduction systems including cylinders, disks, records, reel-to-reel tapes, cartridges, and cassettes. Like other electronic media, the phonograph requires machines to record and playback the

Sound Recording

content, but unlike the others, consumers have direct control over what they use. Individuals buy records and play them when and where they want. Recordings stop time in the sense that the event can be repeated because it is stored on records and tapes.

In no medium has the consumer been more fickle and erratic than in the sound-recording medium. The music may go round and round, but the business goes up and down. Sound-recording history shows it to be the least predictable of the mass media.

There are three major periods in the history of sound recording: (1) 1877–1923, a time of discovery, experimentation, and exploitation; (2) 1924–45, a time of technical improvement, financial disaster, and consumer ambivalence; (3) 1946 to the present, a time of technical rebirth, cultural involvement, and big business.

1877–1923. Two men working on different continents contributed to the birth of the phonograph. In April 1877 Charles Cros filed a paper with the French Academy of Science that described a system of sound reproduction, but the French physicist never produced a working model. In the United States, Thomas Edison and his machinist, John Kruesi, actually built a functional sound record-playback device in December 1877. This phonograph used a hand-cranked metal cylinder wrapped in tinfoil for recording purposes, but they applied for patents on a disk system as well as the cylinder. Having invented what he considered to be a dictating machine, Edison did little to exploit his invention. For the next decade, the phonograph was little more than a traveling sideshow, exhibiting the marvels of a "talking machine."

Chinchester Bell and Charles Sumner Tainter in 1881 began work on an improved version of Edison's phonograph using wax cylinders. They applied for a patent in 1885 for a gramophone that utilized wax-coated cardboard cylinders instead of tinfoil. By 1886, however, Edison had returned to work on a reusable solid-wax cylinder called the phonogram. Jesse H. Lippencott's purchase of the business rights to both the Edison and Bell-Tainter devices in 1888 brought an end to what was becoming a serious patent dispute. The dream of Lippencott was that the phonograph would become the major means of business communication by using reusable cylinders that lasted from two to four minutes at a time. In 1889, Edison issued the first commercial recordings, and the Automatic Phonograph Company's "nickelodeon" appeared.

During this same period another American, Emile Berliner, was experimenting with a system that used flat disks instead of cylinders. Berliner's gramophone, which was patented in November 1887, used a governor to control the speed. The advantages of the disk over the cylinder were (1) the disk could be mass-produced from an etched negative master, whereas each early cylinder had to be an original; (2) the shellac record was harder and more durable than the wax cylinder; (3) the disk was more easily stored than the cylinder; (4) the disk produced greater volume and better quality from a simpler machine.

The last decade of the nineteenth century was a time of company warfare with everybody trying to drive everyone else out of business: Edison gained control of North American Phonograph as a part of the Edison Phonograph Company; Berliner formed the United States Gramophone Company; the Columbia Phonograph Company entered the business. In 1901 Eldridge Johnson formed the Victor Talking Machine Company. Johnson made the phonograph business respectable and profitable for Victor as well as for the 10,000 dealers who eventually sold Victor's wares.

Victor, using the Berliner-Johnson system, and Columbia, operating under Edison and Bell-Tainter patents, dominated the phonograph industry for the first 20 years of the twentieth century. Assets for Victor grew to over $30 million by 1917 with Americans buying 25 million shellac two-sided disks (introduced by Germany's Odeon Company in 1905) a year. As prices came down, audiences increased. After an initial coolness toward the medium, famous artists turned to the phonograph as a means of expanding their audiences, and millions of their records were sold. Enrico Caruso did more than any other artist to legitimize the medium; over the years, record fans rewarded him with over $5 million, tax-free. The industry was worldwide; interlocking patents permitted the sale of records everywhere.

From 1905 to 1923, few significant technical changes took place in the medium, and only minor changes were made in the recording device. Although the speaker horn was enclosed in the cabinet of the first Victrola (1906), the tone arm was modified, and frequency range of the disk was improved, the scratchy quality persisted. Many musical instruments could not be used because they did not record well. Artists stood in front of a huge bell or horn and shouted their songs onto masters. It was a far cry from the concert hall. Nevertheless, in 1921, 100 million records were sold.

By 1922, however, there were over 500 radio stations on the air giving audiences "free music." The handwriting was on the wall.

1924–45. Economically, the 1920s were expected to be a boom time: low-cost, reliable sets were available, and people had the money to buy them. But the development of radio broadcasting had two major influences on the recording industry: (1) developments in electronic-radio technology (microphones and speakers) led to significant improvements in the technical quality of the phonograph; (2) the public acceptance of radio created an economic recession for the recording industry. Radio provided "live" rather than recorded music, and radio produced a better sound. The recording business was rapidly disintegrating. Then Western Electric patented an electrical recording process and demonstrated the system for Victor, but Eldridge Johnson declined to participate in a project that had anything to do with radio, the medium that was destroying his business. Finally, in financial desperation, the phonograph industry moved into "radio recording."

The first commercial, electrically produced recordings were marketed by both Victor and Columbia in 1925. The new process opened an entirely new aural dimension. The electrical recording process expanded the frequency range, could be played back louder without "blast," allowed musicians to work in a studio setup approximating the physical arrangements of live performances, and improved the home phonograph with a dynamic loudspeaker. That same year the Brunswick Company marketed a low-cost electric phonograph with speakers of brilliant quality compared to previous mechanical horns. By 1926, whole symphonies and operas were being recorded on albums of up to 20 disks.

Despite the technical progress, the medium continued to lose ground—first to radio, then to talking pictures. In 1928, RCA purchased Victor and discontinued production of record players in favor of radio receivers. Edison had previously stopped all phonograph production in 1927. The depression hit the recording industry harder than it did any other medium. Record sales dropped to a tenth of what they had been, and few playback devices were marketed. In 1932, only 6,000,000 records were sold and 40,000 machines produced. The phonograph seemed headed for extinction.

The one bright spot in the mid-1930s was the development of the jukebox. By 1940, more than 250,000 "jukes" were using 15 million records a year made by bands of the "swing era." Despite this public consumption of popular music, the record business was still dominated by classical music, limited by drained financial resources, and hindered by unimaginative marketing.

Several business changes also stimulated medium growth. Jack Kapp and E. R. Lewis bought and reorganized U.S. Decca. They produced 35-cent records to compete with the 75-cent versions of their major competitors. By 1939 Decca was the second-ranking company (behind RCA Victor) and sold 19 million units. In 1940 RCA and Decca sold two of every three records.

Columbia, in serious financial difficulty, was purchased by CBS in December 1938. Edward Wallerstein, a former RCA executive, was hired to rebuild Columbia's fortunes. Wallerstein signed a large number of successful pop musicians and almost cornered that market. He cut the price of Columbia's classical albums to $1 and, overnight, sales jumped 1,500 percent. By late 1941, a revitalized Columbia had helped the industry sell 127 million disks. Radio-phonograph combinations were also selling well.

World War II destroyed all hope for the industry's immediate rebirth. Shellac, required for disk production, became unavailable, and electronics manufacturers turned to war work. And on July 31, 1942, the American Federation of Musicians (AFM), headed by James Caesar Petrillo, refused to allow its members to cut any more records. The AFM was concerned that "canned" music would cut back employment opportunities. The record companies initially refused to negotiate, but a year later, economic pressure forced Decca Records to allot up to five cents per record sold to the AFM's fund for unemployed musicians in order to bring out the first original-cast album, *Oklahoma*. In mid-1944 RCA and Columbia accepted similar terms. AFM's gains were wiped out in 1947 when the Taft-Hartley Act made it illegal to collect royalties in this fashion. That year was the best ever for the recording industry—$200 million.

1946 to the Present. During the period following World War II, five major forces revolutionized the phonograph industry: (1) technical achievements in electromagnetic recording, (2) improvements in records and playback systems, (3) television's destruction of radio's old format, (4) changes in marketing procedures, and (5) a revolution in the content of the medium.

ELECTRICAL MAGNETIC RECORDING. Electromagnetic recordings had been experimented with as early as 1889, when a Danish engineer, Vladimir Poulsen, produced a recording on steel wire. Later, paper was used; later still, plastic tape.

In July 1945 John T. Mullin, then in the Army Signal Corps, came across a sophisticated magnetic tape recorder in a Radio Frankfurt station in Bad Nauheim, Germany, where the American Armed Forces Radio Network was supervising a German staff. This *Magnetophone* was a truly superior sound system, without the background noise so typical of phonograph recordings. Mullin brought two machines and 50 rolls of tape back to the States and in May 1946 demonstrated the system to a meeting of engineers. In June 1947 Mullin and a partner were invited to show the system to Bing Crosby and the staff of his ABC radio show. Mullin was hired, Ampex duplicated and improved the machines, and the 3-M Company started producing tape.

Tape recording revolutionized the record business. Real-time performances gave way to multitrack, engineered-time performances, with Capitol and Decca the first record companies to take advantage of the new system. By

1949, most major studios were using noise-free tape recordings for masters; these were then edited and transferred to disks.

The 1950s saw extensive use of reel-to-reel tapes, and technical experiments during these years led to a tape bonanza in the 1960s. Today there are three basic tape systems:

1. Reel-to-reel systems, which can be edited and have both playback and record capability. High-quality units are fairly large even in portable models.

2. Cartridge systems (1958). These are compact, have great selectivity in 8-track models, but do not usually have record capability.

3. Cassette systems (1964), which are portable but cannot be easily edited. They have record capability, however. Blank cassettes cost less than $1, and dubs are easily made.

The introduction of tape improved sound quality, provided detailed aural separation of instruments, allowed for the most minute editing (e.g., coughs, miscues), and led to the engineer becoming a vital force in "mixing" the final product. The Beatles' *Sgt. Peppers Lonely Hearts Club Band*, Stevie Wonder's *Songs in the Key of Life*, and the albums of every artist from Diana Ross to the Electric Light Orchestra used tape recording creatively.

RECORD AND RECORD-PLAYER IMPROVEMENTS. In 1948, Columbia introduced the microgroove 33⅓-rpm. long-play (LP) record developed by Peter Goldmark. This was far superior to the 78-rpm. shellac record. The 33⅓ could handle nearly 25 minutes of music per side because of its slower speed, larger size, and narrower grooves; the 78 produced only three to five minutes of music. The 33⅓ records were made of plastic "biscuits" and were so resilient that LPs were called "unbreakable."

Rather than submit to a coup by Columbia, RCA Victor in 1949 brought out its seven-inch 45-rpm. records in both single and extended-play (EP) versions. The center hole was far larger than that on either the 78s or 33⅓s. This meant that the consumer needed both a larger spindle and slower speed to adapt to the 45s.

The "Battle of the Speeds" lasted two years, and both Columbia and RCA spent a great deal promoting their products. RCA produced record players for their 45s and sold them for less than cost. By 1950, when the speed war ended, record sales had dropped $50 million below the 1947 level. The consumer, uncertain as to which system would be adopted, bought neither one. The companies reached a compromise that established the 33⅓ LP album as the means of recording classical works and collections by pop artists; the 45-rpm. record was for pop singles. By 1955, 78-rpm. records were no longer in production.

During this same period, significant improvements were made in the sound quality of record players, and high-fidelity recordings became possible with advances in electromagnetic recording-studio techniques. The hi-fi boom lasted nearly ten years. Stereophonic, or multichannel, sound systems, demonstrated in 1957 and marketed in 1958, made monaural systems obsolete. An equipment boom has continued for phonograph manufacturers. Today, all LPs produced by the major companies are hi-fi stereo albums, and even the 45 is a total stereo production.

The home quadraphonic sound-recording unit of today may be composed of a variety of playback units including a stereo phonograph, a cassette, cartridge or reel-to-reel tape system, and an AM-FM radio, with speaker sets throughout the house. In addition, 8-track units have become important accessories in automobiles. The component system is now a major part of the international electronics business.

THE EMERGENCE OF TELEVISION.   From 1946 to 1952 television began to emerge as the dominant mass entertainment medium. Both radio and films were forced to adapt to survive economically. Once the Federal Communications Commission lifted the "freeze" on local TV-station allocations in 1952, there was no holding back video broadcasting. Financial conditions forced network radio to cut back operations, and local radio stations had to develop a new source of programming. The music, news, talk, and sports format evolved as the program policy of most U.S. radio stations. *Music* was the dominant element in the mix. Since the recording industry *is* popular music, the phonograph record became the content of radio. This provided free exposure of the record industry's products to a huge, affluent young audience of potential buyers, and the boom was on. It is ironic, considering past history, that the radio and recording industries are such good "bedfellows" now.

MARKETING PROCEDURES.   At the end of World War II, the majors controlled the industry and released 40 to 100 new records each week; local dealers marked up the records about 40 percent. There was a "straight-line" marketing system from manufacturer to distributor to retailer to consumer. It was a tight, profitable system for everyone except those outside the system.

Independent producers, however, produced records and made "stars" of unknowns. This meant that not only were small retailers faced with the speed war and with pricing and stock-duplication headaches, but an increasing number of "off-brands" and a widening variety of musical types forced larger investments or an inadequate inventory. In addition, promotion people replaced salesmen. The promotion staff worked with radio stations, and the retailer was left to his own devices. The shift in emphasis was from a push to a pull marketing strategy.

The real crack in the majors' armor was the profit motive. The majors controlled the talent and the music, the studios and the manufacturing, as well as distribution. They were secure, so they rented studios to the independents. These were the only studios the new labels had available, and even though they paid high prices—it was the only game in town—it taught them the tools of the trade. In order to "cover" hits (record a song first issued by another company with your artist) of the independents, the majors each set up a subsidiary: RCA (Bluebird), Columbia (Okeh), Decca (Brunswick), and so forth.

The ways of selling records changed in the mid-1950s: (1) discount outlets (low-margin retailers) offered significantly reduced prices on all popular records; (2) the major record producers, noting the success of small record societies, started their own record clubs; (3) rack-jobbers rented space in dime stores, drugstores, grocery stores, and anywhere else one would be likely to buy a record on impulse. All these marketing innovations hurt traditional retail-sales outlets—record and department stores. But business was so brisk that the traditional dealers' complaints carried little weight with the record companies. Today, rack-jobbers and national record-store chains dominate retail record sales.

The "shelf price" for a $7.98 album may run from $5.50 to $7.00, and "specials" drop prices even lower. Singles retail for about $1 in most discount outlets. The consumer who shops selectively can still get a relative bargain.

In 1965, Paul Kives founded K-Tel, a television merchandiser of other companies' older hits through the mails and selected retail outlets. Over 225 labels have leased cuts for the 325 albums released worldwide by K-Tel. They sold 15 million units in 1976 for sales of $39 million, and over the years have paid $15 million in royalties to record companies. The television merchandiser is a low-cost force in the industry.

THE REVOLUTION IN CONTENT.   Popular music in the United States today reflects the diversity of America's "melting pot" culture. Thirty years ago, this was not the case. The four majors (RCA Victor, Columbia, Decca, and Capitol) and three emerging companies (MGM, Mercury, and London) produced essentially three kinds of music: (1) white popular, (2) classical, and (3) show (theatrical). Each company had an all-powerful artist and repertoire (A&R) person, who was in effect the company's record producer. This individual selected all the songs and the artists to record them. Performers were *told* what they would record and when a "take" was acceptable. Each major also told their artists which potential hits on the other labels they would "cover." In effect, a very small number of people controlled the music. It was the independent record producers who generally spearheaded new musical trends. As a result, they were responsible for many structural changes in the business. As minority musical tastes were identified as economically viable, independents found the talent to serve them.

Rock music is the only musical form that is indigenous to the electronic media. In fact, rock is the only music where the recording is the original, and the live performance is the imitation. *Rock and roll* is a four-letter word that has been defined best by the music critic Richard Penniman as *Awop-bopaloobopalopbamboom,* which translated means there is no satisfactory definition of this musical form. Rock is heavy, loud, electric, blatant, simple, immediate; it is a rejection of parts of adult society, often committed to social change; it is pop culture, "people music." It comes from and to young people. Every teen-ager is a potential "star," and the young listener is an active participant in the musical experience.

Rock music is and always has been a direct assault on adult sensibility. It purposely alienates adults and that is one reason young people respond to it—it is their culture. In the beginning there was no content; it was intentionally meaningless. The lack of meaning, the crudeness, the heavy-handed beat, and the obvious lack of respect angered some adults. Many young people understood that fact and loved it. Parents might think that the performers are punk kids with no training and experience—that might be why it is irrationally beautiful to teen-agers. Punk rock attempted to re-create that atmosphere of rejection.

The loudness of rock encapsulates the listener. One physically, tactilely, feels rock as well as listens to it. The phonograph creates a sound barrier that insulates an individual; it is a self-contained, mentally isolated environment. It is a means of escape from other individuals in the same physical space.

Rock music dominates the content of the recording medium. Young people select the content and perform it. But most important, the young *buy* it. Youth dominate the medium economically.

Rock comes out of five traditions in American music:

1. *Rhythm and blues* (R&B) provided the horns, the black beat, and a frank approach to the sexual experience. R&B was rural music urbanized for southern blacks who migrated to northern cities. The form was influenced by jazz, boogie, and the blues. Gospel traditions of "rocking and reeling" were critical in its development. The independents were the major source of R&B records because it was "race" music to the majors. Chess, Atlan-

tic, King, Imperial, and others cut the R&B originals, which were "whitewashed" by the majors who covered their records. But it still introduced white kids to the black R&B sound.

2. *Country and western* (C&W) provided the first "stars," the basic instrument (the guitar), and "songs of life and pain." Jimmy Rodgers, "the father of country music," fused the blues with country. Then western swing bands took the "hillbilly" out of it. The music spoke to the lower class (now the middle class) about the traditions of poverty, a hard life, and the sadness of "sneakin' around." It held to traditional values and was slow to change.

3. *White popular ("pop") music* provided sentimentality, the "crooner" sex symbol, and industrial knowhow. "Pop" was money, power, status, and respectability; as well as in the control of the establishment that merchandises artists and music. It was *the* music for most Americans until the rock-'n'-roll revolution.

4. *Folk* provided the tradition of untrained writers performing their own music, the participation of the audience, and the rebellion against those in power. Folk music was "people" music, by and for them. It held that the "amateur" professional had to be close to his "roots." For years, folk had been integrated with the blues, country, and gospel traditions.

5. *Jazz* provided musicians with instrumental skills and a tradition of racial integration. Jazz came upriver from rural southern America. It developed from a fusion of both black and white musical traditions and innovations which spawned "swing," "bop," "cool," and so forth.

All five forms have since the early 1950s been integrally involved in the rock mainstream.

Rock music was an inevitable outgrowth of both white and black musical traditions and social conditions. The two media most responsible for its development, the phonograph and radio, were colorblind; rock 'n' roll was a part of desegregation in the United States.

Alan Freed, a disk jockey, is credited with coining the phrase "rock 'n' roll" in the early 1950s. But rock did not crystallize until 1955 when one monster record, Bill Haley and the Comets' "Rock Around the Clock," sold over 15 million copies. In three areas—pop, R&B, and C&W—there were consistent hits that bordered on rock 'n' roll, including Johnny Ray's "Cry" (1951), Tennessee Ernie Ford's "Shotgun Boogie" (1950), and Lloyd Price's "Lawdy Miss Clawdy" (1952).

The first superstar of rock 'n' roll was the late Elvis Presley, a hip-swinging, greasy-looking, brilliant performer. The period from 1956 to 1958 was the "age of Elvis." He was James Dean's and Marlon Brando's rebels set to music. Elvis had 14 straight million-seller 45s. Presley was RCA's best $40,000 investment, which was the price they paid Sun Records for his contract. Sam Phillips, the founder of Sun Records, used that $40,000 to create "rockabilly." The "sale of Elvis" made it possible for him to develop Carl Perkins, Jerry Lee Lewis, and Gene Vincent.

The music field became racially integrated from 1954 to 1960. White performers sang black music and sold it to white consumers. This later made it possible for black singers to sing black music and sell it to white consumers. Previously, blacks like Nat "King" Cole, the Ink Spots, and Lena Horne had sung white music for "white folks." Rock helped legitimatize the black beat and black themes.

Elvis Presley, Jerry Lee Lewis, the Everly Brothers, and Buddy Holly sang rock that had black roots. This opened the door for blacks doing rock. Little Richard (Penniman) sold a million copies of "Tutti Frutti" and "Long Tall Sally"; Fats Domino sold 50 million records to youngsters before 1960; Larry Price did "Bony Maronie"; the Coasters and the Drifters opened the door for other stylized black groups to reach white audiences. Most important was Chuck Berry, an extraordinary writer as well as performer, whose "Maybelline" was one of the first black monster rock hits.

In the late 1950s, rock created a whole series of noncontact sports, starting with Chubby Checker's "twist," then the "monkey," "frug," "mashed potato," ad infinitum. Nobody touched anybody—the body movement was detached yet sensual. As soon as a dance was adopted by adults, it was often discarded by their children. The discothèque became the nightclub based on recorded music and recorded dances. *Saturday Night Fever* (1977) legitimized the form and created a sociodrama or a "rebel without a cause a go-go" movie.

The biggest fad of the early 1960s was strictly white middle-class surfing music that rejected the corporation life for the beach buggy, bikini, and surfboard. Brian Wilson and the Beach Boys made hot rods, motorcycles, and beach bums into national symbols. The teen-aged pop stars of that era—Frankie Avalon, Neil Sedaka, and Paul Anka—are alive and well and living in Las Vegas. Pat Boone, who "covered" more R&B hits than anyone else, is making middle-of-the-road commercials. Ricky Nelson, who had real talent, is living off television royalties.

During 1959–60, the government investigated rock music. The record companies regularly paid disk jockeys for plugging records; this "payola" and other overt types of "hype" were stopped, but "hype" is so integral a part of the entertainment industry it is almost impossible to stop. Stopping payola did not stop rock because rock was a significant cultural force with young people.

By the 1960s rock was also an economic force, although the music establishment and rock 'n' roll were still at odds. Several song publishers attempted to bridge that gap. The Motown sound of Barry Gordy, through his talented writers and the great artists who recorded on his labels, served as a black bridge between middle-class musical taste (the music establishment) and rock-'n'-roll America. By the mid-1960s, three of every four songs recorded by Motown artists made the charts.

The white transitional team was Don Kirshner and Al Nevins of Aldon Music, a Philadelphia-based publishing company, who supplied songs to the majors using then unknown writers, such as Neil Sedaka, Carole King, and Neil Diamond. They developed a style called the "Brill Building Sound" that came to cover all the music of the urban east. It was, in effect, Tin Pan Alley music for teen-agers. Aldon Music was swallowed up by Screen Gems. It all culminated in the manufactured supergroup and sound of The Monkees.

Although rock is an American creation, it reached fruition under the English. If the late 1950s belong to Elvis, the late 1960s belong to the Beatles. This shaggy bunch of household words (John, Paul, George, and Ringo) had the top five records in America in April 1964. Every album they cut was a million seller. They were a cultural phenomenon as well as a musical phenomenon. They were artist-poet performers. Without a doubt they influenced the rock scene more than anyone in the 1960s with the possible exception of Bob Dylan. Their uniqueness, however, was not only the quantity of their work and its financial success; it was the quality of the Beatles' music that set them apart.

The Beatles reached perhaps rock's highest artistic summit in June 1967, when *Sgt. Pepper's Lonely Hearts Club Band* was released. That it would be a gold mine was a foregone conclusion; but it was the innovation, vision, beauty, and expertise that set off the musical reaction that is still with us. The Beatles' quarrels, Apple failures, lackluster *Let It Be* movie, fratricidal Klein war, breakup, and various personal problems and idiosyncracies cannot dim the contribution of "Sgt. Pepper" and the great musical cartoon, *Yellow Submarine*, that it spawned. They *are* "the once and future" Beatles.

Mick Jagger, the ultimate rock showman with the pouting satanic style, drove the Rolling Stones to the forefront. Their personal hassles with drugs, the law, and the Altamont concert killings somehow added to the mystique their hard-core followers loved. They remain the best rock "touring show."

Tommy, the milestone recorded by The Who and rerecorded by everybody else, and then made into a movie, is the rock opera achievement, along with *Jesus Christ, Superstar*, which became a show-business phenomenon that only *Hair* could approach in the late 1960s.

In the mid-1960s Bob Dylan was the most influential American pop musician. His music was socially conscious; since 1966, many pop singles in the "Top 100" have become committed to social causes. Many young people are interested in peace, ecology, race relations, loneliness, and love. Their music has reflected it. Rock music is part of a cultural life style. The 1970 Woodstock Music and Art Festival was a celebration of this rock-youth culture. Rock music is, in effect, rock politics, rock economics, and rock sociology. Rock is so powerful that nationalities have become sublimated in the new rock-youth culture.

As the 1970s broke, three deaths in rapid succession hit the industry. Jimi Hendrix choked to death on barbituate-induced vomit while asleep. Janis Joplin died of a heroin overdose. Jim Morrison (The Doors) had a heart attack in a bathtub after a series of drunken-lewd performances that lacked professionalism and destroyed his career. It was as though rock stars, like movie stars before them, could not control their success.

The war in Vietnam and the social protest movements set in musical motion by Bob Dylan in the 1960s continued through the end of America's most unpopular war and Nixon's "Watergate" administration. In the 1970s, James Brown's support of Hubert Humphrey and the Allman Brothers concert for President Jimmy Carter have, along with other rock-politic moves, legitimized the form. In the mid-1970s the heavy metal sounds were dominated by Led Zepplin and Bad Company. The glitter rock of Kiss and the rock theater of Alice Cooper held sway as rock became "show biz." Stevie Wonder was in command of the Grammy's every time he cut an album. The "wars" were over. Young and old kids were dancing again to the reggae, salsa, and the white-black, black-white disco sounds. Bruce Springsteen made the cover of *Time* and *Newsweek* as the establishment proclaimed the great white hope of rock. But Barry Manilow wore the crown, and Elton John and Bernie Taupin, a great singer-showman and his songwriter, made the million-dollar deals. Happy times were here again.

Music has gone into and come out of a rock-'n'-roll dynamic. Rock music was created out of rhythm and blues, country and western, folk, jazz, and white pop, but rock has also had an impact on each of its parent forms and spawned:

1. *Soul rock*, typified by James Brown, Joe Simon, Wilson Pickett, Al Green, and Boz Scaggs.

2. *Country rock*, typified by Kris Kristofferson, The Band, Waylon Jennings, and Jimmy Buffet.

3. *Folk rock*, typified by Donovan, Buffalo Springfield, and Gordon Lightfoot.

4. *Jazz rock*, typified by the Brothers Johnson; Chicago; Blood, Sweat, and Tears; George Benson; and the Blackbyrds.

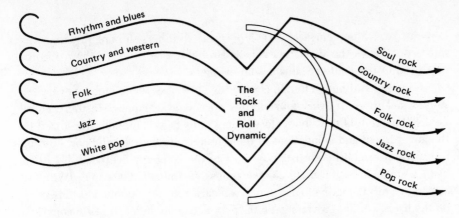

FIGURE 19.1. *The Rock-'n'-Roll Dynamic*

5. *Pop rock*, typified by Bary Manilow, Elton John, Steely Dan, and David Bowie.

The older forms remain in both the pure state as well as the hybrids. But the crossovers have been phenomenal. Olivia Newton-John, a pop singer, is a country star; Glen Campbell's albums are on both the C&W and pop charts; Boz Scaggs sings soul but is a white rock star; Chick Corea is a jazz musician followed by everybody. Pop music is rock music, so much so that it is hard to find it anymore.

A rock is something to throw in order to smash. Roll means turn over. Rock 'n' roll has smashed and turned over many musical traditions. Many depression-reared adults cannot fathom rock's style; that is why, for young people, it is important to smash their instruments, and that is why Mick Jagger's life style is so important to young rockers. Rock is a raw, sexual, antisocial, young experience, and it is the economic backbone of the recording industry.

The Scope of Sound Recording

Today the sale of records and tapes is about $3 billion per year. The public, with money to spend, spends more of it on records than it does on textbooks. In terms of dollar distribution consumers spend: 70 percent of their money on records and 30 percent on tapes; 90 percent on albums and 10 percent on singles. The sale of singles has gone down, albums up; tapes have stabilized over the past few years. Rock sounds account for most sales: contemporary rock-soul, 61 percent; country and western, 12 percent; middle of the road, 11 percent; jazz, 5 percent; classical, 5 percent; all others, 6 percent. American music dominates the world market; and roughly one of every three records produced in the United States is sold overseas.

Sound recording is a tough, competitive business where eight of every ten singles and three of every four albums do not make money. In the classical field, 90 percent of the albums lose money; this field is literally subsidized by the government and foundations in their grants to orchestras. Big new hits and the work of established artists pay most of the company overhead. To break even, a single must sell about 25,000 copies, an album 85,000 copies. When an artist has a hit, the individual or group can earn a royalty of from 5 to 15 percent on the list price. Songwriters get $.0275 for each sale under the 1976 copyright law. A single that sells a million copies can earn the writer $27,500. One measure of success is the charts of the leading hits in trade magazines such as *Billboard, Cashbox,* and *Record World.*

It is crucial for a company to keep a stable of successful artists. Since the lifetime of performers as well as music is relatively short in rock, new talent is constantly being recruited. One supergroup can make a company. In 1970 Apple Records ranked tenth in albums (3.4 percent of the slots on the "Top 100" lists), and all but one entry belonged to the Beatles. In 1977–78, Fleetwood Mac's album *Rumors* was in the Top 10 albums for over a year and made its artists millionaires.

The economics of the industry work out so that the producer earns from 40 to 50 percent of the retail price; distributors get from 15 to 25 percent; the retailer gets the remaining 20 to 30 percent, depending on his markup. The rack-jobber pays the record company 40 to 50 percent and the retailer a flat fee of 10 to 15 percent of total sales, which means that the jobber keeps 35 to 40 percent of every record he markets.

Table 19.1 illustrates the relative position of the 10 top corporations in the record business in 1976. Although independents and small labels are viable, the large majors dominate the market.

The individual artist or group is usually advanced money to produce an album; that advance must also take care of touring expenses, however, which for groups can cost $5,000 per week. For example, say that a group gets $70,000 for an album. Production costs are roughly $50,000, which leaves $20,000 to tour an average of ten weeks. If the group is new, it can expect only $1,000–$3,000 a week in pay. If the album sells 50,000 copies, the group's royalty is $31,500, which the company keeps to pay back part of the advance. This leaves the group in arrears $38,500 for the advance, in debt for the tour, and in need of money to produce a second album. The company does a bit better. It earns ($.94 per album) $47,000 on album sales plus $31,500 in artist royalty for a total

TABLE 19.1.

THE TOP 10 RECORD CORPORATIONS

CORPORATION	% OF SHARE	NUMBER
WEA	24.2	307
CBS	16.1	194
Capitol	8.3	117
RCA	7.5	101
A&M	7.0	80
Motown	4.9	59
ABC	4.3	82
Polygram	4.3	83
United Artists	3.8	46
Arista	3.4	49

SOURCE: *Billboard* February 26, 1977.

of $78,500, which gives them $8,500 above the advance. These facts notwithstanding, the superstars earn from $2 million to $6 million each year from song royalties, concerts, singles, albums, promotions, and tours.

Nobody can become a rock star without recordings, and no record can be a hit without airplay. Payola, although it is more subtle, is still prominent. The money is so attractive that the "mob" has moved in and is pirating records and wholesaling them. Small-timers dub tapes from records and make a profit. Payola and piracy are two problems that seriously affect the industry.

The Structure and Organization of Sound Recording

Many individuals and groups affect the creation, development, and sales of recorded music. Essentially there are 14 categories of persons under four major subheadings that determine the success of a given record (see figure 19.2). Before a record can be a success, four groups must support it: (1) the creative element, (2) the business element, (3) the information-distribution element, and (4) the consumer element. No single element can create a hit or prevent one.

The Creative Element. The artist-musician creates the material; many successful rock performers write as well as perform their own material. The engineer-mixer-technician manipulates the inherent qualities of the medium to create recorded music. Performers are aided, guided, and supervised by a business consultant, generally called an agent. Performers also have managers to handle details and run concert tours. Both agents and managers are paid a percentage of the performer's income, usually 10 percent. Artist and repertoire

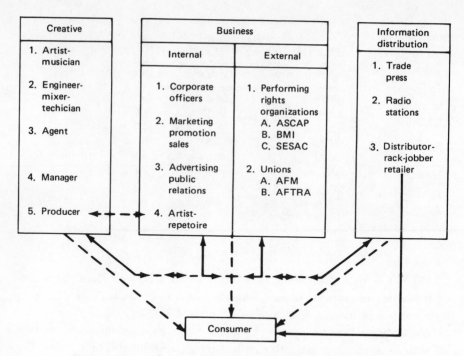

FIGURE 19.2. *The Structure of the Music-Recording Industry*

(A&R) people serve a similar function for production companies. The record producer often also serves an A&R function; the task here is not to select the groups, but to get them taped in a satisfactory manner.

The Business Element. There are two subcategories: (1) internal, individuals within the record company; and (2) external, groups outside the record company that have a significant impact on the music business.

INTERNAL. Decisions to exploit the creative element are made by high-level corporate officers who approve the financial appropriations considered essential to the successful marketing of the record. They provide the capital and reap the greatest portion of the profits. The marketer-promoter-sales representative devises the best way to get visibility for the record. If an established star or group makes a record, there is less difficulty than if it is made by an unknown. The field representative can promote only what his company puts out, and there is no way to force radio stations to play the company's product. Since all the company's records cannot be pushed with equal effort, the field representative must promote one unit in preference to another. The advertising and public relations staffs prepare trade announcements for radio stations, distributors, and retailers, as well as consumer advertising for the general public. Most of the effort and money is spent on trade materials. In effect, records are "pushed" through the distributor-retailer by the trade press and airplay, rather than "pulled" through by consumer demand. The A&R person is a talent scout who seeks the next "stars" in the field. Other A&R people, not associated with established companies, act as go-betweens for the artist and the producer.

EXTERNAL. Publishing-rights organizations collect performance payments, which come primarily from radio and television stations. Under the copyright law of 1976 each jukebox pays an annual tax of $8 (which is over $4 million additional income to songwriters). The three organizations handling publishing rights are (1) The American Society of Artists, Composers, and Publishers (ASCAP), which has about 18,000 members and collects 67 percent of the fees; (2) Broadcast Music, Incorporated (BMI), which has over 21,000 writers and 9,500 publishers as clients and accounts for 32 percent of all fees; (3) Sesac, a small family-owned company that does about $2 million business annually for its 200 publishers and 375 catalogues. Broadcasters normally subscribe to both ASCAP and BMI.

The two major labor unions in the recording business are the American Federation of Television and Radio Artists (AFTRA) and the American Federation of Musicians (AFM). Record companies are "closed shops": vocalists and musicians must join a union in order to record. Union "scale" is set for every aspect of the business from studio sessions to club appearances to concert tours. The unions are a real power in the music business.

The Information-Distribution Element.   This area has three participants: the trade press; radio-station programmers; and the distributors, rack-jobbers, and retailers. The trade press serves as a general information and evaluation source. Four major publications serve this function. *Billboard* is considered the most reliable source for business and creative information. *Cashbox* and *Record World* are less important but serve the same function. *Rolling Stone* concentrates on creative evaluation and has a wide public as well as trade readership. All four aid in the selection process by featuring articles on what records are expected to be successful. Radio-station programmers greatly affect the sales performance of many records—if the local D.J.s do not play the records, the public cannot become acquainted with them, and audiences are less likely to buy them. Stations must choose a limited number of songs each week to add to their play list. Only four or five of the 200 singles and 100 LPs received each week ever get extensive airplay, which is more valuable than any advertising. The distributors, rack-jobbers, and retailers are also crucial to the whole process. If a record is not in stock, it cannot be bought. And since the life of popular music, especially singles, is short, it is crucial that the record be available immediately upon public demand.

The Consumer Element.   Finally, there is the audience, the consumer of phonograph records. This individual makes the final decision as to whether a record will be a success. A million seller is, in the end, determined by audiences. The gold record presented to an artist attests to the fact that a million consumers bought a single or that 500,000 people bought an album. Platinum awards have been added for "supersellers" (2 million singles—1 million albums).

The audience can select only from what is available. Therefore, each of the above elements serves as a gatekeeper in phonograph communication. The artist, the manager, the A&R person, the producer, the policy maker, the publicist, the promoter, the unions, the trade press, the station, and the distributor-retailer can hinder success by not doing the job. Nevertheless, even if they all support a given record, the public can and often does prefer to buy something else.

The "Music Flow" of the Music Business.   In order to understand how records get into the hands of consumers, the flow chart in figure 19.3 is helpful. The record companies send copies of records to the trade press and radio stations for publicity and airplay. They also take out ads and get stories about artists printed and broadcast. Performers hit the road to push their recording. These road shows or concert tours are covered by the press and stations and attended by consumers. Records are distributed by the company distribution system or general distributors to rack-jobbers, who sell their units in nonrecord store outlets; record store chains; and one-stops, which service jukebox operators as well as consumers. Record clubs are another source of sales for the company.

The consumer is influenced by concerts, radio plays, jukeboxes, and the press; and then buys records from clubs, one-stops, chains, and low-margin retailers.

Each year the consumer makes selective purchases from the 6,000 singles and 4,000 LPs released annually by the record companies.

Characteristics and Roles of Sound Recording

The record industry is a mass media institution that has grown around a physical reproduction system. And there are very specific characteristics of this medium.

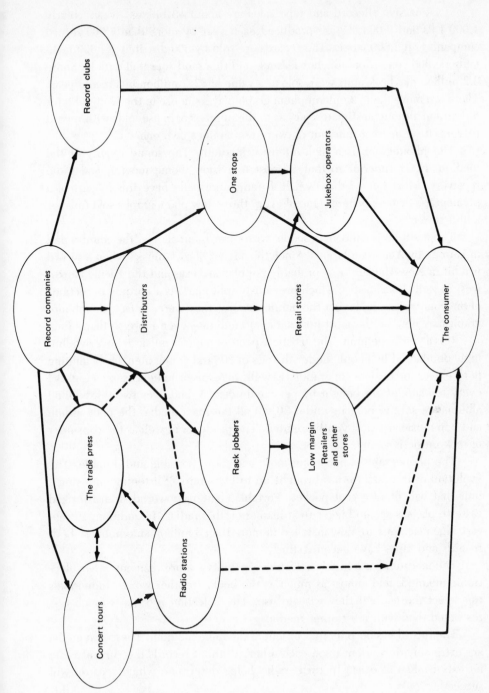

FIGURE 19.3. *Flow Chart of Records to Consumers*

Nodes: Record clubs, One stops, Jukebox operators, Record companies, Distributors, Retail stores, The consumer, The trade press, Rack jobbers, Low margin Retailers and other stores, Concert tours, Radio stations

It is massive. Record and tape sales are about $3 billion a year. Nearly 4,000 LPs and 6,000 45s are produced each year by more than 1,500 record companies on 2,500 labels. The records are sold by 500 distributors, 300 rack-jobbers, 300 "one-shot" jukebox leasors, and thousands of retail outlets. Some 3.2 million playback units were sold at a value of $247 million in a recent year. There are more than 73 million phonograph players in use in the United States today, and although estimates vary as to the number of households with record players, it seems that nine out of every ten families own one.

The phonograph is a high-intensity medium. The sound quality of the medium is far superior to that of most television, home movies, and radio receivers. Most homes that own hi-fi radios normally have this as part of a phonograph or tape system. One of every three new phonographs sold today is a hi-fi stereo.

The medium is national in scope, with records cut all over the country and in Europe by American groups. Since the advent of rock music, when a record is a hit in New England it is probably popular in Texas and the Pacific Northwest as well. Local tastes, which previously split markets according to sections of the country, are no longer the dominant force they were. In fact, the phonograph may now be the most international medium—even more so than film.

It is a youth medium. The artistic aspects of popular music are overwhelmingly dominated by people under the age of 30, and young men are beginning to take over the business operations as well. In terms of audiences, over eight of every ten singles are bought by persons under 25, and over two-thirds of all albums are sold to persons under 30. Of all the mass media, the phonograph and pop music are most youth oriented. The producer as well as the consumer of rock music is young.

The phonograph is becoming more and more portable and durable. The evolution of the cassette has brought up to two hours of listening on a single unit that will fit in a coat pocket. Portable, battery-powered, transistorized cassette players are no bigger than many portable radios. In addition, stereo-cartridge machines are now installed in more than 3 million automobiles. Both records and tapes have become sturdy.

The medium has a highly selective capability—more than any other electronic medium, and almost as much as the book. In other words, individuals can select the content they wish to use. This selection process is much less restricted than with most other media.

The record has become the content of the radio medium. These two media are extremely dependent upon each other. Without records the current radio formats could not exist. In turn, radio helps determine which records will succeed.

The sound-recording medium is a means of socialization of the young. It is a medium that is danced to, which is essential in the dating-mating process; it is a medium committed to young social, political, and economic causes; it insulates young individuals within the household from parental moral values. It has become a crucial element in the development of a youth culture.

The medium provides cultural variety in that, although it is dominated by rock music (six of every ten dollars spent on records buy rock music), other forms of musical expression are available for limited consumption.

And, like the book, the phonograph stores the culture of today for future examination.

In addition to the seven media covered in previous chapters, there are other established means of mass communication. Our discussion here is limited to some of the new media that emphasize personalized or specialized media communication, rather than mass communication. Although they may utilize the production and distribution techniques of mass media, these new media are often used in a new way because of recognition of the impersonality of newspapers, magazines, radio, television, books, and motion pictures.

These new media attempt to individualize the communication process, to provide more intimate communication, including audience response and participation, interaction between medium and audience, and immediate feedback for more effective dialogue, which alone can make communication truly meaningful.

The Newsletter

The rise of the newsletter is a twentieth-century journalistic phenomenon, even though the newsletter is one of the oldest forms of journalistic communication. Letters were used for news and general communication in ancient Greek and Roman civilizations and throughout the Middle Ages. The Fugger newsletters, produced in several German city-states in the fifteenth and sixteenth centuries by the Fugger banking house, were among the forerunners of the

20

Other Media

modern newspaper. Written in letter form, they were reproduced and circulated among merchants and businessmen and contained financial and economic information that helped spread the mercantile revolution. The modern newsletter is often used for a similar purpose.

The father of the modern newsletter was probably Willard M. Kiplinger, who started the *Kiplinger Washington Letters* in 1923. He had been a Washington reporter for the Associated Press and was hired by a New York bank to send reports on government information vital to banking and business interests. Kiplinger put this information in a letter that he regularly sent to the bank. He reasoned that he might sell the information in his letter to other banks as well, and then he saw he could sell it to businessmen too.

He typed the four-page letter on his own typewriter, had it mimeographed and later printed by offset, without any fancy makeup or advertising. Underscoring and capital letters were used to provide some graphic effects, but Kiplinger was primarily interested in distilling information to its essence. He wrote so that each typewritten line carried a complete thought, putting it into good meter so each line would be easy to read and readily remembered. He did not feel constrained to follow normal journalistic restrictions of objectivity and attribution. Kiplinger made interpretations, analyses, and predictions for his readers, taking them into his confidence.

In reality, Kiplinger was writing a personal letter to each of his subscribers, telling them his version of the truth. He started his letter with "Dear Reader" and closed it with his own signature, in his handwriting, printed in blue ink. This feature alone cost him thousands of dollars in postage because he had to send his letter as first-class mail, rather than second-class as a news publication. But the extra cost was worth it to Kiplinger; he wanted to have a form of communication that was warm, personal, and intimate.

The *Kiplinger Letters* have been widely imitated. Others preceded them and others followed them, but none has been as successful or as widely copied. By the late 1970s there were nearly 4,000 commercial newsletters.

A commercial newsletter, as defined by the Gale Research Company, publisher of the newsletter directory, is a publication that is usually reproduced as a typewritten page, without elaborate makeup or printing. Equally important, it does not carry advertising, since its essential feature is the personal relationship it attempts to develop between author and reader, without any middleman to sponsor or subsidize the communication. Thus, the commercial newsletter must charge a subscription, and sometimes the rate may be very high. Some newsletters cost as much as $1,000 a year, if there are few subscribers and the information is of vital importance. The *Kiplinger Letters* cost about $28 a year, an average for the field.

Not counted in the 4,000 commercial newsletters are the many thousands of subsidized newsletters used to promote or persuade, or as internal organs of communication within an organization or a group. Nearly every congressman today uses some form of newsletter to communicate personally with constituents. Newsletters are used by professional associations, church groups, factory workers, fraternal organizations, university administrations, alumni associations, labor unions, and most other organized units in our society.

Newsletters have become so well established that there is now a *Newsletter on Newsletters* and a Newsletter Clearinghouse. In 1977 a new group was founded in Washington, D.C., the Newsletter Association of America, to serve the special interests and needs of those who write, edit, and publish in this special medium.

A typical newsletter publishing company is Plus Publications in Washington, D.C., headed by Ray Henry, a former Associated Press reporter. He started with one newsletter in 1971 and by the late 1970s had eight, all highly specialized, with subscription rates running from $80 to $237 a year. They included *National Health Insurance Reports, Health Planning and Manpower Reports, Health Labor Relations, Election Administration, Daycare and Child Development, Campaign Practices and Access Reports.* The last one, selling for $237 a year, has more than 1,200 subscribers; it grosses nearly $300,000 a year with very small production costs.

The newsletter is quick, inexpensive, simple to produce, and useful. Just about anybody with a typewriter, a copying machine, and a mailing list can get into the newsletter business. Succeeding at the business is not so simple, however. Many newsletters have short lifetimes and make only a fleeting impression.

The "Alternative" Press

Like the newsletter, the "alternative" press has become a new medium of communication that has a direct and personal appeal to select subcultures within our society. The newspapers are not "underground," as they are sometimes called, but are publicly available. They came into vogue during the 1960s, and by the end of that decade several hundred were in existence.

Today there is considerable flux in the fortunes of the alternative press. Many of the papers that were started during the rebellious years of the 1960s by flower children, hippies, war protestors, social and sexual reformers, and college rioters have died. Others, such as *Rolling Stone* and the *Village Voice*, have become so successful that they can hardly be considered alternatives anymore; they are now part of the establishment press.

These papers are printed by inexpensive offset methods, are often sold on the streets rather than by subscription, and usually deal with sensational materials, either sexual, social, or political.

In order to divorce themselves from the traditional press, the young people who ran the alternative press often deliberately cast off accepted newspaper forms. The papers were sometimes garish, obnoxious, gaudy, biased, amateurish, vulgar, crude, slanted, and obscene. These tabloids specifically sought to combine unorthodox style with their content of dissent. The rejection of newspaper conventions, said the editors, like the rejection of American society, is vital—style and content are inseparable and must reject present societal and press conventions.

Five factors contributed to the rise of the alternative press:

1. In the United States in the mid-1960s a climate of dissent was nurtured by an increased awareness of negative aspects of society and knowledge that involvement and protest could change existing evils. First the civil rights movement and then the anti-Vietnam war demonstrations involved young people in political action. The alternative press came to serve as the medium of the protest movement.

2. Although there were attempts at repression of alternative newspapers in some communities, recent court decisions and the changing morality of society have liberalized views on such matters as obscenity. In general, local governments and society as a whole became more permissive in the 1970s.

3. Very important in the rise of an alternative press was the development of less expensive means of printing. Photo-offset printing, which could use inexpensive typesetting, even typewriting, contributed to the proliferation of newspapers in the 1960s and 1970s.

4. The staffs of alternative newspapers seemed willing to work for small salaries and to perform any task, from writing the copy to selling the paper on street corners. Their commitment to social-political movements was critical for these papers, most of which were started with little capital.

5. Perhaps most important was the fact that the alternative press served a growing subculture dissatisfied with traditional forms of journalism. The readership as well as editorial staffs were often openly hostile to the establishment and its press.

The alternative press appears to satisfy a need not fulfilled by the usual news media. These papers' editors argue that traditional "objective" reporting is impossible, and, indeed, that subjective reporting should be the norm. Although some of the content is designed simply to shock, much of the "news" in these papers simply cannot be found in regular newspapers. The success of some of these papers cannot be discounted. Alternative papers are found on some military bases, college campuses, and in high schools.

The Suburban and the Specialized Press

The development of photo-offset printing and cold-type composition, plus the automation and computerization of typesetting, enabled reporters to set their copy in type and made small newspapers for a specialized audience economically feasible in the 1970s. The result has been the growth of small weekly newspapers to serve the local community and specialized weekly newspapers to serve distinct ethnic, cultural, or language groups. In fact, the suburban press was the fastest growing form of journalism in the 1970s.

As people moved out of the central city and into the suburbs they continued to rely on their metropolitan daily until cheaper forms of printing made local newspapers possible. In the typical suburban communities of Washington, D.C., for example, dozens of new weeklies emerged in the 1960s and 1970s. One company, the Army Times Publishing Company, by using a central plant with automated equipment, was able to start five new suburban weeklies in the Washington area in a short period of time—the *Montgomery Journal, Prince George's Journal, Alexandria Journal, Arlington Journal,* and *Fairfax Journal*—each serving a specific Washington suburb with news about the local community that could not be provided by the *Washington Post* or the *Washington Star.*

Other specific groups in our society have been able to develop their own newspapers. Foreign-language papers—Spanish, German, even Korean—are flourishing. Newspapers serving specific ethnic groups are also thriving.

Even within a community, the lowering of publication costs has made a proliferation of specialized publications possible. This is true within a corporation, an association, a university, and other institutions. At the University of Maryland, for example, until the mid-1960s the campus was served by only one newspaper, the *Diamondback,* a student daily. Since then cheaper printing has brought into existence dozens of newspapers on campus, each serving a specialized audience. The faculty and administration have their weekly newsletters; the black students have a weekly newspaper; the fraternities and sororities, the commuter students, some of the dormitories, and some schools and departments have their regular means of communicating information to special groups.

Special-interest groups are also producing newspapers for mass circulation, carrying the news from their perspective rather than a general, objective point of view. For example, in 1977 a daily newspaper called the *News World* was started in New York. It was published by a group with backing from Sun Myung Moon, the Korean religious leader who has stimulated a growing religious movement. The *News World* was a professional-looking newspaper with news stories, color photographs, editorials, features, and advertising; but its general slant was toward Moon's philosophy.

The Black Press

An exception to the growth of a specialized press has been the black press, which has been declining. Nevertheless, in the late 1970s it was still a potent voice. The black press was started in America more than 150 years ago when John B. Russwurm and the Reverend Samuel E. Cornish published the first issue of *Freedom's Journal* in 1827.

Prior to the Civil War, more than 40 newspapers were published for blacks. Many of them were short-lived; all suffered extreme pressures. The most prominent was the *North Star*, founded and edited by Frederick Douglass to "attack slavery in all its forms." By 1890 there were 575 black newspapers in America. Many of them became great voices of the black community, especially newspapers such as the *Chicago Defender*, the *New York Amsterdam News*, the *Baltimore* and *Washington Afro-Americans*, the *Milwaukee Courier*, the *San Francisco Sun*, the *Columbus Times*, the *Philadelphia Tribune*, the *Cincinnati Herald*, the *Houston Forward Times*, and the *Los Angeles Sentinel*.

The black press established its own organization in 1940, the National Newspaper Publishers Association, and by the end of World War II the combined circulation of more than 100 leading papers in the black press was more than 2 million copies a week.

But the black press declined in the decades after the war, as blacks became increasingly assimilated into white culture. James D. Williams, director of communications for the National Urban League, in a booklet *The Black Press and the First Amendment*, wrote that "there were other factors that also began to operate against the black press; the general decline in newspaper readership as more and more people turned to television; the dispersal of black persons outside the central-city where the black papers were available; the continued indifference of major advertisers to black media (in 1974 black media received less than one percent of the $13.6 billion in advertising agency billings); and a decline, in some instances, of the quality and quantity of the reporting."

Direct Mail

The personal letter can be used as a form of advertising for persuasive communication, and with the development of robotypewriters and computers, the personal letter has become a form of mass communication. A robotypewriter is a machine that can be programmed to type the same letter many times, leaving spaces for individualized names, addresses, and salutations. Direct mail is based on sending a message through the postal system to a mailing list of potential readers who have something in common. The gathering of such mailing lists has itself become a big business, and one can rent or buy the list of names from a mailing-list company to reach almost any desired audience.

Direct-mail letters in the past have been printed and sent out to anonymous recipients, but today, with sophisticated computer capability, the letters can be individually addressed, with individual messages inserted at key points in the letter, and personally signed by the sender. That is, the letter can be signed with pen and ink, by a signature machine that can produce an exact copy of the original handwritten signature. Letters from the President, congressmen, or political, governmental, or business officials are now often handled in this manner, with thousands of letters sent to individuals; they appear to be personal letters but in fact are mass-produced by machine.

A typical congressman's office, which might receive a heavy volume of mail on a political issue, might program into the computer half a dozen stock replies; each incoming letter is simply marked for a particular response. Names and addresses and any variations can be inserted in the program and the robotypewriters automatically do the rest, even signing the congressman's name.

Thus, direct mail has become a new mass medium, capable of reaching millions of people with direct messages, more personally and more intimately than newspapers, magazines, books, or electronic media.

Graphic Materials

The volume of other printed materials is increasing so rapidly that mention should be made here of the nonperiodic graphic media as well.

Display graphics, one of the oldest forms of communication, are increasing. Earlier societies used bulletin boards and wall postings for information and persuasion. Many countries, particularly China and Russia, still use wall newspapers and posters, as well as open-air radio and television, to inform and exhort their people. In America, posters have experienced a rebirth and revitalization with the advent of psychedelic colors and images. Poster-publishing companies have come into existence to produce posters in volume for decora-

Drawing by Ziegler; © 1978 The New Yorker Magazine, Inc.

tion and information. Billboards have been a fixture in graphic display for as long as America has had highways and automobiles. Equally ubiquitous but even more effective, according to research findings, are car cards on streetcars, subways, and buses. Even the automobile bumper sticker carries a message, often political, and so can matchbook covers and even restaurant menus.

The National Institute of Mental Health, a U.S. government agency fighting drug use among young people, decided to tell its message about the abuses of drugs, not through the traditional media but through new display graphics. As a result, it produced brilliant posters for bedroom as well as classroom, eye-catching billboards, striking car cards, bumper stickers, and even clever matchbook covers. These media carried a message to many people who would not otherwise be reached.

Printed matter other than books and periodical publications are also expanding. Again, these are not new media, but they are being put to new use. They include tracts, leaflets, flyers, pamphlets, brochures, and booklets. Their proper distribution has always been a problem; the government alone produces many thousands of such printed materials each year, ranging from booklets on legislative actions to leaflets on rat control in inner-city slums. But many of these in the past have remained in literature racks in public post offices or stored in government warehouses. The use of direct-mail techniques to distribute these reading materials to appropriate mailing lists, however, has vastly increased their utility.

Audiovisual Materials

Audiovisual materials have been so fully developed and widely used that we might consider them a new kind of communication medium. Most of the equipment is built for small-group usage, but the equipment itself is standardized, and programs are being mass-produced to the extent that audiovisuals almost qualify as mass media, yet they retain their personal intimacy and allow for easy and inexpensive production of audiovisual presentations even by amateurs.

Most audiovisual equipment falls into two categories. Filmed materials for visual presentation include still photographs, either for display or projection through opaque or overhead projectors; slides and film strips, usually 35-mm, for projection; and motion pictures for projection.

Audio materials for sound reproduction include disk recordings, audiotape recordings, and videotape recordings. Videotape, of course, includes sound and picture. Most sound reproduction is now made to synchronize with visual presentation, even with slides and film strips, and simple systems are now available to program, synchronize, and mix sound and sight. The development of stereo tape and tape cassettes has also enlarged the potential of the entire audiovisual field, providing compact and convenient packages of sound that rival the convenience of books for storage, retrieval, and easy access.

Closed-circuit broadcasting is another form of audiovisual presentation, one that is finding increased use in large meetings, conventions, and educational institutions to augment the communication process. Both closed-circuit radio and televison are being used in home and office, in shops and factories, and for personal communication.

Finally, audiovisual tools of all kinds are being programmed and computerized to become teaching machine , capable of individualized communication and instruction. Large collections of instructional programs and programmed courses are now available in slides, film strips, motion pictures, videotape, and tape cassettes. These collections are certain to expand in the future, making individualized instruction more possible through use of the technical equipment of mass communication. Some educational institutions have developed multimedia libraries so that these materials can be stored, retrieved, and used in the same manner as printed materials.

Mixed-Media Presentations

Since person-to-person communication is still the most effective way to send a message, eyeball-to-eyeball confrontation has become institutionalized in our mass society. It has long been the dominant form of communication in the classroom, church, synagogue, or town hall. Now person-to-person meetings are widely used and fairly standardized in format to inform, persuade, educate, and even entertain us in business, trades, professions, associations, and even religious and social groups.

Meetings, seminars, conferences, and institutes have become such successful media for communication that they are now regularized affairs for most groups, at the least on an annual basis, although some are semiannual, some quarterly, others monthly or weekly, and, not inconceivably, some even daily. Most such meetings bring together people from diverse geographical locations for personal communication; hotels have become common meeting grounds, and new hotels are being built today with a great variety of auditoriums and meeting and seminar rooms equipped with the latest audiovisual apparatus. Such facilities can almost be classified as communication media.

Sometimes the message rather than the audience is moved from place to place for different meetings. The display and exhibit have become new communication media for such a purpose. Here again, techniques of display and exhibit production have been formalized and standardized to the point where these new forms of communication might almost be considered mass media, although they too provide for direct confrontation with their audience and lend a personal approach to the message.

The traveling display or exhibit has been used effectively for communicating across cultural barriers. The United States makes wide use of such shows in its overseas information programs. The Soviet Union made effective use of this technique in a traveling exhibit of photographs, including hundreds of black-and-white and color pictures of life in Russia. This exhibit was displayed in hotels in major cities around the United States and received an enthusiastic American response.

In many of these person-to-person communication efforts, mixed-media presentations are used to enhance the communication effectiveness. But nowhere is the mixed-media presentation so varied as at a fair, with color, lights, sound, pictures, sights, people, smells, and even tastes—all designed to communicate a message. The fair, which started out as a way for farmers to get together and show their wares, has become a mass medium in modern times.

The grandest expression of multimedia, mixed-media presentation is probably a world's fair. Here nations and cultures communicate with each other—through sight and sound and smell and touch—the way neighboring farmers might at a county fair. New forms of multimedia presentations, developed at world's fairs, have furthered the effective techniques of communication. Such presentations have ranged from posters and brochures to light and sound shows, from multimedia-screen projections to complicated, all-encompassing exhibits through which one might ride in a special car fitted with audiovisual-olfactory-sensory mechanisms to massage all the senses and provide for total communication.

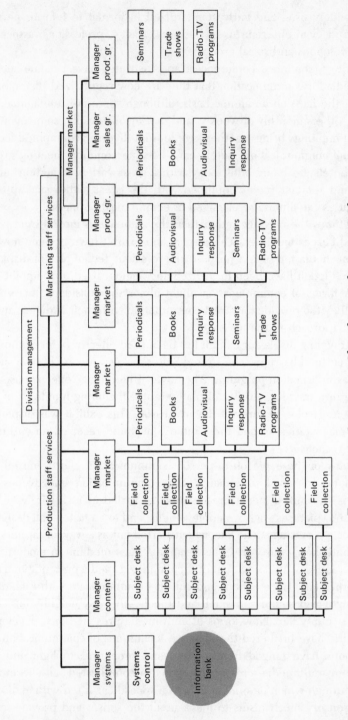

FIGURE 20.1. *Organization Chart for an Information Bank*

SOURCE: Book Production Industry, February 1969.

The communication techniques developed for world's fairs have had wide application in other areas as well, including higher education and popular entertainment, from the multimedia center at the University of Texas to Disneyland in California.

Data Banks and Information Centers

Increasingly, American institutions—business, professional, or educational—are finding it necessary to provide for multimedia information centers, data banks, and libraries to ensure effective communication. These, too, are new media. A number of organizations now use a multimedia information center complete with central projection core, control lectern, multiple rear and front projection screens, contoured chairs, and specially designed lighting and acoustics. The aim is to provide a total environment in which messages can be transferred with great effectiveness.

At the same time, our concept of information storage is changing. Libraries are no longer viewed only as places in which to shelve and store books and papers, but rather also as information systems. When storage and retrieval of the library's contents are fully computerized, the library is really a data bank, and as such it is a new medium of communication (see figure 20.1).

Such data banks are in effect publishers or broadcasters, not of mass communications but rather of individualized reports and communiqués to fulfill the specific needs of the person who seeks specific data. These data banks are organized more like modern newspapers, magazines, and book publishers than like libraries. That is, they are engaged in data gathering, data processing, data editing, and data sales. The staff is organized much like a modern newspaper's staff. Such data banks may well become the newspapers, magazines, and book publishers of the future, producing materials on demand to fit individual needs.

While most of this book discusses mass media, we have seen in this chapter how the techniques and mechanisms of mass communication are increasingly being used by new media for a more personal communication experience. Without a doubt, more eyeball-to-eyeball communication is needed in human discourse in our mass society. These new media that can achieve some greater measure of dialogue and mutual response may well provide important areas of communication development in the years ahead.

Part Four
Uses
of Mass
Communication

The media are used for a variety of purposes—to educate, to entertain, to persuade, to interpret, and to sell—but probably the most important use is for the dissemination of news and information. We describe secondary functions in later chapters in this section, but here we want to discuss the key function.

For the most part, the media do not cause the events that become news. They merely record them, interpret them, or express opinions about them. Other forces in society—political, economic, sociological, meteorological, personal—cause events to happen: media react to those events. As human beings acquire greater control over their environment, they can also exercise greater control over communication by manipulating people, events, and environment to make news.

Obviously the media are not simply passive agents manipulated by other agencies. By making judgments about what is newsworthy, about what is important and unimportant, about what is true and false, reporters and editors in the mass media play a key role in shaping the course of events.

Why Do We Need News?

The need for information is basic to nearly all human groups. Even in primitive societies someone acts as a watchman for the tribe. The best climber might be dispatched to climb the tallest tree and look out over the horizon for dangers and portents, for rain or fire, for animal food or tribal enemies. The tribe depends upon such reports for survival.

News and Information

In modern society we sometimes employ private informers, such as detectives or investigators, to perform informational services. But for the most part we depend upon mass media to keep us aware of dangers and potentials on the horizon. We need journalists to provide a check on government and business as well as neighbors and friends. The journalist is, indeed, a tree climber, a person who knows how to get the broadest view of what is happening in the world in order to report the important news and information for a particular audience.

In the terminology of the journalist, news is that which an individual is willing to pay for with time or money in order to read or hear or watch. In other words, news must have some intrinsic value to the individual. News is different from information. A great deal of information about many subjects is available in the world, but information does not become news until a disinterested journalist selects it for presentation via news media to an interested audience.

Before information can become news, it must be made to fit the quality and criteria of news; it must be an accurate, fair, balanced, and objective presentation, and it must have a relatively high degree of news value based on such criteria as prominence, proximity, consequences, timeliness, and human interest. We return to these qualities and values shortly.

Relativity and Relevance

The only area where the journalist's role is active rather than passive is in making judgments about what is news. Literally millions of events occur on any given day, and it is news media gatekeepers who determine which events are newsworthy and which are not.

Newsworthiness depends upon those judgments. Gatekeepers select and evaluate facts, ideas, and events that make up the news. Selection and evaluation depend upon many factors, not the least of which is the nature of the group to which the journalist is reporting.

News and information are, therefore, relative matters; only those people and happenings that are relevant to the audience become newsworthy. We might say, then, that news is that which gatekeepers decide should go into the stream of communication on any given day on the basis of what the audience is willing to read, hear, or watch. Today's news may not be relevant tomorrow, for news values are relative.

Elements of News Quality

Perhaps the most dominant principle of news in America is the idea of objectivity. News is supposed to be a factual report of an event as it occurred, without the bias of the reporter or an attempt on the part of the journalist to make any one view more influential than another. In America, the journalist plays a nonpartisan role—taking the part of a teacher, passing on facts for their own sake, allowing the individual to draw conclusions and make interpretations. The journalist disavows the role of promoter, to pass on information in order to persuade or influence an audience.

Objectivity is a difficult quality to measure and a difficult standard to attain. Journalists can never really wholly divorce themselves from their work; their emotions and opinions are apt to be tied into their perceptions of facts and events whether they think they are or not. Moreover, no journalist ever sees the whole of any situation; and as events become more complex in our complicated world, the journalist necessarily sees a smaller portion of any set of facts.

A growing school of thought in American journalism argues against the principle of objectivity for these reasons. This "new journalism" is devoted to the idea that reporters should be more than messengers delivering a message; this concept holds that they are involved in the message itself, and their reporting will be better if they openly and honestly admit their biases and clearly label their reports as their views of the situation.

In any case, the goal of any news operation is to keep people fully informed about vital events and information, knowledge of which is essential to full citizenship in a democratic society. The people have a right to know; that is a basic tenet of free men, and news must provide the necessary factual basis for forming sound opinions. The reporter who wishes to fulfill this responsibility through objective reporting must work at it diligently.

Objectivity is enhanced by proper attribution of facts and opinions. The news reporter, following the basic principles of objectivity, must attribute to an authority—an eyewitness, an official, a participant, an expert—anything that is not routine and readily verifiable knowledge.

Accuracy of reporting is another basic quality of news. Reporters must train their eyes to see and their ears to hear as accurately as possible. They must be constantly vigilant for detail and perpetually skeptical of those who would deceive, exaggerate, or hide in order to twist and distort the truth.

Finally, balance and fairness in reporting are crucial standards by which the quality of news should be judged. Both sides of the story must be told; all arguments fairly represented. A report of a football game may be accurate and factual, but it could be unbalanced and unfair if only the play of the home team were noted.

Telling both sides of the story is so much a part of American journalism that reporters sometimes seem unpatriotic, unwilling simply to accept the pronouncements of presidents or bureaucrats as the only statement on a matter. In war this becomes particularly difficult for leaders to understand, as the press and news media seem bent on reporting the successes of the enemy as well as the failures of compatriots. But the journalist is dedicated to the proposition that only from balanced reporting of both sides will the people be able to discover the truth.

Criteria for News Selection

On what basis do journalists for the mass media make judgments about people and events that turn information into news? In the past, those decisions have often been made from seasoned intuition. The editor could say, this is news and that isn't because my past experience tells me so, but he or she could not rationalize and quantify criteria for the selection.

This is a little like flying by the seat of one's pants, as the old pilots' saying goes. And it might be perfectly well to guide an ancient flivver by feeling the tug of gravity in one's bowels, but one would not dream of piloting a multimillion-dollar jet with hundreds of passengers without using a computer to aid in the thousands of decisions and judgments necessary to make the trip as scientifically safe and sound as possible.

In mass communication, too, where hundreds of thousands of people depend upon the information that journalists decide to publish and broadcast, the decision about what is news and what is not must be made as rationally as possible. We need to develop better criteria for the selection of news, and in the future it may well be that media will use computers to aid in making these judgments as much as we now do in other fields. Meanwhile, we depend upon a few standard bases of news judgment.

Timeliness. Certainly one of the most important criteria for news is its newness. We say that nothing is as old as yesterday's newspaper, but actually the length of time for which a piece of information continues to be newsworthy depends upon the medium. For radio, a story may lose its timeliness after one hour. Television news, because of the longer time it takes to provide film than tape, may have a slightly longer lifetime, from an hour to a day. Newspaper news has a one-day lifetime; after that the story must be rewritten with new information. Weeklies have a week, monthlies a month, and so on.

Proximity. Geographical factors are also important to news judgment. Relatively speaking, the nearer an event occurs to the people who read about it, the more newsworthy it is. The election of the governor of New York is much more important to New Yorkers than it is to those who live next door in

Pennsylvania. A two-car accident killing two local people might be more significant to the audience in their community than a major earthquake in Peru taking the lives of thousands on the same day.

Prominence. The more widely known the participants in an occurrence, the more newsworthy the happening. If the President of the United States hits a hole-in-one on the golf course, it could be national news. If the mayor does the same, it might be news in his town. If the golf pro does it, it might make the newsletter at the country club. Actually, prominence has a snowballing effect on newsworthiness since mass media make famous people more prominent through constant reference to them in the media.

Consequences. The consequences of an event have a direct bearing on its newsworthiness. Even the most inconspicuous and anonymous human being might suddenly become newsworthy by inventing a better mousetrap or assassinating a President, acts that could have widespread ramifications. The earthquake in Peru might be more newsworthy to the small community where the two-car accident occurred if the tremor will cause a shortage of Peruvian tin at the local factory.

Human Interest. Finally, we can identify a criterion that we only vaguely refer to as human interest, matters that catch and hold our attention because of physical and emotional responses that are built into human beings. Mitchell Charnley, in his book *Reporting*, notes a number of elements that provide human interest, including adventure and conflict, humor, pathos and bathos, sex, the odd and the unusual, and self-interest. A high percentage of each day's news is selected on the basis of these factors.

Categories of News

News covers a surprising range of subject matter, although some categories obviously receive more coverage than others. A national survey by the American Newspaper Publishers Association found more than 40 general categories of news in daily newspapers. The survey found some interesting aspects of news: more space is devoted to sports than to international news, more space is given to crime than to cultural events and reviews, and more space is given to news of interest to men than news of interest to women (see table 21.1).

The percentage of news in these various categories probably matches the profile of interests by the news reader. But interests do vary by sex, age, and

TABLE 21.1.
DISTRIBUTION OF NEWS AND EDITORIAL CONTENT BY CIRCULATION
(All percentages based on items of 5½ column-inches or longer.)

	ALL DAILY NEWSPAPERS	50,000 OR LESS	50,001 250,000	250,001 OR MORE
General Interest	**66.8%**	**67.0%**	**66.6%**	**67.2%**
State and Local News	**12.7**	**15.2**	**12.0**	**9.5**
General local news	7.3	9.6	6.8	4.1
State and local government	5.4	5.6	5.2	5.4
International News	**10.2**	**9.5**	**10.2**	**11.5**
Vietnam (not U.S. Govt.), other wars, rebellions	4.4	4.4	4.2	4.9
U.S. Government (Vietnam), armaments, defense	2.8	2.6	2.7	3.4
International, diplomatic news (U.S. and foreign)	3.0	2.5	3.3	3.2
U.S. Government, Domestic	**6.9**	**6.6**	**6.9**	**7.7**
Other General Interest	**37.0**	**35.7**	**37.5**	**38.5**
Crime	3.9	3.3	4.3	4.6
Education, school news	3.3	3.5	3.6	2.6
Comics	2.6	2.7	2.5	2.6
Cultural events, reviews	2.6	2.6	2.3	3.0
Public health, welfare	2.4	2.3	2.4	2.6
Puzzles, horoscopes	2.4	2.8	2.3	1.8
Accidents, disasters, natural phenomena	2.4	2.5	2.3	2.2
Social problems, protest	2.1	2.1	1.9	2.3
Obituaries	2.1	2.2	2.1	1.8
Labor, wages	1.8	1.3	1.9	2.7
Environment	1.6	1.5	1.5	1.7
General non-local human interest	1.2	1.3	1.3	1.1
Other General Interest				
Racial news, minorities (peaceful)	1.2	1.0	1.5	1.2
TV/radio logs	1.2	1.0	1.1	1.5
Weather	1.1	1.1	1.1	1.1
Science, invention	1.0	1.0	1.1	0.9
Travel	1.0	0.9	1.0	1.1
Taxes	1.0	0.8	1.1	0.9
Entertainers, Hollywood	0.9	0.6	0.8	1.7
Letters to the editor	0.6	0.5	0.7	0.8
Religion	0.6	0.7	0.7	0.4
Men's Interest	**21.1**	**19.6**	**21.7**	**22.9**
Sports	14.2	14.0	15.2	12.9
Business, finance	6.9	5.6	6.5	10.0

TABLE 21.1. *continued*

	ALL DAILY NEWSPAPERS	50,000 OR LESS	50,001 250,000	250,001 OR MORE
Women's Interest	**5.4**	**6.9**	**5.0**	**3.2**
Fashion, society, etc.	3.9	5.3	3.6	1.9
Food, home, garden	1.5	1.6	1.4	1.3
Columns	**5.3**	**5.4**	**5.4**	**4.8**
Advice columns	3.1	3.2	3.2	2.5
Political columns	1.1	1.2	1.0	1.0
Humor columns	0.8	0.8	0.8	0.7
Gossip columns	0.3	0.2	0.4	0.6
Other Items Not Classified Elsewhere	**1.4**	**1.1**	**1.3**	**2.0**

SOURCE: *News and Editorial Content and Readership of the Daily Newspaper* (American Newspaper Publishers Association Research Center, 1973).

education, as the ANPA survey showed. The newspaper tries to be all things to all people, which is obviously impossible, and for that reason specialized news media have increasingly developed to serve special needs for news and information (see tables 21.2 and 21.3).

TABLE 21.2.
READERSHIP OF NEWS AND EDITORIAL TOPICS BY SEX

How to read this table: The first item listed under "Men" indicates that the average item dealing with an accident, disaster, or natural phenomenon is seen or read by 37% of all male readers.

MOST WIDELY READ TOPICS

Men:
Accidents, disasters, natural phenomena (37%)
U.S. Government, Vietnam, armaments (36%)
Taxes (34%)
Crime (33%)
Letters to the editor (31%)

Women:
Accidents, disasters, natural phenomena (41%)
Letters to the editor (38%)

Advice Columns (38%)
Obituaries (37%)
General non-local human interest (35%)

LEAST WIDELY READ TOPICS

Men:
Puzzles, horoscope (13%)
Entertainers, Hollywood news (14%)
Fashion, society, etc., (15%)
Food, home, garden (17%)
TV/radio logs (19%)

Women:
Sports (7%)
Business news, commerce (15%)
Political columns (17%)
Education, school news (21%)
Cultural events, reviews (21%)

SOURCE: See table 21.1.

TABLE 21.3.
READERSHIP OF NEWS AND EDITORIAL TOPICS BY AGE

MOST WIDELY READ TOPICS

18–24 years:
Comics (42%)
Accidents, disasters, natural phenomena (32%)
Letters to the editor (29%)
General nonlocal human interest (28%)
Entertainers, Hollywood news (26%)

35–49 years:
General nonlocal human interest (39%)
Accidents, disasters, etc. (37%)
Letters to the editor (37%)
Public health, welfare (36%)
Travel (35%)

25–34 years:
Taxes (39%)
Accidents, disasters, etc. (38%)
Labor, wages (35%)
Weather (33%)
Crime (32%)

50 years or more:
Accidents, disasters, etc. (43%)
Letters to the editor (42%)
Obituaries (41%)
Crime (36%)
Public health, welfare (35%)

LEAST WIDELY READ TOPICS

18–24 years:
Gossip columns (6%)
Business, commerce (9%)
Taxes (12%)
Education, school news (14%)
Obituaries (15%)

35–49 years:
Puzzles, horoscope (17%)
Sports (17%)
Weather (17%)
Entertainers, Hollywood news (18%)
International, diplomatic news (19%)

25–34 years:
Puzzles, horoscope (13%)
Political columns (15%)
TV/radio logs (16%)
Cultural events, reviews (17%)
Science, invention (18%)

50 years or more:
Sports (12%)
Puzzles, horoscope (18%)
Entertainers, Hollywood news (18%)
Business, commerce (19%)
Comics (21%)

SOURCE: See table 21.1.

Immediate and Delayed Rewards

All news in American journalism is selected by media gatekeepers because it fulfills some audience need. People are willing to spend time and money on it. The basic criterion is, will it sell? Will people pay attention to it? Do they want it and need it? To catch and hold attention, information must fulfill a need, whether for self-preservation, self-advancement, ego satisfaction, sexual stimulus and gratification, or for vicarious resolution of thwarted desires for adventure and conflict.

Wilbur Schramm, formerly professor of communication at Stanford University, has categorized news as providing either an "immediate reward" or a "delayed reward" to a felt need. The immediate-reward type of news provides instant satisfaction for the recipient, who laughs, cries, sympathizes, thrills, or muses. Schramm places in this category such news as "crime and corruption, accidents and disasters, sports and recreation, and social events."

Delayed-reward news has an impact that does not affect the consumer until later. Such news includes information about "public affairs, economic matters, social problems, science, education, weather, and health." Often, delayed-reward news may bring an unpleasant consequence for the reader, listener, or viewer, while the immediate reward can bring instant gratification. Schramm concludes that most news consumers spend more time with, find more satisfaction in, and give greater attention to immediate-reward news than delayed-reward news.

Consequences of News Selection

Judgments about news may constitute the most important decisions made in our society, with wide significance and deep consequences. It is important to examine the problems that have arisen in the past and that loom on the horizon of the future as a result of news selection.

First, since news decisions are consumer-oriented, in order to sell media, news usually overemphasizes immediate-reward types of information. Crime and violence almost always outweigh and outdraw stories of good deeds, constructive action, peaceful progress, and orderly dissent. Sex is not as large an element in news as it is in advertising, but it is nonetheless a significant factor. The aberrations of society—the odd, the unusual, the unique—are more often the subject of news than the normal.

One result can be a gloomy view of the world. Dr. Glenn T. Seaborg, Nobel-Prize-winning nuclear scientist and former chairman of the Atomic Energy Commission, warned that the last decades of the twentieth century may usher in a worldwide doomsday depression. People, he said, are so constantly reminded of evil and corruption in the world by the news media that they may sink into a hopeless morass of gloom and despair, not realizing that the world is still a beautiful place with much more good about it than bad.

Indeed, fright and hysteria can sometimes result from a small detail of news. The famous Orson Welles broadcast in 1938 about an invasion from Mars brought such a reaction. The Welles radio program was a dramatization of a science-fiction story about Martians coming to earth, told in the form of a news program, with bulletins interrupting a music show. Dr. Hadley Cantril, a psychologist who studied the event, summarized his findings in his book *The Invasion from Mars:* "Long before the broadcast had ended, people all over the

United States were praying, crying, fleeing frantically to escape death from the Martians. Some ran to rescue loved ones. Others telephoned farewells or warnings, hurried to inform neighbors, sought information from newspapers or radio stations, summoned ambulances or police cars. At least six million people heard the broadcast. At least a million of them were frightened or disturbed."

As a result, the NAB code adopted a resolution forbidding dramas to be presented as news programs. Yet other straight news stories continue to have such an effect. A massive publicity effort by the federal government to tell people that smoking might cause lung cancer had the effect of sending thousands of smokers to their doctors for hypochondriacal ailments.

One news reader in Washington, D.C., expressed the feelings of many consumers when she wrote to the *Washington Post:*

> Isn't there such a thing as *good news* any more? Every morning after reading the newspaper (yours) I am left depressed for the rest of the day. Is it that I am too weak to cope with the cruel realities of the world or is it that *you* are too weak to deny the sensationalism that brings your paper its profit and salaries? Can you never print just *one* happy or amusing or heart-warming story on the front page? Or for that matter, on *any* page? Even the food advertisements on Thursdays are psychologically devastating, but that, in short, is not your fault—I guess none of it is. I guess, too, that you are just printing things as you see them.
>
> It's a vicious cycle, though: the world is sick, which makes the people sick, which makes the sick people make a sicker world. If everybody gets as depressed as I do after reading or seeing the news, there's only one destiny for all of us—an insane asylum. (Letters to the Editor, *Washington Post*, 4 July 1970)

Journalists have traditionally defended the publication of "bad" news and "unusual" information by saying, first, that people prefer to read such stories, and second, that exposing evil and corruption does more good for society than praising constructive action. But here, too, greater balance is desirable to tell the whole story to the news consumer.

A second consequence of news selection is the distortion caused by the attempt to be objective and fair. The unprincipled person can tell a lie to make news and have it reported with the same weight as the honest person who tells the truth.

Perhaps the best historical example of this is the story of the late Senator Joseph McCarthy of Wisconsin, a man who used the exposure of communists in government for his own political ends. The senator made charges, most of which he was never able to substantiate, sometimes ruining people's careers and lives. The news media would objectively report the fact that the senator had charged Mr. A with being a communist, and Mr. A would, if available, deny the charges. Both sides of the story were told, so the news media were giving a fair and balanced coverage of news. But the reporters could not inject their opinion that the senator was lying, and irreparable public damage was thus done to the accused.

Ultimately the truth will win out, if we believe John Milton's theory about putting truth to the test in the open marketplace of ideas. And ultimately, in the case of Senator Joseph McCarthy, it was the news media that continued to give coverage to the senator until his distortions were so apparent that his colleagues in the Senate finally censured him.

In the end we must say that news is a two-edged sword that cuts both ways. Those who would use it purposely to depress or deceive the world will, sooner or later, be exposed by the same media that allow them expression. The consequences of news, however, are enormous, and no one should undertake to deal with news who does not want to accept the awesome responsibilities for making such decisions.

News Services and News Gathering

Thorough coverage of news requires a complex organization of well-trained professionals who follow a scrupulous routine to uncover not only that which has happened and is happening but also that which is going to happen. News coverage is not accidental, in other words, but well planned and carefully managed.

The newspaper organization, described in chapter 14, provides the basic plan for news coverage, with editors to supervise and make final decisions; reporters and legmen to gather facts, usually on the basis of permanent beats at routine sources of news; reporters and rewrite people to write the news into readable prose; copyreaders and proofreaders to edit and check that prose. Magazines, radio and television stations, and network news organizations simply provide variations on the basic newspaper organization for the gathering and processing of news.

Most news media also have some small network outside their local communities for gathering news. Some employ housewives or students as part-time stringers in suburban communities or outlying towns. Some have bureaus in their state capitals or county seats to report local governmental news. A few large stations and publications have bureaus in New York City, particularly to report business and financial news. An increasing number of media of all sizes have correspondents or bureaus stationed in Washington, D.C., to provide news coverage of the nation's capital, often called the news center of the world. And the larger media have their own foreign correspondents, people who are usually stationed on one continent or another with roving assignments to follow the international news of particular interest to their audiences.

Most news media, however, have as their primary purpose the processing of local news. No one newspaper (even the *New York Times*), no magazine (even *Newsweek* or *Time*), no radio or television station or network (even NBC, CBS, or ABC) could provide worldwide coverage of news on an efficient basis. Increasingly, the news media have turned to independent news services or wire services for such coverage.

The wire services today are the world's news brokers, providing the vast bulk of nonlocal news for most media. Their news and information usually goes out to their subscribers by telegraph wire. In America the important services are the Associated Press and United Press International; in England it is Reuters; in France, Agence France-Presse; and in Russia, TASS, which is part of the Soviet government.

The Associated Press is a cooperative, started in 1848, and owned by the newspapers and other media that subscribe to its services. UPI is an amalgam of the old Hearst International News Service, begun in 1909, and the Scripps-Howard United Press, started in 1907. AP now serves more than 8,500 newspaper, magazine, television, and radio clients around the world; more of its clients are now in broadcast than print media. UPI has more than 7,000 subscribers.

Each of these wire services operates in more than 100 countries around the world. Together they lease more than a million miles of telephone wire and make extensive use of radio-teletype circuits and transoceanic cables for reports around the globe. Together they employ more than 12,000 journalists full- and part-time, who operate nearly 400 bureaus. They send out nearly 10 million words a day, thousands of pictures, and hundreds of special broadcast reports.

News services provide a variety of types of coverage, such as a national wire, a state wire, a local wire, or a special radio wire written for broadcast. They charge the media a fee based on circulation or station size. A small newspaper of 25,000 circulation may pay from $100 to $400 a week, while a large metropolitan daily might be charged as much as $6,000 a week. Both AP and UPI have annual budgets in excess of $50 million.

The wire services are staffed by seasoned reporters who work out of bureaus organized much like the city staff of a daily newspaper, again with legmen, reporters, copyreaders, and editors. Nearly every state capital, all major cities, and most foreign capitals of the world have wire-service bureaus;

one of the largest of all is in Washington, D.C., where more news is made than in any other city of the world; New York is the headquarters and houses the largest operation for AP and UPI.

The wire services are basically news-reporting organizations. Their staffers are professional news hounds; they know where to get the news and how to get it. When anything important happens, they are sure to be there. No better training for news work could be obtained than at one of the wire-service bureaus.

Investigative News Reporting

One of the most important developments in news and information in the 1970s has been the increase of investigative reporting. Indeed, investigative reporters such as Robert Woodward and Carl Bernstein, the *Washington Post* team that cracked the Watergate story, have become the modern heroes of American journalism. Others, such as Don Bolles of the *Arizona Republic*, have been assassinated because they knew too much inside information.

Investigative reporters cover more than apparent events; they often make news by going beneath the surface situation to find the real cause or purpose. At times, they are almost a combination of police detective, spy, and gossip columnist. In their book *All the President's Men*, Woodward and Bernstein provide an unusual inside glimpse at the world of investigative reporting, sleuthing secrets from confidential sources, wheedling their way into private homes and offices for a few tidbits of facts, holding clandestine meetings in dark basement garages for morsels of information, and building a case piece by piece until the larger picture is formed.

Investigative reporting is often done best by teams of reporters, for both speed and thoroughness. Jack Anderson, who bills himself as an investigative reporter in Washington, employs a small staff of aides that serve as his researchers and investigators for his column. A number of newspapers have set up investigative teams, as have the wire services.

The Style and Structure of News

Since the purpose of news is to transmit information as efficiently as possible, it must have a style and structure that permit quick and effective communication. Language must be clear, simple, and to the point. Syntax must be direct and concise. Organization must be logical. Above all stands clarity and brevity.

The news story must be organized and written in such a way that others who work on it can do so easily; it might be compared to a racing car with easily accessible parts for rapid repair by all mechanics at the pit stop. Copyreaders, printers, announcers, editors, directors—all must be able to work with the news copy quickly and cooperatively.

The inverted pyramid structure is usually used to organize the news story, telling the most important part of the story at the beginning, the less significant material in the middle, and the least meaningful at the end. News is usually not told chronologically or dramatically, for the most important things usually happen at the end of an event or a drama, not at the beginning. If we were writing fiction about a baseball game we might start our story with a description of the weather and an investigation of the butterflies in the stomach of the pitcher. But in news the story begins with the final score of the game.

This method of reporting serves two important functions. First, it gives the hurried news consumer the most important information immediately. The consumer need not learn more about the event unless he or she has time or special interest. Second, it allows the news processors to cut a story at the end, if there is competition for time or space (as there usually is) without losing the essential facts of the story.

Since the beginning of the story is the most important, the usual lead, or opening paragraph, is used to summarize the significant facts of the event. In the past, reporters spoke of the five *w*s and the *h*—who, what, when, where, why, and how. If these questions about each event were answered in the lead, the main points of the story would be summarized. Today there is less emphasis on the five *w*s and the *h*, and yet the basic principle remains—that the first paragraph must summarize the most important elements of any news situation.

Finally, news must be presented in a style that is attractive and interesting. Factual writing that is clear, direct, and concise need not be dull. Often the facts are the most arresting aspect of good style; an individual who has done a good job of reporting, interviewing, investigating, and researching need not worry about drab writing. Some of the most forceful literature of the twentieth century is the product of men and women who mastered news style, including former reporters such as Ernest Hemingway, John O'Hara, Mary McCarthy, and John Gunther.

Radio and Television as News Media

Radio and television have become increasingly important as media for reporting news and information. The number of people who depend upon the broadcast media for their news has risen steadily; today, the majority of the people in the United States fall into this category (see table 21.4).

TABLE 21.4. SOURCES OF NEWS

"First, I'd like to ask you where you usually get most of your news about what's going on in the world today—from the newspapers or radio or television or magazines or talking to people or where?"

Source of Most News	12/59 %	11/61 %	11/63 %	11/64 %	1/67 %	11/68 %	1/71 %
Television	51	52	55	58	64	59	60
Newspapers	57	57	53	56	55	49	48
Radio	34	34	29	26	28	25	23
Magazines	8	9	6	8	7	7	5
People	4	5	4	5	4	5	4
Don't know or no answer	1	3	3	3	2	3	1
Total mentions	154	157	147	153	158	145	140

Analysis of Multiple Responses	12/59 %	11/61 %	11/63 %	11/64 %	1/67 %	11/68 %	1/71 %
Television only	19	18	23	23	25	29	31
Newspapers only	21	19	21	20	18	19	21
Both newspapers and television (with or without other media)	26	27	24	28	30	25	22
Newspapers and other media but not television	10	11	8	8	7	6	5
Television and other media but not newspapers	6	7	8	6	8	5	7
Media other than television or newspapers	17	15	13	12	10	13	13
Don't know or no answer	1	3	3	3	2	3	1

SOURCE: The Roper Organization, Inc., *An Extended View of Public Attitudes toward Television and Other Mass Media, 1959–1975.*

The major networks have large news operations, with correspondents covering the world in the same way the wire services do, although not nearly so extensively. The networks concentrate their news coverage on major news centers such as Washington, D.C., New York, Los Angeles, and foreign capitals.

Local radio and television stations have increased their news operations as well. Indeed, local news has become one of the most important functions of individual stations. The average TV station now spends more than $500,000 a year on news and public affairs programming, with an average payroll of nearly $300,000 a year.

Both network and local broadcasting have been increasing the amount of time devoted to news. The number of radio stations has increased, although most other radio has turned to the five-minutes-on-the-hour headline news. Television news has settled into a format of network news in the morning, some local news at noon, network and local news in the evening, and local news in the late evening.

Electronic News Gathering

One of the most important developments in broadcast news has been the introduction of electronic news gathering, or ENG, as it is called in the trade. Electronic news gathering is based on the use of video cameras rather than film cameras. ENG is possible because of the perfection of minicams—miniature hand-held television cameras that replace motion-picture cameras and film. Minicams can be used either for videotape or for live transmission, doing away with the time-consuming problem of developing and editing movie film.

Electronic news gathering enables the television station to send out a crew for live coverage of a news event. The station can be equipped with a van that has a microwave relay dish on top of it. The ENG crew goes in the van to a news event, say a fire. They use the minicam to get a video picture of the fire and maybe an interview with the fire chief or a fire victim. The relay dish on the van sends the signal directly to the TV station, and the station in turn puts the live picture on the air. The viewer at home can see the fire while it is happening.

ENG is greatly changing the nature of television news. For one thing, it is expanding the news day of the television station. With movie film and the problems in setting up equipment, a TV station could cover events only from, say, ten in the morning to two in the afternoon. With ENG requiring a minimum of setup time and no film-development time, the news day can run from early morning to late at night. ENG poses some new problems for broadcast journalism, too, such as the ethical problems of live coverage. When ENG reporters go on the air live, they have no editors to prepare the news for the viewers. Whatever happens live happens on the screen as well. This is the excitement but also the danger of this new kind of news presentation.

Media Differences in News

News is not treated the same by all the mass media. For one thing, communication designed for eye reception must be structured in quite a different way from communication designed for the ear.

In writing for the print media, an important principle to note is that the eye is apt to be attracted to the first part of the page or the story or the paragraph or the sentence; the eye then trails off or is attracted elsewhere. Thus, the most important element is usually placed at the beginning. A newspaper lead would begin: "Jimmy Carter has won the election, according to the latest figures."

Writing for the broadcast media, however, requires attention to ear reception. Unlike the eye, which focuses immediately, the ear needs time to become accustomed to sound. So radio and television news copy generally backs into a story, giving the ear time to warm up for the important element of the sentence. Our lead for radio or television might begin: "According to the latest figures, Jimmy Carter has won the election."

In addition, print media have more space to develop stories in depth, while the broadcast media usually have time only to skim the surface of the news. Broadcast news must use fewer words and transmit fewer stories. A 15-minute newscast contains only about 1,800 words and about 25 different stories. An average daily newspaper has more than 100,000 words and dozens of different news items.

Differences in mechanics of news gathering also cause differences in media handling of news. Print media reporters still need only pad and pencil to gather news, although they may be accompanied by photographers and may carry tape recorders to help them with note taking. Radio reporters depend heavily on the tape recorder, although they may still do most of the legwork with pencil and paper. The television news operation requires heavier equipment—motion-picture and video cameras as well as complex sound equipment. A mobile unit is usually transported in a van, giving television quicker and more manueverable coverage of more news than it used to have. Nonetheless, many events are inaccessible to such equipment, including courtroom sessions, legislative meetings, and even Sunday sermons.

In the future, media news coverage may become even further differentiated, with the media complementing each other with various types of coverage rather than competing for the same facts and using the same methods. The print media will no doubt increasingly stress in-depth coverage, interpretation, explanation, and analysis, while the broadcast media will assume the headline and spot-news responsibilities, the extra editions, and perhaps more of the light, dramatic, and human interest elements of the news.

The man who climbs the highest tree and looks out over the horizon, no matter how accurately he observes and how carefully he reports, by giving the facts alone may not communicate all that his tribe needs to know. A black cloud may turn out to contain locusts, not rain. A friendly-looking tribe may turn out to be hostile. A promising supply of fruit or game may not be edible. As we have seen in the preceding chapter, even a fair and objective account of an occurrence may be misleading.

During World War II it became apparent that propaganda activities by Allies and Axis alike could and did color the news reporting of the war. American concern about the effect of international propaganda prompted the establishment of a high-level group to study the problems of free communication in modern society. The Commission on Freedom of the Press carefully investigated and analyzed the passive objectivity of news and concluded, among other things, that "it is no longer enough to report *the fact* truthfully. It is now necessary to report *the truth about the fact.*"

Why Interpretation Is Needed

Many indications from the world around us confirm the notion that straight reporting of the facts, while essential, may not always be enough. Observe, for example, how news can be abused. Tom Hayden, one of the "Chicago Seven"

Analysis and Interpretation

defendants convicted of conspiracy in starting riots at the 1968 Democratic convention, described the tactics of his colleagues in disrupting the courtroom during the trial:

> Part of the Yippie genius is to manipulate the fact that the media will always play to the bizarre. Even the straightest reporter will communicate chaos because it sells. The Yippies know this because their politics involve consciously marketing themselves as mythic personality models for young kids.
>
> Now, almost entirely media personalities, Abbie [Hoffman] and Jerry [Rubin] would spend much of their courtroom time analysing trial coverage in the papers, plotting press conferences, arranging for "Yippie witnesses" to get on the stand in time for deadlines, even calculating which of the defendants was getting most of the media attention. They knew that the smallest unconventional act would spread an image of defiance and disorder in the country.

On completely the opposite side of the spectrum, a respected scholar and statesman, Andrew Cordier, former president of Columbia University, makes the same point:

> I am convinced that there is increasing confusion on the part of the older generation regarding the youth of our day. Part of the difficulty can be attributed to the news media, whose field reporters seek out news regarding every shred of tension, crisis, and disruption on campus after campus . . . [creating] a sadly distorted picture of American campus life.

Those who wish to express a particular point of view, from the right to the left, from the old to the young, can use the news function of the media to communicate their one-sided ideas. To balance the use and abuse of news, the media must also be used to fulfill the need for analysis and interpretation, to put facts into perspective, to tell what it all means, to explain, to argue, to persuade, to express expert opinion about what happened, and to provide a forum for the expression of other opinions, as well.

Actually, the role of persuader, the act of molding opinion, came earlier in the historical development of media than the role of informer. Early newspapers and magazines were often more a collection of editorials and advertisements than news stories. It was not until the middle of the nineteenth century that news assumed great importance in mass communication.

The Separation of Fact and Opinion

When news became a part of American journalism, the tradition grew that news and opinion should be communicated separately. The reporter has been taught not to editorialize, not to express ideas and opinions and feelings about what happened, but rather to tell simply what happened. This practice is not followed by journalists in all countries. In many European countries, journalists are expected to bring their interpretation to the news they report.

The usual practice among American newspapers is to place editorial comment and opinion on a separate editorial page, often printed toward the end of the first section of the paper, leaving the front page and first inside pages for the publication of straight news. Another practice is to label clearly interpretative analysis or comment. Often the newspaper will publish a straight news account of a major story on page one, followed by an interpretative report as a sidebar feature, either on the same page or the inside pages. An editorial might then be written, on the same day, but more often on succeeding days, telling what the newspaper management's opinion is about the occurrence.

Much criticism is frequently directed at the news media for injecting editorial remarks into the presentation of news. The political affiliation of a newspaper or the bias of its staff may sometimes seem to affect its political news coverage. News magazines such as *Time, Newsweek,* and *U.S. News & World Report* have a particular problem because, while they conceive of their mission as a weekly "interpretation" of the news, their stories are not individually labeled as interpretation and many readers accept these stories as unbiased news accounts. The blurring of fact and opinion in the news media has become an increasing problem, requiring more critical attention on the part of the consumer.

Broadcasting and Editorializing

Radio and television also have a special problem in being used for interpretation and analysis. For many years, the FCC prohibited editorializing on the somewhat nebulous ground that broadcasting was such a powerful medium that it should not be allowed to influence opinions; it should only report facts.

Happily, that situation no longer exists, but the FCC still regulates the editorial function of broadcasting, particularly through the so-called Fairness Doctrine and the "equal time" provisions of section 315 for political candidates.

The Fairness Doctrine requires that when a station presents one side of a controversial issue of public importance, a reasonable opportunity must be afforded for the presentation of contrasting views. For example, station KING in Seattle, Washington, aired 24 editorials for 20 seconds each, endorsing certain candidates for public office. It offered all the other candidates not endorsed six 20-second time periods in which to respond. The FCC ruled that six replies were not a "reasonable opportunity" for rebutting 24 editorials. When KURT in Houston, Texas, expressed the opinion that the John Birch Society engaged in "physical abuse and violence" and "local terror campaigns against opposition figures," the FCC ruled that the station must give the society equal opportunity to express its views. Many such rulings have been made.

The equal-time provisions of section 315 of the FCC code require broadcasters to give all major candidates running for the same political office the same amount of air time to present their platforms. In 1967, when President Lyndon Johnson made a speech with heavy political overtones, Senator Eugene McCarthy, then a candidate for the Presidency, asked for equal time on the networks to present a different political point of view. The FCC commissioners, reviewing the request at length, ultimately voted against it on the grounds that President Johnson was not a presidential *candidate*. On many other occasions the FCC has ruled that candidates must be afforded the same air time as incumbents, and vice versa.

How the Media Interpret and Analyze

It is useful to examine the variety of ways in which mass media are used to provide interpretation and analysis of the world in which we live.

Interpretative and Background Reports. An increasing emphasis is being placed on reporting that attempts to tell more about an occurrence than the fact that it happened today. Historical background and perspective is needed. Many facts need further explanation, amplification, and clarification. The news media are increasingly developing specialists among their reporting staff, people who know as much about their subjects as the experts, and in reporting about a complex or controversial matter they can add their own expert opinions to give their audiences fuller understanding of the situation.

Even the wire services, long the staunchest defenders of straight, objective news reporting, are making more use of background and interpretative reports. In Washington, D.C., the Associated Press now employs a team of special reporters who carry out in-depth investigations of complicated yet vital concerns and practices. They are under no deadline pressures that would force them to write a quick and superficial report of the facts. They can get behind the facts, explore the ramifications and meanings of the facts, and reveal the "truth about the facts."

Editorials.   These have become a standard feature on the editorial pages of American newspapers and in some magazines as well. At times they are placed on the front page when they concern an issue that is extremely important to the publisher, but the responsible practice is to put the editorial in a box, set it in larger type, or in other ways make it appear separate from news coverage.

Generally, editorials are written anonymously by editorial writers, persons who specialize in persuasive rather than informative writing. The editorial-page staff begins each day by deciding the issues that require editorial statements. Editorial staff members discuss the general treatment of these issues and, with guidance from management on crucial issues, determine the stand the newspaper will take. Others may write editorials, too, including the editors and publisher as well as reporters who might develop strong opinions about the news they are covering and feel compelled to make a relevant editorial judgment.

Unlike the print media, which have enjoyed freedom of expression for centuries, the broadcast media have not yet unanimously embraced their right to air their opinions. In a survey by the National Association of Broadcasters it was indicated that only slightly more than half the stations in the country (57 percent of radio and 56 percent of television) regularly broadcast editorials (following the NAB's definition of an editorial as an "on-the-air expression of the opinion of the station licensee, clearly identified as such, on a subject of public interest").

But the editorial function is growing in broadcasting. The larger stations are more apt to editorialize, which bears out the journalistic theory that the stronger the medium, the more courageously it can accept its responsibilities. Four out of ten television stations now put editorials on the air every day; two and a half out of ten radio stations do the same.

Weekly Summaries and Interpretations.   Weekly news magazines, Sunday newspaper supplements, and some weekly newspapers also fulfill the need for interpretation and analysis. News magazines, particularly *Time, Newsweek,* and *U.S. News & World Report,* have had a major impact on interpretative journalism. They see their role as weekly summarizers and explainers, putting the news of the week into historical, political, or scientific perspective, to express the meaning in the news. *Time,* especially, has perfected the technique of "group journalism," where facts are sent to New York headquarters from many different persons and many different angles on a given story. These facts are chewed over and digested at the Olympian heights by editors and specialists, who then put together a final summary, synthesizing, interpreting, and analyzing the facts in some perspective.

Most major metropolitan newspapers are now also publishing special weekly reviews for their Sunday editions; here, news for the past week in various fields—politics, education, finance, culture—is reviewed and interpreted. A few publications, in weekly newspaper format, have been started for this purpose alone, such as *Barron's* a national weekly financial review published by Dow Jones & Company.

Editorial Cartoons. The editorial cartoon may be the most widely communicated interpretation or analysis of all. It has been a force on the editorial page in American journalism since 1754, when the first cartoon appeared in the *Pennsylvania Gazette* accompanying an editorial written by Benjamin Franklin. It pictured a snake, cut into 13 pieces, representing the British colonies, and it was entitled "Join or Die."

Effective editorial cartoons use the art of caricature, employing a few swift lines to exaggerate a character, personality, or feature to make a point. Bill Mauldin's "GI Joe" came to represent the attitudes and feelings of servicemen for an entire generation, and a few strokes of the pen could communicate much meaning. Herblock's grim, five-o'clock-shadowed hydrogen bomb expressed widely shared opinions about banning nuclear warfare. The economics of time and space that are permitted by the editorial cartoon give it particular force for mass communication; but by the same token the editorial cartoon is often a superficial and exaggerated statement about people or issues.

Documentaries. The broadcast media have combined interpretative reporting, analysis, and even editorial comment into one of the best vehicles for getting at the truth behind the facts; but the documentary has not been used nearly enough. When it has been used, however, the resulting product has been a powerful force for interpretation and analysis of events that often cannot be better communicated in any other way.

Most news on radio comes in five-minute segments, while television usually offers half-hour or hour news programs. Some interpretative programs and documentaries have often been "tucked away at unwanted hours" of Sunday mornings or afternoons, the so-called Sunday ghetto of broadcasting, says William S. Small, executive vice-president of CBS news, in his book, *To Kill a Messenger: Television News and the Real World.* The networks use special documentaries that preempt regularly scheduled shows whenever an event of major consequence occurs—an earthquake, a moon shot, a riot, or the death and funeral of a great person. Using sight and sound, television has been able to probe, capture, and communicate such events with great effectiveness.

The same techniques have been used to probe, analyze, and interpret great issues as well as events. The networks have produced documentaries on race relations, drug addiction, court procedures, political campaigns and elections, spy flights, island invasions, and war. Local news staffs of both radio and television stations have used the documentary to expose local police corruption, housing ills, poverty, hunger, and education problems.

The documentary can have a powerful effect because it can use sounds and pictures together to move people. Small describes one of the most impressive CBS News efforts, a documentary on "Hunger in America," a moving hour of broadcasting that opened with film of a baby actually dying of starvation as the camera took its picture. "The broadcast had tremendous impact," says Small, "particularly on the Secretary of Agriculture, Orville Freeman, who bitterly attacked it and demanded equal time. He called it 'shoddy journalism' that blackened the name of the Agriculture Department. Even as Freeman attacked, he was taking official steps that CBS interpreted as conceding the broadcast's main points: The Department abandoned its ceiling on food stamp programs, sharply expanded the number of counties with such programs, enlarged the quantity and variety of surplus food and sought (and won) Senate approval for an additional $200 to $300 million for food programs."

In 1971 CBS's "The Selling of the Pentagon," a documentary on the public relations efforts of the military, in turn became an editorial issue. Supporters and detractors used the media to praise or attack the production. The program's format eventually caused an attempt by the House of Representatives' Commerce Committee, led by Chairman Harley O. Staggers, to force a contempt citation against CBS president Frank Stanton. Dr. Stanton refused to submit "out takes" (film not actually used in the program) for committee analysis. The committee was concerned over whether two personal interviews shown in "The Selling of the Pentagon" were used out of context. Eventually, the issue settled on whether Congress should become the arbiter of what is *truth* in programming. The FCC ruled that the program met all criteria under the Fairness Doctrine. Some cynics saw the criticism of the documentary as an attempt by Pentagon supporters to cloud the issue or prevent future media disclosure of military-industrial activities for fear of reprisals.

Crusades. In some ways the print media counterpart to broadcast documentaries is the crusade. A newspaper might undertake a crusade for an issue on which it feels public interpretation and analysis is vital. The *Washington Star* undertook a crusade against fraudulent used-car sales practices and forced the government to improve regulations. The *Washington Post* crusaded against deceitful savings-and-loan-bank operations and brought about new legislation curbing such activities. Crusades have been the hallmark of courageous journalism and often have led to media prizes.

A crusade often starts with a news story that uncovers some illness in society that the editors feel should be exposed. A reporter or a team of researchers and writers might be assigned to dig into the facts. After the newspaper knows the facts, it decides how it will treat the story; it might publish the material in a series of news stories or interpretative reports, sometimes following up with sidebars and features on various aspects of the problem, and finally nailing down the crusade with an editorial or series of editorials in which the newspaper presents its conclusions and recommendations.

Columnists and Commentators. The media provide an opportunity for experts and specialists to analyze and interpret public problems in their fields regularly through the column, a by-lined feature. Many newspapers and magazines have staff columnists who write on local or special interests. But most columnists are handled by national syndicates, to which the publications subscribe. Columnists have great latitude to handle material in their own way, with a light or heavy touch, as reporters or essayists, with sarcasm, satire, or humor, as a critical review or exposé.

A typical newspaper publishes an amazing variety and number of columns. On an average Sunday, selected at random, the *Washington Post* published about two dozen columnists, covering a wide range of topics. Among them were four nationally syndicated political columnists representing a variety of political viewpoints: Joseph Kraft, liberal; George F. Will, conservative; David S. Broder, moderate; and Jack Anderson, investigative. A fifth, Henry Fairlie, a British journalist, wrote on international topics. The *Post* also ran a variety of columns on cultural subjects, including Sander Vanocur on television; David Hume on music; Joseph McLellan on records and paperback books; and Norman Eisenberg on hi-fi.

Syndicated columnists dealt with personal problems for the *Post:* Ann Landers' advice on sex, love, marriage, and almost anything else (the modern version of the old "advice to the lovelorn" columns); Dr. Jean Mayer and Dr. Johanna Dwyer's advice on nutrition; and Dr. Timothy Johnson's advice on health. The *Post* also carried four columns on a variety of sports in this particular issue: two on local sports, one on motor sports, and one on outdoor sports. Sports columnists' coverages vary from day to day, taking in almost every sport imaginable.

Other columns dealt with hobbies and helpful hints, and in this particular

"Hold on there, Tom. That's not cracker-barrel, that's 'Dear Abby.'"

issue there was a column on stamp and coin collecting, needleplay, gardening, and consumer problems. Columns on humor and "just plain easy reading" are also carried. This issue of the *Post* carried Art Buchwald's "Capitol Punishment," a column of Washington satire that often has more political bite than the work of some serious writers.

The Sunday *Washington Post* contained special sections with news reports and comments, too, including a book-review section and sections on business and travel; *Parade*, a national Sunday supplementary magazine; *Potomac*, a local magazine; a TV guide for the week; and 16 pages of comics in color.

Radio and television also utilize commentators who play a similar role for electronic audiences. The old format of 15-minute radio commentaries by strong personalities has vanished: individuals with strong political commitments, like Gabriel Heatter, Raymond Gram Swing, and Fulton Lewis, Jr., or persons with strong interpretative reporting talents, such as Elmer Davis, H. V. Kaltenborn, and Edward R. Murrow, are gone and have not been replaced.

Most stations now use a variety of newsmen and correspondents, some of whom might comment upon and analyze local news, but not as personalities. The networks have commentators, but they too are more likely to be reporters than persuaders, people like CBS's Walter Cronkite, NBC's David Brinkley, and ABC's Frank Reynolds. Only Mutual's Paul Harvey still falls into the category of strong personality with definite political commitments.

Criticism and Reviews. The mass media assume a responsibility to provide critical analysis of public performances, particularly in the popular arts. Books, movies, concerts, recordings, and dramas are all public performances that need comment. Such public review helps the audience find the right performance and the performer find the right audience and aids the artist in perfecting a craft and the public in making decisions.

In the past most mass media commentaries on popular arts were reviews rather than criticisms; they were reports of what happened, and only sometimes critical reports. The reviewers were more likely to be news reporters who had been given the book beat, the movie beat, or the music beat. There is now a general trend on the larger newspapers, at the networks, and certainly among national magazines, for these reviewers to be critics, expert and trained judges of literary, dramatic, or aesthetic performances, who can make authoritative evaluations.

About 33% read letters to the editor "almost always" while 12% read them "often" found Michael Singletary, chairman of the department of communication/journalism at Shippensburg State College, Pa. He also found that another 33% read letters to the editor "occasionally" and that 21% "almost never" read them.

Singletary found that 7.1% had sent one or more letters to the editor and that 65% of the writers were men. The survey was conducted near Harrisburg, Pa., where 368 persons were interviewed by telephone.

Letters to the editor apparently had a high degree of acceptance. Only 6.3% felt the letters were "unreliable" as to content and about 41% felt letters were "reliable." Given a hypothetical situation in which the letters were one of five features which might have to be eliminated, 24% said letters should be "the last to go" while 3.4% said they should be "the first to go."

As to why people read the letters, half the sample gave open-ended responses which were categorized as "testing public opinion on issues." Another 20% thought the letters were a mechanism for "letting off steam."

FIGURE 22.1. *Who Reads Letters to Editor?*

Letters to the Editor. Finally, it is the responsibility of the mass media to provide a forum for the expression of audience opinion as well. This function increases in importance as the ability of the masses to communicate publicly decreases because of the rising costs of printing and broadcasting. The people who write letters to the editor do not represent a true cross section of the public, nor can the media publish or broadcast all the letters that come into their offices. Selection and judgment are key elements in publishing the public's letters, as in all other phases of mass communication.

Public Access

The analysis and interpretation of information raises the issue of the right of access to the mass media by the public. Do only media analysts and interpreters have a right to comment on and pass judgment on facts and events and ideas? What right do outsiders have to express their opinions in the mass media? The mass media are privately owned institutions, but do they have an obligation to make their air time and pages available to nonowners who want to express themselves?

Public access to the mass media has become a critical issue at the present time. Some forceful pressure groups advocate open access to the media. In his book *Freedom of the Press vs. Public Access* (Praeger, 1976), Benno C. Schmidt, Jr., describes some of the rights claimed by those who advocate access: the right to defend oneself from defamation or to correct inaccuracies; the right of political candidates to advertise or appear in the media in which their opponents appear; the right of a person to respond to an attack or criticism; the right to advertise competing goods, services, or ideas in a medium that accepts advertising; or the right of anyone to have his or her views published or news covered on subjects about which the medium has carried its views or news.

In broadcasting, FCC regulations such as the Fairness Doctrine and the equal-time provision have made access a fact of life. The 1969 Red Lion ruling of the Supreme Court not only upheld the notion that broadcasters should provide reasonable opportunity for contrasting views to be heard on a subject; it also supported the idea that all media have an obligation to preserve an uninhibited marketplace of ideas.

The FCC regulations on cable television, adopted in 1972, require each new cable system in the top 100 markets to keep available one access channel for the general public, educational institutions, and local government. This channel must be available without charge at all times on a first-come, first-served nondiscriminatory basis. Live studio presentations of less than five minutes must be subsidized by the cable system, but other production costs must be paid by the user. The public-access channel has caused some problems in cities where it is already in use, such as New York, where the programs have tended to appeal to narrow and special-interest groups such as homosexuals or transcendentalists, and the channel has had trouble attracting audiences and financing.

Cable is the only area of mass media where the owner is actually required to open the doors to outsiders and permit them to come in and use the property for the expression of their views. No one can walk into a regular radio or television station and demand to go on the air with his or her version of the news or opinions. And no one can demand that any newspaper, magazine, or book publisher accept his or her ideas and put them into print.

The access philosophy accepted by the FCC in the area of cable television has been suggested for other media, but it has not been implemented. Further definitions of access rights came about as a result of the most celebrated access case of the 1970s, *Miami Herald Publishing Co.* v. *Tornillo.* In 1972, the *Miami Herald* ran an editorial opposing the candidacy of a Florida union leader who was running for the nomination for the state house of representatives. The candidate, Pat L. Tornillo, Jr., wrote a reply, which the *Herald* refused to publish. The case ultimately reached the U.S. Supreme Court, which ruled that the newspaper did not have to publish the reply. The Court's decision in the *Miami Herald* case constituted a firm rejection of the idea that anyone has a constitutional right to force a publisher to print something against the publisher's will. The Court held that such a ruling would do greater damage to freedom of the press than access would help freedom of expression.

Nevertheless, the mass media have an obligation to encourage uninhibited public dialogue and freedom of expression for everyone. And today the mass media have voluntarily accepted this responsibility in larger measure than ever before. For example, newspapers are providing more space for letters to the editor. Some newspapers, such as the *Salt Lake City Tribune*, have a "common carrier" column for outsiders, and pay a community panel to screen the contributions. Bill Monroe, executive editor of NBC's "Meet the Press" and former Washington editor of the "Today" show, has advocated a "letters to the editor" feature for radio and television stations as well, and a growing number of stations are moving in this direction. Other media have appointed ombudsmen to deal with reader and listener complaints. Many newspapers are giving greater visibility to their published corrections than they used to. These are all signs that mass media leaders are concerned about public access without giving up their essential rights to use freely their own franchise.

Syndicates

As news services provide for the centralized gathering and distribution of news and information, so syndicates serve as central agencies for the analysis and interpretation function for the media. There are 400 agencies that sell feature and editorial material to the media, both print and electronic. The small, independent weekly and daily newspapers or radio and television stations are the most likely customers for the syndicated material.

Syndicates hire writers and commentators and market their work to the individual media. Like the wire services, they charge the media on the basis of circulation or size. A widely syndicated columnist, such as political humorist Art Buchwald, can earn well over $100,000 a year through syndication.

Editor and Publisher's Yearbook lists more than 2,500 features that could be purchased from syndicates in the following categories: astrology, automotive, aviation, beauty, books, bridge, business-financial, cartoons and panels, chess, checkers, farming, health, history, household, maps, motion pictures, music, nature, patterns, photography, puzzles-quizzes, radio and television, religion, science, serials, short stories, special pages, sports, stamps, travel, veterans, women's pages. These are main features. Other classifications include agriculture, bedtime stories, dogs, foreign news, labor, manners, politics, questions and answers, schools, and verse.

The Impact of Analysis and Interpretation

Finally, we must ask the question, how effective are the media in fulfilling a role as interpreters and analysts in our society? Most readership studies show that more people read comic strips than editorials. Wilbur Schramm and David Manning White have reported surveys that show that 46.8 percent of college-educated males read the comics, while only 36.6 percent of college-educated males read editorials. The percentage of comic-strip reading decreases with increasing education, age (until age 59; after 60 it increases), and economic status, while the reading of editorials increases with age, education, and economic status.[1] Editorials thus may not reach as many people as comics, but they no doubt reach more important people, the doers and the thinkers who influence the masses.

In its study of the impact of broadcast editorials, the National Association of Broadcasters also concluded that awareness and actual exposure to editorials are more prevalent among certain types of people:

[1]Wilbur and David M. White, "Age, Education, and Economic Status as Factors in Newspaper Reading," in *Mass Communication*, ed. Wilbur Schramm (Urbana: University of Illinois Press, 1960).

They're apt to be found in three segments of the population: men; young adults; and college-educated people. In these groups there is greater awareness that stations editorialize... and that an editorial is the viewpoint of the station itself. Moreover, these are the people most likely to have been exposed to television and radio editorials (which may be why they are better informed on the subject to begin with). And, finally, they are the ones most inclined to want to see and hear more editorials than they do now.

The NAB's survey showed that about two-thirds of the public felt that broadcasting stations should editorialize. A large majority of those who have seen or heard editorials (83 percent for television, 73 percent for radio) remembered instances in which an editorial made them think more about a particular issue. And about half (54 percent for television and 47 percent for radio) reported that these editorials helped them make up their minds about issues.

Do editorials change minds? Probably not as much as editorial writers would like. During political campaigns, editorial endorsement of political candidates does not seem to have made a great impression on voting, according to most studies. Frank Luther Mott's analysis of the power of the press in presidential elections showed that newspapers had been beaten more frequently than they had triumphed.

On the other hand, there is much tangible evidence of the immediate impact of the mass media's analysis and interpretation, from editorials, columns, commentaries, crusades, and documentaries, including legislation passed, injustices corrected, individuals aided, tasks completed, and political victories won.

In summary, well-informed citizens, who alone can make democracy work, require news, information, analysis, and interpretation. They should get their facts, and the truth about the facts, from as wide a selection of media as possible. They should not depend upon any one radio or television station, or any one newspaper or magazine. They should have access to as many different reporters and interpreters for any given event or issue as possible. Otherwise, they will be like the blind men who touched only one part of the elephant and interpreted it as the whole.

A boy is roused a little early so that he can finish an assignment in his programmed-instruction sheets. After breakfasting with "Captain Kangaroo" he rushes out to the school bus, and shares a copy of *Mad* magazine with the older boys.

When he gets to his third-grade pod, a large open area containing four classes, he goes directly to the media center, puts on the head set, and pushes a button. A voice tells him about fractions, and slides come up to illustrate the points being made. Then he begins reading a fifth-grade book and responds to questions on reusable acetate pages in his workbook. Each third-grader works from a daily prescription that meets his special needs. After this he picks up a cassette tape and walks down the hall to the place where he will practice his French drill, imitating the narrator. When the practice drill is completed, he plays back the recording so he and the teacher can assess his progress. Back in the pod, a friend is watching an enrichment film on farm animals. In another part of the pod, an intern is working with several slow readers while being videotaped for evaluation by a master teacher later in the day.

On the way home from school the same boy reads a section in *Sports Illustrated* on "red-dogging" to his little brother. After dinner he settles down to some television entertainment; Jacques Cousteau is investigating sharks. After he goes to bed, he listens to his record player as Maurice Evans reads *Winnie-the-Pooh*.

23

Education and Socialization

This is not an unusual day for an American child, at least for one from a middle-class home in a suburb with an advanced public school system. For him the mass media are involved, both in and out of the classroom, with his education. Therefore, it is important to understand the extent to which the mass media have become his teachers.

The Tasks of Education

The mass media perform three major educational tasks: (1) *socialization*, which usually occurs in the home, is the process of reinforcing or modifying cultural norms; (2) *informal education*, which usually occurs outside the school, supplements the educational outlook of the individual; (3) *formal instruction*, which usually occurs in the school, is the process of systematically imparting specialized information and skills in a controlled, supervised environment. These three tasks affect the individual culturally as well as educationally.

The educational media mix is different for each person because of the amounts and types of formal instruction, informal education, and socialization

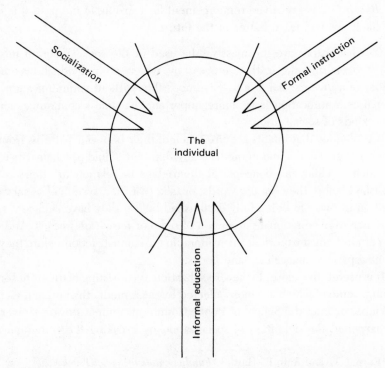

FIGURE 23.1. *The Components of the Educational Media Mix*

each of us experiences. Some schools are better than others. Some individuals read more books or watch more television. Each of us in conjunction with our parents, peers, schools, and the media have created a distinct educational mix for ourselves. But, regardless of the task or the individual, certain factors always affect learning.

1. *Repetition.* The more often we are exposed to something, the more likely it is that we will learn.

2. *Association.* The more a learning event can be associated with other things in the individual's experience, the more likely it is that it will be learned.

3. *Attention-Concentration.* The more effort we put into the learning, the more we will learn.

4. *Approaches.* If we learn in sequential steps from multiple approaches with appropriate content, the chances are better we will retain it. If many media impart the same content, there is a higher probability it will be learned.

5. *Reward.* If we received reinforcement for learning in the past, it is more likely we will learn better in the future.

To what extent are the mass media used in the socialization of modern society? Socialization, or the "process by which an individual becomes a member of a given social group,"[1] is impossible without communication. But personal communication is far more important than mass communication for certain kinds of socialization.

It is obvious that infants acquire much of their behavior patterns from the mother, father, family, and immediate environment. Child psychologists tell us that much of children's concepts of themselves in relation to others is well established before they can use words, or talk; that their system of social values is well on the way to being fully established before they have sufficient social experience to have rational perception of radio or television images. And children certainly must experience considerable formal instruction before they can read newspapers, magazines, and books.

It is useful, therefore, to view socialization as consisting of different sorts of learning, some of which are more affected by mass media than others. Gerhart D. Wiebe, dean of the School of Public Communication at Boston University, has sharpened the definition of socialization by breaking the communication

[1]Eugene L. and Ruth E. Hartley, *Fundamentals of Social Psychology* (New York: Alfred A. Knopf, 1952), p. 202.

process into three zones in a continuum. He refers to these as directive media messages, maintenance media messages, and restorative media messages. In other words, Wiebe proposes, some media messages direct or change human behavior, some serve to maintain or provide norms for human behavior, and some restore or release pent-up behavior.[2]

Directive messages are those that command, exhort, instruct, persuade, and urge in the direction of learning and new understanding. They must, says Wiebe, come from authoritative figures and call for substantial and conscious intellectual effort by the learner. Those kinds of messages that intend to direct performance or change behavior, most studies show, do not succeed unless they tie in to a structured, face-to-face, teacher-pupil relationship. Since the mass media cannot provide this sort of relationship, they are not important bearers of directive messages. They may supplement and enrich the direct learning process but they cannot replace it. In classrooms, from kindergarten to college, teachers having a direct relationship to students cannot be replaced by books, television sets, or computerized learning machines. As Wiebe says, "the printed Bible has not made the church obsolete nor has it reduced the role of the clergy."

Maintenance messages are those needed to tell us what to do in the every-day business of living. They tell us where we can find food, what dangers we should avoid, when we should pay our taxes, how we can get a driver's license, who we should regard as friend and foe. Such messages call for relatively little conscious intellectual effort. Here the mass media play an extensive role, through the communication of news, information, analysis, interpretation, per-suasion, and sales promotion. Wiebe maintains, however, that three conditions must exist before mass communication messages will have an impact in main-taining social norms: (1) the audience must be predisposed to react along the lines indicated in the message; (2) social provisions must exist for facilitating such action; and (3) the message itself must have audience appeal.

Restorative messages are those that renew and refresh the human capacity for productive social relationships. These include fantasies, which allow us to escape the harsh realities of life; humor, which allows us to relieve the tensions of the day; and drama and violence, which can provide catharsis for frustrations and anxieties. Here the mass media play perhaps the most important role in the socialization process, not only in the dramas of dime novels and soap operas, but also in the escapist TV serials and televised sports events, the violence of rape and robbery news, and even the fright in the stories of riot and war.

[2]Gerhart D. Wiebe, "The Social Effects of Broadcasting," in *Mass Culture Revisited*, ed. Bernard Rosenberg and David Manning White (Princeton, N.J.: D. Van Nostrand, 1971), pp 154–68.

If we run a personal inventory of the media socialization process, it becomes clearer. Did you go to church last Sunday? How long is your hair? What are you wearing? Where do you go on dates? Which of the new dances can you do? What records, books, magazines do you buy? What movies or television do you watch? To which radio station do you listen? Are the answers the same ones your parents or grandparents would have given?

To the last question, your answer is, probably not, because you have been socialized by your peers and the media as well as your parents. And often your peers and the media do not agree with your parents. There is a definite mix of interpersonal and media socialization.

For young people, the electronic media are truly significant in modifying attitudes about life styles. Radio-television-film-sound recording also affect other age groups. But the print media assume greater impact as age, education, and income *rise*. If the media pick up an issue (as they have with minority rights and women's rights), resocialization in this country can be slowly accomplished. The length of time required for the modification to occur depends on the complexity and importance of the issue as well as the exposure given the issue in the mass media.

Informal Education

All mass media provide content that is designed for neither socialization nor formal instruction. *National Geographic* magazines and specials on public television; the "Schoolhouse Rock," "Multiplication Rock," and "Grammar Rock" episodes in ABC-TV's Saturday morning lineups; the recordings of children's literature; and a variety of other content are used both in the home and in the school for learning purposes.

Perhaps the most visible and successful examples of informal education are "Sesame Street" and "The Electric Company" series produced by the Children's Television Workshop (CTW). Both were funded with initial production budgets of $7 million to $8 million a year, which allowed for quality planning, production, and research using commercial techniques and personnel. These projects were designed to "enterteach" children language, mathematics, problem-solving, and perception skills as well as dealing with the affective areas of moral and social development. These series were designed to compete for audiences. Both series were entertaining as well as educationally satisfying experiences. But *they are the only significant series to have been produced to date.*

Research in the area of informal education is limited, but all of us have learned about sharks, whales, seals, and other creatures of the sea from the televised programs of Jacques Cousteau. We have learned about the world we live in from books and magazines. Informally, we educate ourselves about food, wines, travel, and art from all media. In effect, our informal education occurs before, during, and after our school years. It is the means by which we stay intellectually alive.

Television and movies have become our teachers of history with films and series such as "The Adams Chronicles," "Eight Who Dared," "Eleanor and Franklin," "Lawrence of Arabia," "The Miracle Worker," and many others. "Civilisation" and "Alistair Cooke's America," as cultural evaluations of artistic and cultural heritage, have expanded our total education about the world and improved the quality of our lives. The docudramas of the lives of Lee Harvey Oswald, Martin Luther King, Jr., Lou Gehrig, Amelia Earhart, and others document social issues as well as dramatize personalities.

All these experiences occur in the "home (nonschool) environment," and have an impact on and broaden our educational horizons. Informal education is a critical learning force in America. It is the "high culture" of our mass media system.

Formal Instruction

Education in the United States involves the more than 54 percent of our population that enrolls in some type of formal instruction in nursery schools, kindergartens, elementary schools through senior high schools, junior and community colleges, postgraduate degree-granting institutions, professional schools, vocational and technical schools, correspondence schools, and continuing education. Over 70 million children and adults attend school every day; the schools are supported by $.40 of every city and state tax dollar, or over $120 billion, 8 percent of the GNP. There are over 2 million teachers in 95,000 public schools in 16,000 school districts. Another 11 million students go to college and universities taught by 670,000 faculty.

Books in Education

The most influential medium in formal instruction is the book, which also plays an important role in socialization and informal education. Books are successful largely because they adapt so well to individual needs and habits of students who use them.

Drawing by Schoenbaum; © 1978 The New Yorker Magazine, Inc.

"Read me."

Three crucial elements interact in the classroom: the student, the book, and the teacher. In many situations the book is the central reference point for both students and teachers. For example, books may be the only common, shared intellectual experience most white middle-income teachers have with their black low-income pupils in ghetto schools.

A specialized form of the book has evolved in the school environment. The textbook, by definition, is a book prepared specifically for classroom use; it provides an exposition of one subject area; and it serves as the content core of a given class. Several other types of books are specifically designed for the classroom; these include teacher editions of the text, consumable workbooks (the student writes directly in the book) to be used in conjunction with the text, standardized tests to evaluate student performance on the text, and manuals and trade books that are used to supplement and reinforce textbooks. The paperback, a softbound, less-expensive form of trade book, is used for a variety of classroom purposes, largely in higher education. Two kinds of textbooks are of primary importance. First are authored books, which focus on a special topic within the general subject area; second are edited books, which provide a general survey of materials written by a large number of specialists on their area of expertise.

Before a textbook gets into the hands of elementary school children, it must pass through the hands of a series of gatekeepers.

1. The book must be selected and printed by a publisher, who either solicits someone to write it or accepts a manuscript submitted by the authors.

2. The book must be adopted by both the state and local school boards; competition here is intense, because these adoptions are crucial economically. Unfortunately some boards exercise their power not only to modify the style of textbooks, but to censor the content as well.

3. The book must be chosen by the total school faculty, although some individual teachers have some degree of latitude in the use of supplementary material.

The selection process is similar at the secondary school level, but professional organizations, such as the National Council of Teachers of English, exert considerable influence. At most universities the individual teacher makes the selection of most books. This has led to the procedure of individual salesmen contacting individual professors, not only to sell books but to procure future manuscripts. Many college bookstores serve as little more than clearing houses for course materials, but the more progressive serve a critical role of carrying an extensive stock beyond course demands.

Although most of the publicity goes to best sellers, much of the income in the publishing industry comes from the sale of textbooks and reference works. If you consider all the educational possibilities of books, over 60 percent of all book sales are education related. In terms of learning materials sold and the percent of the educational budget spent on them, five categories are identifiable: (1) elementary textbooks, 29.4 percent; (2) high school textbooks, 16.9 percent; (3) college textbooks, 40.7 percent; (4) standardized tests, 2.8 percent; (5) audiovisual hardware and software, 10.2 percent. Interestingly, the audiovisual share of the market is decreasing, which is a critical indicator of the value of these materials compared with books. If we examine only textbook sales, 47 percent are sold to college students, 34 percent to elementary schools, and 19 percent to high schools. The average per capita sale of books to students is $11.83 per elementary pupil, $14.84 per high school pupil, and $58.22 per college student.

Textbooks cost Americans more than $1.2 billion annually, and they account for almost 30 percent of all book sales. Of this amount, 34 percent is spent on books for the 34 million elementary students; 19 percent for the 15.6 million high school students; and 47 percent for the 11 million college students.

Textbooks have a relatively low profit margin and are expensive to market. It costs from $1 million to $2 million to launch a new elementary school series. For the individual high school text, preparatory costs can run as high as $250,000; for one college text, $100,000. To compound the problem, many textbooks have life spans of only three to five years before revisions are necessary.

Societies have created a separate institution just to house their books. The primary purposes of the library are to provide long-term storage and easy retrieval of information. There are approximately 8,500 public libraries (plus 5,477 branch libraries), 4,267 college libraries, and 6,563 special libraries. Over $1 billion is spent on university libraries alone, and total U.S. library costs for all areas and activities are over $2 billion a year.

In order to make efficient use of the information stored in the library, a new class of books has been developed. Reference books, despite their limited numbers, account for 7 percent of all book revenues each year. This group includes general references, indexes, annuals, encyclopedias, handbooks, and many other subcategories. The reference book is crucial to the retrieval of data from large, complex library systems.

The book is a useful learning device because it is compact, portable, low in cost, and reusable; does not require special equipment to use; does not disrupt nonusers; provides individualized learning experiences as people set their own rate of learning; has easy reference capacity; and the reader can reread those portions that at first were not mastered.

Without doubt, the book is the best medium for many kinds of classroom instruction. Its inherent characteristics, and the schools' predisposition to exploit them, make the book an important information source in the classroom, library, and bookstore. Books are important for providing insights into a variety of activities and skills.

Magazines in Education

The *Standard Periodical Directory* lists more than 62,000 titles of periodicals other than newspapers. The education system uses a wide variety of these magazines and other serials, but two types of periodicals are more important than the others: (1) the 5,000 or more scholarly journals, which print the latest research and other information in a given field; (2) the 20,000 or more trade journals, which offer the latest information about the application of new research.

These two types of magazines provide important learning tools, especially at the university level. As a field expands, the number of scholarly and trade journals proliferate as well. For example, there are almost 2,000 periodicals that deal with education; about 1,000 cover library science; and over 450 that deal with media and media-related activities. It is almost impossible to stay abreast of the information in these fields, so special reference services, which cover a given area, have emerged—for example, *Topicator* is a periodical guide to a select group of magazines that deal with radio and television.

The scholarly magazine provides an open review by peers of a scholar's work. These scholarly journals usually contain original research, surveys of research literature, abstracts, reviews of research, news about the field, and book reviews.

The magazine plays a minor role in the primary grades of public schools because few magazines of the quality of *Highlights* are published for elementary pupils. Publishers find that subscribers outgrow their material rapidly, and it is too expensive to resell their product to each generation. Also, many classes of advertising are not considered suitable for children's fare. Most school libraries fill the void by subscribing to general adult periodicals like *National Geographic, Popular Science,* and *Popular Mechanics* that are used by children. Since few school libraries can afford to bind back issues, however, these periodicals are usually used for recreation rather than instruction or research. Even in high school, when term papers become part of the assignments, most students who want to search periodical literature must use the public library.

Thus, students making the transition from high school to college sometimes have difficulty adjusting to the increased emphasis placed on the magazine medium. Although the book is easier to find and use, the large library's periodical collection can and should expand the amount of recent data available.

The popular magazine is obviously a more important force for socialization than formal instruction. But many popular magazines such as *Popular Mechanics, Consumer Reports,* and *Better Homes & Gardens* provide specific information and teach new skills or improve old ones.

Newspapers in Education

Although the newspaper is heavily used for the socialization of society, especially for the communication of maintenance and restorative messages, it is the least used of the mass media in formal instruction. Newspaper organizations are making increasing efforts to have newspapers used in classrooms, but despite a few exceptions such as *My Weekly Reader*, newspapers are not yet as widely used as the other media.

Curiously, however, newspaper organizations are increasingly thinking of themselves as educational institutions rather than merely businesses. The editorial staff of the daily newspaper is essentially in the business of developing and communicating knowledge, researching facts, and packaging them for their audience. Some newspapers approach this task with the same seriousness that universities bring to the development of knowledge, allowing their staffs the time, freedom, and security necessary to pursue knowledge, even providing a sort of tenure and sabbatical leave system for expert writers and specialists on the staff.

Without a doubt, newspapers provide a wide variety of information necessary for carrying out day-to-day living as well as an increasing amount of facts and ideas to round out a well-informed citizen. Newspapers have also increasingly become source materials for some academic disciplines, particularly the social sciences, such as history, sociology, and cultural anthropology.

The Electronic Media in Education

Before analyzing the electronic media, it is important to understand that despite the potential educational impact of television, film, radio, and the phonograph in classroom instruction, there is—in comparison to print—little use of electronic media in most classrooms.

A variety of forces have affected attitudes about using the new media for instructional purposes, but six major issues have had a negative impact on electronic media usage in the schools:

1. Society's general attitude is that electronic media are for entertainment, not education.

2. Teachers often are print oriented and have little free time to develop the skills and attitudes necessary to use electronic media in the classroom.

3. The decision to use electronic media in schools is often made at the administrative level and forced on teachers, who resent this imposition.

4. Most of the materials available do not exploit the inherent qualities of these media.

5. The electronic media are prohibitively expensive unless they are used for a large number of students.

6. The "software" (content) is a threefold problem: (a) the traditional suppliers of materials have not moved vigorously to provide it; (b) local "in-house" materials do not reach the production standards children have become accustomed to in commerical radio-TV-films; (c) the content ages rapidly and is difficult to maintain professionally and economically.

Judith Murphy and Ronald Gross observe in *Learning By Television*:

Education is slow to accept innovation. It is a widely accepted fact that, on the average, an educational innovation takes fifty years to trickle down to the mass of schools and colleges. Earlier technological tools of communication, with obvious implications for learning, have not to this day become an intrinsic part of education. Films, radio, recordings, etc., play little more than token roles in instruction. Acclaimed in their day as TV is today, these devices have for the most part never been used with any real imagination.

The book is the *essential* classroom tool, and if the electronic media are to find a place in the current education structure, it will more than likely be as a supplement to the teacher and the book.

The development of our educational system is closely tied to the economics of student enrollment. The flow of all levels of government funding for education mainly determines the level of activity individual schools have in media education. With the leveling off of student population and financial support, educators have sought to protect teachers, physical plants, and the print materials. The new media are the first to go in difficult times because they are viewed as supplementary rather than central to the educational mission.

Purchases of educational media are literally at a standstill: total expenditures for educational equipment and materials dropped almost 10 percent in the late '70s; with continued strain on school budgets, the newer media will continue to suffer.

Sound Recording.   Recordings are seldom used in classroom instruction. Some use of tapes and records is made in music-appreciation classes, but few if any teachers have been able to obtain a sophisticated, stereo-equipped, accoustically satisfactory learning environment. Teachers use the old, worn "industrial" phonograph and then are amazed when their students are not overwhelmed by the classical-music experience. Many young people have sophisticated sound systems at home and are musically adapted to a culture out of touch with classical music. The aural books for the blind are, however, a major contribution in the field.

Foreign-language teachers have been able to develop expensive language laboratories to handle rote learning of pronunciation (a Berlitz approach). Unfortunately, some teachers and students have not learned how to function efficiently in these labs.

Audiotutorial systems based on programmed instruction are one bright area for the future. This process uses cartridge and cassette tapes, sometimes with auxiliary slides or film strips, for individualized instruction. At a few universities dial-access systems have been installed in library carrels or dorm rooms so that students can dial a given number and taped lessons can be obtained as frequently as needed.

Radio.   Using phonograph music for the bulk of its content, radio serves a significant role in socialization. The general education function of radio in the United States is expensive and fairly ineffective. For a number of years, many of the more than 870 public radio stations served as little more than classical jukeboxes for an elite audience within the total society. National Public Radio (formed in 1969 and government and foundation subsidized), however, is attempting to change the educational-radio service. Public radio now serves as a training ground for students planning careers in broadcasting, and many educational-radio facilities are used to teach broadcast courses within the university curriculum. Attempts have been made to use educational radio as a means of formal instruction, but, in general, this use has met with only minimal success. Despite its potential, radio is not deeply involved in classroom education in most U.S. schools.

Film.   Film is used extensively in socialization, and along with radio and the phonograph, is a crucial molder of youth culture. Film is used in formal instruction but in limited amounts. Unfortunately, many films supplied by audiovisual centers are either commercial films from television, which require modification of the course content in order to be used successfully, or they are poor-quality films designed for specific classes. When the commercial film is used, often little attempt is made to integrate it into the course. Student reaction to films in class is that screenings mean a day off from learning. Many specially developed, low-budget films are poorly produced. They become adverse experiences, which reinforce both the teachers' and students' negative attitudes about electronic instruction.

The major suppliers of educational films fall into two groups: (1) companies that produce their own films, such as Encyclopaedia Britannica and Coronet; (2) companies that distribute films produced by other companies for initial use in situations other than the classroom (McGraw-Hill distributes films produced by the television networks). At the present time there are more than 50,000 educational films, and too many of them are classroom-instruction disasters. Film production budgets, when they exist, range from $500 to $1,000 per running minute of an instructional film, compared to a budget that can run up to $70,000 a minute for television and theatrical films.

Future movies in the classroom will probably use the super-8-mm, cartridge, single-concept film. The function of such films is to teach one idea or operation in a few minutes. The film can be repeated until the student has mastered that body of information. The equipment is fairly inexpensive, and, once the cartridge is assembled, the loading and unloading of the projector can be handled by the student without difficulty. But there is a problem with "software." The ready-made cartridge films are few in number, and many are poorly made.

The film may have had more impact on classroom than any other electric medium, yet the impact is still really minimal. Many teachers cannot even thread projectors, and a large number of schools do not have an adequate equipment supply. The person responsible for audiovisual equipment is generally a classroom teacher with a part-time audiovisual job. If film is to become a significant part of classroom instruction, motion pictures must be integrated into the total curriculum and cease to be used as vicarious experiences and classroom entertainment.

Television. Television is the medium that contributes most to the socialization of Americans because it is the medium used by more people more of the time. Both commercial and public stations and networks contribute significantly to general education.

In 1952, the Federal Communications Commission set aside 242 (later increased to 309) station allocations for educational television (ETV). This was done in spite of considerable indifference toward the idea on the part of most educators. Four years later, fewer than 30 ETV stations were in operation. Educational institutions were not willing to invest the capital necessary to build the facilities. Thanks to an investment of more than $100 million by the Ford Foundation and extensive federal grants, 256 public television (PTV) stations are now on the air. Well over 60 percent, unfortunately, use the less desirable UHF channels. Despite tremendous dollar investments, plus extensive interconnection, the successes have been few in number, although in recent years the track record is improving as the result of federal funding of the Corporation for Public Broadcasting (CPB). Most public stations are on the level of paupers compared with the commercial stations and their resources.

A task force under the auspices of the Carnegie Foundation analyzed the ETV field. Because of this report and actions by the National Association of Educational Broadcasters (NAEB), Congress passed the Public Broadcasting Act of 1967, which provided the ludicrously small sum of $9 million to establish the Corporation for Public Broadcasting (CPB). The 1967 act also stipulated that Congress may appropriate additional sums each year if public broadcasters request such funds from Congress. Once again, the Ford Foundation came to the rescue, putting up the $10 million needed to air the first two-hour Sunday-evening broadcast of CPB; but that programming was less than successful and is no longer on the air.

To date, there have been two truly superior series achievements of American educational television, the Children's Television Workshop's "Sesame

Street" and "The Electric Company." Despite some carping from special interests in the school community, both series are considered to be the best educational programs yet produced. The two series used the unusual approach that learning can be pleasurable. These programs succeeded because they used flashy, commercial, TV techniques to "enterteach" youngsters.

Classroom use of television or instructional television (ITV) has been less than a complete success, especially when money spent and successful results are compared. Most of the research literature indicates that telelessons are no more effective than other methods of teaching.

Two generalizations become evident after a review of the research literature: (1) most ITV materials are developed without adequate consideration of learning theory and the inherent qualities of the medium; (2) the experimental situation has been unable to assess the complex nature of television learning. Most studies examine *how much* was learned, a few assess user attitudes, but longitudinal studies over periods of time have not been made.

The current state of educational uses of TV is limited.

> That televised instruction has achieved even its present modest success is, perhaps, a miracle. The achievement has taken massive pump-priming from private foundations and government. The Ford Foundation alone has made grants in the neighborhood of $100 million to all phases of educational television, at first through the Fund for Adult Education for educational television stations and programing, and later through the Fund for the Advancement of Education to schools and colleges. The federal government's support has added approximately another $100 million in equipment to the country's ETV facilities.
>
> The outlays of money and effort were expended for a variety of objectives: first, to put educational programs on commercial stations; later to stimulate in-school programs, both by broadcast and closed circuit; then to establish, equip, and staff noncommercial TV stations and to provide evening and out-of-school programs.[3]

Although educational researchers have spent millions of dollars of government money, little of their findings have been put to use by administrators and teachers, even at the institutions that have done the research.

"Most important is the point, rarely made, that the major—possibly only major—practical attempts made to use TV as a teaching tool have not come from conventional innovators in education (that is, from schools of education, administrator's groups, educational specialists' organizations or even the gen-

[3]Judith Murphy and Ronald Gross, *Learning By Television* (New York: Fund for the Advancement of Education, 1966), p. 11.

eral public). Neither... have teachers... or students shown much spontaneous impetus in demanding TV...."[4]

In effect, the single major problem for the condition of educational content of television is lack of funding. "The situation can be summed up in the fact that in a country where we spend almost $14 per capita each year for commercial television, we spend less than 70 cents on public television...."[5] And public television suffers because of this. In the mid-1970s fewer than three of every four American homes could receive a public TV signal, and despite the low cost public radio reception is even lower.

In the United States ITV services are provided to schools using four major distribution systems: (1) open-air broadcasting over existing ETV stations; (2) Instructional Television Fixed Service (ITFS), a 2,500-megahertz system for short-distance, point-to-point systems within a school district; (3) closed-circuit systems (CCTV) over telephone lines; (4) portable videotape recorders (VTR) in the classroom.

Open-air broadcasts provide the largest class audiences and revenue bases, but have the least flexibility as far as classroom usage is concerned. The ITFS systems are not widely exploited at the present time but have the potential of school-district autonomy and some flexibility in scheduling. Closed-circuit systems are widely used and have good technical transmission capability and considerable scheduling flexibility. The VTR units have flexibility in terms of scheduling, multiple use by instructors for recording class activities, and playbacks of materials produced elsewhere for individual student use.

At this time in history, educational research indicates the best course of action may be to move away from entire courses taught via television. The lightweight VTR units in production and the future cartridge-TV systems seem to be the best means of integrating television with other media and teaching techniques in the classroom. The TV instructional experience can be based on individual needs and personalized learning.

Three kinds of people are needed to create a major ITV project—a content specialist, a media specialist, and a learning-theory specialist. The content specialist is responsible for *what* is taught. The learning-theory specialist is responsible for *how* it is taught. The media specialist is responsible for translating both the *how* and the *what* into television techniques. It is better when each person knows a little about the others' jobs so that the interaction can be more fruitful.

The most innovative uses of media instruction have occurred in the United

[4]George N. Gordon, *Classroom Television* (New York: Hastings House, 1970), p. 3.
[5]George W. Tressel, Donald P. Buckelew, John T. Suchy, and Patricia L. Brown, *The Future of Educational Telecommunication* (Lexington, Mass.: D. C. Heath, 1975), p. 3.

States military. These include traditional A-V equipment, television, film, computers, and individualized programmed learning. Each branch of service requires training of instructors in media usage. The typical uses of visual media include (1) demonstration on specific manual tasks, (2) introductory units in technical and nontechnical subjects, (3) image enlargement of detailed demonstrations, and (4) playback of dangerous or nonnormal activities. The military establishment has 7,075 films, 15,516 audio tapes, and 1,220 video tapes in annual use. The service academies are also actively involved in mediated instruction to improve teacher-student ratios, standardize instruction, keep faculty and students up to date on weaponry, and train future officer-teachers to use electronic media when they enter the military classroom.

On the other hand, the problems within military education and training are generally the same sort of problems that plague civilian education. An "establishment" comes into being, with all its conservatism and resistance to improvement which that sometimes odious term implies. On an individual basis, people themselves tend to become bureaucratic and resistant to change. Innovation, where it occurs, depends a great deal on the "climate" created by the leaders and managers of training. The military establishment knows its mission—it therefore can design the training process with a great deal more specificity than can civilian education. With this realization, the trend is clearly established toward even more systematic design to insure the desired training outcomes. Systems engineering is no longer applied just to the development of hardware or weapons systems. The techniques of systems engineering are being applied to the instructional process and much needed instructional design techniques are evolving. Military training activities are beginning to package segments of courses for the training consumer. Significantly, military trainers are reexamining the traditional audiovisual communication media with the hope of developing some *strategy* for their employment in the instructional process.[6]

In effect, the military has identified problems, moved to solve them and, most importantly, attempted to socialize both teachers and students so as to help the media have an impact on the educational process.

There are many advantages to the television medium: it can serve as content specialist, relieve teachers of repetitive tasks, provide supplementary data, improve close-up visual demonstrations, and record performances of children and teachers for evaluation.

[6]H. B. Hutchins, Jr., "Instruction Technology in the Armed Forces," in *To Improve Learning* (New York: R. R. Bowker, 1970), 2:717.

The major disadvantages are lack of feedback and interaction, lack of integration of television into the total classroom experience, significant negativism toward it on the part of teachers, and inability to use the best techniques available because of high costs.

The future success of television instruction depends on intelligent use of the inherent characteristics of the medium. Too much ITV has been the "great talking face," which is an electric extension of the lecture method. Television is a tool to be exploited to solve educational problems, but an instructor must always consider carefully whether television is the best learning strategy to use in a given situation. Economic resources must be brought to bear on ITV, and it is absolutely essential that the classroom teacher be involved in such a project and receive in-service training. Considerable flexibility has to be built into the ITV system so that the teacher and students can use the material at their convenience.

The value of every technology is in terms of what it can do to improve the learning process. The book remains the essential tool of the classroom, and if television and the other technologies are to find a place in the current educational system, *it will be of a supplementary nature.* Newspapers will remain essentially a source of historical research and the scholarly journal a major source of current information and an important part of the "publish or perish" syndrome for university faculty.

New technology has tremendous relevance in the home but practically none in the classroom because it is breakable, costly, and unreliable; and because most teachers and students do not understand how to use it for instruction. Changes are going to have to come, but they will be slow. Perhaps, someday, former Secretary of Health, Education, and Welfare Robert H. Finch's observation will be invalid.

> The establishment in lower and secondary education is probably the most encrusted in the entire world. They still are teaching children as we were taught thirty years ago. A child today who comes into kindergarten has had from 3,000 to 4,000 hours sitting in front of that television tube, absorbing unstructured data that takes him way past Dick and Jane. And the system just doesn't respond to that.

There are serious problems in education, and the mass media alone cannot solve them. If the media are intelligently developed and used by teachers and learners, however, the educational process can most certainly be improved.

What is the difference between education and propaganda? While people usually respond positively and enthusiastically to the word *education*, they often react negatively and reluctantly to the term *propaganda*. Communication is essential to both, but a distinction needs to be made between these two concepts.

Education, traditionally, is the communication of facts, ideas, and opinions for their own sake, because they have an intrinsic value to the receiver of the message. The educator should be interested only in teaching Johnny to read because reading has some value to Johnny. The teacher should be interested in teaching the methods whereby Johnny can discover truth for himself and apply it to his own needs; the teacher should not be concerned with dictating the nature of that truth.

News media reporters and editors, in providing news, information, interpretation, and analysis for their readers, serve more as educators than propagandists. That is, journalists are educators in the sense that they usually attempt to provide in a balanced, fair, objective, and accurate manner a broad array of facts, ideas, and opinions from which readers or listeners can select those that serve their own needs.

Propaganda, on the other hand, is the communication of facts, ideas, and opinions, not for the audience's sake but for the benefit of the communicator, to further the communicator's purposes, whatever they might be. Propaganda has

24

Persuasion and Public Relations

had many definitions; the word comes from the Latin *propagare*, meaning the gardener's practice of pinning fresh roots of a plant into the earth in order to reproduce new plants. The Roman Catholic Church took this meaning when it established its College of Propaganda in 1622, considering its mission one of propagating the Christian religion.

Most students today have accepted the definition of propaganda given by the Institute for Propaganda Analysis and inspired by Harold Lasswell: "Propaganda is the expression of opinions or actions carried out deliberately by individuals or groups for predetermined ends through psychological manipulation."

Carried to an extreme, any attempt to persuade another person is propagandistic, whereas any attempt to inform is educational. Of course, propaganda contains a good deal of information, and there is much persuasion in education. People's minds are changed by both education and propaganda; the difference between the two often lies in the purpose of the communicator.

The Right to Persuade

Human beings are more often persuaders than teachers. Most communicate only when they want someone to do something for them. Early in life, babies communicate to get their diapers changed or to have someone bring food or warmth. Most private communications are purposive. In most democratic societies, it is a basic right of individuals freely to express themselves so that they can get others to serve their needs or believe in their ideas. The right of each person to persuade others is certainly basic to the American political system.

Public relations uses mass media for purposive, persuasive, or propagandistic communications. The practice of public relations is based on the assumption that we each have a right to our own point of view, and on the knowledge that there is no one right point of view. As Walter Lippmann argued persuasively in his book *Public Opinion*, we all see the world as pictures in our heads, from our own frame or reference. Each one of us sees a slightly different version of the world, and only through a free exchange of views about our version of the world can human beings reach some consensus about truth.

Our own society has traditionally been libertarian in its attitudes toward public communication. We have sought a dynamic and progressive order. We have argued that growth can only come from the open marketplace of ideas. We have felt that stability could be achieved not by curbing public communication but by allowing each individual to express personal ideas and opinions. Laws to preserve freedom of expression ideally should provide the best means to bal-

"Excellent, excellent. A fine blend of truths, half-truths, and blatant falsehoods."

ance power in society. They should prevent authority from getting into the hands of only a few, who would then control public communication to extend and preserve their own powers.

Thomas Jefferson reasoned that a free press could be a fourth branch of government to check on and balance the powers of the executive, legislative, and judicial branches. If the press were free, the truth would emerge in the open marketplace of ideas. And the truth would keep people free. But America grew to be a mass society, with industrial megalopolises in the place of pastoral villages and communication satellites in place of soapboxes in village squares.

By the middle of the nineteenth century, industrial power had become so strong that "big business" dominated public opinion at the polling places. It would have been difficult then to prove that each man was sharing in democracy by voting his own individual version of the truth.

Less than a decade after Jefferson's death, the development of the penny press gave rise to mass communication for the first time. By the end of the nineteenth century, the high cost of mass publishing, the beginning of newspaper chains, and the rise of communication empires made it difficult for the common person to use the press for personal expression.

The Dilemma of Mass Persuasion

In the twentieth century, the mass media have often been used for persuasion by the state, and in some societies propaganda is the chief function of media. Hitler used radio in Germany to arouse an entire nation to his ideas. Franklin D. Roosevelt, too, used radio in his famous "fireside chats" to persuade America to approve of his solutions to the problems of economic depression. In the 1960s and 1970s television became the chief means of political persuasion in America, and for a generation motion pictures have been one of the most effective weapons of international persuasion.

The growth of mass media as powerful and complicated institutions has made it increasingly difficult for individuals outside the media to protect themselves from massive propaganda and to raise their voices to persuade others. Must those who do not have access to the mass media be denied the right to influence others? Must they content themselves with being victims of the persuasive force of those who do have such access? This question poses one of the basic dilemmas of modern democracy.

John Milton's ideas about truth emerging in the free marketplace of ideas, and Thomas Jefferson's ideas about the free press as the bulwark to check and balance the power of government, seem insufficient in our modern, complex society.

The Role of Public Relations

The function of public relations developed as a result of this insufficiency in modern society. The profession of public relations came into existence in the democracies of the West at the very time that the Industrial Revolution had caused the breakdown of the old agrarian democracy espoused by Thomas

Jefferson. Public relations provided a way to adjust relationships in a mass society where power no longer seemed to be spread equally among all.

Public relations professionalizes and systematizes the persuasive efforts of individuals and organizations that stand outside the media, because access to the media requires expert techniques and knowledge. These individuals and organizations seek ways to use the media for their persuasion. The practice is based on the simple proposition that in a democratic society it is essential for anyone to win public acceptance, for nothing can succeed without the approval of the people.

The public relations person is thus an advocate of an idea or point of view, much as an attorney is an advocate of a client. Public relations practitioners have a right and responsibility to defend their client's point of view before the court of public opinion as much as attorneys have a right and obligation to defend their client's actions before a court of law.

In this book, we are primarily concerned with the media or communication functions of public relations. But public communication is only one part of the work of public relations, just as courtroom activity is only one part of the role of a lawyer; and in both professions, the public work may be the smaller role. The public relations professional also spends much time on counsel and advice, helping guide the client in ways that will be acceptable to public opinion.

Defining Public Relations

Public Relations.   This is a most difficult term to define because it has been so abused and misunderstood. It has taken half a century to come to some agreement about the definition of the term. But in 1976, Dr. Rex Harlow, a social scientist and public relations practitioner, through a definitive survey of professionals in the field, finally devised the following definition:

> Public relations is a distinctive management function which helps establish and maintain mutual lines of communication, understanding, acceptance, and cooperation between an organization and its publics; involves the management of problems or issues; helps management to keep informed on and responsive to public opinion; defines and emphasizes the responsibility of management to serve the public interest; helps management keep abreast of and effectively use change, serving as an early warning system to help anticipate trends; and uses research and sound and ethical communication techniques as its principal tools.[1]

[1]Rex F. Harlow, "Building a Public Relations Definition," *Public Relations Review* 2, no. 4 (Winter 1976): 36.

Organizationally, public relations is perhaps best conceived as the total public-communication effort of an operation, the overall umbrella under which would come advertising, marketing, promotion, publicity, employee communication, community relations, press relations, public affairs, and other such functions, including public relations counseling. Of course, not all organizations follow this formula.

Advertising.   For our purposes, advertising should be defined as a very specific type of communication effort, one that is based on purchased time or space in the communication media in order to send out a message. Institutional advertising plays a very important separate role in public relations.

Publicity.   This should also be defined in specific terms as free time or space in the communication media to send out a message. In order to get free space in the newspaper, for example, the message must contain some element of news or human interest. To get free time on radio, for instance, the message must contain some element of news or human interest, or some element of public service, because of FCC requirements for radio-TV stations.

The main difference between advertising and publicity is that, since the message sender pays for the time or space in advertising, he or she has more control over what is said. In publicity, since the message is free, the final shaping of it is left in the hands of the communication media gatekeepers. Publicity might be more effective, however, because it carries the tacit endorsement of the media.

Promotion.   Generally, promotion means the use of both advertising and publicity over an extended period of time to communicate a specific point. We speak of "promotional campaigns," implying that a longer period of time is involved over which message senders wage efforts to get their views into the public consciousness.

Public.   The term *public* has two meanings. There is, of course, a general public, meaning all the human beings in the universe. But more often we use the term to mean some specific public, such as American citizens, or more specifically, employees, stockholders, customers, and so forth.

The Growth of Public Relations

J. A. C. Brown, in his book *Techniques of Persuasion*, shows how the development of the printing press enhanced man's ability to persuade others.

The first printed books, bibles and missals, were used not only to win souls but to reform and revolutionize the Church. Printed tracts were used to persuade Europeans to migrate to the New World. Early newspapers quickly became used as organs of propaganda for economic, religious, and political causes, persuading people of the New World to break with the old, to revolt, and to adopt a democratic form of government. When the mass magazine appeared in America in the late nineteenth century, it was quickly put to use to persuade readers of the ills of society.

The forerunner of the modern public relations practitioner was the individual who worked as a press agent, publicity stunt man, and promoter. He became a character common in nineteenth-century America associated with the penny press. He promoted ideas, gimmicks, schemes, gadgets from the assembly line, land-speculation deals, theater personalities, and carnival freaks. Men like P. T. Barnum, the circus entrepreneur who made Tom Thumb and Jenny Lind the Swedish Nightingale into the sensations of the century, and Buffalo Bill, who made a hero out of the ruffians of the West, used press agents and promoters to get newspaper headlines for their stunts.

The first professional public relations man was Ivy Lee, a former *New York Times* and *New York Journal* reporter. He opened a publicity firm in 1904, which was involved not in simply promoting his clients but in guiding their total public communications. He saw an analogy between the court of law and the role of public opinion, and saw himself as a new kind of lawyer, one who would represent his client before the court of public opinion by counseling the client on his public communications. He saw his job as one of "adjusting relationships between clients and their publics"; he spoke of "public relationships," and so the phrase "public relations" came into use.

Ivy Lee counseled such important men and groups in America as John D. Rockefeller, the Pennsylvania Railroad, Standard Oil, Bethlehem Steel, Chrysler, the American Red Cross, Harvard, and Princeton.

Before long, many others were engaged in similar practice. During World War I, the United States government officially recognized, for the first time, that it had to organize persuasive efforts in its behalf in winning the war. It had to use communication to advocate its position before the American public and the world. President Woodrow Wilson employed a Colorado newspaper editor, George Creel, to head a Committee on Public Information. Creel's committee advertised, publicized, and promoted America's role in the war through all the media.

Although Creel's committee was disbanded after the war, America's increasing role in international affairs led to the realization that the nation needed to defend itself before the world court of public opinion, to express its national views before the other countries of the world. Nothing of this sort was done, however, until World War II had been declared. The government then established an Office of War Information, headed by Elmer Davis, a radio-news commentator.

After World War II, the Office of War Information evolved into the United States Information Agency, the official public relations organization for the United States government in its relationships with other nations and foreign peoples.

Between World War I and II, private public relations firms multiplied and grew to maturity in the United States. Chief among those who pioneered in the maturation of public relations during this period was Edward Bernays, a double nephew of Sigmund Freud. Bernays attempted to take public relations out of the realm of art and make it systematic and scientific.

In 1922 Walter Lippmann, newspaper editor and political philosopher, aided that task. His book *Public Opinion* was a carefully reasoned philosophical statement of the role of public opinion and public persuasion in democratic society.

Systematic and scientific persuasion required accurate measurement of public opinion. In the 1930s and 1940s the practice of public opinion polling emerged, pioneered by such men as George Gallup, a former journalism professor, and Elmo Roper, a social scientist. Polling not only provided a mechanism for the media to obtain feedback from their messages, but it also became a necessary adjunct to communication efforts of those who used the media to persuade the public.

In the 1950s and 1960s, public relations professionals turned increasingly to social and behavioral scientists to help measure public attitudes and test the effects of different ideas and messages on public opinion. Yet most public relations activities in the 1970s still centered on communication efforts and utilized basic communication skills, using the mass media to send messages to persuade millions.

At this time it is estimated that more than 100,000 people directly engage in public relations activities worldwide, with more than 50,000 in the United States alone. Several hundred independent public relations consulting firms provide advice and counsel to clients. Most of these are headquartered in New York, often with branch offices in the other large American and foreign cities. But almost every sizable organization in America has its own public relations representative, whether business corporation, labor union, political party, educational institution, or religious group; show-business personalities and other influential public figures also utilize the services of such representatives. Governments, too, at local and national levels, employ public relations experts to help get government facts and opinions expressed in the mass media, since in American society, the government does not own the mass media.

J. A. R. Pimlott, in his book *Public Relations and American Democracy,* says:

> Public relations is not a peculiarly American phenomenon, but it has nowhere flourished as in the United States. Nowhere else is it so widely practiced, so lucrative, so pretentious, so respectable and disreputable, so widely suspected and so extravagantly extolled.[2]

Public Relations and Politics

Nowhere is public relations more important than in American politics. Politicians are most often persuaders of public opinion, and increasingly they employ the mass media to influence the electorate. They often use the techniques of public relations, and they sometimes hire professional public relations firms to help them win election to public office and guide their relationships with constituents.

The process of legislation itself require publicity and promotion through the mass media. Bills that cannot capture the attention of the public through mass communication rarely reach the floor of Congress or state legislatures. Former Senator Joseph Tydings of Maryland expressed a growing sentiment when he charged that congressmen who could win media publicity were more likely to get their bills signed into law than those who were ignored by the press.

Extensive use of public relations has also been made in the process of electing public officials. A growing group of consultants who specialize in political persuasion have tried to make election campaigning more sophisticated, systematic, and scientific. They use survey research and polling to determine voter interests, to gauge the popularity of issues, and to test the public image of their candidates. They use computers to analyze the research and to aid in targeting the audience for the candidate's message. They advise the candidate, on the basis of research data, on the platforms to adopt and the personality aspects to emphasize or conceal. And they prepare the messages—through speeches, television commercials, press conferences, news releases, and such—to reach the voter.

Interestingly, these new techniques of political persuasion can make the

[2]J. A. R. Pimlott, *Public Relations and American Democracy* (Princeton, N.J.: Princeton University Press, 1951), p. 3.

election process more democratic. Politicians can take their candidacy directly to the people, through the mass media, particularly through television. They can bypass the traditional party structure, the political boss, and backroom politics. The public can be brought more directly into political decision making.

Unfortunately, however, the new public relations techniques in electioneering require money and a new kind of talent. The costs are high for public relations advice, polling, computers, advertising preparation, and media time and space. More than $400 million was spent on such electioneering in the 1972 presidential campaign. But expenses were far less in 1976, as a result of federal laws limiting the amount of money that can be contributed to and spent on a political campaign. For a time in the 1960s and early 1970s, much concern was expressed that the "new politics" of public relations campaigning through mass media would result in only very wealthy candidates being able to run for political office. But the election of Jimmy Carter, a farmer of relatively modest wealth from rural Georgia, proved that the new campaign reform laws were working and dispelled many fears.

A new kind of political talent is often required, too. Politicians who use media—particularly the television medium—to reach the voter must have a new kind of charisma. They must be able to captivate an audience through media. This could lead to a situation in which handsome, low-keyed, youthful, energetic candidates would have the edge over the more mature statesmen or political professionals.

Again, the Campaign Reform Act of 1972 helped to mitigate some of these dangers, by placing limits on the amount of money each candidate can spend on television campaigning. The televised debates between Jimmy Carter and Gerald Ford in the 1976 presidential election proved that television is not the only medium that people use to make up their minds about political candidates. The televised debates proved to have relatively little effect on changing voter attitudes.

The Government and Nonprofit Public Relations

Although public relations is most often viewed in terms of corporate and business interests, most areas of our society use public relations as a way of maintaining and adjusting relationships with their various publics, including local, state, and federal governments, hospitals, schools, religious organizations, the arts, the sciences, and even the mass media themselves. The federal government increasingly uses public relations people and public relations techniques. At this time, it is estimated that more than 10,000 federal government employees are directly involved in the practice of public communication.

There is a long-standing tradition in America that government should not be directly involved with public communication. The government does not own or publish any daily newspapers or own and operate any radio or television stations in the United States. The philosophy has been that government should not use media to propagandize citizens in a free society. Rather, the media should be privately owned and unrestricted so they can report the activities of government and keep the bureaucracy from growing too powerful.

Nevertheless, it has become increasingly clear that even the government in a free society must communicate vital information to the public and must be sensitive to the attitudes and opinions of the people. So government employs public relations practitioners, both to counsel government on its public relations and to inform people through the media, by using press releases, press conferences, media events, films, brochures, magazines, newsletters, and any other means that would prove effective.

At the federal level, government has not permitted the use of the term "public relations" because some politicians and legislators in Congress still feel that government should not be engaged in "propaganda" and that only elected officials should be in direct contact with the public. The executive and judicial branches should only carry out the laws created by Congress; they should not be responsive to their publics. So the public relations function in the executive branch of the federal government is called "public information," and public information personnel are supposed to "inform the public," not respond to the public.

The same attitude does not apply to our international communication efforts. Congress long ago recognized that America must communicate its policies and point of view to other nations. After World War II, Congress set up the United States Information Agency to inform and persuade the people of the world about America. The Voice of America is the broadcasting station of the United States to the rest of the world, but the VOA cannot be heard in America because of our tradition of keeping the government out of direct communication with our own people.

The Organization of Public Relations

Today most large business concerns, corporations, associations, and institutions with their own in-house public relations activities have a person in charge of these activities at a high level in the organization, often equivalent to that of a vice-president. This person's job is to help the organization with its communication, making use of the mass media wherever possible. Communication with and between employees is an essential element, of course, so the person in charge of public relations might have a staff of people who specialize in internal communication, producing employee newspapers, magazines, or other house organs. Public relations chiefs are also concerned with the owners or principals of their organizations, for whom they might produce stockholders reports or annual reports. The larger the organizations, the more publics they must deal with, and the more they must have specialists on their staffs to deal with those publics or the special media needed to communicate with them.

Perhaps most important, the public relations executive is concerned with the public at large, the customer, consumer, voter, and the person who makes up "public" opinion. Reaching this audience means using publicity, institutional advertising (which seeks to promote the institution rather than its by-products), promotional materials, and special events to establish communication channels to the mass public. Here public relations makes greatest use of mass media.

To use the media, the public relations expert must put the intended message into terms acceptable to the media—that is, must make the message newsworthy, compellingly vital for human interest, or of public service for the broadcast media. The public relations person puts messages in the form of news releases, public service announcements, or other means to get communications into the media.

The other side of public relations is the external public relations counsel. Counseling firms, like legal firms, exist to provide independent advice and counsel on public relations problems for clients. Some of these firms undertake the entire public relations effort of their clients, producing their internal communications as well as providing direction for achieving their overall public image. Hundreds of such public relations counseling firms exist. Table 24.1 lists the 40 largest in the United States.

We have discussed here mostly the public communication aspects of public relations, the "outbound" communications. But there is also a very large "inbound" communication aspect, where the public relations practitioner is concerned with public attitudes, opinions, and conceptions, and it is a large job to report these to the client. This part of the task involves analysis of the media as well as analysis of public opinion, through polls, surveys, and other measurement instruments.

The Public Relations Society of America (PRSA), an association of about 9,000 professional members, maintains a program of accrediting public relations practitioners through a series of written and oral examinations on the body of public relations theory and practice. The society also maintains a code of ethical and professional standards. Such programs have increased professionalism in the field.

TABLE 24.1. 50 LARGEST U.S. PUBLIC RELATIONS OPERATIONS, INDEPENDENT AND AD AGENCY AFFILIATED

	1977 NET FEE INCOME[1]	TOTAL EMPLOYEES
1. Hill and Knowlton	$20,071,673	602
2. Burson-Marsteller*	17,625,000[2]	605
3. Carl Byoir & Associates	—	293
4. Ruder & Finn	7,040,000	240
5. Manning, Selvage & Lee	4,398,795	111[3]
6. Harshe-Rotman & Druck	4,324,000	146
7. Daniel J. Edelman	3,929,449	148
8. J. Walter Thompson Company PR Department*	—	232[3]
9. Doremus & Company*	3,701,487	118
10. The Communications Board[4]	3,503,002	118
11. Ketchum, MacLeod & Grove*	3,300,000	95
12. Rogers & Cowan	2,870,608	94
13. Booke and Company	2,800,460	74
14. Sydney S. Baron & Company	2,780,400	40
15. The Rowland Company	2,524,848	68
16. Foote, Cone & Belding PR Companies*	2,416,000	99
17. ICPR	1,968,000	58
18. Robert Marston and Associates	1,913,000	36
19. Dudley-Anderson-Yutzy	1,749,924	59
20. Ayer PR Services*	1,602,000	40
21. Creamer Dickson Basford*	1,546,000	40
22. Fleishman-Hillard	1,466,059	31
23. Bozell & Jacobs PR*	1,425,000[2]	30
24. Underwood, Jordan Associates	1,355,000	31
25. Hank Meyer Associates	1,325,046	21
26. Aaron D. Cushman and Associates	1,179,000	31
27. Gibbs & Soell	1,117,379	30
28. Barkin, Herman, Solochek and Paulsen	1,021,124	33
29. The Softness Group	1,017,500	25
30. Golin Communications	1,000,000	34
31. Padilla and Speer	982,767	28
32. Edward Howard & Company	965,722	25
33. Anthony M. Franco	901,000	26
34. Lobsenz-Stevens	890,000	24
35. Sontheimer and Company	735,670	21
36. Cunningham & Walsh*	710,020	20
37. Gray & Rogers*	702,392	18
38. Anna M. Rosenberg Associates	700,652	13
39. Woody Kepner Associates	678,778	23
40. Richard Weiner	650,000	14
41. Grey & Davis*	600,000	16
42. Gross and Associates/Public Relations	581,000	15
43. Public Communications	550,000	25
44. Drucilla Handy Company	538,080	15
45. Ray Josephs-David E. Levy	471,122	15
46. Jay DeBow & Partners	445,935	11
47. Kanan, Corbin, Schupak & Aronow	436,515	15
48. Fred Rosen Associates	400,000	8
49. T.J. Ross and Associates[5]	—	16
50. Earl Newsom & Company[5]	—	12

*Advertising agency PR department or partner. [1]For 12 months ended June 30, 1977, unless otherwise indicated. [2]Year ended Sept. 30, 1977. [3]Includes 85 employees in U.S. and 147 abroad. [4]Includes Financial Relations Board and Public Relations Board. [5]T.J. Ross and Earl Newsom probably rank higher, but don't supply dollar figures.
SOURCE: © 1978 The J.R. O-Dwyer Company Inc.

The Work of Public Relations

In its occupational guide, *Careers in Public Relations,* PRSA outlines eight major functions for PR personnel. Most PR positions involve one or more of these eight functions: (1) writing and editing; (2) placement, meaning knowledge of and work with mass media; (3) planning and coordination of special events; (4) speaking; (5) production, meaning typography, layout, and the technical end of broadcasting and film; (6) programming, meaning the work of counseling and advising for long-range communicative effort and public image; (7) research and evaluation, both in planning a program and in measuring its effectiveness after implementation; and (8) coordination, meaning working with and sometimes through other staffs, such as personnel, legal and marketing.

The public relations job includes other elements as well. Public relations professionals must be experts on the subject about which they are relating. They must be the information center for their field, the central clearinghouse. They must also be versed in public affairs and current events, with a sensitivity to the forces that are shaping the world and public opinion, so that they can be the eyes and ears of their organization and respond with advice about goals and directions. Therefore they must increasingly understand the social and behavioral sciences and be able to apply statistical analysis and the use of the computer to their work.

PRSA's *Careers in Public Relations* lists five attributes for public relations: imagination; verbalizing skills, for writing and speaking; extraversion, for contact with people; sensitivity to people and events; and organizing and planning skills, including leadership and administrative ability.

While writing and speaking skills are essential to public relations, more emphasis should also be given to seeing and listening abilities. Communication, as we have said throughout this book, is a mutual act, requiring a receiver as well as a sender. Communication is a two-way process. In fact, public relations pioneer Ivy Lee long ago spoke of public relations as a "two-way street." The message sender must be a message receiver to make communication effective. The best persuader is often the best listener, one who is sensitive and compassionate.

A good example of this was the war in Vietnam. President Johnson believed he was doing the right thing in bombing Hanoi. But he could not persuade the majority of Americans to agree with him. A good public relations practitioner, listening to the will of the people, could perhaps have helped the President by either advising a more acceptable course of action or preparing a more persuasive argument for the final decision.

Rights in Conflict

Unfortunately, not all that is sent to the mass media from public relations offices is legitimate news or genuine human-interest material. Much of it is puffery, self-promotion, or a cover up of damaging facts. One cannot blame the public relations person for putting the client's best foot forward. That is not only a natural human tendency; it is a human right. We cannot expect the public relations practitioner to have the objective judgment about his or her message that the journalist should have.

Even more unfortunately, however, journalists often fail in their role as objective judges of the competing messages of various vested interests. Too often, the public relations professional's news release provides an easy way out for reporters or editors. It gives them a story for which they do not have to do extensive digging and research. The lazy journalist, the hurried journalist, the untrained journalist too often fall victim to the messages of public relations.

How much of today's news starts in a public relations office? No authoritative answer has been given to that question. Obviously, the answer depends upon the medium. Those newspapers and news broadcast offices that maintain large, well-trained, and well-paid staffs are less likely to depend upon the messages of outsiders than are small, economically weak and marginal news operations. Some studies of some media have shown that more than 50 percent of the editorial matter originated in press releases or promotional material.

Clearly, two rights are involved and are sometimes in conflict here. One is the right of each individual or group to express its point of view and tell its version of the truth. The other is the right to know, the right of individuals and groups to have access to accurate information about any subject of immediate concern. When these two rights are in conflict, it is difficult to know which has supremacy over the other, if at all. Perhaps the best that can be done in a democratic society is to maintain a balance between the two; the tension resulting from the effort to maintain such a balance should help preserve a healthy society.

The Future

Without doubt, the role of public relations will grow more important in the 1980s and beyond. As the population of the world grows and as the size of the planet shrinks (with supersonic jets and instantaneous global electronic communication), the relationships among people will become more crucial.

Communication, indeed, is essential to world peace. Understanding is essential to satisfactory relationships. Increasingly, more people in the world will need expert advice and counsel on how they can make themselves understood, or how they can change their ways to make themselves acceptable. This can be, and should be, the work of public relations, making use of mass media for human persuasion, through two-way communication, to achieve consensus and concord.

Consider the items the American family buys and uses—toothpaste, automobiles, canned goods, cigarettes, clothing, hardware, frozen foods, beer, tires, deodorants, watches, ready-to-eat cereals, paper products, cosmetics, patent medicines, and so on and on, ad infinitum. *Why* does the consumer spend his money on these items? Yes, they must have some value, but how does the buyer distinguish between brands when there is a great deal of similarity?

For example, what makes Green Giant vegetables preferable to those of another food processor? Part of the answer is the "Jolly Green Giant," his sidekick "Sprout," and the Giant's "helpers." Adults and children alike know these characters are fictitious, yet the identities created for them are important factors in the competitive canned-and-frozen-vegetable business. The Green Giant and his helpers inform the consumer as to the availability of Niblets Corn, convince the buyer of the value of the product, and persuade the shopper to buy Niblets rather than other canned corn in the supermarket. All these steps are a part of the advertising-communication process. Above all, these characters are communicators in the sales function of the mass media—"Ho, ho, ho . . . Green Giant."

25

What Is Advertising?

Advertising's increasing importance in the economy since the turn of the century can be easily demonstrated by noting that billings have grown from

Sales and Advertising

1. SONG: Up in the Valley...

2. ...of the Jolly Green Giant.

3. (Music under) HELPER: Why Sprout--...

4. ...you leaving the Valley?

5. SPROUT: Why not?

6. I'm big enough to be on my own.

7. HELPER: Yeah? Won't you miss the Giant's frozen Niblets Brand Corn?

8. (VO) Delicious sweet corn frozen in a pouch.

9. So you cook it in a butter sauce, not water.

10. SPROUT: Huh?

11. (Helper VO) Won't you miss that sweet, buttery, fresh corn flavor?

12. SPROUT: Frozen Niblets corn...?

13. (Helper VO) Yep. SPROUT: I'll stay.

14. This Valley's big enough for both of us.

15. SONG: Ho, ho, ho... Green Giant.

FIGURE 25.1. *Selling Niblets Corn in the Valley*

Used with the permission of the Green Giant Company.

about $500,000 in 1900 to $33 billion today. Significantly, most of that growth has occurred since World War II, and advertising now accounts for approximately 2 percent of the gross national product (GNP). Advertising supports commercial broadcasting entirely and pays for over half the costs of newspapers and magazines. In turn, the consumer pays for this advertising when he buys the goods and services advertised.

In the past the overwhelming concern of American industry has been production. Since World War II, however, distribution—getting goods and services to the public—has become the dominant consideration of many consumer-oriented companies. One of the critical components of the marketing mix, or plan, is advertising.

In order for a message to be classified as advertising, it must have the following characteristics: (1) a medium must be used to transmit the message; (2) money must be paid by the advertiser to the medium for carrying the message; (3) the message must be directed at more than one person, preferably a large number of potential consumers; (4) the message must identify the goods-services, the sender of the message, or both. These characteristics make advertising a different business-communication from personal selling, sales promotion, publicity, or public relations.

With the advent of the 1970s, new technological achievements had their impact on advertising. The computer radicalized many facets of the business. New techniques, new media campaigns, and new message construction has marked this decade.

Rarely, however, is a consumer decision based solely on an advertisement. Consumers are affected by needs, price, familiarity with the product, previous satisfaction, packaging, availability, and other factors. Advertising's job is to help create awareness of the goods-services, create a favorable attitude toward the goods-services, and create action in regard to buying the goods-services.

Advertising decision making is based on multiple forces within and outside the advertiser's organization. It is based on a marketing program that includes (1) distribution, pricing, and brands sold; (2) amount of personal selling involved; (3) nature of the product, its competition, and consumer demand; and (4) the budget. Advertising is only *one* part of the total marketing mix.

Advertising Age described the basic advertising convictions of Proctor & Gamble, the largest advertiser in the United States, as being—

1. *"The advertiser's chief role is selling the consumer."* Ads emphasize the distinctive qualities of the product and reflect the overall cultural values of the society.

2. *"Advertising creates new markets."* Ads suggest new uses for old products and new products to solve old problems. Competition has created new technologies and made better products available in the marketplace.

3. *"Advertising lowers costs to consumers."* Ads increase sales and per unit production costs decrease because of this. The per unit savings far exceed the cost of the advertising which the consumer eventually pays.

4. *"Advertising spurs continual product improvement."* Ads cannot "resell" poor products and the competition will overwhelm those products which do not become "new and improved."

5. *"Advertising forces competition."* Ads are necessary in today's marketplace, where price and quality are essentials in the marketing mix. The sales-distribution system is incomplete without advertising.

6. *"Advertising and scientific research work hand in glove on a vast and amazingly productive scale."* Ads help the consumer profit from inventions by speeding up the diffusion of innovation process.

Many individuals have developed very strong attitudes about advertising as a result of some ad campaigns. But advertising is neither the devil incarnate nor the saviour of our economic system.

Advertising Controls

In order to protect the consumer and counteract public criticism of advertising, a variety of controls have evolved. These controls over advertising come from three major sources: (1) governmental regulation, (2) industry codes of self-regulation, and (3) public pressure groups seeking specific changes from one or both of the above groups.

Governmental Regulation. The primary force in governmental regulation of advertising is the Federal Trade Commission (FTC), which was set up under the Federal Trade Commission Act of 1914 and bolstered by the Wheeler-Lee amendments of 1938. Since that time a variety of laws have increased the FTC's role. Each new law has, in effect, been a compromise between the forces seeking stringent governmental controls and the industry, which feels any additional legislation is unnecessary.

Although the Federal Communications Act of 1934 and subsequent broadcast legislation have never given the Federal Communications Commission direct control over advertisers, the FCC can and does exert some influence over the radio and television stations in advertising matters. In the case of cigarette ads, the commission had no jurisdiction over the tobacco companies. However, this agency forced the radio and TV stations, which it licenses, to refuse to accept cigarette advertising after January 2, 1971, but allowed them to accept ads for cigars and pipe tobacco.

In the end, however, it is the FTC that serves as the major federal watchdog over advertising practices. Most of the current laws and proposed legislation deal with seven basic problem areas:

1. Copyright laws protect original expressions of advertising ideas from being exploited by anyone other than the creator or his agents.

2. The Lanham Trade-Mark Act (1947) protects use of distinctive product names, identifying symbols, and advertising exclusively by the creators and their agents.

3. An individual's "right of privacy" is protected, since the advertiser must obtain written permission for any use of a person's name or endorsement in an advertisement.

4. A lottery is an illegal interstate activity and is also outlawed in most individual states. Advertising contests must not contain these three elements: prize, consideration, and chance. If they do, they are defined as lotteries and are subject to gambling laws.

5. Obscenity and bad taste are difficult to identify because the morals of this country are in a constant state of flux. What is acceptable today would have been obscene ten years ago. Some ads in *Penthouse* could be thought in bad taste by some people if seen in the context of *Jack 'n' Jill*.

6. Truth in advertising is generally agreed to be an absolutely essential item of an advertisement. However, an exact definition of truth is hard to come by. The FTC attacks untruths in advertising because they are "unfair methods of competition."

7. Libel or defamation (the intent to harm a person's reputation) is a legally punishable offense, and advertisers take every precaution against it.

Most of the cases handled by the Federal Trade Commission originate with a business competitor or a consumer. Some cases originate from studies initiated by the FTC or another agency. After investigation a formal complaint may be issued, and the advertiser is then given an opportunity to respond in a hearing. If the advertiser is found guilty, a cease-and-desist order is issued, forcing the advertiser to end the practice.

Besides the FTC and FCC, the U.S. Postal Service, Food and Drug Administration, Alcohol Tax Unit, Patent Office, and Securities and Exchange Commission exert pressures, if not actual control, over advertising at the federal level.

Industry Regulation.   Public and governmental outcries over excessive amounts of advertising, special product advertising (liquor, ready-to-eat cereals, children's toys, etc.), labeling, and other problems have led the industry to devise self-regulations to avoid the passage of new, more stringent laws.

Industry self-regulation of advertising practices comes from three sources: (1) advertisers, (2) advertising agencies, and (3) media. Although this form of regulation is not legally binding, it is effective because internal pressures are applied by the industry on offenders.

ADVERTISERS.   Self-regulation occurs here on both the local-retailer and national-manufacturer levels. Retailers have organized Better Business Bureaus to investigate consumers' and competitors' advertising complaints before legal action becomes necessary. There are approximately 100 local bureaus associated with the National Better Business Bureau, which developed a "Fair Practice Code for Advertising and Selling." In addition, "The Advertising Code of American Business" has been adopted by both Advertising Federation of America and the Association of National Advertisers.

AGENCY.   Self-regulation functions here under the auspices of the American Association of Advertising Agencies. The "4As" endorses "The Advertising Code of American Businesses." This code's major concerns are truthfulness, responsibility, decency, and accuracy.

The Committee on Improvement of Advertising Content of the American Association of Advertising Agencies seeks to evaluate offensive ads and recommends changes in that campaign to its agency. The advertisers individually or through trade associations police advertising practices.

MEDIA.   The media also review advertising and regulate the kinds of products and appeals that appear for public consumption. The stronger a given newspaper, magazine, radio, or TV station becomes financially, the less likely it is to permit marginally acceptable ads. The fleeting quality of the broadcast media makes radio-TV ads more difficult to review, but the National Association of Broadcasters has established a "code" for advertising and other member activities. Not all stations subscribe to the code, however.

The general purpose of self-regulation is twofold: It helps protect the public from false advertising; and it heads off further governmental restriction of advertising.

Public Pressure Groups. The individual's major form of advertising control—the refusal to buy the offending product—could be the most effective ad control, but generally is not because this form of protest is not organized.

The consumer's major success has been in group protests and information campaigns such as the Consumers Union, which publishes *Consumer Report.* Occasionally, crusaders arise to take up the consumer's cause. Under the leadership of Ralph Nader, an increasingly successful group of dedicated young people have committed themselves to consumer protection. Considerable push is being given to the notion of institutionalizing public pressure groups in the form of a major federal consumer-protection department. The reason runs that if both business and labor are cabinet-level posts, the consumer also needs a "Washington bureaucracy."

The Structure of the Advertising Industry

Four distinct business units are involved in the process of advertising communication: (1) the advertiser or company that produces or sells the goods or services being advertised, or both; (2) the advertising agency that represents the advertiser and creates advertisements; (3) the media representative who has three essential duties—to sell a given medium in preference to another; to sell a given market area in preference to another; and to sell one basic media unit in preference to another; (4) the medium that carries the advertisement.

In most cases the local advertiser deals directly with the local media. The ads are usually prepared in one of three ways. First, the local merchant's advertising department can design them. That is the case for most large department stores such as Marshall Field and Company in Chicago, which has an outstanding advertising department. Second, the local merchant can use advertisements provided by the national manufacturer of the goods he sells. Third, the medium can prepare the ad for the advertiser as a part of the total media service. In all three circumstances there is considerable interaction between the advertiser and the medium.

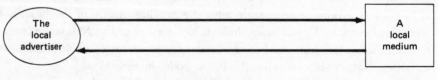

FIGURE 25.2.

Advertisers that use agencies to represent them seldom deal directly with the media. In this situation the agency, the company's advertising expert, prepares ads for, and recommends media to, the advertiser. If the advertiser approves, the agency then deals with the newspapers, magazines, or broadcasting stations involved in that ad campaign. In this case the agency initiates the action with both the advertiser and the medium.

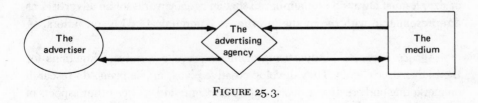

FIGURE 25.3.

At another level of complexity, the media may also have advertising representatives. In these instances the agency devises an advertising campaign and secures the advertisers' approval. Then, the agency contacts the media representative, who makes the necessary arrangements with the media. Under this interaction pattern, the media and advertisers are still farther removed from one another, since the major negotiations are conducted between the advertising agency and the media representative. As the advertising industry has grown more complex, the advertising agencies and media reps have become extremely important communication partners of advertisers and media in the sales-communication process.

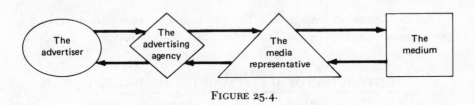

FIGURE 25.4.

The Advertising Process

Perhaps the best way to examine the advertising process is by analyzing the structure and operation of an advertising agency. Most large-budget advertisers employ agencies, but some, usually supermarket chains and large department stores, handle advertising with an in-house staff to merchandise the wide variety of nationally advertised products they sell. These merchants emphasize local availability, price, and service. If the chain handles its own brands as well (Sears, Penney's), then agencies and national campaigns designed and placed by a national agency become a viable alternative or addition.

Agency Structure.   There are approximately 3,400 advertising agencies in the United States. They come in all sizes, from one-man operations to those that are multinational and bill in the hundreds of millions of dollars. Regardless of size, it must always be remembered that an agency works for an advertiser as a representative with the media in order to communicate with consumers.

Agency Formats.   Advertising agencies serve a variety of functions for their advertiser clients. They develop creative plans, media plans, do research on marketing and creative aspects of the campaign, and service other aspects of the client's total marketing mix.

The *full-service agency* provides the total range of activities including creative, media, research, and marketing support for their clients. An alternative system has emerged; it relies heavily on the advertiser's in-house operation, which "jobs out" specific tasks to specialized organizations. These *boutiques* work exclusively in one aspect of the business: creative service, media placement, public relations, marketing research, etc. Part of the rationale for the boutique approach is that the advertiser will save a portion of the traditional 15 percent agency commission and the system will give the client more direct control of the total advertising program. Critics of this approach, however, feel the full-service agency provides more objectivity, more talent, and centralized responsibility.

Fee vs. Commission Systems.   The two payment systems in advertiser-agency-media relationships are (1) *the commission system* (usually 15 percent),

TABLE 25.1.
DISTRIBUTION OF AGENCIES BY U.S. BILLING, 1978

BILLING RANGE	NUMBER OF AGENCIES
$25 million or more	97
$10–25 million	137
$5–10 million	226
$1–5 million	1,299
Under $1 million	1,015
Agencies not listing annual billings	900
Total agencies	3,674

SOURCE: *Standard Directory of Advertising Agencies*, October 1978.

in which the agency keeps a percentage of the money it pays the media on behalf of its client; and (2) *the fee system*, which is a direct payment of a specified amount to the agency by the advertiser to cover manpower, expenses, and overhead, and allow for a reasonable profit. This is fairly standard payment procedure for boutiques and other creative support units.

In general, small advertisers and agencies of large-volume advertisers support the commission system because it is the most economical and best provider of services.

Agencies that work for a small-budget advertiser who desires multiple campaigns or a high-volume advertiser who seldom changes campaigns often prefer the fee system.

Ad agencies on the commission system also receive add-on fees for work that is "jobbed-out" to offset internal management costs for support of the client's publicity, public relations, promotional, and sales operations.

Advertising Classifications

Advertiser-communicators have developed labeling systems to clarify advertising processes. The four basic ways of classifying advertising are (1) by type of advertiser; (2) by audience; (3) by message—content, placement, and approach; and (4) by medium.

These classification systems are important because they identify the who, what, where, when, and how in relation to advertisers' expenditures and media earnings.

Type of Advertiser.   There are two major categories of advertisers: general and retail.

The general advertiser is usually a national or regional producer or distributor of a limited number of product classes who does not normally sell directly to the consumer. Nearly every general advertiser's campaigns are developed and executed by an advertising agency. Some corporations that produce competing brands in the same product class utilize the services of several agencies. Most general advertisers have come to use television heavily but also invest large sums in supplementary advertising in magazines, radio, and newspapers.

The retail advertiser, by contrast, is normally a local or limited regional operation that traditionally does not retain an advertising agency. The retailer's ads are prepared or supplied by the retailer's advertising department, the media in which the ads are placed, or the general advertiser whose products the retailer merchandises. The retail advertiser depends most heavily on local newspapers and radio stations.

Most retail and general advertisers maintain continuing ad campaigns to obtain the positive, cumulative effects of repetitive advertising. However, the most pressing concern of the retailer is immediate sales from specific ads, whereas the general advertiser is more concerned with the long-range effects and future sales of the total advertising campaign. The retailer must reach the consumers seeking immediate gratification of a specific need. The general advertiser is seeking to lay a foundation for purchasing decisions when the consumer need arises.

Type of Audience.   There are two groups to whom advertisers seek to sell their goods and services: other businesses and consumers.

Advertisers who seek industrial buyers, including other manufacturers, distributors, and retailers, are involved in *business* advertising. Most business advertising appears in the industry or trade press and in very specialized direct-mail campaigns.

Advertisers who seek individuals or individual home units are involved in mass, *consumer* advertising. Consumer advertising uses all the available media to varying degrees, depending on the specific thrust of the products' campaign.

The target audiences of business and consumer advertising make significantly different demands on the advertiser, especially in the scope of the media plan and the number of buyers available. The business advertiser sells goods and services that are in turn converted into consumer goods and services. The advertiser of consumer goods is selling items that are used directly by the people that buy them.

By Message.   The content, placement, and approach of advertisements are important because they designate the intent of the advertising communication.

The *content* of an advertisement-message may be either institutional or product oriented. Institutional ads refer to messages that develop the *image* of the advertiser. Institutional messages do not seek the immediate sale of specific products but rather attempt to create a positive attitude of good will in the mind of the public toward that advertiser. Institutional advertising may also seek to correct a negative corporate image, align the company with specific national goals, or, more recently, place the company in the vanguard on a specific social issue, such as race relations. Many industries pool individual, corporate, and financial resources to improve the general image of industry as a whole. America's railroads recently invested great sums in this type of ad campaign. In effect, this type of advertising message serves a function generally assigned to public relations. However, it is hoped that the long-range effect of institutional ads may lead to future sales by creating this positive image.

Product advertising seeks to generate *sales* of a specific commodity. The sales may occur immediately or at a later date when the consumer needs to replace or replenish a specific item. In terms of total dollar volume spent, product advertising overwhelmingly exceeds institutional advertising.

The *placement* category identifies the advertiser placing the message in a given medium, and there are three designations of type of ad placement: national, spot, and local. National advertising refers to ads placed by general advertisers in national media (broadcast networks, magazines, and so on). Spot (or national spot) advertising identifies ads placed in local media by general advertisers. Local advertising specifies messages that retailers place in local media.

When the Oldsmobile Division of General Motors advertises on the NBC radio network, that is national advertising. When Oldsmobile places an ad directly with WSB-TV, an Atlanta TV station, that is spot advertising. When an Oldsmobile dealer buys space in the *Milwaukee Journal*, that is local advertising.

In terms of television, national advertising accounts for nearly 45 percent of every TV dollar, spot 38 percent, and local 17 percent. For radio, local advertising accounts for 68 percent, spot 29 percent, and national only 3 percent.

A hybrid has also emerged in this category, cooperative (co-op) advertising. Co-op advertising refers to ads placed in local media by general advertisers and their retail outlets in combination. They share the costs and reap the benefits of the lower, local-media rates.

The *content* approach is another way of analyzing advertising messages. Advertisements may be *direct* and demand immediate action: "Sale, Today Only!" "Buy Now and Save!" The *indirect* approach is a "soft sell." It seeks action, but is calmer and more reserved or may use whimsy, humor, and informality in its approach. "Now" is replaced by "soon" or "at your convenience," or "when the need arises."

Both are effective, and when handled by experts, neither content approach is insensitive or offensive. But the indirect approach seems to be growing more dominant as time goes by.

Type of Medium. This classification system helps assess the relative strengths of the various media. Radio and television account for practically all advertising revenue for electronic media, although a small amount is spent for

Allstate Insurance Companies
American Bankers Association
Commonwealth Edison Company
The Frame House Gallery, Inc.
General Motors Corporation
Green Giant Company
Harris Trust and Savings Bank
H.J. Heinz Company
Keebler Company
Kellogg Company
Kimberly-Clark Corporation
Lewis/Howe Company
The Maytag Company
Memorex Corporation
The Nestlé Company, Inc.
Philip Morris Incorporated
The Pillsbury Company
The Procter & Gamble Company
RCA Consumer Electronics Division
Revlon Inc.
Schenley Industries, Inc.
Star-Kist Foods, Inc.
Steak and Ale Restaurants of America
Swift & Company
Union Carbide Corporation
Union Oil Company of California
United Airlines
Wilson Sporting Goods Co.

FIGURE 25.5. *Partial List of Leo Burnett Company Clients*

consumer advertising in motion-picture theaters. Five media account for most of the revenue earned by print advertisers: newspapers, magazines, billboards, transit, and direct mail.

Every company's media plan begins with an analysis of alternate classes of media. There is no universal rule as to which medium is best because each medium has advantages and drawbacks. What's more, marketing objectives for most products require an advertising campaign that combines media to provide the greatest degree of flexibility.

The Burnett Agency

In order to clarify issues and relationships, an analysis of the Leo Burnett Company follows. Burnett is a worldwide advertising agency with 33 offices in

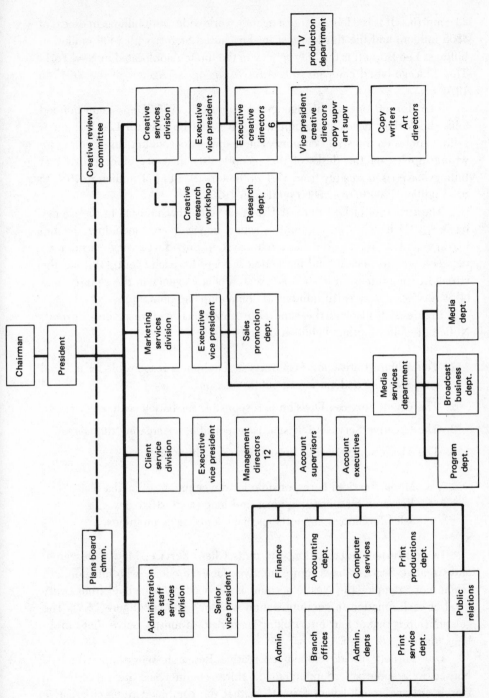

FIGURE 25.6. *Organizational Chart of Leo Burnett, U.S.A.*

23 countries. It is the fourth largest agency worldwide, with billings in excess of $865 million; and the third largest in the United States, with $400 million in billings. Leo Burnett is the only agency in the top ten not located in New York. This Chicago-based company was *Advertising Age*'s "Agency of the Year" in 1976.

Leo Burnett opened his agency on August 5, 1935. Depression-minded folks shook their heads and announced, "It won't be long till Leo Burnett is selling apples on the street corner." The doomsayers couldn't have been more wrong; apples on the desks of the receptionists in every office prove that billings have risen steadily from $7.4 million in 1945 to $71 million in 1955 to $188 million 1965 to over $865 million in 1978.

The structure of Leo Burnett U.S.A. is somewhat unusual in the agency business: (1) it relies on committee action in every area including the top management decisions; (2) it has a team system providing strong consultation between creative, client, and marketing services for each client; (3) it has the strongest commitment to in-house research of any agency in the country; and (4) it services a very small number of "blue-chip" accounts.

Figure 25.6 displays the general organizational pattern at Leo Burnett. Notice the following highlights on the chart:

1. The Administrative and Staff Services Division is responsible for internal housekeeping and corporate public relations.
2. The Client Services Division is responsible for liaison with advertisers.
3. The Creative Services Division is responsible for creating the ads.
4. The Marketing Services Division contains three units:

    a. Media Services is responsible for development of media plans.
    b. Research tests creative ideas and long-range strategies.
    c. Sales Promotion supports special clients' sales programs.

In the Burnett organization, the units Client Service, Media, Research, and Creative Services have representatives for each client, who function as a team. For example, the Nestlé account is serviced by personnel from every level of each function in communication with one another (figure 25.7). The relationship is that of four interlocking rings that, in unison, solve client problems (figure 25.8).

Leo Burnett has developed a Creative Research Workshop, which is housed in a suburban shopping mall. Here, commercials are pretested in storyboard and rough-layout formats so that the combined research-creative team can determine early-on if the campaign is on the right track.

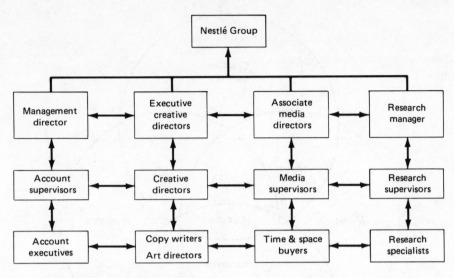

FIGURE 25.7. *Interaction of Burnett Units on the Nestlé Account*

A top-management Creative Review Committee analyses and approves all campaigns. This unusual agency procedure "provides an objective review for new work so that creative people aren't in the position of 'grading their own papers.' It's hard for a creative person to see his own efforts objectively."[1] Creative review also raises standards by challenging people to do their best. The review process builds morale, serves as a training ground, prepares the group for client presentations, and allows for interaction between top management and the young staffers on the creative team.

Creative Services. The process of creative decision making has one goal in advertising, *to help the client,* usually in the form of selling goods and services. Objectivity, avoidance of quick decisions to support cute-clever ideas, and simplicity are essential. Leo Burnett, a great copy writer himself, argued that there are three basic considerations in advertising:

1. What to put in it (copy, art, research, service and mechanical).

2. Where to put it (media and research).

3. How to extend its results at point of sale (research and merchandising).[2]

[1]Bob Noel, "A Few Kind Words for the CRC," *Leo Burnett News from around the World* 2, no. 5 (December 1976): 4.
[2]Leo Burnett memorandum, "What, Where, and How of Advertising," 9 April 1940.

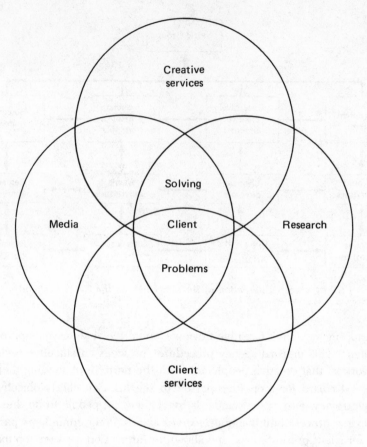

Creative
services

Solving

Media   Client   Research

Problems

Client
services

FIGURE 25.8. *Interlocking Rings as the Solution to Advertising Problems*

Burnett also felt that every advertisement should be (1) simple, (2) remembera-
ble, (3) inviting to look at, and (4) fun to read (see, hear). Above all else, an ad
should sell the client's products.

Dick Stanwood, a creative review chairman at the Leo Burnett Company,
feels that the creative decision maker must ask the following questions:

1. Is this a good, simple idea?

2. Will the reader-listener-viewer be left with the idea? What will they
remember from the ad?

3. Is this a good technique for presenting the idea?

4. How will the audience feel about the product and advertiser? (Most consumers want to do business with people they like!)

5. Is the presentation talking to the right people—people who will buy the product?[3]

The product, the ideas, and the ads have to come from writers, artists, art directors, musical talent, and other creative specialists in art, copy, and production. These creators must be able to conceptualize as well as write or draw or storyboard. The development of ideas is the most valuable contribution a creative individual can offer an agency. The members of the creative team must understand and appreciate every aspect of creative activity as well as their own specialty because the words of the writer must "jibe" with the visuals of the artist and the "music" of the arranger.

Creative ads depend on a select number of considerations in creative development.

SOURCE.   Who is the loneliest man in town? *The Maytag repairman.* Who sends you to the store to buy Starkist? *Charlie the Tuna.* Other product spokespersons are the *Jolly Green Giant,* the *Pillsbury Doughboy, the Keebler elves,* and the ladies in the laundry room who use Cheer. Whether real or created, their attractiveness adds power to an advertisement.

MESSAGE.   "Me and My RC," "Fly the Friendly Skies of United," "You're in Good Hands with Allstate," and "Take the Nestea Plunge" are phrases that focus the message through humor, develop conclusions, and state the product's case. They are central in developing the brand image. The most difficult lesson for advertising students to learn is that they need to create messages that sell. If the messages are *also* witty and clever, all well and good, but selling is the important issue.

PRODUCTION.   The quality and style of an ad depends on the creative talents of those who produce it. The artists, copyeditors, cartoonists, and others make good ideas work.

Copy strategy varies by product conditions; in general, however, new brands seek to create awareness and promote a first purchase, whereas established brands seek to create unique images to expand their market share. The overall objectives of the marketing plan must guide creative work. Copy can (1)

[3]Interview with Dick Stanwood, Chicago, December 1976.

characterize a product by creating an image, (2) provide a description of the type and quality of functions it performs, and (3) serve as a physical description of the product. But ads must at some point increase sales by providing reminders that the product is available and that it has multiple uses, many of which are new or can be used in new situations. The recruitment of new consumers and increased rate of consumption by current users are the two major ways to increase market share.

If we examine Leo Burnett ads for three cigarettes produced by Phillip Morris—Marlboro, Virginia Slims, and Merit[4]—we can identify three different approaches taken by the Leo Burnett Company to create distinct images.

The rugged *Marlboro man* emerged in 1954, after the product had been on the market thirty years as essentially a mild cigarette for women. The image of the prototype American male, the tattooed cowboy, sold Marlboro to those who wanted "filter, flavor, and flip-top box." For television ads, the theme music from the Western film *The Magnificent Seven* and the phrase "Come to Marlboro Country" were added and became a part of pop culture as well as the product. Marlboro has a direct and traditionally masculine image.

Virginia Slims emerged in the early 1960s before many women had their consciousness raised to today's level. The ads predated some aspects of the women's liberation movement and anticipated attitudes that Burnett felt were about to change. The *Virginia Slims woman*, like the *Marlboro man*, is a strong individual who knows her new place in American society. She is career oriented, fashionable, intelligent, and committed. This was one of the last major cigarette advertising campaigns to use television to create an image.

Merit cigarettes use a totally different approach because two factors had to be considered: (1) Merit had to depend totally on print media and (2) Merit had to develop a story that recognized public pressure and awareness about the health hazards of smoking. The Merit ads have detailed print copy rather than phrases, and they deal with the health issue in a print style that resembles a news story. These ads do not use role stereotypes, as do Marlboro and Virginia Slims. Merit promises a technological development that substantially reduces tar and nicotine content, but in blind comparison tests has taste levels that smokers judged equal to brands with much higher tar-nicotine levels. The factual news copy approach capitalizes on these ideas.

[4]There is tremendous concern about tobacco advertising today, and the inclusion of these ads is designed to provide information about advertising and not as an advocacy of smoking. It is imperative that in our free marketplace of ideas, students be allowed to examine all types of ideas; the Marlboro, Virginia Slims, and Merit campaigns are superior examples of advertising and need to be studied because of this.

These three cigarette ads contain:

A. Headlines

1. "Come to where the flavor is" (Marlboro).

2. "You've come a long way, baby" (Virginia Slims).

3. "Tar/Taste Theory Exploded" (Merit).

B. Copy

1. For Marlboro, there is one line identifying the two boxes.

2. For Virginia Slims, there are two lines and one is a second headline.

3. For Merit, the copy is all important; it is an information force in the ad.

C. Visuals

1. The *Marlboro man* is the center of attention; it is a "macho" image.

2. The *Virginia Slims woman* is juxtaposed against a second visual of *older* men and women in *olden* times, both historically and culturally.

3. The *Merit* visual is a small photo of cigarette packs.

In every case the cigarette packages are small but important parts of the total ad. The key, of course, is the integration of the visuals and the copy in the layout of the ad. This includes the design, composition, and appearance, as well as physical rendering of the ad. It is this combination in layout that makes the headline, copy, and visual work.

Compared to print production, the costs of television commercials are astronomical. Production costs have risen to an approximate average cost of $35,000 per 30-second spot. In a United Airlines advertisement two headlines are used, "Call United or your Travel Agent," and "Fly the Friendly Skies of United," which is the major slogan of United's overall advertising campaign. The copy is set to music and sung, adding an aural/oral dimension. Finally the visuals are all in motion, both within individual shots and between shots.

Whether print or television, the creators must ensure that the ad has unity, balance, and eye movement. At Burnett, an advertisement must be orderly, clear, clean, arresting, and inviting.

Client Service. For the general public, the account executive may be the most commonly recognized role in the agency business. He or she is both the liaison and their policy maker, who interprets client needs for the agency and presents agency solutions to the client. Client-service personnel are in the middle and are a key force in the planning, coordination, and evaluation of the total ad campaign.

At the Leo Burnett Company, most individuals move to client service after being trained and serving "apprenticeships" in other areas of the agency. Account executives' training needs to be broadly based so that they can understand and interpret every phase of the campaign for the client. Account group personnel are generalists among the specialists who populate the agency business.

Client-service personnel deal with a wide variety of client advertising departments, but five traditional approaches are most common.

1. The client's advertising department may be organized by media. Under this arrangement, the advertiser has a television-and-radio manager, a newspaper manager, and an outdoor manager. The emphasis of specialization in this case is based on the unique characteristics of each medium.

2. The department may be organized by product. At Proctor & Gamble, each of the company's brands has a complete team to service it, which leads to strong competition between teams as well as with other manufacturers.

3. The advertising director may have assistants for the South, Northeast, Midwest, and West. This geographical pattern of organization works well with companies that produce regional products or use specialized channels of distribution.

4. Some companies base their advertising operations on the kinds of users who buy their products and therefore have a farm manager, an industrial manager, an institutional manager, and a consumer manager.

5. The functional approach is used by many companies. This arrangement has an art manager, a copywriting manager, a media manager, and a production manager.

The client-service department of the agency is literally a part of the marketing staff of the advertiser. The account executive often has a counterpart in the advertiser's organization known as a brand manager, and they are the working contacts or partners or links in the agency-advertiser relationship.

Every advertising campaign should be developed around a set of specific objectives, which serve as operational directives for lower-level management to follow in developing the campaign and as a basis for evaluating the results. Sales, product recognition, public attitudes, share of market, brand loyalty, and other goals are logical objectives or goals of advertising campaigns.

Creative ideas can solve marketing problems and sell the product only if the facts are known. A good agency is more than a copy producer. The full-service agency has to develop a total relationship with its clients that extends to every aspect of the business. One of the clearest examples of this is the relationship between the Leo Burnett Company and Procter & Gamble. Procter & Gamble brought its new cold-water detergent, H-57, to Burnett in 1967. Because the cold-water detergent market was small (less than 10 percent of the total detergent market) but growing, because it was dominated by two well-established brand competitors (each had roughly 50 percent of the nearly 10 percent market), and because H-57 had achieved superior results in cold water and cleaning parity in warm and hot water, Burnett recommended that the product be marketed as an all-temperature product rather than as a "me-too" cold-water detergent. Procter & Gamble agreed, but decided to use the H-57 formula in its 18-year-old detergent Cheer. The product was revitalized, and the All-Temperature Cheer campaign begun in 1969 has doubled its share of the market and made it the second-largest-selling detergent in the marketplace. The turnaround occurred because of the mutual sharing of ideas and information between the advertiser and the agency.[5]

Client service is, in effect, involved in everybody else's business. It is the account group's responsibility to bring to bear all of the resources of the agency to solve the client's problems intelligently and efficiently.

Media Services. The buying of "space" and "time" has value only if it reaches the client's prospective consumers. The selection and buying of media is a highly complex operation that is increasingly research-based. Time and space buyers must be evermore "on target" because the placement of ads has taken on new intensity as ad costs skyrocket.

Advertisers seek out target audiences who use or are likely to buy their products. Advertising research seeks to specify the characteristics of the target audience, to identify the basic media units that reach the target audience most efficiently, and to develop advertisements that persuade that target audience to purchase the product being marketed.

Consumers must work to sort out the thousands of product advertisements that compete for their attention, time, and money. It is estimated that Americans see or hear more than 1,500 ads each day, and as consumers they have created psychological mechanisms that filter out those advertising communica-

[5]"All-Temperature Cheer: A Success Story," *Leo Burnett News from around the World* 2, no. 5 (December 1976): 1, 7.

tions that are of no value to them and have become increasingly aware of products for which they have an immediate need. That is why advertisers must ensure that their ads reach more of the right people and are better communications than those of the competition.

Media Services at Leo Burnett asks eight critical questions about target audiences.

1. Who are our potential customers in terms of demography?
2. Are there geographic differences in consumption? How much of the budget should be allocated to each market?
3. Are there seasonal differences in consumption? Should advertising weight vary across the year, or should it be level?
4. What are competitive brands doing in terms of budget size, and advertising strategy?
5. How do the consumers' demographic characteristics relate to their exposure to the various media?
6. Does the product's sales message lend itself to a particular medium?
7. Is exposure in one medium more valuable than in another in terms of impact on brand preference?
8. In terms of cost-per-thousand persons in the desired target group who are exposed to the advertising, which media vehicles are the most efficient?[6]

Every media plan seeks to enhance the advertising and marketing objectives. A media mix is built to maximize the advertiser's dollars, and to ensure that each medium makes unique contributions.

TELEVISION. There are three types of TV advertising:(1) *local* advertisers buying local time; (2) *spot* advertising bought by national advertisers on local stations; (3) *network* advertising bought by national advertisers. Cost to the advertiser is based on audience size and characteristics, production-distribution costs, and advertiser demand, which has accelerated dramatically. This increase in demand has increased prices paid by national advertisers. Local television advertising is sold by commercial units to local advertisers and by audience units (Gross Rating Points) to national advertisers through local stations' media representatives. Most network advertising plans today are packages or scatter plans, which provide a series of spots spread over a variety of shows at a

[6]*Training Manual for the Media Department* (Chicago: Leo Burnett, 1970), pp. 1–6.

group price. Full or partial sponsorship of programs and specials is relatively rare because of costs, risks, and demand. The 30-second commercial dominates; it was the child of necessity when costs and demand for spots required a change in the 60-second format. The transition began with advertisers "piggybacking" spots (combining two shorter commercials in a 60-second slot). The 30-second commercial delivers about 75 percent of the recall of a 60-second spot. The national advertiser is very dependent on network TV and the high cost and lack of availability of network commercial times is generating considerable interest in the development of "fourth TV network" alternatives. High network costs have also increased interest in other advertising media by traditional heavy users of television.

RADIO.   Radio is classified in the same way as television, but the medium is used in significantly different ways. Radio tends to supplement the media plans of most local advertisers, whose major focus is on newspapers and on national advertisers who emphasize TV. Radio day parts and program formats are key factors in audience size and composition, and because of this, radio audience selectivity has become an advantage to the advertiser with a specialized target audience.

MAGAZINES.   Magazines are generally classified by content, life-style of consumer, trade, and farm periodicals. The trend is toward greater selectivity in audiences, rather than general readership. This has proved to be an excellent development for the advertiser with a narrowly defined target audience that can be provided at a low cost per thousand readers. Regional runs of magazines have increased flexibility for smaller national advertisers, as well as longer local advertisers. Ads can now be run in some periodicals on the basis of zip-code references. Sales reps for magazines sell all advertisers at rates that decrease as advertising volume increases. Size of ad, position in the magazine, use of color, and number of copies in the run all have an impact on the cost.

NEWSPAPERS.   Newspapers are the backbone of retail advertising. This is the largest ad medium in the United States because it offers good geographical flexibility for advertisers seeking general audiences. National advertisers pay higher rates than do local advertisers, and this has led to co-op advertising, where the national advertiser pays most of the cost. Because the ad is placed by the local advertiser, the lower local rate is paid. Costs of advertising are based on rate systems that go down as annual ad volume goes up. Size of ad, type of reproduction, use of color, and position have an impact on newspaper ad costs. Both national and local Sunday supplements are valuable and offer superior reproduction and climate. However, as in magazines, newspaper readership rather than circulation is a true measure of the medium's value. Like magazines, newspapers have *primary readership*, those who purchase the newspaper, and *pass-along readership*, where use is based on casual availability, but readers do not have enough interest to buy. In-home versus out-of-home readership also is important because the out-of-home reader is generally a short-term user and the advertiser must depend on repeated exposure for impact.

DIRECT MAIL. Direct mail is the second-largest medium by dollar volume in the United States and is very selective, based on personalized messages sent to names on specific lists. It is expensive but successful. It can include letters, stuffers, cards, brochures, and anything else that will fit in an envelope. Many companies now include ads with their monthly billing statements; this is an excellent advertising format, which cuts postal costs because the bill has to be sent anyway.

OUTDOOR ADS. Outdoor ads take essentially two forms, the 24-sheet billboard and the painted spectacular (always lighted and sometimes animated). Boards have a life span of one to six months on the average. Outdoor ads are not selective, have to be bought locally, and usually carry reminder messages. This is an excellent supplementary medium for ads that do not rely on extensive copy.

OTHER FORMATS. Other ad formats include car cards, displays at airports and sporting arenas, matchbooks, sky writing, shoppers' specials, sound trucks, and anything else from ballpoint pens to T-shirts.

Like units in other departments at the Leo Burnett Company, media groups are built around accounts rather than function. The Burnett Media Services Department has a reputation for being the best in the business because it usually reaches the greatest number of prospects, as often as possible, to meet marketing objectives within tight fiscal controls.

Research Services. The three major types of research supplied by the Research Department at Leo Burnett support media, marketing, and creative functions of the agency. Traditionally, marketing and creative research is an in-house operation, whereas media research is supplied by outside sources, who survey print and electronic media audiences. The numbers in media research are important and impact on agency decisions. Agencies vary in the amount of research effort they support, but there is a trend of decision making based on supportable facts, rather than the old "seat of the pants" approach. However, suspicion of the "numbers crowd" remains in some areas of the advertising business.

At the Burnett agency, the media research unit is a part of the Media Department but handles problems agency-wide. A distinct Research Department is primarily involved in three activities: (1) evaluating creative ideas and copy in the research workshop to identify and articulate problems early-on so that they can be corrected before huge dollar investments are involved; (2) developing of new up-front marketing research and development funded out of Burnett profits and not the client's budget; and (3) evaluating government, private, or consumer research that might have an impact on client products.

At a time when some agencies were cutting back in research, the Burnett agency expanded and made its research commitment more sophisticated.

Reasons for Success. Leo Burnett has clients who believe in and appreciate advertising. About half of Burnett's annual growth comes from the expanding growth with current clients. The agency has about thirty U.S. clients, yet it annually does $604 million in billings within the United States.

Burnett's success is based on the quality of output constantly reviewed by its personnel. The client-service attitude of participation in solving the client's problems permeates the agency. Burnett has always sought a basic strategy, a basic selling idea, a something extra to help its clients. Burnett ads are simple, memorable, pleasant, and focus on key product qualities. Most importantly, Burnett ads sell clients' goods. How could they miss? Think of all the help Leo Burnett gets from giants, elves, talking tunas, lonely repairmen, and doughboys!

Creative Advertising Communication

Advertising creativity depends on the ability of the advertising encoder to develop advertisements that move the target audience to respond positively by buying the product advertised. With the ever-increasing political, social, and economic pressures of our complex mass society, creative advertisers need to do more than exercise creative freedom. They must constantly improve media plans, research skills, and creative approaches. The competition for consumer attention is growing fiercer, and the truly creative advertising campaign is being forced to assist in the consumer's handling of this information implosion. The target audience must *hear* as well as listen, and *see* as well as watch a given ad, if the ad is to be a creative sales tool.

The creative advertisement has to revolve around consumer needs and the ability of a given product to satisfy those needs. The target audience is not some unthinking mass; it is composed of individual, thinking beings. The few intellectuals who sneer at advertising as some sort of drivel are as foolish as the rare advertiser-communicator who believes that he can consistently mislead the public. David Ogilvy in *Confessions of an Advertising Man* argues most persuasively for intelligent, creative advertising when he states, "The consumer isn't a moron; she is your wife."

People listen to Stevie Wonder, Mozart, or a recording of a Broadway musical; they go out to see *Equus* or the latest Mel Brooks film; or they stay at home to read or watch television. Most of these audience members are seeking entertainment more than anything else. They are seeking respite from their regular work routine, and the mass media add something to their lives.

When that "something" becomes qualitatively valued by the society, the listeners-viewers-readers become involved with art. Are the Beatles' *Sgt. Pepper's Lonely Hearts Club Band*, Orson Welles' *Citizen Kane*, television's "The Ascent of Man," or the novels of John Cheever works of art? Can media content for a massive audience ever be anything other than pure entertainment?

As our society expands, urbanizes, and accelerates, the mass media are being asked to provide more and more entertainment. Much that is art in every society—music, dance, theater, literature, sculpture, painting—is also a major means of entertainment. In effect, much that is art is entertaining, and entertainment can certainly be artistic. As the media are utilized to provide recreation and play as entertainment and art for an ever-expanding audience with increasing hours of leisure time, it becomes more difficult to produce both quantity and quality.

26

Entertainment and Art

The Interaction of Leisure, Entertainment, and Art

Three aspects are relevant to an understanding of the importance of entertainment and art in the mass media: (1) leisure, or free time from work or duty; (2) play, or nondirected, random, spontaneous amusement; and (3) recreation, or diverting pastime for relaxation and rejuvenation. Both art and entertainment are a combination of the mental, emotional, and physical acts that occur during leisure time in the form of play for enlightening and recreational purposes.

Mass Media and Play. Americans formerly had difficulty coping with play because our society was work oriented. Those who followed the work ethic praised labor and achievement and condemned play and idleness. Play was considered worthwhile only when it was evaluated as the *work* of children. Entertainment and nonessential art were often suspect because they occupied time that could be better spent at work. For many Americans, work was the real business of life; the periods between labors were times of guilt. Much criticism of the mass media has been inspired by this work ethic, prompting the feeling that if readers or listeners or viewers are not being informed, enlightened, persuaded, or educated, their time is being wasted.

New Leisured Class. Traditionally, the leisured class was composed of the wealthy and well-educated elite who were expected to use their freedom from work to refine the culture and use their money to encourage artists to improve life. For the rest of society, limited leisure was earned by working; often "leisure" time had to be used to prepare for future labors. Art has flourished under these conditions, as did entertainments, in previous periods of history—the Renaissance, for example.

Today, the Industrial Revolution has forced us to change our attitudes toward leisure. Machines have taken over much of our heavy labor, shortening our workweek and leaving us with more free time. In 1900 the average workweek was 6 days, 72 hours; by 1950, it had been reduced to 5 days, 44 hours; by 1970, less than 40 hours a week was average; and today the 4-day workweek is becoming increasingly popular. One observer computed that the average worker in 1970 had 2,750 hours of "free" time each year, time not spent at work, sleep, eating, or commuting. A large portion of those 2,750 hours was spent with attention focused on the media and the art and entertainment they provide. Consider the average weekday of 8 work hours, 8 sleep hours, 2 personal needs hours, and 2 household activity hours; that leaves 4 leisure hours a weekday plus most of the weekend for recreation.

Also, life expectancy is increasing; the late adult years, which do not usually include a job, must be made worth living. The development of a leisure ethic could imbue individuals with confidence to use spare time. Leisure has worth in learning, self-expression, and personal well-being. A major challenge in this society has become what to do in free time. For too many Americans, it has become a plague.

Mass Media and Recreation.   Today we recognize that recreation is vital to personal happiness and self-development. The human being needs to be restored and rejuvenated through diversion and relaxation. The pressures of society, the pace of modern life, the intensity of competition, and the anxieties caused by increasing change and mobility have made recreation more important than ever.

Much mass media fare has been designed specifically to provide recreation. Television situation comedies, newspaper lovelorn columns, romantic movies, comic strips, magazine features, radio soap operas, and the publishing bonanza of the "erotic historical romances" of Rosemary Rogers (*Sweet Savage Love*) and others have often been criticized by segments of the intellectual community, but they have an important recreational function. They provide emotional escape, create fantasy, and allow for physical catharsis necessary to renewal of the human spirit.

Leisure and Art.   In order for artists to write, direct, and perform in plays, movies, television series, operas, concerts, records, etc., they need "free-time" to be creative. It is difficult if not impossible to work all day at a job and then come home and be creative. B. F. Skinner suggests that leisure time is a prerequisite for the emergence of art both for its creation and enjoyment. This does not mean that everyone who has time will use it to create art or that consumers will use their free time to enjoy that art. But without freedom from care or want, art is an unaffordable luxury.

Leisure and Entertainment.   Time to enjoy life or to relax and prepare for the next work period is essential. Entertainment, whether self-produced or supplied by the mass media, requires leisure time. Think about the difference in your television viewing at school during exam week vs. the winter break back home. This vacation is when you have the time to spend watching television. Only when you have it can you spend it.

A large segment of media audiences use music, film, television, novels, and magazine literature to meet their need for art; and this art literally improves the quality of life in our intense, crowded, increasingly urbanized society. Art brings "beauty" to mankind.

But audiences of the mass media are offered many kinds of entertainment and art. These audiences make conscious choices between various types of entertainments of varying levels of artistry. This choice is based on (1) what audiences have learned to like; (2) what their immediate physical, emotional and intellectual conditions are; and (3) what is available for the time and money they have to spend. The mass media provide both entertainment and art, and many media contents are often both.

The Scope of Entertainment in Media Content

Entertainment is an important element in almost all aspects of mass media. Artists, writers, journalists, teachers, and preachers have long known the value of drama, humor, entertainment, and art in the process of creating, reporting, educating, and promoting. We might speak of entertainment as an "overlaid" use of mass media, because it is an aspect of almost all media content.

News as Entertainment.   Newspapers and news magazines often try to make the news as entertaining as possible. The layout of the page is designed to make information attractive and palatable. News content is often intermingled with humorous features, amusing sidebars, diverting human-interest stories, and clever fillers.

Even writing style can add entertainment to news presentation. David Brinkley's wry, laconic style and Walter Cronkite's sense of humor make their evening news programs entertaining as well as newsworthy. CBS's Charles Kuralt's amusing series of "on-the-road" reports provides information about ordinary citizens and little-known events presented in a low-key, human-interest manner that is packed with insight.

Sometimes news provides unexpected entertainment. One of the most interesting moments in news entertainment came during the NBC-TV broadcast of the 1964 Republican convention, when John Chancellor was carried off the convention floor in semiarrest. As he was being taken away, he signed off with, "This is John Chancellor, somewhere in custody." It was news, and it said something about that convention; but it was also entertaining.

Often publications or productions designed primarily to be entertaining also provide news and information. "Roots," the most widely viewed television miniseries in history, attempted to provide information about the history and struggle of Afro-Americans, and it was informational and entertaining. Both

Godfather I and *II* entertained, but they also informed the audiences about underworld operations. Even the comic book provides certain types of information for many of its young readers.

Analysis as Entertainment.   Much analysis contains entertainment. Editorial cartoons take positions on issues, analyze and interpret events, but also entertain audiences. The humor in such cartoons helps attract the reader's attention and becomes important in the analysis of the problems involved. The Marlette cartoons "The Big Apple" and "My Place in History" are humorous as well as comment on the economic problems of New York City and the "Watergate" mentality of the Nixon administration.

The *Peanuts* comic strips, paperback books, television specials, and feature motion pictures are all blatant, unadulterated, good-natured fun. For many fans, *Peanuts* is the ultimate entertainment, and Charlie Brown is a child's version of Everyman. The philosophy of Charles Schulz (creator of *Peanuts*) is that a comic strip that does not say something is valueless. Schulz analyzes, interprets, and editorializes as he entertains.

Persuasion as Entertainment.   Entertainment is an ingredient essential to persuasion and propaganda. One must attract and hold public attention in order to persuade, and entertainment is often more effective than information in

THE BIG APPLE

5/28/75

New York faces bankruptcy.

winning over an audience. Sometimes the most subtle propaganda is that which contains the least haranguing and most entertainment, for example a military concert to promote the Pentagon, or the programming of the Voice of America to promote U.S. interests.

In the brilliant propaganda film *The Triumph of the Will*, director Leni Riefenstahl glorified Adolf Hitler and the Nazi party. Despite our horror of Nazism, the film's ability to entertain still excites and stimulates our imagination.

During World War II, hundreds of feature films supporting the war effort were made, such as *Across the Pacific*, *Bataan*, *Guadalcanal Diary*, *Lifeboat*, *Master Race*, *Mrs. Miniver*, and *They Were Expendable*. In each of these films the enemy was depicted as evil and dehumanized; Americans and their allies, by contrast, were pure, tough, and right. Interestingly, few major films were made in direct support of America's military involvement in Vietnam. An exception was *The Green Berets*, which was entertainment that propagandized in a World War II fashion. It was not very popular, suggesting that factors other than entertainment are involved in effective propaganda. In 1977–78, however, American artist-propagandists released a series of antiwar films set in the Vietnam period: *The Boys in Company C*, *Coming Home*, *The Deer Hunter*, and *Apocalypse Now*. The successful persuasion came in the form of entertainment years after the war was over.

Advertising as Entertainment.   The primary purpose of advertising is to sell products, but to make sales requires audience attention. Entertainment is one way to get that attention; and entertaining ads also sell. One of the best ad campaigns was the Volkswagen series. They were good advertisements because they helped sell VW "bugs" and "rabbits." The same ads were good entertainment because they were interesting, diverting, and amusing. Another campaign entertainingly sold Benson & Hedges 100's despite a growing negative public attitude toward cigarette smoking. The best testimony for the entertainment value of commercials is the fact that children, and some adults, often pay more attention to the television advertising than to the program.

By the same token, the media often advertise as they entertain. All cars driven by the villains and the investigators in "The Streets of San Francisco" were Fords. Fords were provided because the Ford Motor Company benefits from the exposure of their products. An attempt is often made to link well-known entertainers with products. Bob Hope plugged Texaco because Texaco sponsored his comedy specials. Sometimes an attempt is made to link a program with the show's sponsor: "The Kraft Music Hall" (Kraft Foods) and "The Hallmark Hall of Fame" (Hallmark Greeting Cards) are examples.

Education as Entertainment.   "Sesame Street" is an educational TV program that is also highly entertaining. The series was designed to teach preschoolers basic skills that would be helpful when they entered kindergarten and first grade. In order to maintain attention, the program used the most interesting qualities and techniques of film and television. For example, highly sophisticated TV commercial styles are used to teach the alphabet and numbers in ABC's "Multiplication Rock" and "Grammar Rock" inserts in their Saturday morning lineup.

Films like *Rocky, Network, A Star Is Born,* and *Saturday Night Fever,* and radio programming of rock music, are elements in the socialization of young people. Both media are primarily concerned with entertainment but play an educational role as well.

Textbooks are designed to keep the child's attention as they teach reading skills. Much English instruction in the United States is designed to teach youngsters to appreciate entertaining literature. Television, too, can combine entertainment with socialization. "Phyllis," "Rhoda," "The Mary Tyler Moore Show," "Maude," and "Good Times" were TV shows designed primarily to entertain audiences, but they also taught us something about the changing roles and status of women in American society and the problems they face, which were very different when "I Love Lucy," "My Friend Irma," and "Our Miss Brooks" were popular.

Specific Media Roles in Entertainment

Each medium has technical, cultural, and economic limitations that determine how much and what kinds of entertainment it can provide. Some media are essentially purveyors of mass culture and others of elite culture. The media and the audiences tend to be selective and seek each other out.

Television. More than 74 million American households are equipped with at least one television set that is used an average of over six hours per day. We might safely say that watching television has become one of America's major leisure-time activities. People seem to want to use TV to be diverted, interested, amused, and entertained. This does *not* mean that television provides no service to specialized audiences. It does mean that mass culture dominates commercial TV content.

Commercial television provides an array of escapist entertainment. It has been called a "vast wasteland" of programming determined by a "cultural vote" through ratings that are accurate only within specific statistical limits. Network television provides filmed dramas and videotaped variety shows in prime time (8:00–11:00 P.M. EST). Daytime television consists of situation comedies, soap operas, and quiz shows. Local stations provide little more than a news block and syndicated series that were previously on the networks. To many critics, the total impact of television seems to have been designed primarily to be a massive, pop-culture machine catering to the entertainment needs of its audiences.

Unlike the pages in books, the cuts in an album, or the footage of a film, broadcast media cannot increase the hours in a day. Television entertainment is time-bound. In addition, TV is a limited natural resource—only a specific number of channels are available. Our society seems to have charted a course for television; that course is entertainment. But not all television content is popular, mass culture. Significant progress is being made to provide outstanding cultural experiences such as "Eleanor and Franklin," "Roots," "The Adams Chronicles," "King," and coverage of the Olympics.

The Motion Picture. Unlike the situation in television, anyone willing to spend enough money can make a film, and with the technical advances being made in 16-mm production equipment, the cost is coming down. The days of mass production of theatrical films are over. The United States produces only 225 films a year. The masses who used to flock to movie houses now stay at home to watch television. Because of this loss of a general audience, the film medium has begun to turn to specialized entertainment films for minority audiences, which seem to come in topical waves. Films try to provide content that is not available on television.

America is in the midst of a period of rapid social change. Motion pictures are often a reflection of this state of affairs. Three major trends in entertainment and social values are being exploited: (1) the market for films has become youth oriented because some two-thirds of all movie tickets are bought by people under 30—the people in this age group have been called a "film generation"; (2) the presentation of content has become much more explicit, especially in terms of violence and sex; (3) the spectacle and large-budget disaster, horror, and science fiction cycles have emerged.

These three characteristics exist because young people seem to prefer frank, explicit, and fright-oriented films. With the replacement of the old movie code with the new rating system, greater artistic freedom has been afforded film makers. As a result, we have low-budget "nudies," sadistic motorcycle-gang films, and horror "flicks." But this same freedom has also produced outstanding films. The violence in the statements of Sam Peckinpah in *The Wild Bunch,* Francis Ford Coppola in both *Godfathers,* and William Friedkin in *The French Connection* is integral to the manhood of the dying breed of the wild bunch and their place in history, to the insidiousness of organized crime, and of the nature of police work and what it does to men. The sex and nudity in Federico Fellini's *Casanova,* Bob Fosse's *Cabaret,* and John Schlesinger's *Midnight Cowboy* are valid in the human dramas they present.

Of all the electronic media, the motion picture seems to serve specialized tastes most satisfactorily. It has been discarded by most general audiences, and criteria to evaluate films have been institutionalized. Nevertheless, although film is the most socially conscious of all the electronic media, it is still *primarily* an entertainment medium.

The Phonograph and the Radio. These two media are closely linked in the entertainment function because recorded music constitutes the bulk of most radio stations' programming. A wide range of musical tastes is served, but most markets are dominated by a "Top 40" or rock music station.

The phonograph has great flexibility and provides almost any kind of music desired. Although classical music does not dominate, classical records continue to be produced, and most university towns and metropolitan areas are served by at least one FM classical "jukebox." The primary cultural thrust of these media, however, is to provide music for specialized audiences.

The Print Media. Of all the mass media, the newspapers provide the greatest amount of information and perhaps the smallest amount of pure entertainment. But mass entertainment is an essential part of the daily newspaper fare. The *Washington Post,* for example, which prides itself on being the equal of the *New York Times* as a national newspaper, for years published the largest number of comic strips of any newspaper in the country. It claimed that those comics helped build its circulation to make it the largest newspaper in the nation's capital. Almost every newspaper publishes comics and cartoons, as well as features and human-interest stories, to entertain as well as inform and instruct.

Magazines are able to provide a more specialized form of entertainment for special audiences. The comic book itself is a form of entertainment for a specific type of reader. The range of such entertainment in magazine form stretches as far as the imagination will allow, from the most mundane, such as comic books and titillating sex-violence magazines, to esoteric journals on jazz, poetry, folk art, or classical drama.

Books also appear on the surface to be a primary medium for an elite audience, useful more for education and art than entertainment. But books are being expanded into informational and entertainment uses as well. The paperback revolution has brought the book to the economic level of mass audiences, which has allowed books to be used for popular entertainment ranging from best-selling Gothic romances to such entertainment as *The Joy of Sex.*

In effect, entertainment is the "overlay" function of every mass media. It is the reason many people are willing to be informed, editorialized, persuaded, educated, and advertised at by the mass media.

The Place of Art in Media Content

Dramatists, actors, writers, dancers, musicians, and other artists use the mass media as marketplaces to display their wares. The movement arts, practical arts, theater arts, musical arts, applied arts, martial arts, verbal arts, and literary arts are no better or worse than the skill of the artist who practices them. Media artists are not all of the same caliber and not all television series or movies or novels or recordings are of the same quality. In addition, artists using mass media skills differ one from the other in their creative processes and we know practically nothing about the psychology or neurology of creativity.

Consider the opportunities the mass media have created for artists to write novels, films, and television series; to compose music for records, films, and radio; to perform as actors, dancers, and singers. Media and their audiences have insatiable appetites. The vast amount of time and space to be filled requires large artistic work forces of varying levels of ability. Who is to say what the next century will remember of our art and our artists? It may well be that the Lucille Balls, Archie Bunkers, Rhodas, and the Fonzies will be the *commedia d'elle arte* of tomorrow.

The Nature of Mediart

If art is the application of skills in various modes of expression with the intent to please, involve, and arouse consumers, then the products of these doers can be referred to as art. Media artists use machines as tools, and extensions of their minds and hands to produce content of skill and imagination. This is *mediart,* and its quality depends on the combined skills of the artists involved.

As in other arts there are no exact rules in mediart or in its evaluation. The shared perceptions that determine what is "good" in the "good art" in television, film, records, books, magazines keeps changing. Taste in mediart content changes by discarding established values and readopting values previously discarded. Taste in mediart is learned, and mediartists do the teaching.

Mediartists are also bound up with audiences; the rise in audience expectations requires a requisite improvement in the content that artists display in the media. The customer has affected artists throughout history. Demand for an artist's product is one measure of artistic success. Audiences, like the other facts of a mediartist's life (e.g., training, media availability, cost), have an impact on the quality and kind of the content produced.

Everyone knows something about mediart, because it is an important fiber in our everyday cloth of life. "We know what we like and we like what we know." Audiences respond to a variety of content in ways different from critics. Many feel that something is wrong with mediart if it needs to be explained to audiences. But audiences learn to appreciate better mediart by exposure to it. Goethe argued that critics need to consider (1) what is the artist attempting to do? (2) did he do it? (3) was it worth doing? Audiences need to understand (1) how a work is created, (2) how to see or hear it, (3) how to interpret it, (4) how to let it affect them in ways they want to be affected.

There is almost always a difference in mediart between what was the artist's intention and what is the audience's perception. The artist's craftsmanship and skill are a part of mediart but do not guarantee high quality. The audience must join in leaps of the imagination with the artist so that meaning can be shared.

Nearly all mediart is immersed in entertainment. The television play, film, recorded music, novel, or magazine mediart is designed to entertain, but art through the ages has served this purpose. Michelangelo's *David* is entertainment. Aristophanes' *The Birds* is entertainment. Beethoven's *Ninth Symphony* is entertainment. All had audiences of various levels of skill in understanding, but all these works of art were created, like mediart, to entertain.

Levels of Mediart

Considerable debate has taken place over the value and effects of mass media entertainment-art on our culture and society. Cultural anthropologists, sociologists, and critics have tended to group cultural artifacts into three categories, and these have been given various terms. Van Wyck Brooks coined the phrases "highbrow, middlebrow, and lowbrow," to describe these categories.

Highbrow, or high culture, is composed of the cultural artifacts that can be appreciated only by an educated and intellectual elite; examples might include Shakespeare plays, T. S. Eliot's poetry, Schoenberg sonatas, Matisse paintings, the *Economist, Daedalus,* and Bergman movies.

Middlebrow culture has pretensions of being refined and intellectual but also has wider human appeal; examples might include *Horizon* magazine, the *Washington Post,* plays by Neil Simon, paintings by Modigliani, the poetry of Ogden Nash, and novels by Norman Mailer.

Lowbrow culture consists of those artifacts that have massive appeal to the largest possible audience, an appeal that is usually visceral rather than cerebral, emotional rather than rational, brutal rather than aesthetic; examples might include radio soap operas, television situation comedies, confession magazines, lovelorn newspaper columns, sex-violence movies, and pulp novels.

There is in this analysis an elitism that verges on snobbery. It seems more reasonable to adopt a method of analysis that is more objective and a classification based on (1) the medium used, (2) the techniques used, (3) the function of the content, and (4) the success of the content.

Originality and tradition are in conflict in many works. *Barry Lyndon,* a brilliant film by Stanley Kubrick based on a minor novel by William Makepeace Thackeray, goes against the grain of Kubrick's traditional films; and his originality was misunderstood by his movie audience. The beauty, elegance, and grace of *Barry Lyndon* is a joy. The photography, sets, music, acting are remarkable; but audiences were less responsive because it lacked the story, liveliness, and "hype" of *2001: A Space Odyssey* or *A Clockwork Orange.* But mass audience rejection or acceptance of a film is not necessarily the measure of its worth. Beauty can be learned over time or, in some cases, instantly realized.

If we use highbrow, middlebrow, and lowbrow over a period of time to measure film as a medium, its techniques, function, and success, the motion pictures have moved from lowbrow in the 1890s to middlebrow in the 1940s to

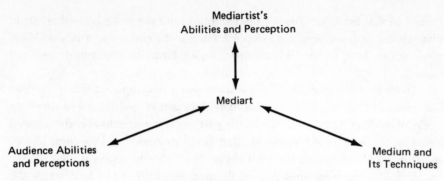

FIGURE 26.1. *Interactions in Mediart*

highbrow in the 1970s. It is the interaction of the mediartist, the mass medium and its techniques, with the audience that creates its worth (see figure 26.1).

Criticism of Mass Culture. On one side of the debate are those who argue that the purveyors of entertainment-art through the mass media are little more than panderers, catering to the lowest common denominator in the mass audience. These critics maintain that most mass media entertainment has a degrading effect on our culture. The mass media, these critics say, by emphasizing that which is popular and salable, ruin standards of style and taste, leading to a "cultural democracy" where "the good, the true, and the beautiful" are decided by the vote in the marketplace of mass media rather than by sensitive, refined, and knowledgeable authorities.

In *Mass Culture Revisited*, Bernard Rosenberg sums up the argument for the many critics on the side of an elite culture. He sees "the masses as victims of a merciless technological invasion that threatens to destroy their humanity. . . . Hardly anyone is unaware," he notes, "at least viscerally—that ninety-nine percent of the material conveyed to us by the mass communications media is aesthetically and intellectually trivial." He takes the position that "the only antidote to mass culture is high culture, that high culture means art and learning, and that these goods are potentially accessible to every person not suffering from severe brain damage."

"Popular culture," or "popular arts," might best be called "current culture," or "current arts." These arts have massive audiences and therefore are rejected out of hand by some critics. The popular arts are designed to entertain and, hopefully, to earn large returns on the dollar investment. Popular culture is big business and therefore suspect, yet artists have always had patrons and tried to sell their work. The popular arts are democratic rather than elitist arts.

Traditionally, art criticism has been based on value judgments of others trained in that art form. Today's media critics tend not to be trained artists in film, music, or television, but people trained in English or journalism. Many good writers have an inordinate impact on art forms in which they were not trained.

There is also a tradition of some widespread development where mediart historians feel much closer to historians than artists and therefore dwell on works of mediart that were made in the past and are understood and evaluated based on the lessons of history. Mediart is not grounded in long-term history and thus media historians have not always been able to cope with it.

Kitsch is the term most commonly used by elitist critics to describe the popular arts and entertainments of the mass media. The word comes from the German expression for scraping mud from the streets or slapping together products such as artistic or literary material produced to appeal only to popular taste and marked by sentimentalism, sensationalism, and slickness.

Not all media entertainment is mediart. There is no reason or possibility for that because of the volume produced. And the current state of the art is changing so fast that it is difficult to make judgments as to what is mediart and what is just fad. Instead of changing every century, mediart changes every few years. By the time you have learned to enjoy it, you may be out of date.

In Defense of Mass Culture. The crass statement of the mass culture position is that of the media entrepreneur who says, "Give the fools what they want. If people will pay for comic books but not poetry, give them comics. If the audience demands burlesque and will not attend tragedy, give them Gypsy Rose Lee and not Lady Macbeth." Most media owners are, first and foremost, businessmen who must sell a product to as many customers as are necessary to make a profit.

But there is an intellectual side to this argument, and it is perhaps best summed up by David Manning White in *Mass Culture Revisited.* He argues that the lowbrow culture of the mass media is important to the overall soothing and comforting of an anxious and complex society. "Throughout recorded history," White says, "most men have sought anodynes from the deepest anxieties about their existence. They did so before any aspects of mass culture pervaded society; they would continue to do so if every vestige of mass culture were to disintegrate and disappear tomorrow."

White proposes that the mass entertainment of the mass media makes news, information, and education digestible. "If I couldn't read Charles Schulz's *Peanuts* every morning in my newspaper," he writes, "I don't know if I could tolerate the grim tidings of the front page. But that doesn't mean that I read only comic books all day long."

Most people do not read comic books or watch situation comedies all day long, White argues; but even for those who do, their attention to the mass media helps to involve them in other uses of media. Thus, he says, "slowly the level of our cultural life in the United States is rising. There are, naturally, many millions who will continue to extract from the media the least demanding aspects of artistic rewards." But, White maintains, the mass media are more influenced over the long run by "middle America"—the middlebrow—than they are by the lowbrow. "The emerging pattern of motion pictures, the paperback book revolution, the hundreds of cultural television programs (scores of them on network programming), all attest to the quality of this growing audience."

Mass and Class as Interdependent. An argument similar to White's but perhaps more meaningful maintains that both good and bad exist in "class" culture and in mass culture, and that class and mass do not only coexist in a society, but also enrich and enliven one another. There are pretentious elements of class culture, just as there are products of genuine quality that emerge from mass culture.

Because these art forms enliven and enrich one another, Eric Larrabee argues, it is as important for students to study the popular arts as it is for them to give serious attention to sculpture, sonnets, and sonatas. This broadening of the critical perspective to include mass culture also has a potentially beneficial effect on classical studies, Larrabee says, because it provides a continual test of relevance. Artifacts that acquire no audience at all perhaps deserve their fate.

"Class" products and artifacts that reach a mass audience through the mass media—Paddy Chayevsky's TV plays, Walter Lippmann's newspaper columns, or Stanley Kubrick's films—prove that a growing number of people have a taste for quality at a price they can afford. By the same token, mass produced or communicated culture that acquires unexpected quality—Charlie Chaplin's little tramp, Red Smith's sports columns, The Beatles' rock recordings, or Mahalia Jackson's gospel hymns—prove that what moves the masses often has genuine and long-lasting quality.

The Place of Entertainment and Mediart in Society

Popular art is in effect folk art aimed at a mass audience. It is a product of current technology. Tradition and originality are caught up in the speed of the times, and qualitative evaluation is difficult. Several basic conclusions can be offered, however.

1. Entertainment has long been the basis for art, and mediart does emerge from mass entertainment.

2. Mediart exists to be enjoyed by the largest possible audience because we live in a mass society.

3. To enjoy mediart fully, audiences need to learn to understand it.

4. Mediart exists for audiences as well as artists and critics, and educated audiences should be and are sought.

5. There are various audiences for various media; it should not be necessary for every medium to provide every form of mediart at every cultural level. Trained audiences will find what's *good*.

6. Artists have always needed patrons, and the patrons of mediartists are big business and big audiences.

7. There will always be tension between media artists and media audiences. The greater the originality, the greater the tension; but this tension leads audiences to "better" preferences in future selection of media content.

8. Mediart is what you "like," and you learn to like it. Media appreciation can be learned although it is difficult because audiences are so close to it and, as always, there are levels of enjoyment.

Value judgments in mediart come from the paying customer. What we are willing to pay for now will determine the quality of media entertainment and art that the mass media will provide in the future. The advance of culture depends on the education of the public. Beware the critic.

Part Five The Impact of Mass Media

Does violence on television make monsters of children? Do newspaper stories of rape and robbery lead readers to commit crimes? Has the *Playboy* philosophy revolutionized our sexual mores? Have Hollywood movies lowered the general level of American culture? Do political reports, editorials, and advertisements in the mass media change our political views or influence our decisions in the voting booth?

These are all questions dealing with effects of mass media on our lives. This is, surely, the most important aspect of mass media—how they influence us. But it is also the most complex aspect of the study of mass media. Adequate answers to the questions posed above cannot be made without sophisticated research, taking into account many complicated factors.

Even a superficial analysis will indicate the important role the media play in presenting facts, shaping opinions, and providing us with pictures of a world that we would not otherwise see. Some people have felt that the effects of media are pervasive and all-important, not only in direct, immediate, and observable terms, but also throughout the history of humankind.

What we know about the effects the mass media have on our society is derived from three basic kinds of research: (1) historical research investigates past and current media events in order to make comparisons; (2) experimental research is done in the controlled environment of the laboratory on specific behavioral problems; (3) survey research assesses media effectiveness in the

27

The Effects of Mass Media

diffused environment of the "real" world. Because of differences in research methodology, design, and manipulation of results, there is some disagreement among researchers regarding the effectiveness of the media in our society. But as additional research is completed, considerable consensus is being reached.

An Overview of Media Effects

Although we might agree that the mass media have affected the course of human development, it is still difficult to establish absolute cause-and-effect relationships. Indeed, the effects of the mass media defy most generalizations. In summarizing our current knowledge about these effects, Bernard Berelson and Morris Janowitz have written:

> The effects of communication are many and diverse. They may be short-range or long-run. They may be manifest or latent. They may be strong or weak. They may derive from any number of aspects of the communication content. They may be considered as psychological or political or economic or sociological. They may operate upon opinions, values, information levels, skills, taste, or overt behavior.[1]

There are so many variables, in fact, that some researchers are pessimistic about achieving scientific verification for any kind of mass communication effect. Berelson, in 1948, expressed his own feeling of futility about answering questions of mass media effect by framing the following axiom: "Some kinds of *communication* of some kinds of *issues*, brought to the attention of some kinds of *people* under some kinds of *conditions*, have some kinds of effects."[2]

Others are more optimistic, however, about the use of behavioral research to learn more about the effects of mass media. Joseph T. Klapper, for instance, favors the "phenomenistic" approach, in which mass media are viewed as only one of many factors to be considered in studying the effect of the environment on human behavior. Klapper also feels that some generalizations have already emerged about media effects from these types of studies.[3]

At the present time there is considerable documentation to support the notion that several factors affect the effectiveness of mass communication:

The medium or combination of media used affect mass communication

[1] Bernard Berelson and Morris Janowitz, eds., *Reader in Public Opinion and Communication* (2nd. ed.; New York: Free Press, 1966), p. 379.

[2] Bernard Berelson, "Communications and Public Opinion," in *Mass Communications*, ed. Wilbur Schramm (Urbana: University of Illinois Press, 1949), p. 500.

[3] Joseph T. Klapper, *The Effects of Mass Communication* (Glencoe, Ill.: Free Press, 1960).

effectiveness. The fewer skills required to use a given medium, the more likely it will be for large numbers of people to take advantage of it. If any medium demonstrates real value to the individual, however, that individual will acquire the skills necessary to use it. The effectiveness of a medium with its audience depends on its source credibility and its traditional association with a specific role. For example, books are the most effective medium in the educational process because textbooks have credibility with teachers and students, and that medium has traditionally been the backbone of the educational process in this country.

The presentation of the message affects mass communication effectiveness. The style of presentation of the message influences its effect on the audience. "Sesame Street's" effectiveness with children is the result in large measure of the way in which the information is presented. The amount of information previously provided by a medium in a given content area affects the future receptiveness of the media user to similar messages. The communicator associated with the message (dramatic writer, director, journalist, actor, editor, or singer) affects the way a message is accepted by the audience. Walter Cronkite, for example, has better *ethos* (a form of proof based in part on his personal characteristics such as physical appearance and voice) than a cub reporter with a weekly paper.

The exposure pattern affects mass communication effectiveness. The number of exposures individuals have to a given message affect their willingness to accept an idea. For example, the My Lai massacre was something less than believable when the story first broke because our society had been taught that Americans did not kill unarmed women, children, and old men. For most Americans, repeated exposure to the idea was required before the report was believed. In addition to the number of exposures, the period of time over which this repetition occurs is also critical for maximum effectiveness. Thus, repetitive exposure over extended periods of time is the cornerstone of most advertising campaigns.

The audience experience affects mass communication effectiveness. The physical environment in which a medium is used modifies effectiveness. The home, with its multitude of interruptions, is a far less satisfactory environment for a film than a movie theater because the film environment needs to be carefully controlled to increase message impact. The interpersonal interactions during a given communication experience also affect the process. Talking or holding hands with one's date while trying to read a textbook is often less than a satisfactory educational experience. By contrast, we are accustomed to having conversations with the radio on. Past media experiences condition us to have certain expectations regarding how and where a specific medium is used.

In sum, scientific verification of the effects of mass media on individual behavior has been difficult to achieve because the variables seem to be nearly inexhaustible. But if the media can be seen as part of the total environment that affects man's acts and decisions, a theory for mass media effects might be developed. Melvin L. DeFleur synthesizes various theories to arrive at the most comprehensive statement to date:

> The effects of a given mass communicated message sent over a given channel will depend upon a large number of psychological characteristics and social category similarities among the members of the audience; these effects will depend upon the kind of social groups within which these people are acting and the relationships that they have with specific types of persons within them; they will depend upon the social norms that prevail among such groups in reality as well as upon the "definitions of the situation" which the communicated messages are to suggest.[4]

A Detailed Analysis of Specific Media Effects

Media effects are seldom—if ever—simple, direct, or totally dependent on media exposure because the direct, personal experiences of the individual are constantly modifying the effectiveness of the indirect, vicarious media experience.

The available evidence in all areas of communication indicates that we move from cognition to comprehension to attitude and value change before behavioral change occurs. In addition, we know that it is easier to create cognition than comprehension, that comprehension is a simpler task than attitude modification, and, finally, major behavioral changes are extremely difficult to produce.

To facilitate the evaluation of research as to the specific effects the mass media have on society, the available data have been collated and summarized in the following pattern:

1. There are three *general areas* of mass communication research of great scientific importance:
   a. The effects of the mass communication media on *cognition and comprehension.*
   b. The effects of the mass communication media on *attitude and value change.*

[4]Melvin L. DeFleur, *Theories of Mass Communication* (2nd ed.; New York: David McKay, 1970), pp. 152–53.

c. The effects of the mass communication media on *behavioral change.*[5]

2. There are three *specific problems* that are of intense public concern:
   a. The effects of the mass media on children.
   b. The effects of *violence* in the mass media on American society.
   c. The effects of *erotica* in the mass media on American society.

Each of these six concerns has involved the efforts of a great many researchers, and this section is designed only as an introduction to each problem and a synthesis of available information.

Cognition and Comprehension

How effective are the mass media in making audiences aware of things not in their direct experience? At a more complex level, how effective are the media in making audiences understand the mass communication experience? Cognition is affected by the fact that the individual does not read all pages of the newspaper or listen to every minute of a newscast with equal attention. Audience members expose themselves selectively to media content, but by constant, repetitive exposure the media can become highly effective on a wide variety of issues. Retention of information over a long period of time is least probable when the individual has no personal interest in that information.

Cognition (as with all media effects) is the result in great measure of the interaction of media content with the direct, personal experiences of the audience members. A person's ability to recall a media event is also dependent in large measure on repeated exposure to the stimulus and some reinforcement in interpersonal relationships. If an individual had a brother in a trouble spot in the Middle East, the mention of that specific area would increase awareness on the part of the viewer to that news item because of the direct experience that encouraged awareness. The viewer *needed* that information.

The achievement of comprehension requires more exposure and personal interest. Although Americans have one of the best overall information systems in the world, there is considerable misunderstanding because people misinterpret, fail to hear, or refuse to accept the facts. And there have been times when the media have misinformed their audiences. Evidence also suggests that audi-

[5]The basis of this section is a modification of Walter Weiss's collation of research in chapter 38 of the *Handbook of Social Psychology*. Weiss's summary is one of the best available to date in the field and a must for students interested in media effects. Walter Weiss, "The Effects of the Mass Media of Communication," in *Handbook of Social Psychology*, ed. Gardner Lindzey and Eliot Aronson (2nd. ed.; Reading, Mass.: Addison-Wesley, 1968), 2:77–195.

ence members' predispositions on a given issue create subtle, unconscious misconceptions despite repeated exposure to messages that contradict these notions. In other words, comprehension on a given issue is distorted by personal beliefs. For example, this may account for some reactions—despite all the evidence to the contrary—that the assassination of President John F. Kennedy was the result of a complex plot involving a large group of conspirators, rather than the alleged singular act of Lee Harvey Oswald. Recent information regarding CIA involvement in plots against the life of Fidel Castro, and the possible links of Lee Harvey Oswald with pro-Castro groups, further complicate the issue.

Cognition and comprehension have a direct effect on the emotional reactions of audiences. Any emotional response to mass communication comes in large measure from the setting in which exposure occurs, the repetition of exposures, information prior to the exposure, and the basic cognitive schema (interpretive framework) of the individual. The reaction of a child to a "horror film" is made more intense because the theater is dark, because the child probably has had previous exposure to other "scary" films so he and his companions have preconditioned themselves to the evocation of a set of emotional reactions, and because the whole cognitive schema or the overall way in which the child perceives the film is dependent on that child's personality traits.

One of the best examples of the effectiveness of media in creating emotional public response occurred during Orson Welles's radio dramatization of H. G. Wells's *War of the Worlds* (Halloween week, 1938). The program, concerning a fictitious invasion of earth by Martians, caused panic among those people who could not put the program into a satisfactory cognitive schema, lacked previous information about the show, were preconditioned by the emotional tenor of the times, or could not find other persons who could counteract or clarify the event for them. In short, *other conditions* in an individual's personal experience are important in determining what his or her emotional response will be to a given media stimulus.

Another important aspect of media effects related to cognition and comprehension is *identification*, which refers to the audience members' involvement with an actor or character in a given communication experience. This intellectual-emotional response enables the individual to experience vicariously events in which he or she otherwise could not participate. The depth of individual involvement depends on the satisfaction derived from previous exposures. The attractiveness of a given fictional character depends on the similarity the audience member has to that character or the aspirations and anticipated roles of the book reader, moviegoer, or radio listener. When the opportunity arises, the majority of males select male characters, and the majority of females select female characters for identification. Interestingly, characters that deviate too far from accepted norms—even if they are the antihero of the piece—are less identified with than are the "good guys." Identification affects a child's selection of comics, TV programs, and movies and has been proved to have an impact on the individual's willingness to accept different kinds of information. If the audience identifies with the communicator, cognition and comprehension improve.

Attitude and Value Change

Obviously, all the previously mentioned studies on cognition, comprehension, selective exposure, retention, emotional reaction, and identification are closely related to attitude change. Values depend upon individuals being aware and understanding the communication experience. For example, if selective exposure blots out positive information about the values of rock music, an adult's attitude will remain unchanged.

In media research on attitudes, there is general agreement that the media do have an effect. However, the extent, speed, and longevity of these effects are in question.

Most research evidence supports the hypothesis that mass media can "create new opinions more easily than they can change existing ones." Joseph Klapper points out that mass communication "is highly effective in creating attitudes on newly arisen or newly evoked issues." He underlines the caution that "the efficacy of mass communication in creating opinion . . . can be gauged only in reference to issues on which, at the time of exposure, people are known to have no opinion at all." Communications on such topics "have been found capable of 'inoculating' audience members, i.e., of rendering them more resistant to later communications or experiences suggesting a contrary view."

Wilbur Schramm points out that "the mass media can widen horizons. . . . They can let a man see and hear where he has never been and know people he has never met."[6] Obviously, this is a more important side effect of mass media in developing societies; ostensibly in a sophisticated and civilized society, fewer issues can be raised with which modern men and women have not already come into contact and about which they have not already formed some opinions.

Schramm also says that mass media, in creating opinions, "can raise aspirations." Again, this is more apt to be true in developing societies, where the typical citizen has had an extremely limited view of the world. But we find illustrations of this among America's poor.

[6]Wilbur Schramm, *Mass Media and National Development* (Stanford, Calif.: Stanford University Press, 1964), p. 127.

It should be emphasized, however, that while the mass media might create opinion easily in a situation where no opinions previously existed, there are always many mediating forces—unsympathetic predispositions, group norms, or opinion leaders—which hinder the creation of new opinions by the mass media.

If we already have opinions about issues, such as politics or religion, what effect do the mass media have in changing us? Not much, according to limited research findings. Most studies show that the mass media "reinforce our old opinions more than they convert us to new ones." Klapper says that reinforcement of an opinion is the dominant effect; minor change, such as a shift in the intensity with which we hold an opinion, is the next most common effect.

One reason for reinforcement is the self-protective human process of selective exposure, selective perception, and selective retention. We tend to expose ourselves only to those media that agree with our existing opinions, and we tend to avoid media that are unsympathetic to our predispositions. A socialist is not apt to read the *Wall Street Journal*, as a capitalist is not apt to be a regular reader of the *Los Angeles Free Press*. Psychologists have long shown that even when exposed to other media, we tend to perceive only those elements that fit our preconceptions. And finally, we tend to retain those facts and ideas that agree with our existing opinions.

Leon Festinger has studied this phenomenon and named it "cognitive dissonance."[7] Basically, dissonance replaces the word inconsistency and consonance replaces consistency. Festinger's main hypothesis is that the psychologically uncomfortable existence of dissonance will motivate a person to try to reduce it and achieve consonance. In addition to trying to reduce dissonance, the person will actively avoid situations and information that would increase it.

For example, a man who continues to smoke, despite media information that smoking is harmful, tries to reduce the dissonance. He can rationalize that he enjoys smoking so much that it is worth the chances of ill health, or he can rationalize that if he stopped smoking he would put on weight, which could be equally bad for his health.

Mass media also aid reinforcement rather than change because in a free-enterprise society the media tend to avoid offending any significant portion of their vast audience and tend to espouse attitudes that are already virtually universal. A significant portion of mass media would not be likely to express a point of view that the majority in society were not already willing to accept. A nationally syndicated newspaper columnist or a political commentator on nationwide television would not likely express a radical political idea, for fear of

[7]Leon Festinger, *A Theory of Cognitive Dissonance* (Evanston, Ill.: Row, Peterson, 1957).

alienating vast numbers of readers and viewers. Even the underground press, which might purposely use language and pictures to offend the general public, nevertheless is reinforcing attitudes held by its regular readers.

Not only do the mass media reinforce what we already believe, they also "enforce the normal attitudes and behavior patterns of society." Two sociologists, Paul F. Lazarsfeld and Robert K. Merton, have pointed out the effects of mass communication on organized social action. "Publicity closes the gap between 'private attitudes' and 'public morality,'" they write.[8] The mass media expose deviations to public view, and, as a rule, this exposure forces some degree of public action against what has been privately tolerated.

For example, some individuals may privately tolerate what they would call "polite ethnic discrimination," but they would be apt to reject this attitude if it were called to public attention by the mass media in a society that condemns discrimination. The media tend to present in an approving manner behavior and attitudes that are socially accepted, and to present in a disapproving manner those that are rejected. Through repetition the media reinforce existing social attitudes.

One result is social conformity, weakening of individualism, and decreasing tolerance of differences. Much research has verified the "bandwagon effect," that is, people will adopt opinions because they are the opinions of a large group, or seem to be. This social conformity is most commonly demonstrated in advertising, which frequently uses such phrases as "nine out of ten," "more people use," or "millions recommend." Studies also show that small, deviant minority groups have an unusual amount of resistance to the bandwagon effect; but most people, without the support of a strong minority group, simply go along with the majority.

Thus, in America the mass media have played a role in the melting pot. Except for small and strong minority groups—such as Hasidic Jews in Brooklyn or Amish Mennonites in Pennsylvania—most Americans have lost the special ethnic and cultural characteristics that their ancestors brought from the Old World.

The mass media tend to make individuals, groups, things, or ideas important simply by selecting them for attention or notice. This effect of mass communication was pointed out by Lazarsfeld and Merton:

> The mass media bestow prestige and enhance the authority of individuals and groups by legitimizing their status. Recognition by the press or radio

[8]Paul F. Lazarsfeld and Robert K. Merton, "Mass Communication, Popular Taste and Organized Action," in *Mass Communication*, ed. Wilbur Schramm (Urbana, Ill.: University of Illinois Press, 1960), p. 499.

or magazines or newsreels testifies that one has arrived, that one is important enough to have been singled out from the large anonymous masses, that one's behavior and opinions are significant enough to require public notice.[9]

Charles Lindbergh received so much publicity for his trans-Atlantic solo flight in the *Spirit of St. Louis* that he became an instant and permanent international hero. But Bonnie Parker and Clyde Barrow, small-time bank robbers and killers in the 1930s, also gained status and prestige through headlines in the newspapers. This status was revived in the 1960s by the motion picture *Bonnie and Clyde,* which dramatized their exploits. A similar example has been the reevaluation of General George Patton as a real hero in *Patton* and in references to his ability in other films, such as *A Bridge Too Far.* As Patton's media star ascends, it is usually at the expense of another Allied general, Britain's Lord Montgomery, who is now being presented by films in a less positive manner than has been true in the past.

Status conferral by the mass media has also produced the star system, not only in Hollywood but in New York and Washington as well, where individuals can enhance the prestige of a production, product, or political viewpoint by virtue of their publicity. A long list could be written of movie stars, political figures, society leaders, artistic lions, and even academic giants who attained positions of prestige and prominence based on their ability to get publicity as well as their other talent, genius, or worth.

Do mass media also have the effect of drugging their audiences? Some feel they do, including Lazarsfeld and Merton, who write that the increasing "outpourings of the media presumably enable the twentieth-century American to 'keep abreast of the world.' Yet, it is suggested, this vast supply of communications may elicit only a superficial concern with the problems of society, and this superficiality often cloaks mass apathy."[10]

News, which is by definition almost invariably about deviations and abnormalities in society, may, according to some sociologists and psychologists, actually create anxieties among readers, listeners, and viewers. This anxiety could result in "privatization," where individuals feel overwhelmed by the news and react by turning inward to a private life, over which they have more control.

Mass audiences may suffer from an information overload to the point where they are actually narcotized by communication. They react with apathy

[9]Ibid., p. 498.
[10]Ibid., pp. 501–2.

rather than action. So many voices are heard, so much static and interference are on the line, that they tend to block out everything, and no message comes through loudly and clearly enough for them to participate and be involved in the action. The media can turn us off as well as on.

Many, in fact, turn to the media to be turned off. The escapist function is an important one for the mass media, and has many socially useful results. We turn to soap operas and musicals in "living color" not just to get away from our problems but also to find emotional release, vicarious interaction, a common ground for social intercourse, the stimulation of our imagination, and mental and physical relaxation. All these, in turn, affect our attitudes and values.

Behavioral Change

Do media experiences change the things persons do and the ways in which they act? What are the physical reactions to media experiences, the things people do as a result of media exposure? A considerable amount of research in the area of behavioral change has sought to determine what the media's influences are on specific kinds of behavior—voting, play patterns, aggression, and a number of others.

In the area of the allocation of discretionary or leisure time, the media are a dominant force. The importance of the media can be estimated if you stop to realize that the media dominate leisure time activity in our society. As new media appear there is usually high public interest, if participation requires no skills—e.g., TV viewing, radio listening, and moviegoing. When television became available, it reduced the amount of leisure time spent on other media, but it also required the viewer to give up other practices as well. The average adult spends more than two hours per day viewing television; the average family spends more than six hours. When a family acquires a color set for the first time, the amount of viewing increases substantially until the novelty wears off. In effect, what happens is that media experiences are so attractive and rewarding that the individual consciously gives up or modifies other media and nonmedia activities in order to partake of them.

The media are often employed to stimulate interests in the form of a specific activity such as homemaking, sewing, cooking, or hobbies. The results of most studies indicate that special-interest programs develop passive rather than active behavior on the part of the viewer. Audiences watched Julia Child's "French Chef"; they enjoyed her performance, but apparently few of the audience members ever tried that specific recipe. However, they may go out and buy a cookbook, which they will use.

The media are constantly accused of *changing public taste* as reflected in other kinds of behaviors: reading novels, going to concerts or the ballet, or watching public affairs programs. Most popular argument states that TV and other media degrade public taste by pandering to the lowest cultural denominator instead of educating people to enjoy higher cultural materials. Research indicates, however, that cultural tastes are much more influenced by personal, family, educational, and social determinants than by the media. Those persons who claim the media should influence tastes for high culture normally already are predisposed to such activities as listening to classical music. What seems to be the case is that the media are *not* used to seek out cultural tastes above those the viewer already possesses. Interestingly, limited research into the effects of radio and television in emerging nations seems to indicate that a concentrated programming effort can create a positive interest in the cultural heritage of that nation.

In terms of *family life patterns,* numerous studies have investigated various aspects of home behavior. In general, the media studies—specifically of television—indicate that TV has not had a marked or sweeping effect on family life styles. At a very superficial level, members of a family spend slightly more time together viewing TV as a group until the second set is purchased.

In terms of passivity, the media do not make people more passive, except where the individual has a very strong predisposition to be so anyway. The specific fear that TV viewing negatively affects school work is false. In fact, television viewing may actually contribute to a faster start for most children. The bedtime of children has not been changed markedly by television.

The life style of the family unit is the primary determinant here. There seems to be little support for the contention that TV has a detrimental effect on eyesight. For most individuals, TV is just another style of play, influenced by age and intelligence, values and personality. Evidence exists that family members use TV as a time-killer between other activities. The primary role of media in the household is for "escapist" entertainment—because this is what the family desires. In general, the medium's use is affected more by the family life style than the life style is affected by the medium.

Considerable research has been devoted to the effects of media on *voting behavior.* The media seem to be relatively ineffective in converting a voter from one party affiliation to another. Few voters seem to be influenced by specific political commercials for the candidate they dislike. The critical role of the media seems to be to reinforce existing political attitudes and maintain party-member support.

Rather than attempt to prove or disprove the relative impact of personal influence and mass communication, a more sophisticated approach seems to be to recognize that they complement one another in changing behavior patterns.

In terms of *adopting a specific behavior,* it takes considerable time for this to occur and depends on several factors, including the number of people involved in the decision, the economic and social risk necessary, the future ramifications of action, the extent of departure from current practices, and the compatibility of this behavior with personality, values, and motives of the individual. For example, consider the implications of the simple behavior involving hairstyles in boys. The decision to have long or short hair might involve parents, peer groups, and school personnel. There may be economic risk (loss of a job) or social risk (forbidding of dates by a girl's parents). The future problems include public derision, family squabbles, or possible social ostracism. If the boy is leaving for college, the long-hair style may not be too great a departure from behavior on the campus. Finally, his personal values in regard to grooming may affect his decision. So, despite the hair length of people in the media, other influences may be too strong for the behavior change to occur.

The same factors influence change in purchasing behavior, wearing clothes, using "miracle cleaning agents," joining protest marches, participating in common-law marriages, adopting children of minority parentage, and any other behavior acceptance, modification, or rejection. It is the interaction of media exposure and other personal experiences that become the critical force in behavioral change.

The Effects of Media on Children

In a famous study, Wilbur Schramm, Jack Lyle, and Edwin B. Parker concluded:

> For some children under some conditions, some television is harmful. For other children under the same conditions, or for the same children under other conditions, it may be beneficial. For most children, under most conditions, most television is probably neither particularly harmful nor particularly beneficial.[11]

In England, Hilde T. Himmelweit, A. N. Oppenheim, and Pamela Vance concluded that television had little negative effect on children, except for those who were emotionally disturbed or predisposed to a particular behavior. In other words, the normal child will probably not commit a violent act as the result of watching violence on television.[12]

In very specific terms, television does not overwhelm the child's life style:

[11]Wilbur Schramm, Jack Lyle, and Edwin B. Parker, *Television in the Lives of Our Children* (Stanford, Calif.: Stanford University Press, 1961).
[12]Hilde Himmelweit, A. N. Oppenheim, and Pamela Vance, *Television and the Child* (London: Oxford University Press, 1958).

consciously and unconsciously, children are selective about *what* they watch and the *amount of time* they spend. The important factors in the child's television behavior are age, intelligence, social level, personality, and parental example. In terms of taste the child's TV behavior *reflects* the child's taste in other areas. Television viewing does not lower cultural levels, nor does viewing of adult programs by young children have the negative effect of developing antisocial behavior.

In general, it has been concluded that television has little, if any, negative effect on the health of children. In terms of emotional effect, children love excitement and even enjoy low levels of fright. If the child is mature and intellectually prepared for movies and TV exposures, there is little, if any, detrimental, long-lasting, emotional reaction. In terms of causing behavior patterns, television creates little or no negative behavior in the normal child.

However, there is considerable concern both in the scientific and lay communities about "kid-vid." Purposive systematic TV viewing behavior begins between two and three years of age and impacts on what kind of person that child becomes. The average child under five years of age watches television over 23 hours every week. The "family viewing hour" (8 P.M. to 9 P.M. EST) was a failure both legally and functionally. Both these factors influenced public concern on three issues: (1) the amount of time children spend watching television, (2) the amount and types of advertising found in child-oriented programming, and (3) the impact of violence on the child viewer.

Research continues to show that when a child watches television, *other play activities are reduced.* Another observation is that *the heavy-viewing child is less creative at play and less willing to persevere at learning that is difficult or that fails to have immediate rewards.* Television has certainly become a major socializing agent of children, and, for some children, television rivals the influence of parents and schools on attitudes and behaviors. Television socialization has improved verbal skills, but some research findings indicate that television may be creating a passive child who is becoming an observer of, rather than a participant in, life.

Two central concerns dominate the literature on advertising and children. First, the amount and kinds of advertising in child-oriented programming is largely for "junk foods" and may be creating a generation of "sugar junkies." Second, the studies seem to show that many children move from total belief to total disbelief in ads, rather than developing those skills that would help the child differentiate between "good" and "bad" advertisements. It is estimated the average preschool child sees approximately 5,000 TV ads a year, and there has been considerable pressure on broadcasters to control the amounts of, and types of, appeals in the advertisements.

The impact of violent content on children remains the most emotional issue, but powerful advocates of change are at work. Both the Parent Teacher Association and the conservative American Medical Association have taken strong public stands on the issue. Earlier work by Action for Children's Television and the National Citizens' Committee for Broadcasting was continued in an effort to reduce violent content. And it appears that the National Association of Broadcasters will add a section on violence to the NAB code. Indeed, network studies show that violent incidents have been reduced by one-fourth over the past several years. Advertisers are also cooling in their attitude toward sponsoring extremely violent shows because of concerns about consumer boycotts of products advertised on violent series such as "Baretta," "Starsky and Hutch," "Charlie's Angels," and "Kojak." The problem, of course, is that over 10 million children watch TV every evening between 9 P.M. and midnight. The major concern has shifted from a fear that TV violence creates violent kids to a concern that young viewers are becoming desensitized to violence in real life, because of heavy doses on the tube.

Experiments can show immediate, dramatic impact, and these studies have demonstrated some relationship between children's aggressive behavior and their viewing of televised violence; but longitudinal (long-term) home environment studies are definitely needed to predict long-term effects.

There is, of course, a simple solution to all these concerns—the parent needs to learn to use the *off* switch. Parents must control the amount and kinds of content their children view. If adults view a violent TV program with their children, they need to discuss the unacceptability of that type of behavior. It is literally that easy to keep television from becoming what *Time* magazine calls the "flickering blue parent." A child's use of television is an adult responsibility.

Violence and Mass Media

Considerable concern has been expressed over the violence and aggression depicted in the mass media and their effect on Americans. A "Task Force on Mass Media and Violence" produced a lengthy report for a National Commission on the Causes and Prevention of Violence entitled *Violence and the Media* (1969). The report summarized what is known to date and called for more research. However, the report listed three areas where studies of violence in the media provided the committee with some general conclusions: learning effects, emotional effects, and impulsive aggression.

As to learning effects, the commission reported "... the belief in the effectiveness of aggression in attaining his [a child's] goal while avoiding punishment. The mass media typically present aggression as a highly effective form of behavior."

As to emotional effects, the commission reported the conclusion that "fre-

Drawing by Geo. Price; © 1977 The New Yorker Magazine, Inc.

"How about some sex and violence for poor ol' Granny?"

quent exposure produced an emotional habituation to media violence. There is suggestive evidence that this results in an increased likelihood of actually engaging in aggression."

The commission also concluded that "aggressive impulses may be held in check if the viewer has been made especially aware of the 'wrongness' of aggression or of the suffering that may result from violence."

Other researchers have reported little direct cause-and-effect relationship between mass media and individual behavior when it comes to sex, crime, and violence. Klapper points out that "heavy exposure to such fare is apparently not a sufficient or crucial cause of delinquency. In at least five major studies, heavy consumers were found no more likely to be delinquent than were light users or nonusers."

In other words, there is considerable controversy within the scientific community regarding the results of behavioral research as to the effect media exposure has in triggering aggressive behavior that may lead to violence. Some social scientists argue that media exposure to violence serves as cathartic experiences—the fantasy of emotionally participating in media violence reduces the possiblity of the individual becoming violent because the media provide a means of releasing aggressive tendencies. Other laboratory research, especially the work of Leonard Berkowitz, Albert Bandura, and their respective colleagues, suggests that under certain circumstances media violence can lead to imitative aggressive behavior with other stimuli interacting with media exposure.[13] The critical factor and the matter least studied at the present time is the long-term, cumulative, extended effects of media violence.

The media, however, are just one factor in the total societal picture, where violence has always been a reality in the American way of life.

In 1972 a study on television and violence instigated by Senator John Pastore's Communications Subcommittee was released by the U.S. Department of Public Health. This study sought to gather all findings related to television violence and its effect on children. Three generalizations emerged from this work. Namely, that there is "a preliminary and tentative indication of a causal relation between the viewing of violence on television and aggressive behavior; an indication that any such causal relation operates only on some children (who are predisposed to be aggressive); and an indication that it operates only in some environmental contexts."[14] Media effects in this area then are dependent upon the mix of violent media content, the child, and the environment.

Obviously, there are other contributions to violence in the United States other than mass media. In a report to the National Commission on the Causes and Prevention of Violence, a partial list was compiled.

> Many unique aspects of our society and politics have contributed to the individual and collective violence that troubles contemporary America, among them the psychological residues of slavery, the coexistence of mass consumption with pockets and strata of sullen poverty, the conflict among competing ethics that leaves many men without clear guides to social

[13]Albert Bandura with a variety of colleagues conducted a series of studies between 1961 and 1965 in the areas of learning, imitative behavior, aggression, and their interrelationship wih mass media (specifically film). His research is reported largely in the *Journal of Abnormal and Social Psychology*. Leonard Berkowitz and his research team concentrated their research on filmed violence and aggressive tendencies. This work was published in part in the *Journal of Personality and Social Psychology* from 1963 to 1967.

[14]The Surgeon General's Scientific Advisory Committee on Television and Social Behavior, *Television and Growing Up: The Impact of Televised Violence* (Washington, D.C.: U.S. Government Printing Office, 1972).

action. Other sources of violence in our national life are inheritances of our own past: a celebration of violence in the good causes of our revolutionary progenitors, frontiersmen, and vigilantees; immigrant expectations of an earthly paradise only partly fulfilled; the unresolved tensions of rapid and unregulated urban and industrial growth.[15]

What the media may be doing in fact is heightening our awareness of the violence that has always been a part of the fabric of our way of life. The news media are constantly providing information regarding assassinations, campus protests, fire bombings, ghetto disturbances, civil disobedience against the war in Vietnam, muggings, and police brutality. Since the media are instrumental in creating this intense awareness, they have come to be associated with violence—as its cause—in the minds of a large segment of the public.

The noted sociologist Otto Larsen surveyed the various material available, and, in general, has presented the view that too little is known about violence to set up a system of censorship that seeks to control or limit the content of the media. Indeed, the results of such a censoring process seem to be much more dangerous to the United States than the current violence portrayed in the media, Larsen concluded.

Erotica in the Mass Media

Erotica is sexually oriented content in the mass media, which has as its purpose physical and emotional arousal of the consumer. Traditionally, books, magazines, and films have been the major means of mass distribution of erotic content, but recently the popular-music industry using the phonograph as a means of distribution has moved into the field. Rod Stewart's "Tonight's the Night" and Donna Summer's "Love to Love You Baby" continue a growing trend of sexually explicit lyrics and grunts and moans.

The intensity of erotic stimuli vary from "mild cheesecake" photos to "explicit stag films." The research in this field is in its infancy because of the social pressures and other difficulties in conducting it, as well as the difficulties obtaining financial support. In general, mild erotica seems to generate a pleasurable state in subjects, but there may be a linkage between strong erotica and aggressive behavior. There may also be a systematic sexual excitation transfer to negative kinds of behavior if other release is not possible. Arousal from erotica seems to lead subjects into two major response patterns: if the material

[15]Hugh Davis Graham and Ted Robert Gurr, *Violence in America* (New York: Signet Books, 1969), p. xiii.

is perceived as entertaining, the subjects usually enjoy it; but if they are bored, their response borders on disgust. Interestingly, the higher the arousal level, the more likely it is that the material will be judged to be pornographic. Studies also indicate that satiation occurs with repeated exposure, and the user loses interest. Recent studies also seem to indicate that male and female responses tend to be growing more alike, and that exposure to erotica and the resultant arousal levels affect how the subjects perceive attractiveness in others and others' receptiveness to their own sexuality.

Limited research has been done relating erotica to anxiety, guilt, socially threatening situations, liberalism-conservatism, and intellectual-antiintellectual variables. Without question, additional research is necessary before any firm conclusions can be reached.

As more sexually explicit content has become available, public attitudes about that content have changed over the past decade as to what is permissible and socially acceptable content in the media. In fact, there is some opinion that the "girl next door" nudity in *Playboy* may have become "humdrum" compared to the more intense poses in *Hustler*, *Chic*, and *Club*. General attitudes toward what is or is not offensive have changed. The acceptance of nudity in PG-rated films such as *Planet of the Apes*, *The Omega Man*, and *Logan's Run* is one measure of the extent of the change since all three of these science-fiction films have large children's audiences. In addition, soft-core films such as *Emmanuelle*, *The Story of O*, and *Madame Claude* are explicit and X-rated, yet play to large audiences throughout the United States. It is a far cry from the late 1960s when *Blowup* was refused the industry seal for what today might well be rated PG. The hard-core industry continues to expand its audience and improve its production standards with films such as *Through the Looking Glass*, *The Opening of Misty Beethoven*, and *Autobiography of a Flea*. Exhibition of these films, however, is limited to larger metropolitan markets. Along with this has come an acceptance of rough language in recent films such as *Slapshot* and *Smokey and the Bandit*.

Nevertheless, the political pressure on intense erotica, which the society deems to be pornographic, is still strong in most areas of the United States outside the major "liberal" urban centers.

Pornography is any obscene material, and obscenity is based on three legal criteria: (1) the dominant theme, taken as a whole, must appeal to a prurient (morbid and unhealthy) interest in sex; (2) the material must be patently offensive and affront contemporary community standards; (3) the material must be without redeeming social value. If a book or movie is shown to possess all three characteristics, it is legally obscene and in some communities the distributor, exhibitor, and seller are liable for prosecution. The major change in this area was the redefinition by the U.S. Supreme Court in 1973 that "community standards" were *local not national*. This means that something could be erotica in San Francisco but pornography in a small town in the Midwest.

In 1967 Congress established through Public Law 90-100 the Commission on Obscenity and Pornography, which on September 30, 1970, submitted its report contradicting many strongly held beliefs of politicians and citizens alike. The commission's majority report has gone the way of many other scientific-bureaucratic undertakings. The findings of the commission have been attacked, and the report's proposed legislation has been ignored.

The financial scope of pornography in the United States is estimated to be between $500 million and $2 billion a year. The major media involved are paperback books, magazines, and films; however, with the advent of the new cassette videotape units pornographic materials might be expected to become more readily available.

The Commission on Obscenity and Pornography was unable to reach unanimous agreement on the effects of obscene material. The findings of the majority are:

1. In the nonlegislative area, the major media involved in providing pornographic materials are paperback books, magazines, and films; however, with the advent of the new cassette videotape units, pornographic materials might become available more readily for use in the home.

2. In the legislative area, all local and state laws as well as federal statutes (Statutes 18 U.S.C. Sec. 1461, 1462, and 1465; 19 U.S.C. Sec. 1305; and 39 U.S.C. Sec. 3006) prohibiting the sale of pornographic materials to consenting adults should be repealed, because:

a. There is no empirical evidence that obscene materials cause antisocial attitudes or deviant behavior, although the material is sexually arousing.

b. Increasingly, large numbers of persons (most frequently middle-aged, middle-income, college-educated males) use pornography for entertainment and information, and these materials even appear to serve a positive function in healthy sexual relationships.

c. Public opinion studies indicate that the majority of Americans do not support legal restriction of adult uses of pornography and legal attempts to control the distribution of obscene material have failed.

d. Obscenity laws are an infringement on Americans' constitutionally guaranteed right to freedom of speech.[16]

[16]*The Report of the Commission on Obscenity and Pornography* (New York: Bantam Books, 1970).

"Although the empirical evidence suggests that pornography is in no way harmful to children, the commission, on ethical grounds, felt that obscene material should not be made available without direct parental consent to persons under eighteen. The commission also argued that unsolicited mailings and public displays should be prohibited.

"In other words, the majority of commissioners believed that there is *no empirical evidence* that pornography is harmful and that government at all levels should repeal obscenity laws for consenting adults. Three members of the commission objected to the findings on moral grounds (as did the Nixon administration) and questioned both the scientific studies and legal interpretations of the majority report of the Commission on Obscenity and Pornography."

Four events in 1976–77 were of political significance. First, Democratic presidential candidate Jimmy Carter was interviewed in *Playboy* and created quite a stir, but the former governor of Georgia was still elected to the White House. A year later, Ambassador to the United Nations Andrew Young was also interviewed in that periodical, with little political fallout. Second, the Memphis-based trial of people associated with the production of *Deep Throat* led to a conviction for transporting obscene material across state lines by individuals not involved in the film's distribution. Vigorous prosecution can still lead to convictions years after production for anyone associated with the film in Tennessee. An optional class screening of the same film at a university in Florida led to an amendment to another bill that set up censorship committees on all state university campuses. The complete bill was vetoed by the governor. Third, Larry Flynt, the publisher of *Hustler*, was convicted under an organized-crime law in Cincinnati. The Flynt trial was a bizarre interpretation of a law banning illegal activity for profit by five or more people. Everyone but Flynt was found not guilty, and the conviction of Flynt is being appealed. It was a classic confrontation between admittedly "bad taste" and the First Amendment protection of the free press. Recently, during a recess at a trial in Georgia for alleged pornography, Flynt was shot and crippled. Fourth, "child pornographers" have come under attack, and the traditional defenders of civil liberties have not closed ranks on this issue. The attack is not on the consumption or sale of "kiddy-porn," but rather the damage that it does to the children forced to perform in the magazines and films. There are community standards, and this appears to be one point on which convictions can be made to stick.

Behavioral research indicates that mass media can have short-term effects on individuals, and this type of evidence is important in developing media policy. But in the long run, what part have the various media played in modifying social conditions during the past few decades? What was media's role in the civil rights movement? Did news coverage of the war in Vietnam and antiwar demonstrations at home affect public policy? How are women, homosexuals, and other activist groups—and their opponents—using mass media?

One difficulty in dealing with the social impact of mass media on the United States is that there are few facts. Observations are made by trained researchers, but their statistics are open to several interpretations. As a consequence, this chapter cannot describe *the* way things are, but can merely offer some observations about how mass media interact with society. Another difficulty arises because events such as the Vietnam war, Watergate, and the various activist movements can be interpreted from a variety of political and cultural standpoints. In fact, one of the pleasures of analyzing mass communication is that everyone has an opinion to offer. This chapter therefore provides a jumping-off point for students who want to observe media events and form their own conclusions.

Historical Perspectives

Harold A. Innis, a Canadian economic historian, was a pioneer in examining the effects of mass media on humankind. His concern with the impact of

28

The Impact of Mass Media on Social Movements

printed money on the economy led him to study the effect of communication on political and economic institutions. Innis concluded that "Western civilization has been profoundly influenced by communication."[1]

Both Innis and Marshall McLuhan have shown that people adapt themselves and their institutions to the available media, whether they be clay and stylus, paper and printing press, microphone and loudspeaker, or celluloid and movie projector. Each invention has marked a stage in our institutional and societal development.

The United States has the most complex mass media system in the world. To what effect? Wesley C. Clark, former dean of the Syracuse University School of Journalism, says that "mass communications and the mass media have played a major role in changing the face of America. They have given us instant nation-wide fashions and modes, and perhaps instant heroes, or nonheroes, both political and nonpolitical."[2]

Indeed, without mass media, America as we know it would not exist. It was the printed word—broadsides and pamphlets—that first induced masses of Europeans to emigrate to the New World. Without colonial weekly newspapers, as Arthur M. Schlesinger, Sr., shows in his *Prelude to Independence*, the war against the British Crown would probably not have been fought or, if fought, would probably not have been successful. He quotes David Ramsey: "In establishing American independence, the pen and the press had a merit equal to that of the sword."

Another American historian, Allan Nevins, has shown that the newspapers of the newly independent nation, carrying essays known today in their collected form as *The Federalist Papers*, persuaded the new Americans to ratify the Constitution and adopt a democratic form of government.

From the founding of the country to the present day, mass media have played an important role in nearly all the important events of the nation. Antislavery publications, such as William Lloyd Garrison's *Liberator* and Harriet Beecher Stowe's *Uncle Tom's Cabin*, did much to foment the Civil War, as did the newspaper editorials of Horace Greeley and James Gordon Bennett. William Randolph Hearst's sensational headlines helped spark the Spanish-American War. Crusading newspaper and magazine reporters and editors at the turn of the century—often called "muckrakers"—brought much-needed political reform and social legislation to America.

In the twentieth century, electronic media added their impact to the

[1]Harold A. Innis, *The Bias of Communication* (Toronto: University of Toronto Press, 1951), p. 3.
[2]Wesley C. Clark, "The Impact of Mass Communications in America," *Annals of the American Academy of Political and Social Science* 378 (July 1968): 69–70.

printed word, and mass media became big business. In October 1969 George Gerbner, dean of the Annenberg School of Communication at the University of Pennsylvania, stated in testimony before the National Commission on the Causes and Prevention of Violence:

> In only two decades of massive national existence television has transformed the political life of the nation, has changed the daily habits of our people, has molded the style of the generation, made overnight global phenomena out of local happenings, redirected the flow of information and values from traditional channels into centralized networks reaching into every home. In other words, it has profoundly affected what we call the process of socialization, the process by which members of our species become human.

One historian, David Potter, has theorized that the basic element in the development of an American national character has been economic abundance, and, he declares, advertising in mass media is the institution of that abundance. Advertising "has vast power in the shaping of popular standards, and it is really one of the very limited group of institutions that exercise social control."

Historically, a kind of technology of opinion making has emerged, and with it has come an aristocracy of opinion leaders. Some scholars now argue that the media performer-newsperson has become both oral historian and influence peddler. Instead of seeking out the tribal chief, medicine man, local politician, priest, or scribe, modern Americans look to Walter Cronkite, John Chancellor, or Barbara Walters for "fast, fast, fast relief" from the burden of independent sociopolitical decision making. In effect, an important new set of "lawgivers" have had status conferred on them by their appearance in the media, especially television. The impact of this phenomenon is not yet clear, but electronics journalism has become one of the most attractive career goals of today's college students.

The Comparative Effectiveness of the Media

Which medium is most effective? Which has the greatest impact? These questions have been much discussed, and many studies have been devoted to finding adequate answers. The findings are far from complete. Different studies have reached different conclusions, partly because of the way the questions have been asked. A point that should be made is that different media have different effects—different advantages and disadvantages in effective communication.

"Remember, my boy, never trust anyone."

"Not even Walter Cronkite?"

Print, for instance, allows the reader to control the occasion, pace, and direction of exposure and permits easy reexposure. Broadcast media provide a sense of participation, personal access, and a "reality" that approximates face-to-face contact. Films command more complete attention from their audiences than do other media.

Mass Media Acculturation

What we see in the movies and on television and read in our newspapers and magazines about current styles affects us. The length of our hair was a political as well as a fashion issue in the late 1960s because mass media made it an issue. Hair was given media exposure, and young people all over the country reacted to it. An off-Broadway musical moved to Broadway and then to our living rooms glorifying *Hair*. The movie version of *Hair* turned the immediate past into nostalgia. Young blacks bought "blowout kits" for their "natural" and "Afro" hairdos. Eventually, with continued exposure and the adoption of longer hairstyles by adults, hair as a symbol lost much of its clout.

In the 1970s platform shoes, maxiskirts, vested suits, the "punk-rock" look, and many other fashions and fads were disseminated via the media. Mass media have participated in a new kind of hyperconsumerism. Rapid change in styles has accelerated to the point where what's "in" is "out"; but because it is "out," it is back "in." Only denim will live forever.

Toys from *Star Wars* are adopted by children along with ready-to-eat cereals and flouride toothpaste as a result of media sales pitches that offer a life style along with the product. Fast-food chains have garnered 40 percent of American food dollars, in part because of a change in leisure-time activities developed in the media.

How often do you eat a TV dinner, go to a drive-in movie, or imitate a character in a network series? Americans are media-acculturated; our views of who we are and what we want to be are often determined by what the media tell us we are or should be.

Are you overweight? Mass media have terrorized the fat people of the United States. Peter Paul Rubens glorified pudgy women in his eighteenth-century paintings. Today, fat is "out" because of visual images in the media. Nobody "ain't gonna bump no more with that big fat woman." Diet drinks, low-calorie foods, and the image of "good-looking" men and women in the media shape what we think is beautiful. The worst question you can ask an audience in America is: "Will those of you who are overweight please raise your hand?" Even the skinniest college freshman wants to lose a pound or two. Thin people look better on TV, in movies, and on the fashion pages.

It is difficult to measure media acculturation, but observation confirms that "images" in mass media affect us. These are *real* effects because we buy them—we eat them, wear them, spray them, and drive them. We may even "become" them. When you dream about the perfect mate, is it the boy or girl next door—or John Travolta or Cheryl Tiegs? Why not just marry your TV set?

Political and Cultural Movements

The frantic speed of change in our society is phenomenal. Think about your attitude toward the Middle East situation. Has your attitude changed lately about who the good guys are? How do you react to the Israelis, to the PLO, to Anwar Sadat? Events reported in the media change our attitudes.

The political and social progress of minorities is in some measure due to media coverage and changes in image effected by the media. Rights activists even stage media events to help bring about change.

Civil Rights and Mass Media

If you are white, compare your feelings about blacks with those of your parents and grandparents. If you are black, how does your self-concept differ from that of your parents and grandparents? The television spectacle "Roots" opened the eyes of many white Americans and encouraged black Americans to take justifiable pride in their African heritage. Kunta Kinte did not come "shufflin' and dancin'" to America; he was dragged and beaten here. "Roots" is light-years away from slave images in *Birth of a Nation* and *Gone With the Wind*. This is so because films and other mass media reflect their times rather than the historical period they cover. Black images in media are both agents of change and reflections of what the society wants to believe at a particular time. The political-economic groups who control the media also control the images on the screen.

The past three decades have been a "thirty years' war" for civil rights, and mass media have been a major weapon. Events in the news and entertainment media have become the conscience of America. Covert discrimination may continue in some parts of our society; but lynchings, segregated public facilities, and attacks on peaceful demonstrators are over because the media exposed them.

Television was the major news instrument used by black Americans to carry their grievances to the American body politic. Events—parades, speeches, protests, sit-ins, marches, freedom rides—were staged for the media and the white power structure.

A blossoming television news industry was ready to bring dramatic events into eight of every ten American homes when a black woman, Rosa Parks, refused to surrender her seat on a Montgomery, Alabama, bus to a white man. The Montgomery bus boycott was one of the first successful mass challenges to public segregation. It also produced a black leader for the news media, especially television. Dr. Martin Luther King, Jr., was a master propagandist. His low-key, reasoned, Gandhi-inspired approach to nonviolent protest was perfect for the news. Television helped make Dr. King a tremendous symbol of change.

Because these events were covered by the media, the federal government as well as the people of America was moved to action in the 1960s. A protest is absolutely worthless unless the people and the power structure know that it is happening. The "freedom rides" of the Congress of Racial Equality (CORE); the marches of the Southern Christian Leadership Conference (SCLC); the manifestoes, posturings, and programs of the Black Panthers; the urban riots in Harlem, Watts, Newark, and Detroit: mass media highlighted them and pressured politicians to act.

Murdered whites and blacks, and ultimately the murdered Dr. King, became martyrs under the glare of television. The violence of riots and the senseless stupidity of beatings and killings were given full media treatment. The civil rights movement was a media movement; and because of news coverage, civil rights legislation was passed. The power of the media was in their ability to focus society's attention on events and make visible the cancer of a racist society.

The entertainment industry (sound recording, motion pictures, and television) was also a powerful change agent. The blatant racism of *The Wooing and Wedding of a Coon*, the "Sambo" and "Rastus" series, *The Nigger*, and *The Birth of a Nation* was supplanted in the 1920s and '30s by black "fools" and "mammys." The tragedy of such great talents as Stepin Fetchit, Willie Best, and Mantan Moreland was not that they played buffoons but that these stereotypes were the only roles available to them and the only blacks that movie audiences saw. With a few notable exceptions (e.g., *Hallelujah*, *Hearts in Dixie*, *Green Pastures*, and *Cabin in the Sky*), the screen was lily white. Few white Americans knew that a black B-film industry was flourishing under the talents of Oscar Micheaux and other independents throughout the 1940s.

The watershed year for black images in white media was 1949, when four problem films were released: *Home of the Brave*, *Lost Boundaries*, *Pinky*, and *Intruder in the Dust*. This last film is notable as the first Hollywood portrayal of an independent black man. In the 1950s one black star, Sidney Poitier, saved dozens of whites and emerged as a visible hero and improved white impressions of blacks. He is the first and only black to win an Academy Award for best actor (in *Lilies of the Field*). By the mid-1960s, the "age of Poitier" had paved the way for a number of black talents.

An economically viable black urban audience made it possible for "black exploitation" films to emerge. The superbad heroes of *Shaft*, *Superfly*, and *The Legend of Nigger Charlie* were important because black talent was providing black entertainment for black audiences. The 1970s produced a number of quality films—*Sounder*, *Lady Sings the Blues*, *Conrack*, *Blazing Saddles*, *Claudine*, *Mahogany*, *The Wiz*, *Blue Collar*—by both black and white directors, some of which centered on black living conditions in America.

A television breakthrough came in 1965. After a virtual "whiteout" since the early 1950s, Bill Cosby starred in "I Spy." Cosby proved that black stars could attract high ratings, and he won two Emmy awards doing it. Today, many TV shows feature black characters; and such shows as "Sanford and Son," "The Flip Wilson Show," "Room 222," "Good Times," and "The Jeffersons" point to the acceptance of a black style on television. "Julia," an often maligned series that starred Diahann Carroll, was important because it offered the example of a black professional woman making it in a white man's world.

The key in both motion pictures and television was the presence of blacks in the shows and their acceptance by white audiences in a wide variety of roles. Blacks were no longer invisible. They lived and breathed and saved white folks. It was not a revolution, but it was a step forward; and the entertainment media were a part of the process of change.

Black ownership of newspapers and broadcasting stations increased in the 1970s, and black radio became a viable instrument in the advertising marketplace. In addition, special-interest magazines such as *Ebony, Essence, Black Enterprise,* and *Players* have continued to serve their black readers. More and more job opportunities in all phases of the communication industry have also opened for blacks.

Perhaps in no other medium does black artistic input dominate as it does in the recording industry. Traditionally the entertainment entry point for blacks, records made by blacks now reach most white home audiences.

In all media, the fact that blacks appear as part of "the system" is a major change of the past ten years. Tokenism still exists in mass media, but affirmative action is becoming a reality.

Without mass media, the progress made in civil rights may still have occurred, but not with the speed and impact that it did. Mass media have access to, and influence on, the power elites of this society. The media have literally disproved the old saw that you cannot legislate cultural change. Mass media have not done it on their own, but attitudes and behaviors have changed on racial issues because of what all of us read, heard, and saw in the media.

Women's Rights

Mass media are in the process of overhauling their presentation of women in America. It is somewhat fruitless to argue over whether mass media changed society's attitudes toward women or whether a changed society modified media's portrayal of women. The best approach may be to accept the fact that a vital interaction took place. Most assuredly, a relationship exists between how men and women view themselves and one another and what media culture holds up as role models. There are those who feel the media are moving too fast in changing sex-role stereotypes; there are others who accuse the media of foot-dragging on the issue. Whatever the pace of change, change is in the air in the media's depiction of women.

For the most part, the women's movement has made better use of print media than it has of electronic media. Women have had easier access to print, print costs are lower and offer a wider range of media vehicles, and more women are trained to write than are trained to use radio-television-film. Books and magazines have been by far the most successful information and propaganda instruments of feminists.

Simone de Beauvoir's *The Second Sex*, Betty Freidan's *The Feminine Mystique*, Kate Millett's *Sexual Politics*, magazines such as *Ms.* and *Working Woman*, and myriad other media vehicles are involved in observing, redefining, and advocating. Even such traditional magazines as *Cosmopolitan*, *Redbook*, and *Woman's Day* have moved in new directions. Counterproposals to women's liberation ideas also have been mounted in the print media, most notably *The Total Woman*, which advocates a more conservative approach to male-female relationships.

The news media have assisted and resisted women's groups when staged events and other protests have occurred. By any measure, women's rights events are covered more sparingly and less enthusiastically than were civil rights stories in the 1960s. This is in part because the women's movement is (1) *decentralized*, which makes it difficult for journalists to cover several groups that often appear to be at ideological odds; (2) *localized*, made up of essentially independent local groups, so that the news media cannot always identify important issues; (3) *nonhierarchical*, which does not give media a leader to focus on; (4) *nonritualized*, so that mass media sometimes cover events that make "poor news," such as conferences, women's studies, and women's centers; and (5) *internally opposed*, with some women's groups in public opposition to the goals of the movement, for example, passage of the Equal Rights Amendment.

The most significant progress in electronic journalism has been the increasing numbers and responsibilities of newswomen. The cumulative effect of daily TV appearances by Barbara Walters, Catherine Mackin, Carol Simpson, Connie Chung, Nina Totenberg, Jane Pauley, and Jessica Savitch on the news is very important in consciousness raising, and affects the attitudes of men as well as of women on a wide range of issues.

Some of the better TV series in the 1970s came from MTM Productions, which created "Mary Richards" and her two spinoff friends, "Rhoda" and "Phyllis," all once part of "The Mary Tyler Moore Show." These independent, bright women were a far cry from the earlier stereotypes of TV women in "I Love

Lucy," "My Friend Irma," and "Father Knows Best." The new TV women could take care of themselves and, if they had to, could handle the bad guys in "Police Woman," the first successful adventure series with a woman (Angie Dickinson) in the title role. One of the biggest hits on television today is "Charlie's Angels," which stars three rough-and-tumble beauties catered to by an affable male back-up who is constantly in need of their help. This show's basis is sex, but it does present a new-for-television stereotype of women.

Even daytime soap operas and the television commercials that sponsor them are rapidly changing their appeal for the stay-at-homes. The "soaps" are now peopled with career women involved in the business and professional worlds. Commercials project an image of women as attractive, childless, and wage earning, with male friends and husbands who are "liberated" as well as good-looking. Norman Lear's "Mary Hartman, Mary Hartman" poked fun at a spaced-out housewife in a world peopled with bizarre characters. Lear's "All That Glitters" created a world of total male-female role reversal.

Even if the TV characterizations of women have not come of age, signs of change exist. Women on TV "have come a long way, baby."

In the motion-picture and sound-recording industries the opportunity to express opinions corresponds with the ability to sell tickets and records. No woman at present can match the success of Barbra Streisand, an accomplished singer and actress who was also the executive producer of the rock remake of *A Star Is Born*. Her dominance of that film and her performance of "The Woman in the Moon" is a political message as powerful as Helen Reddy's "I Am Woman." These songs may have had more cultural impact than the amateur "librock" bands of the 1960s because Streisand and Reddy reach audiences outside the women's movement.

The interpersonal group process has been central to the development of issues and platforms of the women's movement. For most women, the key means of dissemination in mass media was print. Although the electronic media as a whole were far less supportive of women's crusade for equality than they were in the quest of black Americans for civil rights, media images and media opportunities for women are growing at a rapid rate.

Gay Rights

As with the women's movement, the print media have served as the major change agent for the gay community. The film industry has produced some feature films with gay central characters—*Suddenly Last Summer, The Fox, The Boys in the Band, Reflections in a Golden Eye, Fortune and Men's Eyes, The Ritz, Outrageous*. In the 1977–78 television season the ABC series "Soap" featured the first homosexual continuing character in a prime-time series. In most television shows only a very infrequent episode will allude to "the problem." With the exception of "That Certain Summer," television has not concerned itself with the gay issue in any significant drama. A sizable portion of the erotic film industry, however, does exploit this sexual preference in films produced for urban markets.

Until 1977, the gay rights question was still in the closet. In January 1977, the Dade County, Florida, Metropolitan Commission passed an ordinance that banned discrimination in housing and employment on the basis of sexual preference. As the issue came to a vote, two competing groups engaged in a media battle that brought gay rights before a national news audience.

The two factions—"Save Our Children," led by Flordia citrus industry spokeswoman Anita Bryant, and the Dade County Coalition for Human Rights, led by gay rights activist and businessman John W. Campbell—solicited and received nationwide financial support for their large media budgets, which mounted slick ad campaigns. The gay rights activists lost when the people of Dade County voted to repeal the ordinance.

Perhaps no other current media issue carries the emotional impact for audiences as does the issue of gay rights. With increasing numbers of activists, the gay rights issue is bound to receive interesting coverage in mass media. Unlike resistance to civil rights and the women's movement, which is subtle and diffuse, open resistance to gay rights is a reality.

Vietnam and Watergate

No recent political events have been more influenced by media than the war in Vietnam and the political scandal that destroyed the Nixon administration. Mass media participated in large measure in the decision to withdraw American troops from Vietnam and in the resignation of Richard Nixon.

In the past, the entertainment industry always rallied to a national war effort. During the Vietnam war only three war stories were produced: John Wayne's *The Green Berets;* a TV drama, "The Private War of Ollie Winter"; and one episode of the TV series "The Lieutenant." Vietnam was television's first war; it was fought in living rooms across the United States during the evening news. It was a war without battle lines and a war that defied traditional reporting. The Vietnam conflict seemed without form, goals, or end. The television eye burned pictures of downed helicopters and plastic-sheeted bodies into the memory of each member of its audience.

The news media also served as a forum for protest. The events in Chicago at the 1968 Democratic National Convention, the murder of graduate students by political terrorists at the University of Wisconsin, and the tragic shooting of students by Ohio National Guardsmen at Kent State were played and replayed in American homes. Citizens saw the results of the massacre at My Lai and the brutality of the Tet offensive. The home front watched Americans being slaughtered by the Viet Cong, and Americans in turn brutalizing noncombatants. The reality of war opened a political battle at home that led to the retirement of a President and the defeat of the previously popular Senator Hubert Humphrey. It created a climate that contributed to the excesses of Watergate. America's resolve to fight what some called an "immoral war" sapped our national will.

Battle coverage of the war in the news media was chaotic and incomplete, the neutrality of the entertainment industry was obvious, and the feelings of the rock-music industry were intensely antiwar. Today, the media scars are still visible; it will be years before they disappear.

The specter of President Richard Nixon choking back his emotions as he left the White House is unforgettable. The news media, especially the journalistic tenacity of Carl Bernstein and Bob Woodward of the *Washington Post*, and the seemingly limitless coverage of the unbelievable mess by television, literally allowed the Nixon administration to destroy itself. Even Congress was moving toward impeachment, prodded by Watergate events exposed in the media. The David Frost–Richard Nixon interviews in 1977 intensified the seemingly unending public interest in political corruption. Books continued to explore the issue, many of them written by individuals convicted in the courts for their part in the scandal.

Mass media have tremendous impact on our culture and on what we think about ourselves.

Public-relations campaigns mounted in mass media by the Kennedy and Johnson administrations mustered the political support needed to put you and the astronauts on the moon in the 1960s.

You were present at the assassinations and funerals of John Kennedy, Martin Luther King, and Robert Kennedy. Television coverage of these events served as a national outlet for grief.

You attended the Democratic and Republican conventions that preceded our national elections in the past decade and a half. Beyond question, television has altered how we elect public officials.

Out of all this, one has to take heart. We, you and I, control mass media. We must learn to use them well, or watch those who do learn use them in ways we may not wish. The mass communication industry is only what we allow it to become. It can and does influence us, but in turn we set the rules by which the media function. On important issues, cultures change slowly, but mass media are major agents in that process and affect every facet of our society. Mass media are the most important tools in modern communication.

This section is designed to provide a survey of materials used in the preparation of this book and sources of information for additional study in mass communication. Rather than provide the standard bibliographic list, an attempt has been made to annotate major works, describe important periodicals, and provide a list of organizations involved in various phases of media operations.

It is difficult to produce an up-to-date bibliography in a field that is changing as rapidly as mass communication. Therefore, this section is designed to provide major sources useful for the student interested in independent study. This text is designed as one learning resource within a total course in mass communication to be used in conjunction with lectures, videotapes, films, supplementary readings, and other materials. One important, if not critical, means of learning about mass communication is independent study and research.

Types of Independent Study and Research

For the beginning student, three areas of research offer excellent opportunities to discover valuable information through independent study:

1. *Historical-Critical Research* involves the student in describing and evaluating past events that help to explain current situations and may even suggest possible changes for the future.

Research Materials and a Selected Bibliography

2. *Survey, Field, or Descriptive Research* helps the student discover and evaluate public attitudes and opinions and answer the who, what, when, where, why, and how of policy decisions affecting our media system. Surveys and opinion polls assess how groups feel about and use mass media.

3. *Experimental or Laboratory Research* provides students with experiences in observing and assessing individual responses and small-group reactions to media content and use patterns. Observation, psychological or attitude scales, and physiological measures can be used to obtain this type of data.

Research, by definition, is the systematic, controlled, and critical investigation of hypotheses about presumed relationships. Historical, survey, and experimental methods of research seek answers to questions and evidence to support suppositions. Although there is no *one* way to design research investigations, the following procedure may prove helpful to individuals new to independent study. These steps are essential for all types of independent study:

1. Students must select the idea or problem area they wish to study.

2. Students must limit the scope of the topic area so that it can be accomplished in the allotted time period and based on the availability of source materials.

3. Students must initiate a literature search or in some way assess previous research in that subject area.

4. Once this is done, it should be possible to develop a problem statement or hypothesis that can be tested. This process intellectually establishes the scope, importance, and anticipated results of the project at hand.

5. Students must now specify the design of their hypothesis and operationalize it. Reliable indicators must be found to represent the more abstract concepts. More simply put, students need to determine *how* they are going to collect and evaluate information. Obviously, observation, reading previous work, testing, experimenting, or some other means of collecting data is the next logical step.

6. After students have collected all the available information, they must describe and evaluate these data. However, it is important that they do more than *report*—they need the opportunity to assess the *meaning* of what they have collected. Certainly all students may not reach the same conclusions, but this is a minor failure when compared to the major

success of students actually attempting to make a creative assessment of what it is they have done. It is also important to remember that disproved hypotheses are often as important in advancing knowledge as those that are supported.

It is vital that the public become critical consumers of mass communication so that they can actively affect the media rather than simply be affected by the media. Independent study and research seeks to involve students in controlled, reflective thinking, inquiry, and evaluation.

Materials for Use in the Study of Mass Media

This section attempts to provide a variety of sources of information for research in mass communication. It is designed to assist the beginner, and in no way purports to be *the* final word in research possibilities.

Four divisions have been established to help speed up the source-selection process: (1) general reference materials, (2) organizations involved in mass-communication activities, (3) a selected bibliography of periodicals, and (4) a selected bibliography of books. The bibliography of periodicals and books is divided according to medium (i.e., books, newspapers, magazines, radio, television, motion pictures, recordings).

GENERAL REFERENCE SOURCES. Part of the beginner's horror of research derives from a lack of knowledge concerning where to start. The teacher can ease the situation by identifying materials paramount to the successful completion of the project. If that information is not forthcoming, start with the available encyclopedias and almanacs and the library's card catalogue (subject headings) and then turn to this list.

Ayer Directory of Newspapers, Magazines, and Trade Publications edited by Leonard Bray for N. W. Ayer and Sons of New York on an annual basis provides excellent information on print media.

Bibliography Index (H. W. Wilson, 950 University Avenue, New York, NY 10452) is an index of current bibliographies arranged in alphabetical order.

Books in Print is published by R. R. Bowker Co., 1180 Avenue of the Americas, New York, NY 10036, on an annual basis. This source, available in libraries and bookstores of most educational institutions, annually lists all available books from 1,600 publishers by author and title. The *Subject Guide to Books in Print* is also produced annually by R. R. Bowker and is the subject index to *BIP;* it is most important to researchers. It uses the subject headings and cross references established by the Library of Congress. *Paperbound Books in Print,* another Bowker publication, is divided into three sections: (1) subject, (2) author, and (3) title, to facilitate access to paperbacks.

Broadcasting Yearbook (Broadcasting Publications, Inc., 1735 DeSales Street, N.W., Washington, DC 20036) is *the* sourcebook for the broadcast industry.

Business Periodical Index (H. W. Wilson, New York) provides a cumulative index of approximately 170 advertising, communication, marketing, public relations, and other business periodicals.

Dissertation Abstracts (University Microfilms, 300 North Zeeb Road, Ann Arbor, MI 48106) lists all dissertations written in the fields of journalism, mass communication, and speech. Copies of dissertations of interest can be ordered by writing the company. Prices are listed for a copy of each citation.

Editor and Publisher (850 Third Avenue, New York, NY 10022) provides statistical data on the newspaper industry.

Education Index (H. W. Wilson, New York) is a subject index to approximately 200 English-language periodicals, proceedings, yearbooks, bulletins, and series.

Encyclopedia of Associations (Gale Research Co., Book Tower, Detroit, MI 48226) is an annual directory listing national and international organizations by category of interest.

Facts on File (119 West 57 Street, New York, NY 10018) provides a biweekly digest of events and is an excellent source for historical research.

Federal Communications Commission Orders, Opinions, Rules, and Statutes (Pike and Fisher, 1735 DeSales Street, N.W., Washington, DC 20036) is an expensive but invaluable source for research in broadcast law. Most law schools have this source in their libraries. It provides a complete set of *all* legal decisions made by the FCC, case by case.

Film Literature Index (R. R. Bowker Co., New York) is an annual cumulative index to the international literature of film.

International Literary Market Place (R. R. Bowker Co., New York) is a general, annual analysis of publishing internationally.

Motion Picture Almanac (Quigley Publications, 1270 Sixth Avenue, New York, NY 10036) is an annual industry review with a great deal of data and information.

New York Times Index (New York Times Company, 229 West 43 Street, New York, NY 10036) provides a cumulative index to all articles printed in that newspaper.

Public Affairs Information Service (11 West 40 Street, New York, NY 10018) provides a cumulative index to government-oriented periodicals.

Readers Guide to Periodical Literature (H. W. Wilson, New York) is the largest cumulative index of general-interest magazines.

Social Sciences and Humanities Index (H. W. Wilson, New York) is a cumulative index of over 200 periodicals that emphasize materials in the social science and humanities areas.

Standard Periodical Directory. Annual edited by Leon Garry for the Oxbridge Publishing Company, 1345 Avenue of the Americas, New York, NY 10036, provides excellent data on all periodicals.

The Standard Rate and Data Service (5201 Old Orchard Road, Skokie, IL 60077) publishes directories for media advertising rates plus marketing data. Libraries can obtain the following volumes by writing SRDS: *Business Publications Rates and Data; Canadian Advertising Rates and Data; Daily Newspaper Rates and Data; Direct Mail Rates and Data; Network* (TV and Radio) *Rates and Data; Outdoor Advertising Circulation Rates and Data; Spot Radio Rates and Data; Spot Television Rates and Data; Transit Advertising Rates and Data; and Weekly Newspaper Rates and Data.*

Television Almanac (Quigley Publications, New York) is an annual review of the television industry.

Television Factbook (Television Digest, Inc., 2025 Eye Street, N.W., Washington, DC) is a major trade reference for the broadcasting industry and is published annually.

Topicator (Thompson Bureau, 5395 South Miller Street, Littleton, CO 80120) is a cumulative index of magazines in the advertising and broadcasting trade press.

ORGANIZATIONS INVOLVED IN MASS COMMUNICATION ACTIVITIES. There are times during research when standard printed sources do not provide needed information, and the student may want to turn to professional or educational organizations for assistance. Most groups are willing to help if the *specific* question asked does not require excessive work on their part. It is extremely important that persons seeking information be very clear as to what they are requesting.

The Academy of Motion Picture Arts and Sciences (8949 Wilshire Boulevard, Beverly Hills, CA 90211) is the organization that each year presents awards known as the "Oscar" for meritorious achievement in various areas of film work. It also maintains a 10,000-volume library.

The A. C. Nielsen Company (Nielsen Plaza, Northbrook, IL 60062) is a major marketing- and audience-research organization. It provides industry measurements of local and national television audiences. Nielsen will furnish assistance upon request and supply special publications regarding broadcasting research.

Action for Childrens Television (46 Austin Street, Newtonville, MA 02160) is a consumer action group designed to encourage and support quality programming for children. Maintains resource library.

The Advertising Research Foundation (3 East 54 Street, New York, NY 10022) is designed to further scientific advertising and marketing research to improve the content of advertisements and media plans. It maintains a library of over 2,100 volumes.

The American Association of Advertising Agencies (200 Park Avenue, New York, NY 10017) is an association that promotes the interests of agency owners.

The American Broadcasting Company (1330 Avenue of the Americas, New York, NY 10019) is one of the three major TV networks and provides four network-radio services to affiliated stations.

The American Federation of Television and Radio Artists (1350 Avenue of the Americas, New York, NY 10019) is the major union representing broadcast performers.

The American Film Institute (John F. Kennedy Center for the Performing Arts, Washington, DC 20566) is an important data source for researchers in film.

The American Marketing Association (222 S. Riverside Plaza, Chicago, IL 60606) is a very helpful organization of marketing and market-research executives for students of the mass media.

The American Newspaper Publishers Association (11600 Sunrise Valley Drive, Reston, VA 22091) is an organization representing newspaper management. It maintains a library of over 5,000 volumes.

The American Society of Magazine Editors (575 Lexington Avenue, New York, NY 10022) is an important source of data about current trends in that medium.

The Arbitron Co. (1350 Avenue of the Americas, New York, NY 10019) provides measurement of local radio and television audiences. Special reports and copies of its research are available upon faculty request.

The Association of American Publishers (One Park Avenue, New York, NY 10016) speaks for all aspects of the publishing industry.

The Association of National Advertisers (155 East 44 Street, New York, NY 10017) is an organization of regional and national manufacturers (general advertisers) concerned with company, rather than agency, problems.

The Audit Bureau of Circulation (123 North Wacker Drive, Chicago, IL 60606) provides audited circulation figures for all member publications.

The Broadcast Pioneers (40 West 57 Street, New York, NY 10019) contains the important Broadcast Industry Reference Center for historical research.

The Columbia Broadcasting System, Inc. (51 West 52 Street, New York,

NY 10019) is a national television and radio network and is most helpful in answering academic inquiries.

The Comics Magazine Association of America (41 East 42 Street, New York, NY 10017) is the self-regulation agency of the comic-book industry.

The Congress of the United States holds hearings on a variety of media topics. If you write your congressman and specify the report you need, he/she will normally assist you in procuring it.

The Corporation for Public Broadcasting (1111 16 Street, N.W., Washington, DC 20036) is a major source of programming for educational radio and TV stations and is funded by the federal government.

The Direct Mail Marketing Association (6 East 43 Street, New York, NY 10017) serves that industry as a public-relations and lobbying organization.

The Federal Communications Commission (1919 M Street, N.W., Washington, DC 20554) is the federal regulatory agency of broadcasting and is most helpful in providing specific data for researchers. Most of the FCC's reports and other publications are available through the Government Printing Office at a nominal charge.

The Foundation for Public Relations Research and Education (845 Third Avenue, New York, NY 10022) sponsors and distributes basic research in that field.

International Advertising Association (475 Fifth Avenue, New York, NY 10017) is an organization of international advertisers. It maintains a library of periodicals and reference works.

The International Radio and Television Society (420 Lexington Avenue, New York, NY 10017) is an organization of broadcast executives that conducts student/faculty conferences and awards summer internships.

The Magazine Publishers Association (575 Lexington Avenue, New York, NY 10022) is an organization representing magazine management.

The Motion Picture Association of America (522 Fifth Avenue, New York, NY 10036) is one of the best sources of information on the American film industry.

The Mutual Broadcasting System, Inc. (1755 S. Jefferson Davis Highway, Arlington, VA 22202) is a national radio network.

The National Academy of Television Arts and Sciences (291 S. LaCienega Boulevard, Beverly Hills, CA 90211) serves to promote improvements in television programming and awards the "Emmy" each year for meritorious achievement.

National Academy of Recording Arts and Sciences (444 Riverside Drive, Burbank, CA 91505) serves to promote improvement in the recording field and awards the "Grammy" each year for recording excellence.

The National Association of Broadcasters (1771 N Street, N.W.,

Washington, DC 20036) is an organization representing commercial broadcasters in the United States. It is a powerful group and provides extensive types of information upon specific request.

The National Association of Educational Broadcasters (1346 Connecticut Avenue, N.W., Washington, DC 20036) is an affiliation of educational radio and television stations and teachers of broadcasting. The staff of this organization is most helpful in responding to inquiries.

The National Association of Theater Owners (1500 Broadway, New York, NY 10036) is concerned with chain and local movie-theater operations.

The National Broadcasting Company (NBC) (30 Rockefeller Plaza, New York, NY 10022), a subsidiary of RCA, is one of the three major networks and can assist with research.

The National CATV Association (918 16 Street, N.W., Washington, DC 20006) is an organization that promotes the interests of community-antenna operations in the United States.

The National Newspaper Association (491 National Press Building, Washington, DC 20045) is an organization of publishers and has source materials available to researchers.

The National Newspaper Publishers Association (770 National Press Building, Washington, DC 20045) is an organization of blacks involved in journalism.

National Public Radio (2025 M Street, N.W., Washington, DC 20036) is the network organization for public radio.

The Newspaper Comics Council (260 Madison Avenue, New York, NY 10016) deals with the problems of newspaper comic strips. It maintains a library and information center.

The Newspaper Information Service (American Newspaper Publishers Association, Sunrise Valley Drive, Reston, VA 22070) is the public relations service of the newspaper industry and is very helpful to researchers.

The Office of Communication of the United Church of Christ (289 Park Avenue South, New York, NY 10010) is one of the most active religious organizations in the field of mass communication, especially broadcasting. This organization is extremely helpful to beginning students in the mass media.

The Outdoor Advertisers Association of America (485 Lexington Avenue, New York, NY 10017) deals with the special interests of billboard advertisers and space renters.

The Public Relations Society of America (845 Third Avenue, New York, NY 10022) is a professional association of public relations practitioners.

The Publishers Information Bureau (575 Lexington Avenue, New York, NY 10022) provides data on magazines for consumers and the public as well as researchers.

The Radio Advertising Bureau (555 Madison Avenue, New York, NY 10022) is involved in research as to the effectiveness of radio in ad campaigns.

Radio Free Europe (1201 Connecticut Avenue, N.W., Washington, DC 20036) is a broadcasting service beamed into Eastern Europe.

The Radio-Television News Directors Association (1735 DeSales Street, N.W., Washington, DC 20036) is an organization of broadcast news directors.

Recording Industry Association of America (One East 57 Street, New York, NY 10022) represents companies that manufacture records. Awards gold and platinum records for top-selling songs.

The Television Bureau of Advertising (1345 Avenue of the Americas, New York, NY 10019) provides excellent service for students analyzing TV programming and advertising.

The Television Information Office (745 Fifth Avenue, New York, NY 10022) is sponsored by local television stations and is a good source of TV data.

The Transit Advertising Association (1725 K Street, N.W., Suite 414, Washington, DC 20006) is concerned with the problems of advertising in mass-transit systems.

A SELECTED BIBLIOGRAPHY OF PERIODICALS.   This list of magazines has been developed as a selected core for a library used for research in mass communication. Only those magazines primarily concerned with the media or media-related activities have been included. It is assumed that standard consumer and general-interest magazines are available.

Current prices have been included so that persons interested in subscribing to selected magazines can do so easily and with some idea of the cost. Important sources have been noted in the annotations.

ACT News (1970, $15) is the newsletter of Action for Childrens Television, ACT, 46 Austin Street, Newtonville, MA 02160.

Advertising Age (1930, $12) is a national weekly newspaper of advertising and marketing. Crain Communications, Inc., 740 Rush Street, Chicago, IL 60611).

American Cinematographer (1919, $9) provides articles on motion picture photography and production techniques. 1782 N. Orange Drive, Los Angeles, CA 90028.

American Film (1975, $15) contains popular articles on motion pictures and television. American Film Institute, JFK Center for the Performing Arts, Washington, DC 20566.

ASNE Bulletin (1923, $6) deals with problems of editing a newspaper. American Society of Newspaper Editors, Box 551, 1350 Sullivan Trail, Easton, PA 18042.

Audio-Visual Communications (1961, $11) provides a selection of articles on all phases of media use in education. United Business Publications, Inc., 750 Third Avenue, New York, NY 10017.

Billboard (1894, $50) is the music industry's major trade paper. It also provides an analysis of the practices of the recording industry. 9000 Sunset Boulevard, Los Angeles, CA 90069.

Book Production Industry (1924, $10) provides information on the book-publishing industry. 21 Charles Street, Box 429, Saugatuck Station, Westport, CT 06880.

Boxoffice (1920, $15) contains complete, up-to-date news on the film industry and also includes film reviews from the viewpoint of industry management. Associated Publications, Inc., 825 Van Brunt Boulevard, Kansas City, MO 64124.

Broadcasting (1931, $30) is the radio and television industry's trade journal and is an important source for anyone doing research in the broadcasting industry. Broadcasting Publications, Inc., 1735 DeSales Street, N.W., Washington, DC 20036.

Business Screen (1938, $6) provides news and analysis of films made for educational and instructional purposes. Harcourt Brace Jovanovich, 757 Third Avenue, New York, NY 10017.

Cable Report (1972, $15) concentrates on analysis of cable-TV industry. Association of Working Press, Inc., 6037 N. Monticello, Chicago, IL 60659.

Cashbox (1942, $60) is a recording-industry trade journal. 119 West 57 Street, New York, NY 10019.

Cinema Journal (1961, $4) is the magazine of the Society for Cinema Studies. R-TV-Film Dept., Temple University, Philadelphia, PA 19122.

CTVD: Cinema-Television Digest (1961, $3) provides a current analysis of the foreign TV and film industries. Hampton Books, Route 1, Box 76, Newberry, SC 29108.

Columbia Journalism Review (1962, $12) is a scholarly and professional review of opinion and research. Columbia University, 700 Journalism Building, New York, NY 10027.

Communication Research (1974, $13.50) publishes scholarly articles treating a broad range of communication issues. Sage Publications, Inc., 275 South Beverly Drive, Beverly Hills, CA 90212.

Editor and Publisher (1884, $12.50) provides information on the newspaper business. 850 Third Avenue, New York, NY 10022.

Film Comment (1962, $10) provides critical analysis of the medium's artistic and social influence on our society. 1865 Broadway, New York, NY 10023.

Film Culture (1955, $8) covers aesthetics, criticism, and history of the motion picture. G.P.O. Box 1449, New York, NY 10001.

Film Quarterly (1945, $6) provides criticism of the American and foreign film industries. University of California Press, 2223 Fulton Street, Berkeley, CA 94720.

Fourth Estate (1967, $2) is Canada's national press journal. Box 3184, Station C, Ottawa, Ont., KIX 4J4, Canada.

High Fidelity (1951, $8.95) deals with music, musicians, and sound-recording systems, but is more classical than pop. ABC Leisure Magazines, Inc., Great Barrington, MA 02130.

Journal of Advertising Research (1960, $35) publishes original research on advertising and marketing which emphasizes practical applications of these findings. Advertising Research Foundation, 3 East 54 Street, New York, NY 10022.

Journal of Broadcasting (1956, $17.50) is a scholarly journal that publishes a wide variety of articles on various kinds of research in radio, television, and related industries. School of Journalism, University of Georgia, Athens, GA 30602.

Journal of Communication (1951, $15) is a scholarly journal published by the Annenberg School of Communication Press in cooperation with the International Communication Association. Annenberg School Press, P.O. Box 13358, Philadelphia, PA 19101.

Journal of Marketing (1936, $18) provides a survey of marketing and advertising articles for business and education. American Marketing Association, 222 S. Riverside Plaza, Chicago, IL 60606.

Journal of Marketing Research (1964, $18) is a professional and scholarly journal that reports findings in market research. American Marketing Association, 222 S. Riverside Plaza, Chicago, IL 60606.

Journal of Popular Film (1972, $5) publishes scholarly articles of film as a part of popular culture. Bowling Green State University, Bowling Green, OH 43403.

Journalism Educator (1945, $6) provides articles on journalism education and new developments in professional journalism. American Society of Journalism School Administrators, Department of Journalism, University of Minnesota, Minneapolis, MN 55455.

Journalism Monographs (1966, $10) provides longer reports and studies in journalism. School of Journalism, University of Kentucky, Lexington, KY 40506.

Journalism Quarterly (1924, $12) provides reports of the latest research in journalism and other areas of mass communication. Association for Education in Journalism, 111 Murphy Hall, University of Minnesota, Minneapolis, MN 55455.

Media Industry Newsletter (1948, $58) analyzes and evaluates developments in all phases of magazine publication. 150 East 52 Street, New York, NY 10022.

Millimeter (1973, $10) reviews technical and production aspects of film and television. 12 East 46 Street, New York, NY 10017.

More (1971, $10) is an example of the new genre of critical reviews of the news media. Rosebud Associates, Inc., 750 Third Avenue, New York, NY 10017.

Public Opinion Quarterly (1937, $12) provides articles on survey research and public attitudes toward mass media and other topics related to mass communication. Columbia University Press, Columbia University, New York, NY 10027.

Public Relations Journal (1945, $12) is the monthly magazine of the Public Relations Society of America, 845 Third Avenue, New York, NY 10022.

Public Relations Quarterly (1955, $12) provides articles by leading practitioners, psychologists, and sociologists related to public relations activities. 2626 Pennsylvania Avenue, N.W., Washington, DC 20037.

Public Telecommunications Review (1973, $18) is a scholarly journal concerned with educational broadcasting. Formerly known as *Educational Broadcasting Review*. NAEB, 1346 Connecticut Avenue, N.W., Suite 1101, Washington, DC 20036.

Publishers Weekly (1872, $30) reports and analyzes trends and problems in the book-publishing industry. R. R. Bowker Co., 1180 Avenue of the Americas, New York, NY 10036.

Quill (1912, $7.50) is the monthly magazine of Sigma Delta Chi, the national society of journalists. 35 East Wacker Drive, Chicago, IL 60601.

Rolling Stone (1967, $14) has been called the *New York Times* of the counterculture and reports on contemporary trends in the recording industry. Straight Arrow Publishers, 745 Fifth Avenue, New York, NY 10022.

RTNDA Communicator (1971, $15) is the monthly newsletter of the Radio Television News Directors Association, dealing with the problems of radio-television news. Radio Television News Directors Association, 1735 DeSales Street, N.W., Washington, DC 20036.

Sight and Sound (1932, $6) serves as a source of educational and artistic analysis of film. British Film Institute, 155 West 15 Street, New York, NY 10001.

Television/Radio Age (1953, $20) is designed for commercial broadcasters and advertisers and is an excellent source for student research. Television Editorial Corporation, 666 Fifth Avenue, New York, NY 10019.

Television Digest (1945, $198) is a good statistical source of all phases of the industry and offers data on the CATV operations in the United States. 1836 Jefferson Place, N.W., Washington, DC 20036.

TV Communications (1964 $14) is the professional journal of the cable-television industry. Communications Publishing Corp., 1900 West Yale, Englewood, CO 80110.

TV Guide (1953, $9.50) is the best source of information on TV programming. Triangle Publications, Inc., Radnor, PA 19088.

Variety (1905, $25) is the entertainment industry's trade paper and provides current information regarding business and artistic aspects of the mass media. 154 West 46 Street, New York, NY 10036.

Videocassette and CATV Newsletter (1971, $42) looks at new systems, the market and the future of video cassettes and cable television. Martin Roberts & Associates, Inc., Box 5254, Beverly Hills, CA 90210.

Writer (1887, $10) carries information and advice for individuals interested in writing for publication. 8 Arlington Street, Boston, MA 02116.

Writer's Digest (1919, $12) is a guide for free-lance writers. F & W Publishing Corporation, 9933 Alliance Road, Cincinnati, OH 45242.

A SELECTED BIBLIOGRAPHY OF BOOKS. The books in the following list have been selected to provide the student with a useful survey of materials available in the field of mass communication. Obviously this list will not contain all the materials necessary for every study undertaken, but if the bibliographies in each of the books listed are carefully examined, the student will be well on the way with his literature search.

Adler, Richard, ed. *Television as a Social Force: New Approaches to Television Criticism*. New York: Praeger, 1975. A series of eight essays by various authors on the role of television programming in American life.

Agee, Warren K. *Mass Media in a Free Society*. Lawrence, KS: University of Kansas Press, 1969. Contains a good series of articles by media professionals on the freedom and responsibilities of the press.

ANPA Research Institute. *The Structure and Layout of Editorial-News De-*

partments. New York: American Newspaper Publishers Association, 1970. Analyzes newspaper news operations.

Arlen, Michael J. *Living-room War*. New York: Viking, 1969. Examines the effects of TV news reports on society's attitudes toward the war in Vietnam.

———. *The View from Highway 1*. New York: Ballantine, 1977. A series of essays on contemporary television issues originally published in the *New Yorker*.

Ashley, Paul P. *Say It Safely: Legal Limits in Publishing, Radio, and Television*. 5th ed. Seattle: University of Washington Press, 1976. Broad introductory survey of media law and regulation including coverage of libel, privacy, free speech, and pornography.

Ashmore, Harry S. *Fear in the Air: Broadcasting and the First Amendment: The Anatomy of a Constitutional Crisis*. New York: Norton, 1973. Contends that the dangers to freedom of the press caused by technological and social change are greater than presidential anger against them. He proceeds to analyze these changes, especially in relation to the Watergate crisis.

Baddeley, Walter H. *The Technique of Documentary Film Production*. Rev. 3rd ed. New York: Hastings House, 1973. Analyzes visual communication theory and coding processes in the film-TV documentary.

Bagdikian, Ben H. *The Information Machines: Their Impact on Men and the Media*. New York: Harper & Row, 1971. Provides the first full-scale projection of the technological explosion in communication and conveys both the challenge about the future and apprehension about its dangers.

Balio, Tino, ed. *The American Film Industry*. Madison: University of Wisconsin Press, 1976. A series of 21 articles providing an historical overview of the American film industry.

Barnouw, Erik. *A History of Broadcasting in the United States*. New York: Oxford University Press, 1966 (vol. 1), 1968 (vol. 2), 1970 (vol. 3). Surveys the history of radio and television and is essential for anyone who plans to do historical research in broadcasting.

———. *Tube of Plenty: The Evolution of American Television*. New York: Oxford University Press, 1975. A condensation and updating of his three-volume *History of Broadcasting in the United States*.

Barrett, Marvin, ed. *The Alfred I. DuPont–Columbia University Survey of Broadcast Journalism*. New York: Grosset & Dunlap, 1969–1971; New York: Crowell, 1972 to date. An annual series analyzing how TV reports the news and the various forces that influence broadcast newsmen.

Barsam, Richard. *Nonfiction Film*. New York: Dutton, 1973. An up-to-date history and analysis of the various forms of nonfiction film.

Bauer, Raymond A., and Greyser, Stephen A. *What Americans Think of Advertising*. Homewood, IL: Dow Jones-Irwin, 1969. Reports public opinion studies of ad campaigns.

Belz, Carl. *The Story of Rock*. New York: Oxford University Press, 1969. Traces the history of rock music and the personalities involved in its development.

Berelson, Bernard, and Janowitz, Morris. *Reader in Public Opinion and Communication*. New York: Free Press, 1966. Provides a wide selection of sociological material helpful to students of the media.

Berlo, David K. *The Process of Communication*. New York: Holt, Rinehart & Winston, 1960. Analyzes the interpersonal communication process.

Bernays, Edward L. *Biography of an Idea: Memoirs of a Public Relations Counsel*. New York: Simon & Schuster, 1965. Presents a revealing and insightful account of the development of systematic public relations by one of the pioneers of the profession.

Berstein, Carl, and Woodward, Bob. *All the President's Men*. New York: Simon & Schuster, 1974. The inside story on Watergate by the Pulitzer-Prize-winning team of reporters for the *Washington Post*.

Bleum, A. William. *Documentary in American Television*. New York: Hastings House, 1964. Analyzes and evaluates the documentary's achievement in television.

————, and Squire, Jason, eds. *The Movie Business*. New York: Hastings House, 1972. An anthology of articles on the motion-picture industry by leading professionals.

Bliss, Edward, Jr., and Patterson, John M. *Writing News for Broadcast*. New York: Columbia University Press, 1971. Introduces the student to the essential techniques of writing news for radio and television.

Bloom, Melvyn H. *Public Relations and Presidential Campaigns: A Crisis in Democracy*. New York: Crowell, 1973. Traces the growing complexity and sophistication of the "new politics" and the "new professionals" who have run elections for 20 years—from Eisenhower in 1952 to Nixon in 1972.

Blumer, Jay, and McQuail, Denis. *Television in Politics*. Chicago: University of Chicago Press, 1969. Evaluates and criticizes the role of TV in the American political system.

Bobker, Lee R. *Elements of Film*. New York: Harcourt, Brace & World, 1969. Provides an excellent primer for the beginner in film analysis.

Bogart, Leo. *Strategy in Advertising*. New York: Harcourt, Brace & World, 1967. Analyzes advertising-media plans and audience research evaluation.

Bohn, Thomas, and Stromgren, Richard. *Light and Shadows: A History of Motion Pictures*. 2nd ed. Sherman Oaks, CA: Alfred Publishing, 1978.

———. *A Historical and Descriptive Analysis of the "Why We Fight" Series*. New York: Arno, 1977.

Bower, Robert T. *Television and the Public*. New York: Holt, Rinehart & Winston, 1973. An update of the 1963 Gary Steiner report, *The People Look at Television*.

Braestrup, Peter. *Big Story: How the American Press and Television Reported and Interpreted the Crisis of Tet 1968 in Vietnam and Washington*. Boulder, CO: Westview, 1977. An excellent analysis of how American mass media reported the Vietnam war.

Brown, J. A. C. *Techniques of Persuasion*. New York: Penguin, 1963. Serves as a good short primer in persuasive communication in a modern society.

Brown, Les, *Television: The Business Behind the Box*. New York: Harcourt Brace Jovanovich, 1971. Provides an inside view of the television industry as a business, including the problems of ratings, packaging, and monopoly.

Budd, Richard W.; Thorp, Robert K.; and Donohew, Lewis. *Content Analysis of Communications*. New York: Macmillan, 1967. Provides a broad and basic but thorough introduction to the use of content analysis in mass media studies.

Buzek, Antonin. *How the Communist Press Works*. New York: Praeger, 1964. Provides an evaluation of journalism in the communist bloc.

Chafee, Zechariah. *Government and Mass Communication*. 2 vols. Chicago: University of Chicago Press, 1947. A classic in the field of mass communication law.

Chalmers, David Mark. *The Social and Political Ideas of the Muckrakers*. Secaucus, NJ: Citadel, 1964. Provides excellent material on the influence this movement has had on print institutions and forces that shaped investigative reporting.

Chester, Edward W. *Radio, Television, and American Politics*. New York: Sheed & Ward, 1969. Evaluates the political uses of broadcasting in the United States.

Chittick, William O. *State Department, Press, and Pressure Groups*. New York: Wiley, 1970. Deals with four groups: State Department policy officers, foreign affairs reporters, information officers, and pressure groups. Analyzes the role each group plays in the communication of foreign policy.

Cirino, Robert. *Don't Blame the People: How the News Media Use Bias, Distortion and Censorship to Manipulate Public Opinion*. New York: Random House, 1971. Expresses the growing feeling of anger and disillusionment on the part of the average uninformed media consumer in America.

Clark, David G., and Hutchison, Earl R. *Mass Media and the Law*. New York: Wiley, 1970. Shows how the laws (or absence of laws) bearing on the mass media affect our lives. The dual nature of law as a defender of expression, and as a restrainer of expression, is a basic theme.

Cogley, John. *Report on Blacklisting*. Vol. 1: *Film*. Vol. 2: *Radio-Television*. New York: Fund for the Republic, 1956. Reviews the restrictive employment practices in media during the "red scare" in the late 1940s and early 1950s.

Comstock, George. *Television and Human Behavior: The Key Studies*. Santa Monica, CA: Rand, 1975.

Conant, Michael. *Antitrust in the Motion Picture Industry*. Berkeley, CA: University of California Press, 1960. Evaluates government actions taken against the movies during the first half of the twentieth century.

Copple, Neale. *Depth Reporting: An Approach to Journalism*. Englewood Cliffs, NJ: Prentice-Hall, 1964. Presents a unique approach to investigative and interpretative news reporting.

Cornwell, Elmer E. *Presidential Leadership of Public Opinion*. Bloomington, IN: Indiana University Press, 1966. Describes the way in which American presidents have used public relations techniques to deal with the press and mass media.

Costello, Lawrence. *Teach with Television*. New York: Hastings House, 1961. Evaluates a variety of teaching strategies that can be employed in ETV.

Crouse, Timothy. *The Boys on the Bus*. New York: Random House, 1973. Inside account of how news reporters covered the 1972 election.

Crowell, Alfred A. *Creative News Editing*. Dubuque, IA: Brown, 1969, Provides the best basic introduction to editing techniques, especially for newspapers.

————, and Center, Allen H. *Effective Public Relations*. 4th ed. Englewood Cliffs, NJ: Prentice-Hall, 1971. Provides a basic and comprehensive introduction to professional practices and theories of public relations.

Daly, Charles, *The Media and the Cities*. Chicago: University of Chicago Press, 1968. Analyzes the role of the news media in the cities and provides important insights on news in crisis situations.

Davison, W. Phillips. *International Political Communication*. New York: Praeger, 1965. Analyzes media systems under a variety of political conditions, both in terms of national and international interests.

DeFleur, Melvin, and Ball-Rokeach, Sandra. *Theories of Mass Communication*. 3rd ed. New York: Longman, 1975. Analyzes the social-psychological aspects of the mass communication process.

DeGrazia, Edward. *Censorship Landmarks*. New York: Bowker, 1969. Collects cases of censorship in the mass media.

Denisoff, R. Serge. *Solid Gold: The Popular Record Industry*. New Brunswick, NJ: Transaction, 1974. A survey and critical analysis of the record industry. Stress is on cultural and social aspects of industry.

Dennis, Everette, and Rivers, William L. *Other Voices: The New Journalism in America*. San Francisco: Canfield, 1975.

Deutschmann, Paul J. *Communication and Change in Latin America*. New York: Praeger, 1968. Analyzes the effects of the mass media in underdeveloped nations.

Diamond, Edwin. *The Tin Kazoo: Television Politics and the News*. Cambridge, MA: MIT Press, 1975.

Doob, Leonard. *Public Opinion and Propaganda*. Hamden, CT: Archon, 1966. Provides an early analysis of public opinion and propaganda in mass communication media.

Dunn, Delmer. *Public Officials and the Press*. Reading, MA: Addison-Wesley, 1969. Covers the relationships of reporters with the people and events they cover.

Dunn, S. Watson. *Advertising: Its Role in Modern Marketing*. New York: Holt, Rinehart & Winston, 1969. Textbook for a beginning course in advertising, but helpful for media research because of its chapters on the media used in ad campaigns.

Emery, Edwin. *The Press and America*. Englewood Cliffs, NJ: Prentice-Hall, 1972. Chronicles the history and development of journalistic institutions.

Emery, Walter B. *Broadcasting and Government*. East Lansing, MI: Michigan State University Press, 1961. Basic text in broadcast law.

———. *National and International Systems of Broadcasting*. East Lansing, MI: Michigan State University Press, 1969. Provides a country-by-country evaluation of the structure and format of radio and television communication in terms of legal and operating conditions.

Epstein, Edward Jay. *News from Nowhere: Television and the News*. New York: Random House, 1973. Analyzes the role and impact of networks on television news operations.

———, and Schwartz, Alan U. *Censorship: The Search for the Obscene*. New York: Macmillan, 1964. Analyzes the theoretical and practical implications of censorship in the print media.

Fabre, Maurice. *A History of Communication*. New York: Hawthorn, 1963. Presents a historical and analytical review of the concepts and processes of communication.

Fang, I. E. *Television News*. New York: Hastings House, 1968. Evaluates the production and content problems of TV news.

Fell, John L. *Film: An Introduction*. New York: Praeger, 1975.

Fischer, Heinz D., and Merrill, John C. *International Communication: Media, Channels, and Functions*. New York: Hastings House, 1970. Reviews national and international mass communication systems, both in terms of organizational patterns and theoretical considerations.

Fisher, Paul L., and Lowenstein, Ralph L., eds. *Race and the News Media*. New York: Praeger, 1967. Covers the problems of reporting events involving minority groups, and some of the effects news has on the race-relations problems in the United States.

Flippen, Charles C. II. *Liberating the Media: The New Journalism*. Washington, DC: Acropolis, 1974. Contains essays both pro and con about the various forms of "new journalism" today.

Ford, James L. C. *Magazines for the Millions*. Carbondale, IL: Southern Illinois University Press, 1970. Introduces magazines to anyone interested in almost any aspect of the business.

Friendly, Fred W. *Due to Circumstances Beyond Our Control*. New York: Random House, 1967. Analyzes the operation and problems of television news and public affairs programming at CBS.

Gattegno, Caleb. *Towards a Visual Culture*. New York: Outerbridge & Dienstfrey, 1969. Provides a cultural critique of the content of media.

Gelatt, Roland, *The Fabulous Phonograph*. Des Moines, IA: Meredith, 1964. History of the medium with a look at the music business as well.

Gerald, J. Edward. *The Social Responsibility of the Press*. Minneapolis: University of Minnesota Press, 1963. Places the professional and ethical responsibilities of the press against the economic realities of mass communication in modern society.

Gerbner, George, and others, eds. *Communications Technology and Social Policy: Understanding the New "Cultural Revolution."* New York: Wiley, 1973. Examines the implications of communication technology, economics, education, urban and international communication, and social communication research on industrial, political, and cultural power.

Geyelin, Philip L., and Cater, Douglass. *American Media: Adequate or Not?* Washington, DC: American Enterprise Institute for Public Policy Research, 1970. Provides a brief but incisive argument on both sides of the question by two distinguished Washington correspondents and observers.

Gianetti, Louis D. *Understanding Movies*. 2nd ed. Englewood Cliffs, NJ: Prentice-Hall, 1976.

Gilbert, Robert E. *Television and Presidential Politics*. North Quincy, MA:

Christopher Publishing House, 1972. Analyzes the role of video on the presidential level of politics.

Gillett, Charlie. *The Sound of the City*. New York: Outerbridge & Dienstfrey, 1972. A most comprehensive and complete history of rock music.

Gillmor, Donald M. *Free Press and Fair Trial*. Washington, DC: Public Affairs Press, 1966. Analyzes the problems of the conflict between the First and Sixth Amendments.

————, and Barron, Jerome A. *Mass Communication Law*. St. Paul, MI: West, 1969.

Gordon, George N. *Educational Television*. New York: Applied Research in Education, 1965. Analyzes the potential of the medium and evaluates the success it has had in classroom teaching and general education.

————. *Persuasion: The Theory and Practice of Manipulative Communication*. New York: Hastings House, 1971. Provides a comprehensive treatment of the use of communication for persuasive purposes.

Green, Maury. *Television News: Anatomy and Process*. Belmont, CA: Wadsworth, 1969. Analyzes local-station news operations.

Greenberg, Bradley, and Parker, Edwin. *The Kennedy Assassination and the American Public*. Stanford, CA: Stanford University Press, 1965. Dissects the news coverage and operation in a crisis.

Gross, Gerald. *The Responsibility of the Press*. New York: Fleet, 1966. Provides a good analysis of gatekeeping and regulation of media industries on both theoretical and application levels.

Guback, Thomas H. *International Film Industry*. Bloomington, IN: Indiana University Press, 1969. Analyzes the European and American film industries after World War II.

Hall, Edward T. *The Silent Language*. Garden City, NY: Doubleday, 1959. Pioneers in providing an analysis of nonverbal communication.

Halloran, J. *The Effects of Mass Communication*. Leicester, England: Leicester University Press, 1965. Evaluates the changes that are occurring in industrial societies as a result of the mass media.

Haskell, Molly. *From Reverence to Rape: The Treatment of Women in the Movies*. New York: Holt, Rinehart & Winston, 1972.

Head, Sydney W. *Broadcasting in Africa: A Continental Survey of Radio and Television*. Philadelphia: Temple University Press, 1974. A broad country-by-country analysis of various broadcasting services and functions in Africa.

————. *Broadcasting in America: A Survey of Television and Radio*. 3rd ed. Boston: Houghton Mifflin, 1976. A single-volume history, description, and analysis of the American broadcasting industry with emphasis on the physical base of broadcasting, as well as economics and regulation.

Heighton, Elizabeth J., and Cunningham, Don R. *Advertising in the Broadcast Media*. Belmont, CA: Wadsworth, 1976. A complete overview of broadcast advertising including material on marketing research and media planning buying and selling time and social responsibility in advertising.

Hiebert, Ray Eldon, ed. *Books in Human Development*. Washington, DC: Agency for International Development, 1964. Surveys the role and use of books as medium of education and information in the development of peoples and nations.

———. *Courtier to the Crowd*. Ames, IA: Iowa State University Press, 1966. A biography of Ivy Lee, pioneer public relations counselor. Tells the story of the beginnings of professional public relations.

———. *Trends in Public Relations Education*. New York: Foundation for Public Relations Research and Education, 1971. Survey and analysis of public relations educational courses and programs throughout the United States.

———; Jones, Robert; Lorenz, John; and Lotito, Ernest. *The Political Image Merchants*. Washington, DC: Acropolis, 1971. Examines the activities of political campaign managers, advertising agencies, pollsters, and public relations firms and their techniques, successes, and failures in using mass media for the "new politics."

———, and Spitzer, Carlton E. *The Voice of Government*. New York: Wiley, 1968. Analyzes and describes the way in which the American government communicates with the public.

Himmelweit, Hilde T., et al. *Television and the Child*. London: Oxford University Press, 1958. A classic on the empirical research on the effects of TV on children.

Hirsch, Paul. *The Structure of the Popular Music Industry*. Ann Arbor, MI: Institute for Social Research of the University of Michigan, 1970. Analyzes the business aspects and gatekeeper function in the record industry.

———. *The Professional Journalist*. New York: Holt, Rinehart & Winston, 1961. Introduces the student to basic professional practices in reporting the news.

Hollander, Gayle Durham. *Soviet Political Indoctrination: Developments in Mass Media and Propaganda Since Stalin*. New York: Praeger, 1972. Presents information on the content of Soviet media.

Hopkins, Mark W. *Mass Media in the Soviet Union*. Indianapolis, IN: Pegasus, 1970. Analyzes the media system in Russia.

Huaco, George A. *The Sociology of Film Art*. New York: Basic, 1965. Presents three schools of film art: (1) German Expressionism, (2) Russian Realism, (3) Italian Neorealism.

Huss, Roy, and Silverstein, Norman. *The Film Experience*. New York: Harper & Row, 1968. Analyzes the film communication process.

Hynds, Ernest C. *American Newspapers in the 1970s*. New York: Hastings House, 1975.

Innis, Harold A. *The Bias of Communication*. Toronto: University of Toronto Press, 1951. Precursor of the writings of Marshall McLuhan, this book is an analysis of the effects of media on the history of mankind.

Jacobs, Lewis. *The Documentary Experience*. New York: Hopkinson & Blake, 1971. An anthology of articles providing historical and critical analysis of the documentary film.

————. *The Rise of the American Film*. New York: Teachers College Press, 1967. A basic film history text, which unfortunately only goes up to 1939. To that point it is a very thorough and complete analysis of the American motion picture.

Jacobs, Norman, ed. *Culture for the Millions: Mass Media in Modern Society*. Boston: Beacon, 1964. Presents a series of essays by leading sociologists, psychologists, anthropologists, and historians, who examine the effect of mass media on popular American culture.

Janowitz, Morris. *The Community Press in an Urban Setting*. Chicago: University of Chicago Press, 1967. Sociological analysis of the role and impact of news in the urban areas of U.S. society.

Johnson, Nicholas. *How to Talk Back to Your Television Set*. Boston: Little, Brown, 1970. Series of essays by FCC commissioner on the state of broadcasting in the United States and the ways in which individuals can affect these media.

Kahn, Frank, ed. *Documents in American Broadcasting*. 3rd ed. New York: Appleton-Century-Crofts, 1978. Select legal cases and other materials useful in research in broadcast law.

Kendrick, Alexander, *Prime Time*. Boston: Little, Brown, 1969. Presents the story of Edward R. Murrow and the operations of the U.S. Information Agency and network news departments.

Kent, Ruth. *The Language of Journalism: A Glossary of Print-Communications Terms*. Kent, OH: Kent State University Press, 1970. A dictionary of journalistic terms, preceded by a discussion of the meaning and origins of associated words such as "muckraker," "tabloid," and "yellow journalism," and followed by a list of commonly used abbreviations.

Klapper, Joseph T. *The Effects of Mass Communication*. New York: Free Press, 1960. Evaluates the research on the effectiveness of the media in society.

Kline, F. Gerald, and Tichenor, Phillip J., eds. *Current Perspectives in Mass Communication Research*. Beverly Hills, CA: Sage, 1972. Provides a status report on aspects of mass communication research.

Knight, Arthur. *The Liveliest Art*. 2nd ed. New York: New American Library, 1978. A good short history of the cinema up to the middle '70s.

Koenig, Allen E. *The Farther Vision*. Madison, WI: University of Wisconsin Press, 1967. A useful work on education broadcasting.

Kohlmeier, Louis. *The Regulators*. New York: Harper & Row, 1969. Deals with many different federal agencies and contains good sections on the FTC and the FCC.

Krasnow, Erwin G., and Longley, Lawrence D. *The Politics of Broadcast Regulation*. New York: St. Martin's, 1973. An examination of the regulation of broadcasting as a political process.

————. *Pressures on the Press*. New York: Crowell, 1972. Tells why the mass media do not always give the full news, and discusses what the people can do about it.

Lacy, Dan. *Freedom and Communications*. Urbana, IL: University of Illinois Press, 1961. Presents a summary of the problems of maintaining freedom of the press.

Lane, Robert E., and Sears, David O., eds. *Public Opinion*. Englewood Cliffs, NJ: Prentice-Hall, 1964. Surveys the political aspects of public opinion.

Lang, Kurt, and Lang, Gladys. *Politics and Television*. Chicago: Quadrangle, 1968. Analyzes TV news and its political impact in specific case studies.

Larsen, Otto, *Violence and the Mass Media*. New York: Harper & Row, 1968. Analyzes the empirical research on violence, media, and human behavior.

Lee, John. *Diplomatic Persuaders: The New Role of the Mass Media in International Relations*. New York: Wiley, 1968. Deals with the influential use of mass media by governments and the resulting new breed of diplomatic specialists—the career press and information officers.

Lee, Richard W. *Politics and the Press*. Washington, DC: Acropolis, 1970. Presents eleven experts in communications who examine the problems of press coverage of politics and government, and political and governmental pressures on the mass media.

Lerbinger, Otto, and Sullivan, Albert J. *Information, Influence, and Communication*. New York: Basic, 1965. Presents a variety of articles showing the social science foundations for the theory and practice of public relations.

Lerner, David, and Schramm, Wilbur. *Communication and Change in Developing Countries*. Honolulu: East-West Center Press, 1967. Series of case studies on Asian nations and problems of media systems growth.

Lewis, Colby. *The TV Director/Interpreter*. New York: Hastings House, 1968. Excellent analysis of the TV coding process from the director's viewpoint.

Lichty, Lawrence W., and Topping, Malachi C., eds. *American Broadcasting:*

A Source Book on the History of Radio and Television. New York: Hasting House, 1975. A collection of 93 articles covering various topics in radio-television history.

Liebert, Robert M.; Neale, John M.; and Davidson, Emily S. *The Early Window: Effects of Television on Children and Youth.* Elmsford, NY: Pergamon, 1973. An attempt to explore all research involving the effects of television on children.

Liebling, A. J. *The Press.* New York: Ballantine, 1964. Collects some of the best of the caustic and incisive critiques of the press written for "The Wayward Press" in the *New Yorker* magazine.

Lindgren, Ernest. *The Art of Film.* New York: Macmillan, 1963. Discusses film mechanics, techniques, and criticism.

Lippmann, Walter. *Public Opinion.* New York: Free Press, 1965. Pioneers in presenting the philosophy and psychology of the role of public opinion.

Lyle, Jack. *The News in Megalopolis.* San Francisco: Chandler, 1967. Discusses the factors that influence news gathering in metropolitan areas.

MacCann, Richard Dyer, ed. *Film: A Montage of Theories.* New York: Dutton, 1966. Contains theoretical and critical analyses of the techniques and process of film communication.

MacDougall, Curtis D. *Interpretive Reporting.* New York: Macmillan, 1968. Pioneers in presenting a professional approach to reporting the news.

MacLean, Roderick. *Television in Education.* New York: Barnes & Noble, 1968. Provides a fairly detailed evaluation of the current problems and future potential of ETV.

MacNeil, Robert. *The People Machine.* New York: Harper & Row, 1968. Investigates the role of TV in providing political news and information in America.

Manoogian, Haig P. *The Film-Maker's Art.* New York: Basic, 1966. Analyzes the creative aspects of film communication.

Manvell, Roger, and Jacobs, Lewis. *The International Encyclopedia of Film.* New York: Crown, 1972. Presents a highly valuable one-volume reference to most of the important historical, content, and technical trends in film on a worldwide basis.

Markham, James W. *Voices of the Red Giants.* Ames, IA: Iowa State University Press, 1967. Analyzes media in Russia and China and provides insights into media uses in the nations.

Mattfeld, Julius. *Variety Music Cavalcade.* Englewood Cliffs, NJ: Prentice-Hall, 1962. A complete chronology of music published in the U.S. up to 1961.

McGinniss, Joe. *The Selling of the President, 1968.* New York: Trident, 1969. Discusses the Nixon campaign's uses of TV in 1968 and the implications of the medium for American politics in the future.

McLuhan, Marshall. *The Medium Is the Message.* New York: Bantam, 1967. Primer on McLuhan's basic philosophy.

————. *Understanding Media: The Extensions of Man.* New York: McGraw-Hill, 1964. Complex statement of McLuhan's thoughts. Details the complicated but insightful views about the nature of the medium as the message.

McQuail, Denis. *Towards a Sociology of Mass Communication.* London: Collier-Macmillan, 1969. Reviews empirical research in the fields of mass media and society and attempts to draw significant sociological relationships between them.

Mendelsohn, Harold. *Mass Entertainment.* New Haven, CT: College and University Press, 1966. Defends pop culture as a valuable social activity.

Merrill, John C. *The Elite Press: Great Newspapers of the World.* Belmont, CA: Pitman, 1968. Discusses the top 40 newspapers of the world and the factors which have made them great.

Merritt, Richard L., ed. *Communication in International Politics.* Urbana, IL: University of Illinois Press, 1972. Examines communication in worldwide political discourse.

Meyerholt, Paul. *The Strategy of Persuasion.* New York: Berkley Medallion, 1968. Compares American and Soviet propaganda.

Michael, Paul, ed. *The American Movies Reference Book.* Englewood Cliffs, NJ: Prentice-Hall, 1969. Source book for film historians.

Mickelson, Sig. *The Electric Mirror: Politics in an Age of Television.* New York: Dodd, Mead, 1972. Provides the insights of a pioneer broadcast news executive on the impact of television news, particularly on American politics.

Midura, Edmund M. *Why Aren't We Getting Through: The Urban Communications Crisis.* Washington, DC: Acropolis, 1971. Presents nationally known journalists and experts probing the problems of the role of mass media should play in helping break down the barriers between black and white, rich and poor, urban and suburban dweller in modern society.

Mills, Nicolaus, ed. *The New Journalism: A Historical Anthology.* New York: McGraw-Hill, 1974.

Minow, Newton H.; Martin, John Bartlow; and Mitchell, Lee M. *Presidential Television.* New York: Basic, 1973. Shows how every President from

Roosevelt to Nixon has used television to their advantage to go over the heads of Congress and the opposition party and appeal directly to the people.

Moir, Guthrie. *Teaching and Television*. Elmsford, NY: Pergamon, 1967. Analyzes classroom uses of the medium, with helpful suggestions for the classroom teacher.

Mott, Frank Luther. *American Journalism*. New York: Macmillan, 1964. Provides a comprehensive view of the historical development of American newspapers.

————. *A History of American Magazines*. Cambridge, MA: Harvard University Press, 1957. Presents the most complete and authoritative history of magazines.

————. *Golden Multitudes: The Story of Best Sellers in the United States*. New York: Macmillan, 1947. Surveys the role of best-selling books in American publishing.

————. *Jefferson and the Press*. Baton Rouge, LA: Louisiana State University Press, 1943. Summarizes the views of the father of freedom of the press in America.

Nafziger, Ralph O., and White, David Manning. *Introduction to Mass Communications Research*. Baton Rouge, LA: Louisiana State University Press, 1958. Summarizes the basic concepts and methods for research in mass media.

Nelson, Harold L., and Teeter, Dwight L. *Law of Mass Communications: Freedom and Control of Print and Broadcasting Media*. Mineola, NY: Foundation, 1969. Provides a thorough treatment of statutes and precedents concerning all aspects of media.

Nicosia, Francesco M., ed. *Advertising, Management and Society*. New York: McGraw-Hill, 1974.

Noble, Grant. *Children in Front of the Small Screen*. Beverly Hills, CA: Sage, 1975. A broad review of research concerning the effect of television on children. The book reviews international studies as well as those in the United States.

O'Hara, Robert C. *Media for the Millions: The Process of Mass Communication*. New York: Random House, 1961. Presents a unique view of the impact of mass media on our mass culture.

Paulu, Burton. *Radio and Television Broadcasting on the European Continent*. Minneapolis: University of Minnesota Press, 1967. Offers a nation-by-nation analysis of European broadcast operations.

Perkins, V. F. *Film as Film*. New York: Pelican/Penguin, 1972.

Peterson, Theodore. *Magazines in the Twentieth Century*. Urbana, IL: University of Illinois Press, 1964. Develops the history and presents situation of American periodicals in this century.

Phelan, John, ed. *Communications Control*. Mission, KS: Sheed & Ward, 1969. Analyzes the structure of censorship in the United States.

Phelps, Robert H., and Hamilton, E. Douglass. *Libel: A Guide to Rights, Risks, Responsibilities*. New York: Collier-Macmillan, 1966. Shows what libel is and what it is not, and describes how the mass media can communicate the maximum information with the minimum risk.

Pimlott, J. A. R. *Public Relations and American Democracy*. Princeton, NJ: Princeton University Press, 1951. Provides a thoughtful, provocative, and insightful analysis by a British observer of the role of public relations in America, particularly in government and politics.

Potter, David M. *People of Plenty: Economic Abundance and the American Character*. Chicago: University of Chicago Press, 1954. Hypothesizes that the American culture has been shaped largely by advertising and the mass media.

Powers, Ron. *The Newscasters*. New York: St. Martin's, 1977. A critical analysis of national and local TV newscasts and newscasters.

Quaal, Ward, and Brown, James A. *Broadcast Management: Radio, Television*. 2nd ed. New York: Hastings House, 1975. A completely rewritten version of the 1968 book, providing a broad overview of management principles for radio and television stations.

Randall, Richard S. *Censorship of the Movies*. Madison, WI: University of Wisconsin Press, 1968. Evaluates legal and social sanctions placed on the various aspects of the film industry.

Reddick, Dewitt C., and Crowell, Alfred A. *Industrial Editing*. Albany, NY: Matthew Bender, 1962. Introduces the student to the special problems for journalism and corporate endeavors.

Reisz, Karel, and Millar, Gavin. *The Technique of Film Editing*. New York: Hastings House, 1968. A basic source on film editing which surveys the various characteristics and effects of the editing process.

Reston, James. *The Artillery of the Press: Its Influence on American Foreign Policy*. New York: Harper & Row, 1967. Gives a well-reasoned explanation by the distinguished columnist and editor for the *New York Times* why the press must maintain an adversary relationship with government yet sometimes collaborate with government in the national interest.

Rivers, William L. *The Adversaries: Politics and the Press*. Boston: Beacon, 1970. Describes the relationship between government and press in America as an adversary relationship.

————. *The Opinionmakers: The Washington Press Corps*. Boston: Beacon,

1965. Describes how government officials use reporters, and how reporters use government officials, as part of the mass media system in American democracy.

———; Blankenburg, William B.; Starck, Kenneth; and Reeves, Earl. *Backtalk: Press Councils in America.* San Francisco: Canfield, 1972. Examines the need for press councils.

———, and Schramm, Wilbur. *Responsibility in Mass Communication.* New York: Harper & Row, 1969. Analyzes media service in the public interest in terms of current problems of national interest.

———, and Slater, William T., comps. *Aspen Handbook on the Media: Research, Publications, Organizations.* Palo Alto, CA: Aspen Program on Communication, 1973. A guide to major organizations that produce or subsidize or in other ways aid research. Also includes a list of publications about the media.

Robinson, Edward J. *Communication and Public Relations.* Columbus, OH: Charles E. Merrill, 1966. Attempts to bring a systematic analysis to public relations as an aspect of social and behavioral science.

Rosenberg, Bernard, and White, David Manning, eds. *Mass Culture Revisited.* New York: Van Nostrand Reinhold, 1971. Selects a variety of essays on the role and impact of the mass media on modern American mass culture; updates the earlier anthology, *Mass Culture,* by the same editors.

Rotha, Paul; Road, Sinclair; and Griffith, Richard. *Documentary Film.* New York: Hastings House, 1963. A historical and critical analysis of the documentary film primarily in Britain and the United States.

Roxon, Lillian. *Rock Encyclopedia.* New York: Workman, 1969. Presents information on musicians, groups, and trends in rock music and the recording industry.

Rubin, Bernard. *Political Television.* Belmont, CA: Wadsworth, 1967. Pioneers in showing how TV has been used by politicians to win elections.

Rucker, Bryce W. *The First Freedom.* Carbondale, IL: Southern Illinois University Press, 1968. Analyzes media in terms of ownership patterns and news operations.

Rucker, Frank W., and Williams, Herbert L. *Newspaper Organization and Management.* Ames, IA: Iowa State University Press, 1969. Provides an important analysis of management techniques in the newspaper business.

Sarris, Andrew. *The American Cinema.* New York: Dutton, 1968. Reviews American film directors, 1929–68.

Schiller, Herbert I. *Mass Communications and American Empire.* Boston: Beacon, 1971. Analyzes the military-industrial complex's role in the mass media in U.S. internal and external communications from a Marxist point of view.

Schlesinger, Arthur M. *Prelude to Independence: The Newspaper War on Britain, 1764–1776.* New York: Random House, 1965. Chronicles the exciting story of the role of newspapers in bringing about the American Revolution.

Schmidt, Benno C., Jr. *Freedom of the Press vs. Public Access.* New York: Praeger, 1976.

Schramm, Wilbur. *Mass Media and National Development.* Stanford, CA: Stanford University Press, 1964. Analyzes the effects of media and information campaigns on developing nations.

————. *Men, Messages and Media: A Look at Human Communication.* New York: Harper & Row, 1973. Synthesizes major research and theory intended for the laymen and student rather than the scholar.

————, ed. *The Process and Effects of Mass Communication.* 2nd ed. Urbana, IL: University of Illinois Press, 1971. Revises the earlier version of this classic collection of essays and articles on the development, structure, control, content, audiences, effects, and responsibilities of mass communication.

————, and Rivers, William. *Responsibility in Mass Communication.* New York: Harper & Row, 1969. Analyzes media service in the public interest in terms of current problems of national interest.

————, and Roberts, Donald F. *The Process and Effects of Mass Communication.* Rev. ed. Urbana, IL: University of Illinois Press, 1971. Attempts to define the sociological and psychological influence of mass communication for an international audience.

Schumach, Murray. *The Face on the Cutting Room Floor: The Story of Movie and Television Censorship.* New York: Morrow, 1964. A somewhat folksy account of the history and patterns of movie and TV censorship.

Schwartz, Barry N., comp. *Human Connection and the New Media.* Englewood Cliffs, NJ: Prentice-Hall, 1973. Shows that within the next few decades, it will be possible to receive a lasar communication at a home terminal which will enable the citizen to gather information from radio, teletype, microfilm, telephone, televideo, libraries, satellites, and perhaps even interstellar communication.

Seldes, Gilbert. *The New Mass Media: Challenge to a Free Society.* Washington, DC: Public Affairs Press, 1968. Discusses the implications for the individual and the free society of the artistic and social significance of the new media, including television, radio, and motion pictures.

Servan-Schreiber, Jean-Louis. *The Power to Inform.* New York: McGraw-Hill, 1974. A survey of America's print and broadcast media viewed against a world background by a French expert.

Shanks, Bob. *The Cool Fire: How to Make It in Television.* New York: Norton,

1976. An inside look at television from a former ABC executive. Provides a good sense of realities of television production and programming.

Sharp, Donald B. *Commentaries on Obscenity*. Metuchen, NJ: Scarecrow, 1970. Analyzes landmark cases in obscenity in the United States.

Siebert, Fred S.; Peterson, Theodore; and Schramm, Wilbur. *Four Theories of the Press*. Urbana, IL: University of Illinois Press, 1956. Presents the classic arguments of the authoritarian, libertarian, social responsibility, and Soviet Communist concepts of what the press should be and do.

Small, William. *Political Power and the Press*. New York: Hastings House, 1972. Attempts to show how the news media are used by politicans and public officials to gain political power.

————. *To Kill a Messenger: Television News and the Real World*. New York: Hastings House, 1970. Analyzes the structure, function, impact, and importance of TV journalism.

Smith, Alfred, ed. *Communication and Culture*. New York: Holt, Rinehart & Winston, 1966. Presents an anthology of articles analyzing the process and development of communication in various cultures.

Smith, Anthony. *The Shadow in the Cave: The Broadcaster, His Audience, and the State*. Urbana, IL: University of Illinois Press, 1974.

Sommerland, E. Lloyd. *The Press in Developing Countries*. Sydney, Australia: Sydney University Press, 1966. Analyzes news media systems in underdeveloped nations in Asia and Africa.

Sorenson, Thomas. *The Word War*. New York: Harper & Row, 1968. Provides a history and analysis of the U.S. Information Agency.

Speed, F. Maurice, ed. *Film Review*. New York: Barnes & Noble, 1970. Annual review of film productions in the U.S. and abroad.

Stearn, Gerald. *McLuhan: Hot and Cool*. New York: Signet, 1967. An anthology of articles by various individuals presenting their views on McLuhan's theory and ideas.

Steinberg, Charles S. *The Creation of Consent: Public Relations in Practice*. New York: Hastings House, 1976.

Stephenson, Ralph, and Debrix, J. R. *The Cinema as Art*. London: Penguin, 1969. An analysis of film in terms of its spatial, temporal, and sensory qualities.

Sterling, Christopher H., and Haight, Timothy R., eds. *The Mass Media: Aspen Guide to Communication Industry Trends*. New York: Praeger Special Studies, 1977. A statistical abstract of all media consisting mainly of some 200 tables of data with accompanying text description.

————, and Kittross, John. *Stay Tuned: A Concise History of American Broad-*

casting. Belmont, CA: Wadsworth, 1978. A tight, data-packed chronology of important dates, people, events in American broadcasting.

Stone, I. F. *The I. F. Stone's Weekly Reader*. Edited by Neil Middleton. New York: Random House, 1973. Writings from one of America's top journalists, covering samples from almost 20 years of his work—from Korea through Vietnam, from Joe McCarthy through Eugene McCarthy, from before Suez to after the Six-Day war.

Strauss, Victor. *The Printing Industry*. Washington, DC: Printing Industries of America, 1967. Explains the branches, processes, techniques, costs, and products of print media.

Tebbel, John. *The American Magazine: A Compact History*. New York: Hawthorn, 1969. Analyzes magazines in terms of their historical periods and the changes in magazine roles and audiences.

Tunstall, Jeremy. *Media Sociology: A Reader*. Urbana, IL: University of Illinois Press, 1970. Provides a broad collection of essays, primarily British, dealing with media research, organizations, content, audience, and political role.

Turnbull, Arthur T., and Baird, Russell N. *The Graphics of Communication*. New York: Holt, Rinehart & Winston, 1964. Provides a basic but comprehensive introduction to the principles and practices of typography, layout, and design.

Twentieth Century Fund. *Press Freedoms Under Pressure*. New York: Twentieth Century Fund, 1972. Reports on a special task force investigation of the increasing problems of maintaining freedom of the press in a mass society.

Waldrop, A. Gayle. *Editor and Editorial Writing*. Dubuque, IA: Brown, 1967. Presents the techniques of writing editorials and interpretive articles.

Weisberger, Bernard A. *The American Newspaperman*. Chicago: University of Chicago Press, 1961. Tells the story of the two-and-a-half-century development from the printer-writer-editor-owner of colonial days to the present-day professional reporter for daily newspapers.

Westin, Alan F. *Privacy and Freedom*. New York: Atheneum, 1967. Summarizes the legal arguments and implications of the right to privacy vs. the right to know.

Williams, Francis. *The Right to Know*. London: Longmans, Green, 1969. Provides an excellent analysis of news operation under various political, economic, and social conditions.

Willis, Edgar, E. *Writing Television and Radio Programs*. New York: Holt, Rinehart & Winston, 1967. Introduces the student to the verbal and visual coding systems used in broadcasting.

Winick, Charles, and others. *Children's Television Commercials: A Content Analysis*. New York: Praeger, 1973. Deals with length of commercials, product information, sales persuasion techniques, setting and story elements, language, age, and techniques.

Wood, Donald, and Wylie, Donald G. *Educational Telecommunications*. Belmont, CA: Wadsworth, 1977. A well-organized overview of public broadcasting and instructional media.

World Communications: A 200-Country Survey of Press, Radio, Television, Film. New York: UNIPUB, 1975. Although not revised since 1964, this remains the standard source for a comparative survey of virtually all countries with media systems.

Wright, Charles R. *Mass Communication: A Sociological Perspective*. 2nd ed. New York: Random House, 1975. Pioneers in developing a sociological framework for studying mass media.

Wyckcoff, Gene. *The Image Candidates*. New York: Macmillan, 1968. Investigates the role of television in political campaigns.

Youngblood, Gene. *Expanded Cinema*. New York: Dutton, 1970. An analysis of new and future developments in the technology of film and television.

Yu, Frederick T. C. *Behavioral Sciences and the Mass Media*. New York: Russell Sage Foundation, 1968. Presents a variety of essays and statements by journalists and social scientists on the increasingly important relationship between the behavioral sciences and the mass media.

Zettl, Herbert. *Sight Sound Motion*. Belmont, CA: Wadsworth, 1973. Examines applied media aesthetics of television.

———. *Television Production Handbook*. 3rd ed. Belmont, CA: Wadsworth, 1976. Provides an analysis of TV-production techniques; serves as an excellent text in beginning production courses.

Name Index

Subject Index

Public broadcasting, 59, 64–66, 304–5, 395–99
Public Broadcasting Act (1967), 304–5
Public Opinion, 165, 401, 407
Public relations, 134–35; defining, 404–5; filters, 168; future, 414–15; government, 409–10; growth, 405–8; organization, 410–12; politics and, 408–9; role of, 403–4; work, 413
Public Relations Society of America, 152, 411, 415
Pulse, Inc., 189, 194, 196

Quaker Oats Company, 273

Radio: advertising, 64, 280–83, 288–89, 439; audiences, 181–82; characteristics, 288–92; codes, 104, 106; communicators, 87–90; in education, 394; as entertainment, 451; feedback, 192, 194; government regulation of, 147–48, 279–80; history, 277–83; industry, 130, 284–85; news, 364–66, 370–71; public, 64–65; scope, 8, 283–84; sets, 136; stations, 286–87
Radio Act (1912), 279–80
Radio Act (1927), 280
Radio Advertising Bureau, 291
Radio Corporation of America (RCA), 56, 76–77, 86, 264, 279, 294–95, 299, 317, 319, 321, 323
Ratings: movie, 270; television, 188–89, 192, 194–96
Reader's Digest, 10, 235, 239, 248
Recording Industry Association of America, 138
Record World, 331
Red Star, 50
Regulators: advertisers, 150–51; consumers, 157–59; content sources, 149–50; government, 26, 140–49, 279–80, 296–98; profession as, 151–57
Reviews, critical, 376
Rock music, 322–27
Rolling Stone, 331, 338
"Roots," 109, 170–72, 306, 446

St. Louis Post-Dispatch, 223
Salaries, newspaper, 10, 137
Salt Lake City Tribune, 379
Sampling techniques, 186–87
Satellites, television, 302–3
Saturday Evening Post, 237, 239, 243
Saturday Night Fever, 69
Screen Actors Guild, 137
Securities and Exchange Commission (SEC), 149
"Selling of the Pentagon, The," 374
Selling of the President, The, 301
Sepia, 241
Seventh Seal, The, 109–10
Sex films, 270, 478–80
Silent Language, The, 163
Sindlinger, 194, 196, 300
"60 Minutes," 83, 88, 121
Slapstick comedy, 260, 263

Social-consciousness films, 268–69
Socialization, media and, 383–86
Social movements, media impact on: civil rights, 487–91; gay rights, 491–92; history of, 482–84; women's movement, 489–91
Social-responsibility theory of press, 31–32
Sound of Music, The, 56, 267
Sound recording: audiences, 181; characteristics, 332, 334–35; codes, 106; costs, 71–72; distribution, 136; in education, 393; as entertainment, 451; environment, 182–83; feedback, 191–92; history, 314–27; industry, 130, 329–33; payola in, 324, 329; rock music, 322–27; scope, 9, 327–29; on tape, 318–19
Southern Christian Leadership Conference, 488
Soviet-Communist theory of press, 31
Soviet Union. *See* USSR
Specialized media, 168–70, 181, 241, 248–49, 340–41
Star Is Born, A, 255, 491
Star Wars, 56, 69, 71, 73, 90, 270, 486
Stereotypes, 165–68, 265
Still photograph, 104, 105, 106–10
Syndicates, 89, 133, 310, 380

Talent agencies, 136–37
Tape recordings, 318–19
TASS, 51–52, 362
Techniques of Persuasion, 405
Technology, 206; media systems and, 37–38, 302–3; newspapers and, 232–33
Television: advertising, 61–66, 306, 438–39; audiences, 181–83; cable, 149, 303–4, 378–79; case study, 73–77; characteristics, 312–13; children and, 159, 305, 386, 395, 473–77; codes, 106–11, 152, 154–57; color, 299, 304; commercials, 74–75; communicators, 87–90, 375–76; educational, 304–5, 386–87, 392–93, 395–99; as entertainment, 450; feedback, 194–96; government regulation of, 145–49, 294–96; history, 294–305; impact, 487–94; industry, 130, 306–10; live, 111; news, 364–66, 370–71; pay, 304; public, 59, 64–66, 304–5; ratings, 188–89, 192, 194–96; satellite, 302–3; scope, 8, 305–6; sets, 136
Telstar, 302
Textbooks, 209–10, 215, 387–90, 449
Theories of Mass Communication, 175
Theories of press, 31–32
Third World, 42
Time, 10, 77, 92–93, 101, 104–5, 240, 245, 370, 372
"Today Show, The," 84
Trendex, 194, 196
Triumph of the Will, 107–8, 448
20th Century-Fox, 71, 265, 273

Underground films, 267–69
Understanding Media, 6